S0-BEC-482

Library Statistics of Colleges and Universities
1979 Institutional Data

(U.S.) National Center for Educational
Statistics, Washington, DC

Oct 81

U.S. DEPARTMENT OF COMMERCE
National Technical Information Service

Library Statistics of Colleges and Universities, 1979 Institutional Data

Richard M. Beazley

National Center for
Education Statistics

U.S. Department of Education
T. H. Bell
Secretary

Office of Educational Research and Improvement
Donald J. Senese
Assistant Secretary

National Center for Education Statistics
Marie D. Eldridge
Administrator

National Center for Education Statistics

"The purpose of the Center shall be to collect and disseminate statistics and other data related to education in the United States and in other nations. The Center shall . . . collect, collate, and, from time to time, report full and complete statistics on the conditions of education in the United States; conduct and publish reports on specialized analyses of the meaning and significance of such statistics; . . . and review and report on education activities in foreign countries."--Section 406(b) of the General Education Provisions Act, as amended (20 U.S.C. 1221e-1).

Division of Statistical Services
Forms Management and Publications Branch
Thomas Hill, Editor

50272-101

REPORT DOCUMENTATION PAGE	1. REPORT NO.	2.	3. Recipient's Accession No. PB82 169087

4. Title and Subtitle	5. Report Date
Library Statistics of Colleges and Universities: 1979 Institutional Data	6. 057193

7. Author(s)	8. Performing Organization Rept. No.
Richard M. Beazley	NCES 81-260

9. Performing Organization Name and Address	10. Project/Task/Work Unit No.
U.S. Department of Education National Center for Education Statistics 1001 Presidential Bldg. 400 Maryland Ave. SW. Washington, D.C. 20202	11. Contract(C) or Grant(G) No. (C) (G)

12. Sponsoring Organization Name and Address	13. Type of Report & Period Covered Statistical. Through fall 1979.
Same as above	14.

15. Supplementary Notes

16. Abstract (Limit: 200 words)

The report is based on data gathered in a survey of college and university libraries, part of the Higher Education General Information Survey (HEGIS) conducted annually by the National Center for Education Statistics (NCES). The last previous library survey was conducted in 1977. Of the 3,122 college and university libraries surveyed, 2,945 responded, 1,446 of these public, 1,499 private. The overall response rate was 94.3 percent. This report covers library transactions, expenditures, staff, staff salaries and management data. Institutional data include control and type of institution; number of volumes and titles in stock, and number added; number of government document collections; number of microforms; and number of periodical subscription titles. Among the findings:

- Current periodical subscriptions increased by 2.2 percent;
- Fewer book volumes were added to academic library collections--continuing a downward trend begun in 1972-73;
- Acquisitions of nonprint materials increased at a greater rate than those of print materials;
- Operating expenditures increased by 19 percent, or less than 1 percent when inflation is discounted.

17. Document Analysis a. Descriptors

b. Identifiers/Open-Ended Terms

c. COSATI Field/Group

18. Availability Statement:	19. Security Class (This Report)	21. No. of Pages 185
	20. Security Class (This Page)	22. Price

(See ANSI-Z39.18)

FOREWORD

This report is based on data gathered in a survey of college and university libraries which was a part of the Higher Education General Information Survey (HEGIS) conducted by the National Center for Education Statistics (NCES). HEGIS was initiated in 1966 to provide a continuing data base on higher education institutions. The last previous library survey was included in the HEGIS conducted in 1977.

College and university library surveys not only provide information on a vital component of higher education institutions, they also complement the data gathered from other types of libraries. Accordingly, the college and university library survey is a part of the Library General Information Survey (LIBGIS) which is also conducted by NCES. LIBGIS gathers data on academic, public, school, and special libraries as well as on networks and the library profession. Collectively, these surveys afford an assessment of the status of libraries in the Nation.

This publication continues the series that provides basic data from each of the academic libraries responding to the survey.

We appreciate the continuing cooperation of college and university librarians who supplied the data in this report. The assistance of State Coordinators who assisted in the collection and review of data from their States is also gratefully acknowledged.

Paul F. Mertins
Acting Chief
Learning Resources Branch

David Sweet
Assistant Administrator
Division of Multilevel Education Statistics
October 1981

ACKNOWLEDGMENTS

This report is made possible by the cooperative endeavors of many individuals. VSE Corporation of Alexandria, Virginia under contract with the Department of Education, conducted follow-up of nonrespondents, edited survey responses according to NCES specifications, and produced tabular output. Special recognition is extended to Thomas Shifflett and the computer staff of VSE for their untiring efforts in striving for the highest possible completeness and accuracy in the survey results. Special recognition is also extended to NCES staff members who made valuable contributions to the preparation of this report. They include: John Dusatko, Thaddeus Chmura, Stanley Kwaczala, and Kevin Kwiatkowski who provided data processing assistance; Thomas Hill for editorial review and copy preparation of the manuscript; and Sindy McDowell for typing and clerical assistance.

How to Obtain More Information

Information about the Center's statistical program and a catalog of NCES publications may be obtained from the Statistical Information Office, National Center for Education Statistics, Presidential Building, 400 Maryland Avenue SW., Washington, D.C. 20202, telephone (301) 436-7900.

CONTENTS

Text Tables

Basic Tables

HIGHLIGHTS

- Current periodical subscriptions increased by 2.2 percent.

- Fewer book volumes were added to academic library collections than in 1976-77 to continue the downward trend which began in 1972-73.

- Acquisitions of all types of nonprint materials increased at a greater rate than print materials.

- Circulation increased by 1.3 percent and loans to other libraries increased by 10.2 percent.

- Operating expenditures increased 19 percent in a 2-year period, but this increase was equivalent to less than one percent when inflation is discounted.

- Total FTE library staff increased by 2.3 percent. FTE librarians increased by 3.2 percent.

- Staff salaries represented 60 percent of total operating expenditures as in 1976-77.

- Library expenditures per FTE student increased at about the same rate as enrollment when expenditures are adjusted for inflation.

Collections (Table A)

Acquisitions. Substantial numbers of materials were added to academic library collections in 1978-79. Acquisitions were greater than in 1976-77 among all types of library materials with the exception of book volumes and titles. The decline in acquisitions of book volumes continues the downward trend which began in 1972-73. In 1970-71, 26.4 million books were added to collections compared with 21.6 million in 1978-79. Furthermore, 759,000 more books were added to collections in 1976-77 than in 1978-79.

Current periodical subscriptions in 1978-79 exceeded those in 1976-77 by 105,000. Acquisitions of government documents in separate collections were not included in the previous survey. However, they undoubtedly increased because there was substantial growth in holdings of these materials in the 2-year period.

Acquisitions of all types of nonprint material were greater in 1978-79 than in 1976-77. In fact, acquisitions of nonprint materials increased at a greater rate than comparable print materials. Periodicals on microform doubled while periodical subscriptions increased by only 2.2 percent. Furthermore, book titles on microform increased approximately 8 percent in contrast to a decline of nearly 8 percent in printed book titles.

Holdings. Additions to collections in the 2-year period since 1976-77 resulted in widely varying rates of increase in library holdings. Book volumes and book titles had the lowest rates of increase; 8 and 3 percent, respectively. These comparatively lower rates reflect the downward trend in book volume acquisitions in recent years which was cited above. At the other extreme, periodical titles on microform nearly doubled. Such a large increase in this type of library material is viewed with skepticism because it may be attributable, in part, to inconsistencies in reporting. Probable causes of these inconsistencies are discussed in appendix B.

The rates of increase among the remaining items in library collections varied between approximately 9 and 30 percent.

Transactions (Table B)

Circulation of library materials in academic libraries was 1.3 percent higher than in 1976-77. Interlibrary loans to other libraries increased by 10.2 percent, while loans from other libraries increased by 6.9 percent. The ratio of loans made by academic libraries to the number received from all libraries was 1.6:1 in both 1976-77 and 1978-79. It is apparent that collections in academic libraries are serving needs in other types of libraries as well, since academic libraries are lenders, on balance, rather than recipients.

Reference and directional transactions (per typical week) both increased by approximately 10 percent in the 2-year period. Group transactions were surveyed for the first time in 1979. Data from 2,193 libraries presented in table B represent an average of 15.6 participants per group transaction.

Table A. — Acquisitions and holdings of library materials in college and university libraries: Aggregate United States, 1976-77 and 1978-79

Acquisitions

Item	1976-77	1978-79	Percent change
Periodical subscriptions	4,670, 074	4,774,946	2.2
Book volumes	22,366,931	21,608, 010	-3.4
Book titles	15,751,180	14,508,574	-7.9
Government documents (in separate collections)	–	7,351,198	–
Microform – book titles	3,040,933	3,276,584	7.7
– periodical titles	143,258	287,114	100.4
– physical units	18,378, 043	21,674,807	17.9
Audiovisual titles	1,814,256	2,095,786	15.5
All other library materials	5,006,089	5,328,858	6.4

Holdings

Item	1976-77	1978-79	Percent increase
Book volumes	481,442,026	519,895,257	8.0
Book titles	329,953,073	340,302,086	3.1
Government documents	76,211,936	91,542,002	20.1
Microform – book titles	35,500,753	39,174,697	10.3
– periodical titles	1,305,077	2,503,941	91.9
– physical units	172,975,571	224,334,739	29.7
Audiovisual titles	18,401,386	20,929,651	13.7
Other library materials	109,404,282	118,967,622	8.7

Table B. — Transactions in college and university libraries: Aggregate United States, 1976-77 and 1978-79

Transaction	1976-77	1978-79	Percent increase
Circulation	198,719,411	201,306,592	1.3
Interlibrary loans – to other libraries	2,802,492	3,088,626	10.2
– from other libraries	1,779,908	1,902,546	6.9
Reference transactions (per typical week) ...	927,597	1,018,741	9.8
Directional transactions (per typical week) ..	1,117,690	1,230,884	10.1
Group transactions (per year) – number	–	239,233	–
– participants .	–	3,732,293	–

Expenditures (Table C)

Operating expenditures in academic libraries increased by $242 million; a 19.3 percent increase in the 2-year period. During the same period, the inflation rate as indicated by the Consumer Price Index (CPI) was nearly 17 percent. When inflation is discounted by converting the 1978-79 expenditures to 1976-77 dollars, the increase in total library expenditures is equivalent to $27 million; only 2.2 percent greater than in 1976-77.

Expenditures for periodicals increased at a greater rate than any budgetary item except "all other library materials." The large increase in "all other library materials" may be due in part to some libraries reporting all of their expenditures for library materials in this category because they were unable to report expenditures for each separate item.

Expenditures for staff compensation[1] of $904 million were slightly more than double the amount spent on library materials[2], but expenditures for library materials were 20.5 percent above 1976-77 as compared with a 17.9 percent increase in staff compensation. When adjusted for inflation, the increase in staff compensation is equivalent to 1.0 percent, while the equivalent increase for library materials is 3.2 percent.

Library Staff (Table D)

In the fall of 1979, there were 58,416 full-time-equivalents (FTE) among a total staff of 63,734 persons. Full-time employees represented 84 percent of total employment. The average FTE of a part-time professional was .45 compared with .48 for nonprofessionals.

The total staff, in terms of FTE's, increased 2.3 percent from the number in fall 1977. FTE librarians increased by 3.2 percent. The second largest rate of increase was among nonprofessionals. "Other professionals" virtually remained constant, while FTE administrators declined by 1.8 percent.

Women outnumbered men by a ratio of approximately 3:1 for the total staff, but the ratios varied among the four employment categories. In the administrator category, the numbers of FTE men and women were practically equal. On the other hand, there were more than twice as many FTE women librarians as men and more than five times as many FTE women in nonprofessional jobs as men.

The number of hours of student assistance declined, but was only 1 percent less than in 1976-77.

---

[1] Sum of salaries, fringe benefits, and wages for student assistance.
[2] Sum of expenditures for books, periodicals, microform, audiovisuals, and other library materials.

Table C. – Library operating expenditures in college and university libraries: Aggregate United States, 1976-77 and 1978-79

Item	1976-77	1978-79	Percent change
Total operating expenditures	$1,259,636,773	$1,502,157,203	19.3
Salaries and wages[1]	608,173,322	710,126,820	16.8
Fringe benefits	89,916,974	114,310,859	27.1
Wages for student assistance[2]	68,683,278	79,535,164	15.8
Books	198,464,689	224,471,359	13.1
Periodicals	136,598,718	179,207,105	31.2
Microform	18,722,979	20,085,275	7.3
Audiovisual material	15,364,549	17,123,912	11.5
All other library material	4,547,923	9,292,154	104.3
Binding and rebinding	22,521,114	25,273,715	12.2
All other library expenditures	96,643,227	122,730,840	27.0

[1] Includes salary equivalents for contributed services staff.
[2] Student wages charged to library budgets.

Table D. —   Full-time-equivalent staff and hours of student assistance in college and university libraries: Aggregate United States, 1977 and 1979

Full-time-equivalent library staff	Fall 1977	Fall 1979	Percent change
Total	57,087	58,416	2.3
Men	14,355	14,627	1.9
Women	42,732	43,789	2.5
Administrators	5,601	5,500	-1.8
Men	2,793	2,749	-1.6
Women	2,808	2,751	-2.0
Librarians	14,975	15,449	3.2
Men	4,690	4,864	3.7
Women	10,285	10,585	2.9
Other professionals	2,732	2,727	-0.2
Men	1,140	1,112	-2.5
Women	1,592	1,615	1.4
Nonprofessionals	33,779	34,740	2.8
Men	5,732	5,902	3.0
Women	28,047	28,838	2.8

Student assistance	1976-77	1978-79	Percent change
Hours	39,949,561	39,552,306	-1.0

Library Staff Salaries (Table E)

Average salaries for full-time library administrators were 15.5 percent higher in fall 1979 than in fall 1977. The average salary of librarians increased by 14.1 percent; "other professionals" by 12.8 percent; and nonprofessionals by 16.2 percent. Women's salaries increased at a greater rate than men's in each of the job categories except "other professionals." Still, the average salary for women was substantially less than for men in all cases. The greatest difference was among administrators where the average salary for men exceeded that of women by $5,560. In contrast, the difference among librarians was $1,777.

Management Data (Table F)

The distributions of expenditures by purpose was nearly identical in 1976-77 and 1978-79. Staff compensation and library materials, the two major expenditure items, collectively represented about 90 percent of the total with staff compensation being twice that for library materials.

The proportion expended for staff compensation followed a consistently higher trend over the decade ending in 1976-77. Although 60.2 percent in 1978-79 represents a trivial decline below the 60.9 percent in 1976-77, the difference of only a fraction of a percentage point should probably be regarded as a leveling of the trend rather than the beginning of a reversal.

Library expenditures as a percentage of education and general expenditures, even though nearly identical to the percentage in 1976-77, was lower than it has been in the last 10 years when it varied between 3.8 and 4.0 percent. Although a consistent trend in this statistic has not been evident, the tendency has been downward.

Library expenditures per FTE student were $27.00, or 18 percent, higher in 1978-79 than in 1976-77, but most of this increase was attributable to inflation. When inflationary effects are removed by adjusting 1978-79 expenditures to 1976-77 dollars using the Consumer Price Index as a deflator, the expenditure per FTE student becomes $151.65 in contrast to the $177.04 shown in table F. Thus, in terms of purchasing power, expenditures per FTE student increased by 1.2 percent rather than 18 percent. FTE enrollment increased by 0.9 percent during the same 2-year period; therefore, expenditures merely kept pace with enrollment.

FTE library staff per 1,000 FTE students was virtually unchanged in the 2-year period. At both the professional and nonprofessional levels, the ratios of library staff per student were about the same as in 1976-77.

Table E. — Average salaries of full-time staff in college and university libraries: Aggregate United States, fall 1977 and 1979

Full-time staff	Fall 1977	Fall 1979	Percent change
Administrators	$18,667	$21,553	15.5
Men	21,198	24,304	14.7
Women	16,133	18,744	16.2
Librarians	15,098	17,233	14.1
Men	16,349	18,438	12.8
Women	14,512	16,661	14.8
Other professionals	12,493	14,096	12.8
Men	14,884	16,904	13.6
Women	10,715	12,065	12.6
Nonprofessionals	8,301	9,645	16.2
Men	9,141	10,266	12.3
Women	8,137	9,522	17.0

Table F. — Selected management data on college and university libraries: Aggregate United States, 1976-77 and 1978-79

Selected management data	1976-77	1978-79
Percentage distribution of library expenditures		
Total operating expenditures	100.0[1]	100.0[1]
Salaries, wages and fringe benefits[2]	60.9	60.2
Books and other library materials	29.7	30.0
Binding and rebinding	1.8	1.7
All other expenditures	7.7	8.2
Ratios of library and institutional variables		
Library expenditures as a percentage of education and general expenditures	3.8	3.7
Library expenditures per FTE student[3]	$149.83	$177.04
FTE library staff per 1,000 FTE students"	6.7	6.8
FTE professional library staff per 1,000 FTE students[4]	2.7	2.8
FTE nonprofessional library staff per 1,000 FTE students[4]	4.0	4.0

[1] The detail does not add to the total due to rounding.
[2] Includes estimated salary equivalents of contributed services staff and wages for student assistance charged to library budgets.
[3] Expenditures for the academic year are related to students in the fall of the same academic year.
[4] Staff and students are as of the fall of the following academic year. Library staff excludes student assistants employed on an hourly basis.

Appendixes

Appendix A. METHODOLOGY

Survey Universe and Response

The universe of college and university libraries was derived from the universe of colleges and universities, as defined by the Department of Education, which enumerates individual institutions and each of the branches of multi-campus institutions.[1] There were 3,190 institutions and branches in the college and university universe in the 1979-80 academic year. Some of these institutions and branches had no library facilities, while others were affiliates of a joint library. The universe of 3,122 college and university libraries was established from the college and university universe by: (1) removing the institutions and branches of institutions that had no library or were members of joint libraries, and (2) adding the joint libraries.[2]

The following tabulation shows the derivation of the college and university library universe:

Institutional control	College and university universe	No library	Members of joint libraries	Joint libraries	College and university library universe
Public and private	3,190	33	56	21	3,122
Public	1,488	18	13	7	1,464
Private	1,702	15	43	14	1,658

The list of institutions and branches where the 3,122 libraries are located appears in tables 1 through 3. Completed questionnaires were received from 2,945 of the 3,122 libraries. The following tabulation shows response rates by institutional control:

Institutional control	Library universe	Number responding	Percent responding
Public and private	3,122	2,945	94.3
Public	1,464	1,446	98.8
Private	1,658	1,499	90.4

Imputation Procedure

To obtain national totals for the data items included in this report, it was necessary to impute responses for the 177 libraries that did not submit survey forms and for certain data items that were not provided by respondents. Salaries of library staff were not imputed because the survey response rate was sufficiently high to provide reliable measures of mean salaries.

Data were imputed for libraries that failed to submit a survey form by substituting either: (1) the library's response to the 1977 survey, when available, or (2) the response to the 1979 survey by a library in an institution having characteristics similar to the institution in which the nonresponding library was located.

[1] U.S. Department of Education, National Center for Education Statistics, Education Directory, Colleges and Universities 1979-80. Washington, D.C.: 1980.
[2] Joint libraries and member institutions are listed in Appendix C.

Of the 177 nonrespondents, 77 libraries had responded to the 1977 survey, so those data were substituted without adjustment in lieu of responses to the 1979 survey. Since all of these libraries were relatively small, attempts to estimate changes in data over the intervening 2-year period could have introduced errors. Furthermore, small differences that might have resulted from adjustment would have been insignificant in relation to the universe.

Imputation for the 100 remaining nonrespondents was accomplished by substituting data from a responding library that was located in an institution having characteristics similar to the institution in which the nonresponding library was located. Institutions were judged as being similar if the following characteristics of each were identical or closely approximate:

(1) institutional control (financially supported by: (a) Federal, State, or local governments; (b) a religious denomination; or (c) an independent nonprofit or profitmaking organization)

(2) institutional level (university, 4-year, or 2-year)

(3) enrollment size

(4) highest degree offered

(5) accreditation in specialized subject fields

(6) geographical location

Omitted items were also imputed by substituting responses from the 1977 survey or from a peer institution. Ratios were also utilized for greater precision, when appropriate. For example, the ratio of book titles to book volumes was used to impute book titles for 247 libraries; the largest number of omitted items. In 100 of these cases, book titles and volumes were available for 1976-77, so that ratio was applied to book volumes reported in 1978-79 to obtain an estimate of book titles in 1978-79. In each of the remaining 147 cases, neither titles nor volumes were reported in 1976-77, so ratios of book titles to book volumes in similar libraries in the 1978-79 survey were applied to book volumes reported by libraries omitting book titles in 1978-79.

Tabular Procedures

In basic tables 1 through 3, the 3,190 institutions and branches in the higher education universe, along with 21 joint libraries, are listed in alphabetical order within States. The institutions comprising a system and the branches of multicampus institutions are both designated by brackets in the left margin of the tables.

Data are presented in tables 1 through 3 for each of the institutions, branches, and joint libraries in the higher education universe. Members of joint libraries are identified by a reference to the name of the joint library to which they belong. Institutions having no library facilities are so designated.

The survey items not reported by respondents are indicated by alphabetical symbols in the tables 1 through 3. Data were imputed for the unreported items in tables 1 and 2, and those values are included in the summary figures presented in tables A, B, C, D, and F. Mean salaries of library staff, which appear in table E, were calculated from the data provided by responding libraries and do not include imputation for nonresponse.

Classification of Institutions

The abbreviations in column 2 of basic tables 1 through 3 pertain to the institutional control and level of the institutions or branches, and are translated as follows:

PUB — **Public.** An institution financially supported by public funds derived from Federal, State, or local reveunes.

PRI — **Private.** An institution financially supported by a religious denomination or independently o⟶rated as either a nonprofit or a profitmaking organization.

U — **University.** An institution that: (a) gives considerable stress to graduate instruction, (b) confers undergraduate and graduate degrees in a variety of liberal arts fields, and (c) has at least two professional schools that are not exclusively technological.

FG — **4-year institutions with graduate programs.** A 4-year institution, not classified as a university, offering programs leading to graduate or other postbaccalaureate degrees, including first-professional degrees.

FN — **4-year institutions with no graduate programs.** A 4-year institution, not classified as a university, offering no degrees beyond the baccalaureate.

T — **2-year institution.** An institution offering at least 2 but less than 4 years of college-level education.

13

Appendix B. TECHNICAL NOTES

Survey questions pertaining to microform have been identical since 1975 when librarians were asked to report acquisitions and holdings of book titles, periodical titles, and of physical units of microform other than book or periodical titles. The data from four surveys conducted over a 5-year period are presented in the table below:

Microform acquisitions and holdings (in thousands)

Year	Book Titles on Microform		Periodical Titles on Microform		Physical Units (not included as book or periodical titles)	
	Added	Held	Added	Held	Added	Held
1974-75	4,009	36,415	210	1,689	14,424	129,460
1975-76	3,030	31,552	143	1,345	18,348	156,399
1976-77	3,041	35,501	143	1,305	18,378	172,976
1978-79	3,277	39,175	287	2,504	21,675	224,335

Books and periodicals are expected to constitute the majority of material on microform, yet acquisitions and holdings of physical units (other than books or periodicals) exceeded those of book and periodical titles by 3 to 6 times. This may be indicative of books and periodicals being reported in terms of physical units as well as titles, or the reporting of physical units rather than titles.

The table above shows that acquisitions and holdings of physical units consistently increased in each successive survey year. On the other hand, acquisitions and holdings of both book titles and periodical titles increased in some years and declined in others. While acquisitions would not necessarily increase in each successive survey, holdings would be expected to increase if discards did not exceed acquisitions. Even though data were not collected on discards, it is highly improbable that discards accounted for the wide fluctuations in microform holdings. For example, 36.4 million book titles on microform were held at the end of 1974-75. The addition of 3 million titles in 1975-76 should have increased holdings to approximately 39 million, but only 31.6 million holdings were reported. Similar disparities are evident in other years and among periodical titles as well.

Possible causes of disparities in microform data are as follows:

(1) Misinterpretation of survey definitions in earlier years could have led to adjustments in subsequent years. Fluctuations among book and periodical titles may have been caused by enumerating these items in terms of physical units and later changing to counts of titles.

(2) Records of microform materials, as kept by many libraries, may not permit accurate counts or reliable estimates of these survey items. Periodical titles pose a special problem. Duplicate counting may well result when a periodical is added to a collection at irregular intervals.

(3) Data continuity can be affected by different persons completing the survey form in successive surveys; particularly when the survey interval is biennial or less frequent.

Appendix C. JOINT LIBRARIES AND MEMBER INSTITUTIONS, FALL 1979

Stratton Joint Library, Sitka, Alaska
  Serves: Sheldon Jackson College
            University of Alaska, Sitka Community College

University of Alaska, Anchorage, Alaska
  Serves: University of Alaska, Anchorage Campus
            University of Alaska, Anchorage Community
              College
            Alaska Pacific University

University of Alaska, Juneau, Alaska
  Serves: University of Alaska, Juneau Senior College
            University of Alaska, Juneau – Douglas
              Community College

Graduate Theological Union Joint Library, Berkeley,
California
  Serves: American Baptist Seminary of the West
            Church Divinity School of the Pacific
            Franciscan School of Theology
            Graduate Theological Union
            Jesuit School of Theology
            Pacific Lutheran Theological Seminary
            Pacific School of Religion (associate)
            San Francisco Theological Seminary
            Dominican School of Philosophy and
              Theology
            Starr King School for the Ministry

Honnold Joint Library, Claremont, California
  Serves: Claremont Graduate School
            Claremont Men's College
            Harvey Mudd College
            Pitzer College
            Pomona College
            Scripps College

Mennonite-Pacific Joint Library, Fresno, California
  Serves: Mennonite Brethren Biblical Seminary
            Fresno Pacific College

Auraria Joint Library, Denver, Colorado
  Serves: Community College of Denver, Auraria
            Metropolitan State College
            University of Colorado, Denver

Bethany-Northern Baptist Joint Library, Belleville, Illinois
  Serves: Bethany Theological Seminary
            Northern Baptist Theological Seminary

Jesuit-McCormick Joint Library, Chicago, Illinois
  Serves: Lutheran School of Theology, Chicago
            McCormick Theological Seminary

Mennonite Biblical Seminary Joint Library, Elkhart, Indiana
  Serves: Goshen Biblical Seminary
            Mennonite Biblical Seminary

Saint Meinrad College Joint Library, Saint Meinrad, Indiana
  Serves: Saint Meinrad College
            Saint Meinrad School of Theology

Loyola-Notre Dame Joint Library, Baltimore, Maryland
  Serves: College of Notre Dame
            Loyola College

Worcester Joint Library, Worcester, Massachusetts
  Serves: Central New England College of Technology
            Worcester Junior College

Calvin College Joint Library, Grand Rapids, Michigan
  Serves: Calvin College
            Calvin Theological Seminary

Luther Northwestern Seminary Joint Library, St. Paul,
Minnesota
  Serves: Luther Theological Seminary
            Northwestern Lutheran Theological
              Seminary

Eden-Webster Joint Library, St. Louis, Missouri
  Serves: Eden Theological Seminary
            Webster College

Saint Vincent College Seminary Joint Library, Latrobe,
Pennsylvania
  Serves: Saint Vincent College
            Saint Vincent Seminary

Texas Medical Center Joint Library, Houston, Texas
  Serves: Baylor College of Medicine
            University of Texas Health Science Center,
              Houston

Harold R. Yeary Library, Laredo, Texas
  Serves: Laredo State University
            Laredo Junior College

VC UHVC Joint Library, Victoria, Texas
  Serves: University of Houston Victoria Campus
            Victoria College

Union Theological Seminary Joint Library, Richmond,
Virginia
  Serves: Presbyterian School of Christian Education
            Union Theological Seminary of Virginia

Basic Tables

Table 1. — Collections in College and University Libraries, by State or Other Area and Institution: Aggregate United States, 1978-79, and Fall 1979

STATE OR OTHER AREA AND INSTITUTION	CON-TROL AND TYPE OF IN-STITU-TION	HELD AT END OF YEAR							ADDED DURING YEAR		CURRENT PERIOD-ICAL SUB-SCRIPTION TITLES FALL 1979
		BOOKSTOCK		SEPARATE GOVERN-MENT DOCU-MENTS COLLEC-TIONS (VOLS.)	MICROFORMS			ALL OTHER LIBRARY MATE-RIALS	BOOKSTOCK		
		VOLUMES	TITLES		BOOK TITLES	PERI-ODICAL TITLES	OTHER PHYS-ICAL UNITS		VOLUMES	TITLES	
(1)	(2)	(3)	(4)	(5)	(6)	(7)	(8)	(9)	(10)	(11)	(12)
ALABAMA											
ALABAMA A & M UNIVERSITY	PUB-FG	248,512	207,093	59,864	59,908	457	8,905	151	3,700	3,083	1,170
ALABAMA CHRISTIAN COLLEGE	PRI-T	22,987	18,000	0	0	21	0	800	1,236	1,000	308
ALA LUTH ACAD AND COLLEGE	PRI-T	11,689	11,624	0	0	0	0	0	400	340	97
ALABAMA STATE UNIVERSITY	PUB-FG	170,980	129,338	0	9,661	129	204,856	1,549	12,402	10,585	1,051
ALEXANDER CITY STATE JC	PUB-T	32,240	28,000	35,084	0	43	5,635	0	928	800	489
ATHENS STATE COLLEGE	PUB-FN	62,778	50,067	0	9	2	100	29	1,328	1,054	377
AUBURN U ALL CAMPUSES											
AUBURN U MAIN CAMPUS	PUB-U	1,043,428	489,853	424,340	191,025	7,977	917,238	77,043	62,287	34,791	15,739
AUBURN U AT MONTGOMERY	PUB-FG	97,442	78,820	8,872	268,078	0	22,636	994	8,013	6,784	1,007
BIRMINGHAM STHN COLLEGE	PRI-FN	128,495	102,076	126,660	60	250	7,008	0	3,850	2,830	602
BOOKER T WASHINGTON BUS C	PRI-T	A	A					A	A	A	A
BREWER STATE JR COLLEGE	PUB-T	23,682	23,672	0	1	122	1,200	300	1,292	1,287	219
CHATTAHOOCHEE VALLEY CC	PUB-T	37,459	37,233	62	46	214	682	36	6,799	6,775	360
ENTERPRISE ST JR COLLEGE	PUB-T	31,007	30,958	33,000	0	108	7,341	0	1,449	1,440	378
FAULKNER STATE JR COLLEGE	PUB-T	32,900	30,844	0	0	169	1,821	0	1,168	1,015	282
GADSDEN STATE JR COLLEGE	PUB-T	55,882	43,954	0	0	457	0	65	1,447	1,247	476
GEO C WALLACE ST CC-DOTHN	PUB-T	32,411	32,172	0	0	38	148	39	2,075	2,068	459
GEO C WALLACE ST CC-HNCV	PUB-T	11,520	11,137	9	0	21	80	29	1,700	1,676	192
GEO C WALLACE ST CC-SELMA	PUB-T	21,836	19,803	0	0	86	0	0	1,619	1,300	0
HUNTINGDON COLLEGE	PRI-FN	96,956	90,850	0	0	95	0	0	1,944	1,900	428
JACKSONVL ST UNIVERSITY	PUB-FG	364,844	297,300	0	31,413	228	561,426	3,240	20,859	17,311	1,719
JEFFERSON DAVIS STATE JC	PUB-T	29,755	28,575	0	0	49	0	36	1,528	1,514	327
JEFFERSON ST JR COLLEGE	PUB-T	48,377	47,000	12,683	0	1,532	0	0	1,692	A	355
JOHN C CALHOUN ST, CC	PUB-T	34,391	26,082	0	154	50	535	420	1,452	1,029	350
JUDSON COLLEGE	PRI-FN	52,878	51,878	0	0	79	1,241	0	1,227	1,200	320
LAWSON STATE CMTY COLLEGE	PUB-T	39,550	39,460	3,852	0	95	395	310	550	460	325
LIVINGSTON UNIVERSITY	PUB-FG	111,112	94,601	2,100	25,000	4,351	267,218	4,466	6,276	5,472	728
LOMAX-HANNON JC	PRI-T	11,199	10,574	60	0	0	0	156	85	A	4
LURLEEN B WALLACE ST JC	PUB-T	22,085	20,426	0	0	9	462	1,867	1,889	1,631	192
MARION MILITARY INSTITUTE	PRI-T	26,773	22,569	0	0	0	0	483	389	350	113
MILES COLLEGE	PRI-FN	78,380	77,387	0	18	16	2,537	39	1,097	827	471
MOBILE COLLEGE	PRI-FN	61,152	45,000	0	843	14	0	550	4,297	4,200	353
NTHEST ALA ST JR COLLEGE	PUB-FN	38,113	34,957	0	500	73	1,526	0	1,418	1,218	267
NTHWST ALA ST JR COLLEGE	PUB-T	34,732	31,238	0	7	76	672	61	1,192	1,073	290
OAKWOOD COLLEGE	PRI-FN	81,944	78,500	650	90	90	500	125	2,500	2,350	460
PATRICK HENRY STATE JC	PUB-T	27,011	26,020	0	0	400	0	0	1,016	991	99
S D BISHOP ST JR COLLEGE	PUB-T	29,723	24,534	50	11	36	2,568	416	1,513	1,157	236
SAMFORD UNIVERSITY	PRI-FG	252,570	111,025	90,190	26,920	160	137,949	3,706	14,680	4,892	2,615
SELMA UNIVERSITY	PRI-FN	14,985	13,161	169	20,000	0	0	257	65	326	0
SNEAD STATE JR COLLEGE	PUB-T	35,057	32,257	0	0	34	0	1,955	1,967	1,900	287
STHESTN BIBLE COLLEGE	PRI-FG	25,589	A	0	0	0	0	2,242	892	A	159
SOUTHERN JC OF BUSINESS	PRI-T	A	A					A	A	A	A
STHN UNION ST JR COLLEGE	PUB-T	57,258	56,858	0	859	20	0	0	2,097	1,697	340
STHN VOCATIONAL COLLEGE	PRI-T	A	A						A	A	A
SPRING HILL COLLEGE	PRI-FN	152,500	120,000	80,500	14	71	966	0	3,500	2,500	425
STILLMAN COLLEGE	PRI-FN	74,480	56,560	0	16	286	2,992	400	1,371	1,228	331
TALLADEGA COLLEGE	PRI-FN	68,321	66,450	0	12	2	2,369	186	1,001	929	427
TROY STATE U ALL CAM											
TROY STATE U MAIN CAMPUS	PUB-FG	181,586	150,641	38,186	20,049	277	289,457	13,860	7,606	5,841	2,391
TROY ST U DOTHN-FT RUCKER	PUB-FG	20,424	18,365	241	1,166	325	14,040	94	2,503	2,229	509
TROY STATE U MONTGOMERY	PUB-FG	9,852	7,328	351	0	64	7,286	2,565	1,565	1,281	284
TUSKEGEE INSTITUTE	PRI-FG	234,849	169,437	15,000	0	118	68,152	0	5,266	3,242	1,064
U OF ALABAMA ALL INST											
UNIVERSITY OF ALABAMA	PUB-U	1,051,974	352,000	488,700	10,708	0	683,287	0	32,277	A	12,044
U ALABAMA IN BIRMINGHAM	PUB-FG	619,947	329,742	29,154	0	8	605,765	0	45,012	38,380	4,773
U ALABAMA IN HUNTSVILLE	PUB-FG	248,080	224,580	86,730	5,303	135	130,401	181	14,463	12,774	2,459
UNIVERSITY OF MONTEVALLO	PUB-FG	149,411	145,000	0	0	0	238,566	6,035	4,290	4,200	1,437
U OF NORTH ALABAMA	PUB-FG	153,887	128,620	9,307	38	111	178,930	0	7,298	4,997	1,073
U OF SOUTH ALABAMA	PUB-FG	260,734	176,937	378,837	42,000	488	307,487	91,020	14,294	10,404	2,095
WALKER COLLEGE	PRI-T	19,463	19,108	0	0	0	0	92	533	420	189
ALASKA											
ALASKA BIBLE COLLEGE	PRI-FN	16,221	A	0	76	0	0	0	711	A	101

SEE FOOTNOTES AT END OF TABLE

Preceding page blank

Table 1. — Collections in College and University Libraries, by State or Other Area and Institution: Aggregate United States, 1978-79, and Fall 1979 — Continued

STATE OR OTHER AREA AND INSTITUTION	CONTROL AND TYPE OF INSTITUTION	HELD AT END OF YEAR							ADDED DURING YEAR		CURRENT PERIODICAL SUBSCRIPTION TITLES FALL 1979
		BOOKSTOCK		SEPARATE GOVERNMENT DOCUMENTS COLLECTIONS (VOLS.)	MICROFORMS			ALL OTHER LIBRARY MATERIALS	BOOKSTOCK		
		VOLUMES	TITLES		BOOK TITLES	PERIODICAL TITLES	OTHER PHYSICAL UNITS		VOLUMES	TITLES	
(1)	(2)	(3)	(4)	(5)	(6)	(7)	(8)	(9)	(10)	(11)	(12)
ALASKA	--CONTINUED										
ALASKA PACIFIC UNIVERSITY	PRI FG	SEE U ALASKA ANCHORAGE JT LIB									
INUPIAT U OF THE ARCTIC	PRI-FN	NO LIBRARY FACILITIES									
SHELDON JACKSON COLLEGE	PRI FN	SEE STRATTON JOINT LIBRARY									
STRATTON JOINT LIBRARY	PUB-T	51,566	47,800	354	1,528	24	661	503	976	976	378
U ALASKA ALL INSTITUTION											
U ALAS FAIRBANKS ALL CAM											
U ALASKA FAIRBANKS CAMPUS	PUB-U	436,547		A	107,079	286,902	0	82,976	13,242	A	3,052
U OF ALASKA TANANA VLY CC	PUB-T	NO LIBRARY FACILITIES									
U ALAS ANCHORAGE ALL CAM											
U ALAS ANCHORAGE CAMPUS	PUB FG	SEE U ALASKA ANCHORAGE JT LIB									
U OF ALASKA ANCHORAGE CC	PUB T	12,385	9,800	0	0	272	0	514	1,986	1,840	200
U OF ALASKA KENAI CC	PUB-T			0	0	65	1,600	248	2,382	A	152
U OF ALASKA KODIAK CC	PUB-T	8,296	8,157	338	0	0	0	2,653	2,771	2,771	175
U OF ALASKA KUSKOKWIM CC	PUB-T	10,156	10,000	4,595	13	0	17	2,900	1,329	1,329	147
U ALAS MATANUSKA-SUSITNA	PUB-T	11,225	11,225	350							
U ALASKA STHESTN ALL CAM											
U ALAS STHESTN SENIOR C	PUB FG	SEE U ALASKA JUNEAU JT LIB									
U OF ALAS JUNEAU-DGLS	PUB T	SEE U ALASKA JUNEAU JT LIB									
U OF ALASKA KETCHIKAN CC	PUB-T	26,081		0	668	10	13	14	2,050	0	106
U OF ALASKA SITKA CC	PUB T	SEE STRATTON JOINT LIBRARY									
U ALASKA ANCHORAGE JT LIB	PUB-FG	204,436		90,946	37	0	174,827	0	16,949	A	3,127
U OF ALASKA JUNEAU JT LIB	PUB-FG	33,199	31,351	5,205	51	259	195,074	125	2,792	2,638	1,221
ARIZONA											
AMER GRAD SCH OF MGMT	PRI-FG	69,601	53,589	0	20	1,436	0	0	3,844	2,833	0
ARIZONA C OF THE BIBLE	PRI-FN	12,586	10,811	0	0	0	0	0	444	444	0
ARIZONA STATE UNIVERSITY	PUB-U	1,537,019	A	A	0	12	1,016,317	88,515	92,941	A	18,132
ARIZONA WESTERN COLLEGE	PUB-T	35,044	34,010	200	45	33	9,243	1,361	754	720	460
CENTRAL ARIZONA COLLEGE	PUB-T	71,582	70,720	16,038	973	33,147	3,280	0	6,964	6,345	693
COCHISE COLLEGE	PUB-T	47,858	39,825	0	28	47	2,886	0	2,053	1,642	229
COLLEGE OF GANADO	PRI-T	15,022	12,692	103	0	2	0	A	A	A	A
DEVRY INST OF TECHNOLOGY	PRI-FN	A	A		0	51	8,465	315	5,025	4,785	383
EASTERN ARIZONA COLLEGE	PUB-T	39,056	37,095	0	0	37	2,090	0	40,043	35,000	710
GRAND CANYON COLLEGE	PRI-FN	116,948	110,000	3,090	5	37	2,090				
MRICPA CO CC SYS ALL INST											
GLENDALE CMTY COLLEGE	PUB-T	65,714	59,683	0	0	433	6,077	702	2,794	1,321	691
MARICOPA TECH CC	PUB-T	40,000	30,000	0	0	132	15	500	3,000	2,000	380
MESA COMMUNITY COLLEGE	PUB-T	49,274	43,186	0	276	270	36	0	2,083	A	546
PHOENIX COLLEGE	PUB-T	93,421	65,708	0	0	139	11	410	3,010	2,009	570
SCOTTSDALE CMTY COLLEGE	PUB-T	31,612	29,983	0	0	213	426	1,504	1,836	1,808	491
MOHAVE COMMUNITY COLLEGE	PUB-T	19,139	17,434	0	0	84	0	340	3,550	2,775	296
NAVAJO COMMUNITY COLLEGE	PUB-T	A	A	A	A	A	A	A	A	A	A
NORTHERN ARIZ UNIVERSITY	PUB-FG	483,137	434,823	209,584	392,075	853	9,903	19,771	29,543	27,389	4,718
NORTHLAND PIONEER COLLEGE	PUB-T	14,000	12,000	0	50	60	4,000	300	4,500	2,500	80
PIMA COMMUNITY COLLEGE	PUB-T	97,000	80,800	0	600	585	202,000	2,400	12,825	10,700	1,280
PRESCOTT CENTER COLLEGE	PRI-FN	4,165	4,100	0	0	0	0	50	1,687	1,680	5
STHWSTN BAPT BIBLE C	PRI-FN	16,381	15,827	0	400	0	0	244	831	635	55
UNIVERSITY OF ARIZONA	PUB-U	1,411,264	837,444	795,317	101,255	4,260	1,266,012	187,026	100,355	56,430	15,011
UNIVERSITY OF PHOENIX	PRI-FG	A	A	A	A	A	A	A	A	A	A
YAVAPAI COLLEGE	PUB-T	39,837	33,042	8,922.	3	142	9,753	110	4,956	4,410	562
ARKANSAS											
AMERICAN C OF COMMERCE	PRI-T	A	A					A	A	A	A
ARKANSAS BAPTIST COLLEGE	PRI-FN	A	A	0	300	42	0	1,000	2,012	A	450
ARKANSAS COLLEGE	PRI-FN	64,242	A								
ARKANSAS STATE U ALL CAM											
ARKANSAS STATE U MAIN CAM	PUB-FG	351,559	309,374	160,587	185,142	531	144,226	438	14,005	10,997	1,823
ARKANSAS STATE U BEEBE BR	PUB-T	35,511	35,211	0	12,474	79	10,548	2,674	2,672	2,372	265
ARKANSAS TECH UNIVERSITY	PUB-FG	146,577	131,919	0	0	0	302,987	0	7,394	6,654	927
CAPITAL CITY BUS COLLEGE	PRI-T	5,926	5,814	0	0	0	0	0	612	504	23

SEE FOOTNOTES AT END OF TABLE

Table 1. – Collections in College and University Libraries, by State or Other Area and Institution: Aggregate United States, 1978-79, and Fall 1979 – Continued

STATE OR OTHER AREA AND INSTITUTION	CON- TROL AND TYPE OF IN- STITU- TION	HELD AT END OF YEAR							ADDED DURING YEAR		CURRENT PERIOD- ICAL SUB- SCRIPTION TITLES FALL 1979
		BOOKSTOCK		SEPARATE GOVERN- MENT DOCU- MENTS COLLEC- TIONS (VOLS.)	MICROFORMS			ALL OTHER LIBRARY MATE- RIALS	BOOKSTOCK		
		VOLUMES	TITLES		BOOK TITLES	PERI- ODICAL TITLES	OTHER PHYS- ICAL UNITS		VOLUMES	TITLES	
(1)	(2)	(3)	(4)	(5)	(6)	(7)	(8)	(9)	(10)	(11)	(12)
ARKANSAS --CONTINUED											
CENTRAL BAPTIST COLLEGE	PRI-FN	19,081	15,445	0	6	1	0	59	1,483	1,377	159
COLLEGE OF THE OZARKS	PRI-FN	68,399	46,332	29,344	0	83	5	500	1,820	1,750	A
CROWLEY'S RIDGE COLLEGE	PRI-T	11,950	11,940	0	0	0	0	0	40	30	55
EAST ARK CMTY COLLEGE	PUB-T	7,170	6,100	0	0	82	0	0	668	A	253
GARLAND CO CMTY COLLEGE	PUB-T	13,639	9,008	0	1	318	6,914	0	1,505	1,316	303
HARDING U ALL CAM											
HARDING U MAIN CAM	PRI-FG	147,801	90,316	9,080	12,204	331	16,828	0	5,414	3,247	1,179
HARDING GRAD SCH RELIGION	PRI-FG	58,438	46,438	0	452	117	314	0	2,542	2,442	506
HENDERSON ST UNIVERSITY	PUB-FG	154,860	154,860	0	19,871	1,000	17,651	5,548	5,169	5,169	1,566
HENDRIX COLLEGE	PRI-FN	126,737	89,621	14,686	0	45	1,482	1,186	4,678	3,451	467
JOHN BROWN UNIVERSITY	PRI-FN	69,263	68,000	0	575	3,836	4,411	236	2,705	2,200	393
MISS CO CMTY COLLEGE	PUB-T	7,057	7,000	0	0	200	1,000	142	1,253	1,203	250
NORTH ARKANSAS CC	PUB-T	9,947	9,947	0	0	1,912	0	0	2,297	2,297	200
OUACHITA BAPT UNIVERSITY	PRI-FG	106,604	65,000	40,952	243,847	300	0	0	2,541	2,500	630
PHILANDER SMITH COLLEGE	PRI-FN	60,089	60,089	0	2,092	2,092	0	0	4,209	3,219	300
PHILLIPS CO CMTY COLLEGE	PUB-T	29,219	23,700	0	0	91	2,455	0	1,270	1,100	342
SHORTER COLLEGE	PRI-T	A	A					A	A	A	A
STHN ARK U ALL CAMPUSES											
STHN ARK U MAIN CAMPUS	PUB-FG	102,106	101,042	10,432	95	544	196,358	4,259	4,108	78	1,008
STHN ARK U EL DORADO BR	PUB-T	4,112	4,067	0	3	41	0	162	2,014	1,924	257
STHN ARK U STHWST TECH	PUB-T	11,200	9,208	0	0	0	0	0	1,050	1,050	175
SOUTHERN BAPTIST COLLEGE	PRI-T	47,498	35,624	2,999	36	77	1,615	48	2,142	1,714	286
U OF ARKANSAS ALL CAM											
U OF ARKANSAS MAIN CAMPUS	PUB-U	877,866	702,293	398,515	39,862	1,947	392,784	42,967	36,711	27,533	9,742
U OF ARK AT LITTLE ROCK	PUB-FG	302,789	179,721	25,285	13,026	383	236,898	3,013	22,497	10,988	4,275
U OF ARK MEDL SCI CAMPUS	PUB-FG	116,127	34,407	0	0	63	0	2	4,530	2,446	2,408
U OF ARKANSAS-MONTICELLO	PUB-FN	75,045	48,108	65,000	3	160	3,295	0	5,591	4,875	768
U OF ARKANSAS PINE BLUFF	PUB-FN	120,369	60,134	8,000	27,849	198	0	1,400	5,729	2,868	1,047
U OF CENTRAL ARKANSAS	PUB-FG	277,078	213,700	16,922	6,087	865	575,272	792	17,468	12,371	2,577
WESTARK COMMUNITY COLLEGE	PUB-T	36,942	35,882	0	0	56	3,065	50	1,234	1,060	370
CALIFORNIA											
ALLAN HANCOCK COLLEGE	PUB-T	45,158	43,658	0	0	754	5	53	1,489	1,442	342
AMER ACAD DRAMATIC ARTS-W	PRI-T	707	451	0	0	0	0	567	242	175	12
AMER BAPT SEM OF WEST	PRI FG	SEE GRAD THEOL UN JT LIB									
AMERICAN CONSV THEATRE	PRI-FG	A	A						A	A	A
ANTELOPE VALLEY COLLEGE	PUB-T	39,951	37,000	0	0	25	615	226	1,258	1,258	247
ARMSTRONG COLLEGE	PRI-FG	17,072	10,700	0	0	2	102	0	642	610	186
ART CTR COLLEGE OF DESIGN	PRI-FG	19,830	19,063	0	0	0	0	5,000	1,805	1,738	272
AZUSA PACIFIC COLLEGE	PRI-FG	80,704	78,246	0	191,356	124	0	0	2,961	2,924	520
BAKERSFIELD COLLEGE	PUB-T	61,445	48,518	0	0	122	0	0	3,226	2,762	411
BARSTOW COLLEGE	PUB-T	30,683	30,013	0	0	39	629	0	1,363	1,355	210
BETHANY BIBLE COLLEGE	PRI-FN	45,718	35,250	0	1	75	0	0	1,682	1,300	304
BIOLA COLLEGE	PRI-FG	165,895	157,500	0	483	149	8,569	42	8,071	7,500	1,076
BROOKS COLLEGE	PRI-T	1,500	1,450	0	0	0	0	0	0	0	25
BROOKS INSTITUTE	PRI-FG	3,954	3,260	80	0	0	0	2,500	500	425	105
BUTTE COLLEGE	PUB-T	48,083	42,457	0	0	283	4,024	236	2,083	A	463
CABRILLO COLLEGE	PUB-T	50,121	50,000	0	1,206	75	1,200	350	2,355	2,300	439
CAL BAPTIST COLLEGE	PRI-FN	114,787	113,975	0	700	214	3	132	1,012	1,000	358
CALIFORNIA CHRISTIAN C	PRI-FN	8,975	8,050	0	0	0	0	0	447	410	23
CAL COLLEGE ARTS & CRAFTS	PRI-FG	A	A	A		A		A	A	A	A
CAL COLLEGE PODIATRIC MED	PRI-FG	13,641	8,000	0	0	0	5	1	1,417	435	348
CALIFORNIA INST OF ARTS	PRI-FG	68,649	52,525	0	0	6,808	5,353	0	2,823	1,996	578
CAL INST OF ASIAN STUDIES	PRI-FG	19,000	18,500	0	0	0	0	0	1,000	750	100
CAL INST OF TECHNOLOGY	PRI-FG	338,151	A	171,754	23,296	7,890	57,285	0	11,090	A	5,336
CAL LUTHERAN COLLEGE	PRI-FG	90,714	76,845	55,745	13	139	5,787	335	3,565	3,145	800
CALIFORNIA MARITIME ACAD	PUB-FN	18,333	15,600	0	0	130	13,020	50	376	342	370
CAL SCH PROF PSYC ALL CAM											
CAL SCH PSYC BERKELEY	PRI-FG	15,000	10,000	0	8	0	0	80	1,009	609	210
CAL SCH PROF PSYC FRESNO	PRI-FG	6,350	5,080	0	0	0	528	0	620	496	145
CAL SCH PROF PSYC LOS ANG	PRI-FG	9,846	9,600	530	1	9	10	0	936	906	121

SEE FOOTNOTES AT END OF TABLE

Table 1. — Collections in College and University Libraries, by State or Other Area and Institution: Aggregate United States, 1978-79, and Fall 1979 — Continued

STATE OR OTHER AREA AND INSTITUTION (1)	CONTROL AND TYPE OF INSTITUTION (2)	HELD AT END OF YEAR — BOOKSTOCK VOLUMES (3)	BOOKSTOCK TITLES (4)	SEPARATE GOVERNMENT DOCUMENTS COLLECTIONS (VOLS.) (5)	MICROFORMS BOOK TITLES (6)	MICROFORMS PERIODICAL TITLES (7)	OTHER PHYSICAL UNITS (8)	ALL OTHER LIBRARY MATERIALS (9)	ADDED DURING YEAR — BOOKSTOCK VOLUMES (10)	BOOKSTOCK TITLES (11)	CURRENT PERIODICAL SUBSCRIPTION TITLES FALL 1979 (12)
CALIFORNIA --CONTINUED											
CAL SCH PROF PSYC SN DEGO	PRI-FG	8,083	7,415	0	4	23	0	1	968	888	148
CAL ST U & C SYS ALL INST								263	16,054	12,843	2,439
CAL ST COLLEGE-BAKERSFLD	PUB-FG	196,332	157,066	57,047	8,913	1,274	208,579	43,676	21,058	16,846	1,735
CAL STATE C-SN BERNARDINO	PUB-FG	301,915	241,532	0	159	461	159,000	2,500	12,820	10,776	2,464
CAL ST COLLEGE-STANISLAUS	PUB-FG	193,240	173,916	85,000	0	0	330,742				
CAL POLY ST U-SN LUIS OB	PUB-FG	549,954	460,000	353,339	80,400	3,501	406,872	23,495	26,943	24,800	3,330
CAL STATE POLY U-POMONA	PUB-FG	342,095	223,719	0	31	1,340	720,632	86,924	24,682	22,214	4,201
CAL STATE U-CHICO	PUB-FG	551,794	496,615	229,025	10,845	949	425,762	67,765	17,697	14,900	2,038
CAL STATE U-DOMINGUEZ HLS	PUB-FG	230,440	194,500	38,733	183,600	877		344	24,947	16,683	3,602
CAL STATE U-FRESNO	PUB-FG	576,595	370,401	227,135	0	0	603,114	215,223	19,020	14,571	2,439
CAL STATE U-FULLERTON	PUB-FG	487,910	345,756	275,199	0	0	449,236	91,861	19,955	14,303	4,711
CAL STATE U-HAYWARD	PUB-FG	666,981	436,432	0	0	0	347,042	14,036	26,340	17,382	21
CAL STATE U-LONG BEACH	PUB-FG	718,578	A	150,726	669,826	0	0	51,894	40,360	A	5,245
CAL STATE U-LOS ANGELES	PUB-FG	750,788	500,475	203,571	0	0	213,656	260,188	22,404	14,935	4,654
CAL STATE U-NORTHRIDGE	PUB-FG	691,394	446,998	258,042	18,192	3,488	1,437,395	44,731	30,154	21,027	3,846
CAL STATE U-SACRAMENTO	PUB-FG	635,252	457,381	0	36,022	1,376	754,540	15,216	30,899	22,247	4,321
HUMBOLDT STATE U	PUB-FG	256,384	204,872	243,031	311,002	192	0	12,206	17,565	15,331	2,187
SAN DIEGO STATE U	PUB-FG	755,775	603,290	328,469	128,880	4,713	1,093,818	230	32,099	29,600	8,270
SAN FRANCISCO STATE U	PUB-FG	558,732	356,255	348,685	14,130	595	398,680	77,485	25,410	18,467	3,675
SAN JOSE STATE U	PUB-FG	695,736	494,946	156,504	0	2,067	652,259	59,984	32,937	27,020	5,502
SONOMA STATE UNIVERSITY	PUB-FG	287,121	229,697	46,117	272,393	637	259,206	24,470	17,448	13,958	3,117
CAL WESTERN SCHOOL OF LAW	PRI-FG	68,154	9,291	0	8,361	34	1,411	0	1,938	1,844	1,057
CENTER FOR EARLY ED	PRI-FG	11,102	9,615	0	0	147	5,632	217	1,716	1,622	86
CERRITOS COLLEGE	PUB-T	67,495	59,396	0	0	31	0	4,952	3,152	2,774	409
CERRO COSO CMTY COLLEGE	PUB-T	15,990	14,605	628	0	0	0	0	838	781	179
CHABOT COLLEGE	PUB-T	109,015	107,488	2,793	17	614	14,850	20,232	5,376	5,301	631
CHAFFEY COLLEGE	PUB-T	66,984	57,881	0	122	71	6,343	696	2,503	2,254	386
CHAPMAN COLLEGE	PRI-FG	149,753	133,263	2,453	40	82	183	0	3,902	3,785	966
CHRIST COLLEGE IRVINE	PRI-FN	54,200	47,600	0	8	24	2,250	3,500	11,100	10,800	349
CHRISTIAN HERITAGE C	PRI-FN	35,591	32,032	0	227	0	0	110	9,440	8,596	198
CHURCH DIV SCH OF PACIFIC	PRI FG	SEE GRAD THEOL UN JT LIB									
CITRUS COLLEGE	PUB-T	76,162	70,576	3,950	25	403	395	14,804	1,804	1,703	470
CLAREMONT U SYS ALL INST	PRI FG										
CLAREMONT GRADUATE SCHOOL	PRI FG	SEE HONNOLD JOINT LIBRARY									
CLAREMONT MEN'S COLLEGE	PRI FN	SEE HONNOLD JOINT LIBRARY									
HARVEY MUDD COLLEGE	PRI FG	SEE HONNOLD JOINT LIBRARY									
PITZER COLLEGE	PRI FN	SEE HONNOLD JOINT LIBRARY									
POMONA COLLEGE	PRI FN	SEE HONNOLD JOINT LIBRARY									
SCRIPPS COLLEGE	PRI FN	SEE HONNOLD JOINT LIBRARY									
COAST CC SYS ALL INST											
COASTLINE CMTY COLLEGE[1]	PUB-T	NO LIBRARY FACILITIES									
GOLDEN WEST COLLEGE	PUB-T	86,700	80,632	0	0	134	1,910	4,163	5,042	4,354	704
ORANGE COAST COLLEGE	PUB-T	92,306	80,208	0	0	140	0	8,319	4,073	3,637	702
COGSWELL COLLEGE	PRI-FN	9,400	8,850	200	0	0	10	50	1,100	1,050	325
COLEMAN COLLEGE	PRI-FN	3,669	3,568	0	0	0	0	5	430	405	24
COLLEGE OF THE CANYONS	PUB-T	35,561	35,205	0	180	92	46,249	572	2,200	2,178	242
COLLEGE OF THE DESERT	PUB-T	46,367	A	0		202	5,928	288	1,066	A	379
COLLEGE OF MARIN	PUB-T	74,681	58,000	0	1	155	82	300	2,511	2,400	499
COLLEGE OF NOTRE DAME	PRI-FG	88,516	A	0	7	69	2,883	0	2,607	A	572
COLLEGE OSTEO MED PACIFIC	PRI-FG	1,800	1,500	0	0	0	0	0	1,200	1,000	211
COLLEGE OF THE REDWOODS	PUB-T	58,051	43,640	0	26	224	4,032	100	4,000	3,500	390
COLLEGE OF THE SEQUOIAS	PUB-T	70,598	59,302	1,899	3,542	35	1,677	122	2,102	2,039	540
COLLEGE OF THE SISKIYOUS	PUB-T	28,895	27,221	0	0	8	930	0	1,067	1,030	186
COLUMBIA COLLEGE	PUB-T	28,204	24,868	0	6	187	0	300	2,813	2,690	305
COMPTON CMTY COLLEGE	PUB-T	A	A	A	A	A	A	A	A	A	A
CNTR CSTA CC ALL INST											
CONTRA COSTA COLLEGE	PUB-T	58,038	57,500	18,174	0	78	15,503	3,031	1,837	1,800	427
DIABLO VALLEY COLLEGE	PUB-T	73,353	62,350	0	733	197	0	5,764	3,829	3,638	477
LOS MEDANOS COLLEGE	PUB-T	10,711	8,679	0	0	30	1,371	63	520	343	307
CRAFTON HILLS COLLEGE	PUB-T	66,686	54,000	0	0	14	565	1,513	5,762	5,000	463
CUESTA COLLEGE	PUB-T	33,211	29,868	0	0	54	0	2	1,539	1,192	358

SEE FOOTNOTES AT END OF TABLE

Table 1. — Collections in College and University Libraries, by State or Other Area and Institution: Aggregate United States, 1978-79, and Fall 1979 — Continued

STATE OR OTHER AREA AND INSTITUTION	CON-TROL AND TYPE OF IN-STITU-TION	HELD AT END OF YEAR							ADDED DURING YEAR		CURRENT PERIOD-ICAL SUB-SCRIPTION TITLES FALL 1979
		BOOKSTOCK		SEPARATE GOVERN-MENT DOCU-MENTS COLLEC-TIONS (VOLS.)	MICROFORMS			ALL OTHER LIBRARY MATE-RIALS	BOOKSTOCK		
		VOLUMES	TITLES		BOOK TITLES	PERI-ODICAL TITLES	OTHER PHYS-ICAL UNITS		VOLUMES	TITLES	
(1)	(2)	(3)	(4)	(5)	(6)	(7)	(8)	(9)	(10)	(11)	(12)
CALIFORNIA	--CONTINUED										
CYPRESS COLLEGE	PUB-T	55,895	49,000	0	0	189	3,991	6,400	1,207	1,150	447
D-Q UNIVERSITY	PRI-T	A	A						A	A	A
DEEP SPRINGS COLLEGE	PRI-T	18,000	16,000	0	0	0	0	0	500	450	15
DOMINICAN C OF SAN RAFAEL	PRI-FG	78,374	57,422	0	18	116	1,517	0	1,685	1,170	392
DOMINICAN SCH PHIL & THEO	PRI FG	SEE GRAD THEOL UN JT LIB									
DON BOSCO TECHNICAL INST	PRI-T	16,259	16,136	0	0	0	0	2,135	609	542	150
EL CAMINO COLLEGE	PUB-T	95,662	88,575	0	0	272	0	0	2,010	1,709	769
FASH INST DESIGN & MERCH	PRI-T	A	A								
FIELDING INSTITUTE	PRI-FG	NO LIBRARY FACILITIES									
FOOTHL-DEANZA CC ALL INST											
DE ANZA COLLEGE	PUB-T	73,383	56,150	245	32	212	3,957	8,110	3,651	2,811	594
FOOTHILL COLLEGE	PUB-T	101,878	85,729	0	17	234	2,410	489	3,888	2,826	492
FRANCISCAN SCH THEOLOGY	PRI FG	SEE GRAD THEOL UN JT LIB									
FRESNO PACIFIC COLLEGE	PRI FG	SEE MENNONITE-PACIFIC JT LIB									
FULLER THEOLOGICAL SEM	PRI-FG	112,500	101,000	0	825	50	1,300	0	6,500	6,000	650
FULLERTON COLLEGE	PUB-T	91,833	76,221	0	569	179	142,881	16,332	1,831	1,519	394
GAVILAN COLLEGE	PUB-T	40,900	38,400	0	0	164	0	30	2,400	2,256	404
GLENDALE CMTY COLLEGE	PUB-T	64,451	56,451	2,232	0	115	0	126	4,766	2,266	358
GOLDEN GATE BAPT SEMINARY	PRI-FG	A	A		A	A	A	A	A	A	A
GOLDEN GATE UNIVERSITY	PRI-FG	100,093	90,000	0	635	375	106,908	19,439	5,137	4,500	2,498
GRADUATE THEOL UNION	PRI FG	SEE GRAD THEOL UN JT LIB									
GRAD THEOL UN JT LIBRARY	PRI-FG	531,472	385,962	0	50,684	255	0	25	7,375	6,242	2,084
GROSSMONT COLLEGE	PUB-T	88,118	A	0	87	206	8,045	6,263	4,033	A	780
HARTNELL COLLEGE	PUB-T	66,688	55,200	0	5,700	33	3,811	300	3,003	1,820	546
HEALD ENGR COLLEGE	PRI-FN	A	A		A	A	A	A	A	A	A
HOLY FAMILY COLLEGE	PRI-FN	36,818	27,641	0	8	0	0	382	4,131	2,668	132
HOLY NAMES COLLEGE	PRI-FG	87,629	75,443	0	27	124	0	393	2,033	1,989	533
HONNOLD JOINT LIBRARY	PRI-FG	805,687	A	179,801	614,235	0	0	0	25,364	A	6,453
HUMANISTIC PSYC INST	PRI-FG	A	A					A	A	A	A
HUMPHREYS COLLEGE	PRI-T	14,907	13,772	163	0	7	0	30	395	366	83
IMMACULATE HEART COLLEGE	PRI-FG	147,645	114,289	0	510	62	0	200	1,169	1,109	503
IMPERIAL VALLEY COLLEGE	PUB-T	44,560	39,709	0	143	521	4,392	0	4,326	4,205	523
INDIAN VALLEY COLLEGES	PUB-T	31,596	27,000	0	0	183	0	45	1,593	1,200	316
INTERNATIONAL COLLEGE	PRI-FG	NO LIBRARY FACILITIES									
JESUIT SCHOOL OF THEOLOGY	PRI FG	SEE GRAD THEOL UN JT LIB									
JOHN F KENNEDY UNIVERSITY	PRI-FG	25,388	14,970	0	0	0	3	65	1,907	1,124	261
LAKE TAHOE CMTY COLLEGE	PUB-T	17,556	15,804	0	0	61	576	0	3,034	2,868	288
LASSEN COLLEGE	PUB-T	13,219	12,900	0	0	22	0	0	625	600	230
LIFE BIBLE COLLEGE	PRI-FN	13,751	12,548	0	0	0	0	0	2,401	2,148	62
LINCOLN UNIVERSITY	PRI-FG	32,844	13,684	0	0	49	0	53	1,652	350	88
LOMA LINDA UNIVERSITY	PRI-FG	356,309	A	0	19,074	72	37,887	811	13,571	A	3,179
LONG BEACH CITY COLLEGE	PUB-T	122,933	A	0	41,741	0	0	3,000	6,253	A	540
LOS ANGELES BAPT COLLEGE	PRI-FN	30,270	28,860	0	0	42	0	7	1,414	1,304	387
LOS ANG C OF CHIROPRACTIC	PRI-FG	12,081	9,273	503	0	0	0	15	1,272	1,023	249
LOS ANG CC SYS ALL INST											
EAST LOS ANGELES COLLEGE	PUB-T	76,402	75,000	0	0	2,807	0	0	1,402	A	553
LOS ANGELES CITY COLLEGE	PUB-T	138,750	126,555	0	0	21	3,283	0	4,374	3,918	774
LOS ANG HARBOR COLLEGE	PUB-T	74,622	A	0	0	0	0	0	5,960	A	0
LOS ANGELES MISSION C	PUB-T	25,992	A	0	0	62	2,113	5,511	2,682	A	561
LOS ANG PIERCE COLLEGE	PUB-T	98,676	96,134	4,928	0	196	6,498	322	3,063	3,006	709
LOS ANG SOUTHWEST COLLEGE	PUB-T	62,435	62,416	0	3,054	115	0	30	2,900	2,881	497
LOS ANG TR TECH COLLEGE	PUB-T	88,500	78,250	0	2,550	42	1,850	850	3,200	2,850	700
LOS ANG VALLEY COLLEGE	PUB-T	115,215	105,000	0	599	167	11,343	38,115	4,372	4,000	768
WEST LOS ANGELES COLLEGE	PUB-T	49,196	48,000	0	0	56	0	0	1,451	1,400	383
LOS RIOS CC SYS ALL INST											
AMERICAN RIVER COLLEGE	PUB-T	74,819	A	0	7	420	33,370	30	2,882	A	453
COSUMNES RIVER COLLEGE	PUB-T	61,288	46,500	0	1,749	154	0	151	1,964	1,502	348
SACRAMENTO CITY COLLEGE	PUB-T	84,625	A	0	0	0	0	587	2,035	A	702
LOYOLA MARYMOUNT U	PRI-FG	384,395	191,783	1,000	47,334	244	79,969	500,320	16,517	9,523	6,005
MARYMOUNT PALOS VERDES C	PRI-T	31,871	30,278	0	0	100	12,950	0	1,572	1,493	200
MELODYLAND SCH THEOLOGY	PRI-FG	28,600	23,652	0	400	11	0	2,000	652	652	250

SEE FOOTNOTES AT END OF TABLE

Table 1. – Collections in College and University Libraries, by State or Other Area and Institution: Aggregate United States, 1978-79, and Fall 1979 – Continued

STATE OR OTHER AREA AND INSTITUTION (1)	CON-TROL AND TYPE OF IN-STITU-TION (2)	HELD AT END OF YEAR — BOOKSTOCK VOLUMES (3)	BOOKSTOCK TITLES (4)	SEPARATE GOVERN-MENT DOCU-MENTS COLLEC-TIONS (VOLS.) (5)	MICROFORMS BOOK TITLES (6)	MICROFORMS PERI-ODICAL TITLES (7)	OTHER PHYS-ICAL UNITS (8)	ALL OTHER LIBRARY MATE-RIALS (9)	ADDED DURING YEAR — BOOKSTOCK VOLUMES (10)	BOOKSTOCK TITLES (11)	CURRENT PERIOD-ICAL SUB-SCRIPTION TITLES FALL 1979 (12)
CALIFORNIA	--CONTINUED										
MENDOCINO COLLEGE	PUB-T	14,755	14,313	0	0	28	3,975	60	1,463	1,388	274
MENLO COLLEGE	PRI-FN	43,920	35,000	0	0	0	0	0	1,171	1,122	278
MENNONITE BRTHREN BIB SEM	PRI FG	SEE MENNONITE-PACIFIC FT LIB									
MENNONITE-PACIFIC JT LIB	PRI-FG	66,970	64,500	0	0	15	4,806	0	2,308	2,250	637
MERCED COLLEGE	PUB-T	36,315	33,515	0	0	91	5,173	700	2,809	2,259	426
MILLS COLLEGE	PRI-FG	185,653	111,562	3,000	5,539	94	0	0	4,753	4,022	516
MIRA COSTA COLLEGE	PUB-T	26,590	25,250	0	0	101	5,632	0	2,062	1,950	356
MODESTO JUNIOR COLLEGE	PUB-T	61,000	48,500	0	6	120	0	1,400	1,700	1,400	639
MONTEREY INTRNATL STDIES	PRI-FG	38,888	29,133	0	0	0	196	1,545	2,024	1,567	177
MONTEREY PEN COLLEGE	PUB-T	64,730	64,730	0	2,020	8,571	0	4,745	4,454	4,454	327
MOUNT SNT MARY'S COLLEGE	PRI-FG	129,947	97,460	4,305	128	168	1,552	2	2,445	1,835	619
MOUNT SAN ANTONIO COLLEGE	PUB-T	89,804	71,800	0	0	231	0	175	2,272	1,279	695
MT SAN JACINTO COLLEGE	PUB-T	31,402	30,774	1,927	28	26	1,212	872	1,672	1,639	281
NAPA COLLEGE	PUB-T	43,420	43,420	2,600	0	1	3,725	0	1,050	1,050	356
NATIONAL UNIVERSITY	PRI-FG	9,577	8,776	0	0	22	2,107	5	2,691	2,043	394
NEW COLLEGE OF CALIFORNIA	PRI-FG	15,000	6,700	0	0	0	4,700	22	1,500	700	65
NORTHROP UNIVERSITY	PRI-FG	138,817	122,558	0	28,500	46	2,535	282,725	2,261	1,432	362
NYINGMA INSTITUTE	PRI-FG	A	A						A	A	A
OCCIDENTAL COLLEGE	PRI-FG	329,023	260,000	250,000	1,000	100	40,642	0	10,222	10,000	1,736
OHLONE COLLEGE	PUB-T	48,867	44,000	547	0	64	1,661	150	3,051	300	469
OTIS ART INST PARSON SCH	PRI-FG	A	A	0	0	0	0	0	509	A	211
PACIFIC CHRISTIAN COLLEGE	PRI-FG	41,554	36,000	0	150	6	0	550	1,113	990	239
PACIFIC LUTH THEOL SEM	PRI FG	SEE GRAD THEOL UN JT LIB									
PACIFIC OAKS COLLEGE	PRI-FG	23,800	23,301	0	300	0	1,292	175	1,036	1,025	195
PACIFIC SCH OF RELIGION	PRI FG	SEE GRAD THEOL UN JT LIB									
PACIFIC UNION COLLEGE	PRI-FG	101,285	86,889	0	15,492	26,798	12,903	0	3,498	3,060	765
PALOMAR COLLEGE	PUB-T	125,146	A	2,520	153	196	0	2,557	8,861	A	1,124
PALO VERDE COLLEGE	PUB-T	14,780	14,500	0	0	280	0	1,215	301	291	290
PASADENA CITY COLLEGE	PUB-T	113,680	80,000	0	72	154	4,877	38,000	3,531	2,500	547
PASADENA COLLEGE CHIRO	PRI-FG	5,281	4,500	0	0	0	0	40	900	A	59
PATTEN COLLEGE	PRI-FN	17,509	A	0	0	2	0	96	574	A	200
PEPPERDINE UNIVERSITY[2]	PRI-FG	222,562	170,846	0	26,118	605	64,529	0	11,608	10,003	2,145
PERALTA CC SYS ALL INST											
COLLEGE OF ALAMEDA	PUB-T	37,725	26,427	0	0	142	4,103	0	1,531	1,411	518
FEATHER RIVER COLLEGE	PUB-T	13,424	11,912	0	1	12	157	15	1,636	1,490	58
LANEY COLLEGE	PUB-T	67,885	61,271	0	0	64	4,035	605	2,305	2,005	350
MERRITT COLLEGE	PUB-T	58,811	58,760	251	0	120	1	10,237	1,075	1,025	360
VISTA COLLEGE	PUB-T	A	A	A	A	A	A	A	A	A	A
POINT LOMA COLLEGE	PRI-FG	161,564	81,383	0	0	0	3,152	118	4,723	3,872	669
PORTERVILLE COLLEGE	PUB-T	20,298	20,216	0	1	34	10	15	863	781	257
RAND GRAD INST POL STDIES	PRI-FG	83,794	227,560	0	0	0	0	0	2,470	13,204	1,652
RIO HONDO COLLEGE	PUB-T	74,929	66,230	0	0	64	37,289	145	3,670	2,883	470
RIVERSIDE CITY COLLEGE	PUB-T	73,866	66,480	0	0	167	0	9,000	4,000	3,600	520
SADDLEBACK CMTY COLLEGE	PUB-T	93,000	72,000	0	0	110	1,929	0	5,000	4,860	501
SAINT JOHN'S COLLEGE	PRI-FG	50,501	38,755	500	2	763	0	0	1,500	1,000	175
SNT MARY'S COLLEGE OF CAL	PRI-FG	128,197	123,050	850	2,457	125	4,957	3,050	4,502	4,312	625
SAINT PATRICK'S COLLEGE	PRI-FN	60,000	58,000	0	0	0	0	450	1,700	1,500	190
SAINT PATRICK'S SEMINARY	PRI-FG	56,032	54,382	0	46	5	0	136	616	593	218
SN BERNARDINO VLY COLLEGE	PUB-T	116,502	81,551	0	0	25	4,095	5,831	3,836	3,260	818
SAN DIEGO CC ALL CAMPUSES											
SAN DIEGO CITY COLLEGE	PUB-T	55,904	A	0	0	2,300	2,728	189	3,335	3,704	400
SAN DIEGO EVENING C	PUB-T	NO LIBRARY FACILITIES									
SAN DIEGO MESA COLLEGE	PUB-T	83,318	63,316	0	0	154	0	0	4,676	3,010	805
SAN DIEGO MIRAMAR COLLEGE	PUB-T	3,040	3,010	0	0	25	439	0	592	560	202
SAN FERNANDO VALLEY C LAW	PRI-FG	40,970	7,633	0	10,933	0	14,801	0	1,722	554	202
SAN FRANCISCO ART INST	PRI-FG	22,684	20,200	0	0	0	0	1,200	1,460	1,200	250
SN FRISCO CC DISTRICT	PUB-T	83,862	70,045	2,642	2	137	7,995	1,154	2,066	1,759	540
SAN FRANCISCO CONSV MUSIC	PRI-FG	16,315	15,660	0	0	0	0	400	368	342	56
SAN FRANCISCO THEOL SEM	PRI FG	SEE GRAD THEOL UN JT LIB									
SAN JOAQUIN DELTA COLLEGE	PUB-T	68,283	A	0	0	517	0	3,380	3,149	3,033	731
SAN JOSE BIBLE COLLEGE	PRI-FN	29,149	25,040	0	320	0	0	1,558	857	702	180

SEE FOOTNOTES AT END OF TABLE

Table 1. — Collections in College and University Libraries, by State or Other Area and Institution: Aggregate United States, 1978-79, and Fall 1979 — Continued

STATE OR OTHER AREA AND INSTITUTION	CON- TROL AND TYPE OF IN- STITU- TION	HELD AT END OF YEAR BOOKSTOCK VOLUMES	TITLES	SEPARATE GOVERN- MENT DOCU- MENTS COLLEC- TIONS (VOLS.)	MICROFORMS BOOK TITLES	PERI- ODICAL TITLES	OTHER PHYS- ICAL UNITS	ALL OTHER LIBRARY MATE- RIALS	ADDED DURING YEAR BOOKSTOCK VOLUMES	TITLES	CURRENT PERIOD- ICAL SUB- SCRIPTION TITLES FALL 1979
(1)	(2)	(3)	(4)	(5)	(6)	(7)	(8)	(9)	(10)	(11)	(12)
CALIFORNIA	--CONTINUED										
SAN JOSE CC ALL INST											
EVERGREEN VALLEY COLLEGE	PUB-T	28,878	25,095	0	0	104	2,080	0	2,871	2,903	417
SAN JOSE CITY COLLEGE	PUB-T	67,065	59,879	0	3	102	3,574	6,245	4,107	3,865	632
SAN MATEO CC SYS ALL INST											
CANADA COLLEGE	PUB-T	46,626	45,200		0	4	94	2,382	405	986	792	325
COLLEGE OF SAN MATEO	PUB-T	110,000	100,000	0	0	129	12,000	300	570	475	295
SKYLINE COLLEGE	PUB-T	44,698	33,847	0	6	35	0	5	2,245	1,553	315
SANTA ANA COLLEGE	PUB-T	82,400	80,000	0	0	6	2,208	500	4,045	4,000	686
SANTA BARBARA CTY COLLEGE	PUB-T	78,831	68,550	0	0	0	4,037	327	2,397	A	631
SANTA MONICA COLLEGE	PUB-T	98,067	76,900	0	10,651	10,000	0	200	2,672	2,672	500
SANTA ROSA JUNIOR COLLEGE	PUB-T	83,028	74,573	0	0	305	18,164	951	3,700	3,150	704
SCH OF THEO AT CLAREMONT	PRI-FG	113,883	90,007	0	1,000	15	0	0	3,163	2,871	685
SHASTA COLLEGE	PUB-T	61,114	A	0	4	412	13,685	0	802	A	350
SIERRA COLLEGE	PUB-T	56,474	50,827	0	0	119	3,067	595	2,324	2,092	390
SIMPSON COLLEGE	PRI-FG	48,806	37,659	0	27	7	0	109	888	640	397
SOLANO COMMUNITY COLLEGE	PUB-T	34,000	31,000	55	4	32	1,490	600	800	750	125
SOUTHERN CAL COLLEGE	PRI-FN	58,469	46,628	0	248	228	0	828	1,487	1,381	391
STHN CAL C OF OPTOMETRY	PRI-FG	A	9,699	0	30	3	30	0	A	762	290
STHN CAL INSTITUTE ARCH	PRI-FG	1,544	1,486	2	0	0	0	25	132	130	32
SOUTHWESTERN COLLEGE	PUB-T	58,938	51,545	0	0	63	1,645	34	3,835	3,216	615
STHWSTN U SCHOOL OF LAW	PRI-FG	71,258	12,739	20,845	8,757	0	0	0	5,094	1,062	2,384
STANFORD UNIVERSITY	PRI-U	4,577,827	A	212,801	0	0	1,963,748	29,617,677	89,596	A	0
STARR KNG SCH FOR MINSTRY	PRI FG			SEE GRAD THEOL UN JT LIB							
STATE CTR CC SYS ALL INST											
FRESNO CITY COLLEGE	PUB-T	49,004	48,900	0	0	250	3,412	0	2,156	A	535
REEDLEY COLLEGE	PUB-T	27,881	26,031	0	0	30	9,192	120	580	580	205
TAFT COLLEGE	PUB-T	25,447	23,617	20	0	0	156	0	1,126	1,069	140
US INTERNATIONAL U	PRI-FG	230,126	198,530	0	31,041	338	66,777	235	4,431	4,119	1,034
U CAL SYSW ADMIN ALL CAM											
U OF CAL-BERKELEY	PUB-U	5,439,883	3,885,631	309,424	54,103	4,376	1,211,501	40,969,306	169,857	121,326	94,783
U OF CAL-DAVIS	PUB-FG	1,525,544	686,943	492,287	220,862	334	605,466	579,529	74,421	33,757	19,337
U OF CAL HASTINGS C LAW	PUB-FG	197,393	32,870	36,538	2,748	0	0	87	16,421	1,156	2,487
U OF CAL-IRVINE	PUB-FG	887,213	614,842	254,028	737	325	37,848	21,136	54,315	33,553	11,354
U OF CAL-LOS ANGELES	PUB-U	4,109,146	A	1,362,340	0	0	1,790,737	0	129,752	A	56,316
U OF CAL-RIVERSIDE	PUB-FG	947,698	550,000	288,936	0	0	730,208	64,999	32,748	28,893	17,925
U OF CAL-SAN DIEGO	PUB-FG	A	886,642	213,962	1,750	80	670,090	710,783	A	38,771	25,648
U OF CAL-SAN FRANCISCO	PUB-FG	457,021	211,434	0	43,921	24	0	35	13,998	7,627	3,564
U OF CAL-SANTA BARBARA	PUB-FG	1,325,063	795,000	411,236	627,000	40	1,065,000	270,000	51,922	31,000	18,075
U OF CAL-SANTA CRUZ	PUB-FG	595,042	258,025	48,162	0	0	178,747	107,668	28,069	13,025	9,891
UNIVERSITY OF JUDAISM	PRI-FG	125,000	110,000	0	350	0	0	0	11,000	9,000	450
UNIVERSITY OF LA VERNE	PRI-FG	A	A	0	0	31,124	0	0	16,767	A	1,012
UNIVERSITY OF THE PACIFIC	PRI-U	330,406	239,672	2,000	616	826	277,075	447	11,843	9,369	3,062
UNIVERSITY OF REDLANDS	PRI-FG	256,938	190,017	154,197	0	0	29,503	14,192	6,616	5,462	778
UNIVERSITY OF SAN DIEGO[2/]	PRI-FG	343,929	154,245	5,000	34,946	1,160	9,341	2,089	17,218	12,378	1,760
U OF SAN FRANCISCO	PRI-FG	490,017	282,888	125,194	32,819	242	338,121	0	19,257	10,953	3,994
UNIVERSITY OF SANTA CLARA	PRI-U	359,982	210,573	149,393	14,134	96	373,357	45,000	14,907	9,630	4,056
U OF SOUTHERN CALIFORNIA	PRI-U	1,949,756	988,848	3,113	628,429	578	544,093	17,500	92,379	39,982	26,163
U OF WEST LOS ANGELES	PRI-FG	19,000	1,637	0	8	0	1,761	0	1,600	257	250
VENTURA CO CC SYS INST											
MOORPARK COLLEGE	PUB-T	57,329	55,811	0	0	249	0	0	960	942	286
OXNARD COLLEGE	PUB-T	21,000	21,000	150	0	0	0	50	400	100	205
VENTURA COLLEGE	PUB-T	66,000	48,711	750	0	112	6	0	1,949	1,700	522
VICTOR VALLEY COLLEGE	PUB-T	30,500	25,837	0	0	163	12,200	1,875	1,100	992	735
WEST COAST BIBLE COLLEGE	PRI-FN	22,798	18,548	10	400	1	0	1,538	495	480	0
WEST COAST U ALL CAMPUSES											
WEST COAST U MAIN CAMPUS	PRI-FG	6,548	6,400	0	0	0	0	0	377	377	70
W COAST U ORANGE CO CTR	PRI-FG	2,608	2,550	0	0	0	0	0	52	48	0
WSTN STATES COLLEGE ENGR	PRI-FN	2,038	1,815	0	0	0	0	0	45	35	10
WSTN ST U C LAW ALL CAM											
WSTN ST U C LAW ORANGE CO	PRI-FG	37,150	A	0	0	0	0	0	6,053	A	587
WSTN ST U C LAW SAN DIEGO	PRI-FG	27,221	A	0	0	0	0	5	2,768	A	263

SEE FOOTNOTES AT END OF TABLE

27

STATE OR OTHER AREA AND INSTITUTION	CONTROL AND TYPE OF INSTITUTION	HELD AT END OF YEAR							ADDED DURING YEAR		CURRENT PERIODICAL SUBSCRIPTION TITLES FALL 1979
		BOOKSTOCK		SEPARATE GOVERNMENT DOCUMENTS COLLECTIONS (VOLS.)	MICROFORMS			ALL OTHER LIBRARY MATERIALS	BOOKSTOCK		
		VOLUMES	TITLES		BOOK TITLES	PERIODICAL TITLES	OTHER PHYSICAL UNITS		VOLUMES	TITLES	
(1)	(2)	(3)	(4)	(5)	(6)	(7)	(8)	(9)	(10)	(11)	(12)
CALIFORNIA --CONTINUED											
WEST HILLS COLLEGE	PUB-T	39,880	39,589	10,630	0	3,928	5,620	0	2,870	2,634	620
WESTMONT COLLEGE	PRI-FN	121,227	97,010	0	0	84	8,891	0	4,758	3,820	629
MISSION COLLEGE	PUB-T	A	13,241	0	0	140	0	0	0	0	300
WEST VALLEY COLLEGE	PUB-T	50,000	45,000	0	0	324	1,291	52	2,700	2,600	902
WHITTIER COLLEGE	PRI-FG	188,340	141,017	3,301	5,891	133	92,024	0	12,979	6,359	1,853
WOODBURY UNIVERSITY	PRI-FG	40,611	33,301	0	0	306	2,050	145	7,562	6,448	500
WORLD COLLEGE WEST	PRI-FN	10,000	9,800	0	0	0	0	100	1,000	900	50
THE WRIGHT INSTITUTE	PRI-FG	6,600	3,700	0	0	0	0	0	390	331	22
YESHIVA U OF LOS ANGELES	PRI-FG	A	A					A	A	A	A
YUBA COLLEGE	PUB-T	51,408	A	0	0	54	2	500	2,079	A	310
COLORADO											
ADAMS STATE COLLEGE	PUB-FG	188,766	A	6,006	56,345	113,592	0	761	3,787	2,381	713
AIMS COMMUNITY COLLEGE	PUB-T	31,458	25,107	0	138	110	590	1,243	2,361	1,856	417
ARAPAHOE CMTY COLLEGE	PUB-T	33,078	20,000	0	0	85	2,548	0	1,485	1,350	394
AURARIA JOINT LIBRARY	PUB-FN	340,140	233,521	4,366	4,721	4,965	0	0	29,530	21,386	2,801
BAPT BIBLE C OF DENVER	PRI-FG	24,872	A	0	0	0	0	160	700	A	214
COLORADO COLLEGE	PRI-FG	290,750	185,560	122,478	2	6	0	0	6,843	6,536	1,027
COLO MTN COLLEGE ALL CAM											
COLO MTN COLLEGE EAST CAM	PUB-T	17,731	16,484	202	0	37	0	32	1,554	1,419	204
COLO MTN COLLEGE WEST CAM	PUB-T	27,500	26,800	0	0	11,200	8,500	700	1,910	1,870	173
COLORADO NORTHWESTERN CC	PUB-T	14,013	11,792	0	0	0	1,792	142	1,090	985	223
COLORADO SCHOOL OF MINES	PUB-FG	141,387	59,184	48,751	120	9	76,051	90,000	8,067	3,295	938
COLORADO STATE UNIVERSITY	PUB-U	863,434	348,854	318,595	0	0	488,113	27,459	31,679	21,903	16,854
COLO TECHNICAL COLLEGE	PRI-FN	3,463	2,315	0	0	0	0	84	200	A	30
COLORADO WOMEN'S COLLEGE	PRI-FN	145,012	120,326	0	20	53	3,492	3,100	2,965	2,031	405
CC OF DENVER ALL CAM											
CC OF DENVER AURARIA CAM	PUB T	SEE AURARIA JOINT LIBRARY									
CC OF DENVER NORTH CAMPUS	PUB-T	34,391	28,269	0	0	423	15,664	36	2,965	2,437	472
CC DENVER RED ROCKS CAM	PUB-T	32,954	29,843	1,500	0	88	60,248	0	2,905	2,463	490
CONS BAPTIST THEOL SEM	PRI-FG	59,500	A	0	2,195	20	0	0	4,725	A	442
FORT LEWIS COLLEGE	PUB-FN	128,161	100,884	0	11,954	339	35,432	962	4,693	4,030	917
ILIFF SCHOOL OF THEOLOGY	PRI-FG	104,824	67,848	0	867	104	10,533	114	1,950	1,741	583
INTERMOUNTAIN BIBLE C	PRI-FN	12,000	11,575	0	0	0	0	234	2,039	2,000	53
LAMAR COMMUNITY COLLEGE	PUB-T	21,281	17,999	585	742	74	1,187	39	275	181	179
LORETTO HEIGHTS COLLEGE	PRI-FN	103,000	61,000	0	5	108	0	0	1,709	1,646	642
MESA COLLEGE	PUB-FN	92,994	47,935	4,125	7,119	6	3,655	1,108	4,037	3,362	695
METROPOLITAN ST COLLEGE	PUB FN	SEE AURARIA JOINT LIBRARY									
MORGAN COMMUNITY COLLEGE	PUB-T	10,021	9,970	0	0	0	397	75	2,254	988	76
NAZARENE BIBLE COLLEGE	PRI-T	25,303	21,245	0	1,235	0	0	58	2,723	2,456	201
NORTHEASTERN JR COLLEGE	PUB-T	41,274	A	0	0	6,067	0	97	2,664	A	414
OTERO JUNIOR COLLEGE	PUB-T	A	A					A	A	A	A
PARKS COLLEGE	PRI-T	A	A	0	8,807	300	0	0	2,046	1,483	534
PIKES PEAK CMTY COLLEGE	PUB-T	37,773	A	0	8,807	300	A	A	A	A	A
PUEBLO VOCATIONAL CC	PUB-T	A	A	0	0	87	0	18	1,783	1,010	506
REGIS COLLEGE	PRI-FG	85,945	59,705	34,320	1,280	1	160	0	2,300	2,160	140
ROCKMONT COLLEGE	PRI-FN	26,490	22,544	0	0	230	0	0	4,550	A	434
SAINT THOMAS SEMINARY	PRI-FG	90,300	A	0	1,790	230	0	0	2,730	A	263
TRINIDAD STATE JR COLLEGE	PUB-T	58,641	A	0	7	36	1,135	0			
U OF COLORADO ALL INST	PUB-U	1,811,881	A	0	0	0	1,923,106	112,514	50,250	A	10,990
U OF COLORADO AT BOULDER	PUB-U										
U OF COLO COLO SPRINGS	PUB-FG	122,213	96,054	3,097	5	560	12,065	1,189	11,553	9,569	1,417
U OF COLO AT DENVER	PUB FG	SEE AURARIA JOINT LIBRARY							7,138	3,224	1,635
U OF COLO HLTH SCI CENTER	PUB-FG	156,479	65,706	0	51	0	0	0	31,306	A	9,843
UNIVERSITY OF DENVER	PRI-U	816,054	A	239,990	0	0	398,551	33,000	12,215	A	4,421
U OF NORTHERN COLORADO	PUB-FG	389,562	A	49,065	0	0	490,503	0	4,088	3,900	1,316
U OF SOUTHERN COLORADO	PUB-FG	155,408	126,245	118,573	5,316	155	0	8,062			
WESTERN BIBLE COLLEGE	PRI-FN	19,050	16,386	0	0	0	0	165	725	610	98
WESTERN ST COLLEGE COLO	PUB-FG	127,493	90,000	87,747	820	550	206,566	184	4,443	3,412	1,200
YESH TORAS CHAIM TALMUD	PRI-FG	A	A						A	A	
CONNECTICUT											
ALBERTUS MAGNUS COLLEGE	PRI-FN	83,889	58,620	1,845	1	46	4,124	2,923	2,025	1,920	240

SEE FOOTNOTES AT END OF TABLE

Table 1. — Collections in College and University Libraries, by State or Other Area and Institution: Aggregate United States, 1978-79, and Fall 1979 — Continued

STATE OR OTHER AREA AND INSTITUTION (1)	CON- TROL AND TYPE OF IN- STITU- TION (2)	HELD AT END OF YEAR							ADDED DURING YEAR		CURRENT PERIOD- ICAL SUB- SCRIPTION TITLES FALL 1979 (12)
		BOOKSTOCK		SEPARATE GOVERN- MENT DOCU- MENTS COLLEC- TIONS (VOLS.) (5)	MICROFORMS			ALL OTHER LIBRARY MATE- RIALS (9)	BOOKSTOCK		
		VOLUMES (3)	TITLES (4)		BOOK TITLES (6)	PERI- ODICAL TITLES (7)	OTHER PHYS- ICAL UNITS (8)		VOLUMES (10)	TITLES (11)	
CONNECTICUT	--CONTINUED										
ANNHURST COLLEGE	PRI-FN	45,391	41,000	0	0	11	601	0	3,200	2,500	260
ASNUNTUCK CMTY COLLEGE	PUB-T	20,468	19,620	600	1,500	52	0	78	939	903	0
BAIS BINYOMIN ACADEMY	PRI-FG	A	A							A	A
BOARD STATE ACAD AWARDS	PUB-T			NO LIBRARY FACILITIES							
BRIDGEPORT ENGR INSTITUTE	PRI-FN	10,000	A	0	0	0	0	0	500	A	10
CENTRAL CONN ST COLLEGE	PUB-FG	280,010	252,818	66,476	775	51	59,702	60,964	11,619	7,550	1,685
CONNECTICUT COLLEGE	PRI-FG	342,664	203,820	204,788	96,659	79	0	9	10,303	7,167	1,501
EASTERN CONN ST COLLEGE	PUB-FG	112,754	80,620	600	0	150	236,168	212	6,111	4,304	859
FAIRFIELD UNIVERSITY	PRI-FG	155,743	116,807	0	1,120	829	140,410	60	7,081	5,310	1,367
GREATER HARTFORD CC	PUB-T	37,356	33,579	0	3,222	5,915	0	564	2,437	2,167	300
GREATER NEW HAVEN TECH C1/	PUB-T			NO LIBRARY FACILITIES							
HARTFORD COLLEGE WOMEN	PRI-T	51,120	50,098	0	0	0	0	0	2,307	2,210	106
HARTFORD GRADUATE CENTER	PRI-FG	21,094	20,108	9,413	0	8	14,210	0	554	508	295
HARTFORD SEM FOUNDATION	PRI-FG	A	A		A	A	A	A	A	A	A
HARTFORD ST TECH COLLEGE	PUB-T	8,000	7,500	0	0	0	0	50	50	A	150
HOLY APOSTLES COLLEGE	PRI-FG	31,035	30,182	0	0	33	0	0	2,168	2,115	119
HOUSATONIC REGIONAL CC	PUB-T	29,212	25,955	0	21,455	122	1,537	0	1,030	910	277
MANCHESTER CMTY COLLEGE	PUB-T	39,674	39,000	323	23,237	48	16,816	0	1,097	1,090	228
MATTATUCK CMTY COLLEGE	PUB-T	26,426	22,167	20	313	175	3,900	1	882	846	161
MIDDLESEX CMTY COLLEGE	PUB-T	35,620	30,989	0	2	147	13,168	0	1,564	1,440	201
MITCHELL COLLEGE	PRI-T	45,075	38,226	0	0	12	0	10	1,024	821	136
MOHEGAN COMMUNITY COLLEGE	PUB-T	20,400	18,332	0	0	28	26,927	3,500	942	920	256
MT SACRED HEART COLLEGE	PRI-T	14,208	14,208	0	0	0	0	0	500	500	250
NTHWSTN CONN CMTY COLLEGE	PUB-T	41,736	35,112	315	1	80	1,428	88	2,002	1,684	257
NORWALK COMMUNITY COLLEGE	PUB-T	49,719	A	0	28,000	8	16,040	12,721	1,531	A	227
NORWALK ST TECH COLLEGE	PUB-T	13,570	A	0	0	0	0	50	1,910	A	104
POST COLLEGE	PRI-FN	21,612	20,000	20	0	65	1,770	0	1,900	A	264
QUINEBAUG VALLEY CC	PUB-T	14,532	12,807	5,000	2,681	51	200	0	518	492	145
QUINNIPIAC COLLEGE	PRI-FG	98,631	60,000	0	8,110	393	235	203	4,383	2,860	727
SACRED HEART UNIVERSITY	PRI-FG	112,992	93,754	0	108	7,030	0	110	3,909	2,931	633
SAINT ALPHONSUS COLLEGE	PRI-FN	31,149	A	0	0	0	0	0	A	582	215
SAINT BASIL'S COLLEGE	PRI-FN	17,370	10,385	0	0	0	24	75	865	620	112
SAINT JOSEPH COLLEGE	PRI-FG	96,066	56,299	1,715	140	61	0	1,200	3,576	2,301	534
SAINT THOMAS SEMINARY	PRI-T	49,432	43,219	0	0	2	109	0	810	684	181
SOUTH CEN CMTY COLLEGE	PUB-T	21,910	19,800	0	151	114	5,690	126	2,300	1,840	157
SOUTHERN CONN ST COLLEGE	PUB-FG	372,065	314,220	73,672	36,947	440	238,433	2,988	11,331	6,640	1,206
THAMES VLY STATE TECH C	PUB-T	7,150	6,800	0	0	636	1,050	0	25	A	50
TRINITY COLLEGE	PRI-FG	512,580	386,873	102,486	0	0	68,282	0	11,984	7,429	1,601
TUNXIS COMMUNITY COLLEGE	PUB-T	19,589	A	0	0	121	2	0	1,125	A	234
UNIVERSITY OF BRIDGEPORT2/	PRI-FG	311,794	239,842	0	16,136	989	401,613	0	4,979	3,830	2,490
U OF CONN ALL CAMPUSES											
UNIVERSITY OF CONNECTICUT	PUB-U	1,594,990	A	357,914	0	0	1,096,560	99,388	64,170	A	16,108
U OF CONN HEALTH CENTER	PUB-FG	112,480	33,586	0	4	56	2,100	0	7,175	2,531	2,864
UNIVERSITY OF HARTFORD	PRI-FG	269,755	160,000	0	2,500	250	0	9,195	10,024	6,447	2,245
UNIVERSITY OF NEW HAVEN	PRI-FG	132,700	98,063	78,190	24	208	6,408	3,181	11,310	8,684	1,318
WATERBURY ST TECH COLLEGE	PUB-T	8,500	8,500	50	0	200	0	75	250	250	108
WESLEYAN UNIVERSITY	PRI-FG	788,260	520,000	59,890	0	173	85,935	102,000	18,537	10,018	3,012
WESTERN CONN ST COLLEGE	PUB-FG	139,510	92,342	1,657	5,100	297	275,972	1,426	4,479	4,549	529
YALE UNIVERSITY	PRI-U	7,072,345	4,420,000	0	0	0	1,190,959	175,000	189,195	116,000	57,740
DELAWARE											
BRANDYWINE C OF WIDENER U	PRI-T	36,506	29,110	0	5	134	14,487	0	1,555	1,240	221
DELAWARE STATE COLLEGE	PUB-FN	112,870	106,420	33,132	25,000	3,338	9,235	146	6,500	3,460	0
DEL TECH & CC ALL CAM											
DEL TECH & CC STHN CAM	PUB-T	25,414	23,523	42,027	0	95	1,819	65	1,045	953	329
DEL TECH & CC STANTON CAM	PUB-T	15,818	15,500	0	0	24	0	5	1,755	1,600	242
DEL TECH & CC TERRY CAM	PUB-T	13,280	13,250	0	0	70	18	78	2,542	2,512	221
DEL TECH & CC WILMINGTON	PUB-T	11,427	9,079	0	17	41	0	7	2,866	2,286	293
GOLDEY BEACOM COLLEGE	PRI-FN	9,239	7,560	0	0	2	497	57	504	329	266
UNIVERSITY OF DELAWARE	PUB-U	1,174,002	660,000	303,931	0	0	434,685	73,643	46,889	27,638	11,806
WESLEY COLLEGE	PRI-FN	44,469	41,356	1,035	0	33	2,869	0	1,640	1,617	357

SEE FOOTNOTES AT END OF TABLE

Table 1. — Collections in College and University Libraries, by State or Other Area and Institution: Aggregate United States, 1978-79, and Fall 1979 — Continued

STATE OR OTHER AREA AND INSTITUTION (1)	CONTROL AND TYPE OF INSTITUTION (2)	HELD AT END OF YEAR — BOOKSTOCK VOLUMES (3)	BOOKSTOCK TITLES (4)	SEPARATE GOVERNMENT DOCUMENTS COLLECTIONS (VOLS.) (5)	MICROFORMS BOOK TITLES (6)	MICROFORMS PERIODICAL TITLES (7)	OTHER PHYSICAL UNITS (8)	ALL OTHER LIBRARY MATERIALS (9)	ADDED DURING YEAR BOOKSTOCK VOLUMES (10)	ADDED DURING YEAR BOOKSTOCK TITLES (11)	CURRENT PERIODICAL SUBSCRIPTION TITLES FALL 1979 (12)
DELAWARE	--CONTINUED										
WILMINGTON COLLEGE	PRI-FG	53,561	30,330	0	4	50	865	111	1,209	1,000	260
DISTRICT OF COLUMBIA											
AMERICAN UNIVERSITY	PRI-U	466,837	305,021	0	54,108	30,239	225,709	0	26,675	8,442	4,603
BEACON COLLEGE	PRI-FG	NO LIBRARY FACILITIES									
CATHOLIC U OF AMERICA	PRI-U	1,100,822	743,284	0	16,815	1	253,267	121,831	20,607	9,925	6,755
CORCORAN SCHOOL OF ART	PRI-FN	7,000	A	0	0	0	0	0	300	A	0
DOMINICAN HOUSE STUDIES	PRI-FG	48,949	32,000	0	4	4	0	0	1,453	1,000	263
GALLAUDET COLLEGE	PRI-FG	131,767	84,982	0	215,551	399	7,102	200	6,539	4,893	1,467
GEORGETOWN UNIVERSITY	PRI-U	1,186,546	513,702	91,011	0	0	592,614	116,123	54,578	32,863	15,507
GEORGE WASH UNIVERSITY	PRI-U	829,267	A	0	0	0	499,065	0	42,067	A	8,488
HOWARD UNIVERSITY	PRI-U	1,058,514	772,638	0	0	1,407	802,548	34,859	46,021	A	9,427
MOUNT VERNON COLLEGE	PRI-FN	26,251	23,600	0	2,900	583	2,450	0	1,668	1,400	399
OBLATE COLLEGE	PRI-FG	A	A	0	0	0	0	0	995	955	221
SOUTHEASTERN UNIVERSITY	PRI-FG	A	A		0	0	0	12	916	880	130
STRAYER COLLEGE	PRI-FN	16,151	15,700	95	0	9	75	2,077	4,006	2,700	605
TRINITY COLLEGE	PRI-FG	150,127	96,370					268	8,986	7,338	2,210
UNIVERSITY OF DC	PUB-FG	381,500	200,000	30,032	64,489		1,210	387,447			
WASH INTRNATL COLLEGE [1]	PRI-FN	NO LIBRARY FACILITIES									473
WESLEY THEOLOGICAL SEM	PRI-FG	88,032	A								
FLORIDA											
BARRY COLLEGE	PRI-FG	103,669	80,816	635	145	901	5,780	5,075	3,586	1,350	957
BAUDER FASHION COLLEGE	PRI-T	A	A						187		A
BETHUNE COOKMAN COLLEGE	PRI-FN	93,777	0	1,347	4,664	27	0		3,635	3,147	506
BISCAYNE COLLEGE	PRI-FG	83,580	76,580	23,199	2	110	8,003	24	2,293	1,959	529
BREVARD CMTY COLLEGE	PUB-T	114,471	90,800	0	23	255	1,100	125	8,169	7,700	505
BROWARD CMTY COLLEGE	PUB-T	170,684	138,707	0	3	453	12,151	385	17,936	14,561	604
CENTRAL FLA CMTY COLLEGE	PUB-T	48,263	40,000	0	0	265	3,032		2,574	1,788	344
CHIPOLA JUNIOR COLLEGE	PUB-T	46,233	46,132	0	0	6	535	296	2,151	2,050	331
CLEARWATER CHRISTIAN C	PRI-FN	27,919	21,200	0	1	0	1	1,030	2,408	2,200	92
COLLEGE OF BOCA RATON	PRI-T	27,780	25,933	0	0	8	0		1,600	1,600	201
DAYTONA BCH CMTY COLLEGE	PUB-T	54,200	51,298	0	0	123	4,468	778	2,244	2,200	500
ECKERD COLLEGE	PRI-FN	120,744	96,595	0	33,167	310	0	306	3,428	2,678	1,025
EDISON COMMUNITY COLLEGE	PUB-T	58,291	53,242	0	4	213	16,876	449	3,943	3,056	330
EDWARD WATERS COLLEGE	PRI-FN	75,119	61,172	0	13,290	45	27,180	240	1,992	768	220
EMBRY-RIDDLE AERON U	PRI-FG	35,000	27,500	13,240	132	300	3,000	0	2,900	2,500	480
FLAGLER COLLEGE	PRI-FN	49,537	40,000	72	0	215	10,582	46	4,533	2,600	357
FLORIDA BEACON COLLEGE	PRI-FG	A	A					49	725	552	347
FLORIDA COLLEGE	PRI-T	25,214	20,368	0	325	9	360		6,192	6,100	1,163
FLORIDA INST TECHNOLOGY	PRI-FG	125,880	59,400	59,839	0	4,083	6,361				914
FLA JR COLLEGE JACKSONVL	PUB-T	188,641	149,524	0	3	994	24,024	2,561	11,984	7,841	
FLORIDA KEYS CMTY COLLEGE	PUB-T	25,162	23,680	0	7,915	139	235	337	1,082	1,050	209
FLORIDA MEMORIAL COLLEGE	PRI-FN	73,554	54,130	0	7,460	153	0	430	839	670	252
FLORIDA SOUTHERN COLLEGE	PRI-FN	159,600	88,722	3,316	701	304	9,557	399	4,549	2,939	774
FORT LAUDERDALE COLLEGE	PRI-FN	A	A	0	3	337	10,806	A	A	A	A
GULF COAST CMTY COLLEGE	PUB-T	44,508	38,932					A	2,850	2,123	529
HEED UNIVERSITY	PRI-FG	A	A	0	0	265	A	44	2,027	1,790	544
HILLSBOROUGH CMTY COLLEGE	PUB-T	29,440	26,496	0	A	A	0	A	A	A	A
HOREB SEMINARY	PRI-FN	A	A	0			202	145,116			
INDIAN RIVER CMTY COLLEGE	PUB-T	43,626	38,866	1,416				216	2,659	2,300	409
INTERNATIONAL FINE ARTS C	PRI-T	A	A								
JACKSONVILLE UNIVERSITY	PRI-FG	164,171	A	55,727	8,296	0	0	735	4,303	4,050	641
JONES COLLEGE ALL CAM											
JONES COLLEGE JACKSONVL	PRI-FN	10,720	9,100	0	0	30	177	0	458	350	85
JONES COLLEGE ORLANDO	PRI-FN	6,980	6,447	0	0	0	0	62	601	538	59
LAKE CITY CMTY COLLEGE	PUB-T	28,647	28,072	0	7,903		258	2,350	480	407	214
LAKE-SUMTER CMTY COLLEGE	PUB-T	45,930	0	40,000	4			8,001	1,580	1,564	331
LAKELAND C BUS AND FASH	PRI-T	A	A					20	9,000	8,000	A
LUTHER RICE SEMINARY	PRI-FG	31,000	23,000	25	82	2	0				0

SEE FOOTNOTES AT END OF TABLE

STATE OR OTHER AREA AND INSTITUTION	CONTROL AND TYPE OF INSTITUTION	HELD AT END OF YEAR							ADDED DURING YEAR		CURRENT PERIODICAL SUBSCRIPTION TITLES FALL 1979
		BOOKSTOCK		SEPARATE GOVERNMENT DOCUMENTS COLLECTIONS (VOLS.)	MICROFORMS			ALL OTHER LIBRARY MATERIALS	BOOKSTOCK		
		VOLUMES	TITLES		BOOK TITLES	PERIODICAL TITLES	OTHER PHYSICAL UNITS		VOLUMES	TITLES	
(1)	(2)	(3)	(4)	(5)	(6)	(7)	(8)	(9)	(10)	(11)	(12)
FLORIDA	--CONTINUED										
MANATEE JUNIOR COLLEGE	PUB-T	47,251	45,916	0	0	8,441	0	800	2,107	1,140	309
MIAMI CHRISTIAN COLLEGE	PRI-FN	24,669	20,169	507	3	15	104	431	1,898	1,788	232
MIAMI-DADE CMTY COLLEGE	PUB-T	309,678	247,250	5,580	3	2,688	607,490	19,206	31,280	15,958	3,668
MORRIS C OF BUSINESS	PRI-T	1,158	1,080	0	0	0	0	0	0	0	27
NORTH FLORIDA JR COLLEGE	PUB-T	33,547	23,924	1,685	8	81	10,954	84	940	888	260
NOVA UNIVERSITY	PRI-FG	91,320	31,719	15,328	102	149	27,500	377	6,205	2,856	2,132
OKALOOSA-WALTON JUNIOR C	PUB-T	66,071	58,185	0	0	213	3,845	973	3,445	3,255	507
PALM BCH ATLANTIC COLLEGE	PRI-FN	40,905	32,267	114	0	133	0	0	1,889	1,591	227
PALM BEACH JUNIOR COLLEGE	PUB-T	111,655	107,059	0	0	261	6	46	4,931	4,567	616
PASCO-HERNANDO CC	PUB-T	30,302	28,549	0	0	16,554	0	118	6,282	5,693	390
PENSACOLA JUNIOR COLLEGE	PUB-T	103,992	78,000	0	0	122	4,829	279	8,136	6,000	817
POLK COMMUNITY COLLEGE	PUB-T	69,190	53,462	0	10	145	10,356	642	5,972	4,474	353
RINGLING SCHOOL OF ART	PRI-FN	9,914	8,008	0	0	0	0	1,200	0	0	84
ROLLINS COLLEGE	PRI-FG	183,709	146,967	33,627	14,024	300	0	0	4,482	3,585	940
SAINT JOHNS RIVER CC	PUB-T	49,563	33,051	74,372	0	6	76	450	2,072	1,408	237
SNT JOHN VIANNEY C SEM	PRI-FN	47,000	46,800	0	0	0	0	0	12,500	12,000	92
SAINT LEO COLLEGE	PRI-FN	66,678	50,492	0	1	140	3,155	85	2,101	1,770	628
SAINT PETERSBG JR COLLEGE	PUB-T	179,378	144,134	8,153	356	516	13,430	2,003	11,017	8,523	1,490
SANTA FE CMTY COLLEGE	PUB-T	43,376	33,294	0	0	190	0	58	3,650	3,200	414
SEM SAINT VINCENT DE PAUL	PRI-FG	37,000	37,000	0	0	238	0	50	2,000	2,000	229
SEMINOLE CMTY COLLEGE	PUB-T	60,811	54,730	0	0	225	10,881	1,694	3,923	3,531	826
STHESTN C ASSEMBLIES GOD	PRI-FN	42,065	41,000	0	0	0	0	0	2,394	2,300	176
SOUTH FLORIDA JR COLLEGE	PUB-T	29,727	27,791	0	428	1	0	51	1,441	1,207	303
ST U SYS OF FLA ALL INST											
FLA AGRICULTURAL & MECH U	PUB-U	302,865	250,096	107,147	47,283	489	32,461	23,064	12,874	10,987	2,560
FLA ATLANTIC UNIVERSITY	PUB-FG	527,387	A	171,142	12,114	19,796	496,868	30,185	25,751	16,796	4,905
FLORIDA INTERNATIONAL U	PUB-FG	324,103	253,939	164,559	54,212	823	986,182	56,323	5,121	42,862	4,855
FLORIDA STATE UNIVERSITY	PUB-U	1,353,613	749,663	732,405	34,469	0	2,018,047	121,986	75,655	50,483	13,158
U OF CENTRAL FLORIDA	PUB-FG	299,561	196,978	175,442	16,492	0	242,996	959	33,280	23,447	5,219
UNIVERSITY OF FLORIDA	PUB-U	2,079,344	A	551,023	0	0	1,200,148	395,963	139,413	A	23,080
U OF NORTH FLORIDA	PUB-FG	213,015	160,828	69,336	111	140	295,484	5,228	17,592	11,938	2,525
U OF SOUTH FLORIDA	PUB-FG	775,177	508,577	359,314	1,360	749	2,177,960	53,876	63,693	40,710	11,346
U OF WEST FLORIDA	PUB-FG	333,454	220,952	123,195	376	567	475,315	19,103	19,013	11,177	21,295
STETSON UNIVERSITY	PRI-FG	199,999	166,666	150,000	4,037	150	0	0	6,717	5,598	848
TALLAHASSEE CMTY COLLEGE	PUB-T	54,748	48,407	7,082	769	8,775	0	4,302	2,212	1,810	643
TALMUDIC C OF FLORIDA	PRI-FG	A	A						A	A	
TAMPA COLLEGE	PRI-FN	10,592	9,851	130	0	0	0	45	1,049	944	53
UNIVERSITY OF MIAMI	PRI-U	1,301,100	625,395	0	2,027	6	1,041,301	3,790	47,536	21,364	13,833
UNIVERSITY OF SARASOTA	PRI-FG	37,638	A	0	91	60	167,700	0	0	0	100
UNIVERSITY OF TAMPA	PRI-FG	165,976	120,110	13,687	11,639	711	26,389	3,149	7,820	6,010	732
VALENCIA CMTY COLLEGE	PUB-T	54,041	41,934	3,884	8,659	804	20,308	121	13,332	8,166	959
WARNER SOUTHERN COLLEGE	PRI-FN	51,332	39,818	0	463	9	0	1,002	5,442	3,715	400
WEBBER COLLEGE	PRI-FN	14,391	11,727	0	0	48	4,745	3	748	655	159
GEORGIA											
ABRAHAM BALDWIN AGRL C	PUB-T	53,728	47,446	1,463	215	197	2,547	428	2,134	1,802	524
AGNES SCOTT COLLEGE	PRI-FN	158,506	115,619	0	150	185	0	0	4,923	3,058	773
ALBANY JUNIOR COLLEGE	PUB-T	62,161	60,421	1,376	3,000	195	4,269	0	3,983	3,653	786
ALBANY STATE COLLEGE	PUB-FN	123,970	113,326	0	36,179	839	271,815	0	3,455	1,860	839
ANDREW COLLEGE	PRI-T	23,142	22,648	0	0	264	274	45	1,052	1,035	90
ARMSTRONG STATE COLLEGE	PUB-FG	111,644	88,380	8,310	14,947	205	250,432	526	2,302	1,492	848
ATLANTA CHRISTIAN COLLEGE	PRI-FN	19,550	12,567	0	470	716	1,187	483	641	440	162
ATLANTA COLLEGE OF ART	PRI-FN	9,991	7,810	0	56	0	150	0	420	330	185
ATLANTA JUNIOR COLLEGE	PUB-T	17,447	16,336	63	0	65	2,784	4	1,893	1,485	271
ATLANTA UNIVERSITY	PRI-FG	317,382	259,500	10,965	3,964	375	25,322	11	3,540	2,369	631
AUGUSTA COLLEGE	PUB-FG	234,961	137,119	101,890	20,439	536	212,500	425	20,593	12,150	1,594
BAINBRIDGE JUNIOR COLLEGE	PUB-T	20,412	16,390	0	1	103	2,238	120	2,167	2,003	250
BERRY COLLEGE	PRI-FG	110,026	67,116	22,733	185,058	328	7,000	450	6,219	5,319	841
BRENAU COLLEGE	PRI-FN	50,329	44,000	0	3	35	0	0	1,919	1,850	469
BREWTON-PARKER COLLEGE	PRI-T	22,218	22,201	0	0	18	487	115	1,167	1,150	186
BRUNSWICK JUNIOR COLLEGE	PUB-T	42,800	40,800	0	0	205	17,605	0	1,500	1,336	410

SEE FOOTNOTES AT END OF TABLE

Table 1. — Collections in College and University Libraries, by State or Other Area and Institution: Aggregate United States, 1978-79, and Fall 1979 — Continued

STATE OR OTHER AREA AND INSTITUTION (1)	CONTROL AND TYPE OF INSTITUTION (2)	BOOKSTOCK VOLUMES (3)	BOOKSTOCK TITLES (4)	SEPARATE GOVERNMENT DOCUMENTS COLLECTIONS (VOLS.) (5)	MICROFORMS BOOK TITLES (6)	MICROFORMS PERIODICAL TITLES (7)	MICROFORMS OTHER PHYSICAL UNITS (8)	ALL OTHER LIBRARY MATERIALS (9)	ADDED BOOKSTOCK VOLUMES (10)	ADDED BOOKSTOCK TITLES (11)	CURRENT PERIODICAL SUBSCRIPTION TITLES FALL 1979 (12)
GEORGIA --CONTINUED											
CLARK COLLEGE	PRI-FN	67,565	58,700	640	0	460	0	350	1,424	A	429
CLAYTON JUNIOR COLLEGE	PUB-T	46,981	42,283	1,417	0	0	4,691	3,813	2,793	2,514	518
COLUMBIA THEOLOGICAL SEM	PRI-FG	77,342	60,200	0	25	30	774	10	2,000	1,554	233
COLUMBUS COLLEGE	PUB-FG	138,681	126,200	22,616	13,023	551	239,135	282	12,911	11,749	1,391
COVENANT COLLEGE	PRI-FN	57,606	A	0	15,299	54	0	88	1,231	1,061	535
CRANDALL COLLEGE	PRI-T	1,080	1,000	0	0	0	0	0	84	81	29
DALTON JUNIOR COLLEGE	PUB-T	57,220	57,220	1,958	41,437	271	756	180	5,404	5,404	434
DEKALB COMMUNITY COLLEGE	PUB-T	A	A	A	A	A	A	0	258	256	19
DRAUGHON'S JC BUSINESS	PRI-T	2,980	2,755	0	0	0	0	0			
EMANUEL CO JUNIOR COLLEGE	PUB-T	23,289	21,519	0	0	156	3,112	2,783	2,979	2,750	447
EMMANUEL COLLEGE	PRI-T	26,188	21,832	0	58	1	0	30	879	849	222
EMMANUEL SCH MINISTRIES[3]	PRI-FN	NO LIBRARY FACILITIES									
EMORY UNIVERSITY	PRI-U	1,368,236	838,419	219,922	0	0	838,173	1,156,604	52,258	33,168	14,036
FLOYD JUNIOR COLLEGE	PUB-T	37,780	31,199	209	582	382	0	221	2,136	1,669	264
FORT VALLEY STATE COLLEGE	PUB-FG	154,392	63,612	0	4,301	31	155,064	574	7,156	3,037	1,555
GAINESVILLE JR COLLEGE	PUB-T	42,825	33,264	508	20,607	229	5,540	430	1,707	1,324	360
GEORGIA COLLEGE	PUB-FG	140,409	103,702	27,857	7,502	1,250	238,734	646	3,519	2,364	1,346
GA INST TECHN ALL CAM											
GA INST OF TECHN MAIN CAM	PUB-FG	584,261	245,390	364,312	177	54	1,239,040	186,517	23,581	8,555	12,094
GA INST TECHN-STHN TECH	PUB-FN	66,269	53,894	0	6,591	13	1,699	8,891	4,244	2,756	1,274
GEORGIA MILITARY COLLEGE	PRI-T	28,567	28,567	A	0	10	0	0	1,440	1,440	49
GEORGIA SOUTHERN COLLEGE	PUB-FG	264,893	A	191,130	400,952	0	0	0	16,522	A	2,349
GA SOUTHWESTERN COLLEGE	PUB-FG	117,942	90,655	48,668	17	418	173,542	247	3,836	2,300	975
GEORGIA STATE UNIVERSITY	PUB-FG	635,722	425,898	292,200	0	0	679,940	384	32,085	26,397	10,313
GORDON JUNIOR COLLEGE	PUB-T	39,178	38,856	0	2,718	153	0	403	4,037	3,875	471
INTRDENOMINATL THEOL CTR	PRI-FG	80,098	78,000	650	75	500	0	25	1,960	1,500	297
KENNESAH COLLEGE	PUB-FN	76,135	A	42,457	9,600	412	886	84	6,169	5,700	669
LA GRANGE COLLEGE	PRI-FG	66,594	55,288	167	5	49	3,513	24	1,839	1,748	467
LIFE CHIROPRACTIC COLLEGE	PRI-FG	13,518	11,554	0	5	0	0	3,042	0	0	112
MACON JUNIOR COLLEGE	PUB-T	54,261	A	0	0	197	0	173	2,151	2,151	642
MEDICAL COLLEGE OF GA	PUB-FG	102,272	43,587	0	2,002	18	0	0	5,193	2,390	1,605
MERCER U ALL CAMPUSES											
MERCER U MAIN CAMPUS	PRI-FG	235,038	146,890	55,000	322	97	22,128	1,500	9,189	5,580	2,698
MERCER U IN ATLANTA	PRI-FG	47,708	45,172	0	19,000	319	119,385	1,066	3,622	3,429	509
MERCER U STHN SCHOOL PHAR	PRI-FG	9,672	4,236	0	0	170	0	0	513	439	341
MIDDLE GEORGIA COLLEGE	PUB-T	74,074	66,487	0	2,053	52	86	1,949	2,473	1,889	669
MOREHOUSE COLLEGE	PRI-FG	A	A	A	A	A	A	A	3,896	A	401
MORRIS BROWN COLLEGE	PRI-FN	60,325	A	0	2,372	401	0	0	3,766	3,716	936
NORTH GEORGIA COLLEGE	PUB-FG	117,803	117,753	18,371	32	374	183,309	3,644	3,766	1,768	936
OGLETHORPE UNIVERSITY	PRI-FG	61,551	59,000	0	0	0	122,294	0	1,953	1,768	300
PAINE COLLEGE	PRI-FN	66,110	59,500	0	7	46	4,676	150	3,255	2,930	350
PHILLIPS COLLEGE	PRI-T	A	A					A	A	A	A
PHILLIPS COLLEGE	PRI-T	A	A	A							
PIEDMONT COLLEGE	PRI-FN	62,073	61,885	1,870	0	3	0	951	2,630	2,253	223
REINHARDT COLLEGE	PRI-T	28,813	22,813	49	0	37	0		1,630	1,570	191
SAVANNAH STATE COLLEGE	PUB-FG	130,136	86,576	0	0	0	214,595	395	6,490	5,025	902
SHORTER COLLEGE	PRI-FN	78,000	75,000	0	674	29	461	51	2,950	2,900	953
SOUTH GEORGIA COLLEGE	PUB-T	67,694	56,228	0	4	116	5,084	12,277	3,037	2,446	811
SPELMAN COLLEGE	PRI-FN	47,809	47,699	0	45	98	1,000	377	2,310	2,200	248
THOMAS COUNTY CC	PRI-T	14,577	14,377	110	0	0	0	55	1,648	1,648	63
TIFT COLLEGE	PRI-FN	59,095	48,523	0	459	397	8,202	313	2,193	1,515	472
TOCCOA FALLS COLLEGE	PRI-FN	46,117	42,000	0	0	250	250	2,760	4,393	4,000	380
TRUETT MCCONNELL COLLEGE	PRI-T	25,823	25,823	0	0	26	251	2	641	641	165
UNIVERSITY OF GEORGIA	PUB-U	1,893,897	A	0	1709,004	0	382,928	83,728	A		31,039
VALDOSTA STATE COLLEGE	PUB-FG	205,434	151,001	29,196	2,709	506	348,653	1,220	13,817	8,943	1,765
WAYCROSS JUNIOR COLLEGE	PUB-T	15,218	11,623	0	0	64	4,780	0	2,014	1,921	164
WESLEYAN COLLEGE	PRI-FN	107,608	A	0	10	66	0	200	4,242	A	467
WEST GEORGIA COLLEGE	PUB-FG	216,577	178,410	22,185	9,926	678	456,243	7,351	10,612	4,941	1,568
YOUNG HARRIS COLLEGE	PRI-T	44,700	39,681	0	0	100	0	13	1,098	1,058	239
HAWAII											
CHAMINADE U OF HONOLULU	PRI-FG	50,000	40,000	0	0	94	2,900	0	2,132	1,700	400

SEE FOOTNOTES AT END OF TABLE

Table 1. – Collections in College and University Libraries, by State or Other Area and Institution: Aggregate United States, 1978-79, and Fall 1979 – Continued

STATE OR OTHER AREA AND INSTITUTION	CON-TROL AND TYPE OF IN-STITU-TION	HELD AT END OF YEAR							ADDED DURING YEAR		CURRENT PERIOD-ICAL SUB-SCRIPTION TITLES FALL 1979
		BOOKSTOCK		SEPARATE GOVERN-MENT DOCU-MENTS COLLEC-TIONS (VOLS.)	MICROFORMS			ALL OTHER LIBRARY MATE-RIALS	BOOKSTOCK		
		VOLUMES	TITLES		BOOK TITLES	PERI-ODICAL TITLES	OTHER PHYS-ICAL UNITS		VOLUMES	TITLES	
(1)	(2)	(3)	(4)	(5)	(6)	(7)	(8)	(9)	(10)	(11)	(12)
HAWAII	--CONTINUED										
HAWAII LOA COLLEGE	PRI-FN	35,938	33,000	0	0	108	1,509	175	1,431	1,400	235
HAWAII PACIFIC COLLEGE	PRI-FN	19,494	14,405	0	0	0	0	167	1,428	1,428	404
U OF HAWAII SYS ALL INST											
U OF HAWAII AT MANOA	PUB-U	1,751,142	883,576	66,750	0	0	1,127,650	88,140	71,403	44,620	28,619
U OF HAWAII AT HILO	PUB-FN	133,081	110,900	0	0	262	10,348	669	19,048	15,903	1,457
U OF HAWAII WEST OAHU C	PUB-FN	8,548	6,899	0	0	3	0	73	2,208	A	82
U OF HAWAII HONOLULU CC	PUB-T	38,987	32,023	0	33,939	83	2,548	350	2,703	2,029	271
U OF HAWAII KAPIOLANI CC	PUB-T	29,813	19,000	0	0	26	529	0	1,638	1,402	324
U OF HAWAII KAUAI CC	PUB-T	26,758	20,578	0	0	256	114	603	2,287	1,858	420
U OF HAWAII LEEWARD CC	PUB-T	56,393	44,029	8,121	77	286	2,948	1,983	3,314	2,621	340
U OF HAWAII MAUI CC	PUB-T	32,632	23,168	0	0	184	750	71	1,505	632	344
U OF HAWAII WINDWARD CC	PUB-T	22,108	18,800	0	11	51	1	403	3,918	2,800	391
IDAHO											
BOISE STATE UNIVERSITY	PUB-FG	242,088	201,659	106,278	2,646	611	131,374	109,218	15,869	13,219	3,465
COLLEGE OF IDAHO	PRI-FG	119,733	118,000	75,000	27	130	18,900	529	2,764	2,700	569
COLLEGE OF SOUTHERN IDAHO	PUB-T	89,824	60,000	1,100	19,000	72	2,250	1,089	1,604	1,400	349
IDAHO STATE UNIVERSITY	PUB-FG	289,080	208,380	309,583	1,960	220	760,125	69,278	16,314	13,451	3,686
LEWIS-CLARK ST COLLEGE	PUB-FN	77,852	75,000	0	18,449	1,741	1,670	437	3,495	3,400	375
NORTH IDAHO COLLEGE	PUB-T	29,650	27,834	0	0	98	1	400	1,368	1,348	388
NTHWST NAZARENE COLLEGE	PRI-FG	101,079	73,958	0	19,527	83	1,336	730	7,252	5,227	483
RICKS COLLEGE	PRI-T	103,761	85,400	170,491	8,419	0	46,847	15,941	7,883	5,500	14,434
UNIVERSITY OF IDAHO	PUB-U	555,582	308,003	350,803	0	0	211,475	0	30,933	16,644	5,457
ILLINOIS											
AERO-SPACE INSTITUTE	PRI-FN	4,000	4,000	15	0	0	0	50	1,500	1,500	50
ALFRED ADLER INST CHICAGO	PRI-FG	4,500	4,350	38	0	0	0	0	700	650	58
AMERICAN ACADEMY OF ART	PRI-T			NO LIBRARY FACILITIES							
AMERICAN CONSV OF MUSIC	PRI-FG	5,630	4,427	0	7	0	0	0	2,036	1,747	17
AUGUSTANA COLLEGE	PRI-FG	205,344	141,608	0	39	270	2,495	300	7,532	7,230	1,255
AURORA COLLEGE	PRI-FN	86,777	61,656	0	47	65	60	45	2,517	2,497	385
BARAT COLLEGE	PRI-FN	74,375	49,800	0	113	29	2,843	0	1,675	1,500	422
BELLEVILLE AREA COLLEGE	PUB-T	51,794	43,024	543	5	303	3,000	0	2,938	2,300	467
BETHANY-NTHN BAPT JT LIB	PRI-FG	130,695	104,556	0	0	34	0	0	2,200	2,100	684
BETHANY THEOLOGICAL SEM	PRI FG			SEE BETHANY-NTHN BAPT JT LIB							
BLACKBURN COLLEGE	PRI-FN	69,500	68,000	10,000	18	69	13,000	40	1,455	1,450	0
BLACK HAWK C ALL CAMPUSES											
BLACK HAWK C EAST CAMPUS	PUB-T	12,600	11,900	250	0	164	1,675	1,200	700	640	349
BLACK HAWK C QUAD-CITIES	PUB-T	48,615	48,419	0	0	4,357	0	3,155	1,957	1,761	498
BRADLEY UNIVERSITY	PRI-U	305,167	A	0	0	0	0	0	8,131	A	1,600
BRISK RABBINICAL COLLEGE	PRI-FG	A	A						A	A	
CARL SANDBURG COLLEGE	PUB-T	33,750	26,651	0	5	135	14,663	4,841	1,479	1,350	412
CATHOLIC THEOL UNION	PRI-FG	79,059	78,766	0	0	0	0	0	3,110	2,817	450
CENTRAL YMCA CMTY COLLEGE	PRI-T	31,035	29,994	0	0	133	2,080	95	1,276	1,201	335
CHGO C OSTEOPATHIC MED	PRI-FG	34,041	32,475	0	3	0	0	1,655	2,451	2,240	1,290
CHGO CONSERVATORY COLLEGE	PRI-FG	A	A	A	A	A	A	A	A	A	
CHICAGO STATE UNIVERSITY	PUB-FG	228,957	162,994	50,349	8,113	102	232,293	5,008	10,074	9,485	1,853
CHICAGO THEOLOGICAL SEM	PRI-FG	90,000	70,000	0	0	13	0	0	1,885	1,857	290
CTY COLLEGES CHGO ALL CAM											
CITY C CHGO CITY-WIDE C1/	PUB-T			NO LIBRARY FACILITIES							
CITY C CHGO KENNEDY-KING	PUB-T	A	A			A	A		A	A	A
CITY C CHICAGO LOOP C	PUB-T	46,688	34,645	0	5	95	4,675	0	1,644	1,361	308
CITY C CHGO MALCOLM X C	PUB-T	39,834	38,834	396	0	1	1,407	670	1,255	1,178	362
CITY C CHGO OLIVE-HARVEY	PUB-T	47,669	40,726	0	12	2,529	33	1	1,712	1,305	408
CITY C CHICAGO DALEY C	PUB-T	38,057	31,679	0	0	78	0	19	918	750	292
CITY C CHGO TRUMAN C	PUB-T	51,326	43,992	0	150	214	0	6,000	4,999	4,212	339
CITY C CHICAGO WRIGHT C	PUB-T	70,317	36,893	0	30	545	11,500	2,500	1,951	1,813	540
COLLEGE OF DUPAGE	PUB-T	93,050	87,000	0	20,000	554	4,566	299	7,831	7,750	861
COLLEGE OF LAKE COUNTY	PUB-T	76,040	61,195	0	0	280	64,000	0	4,034	3,890	353
COLLEGE OF SAINT FRANCIS	PRI-FN	109,492	70,972	0	0	9	4	108	4,197	3,341	418
COLUMBIA COLLEGE	PRI-FN	36,728	31,431	0	0	31	0	2	3,837	3,270	267

SEE FOOTNOTES AT END OF TABLE

Table 1. — Collections in College and University Libraries, by State or Other Area and Institution: Aggregate United States, 1978-79, and Fall 1979 — Continued

STATE OR OTHER AREA AND INSTITUTION (1)	CONTROL AND TYPE OF INSTITUTION (2)	HELD AT END OF YEAR — BOOKSTOCK VOLUMES (3)	HELD AT END OF YEAR — BOOKSTOCK TITLES (4)	SEPARATE GOVERNMENT DOCUMENTS COLLECTIONS (VOLS.) (5)	MICROFORMS BOOK TITLES (6)	MICROFORMS PERIODICAL TITLES (7)	MICROFORMS OTHER PHYSICAL UNITS (8)	ALL OTHER LIBRARY MATERIALS (9)	ADDED DURING YEAR — BOOKSTOCK VOLUMES (10)	ADDED DURING YEAR — BOOKSTOCK TITLES (11)	CURRENT PERIODICAL SUBSCRIPTION TITLES FALL 1979 (12)
ILLINOIS --CONTINUED											
CONCORDIA COLLEGE	PRI-FG	125,350	A	0	65	55	230,989	0	2,629	A	645
DANIEL HALE WILLIAMS U	PRI-FN	NO LIBRARY FACILITIES									
DANVILLE AREA CMTY C	PUB-T	29,857	22,266	0	0	231	0	10	922	790	357
DELOURDES COLLEGE	PRI-FN	19,255	19,250	683	0	0	0	731	1,015	1,010	156
DEPAUL UNIVERSITY	PRI-U	343,570	186,467	6,356	15,891	845	56,652	0	16,387	10,523	5,218
DEVRY INST OF TECHNOLOGY	PRI-FN	7,399	7,323	0	0	0	0	0	1,063	987	173
EASTERN ILL UNIVERSITY	PUB-FG	406,600	279,000	37,169	14,200	84	891,704	55,395	22,814	10,972	4,294
ELGIN COMMUNITY COLLEGE	PUB-T	43,988	34,050	0	0	74	20,000	250	3,608	3,168	332
ELMHURST COLLEGE	PRI-FN	132,372	122,317	0	4,691	182	1,113	144	9,662	8,130	798
EUREKA COLLEGE	PRI-FN	75,940	64,339	0	0	205	18	0	1,305	1,090	370
FELICIAN COLLEGE	PRI-T	43,927	34,212	0	16	145	9	0	2,202	1,695	291
GARRETT-EVANGELCL THEOL	PRI-FG	166,584	119,904	0	818	212	2,400	120	3,133	2,860	774
GEORGE WILLIAMS COLLEGE	PRI-FG	87,649	57,324	0	17	79	978	0	5,468	3,908	606
GOVERNORS ST UNIVERSITY	PUB-FG	170,452	115,201	46,647	0	0	261,690	900	11,054	7,357	2,353
GREENVILLE COLLEGE	PRI-FN	95,025	82,243	1,000	5	27	223	75	1,923	1,417	380
HARRINGTON INSTITUTE	PRI-T	A	A					A	425	102	0
HEBREW THEOL COLLEGE	PRI-FG	41,210	18,040	0	230	0	0	0	1,551	1,424	318
HIGHLAND CMTY COLLEGE	PUB-T	33,181	31,525	0	0	72	2,459	0	4,394	A	941
ILL BENEDICTINE COLLEGE	PRI-FG	112,499	A	30,000	236	109	197	0	2,649	2,371	627
ILLINOIS CENTRAL COLLEGE	PUB-T	63,463	48,583	0	0	194	5,039	0			
ILLINOIS COLLEGE	PRI-FN	96,392	89,731	0	18	182	1,520	0	3,369	2,651	673
ILL COLLEGE OF OPTOMETRY	PRI-FG	12,636	5,700	0	2	46	49	0	991	450	140
ILL COLLEGE PODIATRIC MED	PRI-FG	9,075	3,000	209	0	0	0	0	1,283	720	225
ILL ESTN CC SYS ALL INST											
ILL ESTN CC FRONTIER CC	PUB-T	2,100	2,100	0	0	0	0	75	600	550	38
ILL ESTN LINCOLN TRAIL C	PUB-T	19,700	19,400	0	0	6	550	10,000	1,300	1,250	100
ILL ESTN CC OLNEY CEN C	PUB-T	27,370	26,619	0	0	92	12,209	41	404	388	349
ILL ESTN CC WABASH VLY C	PUB-T	17,500	A	11,000	0	159	0	19	2,750	A	266
ILLINOIS INST TECHNOLOGY	PRI-FG	248,372	104,749	490	35,568	58	67,767	200	14,881	7,265	3,596
ILLINOIS STATE UNIVERSITY	PUB-FG	815,638	569,138	264,471	0	328	896,486	292,138	36,359	23,506	5,529
ILLINOIS VLY CMTY COLLEGE	PUB-T	62,385	51,414	72,563	0	63	3	92	1,196	733	665
ILL WESLEYAN UNIVERSITY	PRI-FN	141,000	138,000	20,000	2,500	2,500	1,000	3,000	5,480	4,900	995
JKM JOINT LIBRARY 4/	PRI-FG	368,490	294,792	0	86,267	195	86,786	2,150	5,272	1,054	1,364
JOHN A LOGAN COLLEGE	PUB-T	27,000	22,000	16,000	0	125	1,150	160	1,050	990	345
JOHN MARSHALL LAW SCHOOL	PRI-FG	85,015	8,537	0	0	25,128	0	0	11,803	1,412	1,313
JOHN WOOD CMTY COLLEGE 5/	PUB-T	2,792	930	0	0	0	0	0	700	330	13
JOLIET JUNIOR COLLEGE	PUB-T	49,030	35,300	0	0	101	25,300	0	2,171	1,726	553
JUDSON COLLEGE	PRI-FN	47,245	37,486	0	24,499	747	344	1,220	4,113	3,694	392
KANKAKEE CMTY COLLEGE	PUB-T	19,647	16,069	0	21,500	79	225	247	2,594	2,137	300
KASKASKIA COLLEGE	PUB-T	42,788	21,250	0	0	79	3	37	830	733	500
KELLER GRAD SCHOOL MGMT	PRI-FG	600	600	0	0	0	0	0	50	50	25
KENDALL COLLEGE	PRI-FN	27,000	26,500	0	0	26	0	0	375	317	160
KISHWAUKEE COLLEGE	PUB-T	29,582	24,950	2,000	0	1	67	0	1,768	1,182	285
KNOX COLLEGE	PRI-FN	191,606	139,914	0	30,000	200	0	600	6,504	5,465	625
LAKE FOREST COLLEGE	PRI-FG	171,662	140,577	61,578	1,214	158	0	300	7,284	6,043	886
LAKE LAND COLLEGE	PUB-T	29,835	29,443	0	0	193	0	1,428	1,795	1,703	387
LEWIS AND CLARK CC	PUB-T	32,705	24,123	0	0	91	8,164	329	1,192	931	402
LEWIS UNIVERSITY	PRI-FG	110,334	A	45,454	24,078	124	3,120	8	4,519	A	650
LINCOLN CHRISTIAN COLLEGE	PRI-FG	59,745	29,495	100	189	127	33	0	907	737	338
LINCOLN COLLEGE	PRI-T	37,016	34,591	0	4	4,390	0	131	1,584	1,412	427
LINCOLN LAND CMTY COLLEGE	PUB-T	66,285	55,292	0	1,303	71	2,287	0	2,889	2,246	522
LOYOLA U OF CHICAGO	PRI-U	702,154	432,787	60,000	9,592	1,499	493,259	0	24,035	12,997	5,512
LUTH SCH THEOLOGY CHICAGO	PRI FG	SEE JKM JOINT LIBRARY						A	A	A	A
MACCORMAC COLLEGE	PRI-T	A						A	A	A	A
MACMURRAY COLLEGE	PRI-FN	132,404	92,550	67,373	55	220	9,484	200	1,542	405	667
MALLINCKRODT COLLEGE	PRI-T	27,890	27,836	5,166	0	6	0	4,057	986	932	144
MCCORMICK THEOLOGICAL SEM	PRI FG	SEE JKM JOINT LIBRARY									
MCHENRY COUNTY COLLEGE	PUB-T	25,272	23,500	0	0	446	8,654	4	2,184	1,508	470
MCKENDREE COLLEGE	PRI-FN	55,637	36,295	19,830	5	42	5,296	250	2,736	1,986	400
MEADVL-LOMBARD THEOL SCH	PRI-FG	90,075	85,000	0	58	0	0	72	0	0	127
MIDSTATE COLLEGE	PRI-T	6,847	6,544	0	0	0	0	570	907	892	95

SEE FOOTNOTES AT END OF TABLE

Table 1. – Collections in College and University Libraries, by State or Other Area and Institution: Aggregate United States, 1978-79, and Fall 1979 – Continued

STATE OR OTHER AREA AND INSTITUTION (1)	CONTROL AND TYPE OF INSTITUTION (2)	HELD AT END OF YEAR BOOKSTOCK VOLUMES (3)	BOOKSTOCK TITLES (4)	SEPARATE GOVERNMENT DOCUMENTS COLLECTIONS (VOLS.) (5)	MICROFORMS BOOK TITLES (6)	MICROFORMS PERIODICAL TITLES (7)	MICROFORMS OTHER PHYSICAL UNITS (8)	ALL OTHER LIBRARY MATERIALS (9)	ADDED DURING YEAR BOOKSTOCK VOLUMES (10)	ADDED DURING YEAR BOOKSTOCK TITLES (11)	CURRENT PERIODICAL SUBSCRIPTION TITLES FALL 1979 (12)
ILLINOIS --CONTINUED											
MIDWEST COLLEGE OF ENGR	PRI-FG	A	A					A	A	A	A
MILLIKIN UNIVERSITY	PRI-FN	149,398	102,714	0	10	239	1,505	82	4,034	3,667	679
MONMOUTH COLLEGE	PRI-FN	120,538	84,377	58,241	0	0	17,993	38,231	3,183	3,098	748
MOODY BIBLE INSTITUTE	PRI-FN	102,579	78,390	0	262	34	357	1,400	4,440	3,404	850
MORAINE VLY CMTY COLLEGE	PUB-T	66,129	53,827	10,825	15	268	0	0	4,859	4,211	689
MORRISON INST OF TECHN	PRI-T	2,180	2,150	0	0	0	0	0	0	0	18
MORTCN COLLEGE	PUB-T	36,977	34,688	0	155	188	63	1,080	1,646	1,357	329
MUNDELEIN COLLEGE	PRI-FG	128,211	116,550	0	55	110	4,097	0	4,655	4,230	696
NATL COLLEGE CHIROPRACTIC	PRI-FG	17,741	A	0	0	0	0	0	1,705	942	483
NATL COLLEGE ED ALL CAM											
NATL COLLEGE ED MAIN CAM	PRI-FG	96,133	93,049	0	30	74	283,000	0	1,156	1,090	393
NATL COLLEGE ED URBAN CAM	PRI-FG	23,905	23,569	0	0	1,204	163	0	301	301	134
NATIVE AMERICAN EDUC SERV	PRI-FN	424	388	24	0	0	0	172	0	0	4
NORTH CENTRAL COLLEGE	PRI-FN	96,748	77,398	920	15	14	0	1,000	2,824	2,260	493
NTHESTN ILL UNIVERSITY	PUB-FG	318,547	222,993	39,756	0	900	376,956	1,086	18,017	12,971	2,638
NORTHERN BAPT THEOL SEM	PRI FG	SEE BETHANY-NTHN BAPT JT LIB									
NORTHERN ILL UNIVERSITY	PUB-U	967,971	640,439	570,370	0	0	1,061,784	229,052	43,696	24,044	15,674
NORTH PARK C & THEOL SEM	PRI-FG	146,040	105,090	1,668	2,676	53	16,218	193	2,718	2,019	845
NORTHWESTERN UNIVERSITY	PRI-U	2,505,509	1,671,175	209,429	0	0	825,982	160,569	67,233	44,844	29,087
OAKTON COMMUNITY COLLEGE	PUB-T	49,012	46,000	3,000	100	217	4,000	300	2,500	2,500	650
OLIVET NAZARENE COLLEGE	PRI-FG	115,869	98,388	26,000	14,000	263	890	4,109	4,536	3,706	845
PARKLAND COLLEGE	PUB-T	66,283	A	0	0	7,486	0	0	5,302	A	712
PRAIRIE STATE COLLEGE	PUB-T	47,685	45,092	893	0	62	730	109	4,283	1,976	491
PRINCIPIA COLLEGE	PRI-FN	135,085	112,575	60,000	300	125	0	160	5,000	4,800	1,234
QUINCY COLLEGE	PRI-FN	194,790	192,000	0	15,166	30	55,550	2,050	4,053	3,998	969
RENO LAKE COLLEGE	PUB-T	27,024	23,353	0	0	29	2,017	182	2,451	1,681	437
RICHLAND CMTY COLLEGE	PUB-T	20,284	17,430	0	0	50	5,689	7,100	923	874	294
ROCKFORD COLLEGE	PRI-FG	A	A	A	A	A	A	A	A	A	A
ROCK VALLEY COLLEGE	PUB-T	50,051	49,976	0	0	199	0	367	1,852	1,836	552
ROOSEVELT UNIVERSITY	PRI-FG	A	A		A	A	0	A	A	A	A
ROSARY COLLEGE	PRI-FG	177,867	162,914	58,986	4,854	98	6,528	599	4,835	3,672	1,089
RUSH UNIVERSITY	PRI-FG	85,000	80,000	0	0	0	0	0	5,000	4,354	1,523
SNT MARY OF THE LAKE SEM	PRI-FG	132,778	75,769	0	699	3	545	0	1,237	1,167	421
SAINT XAVIER COLLEGE	PRI-FG	64,903	50,856	0	0	411	8,579	0	4,965	3,504	611
SANGAMON STATE UNIVERSITY	PUB-FG	232,214	158,830	70,129	0	1,945	436,109	990	19,297	12,097	2,898
SAUK VALLEY COLLEGE	PUB-T	41,206	38,206	0	0	52	1,445	81	2,231	2,100	276
SCH ART INSTITUTE CHICAGO	PRI-FG	12,068	134,653	0	3,239	200	10,010	31,721	4,496	1,234	991
SEABURY-WESTERN THEOL SEM	PRI-FG	75,432	54,671	0	55	14	160	20	1,727	1,605	430
SHAWNEE COLLEGE	PUB-T	34,486	34,112	0	0	1,966	1,966	0	823	798	230
SHERWOOD MUSIC SCHOOL	PRI-FN	A	A					A	A	A	A
SHIMER COLLEGE	PRI-FN	A	A		A	A			A	A	A
SOUTHEASTERN ILL COLLEGE	PUB-T	25,000	23,000	0	0	58	0	0	1,450	1,435	235
STHN ILLINOIS U ALL INST											
STHN ILLINOIS U CARBONDL	PUB-U	1,643,598	781,900	238,738	279,695	2,618	1,329,599	197,852	59,008	36,069	21,145
STHN ILLINOIS U EDWARDSVL	PUB-FG	687,127	424,625	343,452	86,186	1,688	183,751	283,121	25,525	13,998	4,961
SPERTUS COLLEGE JUDAICA	PRI-FG	60,110	26,151	0	0	0	1,084	85	744	674	899
SPOON RIVER COLLEGE	PUB-T	23,115	21,093	0	0	179	2,365	29	3,630	3,386	389
SPRINGFLD COLLEGE IN ILL	PRI-T	30,545	28,020	0	0	0	0	150	738	700	147
STATE COMMUNITY COLLEGE	PUB-T	27,505	27,399	0	1	214	0	0	831	725	141
TELSHE YESHIVA-CHICAGO	PRI-FG	A	A						A	A	A
THORNTON CMTY COLLEGE	PUB-T	31,528	31,206	0	0	21	0	125	1,871	1,375	415
TRINITY CHRISTIAN COLLEGE	PRI-FN	43,000	43,000	0	19,000	18	0	0	1,500	1,500	290
TRINITY COLLEGE	PRI-FN	54,917	46,227	0	21,600	112	0	897	2,284	1,023	507
TRINITY-EVANGELCL DIV SCH	PRI-FG	69,534	51,760	0	297	14	1,351	0	4,093	2,698	828
TRITON COLLEGE	PUB-T	75,300	55,000	0	0	216	0	101	6,703	4,960	704
UNIVERSITY OF CHICAGO	PRI-U	4,182,938	A		862	468,647	0	255,000	175,566	A	913
U HLTH SCI-CHGO MEDL SCH	PRI-FG	36,200	16,900	525	0	225	22,250	0	4,200	1,700	1,111
U OF ILLINOIS ALL CAM											
U OF ILL CHICAGO CIRCLE	PUB-FG	680,675	400,236	325,475	0	0	481,178	106,166	27,103	16,017	8,187
U OF ILL MEDL CTR CHGO	PUB-FG	372,048	104,407	12,942	6,614	1	0	640	28,397	20,604	3,439
U OF ILL URBANA CAMPUS	PUB-U	5,759,666	2,117,017	53,000	0	0	1,377,970	1,783,196	161,279	A	81,396

SEE FOOTNOTES AT END OF TABLE

Table 1. – Collections in College and University Libraries, by State or Other Area and Institution: Aggregate United States, 1978-79, and Fall 1979 – Continued

STATE OR OTHER AREA AND INSTITUTION	CONTROL AND TYPE OF INSTITUTION	HELD AT END OF YEAR							ADDED DURING YEAR		CURRENT PERIODICAL SUBSCRIPTION TITLES FALL 1979
		BOOKSTOCK		SEPARATE GOVERNMENT DOCUMENTS COLLECTIONS (VOLS.)	MICROFORMS			ALL OTHER LIBRARY MATERIALS	BOOKSTOCK		
		VOLUMES	TITLES		BOOK TITLES	PERIODICAL TITLES	OTHER PHYSICAL UNITS		VOLUMES	TITLES	
(1)	(2)	(3)	(4)	(5)	(6)	(7)	(8)	(9)	(10)	(11)	(12)
ILLINOIS --CONTINUED											
VANDERCOOK C OF MUSIC	PRI-FG	18,000	A	350	2	10	0	0	700	A	92
WAUBONSEE CMTY COLLEGE	PUB-T	47,169	45,103	39	287	0	0	45	2,152	2,136	364
WESTERN ILL UNIVERSITY	PUB-FG	458,477	407,366	249,139	16,746	1,000	292,243	135,000	16,323	13,123	3,500
WHEATON COLLEGE	PRI-FG	145,863	A	20,735	68	315	38,182	1,232	12,681	A	1,050
WM RAINEY HARPER COLLEGE	PUB-T	95,766	70,174	0	95	43	15,258	293	4,520	2,644	749
INDIANA											
ANCILLA DOMINI COLLEGE	PRI-T	27,290	27,160	80	108	6	0	55	865	765	232
ANDERSON COLLEGE	PRI-FG	166,737	117,185	9,916	4,265	114	18,766	10,177	7,309	5,601	796
BALL STATE UNIVERSITY	PUB-U	1,006,906	641,451	88,950	39,347	1,149	0	114,016	38,536	32,803	5,142
BETHEL COLLEGE	PRI-FN	50,757	A	0	4	36	2,481	3,202	1,764	1,475	359
BUTLER UNIVERSITY	PRI-U	187,761	138,500	37,623	0	36	15,961	0	5,759	3,294	673
CALUMET COLLEGE	PRI-FN	97,118	79,000	0	2	75	2,619	0	4,434	3,332	530
CHRISTIAN THEOLOGICAL SEM	PRI-FG	94,205	72,700	0	170	104	50	0	2,400	2,350	477
CLARK COLLEGE	PRI-T	A	A						A	A	A
CONCORDIA THEOLOGICAL SEM	PRI-FG	96,262	89,500	0	1,364	1,157	0	1,356	5,162	4,800	567
DEPAUW UNIVERSITY	PRI-FG	220,092	146,963	158,274	258	153	6,806	33,683	4,008	2,503	1,213
EARLHAM COLLEGE	PRI-FG	260,746	A	0	0	0	31,097	7,332	13,821	A	1,311
FORT WAYNE BIBLE COLLEGE	PRI-FN	49,463	44,645	0	2	21	478	1,282	1,438	1,301	363
FRANKLIN COLLEGE INDIANA	PRI-FN	99,947	98,948	0	44	44	1,123	3,455	2,310	2,287	476
GOSHEN BIBLICAL SEMINARY	PRI FG	SEE MENNONITE BIB SEM JT LIB									
GOSHEN COLLEGE	PRI-FN	100,664	A	0	22	195	3,302	105	2,433	A	524
GRACE COLLEGE	PRI-FN	84,696	64,399	0	17,115	72	0	230	3,863	2,897	774
HANOVER COLLEGE	PRI-FN	A	A	A	A	A	A		A	A	A
HOLY CROSS JUNIOR COLLEGE	PRI-T	8,474	8,234	0	163	16	0	0	317	279	82
HUNTINGTON COLLEGE	PRI-FG	51,528	49,528	14,700	78	139	198	800	1,061	1,000	572
INDIANA CEN UNIVERSITY	PRI-FG	100,307	72,018	0	268	70	224	0	7,807	7,178	649
INDIANA C MORTUARY SCI	PRI-T	1,432	A	4	0	0	0	5	4	A	10
INDIANA INST TECHNOLOGY	PRI-FN	45,926	36,237	0	0	0	28,665	0	176	136	159
IND NTHN GRAD SCH MGMT	PRI-FG	7,650	7,650	0	0	0	15	0	100	100	70
INDIANA STATE U ALL CAM											
INDIANA STATE U MAIN CAM	PUB-U	801,220	399,076	156,906	0	0	339,261	18,275	34,164	14,145	4,667
INDIANA ST U EVANSVL CAM	PUB-FN	134,033	96,073	41,096	2,574	196	10,793	4,257	9,508	5,995	521
INDIANA U ALL CAMPUSES											
INDIANA U BLOOMINGTON[1]/	PUB-U	3,254,702	2,250,000	480,821	0	0	898,879	4,829,381	112,206	78,000	27,331
INDIANA UNIVERSITY EAST	PUB-T	26,949	24,212	0	3,845	204	9,219	0	3,048	2,780	361
INDIANA U AT KOKOMO	PUB-FN	79,495	55,641	14,397	5,854	383	1,132	945	2,377	1,806	827
INDIANA U NORTHWEST	PUB-FG	140,614	96,321	76,914	59	1,184	4,695	26,724	8,279	5,374	1,095
IND-PURDUE U INDIANAPOLIS	PUB-FG	559,869	217,472	30,108	1,051	211	429,239	32,460	26,497	A	9,935
INDIANA U AT SOUTH BEND	PUB-FG	164,869	A	45,346	7,761	2,452	0	12,898	8,895	A	1,470
INDIANA U SOUTHEAST	PUB-FG	86,499	54,069	25,496	3,986	200	14,478	607	5,307	2,935	678
IND-PURDUE U FORT WAYNE	PUB-FG	204,482	190,169	42,052	0	0	49,590	25,722	16,376	15,236	1,637
IND VOC TECH C ALL CAM											
IND VOC TECH C-CEN IND	PUB-T	7,049	5,088	0	0	0	0	0	789	698	199
IND VOC TECH C-COLUMBUS	PUB-T	1,789	1,282	20	4	0	15	0	56	48	63
IND VOC TECH C-KOKOMO	PUB-T	1,950	A	0	0	0	360	0	263	A	7
IND VOC TECH C-LAFAYETTE	PUB-T	5,870	3,898	0	14	0	0	43	260	219	165
IND VOC TECH C-NTH CEN	PUB-T	7,283	7,100	0	0	0	0	0	168	160	144
IND VOC TECH C NORTHEAST	PUB-T	4,984	4,705	145	1	20	0	0	146	127	112
IND VOC TECH C-STHCEN	PUB-T	3,513	3,493	25	0	0	0	5	1,175	1,155	76
IND VOC TECH C-SOUTHWEST	PUB-T	3,471	3,090	0	0	0	0	32	223	209	136
IND VOC TECH-WABASH VLY	PUB-T	3,761	3,197	100	243	0	243	0	182	153	149
INTERNATIONAL BUSINESS C	PRI-T	2,000	1,600	0	0	0	0	100	200	200	73
LOCKYEAR COLLEGE	PRI-T	7,464	4,911	66	0	1,000	0	332	120	120	108
MANCHESTER COLLEGE	PRI-FG	150,760	108,548	8,000	181	40	8,010	2,800	3,650	3,278	680
MARIAN COLLEGE	PRI-FN	102,142	71,921	0	0	0	0	0	2,985	3,821	617
MARION COLLEGE	PRI-FN	80,986	55,715	0	203	44	3,030	4,921	4,454	3,638	519
MENNONITE BIBLICAL SEM	PRI FG	SEE MENNONITE BIB SEM JT LIB									
MENNONITE BIB SEM JT LIB	PRI-FG	77,817	67,000	0	230	5	1,018	119	2,198	1,900	435
OAKLAND CITY COLLEGE	PRI-FN	61,082	63,157	0	0	398	0	97	2,090	2,075	338
PURDUE U ALL CAMPUSES											

SEE FOOTNOTES AT END OF TABLE

Table 1. — Collections in College and University Libraries, by State or Other Area and Institution: Aggregate United States, 1978-79, and Fall 1979 — Continued

STATE OR OTHER AREA AND INSTITUTION	CON-TROL AND TYPE OF IN-STITU-TION	HELD AT END OF YEAR							ADDED DURING YEAR		CURRENT PERIOD-ICAL SUB-SCRIPTION TITLES FALL 1979
		BOOKSTOCK		SEPARATE GOVERN-MENT DOCU-MENTS COLLEC-TIONS (VOLS.)	MICROFORMS			ALL OTHER LIBRARY MATE-RIALS	BOOKSTOCK		
		VOLUMES	TITLES		BOOK TITLES	PERI-ODICAL TITLES	OTHER PHYS-ICAL UNITS		VOLUMES	TITLES	
(1)	(2)	(3)	(4)	(5)	(6)	(7)	(8)	(9)	(10)	(11)	(12)
INDIANA	--CONTINUED										
PURDUE U MAIN CAMPUS	PUB-U	1,388,152	555,261	140,122	0	0	955,599	104,181	30,377	12,151	14,500
PURDUE U CALUMET CAMPUS	PUB-FG	125,183	92,203	0	0	0	235,324	0	11,391	5,030	1,227
PURDUE U NORTH CEN CAMPUS	PUB-T	39,457	27,457	0	24	4	1,596	17	1,785	1,217	406
ROSE-HULMAN INST OF TECHN	PRI-FG	50,895	49,388	0	0	0	0	0	1,228	1,112	392
SAINT FRANCIS COLLEGE	PRI-FG	67,729	47,927	0	136,054	237	228,437	785	1,356	1,356	572
SAINT JOSEPH'S COLLEGE	PRI-FG	146,177	93,336	81,575	3,148	142	23,316	38	3,180	1,957	727
SAINT MARY'S COLLEGE	PRI-FN	148,774	120,517	0	27	49	353	0	4,500	3,600	770
SAINT MARY-OF-THE-WOODS C	PRI-FN	131,825	82,452	0	14	7	0	5,147	2,234	1,507	404
SAINT MEINRAD COLLEGE	PRI FN	SEE SNT MEINRAD C JT LIBRARY									
SNT MEINRAD C JT LIBRARY	PRI-FN	120,999	81,356	0	500	20	0	100	3,640	2,809	565
SNT MEINRAD SCH THEOLOGY	PRI FG	SEE SNT MEINRAD C JT LIBRARY									
TAYLOR UNIVERSITY	PRI-FN	123,786	122,709	0	38	62	4,539	0	3,511	3,133	695
TRI-STATE UNIVERSITY	PRI-FN	90,268	52,104	0	0	137	2,167	406	3,471	1,332	569
UNIVERSITY OF EVANSVILLE	PRI-FG	195,578	186,000	0	59,699	6,387	16,595	1,137	8,506	8,000	1,230
UNIVERSITY OF NOTRE DAME	PRI-U	1,383,114	584,411	116,077	0	368	670,364	0	41,180	25,293	14,295
VALPARAISO UNIVERSITY	PRI-FG	306,020	177,165	83,514	17,707	294	42,468	76,000	14,162	8,925	1,959
VINCENNES UNIVERSITY	PUB-T	60,290	58,770	0	0	86	0	71	3,434	2,865	415
WABASH COLLEGE	PRI-FN	207,933	A	37,000	0	78	5,300	6	4,474	2,951	742
IOWA											
AMERICAN INSTITUTE BUS	PRI-T	A	A					A	A	A	A
AQUINAS INST OF THEOLOGY	PRI-FG	72,171	A	0	0	0	1,366	0	3,949	A	294
BRIAR CLIFF COLLEGE	PRI-FN	81,295	81,200	0	0	95	14,737	0	1,717	1,622	495
BUENA VISTA COLLEGE	PRI-FN	72,896	72,896	0	131	37	162	498	3,180	3,180	0
CENTRAL U OF IOWA	PRI-FN	120,000	90,000	0	14	27	3,695	193	5,000	3,528	800
CLARKE COLLEGE	PRI-FG	102,112	102,112	0	2,601	858	0	757	2,500	2,500	550
COE COLLEGE	PRI-FN	176,295	131,924	0	68	44	17,742	0	6,015	4,236	610
COLLEGE OSTEO MED-SURGERY	PRI-FG	22,055	7,425	0	0	0	0	0	463	A	350
CORNELL COLLEGE	PRI-FN	116,582	88,385	43,004	102	126	17,872	43	3,429	2,229	550
DES MOINES AREA CC	PUB-T	71,399	63,902	0	0	1,831	3,222	1,108	3,868	3,713	668
DIVINE WORD COLLEGE	PRI-FN	83,903	71,200	0	0	61	2	0	1,557	1,221	426
DORDT COLLEGE	PRI-FN	82,698	80,000	0	67	625	0	0	4,262	4,162	620
DRAKE UNIVERSITY	PRI-U	460,637	296,139	79,669	82,182	494	0	0	19,093	12,403	3,635
ESTN IOWA CC DIST ALL CAM CLINTON COMMUNITY COLLEGE	PUB-T	14,090	13,501	0	0	100	756	0	710	652	167
MUSCATINE CMTY COLLEGE	PUB-T	17,033	16,460	0	0	288	500	162	574	530	201
SCOTT COMMUNITY COLLEGE	PUB-T	22,337	18,452	12,156	0	6	12	16	1,645	1,607	245
ELLSWORTH CMTY COLLEGE	PUB-T	23,994	22,829	0	0	3,413	0	507	1,317	1,291	326
FAITH BAPT BIBLE COLLEGE	PRI-FN	35,256	32,350	0	400	2	0	3,151	2,024	1,013	402
GRACELAND COLLEGE	PRI-FN	88,044	66,065	63,000	111	37	530	93	2,730	1,827	447
GRAND VIEW COLLEGE	PRI-FN	65,350	45,290	0	1,110	179	4,461	169	4,568	2,523	514
GRINNELL COLLEGE	PRI-FN	252,382	179,439	4,500	41	13	0	0	9,900	7,637	1,326
HAWKEYE INST TECHNOLOGY	PUB-T	15,643	9,687	0	0	160	6,898	1,875	1,284	831	546
INDIAN HILLS CC	PUB-T	31,208	27,414	0	3	27	519	189	5,214	4,818	262
IOWA CENTRAL CC	PUB-T	60,687	57,205	245	0	55	1,651	125	1,199	1,058	458
IOWA LAKES CC ALL CAM IOWA LAKES CC NORTH CTR	PUB-T	22,287	20,967	0	0	54	0	374	782	769	186
IOWA LAKES CC SOUTH CTR	PUB-T	10,899	10,174	0	0	24	0	919	533	512	158
IOWA STATE U SCI & TECHN	PUB-U	1,296,074	696,317	0	0	0	982,529	418,920	47,252	29,062	17,212
IOWA WESLEYAN COLLEGE	PRI-FN	93,305	67,461	0	339	53	7,232	509	2,310	1,705	630
IOWA WESTERN CMTY COLLEGE	PUB-T	54,252	48,826	4,765	0	194	5,743	1,140	2,426	2,183	449
KIRKWOOD CMTY COLLEGE	PUB-T	47,244	A	0	0	73	12,781	159	4,326	A	448
LORAS COLLEGE	PRI-FG	196,593	175,000	55,428	45	62	10,110	1,063	3,543	3,300	732
LUTHER COLLEGE	PRI-FN	244,379	148,255	0	1,058	180	15,254	0	5,779	4,024	869
MAHARISHI INTRNATL U	PRI-FG	47,000	40,125	0	500	0	3	250	3,500	3,000	300
MARSHALLTWN CMTY COLLEGE	PUB-T	27,551	26,123	0	0	137	2,920	454	740	720	347
MARYCREST COLLEGE	PRI-FG	94,638	80,443	0	0	2,704	3,396	0	2,660	A	663
MORNINGSIDE COLLEGE	PRI-FG	119,532	92,266	0	1,875	290	13,247	31	1,513	1,474	660
MOUNT MERCY COLLEGE	PRI-FN	62,947	59,800	500	0	51	172	182	1,800	1,710	409
MOUNT SAINT CLARE COLLEGE	PRI-FN	19,403	15,922	0	0	1	0	47	1,450	1,175	180
NTHEST IA TECH INSTITUTE	PUB-T	17,934	6,114	0	0	0	550	0	2,051	1,438	521

SEE FOOTNOTES AT END OF TABLE

Table 1. — Collections in College and University Libraries, by State or Other Area and Institution: Aggregate United States, 1978-79, and Fall 1979 — Continued

STATE OR OTHER AREA AND INSTITUTION (1)	CONTROL AND TYPE OF INSTITUTION (2)	HELD AT END OF YEAR — BOOKSTOCK VOLUMES (3)	BOOKSTOCK TITLES (4)	SEPARATE GOVERNMENT DOCUMENTS COLLECTIONS (VOLS.) (5)	MICROFORMS BOOK TITLES (6)	MICROFORMS PERIODICAL TITLES (7)	MICROFORMS OTHER PHYSICAL UNITS (8)	ALL OTHER LIBRARY MATERIALS (9)	ADDED DURING YEAR — BOOKSTOCK VOLUMES (10)	ADDED BOOKSTOCK TITLES (11)	CURRENT PERIODICAL SUBSCRIPTION TITLES FALL 1979 (12)
IOWA	—CONTINUED										
(continued)							0	547	1,353	1,005	459
N ICWA AREA CMTY COLLEGE	PUB-T	32,920	25,955	1,222	72	507	0	60	939	867	267
NTHWST IOWA TECH C	PUB-T	30,212	27,598	0	0	0	0		2,739	1,917	509
NORTHWESTERN COLLEGE	PRI-FN	81,423	56,996	18,301	2	334	6,942	1	670	663	51
OPEN BIBLE COLLEGE	PRI-FN	15,210	12,911	0	400	121	521	54	2,022	1,555	436
PALMER C OF CHIROPRACTIC	PRI-FG	13,872	10,671				3,465				550
SAINT AMBROSE COLLEGE	PRI-FN	101,600	86,680	0	12	81	2,697	283	2,066	1,939	
SIMPSON COLLEGE	PRI-FN	109,544	87,636	0	36	52	4,588	0	3,124	2,530	395
SIOUX EMPIRE COLLEGE	PRI-T	14,000	12,500	140	0	0	0	189	1,960	1,790	75
SOUTHEASTERN CMTY COLLEGE	PUB-T	40,856	40,383	1,070	0	46	3	88	1,927	1,850	279
SOUTHWESTERN CMTY COLLEGE	PUB-T	16,717	16,717	0	0	42	854	48	938	938	234
UNIVERSITY OF DUBUQUE	PRI-FG	139,489	A	0	17,000	500	23,327	0	5,388	A	769
UNIVERSITY OF IOWA	PUB-U	2,216,970	1,066,719	675,318	310,723	9,943	1,063,163	227,031	89,522	49,788	26,314
U OF NORTHERN IOWA	PUB-FG	502,831	458,602	173,793	3,450	450	288,676	31,148	29,329	20,743	3,044
UPPER IOWA UNIVERSITY	PRI-FN	79,036	55,325	22,710	0	59	2,414	7,524	1,474	1,031	290
VENNARD COLLEGE	PRI-FN	41,676	33,149	0	0	4	228	350	706	660	320
WALDORF COLLEGE	PRI-T	30,764	23,947	0	0	87	300	180	1,117	1,117	266
WARTBURG COLLEGE	PRI-FN	130,510	110,492	0	0	116	3,955	0	3,968	3,155	950
WARTBURG THEOLOGICAL SEM	PRI-FG	72,170	A	0	0	0	1,367	0	3,949	A	295
WESTERN IOWA TECH	PUB-T	10,145	8,627	0	0	79	1,622	416	1,557	1,261	445
WESTMAR COLLEGE	PRI-FN	89,409	A	0	0	0	0	0	1,450	A	362
WILLIAM PENN COLLEGE	PRI-FN	70,043	69,800	1,902	0	2,938	10	358	1,474	1,470	525
KANSAS											
ALLEN CO CMTY JR COLLEGE	PUB-T	38,221	36,712	0	0	42	88	0	1,382	1,356	320
BAKER UNIVERSITY	PRI-FG	96,187	60,000	0	11	52	1,267	5,400	2,547	2,306	270
BARTON CO CMTY JR COLLEGE	PUB-T	24,361	24,361	0	0	30		30	420	420	348
BENEDICTINE COLLEGE	PRI-FN	285,343	159,073	33,792	13	95	5,720	6,479	5,293	2,878	640
BETHANY COLLEGE	PRI-FN	77,513	53,310	0	5	83	0	60	4,809	2,937	376
BETHEL COLLEGE	PRI-FN	97,090	79,248	0	470	9	2,408	410	3,516	2,952	735
BUTLER CO CMTY JR COLLEGE	PUB-T	30,622	24,050	0	0	33	12,419	15	1,708	10	226
CENTRAL BAPTIST THEOL SEM	PRI-FG	65,526	49,298	0	122	42	0	2,494	810	471	266
CENTRAL COLLEGE	PRI-T	18,045	18,002	0	0	8	28	0	670	660	155
CLOUD CO CMTY JR COLLEGE	PUB-T	18,489	14,362	0	0	642	1,648	18	814	720	253
COFFEYVL CMTY JR COLLEGE	PUB-T	25,611	23,800		0	30	4,075	99	662	863	323
COLBY COMMUNITY COLLEGE	PUB-T	27,731	25,256	32,807	0	52	47	2,423	994	882	242
COWLEY CO CMTY JR COLLEGE	PUB-T	18,764	14,974		1	84		7	1,137	1,362	326
DODGE CTY CMTY JR COLLEGE	PUB-T	32,296	30,447	130	0	37	2,400	60	1,412	1,011	129
DONNELLY COLLEGE	PRI-T	30,461	25,500					0	1,116		
(continued)							0	37,891	10,007	2,674	
EMPORIA STATE UNIVERSITY	PUB-FG	619,223	310,586	227,895	141,569	1,772	454,277	19,449	6,805	6,693	1,386
FORT HAYS ST UNIVERSITY	PUB-FG	300,512	281,613	235,000	5,973	116	167,695	120	943	943	228
FT SCOTT CMTY JR COLLEGE	PUB-T	19,751	19,150	0	1,302	39			1,262	877	73
FRIENDS BIBLE COLLEGE	PRI-FN	18,376	12,396	0	400		64	1,000	2,825	2,000	520
FRIENDS UNIVERSITY	PRI-FN	81,603	57,200	0	1	64		2	1,069	293	320
GARDEN CITY COMMUNITY JC	PUB-T	30,612	23,484	0	0	101	1,411	400	1,128	1,017	508
HASKELL INDIAN JR COLLEGE	PUB-T	20,101	15,221	0	310	294	1,747	0	991	985	247
HESSTON COLLEGE	PRI-T	28,660	25,760	0	0	67		42	654	614	195
HIGHLAND CMTY JR COLLEGE	PUB-T	25,012	21,173	0	2	32	214	44	1,902	1,895	255
HUTCHINSN CMTY JR COLLEGE	PUB-T	37,522	36,500	0	6	43		427	1,243	1,100	199
INDEPENDENCE COMMUNITY JC	PUB-T	27,871	20,075	0	0	39		112	3,380	3,250	501
JOHNSN CO CMTY JR COLLEGE	PUB-T	38,500	37,200	0	0	23	226,400	0	2,200	2,174	291
KANSAS CITY KANS CMTY JC	PUB-T	50,853	50,369	0	0	45	4,840	360	2,684	2,500	442
KANSAS NEWMAN COLLEGE	PRI-FN	68,317	66,000	0	7	13		1,436	1,023	910	187
KANSAS ST U AGR & APP SCI	PUB-U	858,845	619,209	507,600	483,249	284			26,853	16,117	7,414
KANSAS TECHNICAL INST	PUB-T	15,531	15,276	0	0	0	574	100	1,874	1,825	481
KANSAS WESLEYAN	PRI-FN	74,867	74,117	173,200	0	6	0		1,312	1,200	266
LABETTE CMTY COLLEGE	PUB-T	19,739	18,500	300	0	14		1,082	813	813	72
MANHATTAN CHRSTN COLLEGE	PRI-FN	22,173	22,173	0	1,430	76	28	1,075	1,937	1,831	550
MARYMOUNT COLLEGE KANSAS	PRI-FN	75,122	73,066	0	2	106	588		1,729	1,400	371
MCPHERSON COLLEGE	PRI-FN	66,844	64,500	0	30	216	7,265	17,000	2,003	1,953	403
MID-AMERICA NAZARENE C	PRI-FN	62,630	62,580	69	17,350	2,850	410	15			

SEE FOOTNOTES AT END OF TABLE

Table 1. – Collections in College and University Libraries, by State or Other Area and Institution: Aggregate United States, 1978-79, and Fall 1979 – Continued

STATE OR OTHER AREA AND INSTITUTION (1)	CONTROL AND TYPE OF INSTITUTION (2)	HELD AT END OF YEAR							ADDED DURING YEAR		CURRENT PERIODICAL SUBSCRIPTION TITLES FALL 1979 (12)
		BOOKSTOCK		SEPARATE GOVERNMENT DOCUMENTS COLLECTIONS (VOLS.) (5)	MICROFORMS			ALL OTHER LIBRARY MATERIALS (9)	BOOKSTOCK		
		VOLUMES (3)	TITLES (4)		BOOK TITLES (6)	PERIODICAL TITLES (7)	OTHER PHYSICAL UNITS (8)		VOLUMES (10)	TITLES (11)	
KANSAS	--CONTINUED										
NEOSHO CO CMTY JR COLLEGE	PUB-T	20,718	20,284	0	0	29	35	140	1,185	1,105	194
OTTAWA UNIVERSITY	PRI-FN	89,479	58,547	0	0	27	4,322	0	980	717	371
PITTSBURG ST UNIVERSITY	PUB-FG	203,528	173,000	132,000	17,400	834	149,000	1,400	5,872	5,402	1,487
PRATT CMTY JUNIOR COLLEGE	PUB-T	23,949	23,230	800	0	24	0	500	874	847	171
SAINT JOHN'S COLLEGE	PRI-T	43,969	41,338	0	0	13	374	0	757	720	267
SAINT MARY COLLEGE	PRI-FN	110,188	73,600	0	860	16	10,220	60	2,084	1,316	493
SAINT MARY PLAINS COLLEGE	PRI-FN	57,472	37,774	0	103	35	2,934	273	1,646	1,400	390
SEWARD CO CMTY JR COLLEGE	PUB-T	20,238	19,238	0	0	428	0	0	1,134	1,134	250
SOUTHWESTERN COLLEGE	PRI-FN	92,679	68,405	0	0	6,316	0	0	3,236	3,100	565
STERLING COLLEGE	PRI-FN	77,572	76,000	0	9	95	0	152	1,724	1,675	461
TABOR COLLEGE	PRI-FN	54,370	53,829	0	4	14	0	14	1,797	1,687	405
U KANSAS ALL CAMPUSES											
U OF KANSAS MAIN CAMPUS	PUB-U	1,958,429	1,250,000	576,393	0	0	886,090	1,500,000	81,349	50,000	25,721
U OF KANS MEDICAL CENTER	PUB-FG	122,557	50,375	0	207	1,501	0	29	6,263	2,327	1,798
WASHBURN U OF TOPEKA	PUB-FG	250,048	167,543	788	20,472	218	117,935	16,604	14,846	8,292	2,609
WICHITA STATE UNIVERSITY	PUB-U	608,735	394,818	405,997	64,170	401	0	11,436	29,587	19,112	6,420
KENTUCKY											
ALICE LLOYD COLLEGE	PRI-T	29,162	29,162	0	0	1,465	0	0	838	838	185
ASBURY COLLEGE	PRI-FN	94,386	71,449	0	510	277	3,505	270	5,957	5,104	641
ASBURY THEOLOGICAL SEM	PRI-FG	118,052	82,637	0	2,163	287	2,450	168	6,241	4,370	675
BELLARMINE COLLEGE	PRI-FG	78,137	71,874	0	33	350	2	433	1,794	1,488	555
BEREA COLLEGE	PRI-FN	230,673	195,771	0	32	231	22,728	193	7,220	5,281	959
BRESCIA COLLEGE	PRI-FN	62,710	61,510	780	395	129	148,837	110	2,437	2,400	510
CAMPBELLSVILLE COLLEGE	PRI-FN	85,352	61,227	3,054	185	1,257	234	5,000	3,816	1,944	548
CENTRE COLLEGE OF KY	PRI-FN	130,284	105,550	417	21	28	6,967	358	3,792	3,272	697
CUMBERLAND COLLEGE	PRI-FN	87,569	79,009	0	802	151	8,155	3,257	3,038	2,955	759
DRAUGHON'S COLLEGE	PRI-T	2,800	1,400	0	0	0	0	10	105	105	51
EASTERN KY UNIVERSITY	PUB-FG	465,928	313,130	149,090	339,727	2,462	572,115	11,486	37,656	16,749	3,544
GEORGETOWN COLLEGE	PRI-FG	127,799	127,511	1,412	11,655	1,849	260	101	2,893	2,605	575
KENTUCKY BUSINESS COLLEGE	PRI-T	3,600	3,200	0	0	0	0	5	0	0	60
KY CHRISTIAN COLLEGE	PRI-FN	23,577	16,403	0	0	12	100	0	909	841	107
KENTUCKY STATE UNIVERSITY	PUB-FG	135,248	129,838	16,099	25,120	2,134	8,852	848	9,115	8,750	1,081
KENTUCKY WESLEYAN COLLEGE	PRI-FN	88,754	62,130	51,605	78	40	11,750	668	3,081	2,619	514
LEES JUNIOR COLLEGE	PRI-T	27,198	25,838	0	3	26	15	220	1,009	958	227
LEXINGTON THEOL SEMINARY	PRI-FG	91,032	80,000	0	0	0	0	0	3,062	2,600	1,044
LINDSEY WILSON COLLEGE	PRI-T	18,859	12,252	400	0	0	0	25	525	425	99
LCUISVL PRESB THEOL SEM	PRI-FG	83,924	82,124	0	156	5	0	0	1,817	1,800	336
LOUISVILLE SCHOOL OF ART	PRI-FN	6,591	6,201	0	0	0	0	3,823	390	390	55
MIDWAY COLLEGE	PRI-T	27,459	25,453	0	0	0	1,384	0	942	884	184
MOREHEAD STATE UNIVERSITY	PUB-FG	375,077	239,760	17,311	187,463	186	0	10,333	16,443	14,860	2,180
MURRAY STATE UNIVERSITY	PUB-FG	474,267	215,938	145,231	10,482	583	257,516	449	32,485	12,064	2,169
NORTHERN KY UNIVERSITY	PUB-FG	251,386	157,908	48,812	69,637	26,574	499,658	340	19,877	11,887	3,912
OWENSBORO BUSINESS C	PRI-T	2,700	2,384	12	0	0	0	0	200	177	31
PIKEVILLE COLLEGE	PRI-FN	85,057	63,864	0	14,501	169	1,921	357	1,467	1,174	284
SAINT CATHARINE COLLEGE	PRI-T	16,576	15,188	756	0	63	828	1,982	704	648	125
SEMINARY OF SAINT PIUS X	PRI-FN	33,090	29,781	50	35	21	0	350	2,024	1,800	215
SOUTHERN BAPT THEOL SEM	PRI-FG	267,347	175,000	0	2,925	221	0	40,400	20,881	7,500	1,257
SPALDING COLLEGE	PRI-FG	108,482	69,099	0	356	76	1,645	317	2,478	1,742	668
SUE BENNETT COLLEGE	PRI-T	35,520	35,510	0	0	0	0	200	1,122	1,112	130
SULLIVAN JC BUSINESS	PRI-T	4,410	4,181	0	0	4	184	0	854	833	61
THOMAS MORE COLLEGE	PRI-FN	79,896	63,000	14,467	13	77	1,727	4,351	1,488	1,300	617
TRANSYLVANIA UNIVERSITY	PRI-FN	93,286	80,412	0	155	20	2,447	0	1,408	1,210	420
UNION COLLEGE	PRI-FG	71,213	68,160	0	3	50	7,815	105	1,863	1,708	380
U KENTUCKY ALL CAMPUSES											
UNIVERSITY OF KENTUCKY	PUB-U	1,244,935	834,910	544,917	111,719	3,084	1,748,310	168,215	56,333	40,723	25,241
U OF KENTUCKY CC SYSTEM	PUB-T	348,592	285,349	2,037	256	5,659	19,356	7,540	15,142	12,139	2,431
UNIVERSITY OF LOUISVILLE	PUB-U	831,537	454,800	173,016	0	0	0	751,601	32,669	17,253	6,392
WATTERSON COLLEGE	PRI-T	A	A						A	A	A
WESTERN KY UNIVERSITY	PUB-FG	468,644	337,930	248,324	355,698	606	254,006	27,010	41,161	19,937	4,118

SEE FOOTNOTES AT END OF TABLE

39

Table 1. — Collections in College and University Libraries, by State or Other Area and Institution: Aggregate United States, 1978-79, and Fall 1979 — Continued

STATE OR OTHER AREA AND INSTITUTION	CON-TROL AND TYPE OF IN-STITU-TION	HELD AT END OF YEAR							ADDED DURING YEAR		CURRENT PERIOD-ICAL SUB-SCRIPTION TITLES FALL 1979
		BOOKSTOCK		SEPARATE GOVERN-MENT DOCU-MENTS COLLEC-TIONS (VOLS.)	MICROFORMS			ALL OTHER LIBRARY MATE-RIALS	BOOKSTOCK		
		VOLUMES	TITLES		BOOK TITLES	PERI-ODICAL TITLES	OTHER PHYS-ICAL UNITS		VOLUMES	TITLES	
(1)	(2)	(3)	(4)	(5)	(6)	(7)	(8)	(9)	(10)	(11)	(12)

LOUISIANA

BOSSIER PARISH CC	PUB-T	18,261	14,964	0	0	0	0	0	2,501	2,425	104
CENTENARY C OF LOUISIANA	PRI-FG	131,918	121,250	0	1,000	469	0	0	4,964	4,368	812
DELGADO COLLEGE	PUB-T	32,278	30,054	54,000	0	113	40	4,153	714	619	250
DILLARD UNIVERSITY	PRI-FN	120,076	116,100	0	8	101	4,641	440	2,144	2,100	687
GRAMBLING STATE U	PUB-FG	177,962	116,386	1,426	18,600	352	110,212	135	9,528	8,409	1,217
LOUISIANA COLLEGE	PRI-FN	96,158	70,470	41,000	2	50	35	200	3,822	2,486	551
LOUISIANA ST U ALL CAM											
LA STATE U AND A&M C	PUB-U	1,767,635	699,562	305,951	16,217	23	861,611	400,000	56,253	27,499	17,765
LA STATE U ALEXANDRIA	PUB-T	100,146	70,324	0	0	107	14,717	367	5,602	3,931	746
LA STATE U EUNICE	PUB-T	75,386	68,000	45,000	128	20	1,990	0	4,528	2,925	750
LA ST U MEDICAL CENTER	PUB-FG	122,048	A	0	0	0	0	0	6,219	A	1,728
LA STATE U SHREVEPORT	PUB-FG	111,104	75,841	7,057	76	135	7,899	0	7,657	4,621	1,614
UNIVERSITY OF NEW ORLEANS	PUB-FG	369,985	218,653	147,895	275,609	490	134,080	11,603	20,060	11,197	5,723
LOUISIANA TECH UNIVERSITY	PUB-FG	242,955	240,525	523,701	0	0	316,131	60,351	10,380	A	2,820
LOYOLA U IN NEW ORLEANS	PRI-U	380,078	270,757	180,000	22,334	124	1,000	39	13,830	7,265	3,236
MCNEESE STATE UNIVERSITY	PUB-FG	197,812	134,435	289,947	1,799	284	223,747	757	11,991	8,000	1,369
NEW ORLS BAPT THEOL SEM	PRI-FG	145,965	109,473	0	545	545	916	246	3,719	2,789	811
NICHOLLS STATE UNIVERSITY	PUB-FG	184,708	119,701	127,820	178,508	96	7,528	754	6,392	4,091	1,520
NORTHEAST LOUISIANA U	PUB-FG	296,187	133,021	85,771	183,990	14,532	0	0	13,600	7,432	3,442
NTHWSTN ST U OF LA	PUB-FG	244,289	151,450	254,636	206,140	500	500	1,230	8,159	6,366	2,870
NOTRE DAME SEM SCH THEO	PRI-FG	73,054	A	0	0	0	123	0	2,111	A	177
OUR LADY OF HOLY CROSS C	PRI-FN	A	A	A	A	A		A	A	A	A
PHILLIPS C NEW ORLEANS	PRI-T	A	A						A	A	A
SAINT BERNARD PARISH CC	PUB-T	20,000	19,960	0	0	0	0	0	845	805	200
SAINT JOSEPH SEM COLLEGE	PRI-FN	63,000	62,500	0	2	18	0	0	2,250	2,145	212
SAINT MARY'S DOMINICAN C	PRI-FN	71,661	48,549	10,000	27	8	27	0	2,040	1,387	435
STHESTN LA UNIVERSITY	PUB-FG	208,534	A	80,604	0	0	183,441	1,336	11,421	10,115	1,688
SOUTHERN U A&M ALL CAM											
SOUTHERN U A&M C MAIN CAM[2/]	PUB-FG	280,787	139,875	16,409	0	257	83,401	365	11,159	4,375	1,700
STHN U IN NEW ORLEANS	PUB-FN	150,946	150,377	71,940	598	8,584	613	0	9,161	8,592	612
STHN U SHREVEPORT-BOSSIER	PUB-T	26,600	18,350	0	1	141	2,520	486	1,035	460	343
TULANE U OF LOUISIANA	PRI-U	1,346,910	595,926	548,256	33,298	91	36,536	53,430	36,889	20,404	8,680
U OF STHWSTN LOUISIANA	PUB-FG	444,235	253,579	185,213	11,683	158	771,700	1,650	18,135	9,897	5,266
XAVIER UNIVERSITY OF LA	PRI-FG	98,194	78,555	0	50	143	90,706	1	4,622	3,698	675

MAINE

ANDOVER COLLEGE	PRI-T	4,655	3,442	0	0	0	0	0	722	700	32
BANGOR THEOLOGICAL SEM	PRI-FG	69,383	A	0	9	21	128	0	1,179	1,100	410
BATES COLLEGE	PRI-FN	237,171	177,940	63,831	9,352	229	28,552	0	14,067	10,768	1,371
BEAL COLLEGE	PRI-T	13,650	9,325	100	0	0	0	35	246	135	82
BOWDOIN COLLEGE	PRI-FN	410,670	298,529	162,528	0	0	32,736	0	12,617	9,012	1,854
CASCO BAY COLLEGE	PRI-T	A	A						A	A	A
COLBY COLLEGE	PRI-FN	358,072	A	44,854	0	0	66,095	0	10,637	8,477	1,430
COLLEGE OF THE ATLANTIC	PRI-FN	12,777	9,794	400	0	0	498	0	800	700	184
EASTERN ME VOC-TECH INST	PUB-T	15,200	13,400	0	74	34	0	60	700	500	96
HUSSON COLLEGE	PRI-FG	28,544	28,528	75	0	6	471	10	1,687	1,681	354
MAINE MARITIME ACADEMY	PUB-FN	46,100	42,300	67,564	16,379	99	16,578	748	2,927	2,827	763
NASSON COLLEGE	PRI-FN	122,058	122,058	4,060	506	17	14	327	3,005	3,005	889
NTHN ME VOC TECH INST	PUB-T	10,854	7,334	0	0	24	56	0	1,247	1,073	186
PORTLAND SCHOOL OF ART	PRI-FN	10,633	9,808	0	0	0	0	2,910	649	607	44
SAINT JOSEPH'S COLLEGE	PRI-FN	49,020	42,000	0	0	201	0	60	2,000	1,800	404
SOUTHERN ME VOC TECH INST	PUB-T	15,574	14,500	0	0	26	0	0	1,037	A	226
THOMAS COLLEGE	PRI-FG	16,304	13,373	0	1	2	670	0	636	614	183
UNITY COLLEGE	PRI-FN	35,798	34,406	0	0	11	203	0	5,662	5,442	453
U OF MAINE ALL CAMPUSES											
U OF MAINE AT AUGUSTA	PUB-T	31,210	27,139	0	133	53	1,846	177	1,452	1,263	277
U OF MAINE AT FARMINGTON	PUB-FN	86,385	65,700	2,916	11,134	198	7,546	4,242	5,460	4,261	817
U OF MAINE AT FORT KENT	PUB-FN	38,563	34,707	0	0	93	2,872	63	2,084	1,876	164
U OF MAINE AT MACHIAS	PUB-FN	59,284	58,000	0	2	10	2,528	368	2,515	2,515	301
U OF MAINE AT ORONO	PUB-U	544,432	A	17,000	2,100	1,800	3,100	0	22,075	A	2,700
U OF ME AT PRESQUE ISLE	PUB-FN	68,356	60,435	1,761	0	114	4,927	0	2,746	2,600	558

SEE FOOTNOTES AT END OF TABLE

40

STATE OR OTHER AREA AND INSTITUTION	CON-TROL AND TYPE OF IN-STITU-TION	HELD AT END OF YEAR							ADDED DURING YEAR		CURRENT PERIOD-ICAL SUB-SCRIPTION TITLES FALL 1979
		BOOKSTOCK		SEPARATE GOVERN-MENT DOCU-MENTS COLLEC-TIONS (VOLS.)	MICROFORMS			ALL OTHER LIBRARY MATE-RIALS	BOOKSTOCK		
		VOLUMES	TITLES		BOOK TITLES	PERI-ODICAL TITLES	OTHER PHYS-ICAL UNITS		VOLUMES	TITLES	
(1)	(2)	(3)	(4)	(5)	(6)	(7)	(8)	(9)	(10)	(11)	(12)
MAINE --CONTINUED											
U OF SOUTHERN MAINE	PUB-FG	276,729	251,629	0	721	331	23,367	0	7,317	5,404	1,665
UNIVERSITY OF NEW ENGLAND	PRI-FG	65,648	49,736	0	0	53	66	2,160	3,34?	1,875	495
WESTBROOK COLLEGE	PRI-FN	A	23,464	0	0	3	0	2	A	1,584	252
MARYLAND											
ALLEGANY CMTY COLLEGE	PUB-T	40,941	40,000	9,326	39	114	3,424	5	901	875	359
ANNE ARUNDEL CMTY COLLEGE	PUB-T	80,816	78,816	1,000	25	13	2,500	0	4,739	4,689	450
BALTIMORE HEBREW COLLEGE	PRI-FG	30,275	23,480	0	370	10	421	0	2,621	674	250
BOWIE STATE COLLEGE	PUB-FG	151,421	84,593	0	78,904	242	198,799	2,330	1,818	1,300	1,220
CAPITOL INST TECHNOLOGY	PRI-FN	8,841	7,297	0	6	0	0	5	360	329	99
CATONSVILLE CMTY COLLEGE	PUB-T	102,575	77,086	0	23	444	0	16,127	3,282	2,233	927
CECIL COMMUNITY COLLEGE	PUB-T	17,771	17,300	0	0	0	0	9	1,000	900	208
CHARLES CO CMTY COLLEGE	PUB-T	32,915	26,601	2,151	2,269	49	715	1,559	2,213	1,539	238
CHESAPEAKE COLLEGE	PUB-T	27,436	26,548	0	'0	3,281	105	510	1,036	750	167
COLLEGE OF NOTRE DAME MD	PRI FN	SEE LOYOLA-NOTRE DAME JT LIB									
COLUMBIA UNION COLLEGE	PRI-FN	105,667	75,132	0	1,039	47	0	53	3,614	2,439	502
CMTY COLLEGE OF BALTIMORE	PUB-T	87,712	70,247	0	1,014	310	15,380	52	6,661	6,167	1,632
COPPIN STATE COLLEGE	PUB-FG	113,303	84,893	0	21,400	200	0	10,502	3,569	1,832	948
DE SALES HALL SCH THEO	PRI-FG	35,817	35,700	50	0	0	0	56	551	434	176
DUNDALK CMTY COLLEGE	PUB-T	17,461	16,545	0	0	177	1,960	6	1,805	1,612	372
ESSEX COMMUNITY COLLEGE	PUB-T	85,870	72,183	0	0	3,492	0	2,174	3,369	3,032	1,638
FREDERICK CMTY COLLEGE	PUB-T	27,916	A	0	0	0	0	0	1,340	1,063	281
FROSTBURG STATE COLLEGE	PUB-FG	167,170	145,000	72,231	30,000	4,500	58,581	27,606	3,817	3,500	875
GARRETT COMMUNITY COLLEGE	PUB-T	20,780	18,446	0	1	4	0	85	2,763	2,318	291
GOUCHER COLLEGE	PRI-FG	203,413	109,700	23,111	45	87	20,923	26,668	4,899	2,395	845
HAGERSTOWN JUNIOR COLLEGE	PUB-T	43,980	43,980	0	0	3,966	24,000	593	1,920	1,920	540
HARFORD COMMUNITY COLLEGE	PUB-T	37,207	32,000	13,015	0	27	1,852	163	1,952	1,721	417
HOOD COLLEGE	PRI-FG	123,833	89,759	0	14	195	12,939	149	4,656	4,190	982
HOWARD COMMUNITY COLLEGE	PUB-T	27,018	23,775	0	0	90	0	3	789	703	325
JOHNS HOPKINS UNIVERSITY	PRI-U	2,214,282	1,409,719	434,789	2,350	530	343,821	166,040	36,795	22,304	14,262
LOYOLA COLLEGE	PRI FG										
LOYOLA-NOTRE DAME JT LIB	PRI-FG	184,391	115,509	0	28	89	199,380	47	6,449	6,121	1,187
MARYLAND C ART AND DESIGN	PRI-T	6,360	6,335	0	0	0	0	0	871	865	24
MD INST COLLEGE OF ART	PRI-FG	39,000	35,000	0	0	2	0	74,000	1,064	1,040	193
MONTGOMERY C ALL CAMPUSES											
MONTGOMERY C GERMANTOWN	PUB-T	22,553	20,299	0	1	134	2,002	50	12,000	A	431
MONTGOMERY C ROCKVILLE	PUB-T	93,898	77,937	0	1,878	450	6,080	180	4,500	3,735	850
MONTGOMERY C TAKOMA PARK	PUB-T	52,591	47,961	0	49	194	4,796	113	3,430	2,970	365
MORGAN STATE UNIVERSITY	PUB-FG	197,271	135,000	92,350	13,166	1,340	79,761	7,351	19,228	0	1,702
MOUNT SNT MARY'S COLLEGE	PRI-FG	125,680	88,000	0	0	5,781	0	0	3,827	A	613
NSR ISRAEL RAB COLLEGE	PRI-FG	16,992	14,305	189	0	0	0	14	176	160	40
PEABODY INST OF JHU	PRI-FG	65,488	27,726	0	9	2	602	0	2,199	1,026	162
PRINCE GEORGES CC	PUB-T	68,675	61,700	650	0	300	0	50	4,275	4,000	520
SAINT JOHN'S C ALL CAM											
SAINT JOHN'S C MAIN CAM	PRI-FG	78,654	37,595	0	57	7	0	1,183	2,150	1,389	150
SNT JOHN'S C SANTA FE NM	PRI-FG	44,293	27,605	0	2	0	2,500	86	1,734	1,184	207
SNT MARY'S COLLEGE OF MD	PUB-FN	77,515	62,012	0	8,003	489	8,575	1,544	4,582	4,215	959
SAINT MARY'S SEMINARY & U	PRI-FG	76,459	A	0	2,356	0	0	0	1,436	A	335
SALISBURY STATE COLLEGE	PUB-FG	169,866	152,879	34,300	13,556	432	185,736	12,500	9,695	8,726	1,740
TOWSON STATE UNIVERSITY	PUB-FG	327,841	A	13,293	306,722	0	0	31,437	15,708	A	2,165
UNIVERSITY OF BALTIMORE	PUB-FG	295,311	198,212	86,067	25,003	1,094	1,250	620	10,623	4,962	2,413
U MARYLAND SYS ALL INST											
U OF MARYLAND ALL CAM											
U OF MD COLLEGE PARK CAM	PUB-U	1,335,018	527,542	383,909	41,221	5,151	1,294,036	63,016	57,712	22,230	16,161
U OF MD BALTIMORE CO CAM	PUB-FG	293,618	223,150	51,467	100,000	141	181,586	292,015	13,689	10,404	3,122
U OF MD BALT PROF SCHOOLS	PUB-FG	367,392	113,772	46,243	3,997	19	80,680	32	16,680	5,624	3,845
U MD UNIVERSITY COLLEGE	PUB-FG	NO LIBRARY FACILITIES									
U OF MD-EASTERN SHORE	PUB-FG	108,630	106,200	17,613	22,899	29	195,311	78	1,171	1,450	971
VILLA JULIE COLLEGE	PRI-T	26,568	15,500	0	0	5	0	5	1,803	515	155
WASHINGTON BIBLE COLLEGE	PRI-FG	28,452	A	0	150	535	0	512	2,898	2,598	325
WASHINGTON COLLEGE	PRI-FG	104,365	90,837	25,000	421	148	0	278	2,787	2,371	656

SEE FOOTNOTES AT END OF TABLE

Table 1. — Collections in College and University Libraries, by State or Other Area and Institution: Aggregate United States, 1978-79, and Fall 1979 — Continued

STATE OR OTHER AREA AND INSTITUTION (1)	CONTROL AND TYPE OF INSTITUTION (2)	HELD AT END OF YEAR — BOOKSTOCK — VOLUMES (3)	TITLES (4)	SEPARATE GOVERNMENT DOCUMENTS COLLECTIONS (VOLS.) (5)	MICROFORMS — BOOK TITLES (6)	PERIODICAL TITLES (7)	OTHER PHYSICAL UNITS (8)	ALL OTHER LIBRARY MATERIALS (9)	ADDED DURING YEAR — BOOKSTOCK — VOLUMES (10)	TITLES (11)	CURRENT PERIODICAL SUBSCRIPTION TITLES FALL 1979 (12)
MARYLAND --CONTINUED											
WASHINGTON THEOL UNION	PRI-FG	A	A		A	A	A		A	A	A
WESTERN MARYLAND COLLEGE	PRI-FG	119,337	85,265	5,627	75	0	138,427	0	3,541	2,716	951
WOR-WIC TECH CMTY COLLEGE	PUB-T	NO LIBRARY FACILITIES									
MASSACHUSETTS											
AMERICAN INTRNATL COLLEGE	PRI-FG	120,506	73,508	0	3	200	12,266	12	1,823	1,736	509
AMHERST COLLEGE	PRI-FN	545,099	296,438	9,402	190	93	98,638	54,477	14,758	7,464	2,263
ANDOVER NEWTON THEOL SCH	PRI-FG	195,034	127,679	0	76	44	286	0	2,564	2,096	569
ANNA MARIA COLLEGE	PRI-FG	47,753	37,086	0	0	48	0	325	1,647	1,357	287
AQUINAS JC ALL CAMPUSES											
AQUINAS JC AT MILTON	PRI-T	8,332	6,556	105	0	536	0	0	456	436	135
AQUINAS JC AT NEWTON	PRI-T	11,070	11,055	117	0	0	0	275	900	885	149
ADL MGMT ED INSTITUTE	PRI-FG	39,000	36,000	6,000	0	65	95,000	1,500	4,000	3,000	2,500
ASSUMPTION COLLEGE	PRI-FG	149,203	83,071	0	19	47	0	564	3,776	2,454	826
ATLANTIC UNION COLLEGE	PRI-FN	96,528	A	0	0	959	3,225	807	2,979	A	619
BABSON COLLEGE	PRI-FG	80,968	57,270	6,813	0	92	58,021	0	3,698	0	867
BAY PATH JUNIOR COLLEGE	PRI-T	28,355	27,000	0	0	51	0	0	775	725	170
BAY STATE JC OF BUS	PRI-T	4,005	3,898	9	0	0	0	52	108	88	48
BECKER JC ALL INSTITUTION											
BECKER JC-LEICESTER	PRI-T	25,474	21,499	0	0	3	0	9	1,046	996	184
BECKER JC-WORCESTER	PRI-T	29,054	21,341	0	0	30	0	9	1,115	1,115	188
BENTLEY COLLEGE	PRI-FG	95,088	76,494	0	2,575	174	24,205	0	5,733	4,912	818
BERKLEE COLLEGE OF MUSIC	PRI-FN	25,917	22,000	0	3,000	5	0	0	1,190	1,000	70
BERKSHIRE CHRISTIAN C	PRI-FN	34,693	28,466	0	4	12	809	242	3,500	3,061	398
BLUE HILLS REG TECH INST	PUB-T	4,731	A	0	0	0	0	0	402	A	81
BOSTON COLLEGE	PRI-U	810,932	561,255	51,514	1,846	305	552,047	10,658	24,097	18,246	6,442
BOSTON CONSV OF MUSIC	PRI-FG	A	A		A	A			A	A	A
BOSTON UNIVERSITY	PRI-U	1,287,618	919,700	25,500	13,000	11,300	200	253	42,098	21,900	23,453
BRADFORD COLLEGE	PRI-FN	54,724	53,167	0	1	2,759	0	200	1,557	217	185
BRANDEIS UNIVERSITY	PRI-U	609,329	403,937	127,735	185,884	217	153,709	3,578	23,175	14,334	3,511
CEN NEW ENG COLLEGE TECHN	PRI FN	SEE WORCESTER JOINT LIBRARY						6	156	156	42
CHAMBERLAYNE JR COLLEGE	PRI-T	25,200	25,000	0			49,154	125,000	11,994	8,000	2,552
CLARK UNIVERSITY	PRI-FG	347,758	208,654		825	51		0	10,518	5,544	1,632
COLLEGE OF THE HOLY CROSS	PRI-FG	364,277	231,468		292	168	10,771	360	2,774	2,158	450
COLLEGE OUR LADY OF ELMS	PRI-FN	69,823	42,349	16,143	189	64	0				
CURRY COLLEGE	PRI-FN	78,957	64,575	38,943	1,936	260	1,100	15	1,684	1,148	654
DEAN JUNIOR COLLEGE	PRI-T	34,083	24,649	0	13,680	198	390	0	1,053	467	287
EASTERN NAZARENE COLLEGE	PRI-FG	83,020	75,548	0	2	236	0	0	2,886	2,583	467
EMERSON COLLEGE	PRI-FG	62,786	51,215	360	267	66	425	0	2,179	1,773	393
EMMANUEL COLLEGE	PRI-FG	119,619	114,463	0	0	5	939	0	2,918	2,618	475
ENDICOTT COLLEGE	PRI-T	47,844	46,193	0	0	0	842	1,550	863	860	192
EPISCOPAL DIVINITY SCHOOL	PRI-FG	102,748	80,604	0	27	26	0	0	1,645	1,257	259
ESSEX AGRL-TECH INST	PUB-T	13,270	10,675	20,377	444	7,705	0	40	1,168	1,094	287
FISHER JUNIOR COLLEGE	PRI-T	22,119	20,603	0	0	0	0	12	1,238	1,109	103
FORSYTH SCH DENTL HYGNSTS	PRI-T	6,996	6,792	0	0	8	12	0	173	156	167
FRANKLIN INST OF BOSTON	PRI-T	7,708	7,686	0	0	0	0	0	281	259	140
GORDON COLLEGE	PRI-FN	117,967	84,727	11,426	6,285	361	0	163	2,766	2,194	637
GORDON-CONWELL THEOL SEM	PRI-FG	94,464	81,000	0	603	99	5,528	0	5,058	4,650	839
HAMPSHIRE COLLEGE	PRI-FN	59,705	48,061	0	30	404	0	0	1,916	1,513	766
HARVARD UNIVERSITY	PRI-U	9,913,992	3,945,800	0	0	0	1,937,315	3,447,000	241,400	107,000	90,000
HEBREW COLLEGE	PRI-FG	64,703	62,269	0	498	85	0	93	1,353	1,110	220
HELLENIC C-HOLY CROSS SCH	PRI-FG	68,857	A	0	0	0	507	0	4,253	A	320
KATHARINE GIBBS SCHOOL	PRI-T	1,795	1,180	0	0	0	0	0	20	20	12
LABOURE JUNIOR COLLEGE	PRI-T	8,592	6,938	0	50	0	40	0	337	301	149
LASELL JUNIOR COLLEGE	PRI-T	48,600	43,900	0	0	31	4,100	100	1,380	877	253
LESLEY COLLEGE	PRI-FG	72,189	65,581	0	25	263	63,765	612	5,089	4,581	484
MASS BOARD CC ALL INST											
BERKSHIRE CMTY COLLEGE	PUB-T	39,214	33,387	0	0	158	7,132	1,193	2,032	1,672	273
BRISTOL COMMUNITY COLLEGE	PUB-T	40,486	33,554	0	0	160	0	107	2,057	1,529	303
BUNKER HILL CMTY COLLEGE	PUB-T	21,015	17,487	0	460	18	2,230	106	2,176	1,839	307
CAPE COD CMTY COLLEGE	PUB-T	48,936	45,998	0	0	297	12,762	98	0	0	383

SEE FOOTNOTES AT END OF TABLE

STATE OR OTHER AREA AND INSTITUTION (1)	CONTROL AND TYPE OF INSTITUTION (2)	HELD AT END OF YEAR							ADDED DURING YEAR		CURRENT PERIODICAL SUBSCRIPTION TITLES FALL 1979 (12)
		BOOKSTOCK		SEPARATE GOVERNMENT DOCUMENTS COLLECTIONS (VOLS.) (5)	MICROFORMS			ALL OTHER LIBRARY MATERIALS (9)	BOOKSTOCK		
		VOLUMES (3)	TITLES (4)		BOOK TITLES (6)	PERIODICAL TITLES (7)	OTHER PHYSICAL UNITS (8)		VOLUMES (10)	TITLES (11)	
MASSACHUSETTS	--CONTINUED										
GREENFIELD CMTY COLLEGE	PUB-T	38,885	34,996	478	0	0	4,508	180	1,117	1,005	360
HOLYOKE COMMUNITY COLLEGE	PUB-T	46,964	29,956	0	1,408	193	23,053	146	1,825	1,450	286
MASS BAY CMTY COLLEGE	PUB-T	40,891	36,802	0	178	185	0	1,068	1,694	1,342	309
MASSASOIT CMTY COLLEGE	PUB-T	60,217	48,174	640	0	220	8,500	32	1,200	960	356
MIDDLESEX CMTY COLLEGE	PUB-T	33,015	32,502	0	0	9	353	124	5,000	4,436	270
MT WACHUSETT CMTY COLLEGE	PUB-T	53,121	47,596	1,670	0	67	122	120	1,923	1,615	254
NTHN ESSEX CMTY COLLEGE	PUB-T	48,576	46,780	500	0	2,904	157,949	1,976	2,984	A	200
NORTH SHORE CMTY COLLEGE	PUB-T	A	A		0	A	A	A	A	A	A
QUINSIGAMOND CMTY COLLEGE	PUB-T	53,284		0	0	10	52	33	2,213	A	276
ROXBURY COMMUNITY COLLEGE	PUB-T	1,449	1,019	0	0	39	0	0	1,449	1,019	223
SPRINGFIELD TECHNICAL CC	PUB-T	43,590	40,000	0	5	20	5,637	8,314	3,058	1,770	248
MASS C PHAR-HLTH SCI	PRI-FG	55,404	23,585	0	19	18	18,300	150	2,584	1,420	773
MASS INST OF TECHNOLOGY	PRI-U	1,759,971	563,190	0	0	213	852,957	683,043	71,388	22,844	18,849
MASS STATE C SYS ALL INST											
BOSTON STATE COLLEGE	PUB-FG	146,723	120,000	0	22,726	1,031	308,870	0	10,756	7,500	1,028
BRIDGEWATER STATE COLLEGE	PUB-FG	176,642	110,941	11,591	74,498	9,335	21,247	4,345	5,250	3,839	1,486
FITCHBURG STATE COLLEGE	PUB-FG	150,000	125,000	0	23,000	15,700	159,648	3,400	6,434	5,000	2,022
FRAMINGHAM STATE COLLEGE	PUB-FG	130,025	108,354	16,066	25,542	272	240,858	4,962	5,940	4,950	774
MASS COLLEGE OF ART	PUB-FG	64,325	53,689	746	240	140	0	10,000	810	500	410
MASS MARITIME ACADEMY	PUB-FN	35,453	27,967	0	0	743	11,544	575	1,556	1,477	370
NORTH ADAMS STATE COLLEGE	PUB-FG	113,856	91,085	2,100	101	337	92,612	943	6,599	5,279	780
SALEM STATE COLLEGE	PUB-FG	180,006	144,006	0	207,083	460	10,130	63,746	6,388	5,112	1,085
WESTFIELD STATE COLLEGE	PUB-FG	122,327	85,675	0	0	0	212,031	447	4,947	A	698
WORCESTER STATE COLLEGE	PUB-FG	146,461	118,982	0	969	322	36,173	745	3,560	2,982	834
MERRIMACK COLLEGE	PRI-FN	117,414	62,315	0	0	27	3,182		3,315	2,351	875
MOUNT HOLYOKE COLLEGE	PRI-FG	437,071	267,827	0	131	25	6,902	0	17,282	9,502	3,588
MOUNT IDA JUNIOR COLLEGE	PRI-T	25,885	22,300	0	1	32	0	0	1,235	713	246
NEWBURY JUNIOR COLLEGE	PRI-T	7,065	6,097	200	15	24	0	15	690	449	140
NEW ENGLAND C OPTOMETRY	PRI-FG	9,034	5,710	0	308	1	0	900	784	600	229
NEW ENG CONSV OF MUSIC	PRI-FG	40,000	27,000	0	121	3	0	0	2,635	1,760	178
NEW ENG INST APP ARTS-SCI	PRI-T	3,422	3,016	0	0	0	0	106	212	156	72
NEW ENGLAND SCHOOL OF LAW	PRI-FG	72,735	11,418	0	0	3,821	48,239	0	5,669	2,258	1,692
NICHOLS COLLEGE	PRI-FG	A	A	118,000	447,558	A	A	A	13,761	7,196	7,604
NORTHEASTERN UNIVERSITY2/	PRI-U	434,225	301,521	0	4	747	1,670	0	1,861	1,704	224
PINE MANOR COLLEGE	PRI-FN	31,190	25,306			39		45			
POPE JOHN XXIII NATL SEM	PRI-FG	A	A	A	0	A	A	A	A	A	A
QUINCY JUNIOR COLLEGE	PUB-T	7,200	7,000	0	0	63	0	0	0	0	195
RADCLIFFE COLLEGE	PRI-FN	24,000	21,800	0	9,000	90	450	22,500	1,748	1,450	274
REGIS COLLEGE	PRI-FG	119,399	115,000	0	2	0	2,489	0	4,252	4,000	885
SNT HYACINTH COLLEGE-SEM	PRI-FN	53,100	22,300	0		0		0	2,300	1,300	150
SAINT JOHN'S SEMINARY	PRI-FG	120,220		0	0	0	0	0	2,227	1,725	350
SCH OF MUSEUM FINE ARTS	PRI-FG	6,706	5,800	0	0	1	0	18,000	737	658	67
SCH WORCESTER ART MUSEUM	PRI-T	31,761	15,399	0	6	5,790	4,656	27	768	760	93
SIMMONS COLLEGE	PRI-FG	157,810	126,248	0	3,391	109		0	8,802	7,041	1,467
SIMON'S ROCK EARLY C	PRI-FN	45,571	44,533	0	1				2,850	2,725	314
SMITH COLLEGE	PRI-FG	866,244	519,734	0	0	25,839	63,817	23,108	12,105	2,800	
STHESTN MASS UNIVERSITY	PUB-FG	225,175	202,660	91,208	42,072	1,594	81,517	40,000	11,117	10,006	1,600
SPRINGFIELD COLLEGE	PRI-FG	135,380	113,719	0	0	0	282,700	10	2,691	1,954	842
STONEHILL COLLEGE	PRI-FN	109,852	74,136	22,814	0	328	1,429	250	5,295	3,274	1,363
SUFFOLK UNIVERSITY	PRI-FG	197,936	120,161	0	21,080	316	0	0	15,675	4,024	1,948
SWAIN SCHOOL OF DESIGN	PRI-FN	12,101	11,200	0	0	0	0	436	724	670	45
TUFTS UNIVERSITY	PRI-U	566,582	400,000	192,629	151,700	943	263,600	150,000	18,874	12,500	4,173
UNIVERSITY OF LOWELL	PUB-FG	279,197	186,706	152,000	10	565	209,869	1,328	16,301	10,625	2,058
U OF MASS ALL CAMPUSES											
U OF MASS AMHERST CAMPUS	PUB-U	1,258,294	1,006,635	377,078	0	0	729,563	100,956	50,940	40,752	7,515
U OF MASS BOSTON CAMPUS	PUB-FG	318,295	193,564	0	3,500	350	1,392	0	18,556	11,050	3,000
U MASS MEDL SCH-WORCESTER	PUB-FG	74,379	14,845	12,321	0	653	16,156	0	4,820	2,120	1,836
WELLESLEY COLLEGE	PRI-FN	541,798	295,082	77,839	177	405	26,322	0	12,498	6,243	5,490
WENTWORTH INST OF TECH	PRI-FN	50,534	36,950	0	14	2,242	0	0	1,691	1,535	400
WESTERN NEW ENG COLLEGE	PRI-FG	167,087	75,144	896	2,696	135	176,995	0	16,547	6,133	2,223
WHEATON COLLEGE	PRI-FN	205,891	129,714	0	103	86	100	925	7,583	4,685	1,805

SEE FOOTNOTES AT END OF TABLE

Table 1. — Collections in College and University Libraries, by State or Other Area and Institution: Aggregate United States, 1978-79, and Fall 1979 — Continued

STATE OR OTHER AREA AND INSTITUTION (1)	CONTROL AND TYPE OF INSTITUTION (2)	HELD AT END OF YEAR — BOOKSTOCK VOLUMES (3)	BOOKSTOCK TITLES (4)	SEPARATE GOVERNMENT DOCUMENTS COLLECTIONS (VOLS.) (5)	MICROFORMS BOOK TITLES (6)	MICROFORMS PERIODICAL TITLES (7)	MICROFORMS OTHER PHYSICAL UNITS (8)	ALL OTHER LIBRARY MATERIALS (9)	ADDED DURING YEAR BOOKSTOCK VOLUMES (10)	BOOKSTOCK TITLES (11)	CURRENT PERIODICAL SUBSCRIPTION TITLES FALL 1979 (12)
MASSACHUSETTS --CONTINUED											
WHEELOCK COLLEGE	PRI-FG	61,319	47,123	0	1,639	30	1,611	1,624	2,605	1,959	501
WILLIAMS COLLEGE	PRI-FG	490,496	236,767	85,053	950	104	112,027	70	16,585	6,793	2,803
WORCESTER JUNIOR COLLEGE	PRI T	SEE WORCESTER JOINT LIBRARY									
WORCESTER JOINT LIBRARY	PRI-FN	31,506	31,476	0	0	60	0	0	755	725	328
WORCESTER POLY INSTITUTE	PRI-FG	175,522	95,873	11,926	49	120	551,707	5,100	12,476	4,620	1,084
MICHIGAN											
ADRIAN COLLEGE	PRI-FN	112,210	A	0	15,377	138	0	90	3,359	2,641	551
ALBION COLLEGE	PRI-FN	218,341	204,600	40,000	20	80	43,000	0	5,576	4,900	1,250
ALMA COLLEGE	PRI-FN	137,429	114,066	90,000	50	40	7,800	0	5,009	4,157	950
ALPENA COMMUNITY COLLEGE	PUB-T	29,053	A	0	4	2,688	0	0	1,082	A	187
ANDREWS UNIVERSITY	PRI-FG	382,986	A	3,302	188,848	208	132,953	3,609	17,431	A	3,066
AQUINAS COLLEGE	PRI-FG	105,835	101,000	0	32	444	9,922	0	2,812	A	705
BAKER JUNIOR COLLEGE BUS	PRI-T	3,000	2,800	0	0	0	0	0	375	350	100
BAY DE NOC CMTY COLLEGE	PUB-T	24,814	21,725	0	1,765	95	973	0	1,557	1,500	220
CALVIN COLLEGE	PRI FG	SEE CALVIN COLLEGE JOINT LIB									
CALVIN COLLEGE JOINT LIB	PRI-FG	308,251	204,135	97,671	19,593	413	514	0	8,970	7,386	1,943
CALVIN THEOLOGICAL SEM	PRI FG	SEE CALVIN COLLEGE JOINT LIB									
CTR FOR CREATIVE STUDIES	PRI-FN	10,400	10,320	0	0	0	0	90,000	1,000	985	74
CENTRAL MICH UNIVERSITY	PUB-FG	536,369	268,576	117,206	137,703	2,212	0	256,057	28,000	20,201	4,975
CHAS S MOTT CMTY COLLEGE	PUB-T	90,806	80,305	0	0	4,202	0	26,756	2,548	2,450	393
CLEARY COLLEGE	PRI-FN	10,708	A	0	0	0	0	0	310	310	184
CONCORDIA COLLEGE	PRI-FN	103,434	75,000	1,192	80	262	0	50	4,000	3,480	324
CRANBROOK ACADEMY OF ART	PRI-FG	20,179	19,728	0	0	0	0	17,125	378	378	149
DAVENPORT COLLEGE OF BUS	PRI-T	12,676	12,476	0	0	9	260	0	602	602	155
DELTA COLLEGE	PUB-T	84,754	84,021	0	0	7,421	0	2,410	3,825	3,805	621
DETROIT BIBLE COLLEGE	PRI-FN	39,264	31,411	0	0	5	127	51	1,157	926	240
DETROIT C OF BUS ADMIN	PRI-FN	18,180	17,574	0	0	0	1,076	0	1,075	1,035	250
DETROIT COLLEGE OF LAW	PRI-FG	52,523	8,955	0	60,646	27,605	0	0	3,147	1,214	1,395
DETROIT INST TECHNOLOGY	PRI-FN	61,424	46,606	0	0	193	103	0	398	332	247
EASTERN MICH UNIVERSITY	PUB-FG	465,299	325,696	110,207	6,750	910	302,471	31,844	16,956	11,869	4,261
FERRIS STATE COLLEGE	PUB-FG	187,038	157,426	15,997	254	524	147,684	6,026	12,587	10,798	1,380
GENERAL MOTORS INSTITUTE	PRI-FN	40,519	40,061	2,586	7,702	204	0	0	2,501	2,043	760
GLEN OAKS CMTY COLLEGE	PUB-T	31,615	28,046	0	0	191	1	9	1,366	A	276
GOGEBIC COMMUNITY COLLEGE	PUB-T	21,883	18,695	0	20	53	9	18	913	817	218
GRACE BIBLE COLLEGE	PRI-FN	25,855	19,511	0	0	6	0	0	977	687	89
GRAND RAPIDS BAPT C & SEM	PRI-FG	65,065	53,150	0	347	16	646	5,255	8,005	1,468	515
GRAND RAPIDS JR COLLEGE	PUB-T	48,866	43,026	0	1	95	1	0	2,138	1,798	338
GRAND RAPIDS SCH BIBLE	PRI-T	12,225	8,225	0	0	0	0	600	1,225	860	129
GRAND VALLEY ST COLLEGES	PUB-FG	207,811	153,364	66,771	6,100	700	178,464	38,130	10,439	7,703	1,921
GREAT LAKES BIBLE COLLEGE	PRI-FN	17,502	14,015	0	113	28	0	73	1,235	1,180	153
HENRY FORD CMTY COLLEGE	PUB-T	87,077	57,553	11,970	0	256	7,365	18,173	2,249	1,040	909
HIGHLAND PK CMTY COLLEGE	PUB-T	A	17,851	0	0	2,374	0	0	A	1,290	133
HILLSDALE COLLEGE	PRI-FN	85,686	A	0	0	0	1,841	0	5,763	A	442
HOPE COLLEGE	PRI-FN	189,134	146,541	0	18,000	14	5,000	0	7,923	5,187	1,184
JACKSON COMMUNITY COLLEGE	PUB-T	39,197	32,358	0	85	142	10,572	0	3,447	1,813	348
JOHN WESLEY COLLEGE	PRI-FN	36,000	35,357	0	789	99	1,112	25	19	19	47
JORDAN COLLEGE	PRI-FN	13,000	11,750	0	0	0	0	0	3,000	2,800	30
KALAMAZOO COLLEGE	PRI-FN	223,303	162,000	0	125	83	4,681	1,104	7,665	5,812	917
KALAMAZOO VALLEY CC	PUB-T	60,352	48,282	0	221	104	0	90	3,659	2,927	475
KELLOGG COMMUNITY COLLEGE	PUB-T	39,143	34,471	0	632	103	0	17,820	3,379	3,091	435
KENDALL SCH OF DESIGN	PRI-FN	6,010	5,126	0	0	0	0	93,650	722	655	87
KIRTLAND CMTY COLLEGE	PUB-T	30,012	24,770	0	15	65	1,424	155	1,493	1,442	250
LAKE MICHIGAN COLLEGE	PUB-T	70,000	45,500	0	0	5	12,500	400	4,000	3,500	350
LAKE SUPERIOR ST COLLEGE	PUB-FN	92,987	69,898	800	2,018	0	3,116	0	3,560	2,599	710
LANSING COMMUNITY COLLEGE	PUB-T	74,277	63,389	0	0	135	6,891	0	6,643	4,811	1,045
LAWRENCE INST TECHNOLOGY	PRI-FN	47,321	44,901	0	0	62	14,546	0	1,796	1,683	389
LEWIS C BUSINESS	PRI-T	2,778	2,514	248	0	0	0	78	345	301	24
MACOMB CO CC ALL CAM											
MACOMB CO CC-CENTER CAM	PUB-T	57,390	33,967	0	413	63	19,666	0	4,131	2,355	498
MACOMB CO CC-SOUTH CAMPUS	PUB-T	94,312	57,132	3,720	157	82	11,224	184	3,746	2,322	693

SEE FOOTNOTES AT END OF TABLE

Table 1. – Collections in College and University Libraries, by State or Other Area and Institution: Aggregate United States, 1978-79, and Fall 1979 – Continued

STATE OR OTHER AREA AND INSTITUTION	CONTROL AND TYPE OF INSTITUTION	HELD AT END OF YEAR — BOOKSTOCK VOLUMES	BOOKSTOCK TITLES	SEPARATE GOVERNMENT DOCUMENTS COLLECTIONS (VOLS.)	MICROFORMS BOOK TITLES	MICROFORMS PERIODICAL TITLES	MICROFORMS OTHER PHYSICAL UNITS	ALL OTHER LIBRARY MATERIALS	ADDED DURING YEAR — BOOKSTOCK VOLUMES	BOOKSTOCK TITLES	CURRENT PERIODICAL SUBSCRIPTION TITLES FALL 1979
(1)	(2)	(3)	(4)	(5)	(6)	(7)	(8)	(9)	(10)	(11)	(12)
MICHIGAN --CONTINUED											
MADONNA COLLEGE	PRI-FN	94,685	94,145	346	0	59	16,884	1,300	3,708	3,381	571
MARYGROVE COLLEGE	PRI-FG	171,147	135,030	1,500	400	42	15,776	0	1,943	1,584	825
MERCY COLLEGE OF DETROIT	PRI-FN	118,000	99,600	0	0	476	0	31	5,074	4,390	570
MERRILL-PALMER INSTITUTE	PRI-FG	18,000	A	0	0	0	10	0	649	A	220
MICH CHRISTIAN COLLEGE	PRI-T	31,638	19,134	0	19,000	73	10	0	3,059	1,850	217
MICHIGAN STATE UNIVERSITY	PUB-U	1,905,583	1,190,989	503,369	81,000	42,500	1,059,867	116,647	70,053	54,617	24,406
MICHIGAN TECHNOLOGICAL U	PUB-FG	455,367	111,173	0	110	145	40,030	81,905	28,259	10,428	3,220
MID MICHIGAN CMTY COLLEGE	PUB-T	18,283	14,821	0	0	85	11,227	2,134	560	392	276
MCNRCE CO CMTY COLLEGE	PUB-T	45,452	40,864	0	4	174	248	0	644	554	299
MONTCALM CMTY COLLEGE	PUB-T	21,261	20,848	0	0	25	2,514	937	645	645	171
MUSKEGON BUSINESS COLLEGE	PRI-T	3,597	3,581	0	0	0	0	0	636	621	65
MUSKEGON CMTY COLLEGE	PUB-T	52,980	43,359	0	3	326	984	700	4,699	3,959	435
NAZARETH COLLEGE	PRI-FN	83,000	55,333	0	0	39	3,600	204	7,709	5,139	484
NCRTH CEN MICH COLLEGE	PUB-T	21,239	21,000	2,744	0	40	3,456	20	348	450	138
NORTHERN MICH UNIVERSITY	PUB-FG	347,782	225,926	145,069	0	0	297,645	169	18,053	11,748	2,281
NORTHWESTERN MICH COLLEGE	PUB-T	44,390	44,280	3,000	1,150	568	6,837	1,200	2,110	2,000	380
NORTHWOOD INSTITUTE	PRI-FN	45,059	14,000	0	0	23		28	1,633	99	620
OAKLAND COMMUNITY COLLEGE	PUB-T	146,673	69,581	72,904	0	838	19,239	10,196	3,228	2,787	720
OAKLAND UNIVERSITY	PUB-FG	290,345	A	155,564	0	0	402,195	0	10,930	A	1,981
OLIVET COLLEGE	PRI-FG	74,293	68,308	30,000	122	55	7,000	2,000	5,125	3,999	723
REFORMED BIBLE COLLEGE	PRI-FN	34,465	27,700	0	830	12	30	2,100	1,675	1,500	182
SACRED HEART SEMINARY C	PRI-FN	50,956	50,400	0		708		175	1,059	1,050	322
SAGINAW VLY STATE COLLEGE	PUB-FG	87,524	73,796	0	8,559	0		923	5,549	2,373	572
SNT CLAIR CO CMTY COLLEGE	PUB-T	41,871	41,632	0	77	453	11,108		2,044	2,032	697
SNT JOHN PROVINCIAL SEM	PRI-FG	A	A						A	A	
SAINT MARY'S COLLEGE	PRI-FN	48,653								A	
SCHOOLCRAFT COLLEGE	PUB-T	69,765	66,278	42,673	0	2	0	20	2,200	29	455
SHAW COLLEGE AT DETROIT	PRI-FN	89,668	81,397	0	0	66	3,520	0	2,523	2,420	609
SIENA HEIGHTS COLLEGE	PRI-FG	76,469	68,910	25,380	0	900	0	66	865	937	312
SOUTHWESTERN MICH COLLEGE	PUB-T	24,986	25,000	11,049	0	64	4,578	0	3,189	2,470	355
SPRING ARBOR COLLEGE	PRI-FN	64,423	57,355	0	0	11	0		3,549	3,200	335
SUOMI COLLEGE	PRI-T	22,348	A	0	8	1	23	431	511	A	411
THOMAS M COOLEY LAW SCH	PRI-FG	A	A	A	A	A	A	47,274	763	A	
UNIVERSITY OF DETROIT	PRI-U	449,958	334,462	302,800	131,657	350	27,866	1,600	13,612	7,459	3,451
U OF MICHIGAN ALL CAM											
U MICHIGAN-ANN ARBOR	PUB-U	5,076,602	3,227,855	4,496	490,127	5,041	458,264	287,452	118,478	74,052	47,438
U OF MICHIGAN-DEARBORN	PUB-FG	211,130	A	0	229,186	0	0	329	10,065	A	1,601
U OF MICHIGAN-FLINT	PUB-FG	94,892	A	40,290	0	0	154,635	2,306	12,530	A	963
WALSH C ACCTY & BUS ADMIN	PRI-FG	12,500	10,000	0	5	0	400	20	756	700	90
WASHTENAW CMTY COLLEGE	PUB-T	48,219	38,971	0	3	119	0	50	2,831	2,442	536
WAYNE COUNTY CMTY COLLEGE	PUB-T	42,192	13,875	2,490	0	0	0	55	21,200	6,000	490
WAYNE STATE UNIVERSITY	PUB-U	1,804,932	656,800	415,775	0	0	803,505	57,033	49,371	23,327	13,407
WESTERN MICH UNIVERSITY	PUB-FG	753,870	400,070	342,609	0	0	424,763	149,505	36,631	21,669	10,705
WESTERN THEOLOGICAL SEM	PRI-FG	74,977	52,885	0	100	47	201	0	1,858	1,675	476
WEST SHORE CMTY COLLEGE	PUB-T	11,349	10,752	0	0	23	1,054	25	450	450	240
MINNESOTA											
AUGSBURG COLLEGE	PRI-FN	131,506	107,835	3,000	7	28	12,472	2,591	3,807	3,122	626
BETHANY LUTHERAN COLLEGE	PRI-T	A	A	0	0	A	A		1,000	826	225
BETHEL C & SEM ALL CAM											
BETHEL COLLEGE	PRI-FN	125,000	112,000	0	26	105	2,250	0	6,653	6,048	560
BETHEL THEOL SEMINARY	PRI-FG	85,775	62,700	0	215	63	0	1,820	3,900	3,300	505
CARLETON COLLEGE	PRI-FN	260,021	190,837	111,600	20,449	1,274	0	1,820	11,000	8,601	1,380
COLLEGE OF SAINT BENEDICT	PRI-FN	101,760	78,544	0	165	400	0	643	5,321	5,040	685
COLLEGE OF SNT CATHERINE	PRI-FN	206,382	205,492	18,063	333	42	4,803	576	6,005	4,168	943
COLLEGE SAINT SCHOLASTICA	PRI-FG	81,241	76,000	0	117	74	3,081	0	3,031	2,900	556
COLLEGE OF SAINT TERESA	PRI-FN	130,583	130,476	0	0	857	0	1,076	3,282	3,175	698
COLLEGE OF SAINT THOMAS	PRI-FG	196,110	108,741	0	68	40	113,759	474	5,212	3,733	1,113
CONCORDIA C AT MOORHEAD	PRI-FN	204,121	186,686	0	25,596	195	2,631	481	6,627	6,374	1,506
CONCORDIA C-SAINT PAUL	PRI-FN	82,741	78,128	0	158	31	1,720	500	2,968	2,878	460
CROSIER SEMINARY	PRI-T	20,000	19,800	0	0	25	5,000	5,000	1,000	900	117

SEE FOOTNOTES AT END OF TABLE

Table 1. – Collections in College and University Libraries, by State or Other Area and Institution: Aggregate United States, 1978-79, and Fall 1979 – Continued

STATE OR OTHER AREA AND INSTITUTION	CONTROL AND TYPE OF INSTITUTION	HELD AT END OF YEAR							ADDED DURING YEAR		CURRENT PERIODICAL SUBSCRIPTION TITLES FALL 1979
		BOOKSTOCK		SEPARATE GOVERNMENT DOCUMENTS COLLECTIONS (VOLS.)	MICROFORMS			ALL OTHER LIBRARY MATERIALS	BOOKSTOCK		
		VOLUMES	TITLES		BOOK TITLES	PERIODICAL TITLES	OTHER PHYSICAL UNITS		VOLUMES	TITLES	
(1)	(2)	(3)	(4)	(5)	(6)	(7)	(8)	(9)	(10)	(11)	(12)
MINNESOTA	--CONTINUED										
OR MARTIN LUTHER COLLEGE	PRI-FN	46,585	44,256	3,744	73	5	255	14,120	3,012	2,861	402
GOLDEN VLY LUTH COLLEGE	PRI-T	25,195	21,808	0	0	0	0	650	1,990	1,652	244
GUSTAVUS ADOLPHUS COLLEGE	PRI-FN	174,182	155,67C	82,160	25,055	0	0	0	11,250	10,116	1,425
HAMLINE UNIVERSITY	PRI-FG	238,500	148,000	0	0	98	208	0	5,551	5,200	1,078
LUTHER NTHWSTN SEM JT LIB	PRI-FG	167,230	A	0	0	0	410	170	3,552	2,960	670
LUTHER THEOLOGICAL SEM	PRI FG	SEE LUTHER NTHWSTN SEM JT LIB									
MACALESTER COLLEGE	PRI-FN	271,332	169,021	5,311	306	116	7,153	0	4,846	3,899	849
MAYO MEDICAL SCHOOL	PRI-FG	2,574	1,225	0	0	0	0	12	402	227	33
MINNEAPOLIS C-ART DESIGN	PRI-FN	45,671	27,316	0	0	0	0	50,500	1,613	1,216	178
MINNESOTA BIBLE COLLEGE	PRI-FN	17,022	15,144	0	0	44	137	18	907	904	103
MINN CC SYSTEM ALL INST											
ANOKA-RAMSEY CMTY COLLEGE	PUB-T	29,089	29,040	0	0	84	2,486	529	1,145	1,096	229
AUSTIN COMMUNITY COLLEGE	PUB-T	21,428	20,132	0	2,900	49	3,878	0	803	782	256
BRAINERD CMTY COLLEGE	PUB-T	15,340	15,180	1,200	0	26	2,529	1,125	450	160	320
FERGUS FALLS CMTY COLLEGE	PUB-T	29,663	24,101	0	0	42	0	0	850	802	358
HIBBING COMMUNITY COLLEGE	PUB-T	23,525	16,500	0	0	11	1,509	76	696	525	190
INVER HILLS CMTY COLLEGE	PUB-T	29,100	27,600	450	0	129	1,784	750	1,690	1,592	354
ITASCA COMMUNITY COLLEGE	PUB-T	19,384	16,381	0	0	39	3	579	609	45	250
LAKEWOOD CMTY COLLEGE	PUB-T	26,791	25,790	0	1	110	2,130	60	1,159	950	324
MESABI COMMUNITY COLLEGE	PUB-T	28,136	27,666	0	1	9	1,665	250	577	470	192
METROPOLITAN CMTY COLLEGE	PUB-T	A	22,297	0	0	0	0	10	A	1,112	121
NORMANDALE CMTY COLLEGE	PUB-T	51,077	39,136	0	17	96	0	0	6,911	5,057	371
N HENNEPIN CMTY COLLEGE	PUB-T	27,003	24,302	0	0	154	1,014	846	1,234	1,110	383
NORTHLAND CMTY COLLEGE	PUB-T	12,250	11,750	0	0	7	185	3,467	500	475	147
RAINY RIVER CMTY COLLEGE	PUB-T	15,354	13,880	0	0	2	0	1	785	747	116
ROCHESTER CMTY COLLEGE	PUB-T	46,590	43,000	0	0	24	680	0	2,167	2,000	430
VERMILION CMTY COLLEGE	PUB-T	16,000	15,355	0	0	55	0	7	1,056	1,008	267
WILLMAR CMTY COLLEGE	PUB-T	18,395	18,380	0	0	0	988	260	844	834	222
WORTHINGTON CMTY COLLEGE	PUB-T	31,174	28,674	0	157	72	1,078	0	924	893	191
NORTH CEN BIBLE COLLEGE	PRI-FN	25,252	21,000	0	15	3	0	0	1,161	1,000	212
NORTHWESTERN COLLEGE	PRI-FN	48,208	39,988	0	53	13	178	317	1,191	1,191	368
NTHWSTN C CHIROPRACTIC	PRI-FG	6,100	6,036	0	0	1	0	44	702	638	206
NTHWSTN LUTH THEOL SEM	PRI FG	SEE LUTHER NTHWSTN SEM JT LIB									
SAINT JOHN'S UNIVERSITY	PRI-FG	283,358	182,065	91,485	26,045	1,375	0	27,330	6,254	5,183	1,079
SAINT MARY'S COLLEGE	PRI-FG	137,388	137,388	0	800	6	0	1,000	3,848	3,848	590
SAINT MARY'S JR COLLEGE	PRI-T	24,529	22,075	0	0	0	0	0	1,212	998	228
SAINT OLAF COLLEGE	PRI-FN	319,440	219,584	60,000	839	12	7,417	2	10,566	7,682	1,200
SAINT PAUL BIBLE COLLEGE	PRI-FN	64,795	62,694	0	3	56	0	540	11,057	10,121	365
SAINT PAUL SEMINARY	PRI-FG	62,450	53,000	0	0	4	0	0	850	500	350
STATE U SYS MINN ALL INST											
BEMIDJI STATE U	PUB-FG	204,511	194,205	60,660	0	0	440,614	1,820	5,762	5,472	854
MANKATO STATE UNIVERSITY	PUB-FG	369,281	351,895	170,207	0	0	960,831	0	14,739	7,839	2,463
METROPOLITAN STATE U	PUB-FN	NO LIBRARY FACILITIES									
MOORHEAD STATE UNIVERSITY	PUB-FG	248,750	A	67,619	0	0	290,161	0	13,027	A	1,250
SAINT CLOUD ST UNIVERSITY	PUB-FG	477,305	316,000	602,262	0	0	290,573	50,323	14,654	9,671	2,024
STHWST STATE UNIVERSITY	PUB-FN	144,653	120,732	0	0	0	22,446	450	3,579	3,163	750
WINONA STATE UNIVERSITY	PUB-FG	170,209	109,789	0	0	0	471,529	0	5,855	4,883	1,082
UNITED THEOLOGICAL SEM	PRI-FG	53,148	53,106	0	70	3	374	49	1,284	1,242	324
U OF MINNESOTA ALL CAM											
U OF MINNESOTA DULUTH	PUB-FG	257,321	166,410	0	80	380	220,611	600	9,491	6,120	3,418
U MINN MAYO GRAD SCH MED	PRI-FG	219,692	66,317	1,300	2,174	30	1,250	500	4,963	4,800	2,995
U OF MINN MNPLS SNT PAUL	PUB-U	3,738,168	3,738,168	2,006,493	0	0	1,126,011	453,383	92,338	78,920	44,450
U OF MINNESOTA MORRIS	PUB-FN	111,957	100,759	15,591	8	100	155	103	5,153	4,377	732
U MINN TECH COL CROOKSTON	PUB-T	19,037	16,056	0	0	98	215	216	965	921	811
U OF MINN TECH C-WASECA	PUB-T	21,081	18,340	5,702	0	369	1,103	11,149	1,679	1,679	600
WM MITCHELL COLLEGE LAW	PRI-FG	71,463	17,383	0	0	0	35,940	0	5,327	1,243	2,030
MISSISSIPPI											
ALCORN STATE UNIVERSITY	PUB-FG	125,434	109,073	75,683	11	157	95,429	1,093	6,323	4,424	1,007
BELHAVEN COLLEGE	PRI-FN	56,184	55,500	0	18	4	183	375	2,655	2,655	356

SEE FOOTNOTES AT END OF TABLE

Table 1. — Collections in College and University Libraries, by State or Other Area and Institution: Aggregate United States, 1978-79, and Fall 1979 — Continued

STATE OR OTHER AREA AND INSTITUTION	CON-TROL AND TYPE OF IN-STITU-TION	HELD AT END OF YEAR							ADDED DURING YEAR		CURRENT PERIOD-ICAL SUB-SCRIPTION TITLES FALL 1979
		BOOKSTOCK		SEPARATE GOVERN-MENT DOCU-MENTS COLLEC-TIONS (VOLS.)	MICROFORMS			ALL OTHER LIBRARY MATE-RIALS	BOOKSTOCK		
		VOLUMES	TITLES		BOOK TITLES	PERI-ODICAL TITLES	OTHER PHYS-ICAL UNITS		VOLUMES	TITLES	
(1)	(2)	(3)	(4)	(5)	(6)	(7)	(8)	(9)	(10)	(11)	(12)
MISSISSIPPI	--CONTINUED										
BLUE MOUNTAIN COLLEGE	PRI-FN	44,722	27,737	0	1	6	0	0	996	914	220
CLARKE COLLEGE	PRI-T	17,980	15,652	133	0	45	7	101	838	807	213
COAHOMA JUNIOR COLLEGE	PUB-T	26,143	23,141	0	0	255	0	0	1,161	971	264
COPIAH-LINCOLN JR COLLEGE	PUB-T	39,162	38,005	0	1	67	4,058	0	2,191	1,999	185
DELTA STATE UNIVERSITY	PUB-FG	210,157	176,810	29,789	5,231	443	295,387	819	10,707	8,851	1,303
EAST CENTRAL JR COLLEGE	PUB-T	26,471	24,266	0	0	0	0	4	1,177	1,079	123
EAST MISS JUNIOR COLLEGE	PUB-T	20,498	17,483	0	3	32	0	120	978	846	309
HINDS JUNIOR COLLEGE	PUB-T	71,231	51,657	0	477	210	18,527	84	6,878	4,205	644
HOLMES JUNIOR COLLEGE	PUB-T	35,534	35,480	0	351	18	0	405	1,350	1,296	258
ITAWAMBA JUNIOR COLLEGE	PUB-T	36,416	34,830	0	0	192	1,100	3	2,487	2,405	369
JACKSON STATE UNIVERSITY	PUB-FG	315,184	315,149	50,162	130,553	517	19,496	1,199	16,683	16,648	2,127
JONES CO JUNIOR COLLEGE	PUB-T	49,569	49,000	0	0	69	1,169	70	1,800	1,700	550
MARY HOLMES COLLEGE	PRI-T	23,058	22,433	0	0	0	976	4	1,442	1,306	109
MERIDIAN JUNIOR COLLEGE	PUB-T	37,068	35,209	0	3	196	94,435	0	2,751	2,614	607
MILLSAPS COLLEGE	PRI-FN	95,987	85,000	31,236	0	0	10,016	0	2,856	2,000	538
MINISTERIAL INST AND C	PRI-T	7,000	6,706	0	0	0	0	15	0	0	47
MISSISSIPPI COLLEGE	PRI-FG	223,739	200,059	5,750	0	599	1,646	0	12,618	6,181	2,741
MISS DELTA JUNIOR COLLEGE	PRI-T	25,377	24,397	0	12	54	1,298	474	820	780	237
MISS GULF CST JC ALL CAM											
MISS GULF CST JC JACKSON	PUB-T	25,202	25,132	0	0	117	0	28	1,595	1,525	269
MISS GULF CST JEFF DAVIS	PUB-T	33,028	32,148	0	0	86	4,571	195	1,885	1,802	327
MISS GULF CST JC PERKNSTN	PUB-T	21,017	20,902	360	0	60	0	300	A	2,093	160
MISS INOUSTRIAL COLLEGE	PRI-FN	38,549	36,549	0	1,857	220	0	325	629	A	0
MISSISSIPPI ST UNIVERSITY	PUB-U	622,769	255,721	158,561	2,670	490	1,076,434	57,239	27,380	14,002	8,281
MISS UNIVERSITY FOR WOMEN	PUB-FG	220,893	131,321	21,531	0	0	58,670	33	8,098	5,445	1,970
MISS VLY ST UNIVERSITY	PUB-FG	98,363	55,005	0	32,892	10,930	3,456	38	2,729	A	418
NORTHEAST MISS JR COLLEGE	PUB-T	32,262	25,491	0	1	101	3,050	0	2,254	1,178	416
NORTHWEST MISS JR COLLEGE	PUB-T	28,873	27,429	0	0	0	0	0	1,715	1,700	183
PEARL RIVER JR COLLEGE	PUB-T	A	A	0	0	A	A	A	A	A	A
PHILLIPS COLLEGE	PRI-T	1,149	1,133	1	0	0	0	0	352	347	17
PRENTISS NORM-INDUS INST	PRI-T	6,307	5,083	390	5	0	4	14	832	638	128
REFORMED THEOLOGICAL SEM	PRI-FG	46,616	A	0	0	0	7,426	0	3,076	A	600
RUST COLLEGE	PRI-FN	64,658	58,695	0	0	2,454	0	5,432	5,957	4,766	307
SOUTHEASTERN BAPT COLLEGE	PRI-FN	9,475	A	0	0	62	0	0	575	A	0
SOUTHWEST MISS JR COLLEGE	PUB-T	25,071	17,583	0	1	94	819	627	1,127	866	217
TOUGALOO COLLEGE	PRI-FN	A	84,854	542	0	82	3,948	0	A	2,655	397
U OF MISSISSIPPI ALL CAM											
U OF MISSISSIPPI MAIN CAM	PUB-U	602,203	260,744	71,380	15,909	0	0	0	21,111	13,573	4,261
U OF MISSISSIPPI MEDL CTR	PUB-FG	107,019	27,251	0	222	88	852	555	4,236	1,104	2,569
U OF SOUTHERN MISSISSIPPI	PUB-FG	427,652	266,014	530,130	174,977	734	475,170	989	21,278	15,301	4,416
UTICA JUNIOR COLLEGE	PUB-T	25,678	25,178	0	0	592	7,008	2,673	1,047	A	160
WESLEY COLLEGE	PRI-FN	17,093	15,383	0	0	0	0	96	2,707	2,436	115
WHITWORTH BIBLE COLLEGE	PRI-FN	8,337	8,337	0	0	0	0	0	267	267	25
WILLIAM CAREY COLLEGE	PRI-FG	77,076	52,000	0	0	22,312	62	0	3,861	3,000	569
WOOD JUNIOR COLLEGE	PRI-T	25,229	24,016	0	0	0	0	0	517	474	153
MISSOURI											
ASSEMBLIES GOD GRAD SCH	PRI-FG	29,029	26,908	0	233	1,727	29,244	154	3,178	2,644	437
AVILA COLLEGE	PRI-FG	66,007	59,903	37	5	224	49	0	1,369	1,302	416
BAPTIST BIBLE COLLEGE	PRI-FN	29,727	A	0	75	0	0	84	2,282	2,100	145
CALVARY BIBLE COLLEGE	PRI-FG	32,938	A	0	1,606	0	0	112	1,119	A	130
CARDINAL GLENNON COLLEGE	PRI-FN	62,835	A	0	0	0	0	0	1,222	A	191
CARDINAL NEWMAN COLLEGE	PRI-FN	5,987	4,957	0	0	2	179	127	2,267	2,644	86
CENTRAL BIBLE COLLEGE	PRI-FN	85,533	A	587	67	218	8,467	614	8,562	A	0
CEN CHRSTN C OF THE BIBLE	PRI-FN	16,945	11,281	0	89	3	0	200	792	699	111
CENTRAL METHODIST COLLEGE	PRI-FN	136,634	62,017	45,232	2,500	165	4,434	0	1,675	1,300	203
CENTRAL MO ST UNIVERSITY	PUB-FG	312,704	250,163	168,502	5,276	247	315,523	31,277	13,516	10,812	2,758
CHRIST SEMINARY-SEMINEX	PRI-FG	28,111	24,110	0	262	55	1,485	2	2,791	2,475	345
CLEVELAND CHIROPRACTIC C	PRI-FG	3,880	3,825	0	0	0	0	0	212	197	100
COLUMBIA COLLEGE	PRI-FN	37,842	29,886	0	19,000	199	0	100	2,761	2,639	422
CONCEPTION SEM COLLEGE	PRI-FN	87,015	74,746	0	0	0	126	1,220	2,591	1,967	304

SEE FOOTNOTES AT END OF TABLE

Table 1. — Collections in College and University Libraries, by State or Other Area and Institution: Aggregate United States, 1978-79, and Fall 1979 — Continued

		HELD AT END OF YEAR							ADDED DURING YEAR		
		BOOKSTOCK		SEPARATE GOVERN-MENT DOCU-MENTS COLLEC-TIONS (VOLS.)	MICROFORMS			ALL OTHER LIBRARY MATE-RIALS	BOOKSTOCK		CURRENT PERIOD-ICAL SUB-SCRIPTION TITLES FALL 1979
STATE OR OTHER AREA AND INSTITUTION	CON-TROL AND TYPE OF IN-STITU-TION	VOLUMES	TITLES		BOOK TITLES	PERI-ODICAL TITLES	OTHER PHYS-ICAL UNITS		VOLUMES	TITLES	
(1)	(2)	(3)	(4)	(5)	(6)	(7)	(8)	(9)	(10)	(11)	(12)
MISSOURI	--CONTINUED										
CONCORDIA SEMINARY	PRI-FG	145,963	97,000	0	0	0	12,306	57	3,678	2,781	1,111
COTTEY COLLEGE	PRI-T	A	A				A	A	1,614	1,426	A
COVENANT THEOLOGICAL SEM	PRI-FG	35,790	30,128	0	1,040	12	0	0	1,614	1,426	336
CROWDER COLLEGE	PUB-T	26,454	23,923	0	4	28	69	2,954	1,135	1,053	265
CULVER-STOCKTON COLLEGE	PRI-FN	100,656	94,000	0	0	983	0	0	2,173	2,000	313
DRURY COLLEGE	PRI-FG	110,870	A	153,345	37	116	11,977	0	2,537	A	958
EAST CENTRAL MO DIST JC	PUB-T	18,886	17,798	0	0	38	24	0	1,030	1,000	247
EDEN THEOLOGICAL SEMINARY	PRI FG	SEE EDEN-WEBSTER JT LIB									
EDEN-WEBSTER JT LIBRARIES	PRI-FN	156,173	149,888	525	25	89	4,896	0	5,036	3,255	1,195
EVANGEL COLLEGE	PRI-FN	87,950	86,191	0	0	18	36	0	2,957	2,957	600
FONTBONNE COLLEGE	PRI-FG	85,873	85,843	0	20	25	1,007	783	1,384	1,354	510
HANNIBAL-LAGRANGE COLLEGE	PRI-FN	25,000	18,300	0	0	90	3	0	1,140	800	265
HARRIS-STOWE STATE C	PUB-FN	55,604	54,398	0	11,765	4,289	3,100	620	1,404	1,362	332
JEFFERSON COLLEGE	PUB-T	39,775	37,372	0	0	21	0	355	1,369	1,170	235
KANSAS CITY ART INSTITUTE	PRI-FN	28,403	A	0	0	0	0	0	1,200	A	79
KANSAS CITY C OSTEO MED	PRI-FG	32,424	20,195	0	0	0	27	9	4,570	2,269	542
KEMPER MILITARY SCH AND C	PRI-T	20,662	20,210	0	0	14	1,128	12	694	535	144
KENRICK SEMINARY	PRI-FG	62,232	60,054	0	56	277	10	826	968	934	341
KIRKSVL COLLEGE OSTEO MED	PRI-FG	50,113	18,856	751	0	36	277	17	2,585	1,000	745
LINCOLN UNIVERSITY	PJB-FG	131,001	114,721	37,081	55,445	8,717	30,205	22,088	2,946	1,936	1,044
THE LINDENWOOD COLLEGES	PRI-FG	87,457	75,717	6,979	0	227	8,119	0	3,942	3,376	614
LOGAN C OF CHIROPRACTIC	PRI-FG	13,795	13,760	0	0	0	0	297	735	710	120
MARYVILLE C-SAINT LOUIS	PRI-FG	93,000	92,750	12,000	2	124	0	316	3,000	2,750	556
METRO CC ADMINV ALL INST											
LONGVIEW CMTY COLLEGE	PUB-T	23,061	22,811	5,000	1	31	1,148	3	929	925	211
MAPLE WOODS CMTY COLLEGE	PUB-T	18,228	10,593	2,350	3,500	45	0	75	362	300	329
PENN VALLEY CMTY COLLEGE	PUB-T	58,956	A	0	980	8	1,001	0	443	A	185
PIONEER COMMUNITY COLLEGE	PUB-T	727	727	0	0	0	0	0	82	82	26
MIDWESTERN BAPT THEOL SEM	PRI-FG	A	A		A	A			A	A	A
MINERAL AREA COLLEGE	PUB-T	23,075	18,776	3,893	7	110	30	100	1,569	1,562	180
MISSOURI BAPTIST COLLEGE	PRI-FN	33,747	28,867	0	2,607	206	5,717	1,252	2,149	1,942	371
MISSOURI INST TECHNOLOGY	PRI-FN	1,217	1,074	0	0	0	0	0	49	49	79
MISSOURI STHN ST COLLEGE	PUB-FN	129,204	128,000	67,933	250,123	651	0	13,790	6,775	6,550	1,188
MISSOURI VALLEY COLLEGE	PRI-FN	84,754	57,079	2,000	0	2	0	60	1,051	679	274
MISSOURI WSTN ST COLLEGE	PUB-FN	104,154	72,993	3,016	0	0	13,899	222	7,806	5,815	1,163
MOBERLY JUNIOR COLLEGE	PUB-T	14,392	13,052	0	0	41	11	508	344	290	176
NAZARENE THEOLOGICAL SEM	PRI-FG	53,923	43,000	0	71	4	265	34	2,638	2,102	412
NTHEST MO ST UNIVERSITY	PUB-FG	236,141	189,900	43,861	0	105	540,066	4,700	15,876	13,400	1,661
NTHWST MO ST UNIVERSITY	PUB-FG	206,254	127,861	14,139	2,882	15,266	12,034	935	7,057	5,988	1,811
PARK COLLEGE	PRI-FN	A	A		A	A			A	A	A
ROCKHURST COLLEGE	PRI-FG	101,887	A	102,576	0	277	1,149	0	3,231	2,961	584
SNT LOUIS CHRISTIAN C	PRI-FN	21,253	20,434	0	14,282	0	0	98	577	120	117
SNT LOUIS COLLEGE OF PHAR	PRI-FN	31,750	21,575	0	0	28	6,775	40	1,252	1,060	389
SNT LU CC CENTER ALL CAM											
SNT LU CC-FLORISSANT VLY	PUB-T	60,927	49,550	0	125	129	3,387	697	3,755	3,380	455
SNT LU CC-FOREST PARK	PUB-T	49,683	46,206	0	137	215	12,543	0	2,404	2,136	478
SAINT LOUIS CC-MERAMEC	PJB-T	58,679	49,609	0	71	136	3,223	7,810	3,454	3,109	557
SNT LOUIS CONSV OF MUSIC	PRI-FG	7,511	4,022	0	13	0	2,251	0	1,086	758	37
SAINT LOUIS RAB COLLEGE	PRI-FG	A	A						A	A	
SAINT LOUIS U ALL CAM											
SAINT LOUIS U MAIN CAMPUS	PRI-U	780,226	446,336	187,305	791	32	111,931	89,517	18,806	12,170	9,319
SAINT LOUIS U-PARKS C	PRI-FN	33,794	18,550	18,166	0	23	1,555	0	816	660	253
SAINT MARY'S C O'FALLON	PRI-T	43,665	36,936	0	10	0	5,900	0	1,298	1,100	194
SAINT MARY'S SEM-COLLEGE	PRI-FN	56,919	37,811	0	0	0	0	0	1,467	933	225
SNT PAUL SCH OF THEOLOGY	PRI-FG	60,381	A	0	25	100	0	0	1,708	A	335
SAINT PAUL'S COLLEGE	PRI-T	32,516	29,844	0	1	17		17	845	795	266
SCHOOL OF THE OZARKS	PRI-FN	81,000	76,725	0	0	106	5,460	500	2,424	2,152	555
STHEST MO ST UNIVERSITY	PUB-FG	249,882	208,650	158,285	57,973	478	205,619	67	10,218	8,650	2,496
SOUTHWEST BAPTIST COLLEGE	PRI-FN	74,253	51,914	0	81	31	1	733	2,278	1,882	1,078
STHWST MO ST UNIVERSITY	PUB-FG	324,662	247,021	262,817	228,888	2,107	45,850	417	18,151	14,310	4,714
STATE FAIR CMTY COLLEGE	PUB-T	24,268	23,055	0	111	74	5,128	635	1,799	1,710	365

SEE FOOTNOTES AT END OF TABLE

STATE OR OTHER AREA AND INSTITUTION	CONTROL AND TYPE OF INSTITUTION	HELD AT END OF YEAR							ADDED DURING YEAR		CURRENT PERIODICAL SUBSCRIPTION TITLES FALL 1979
		BOOKSTOCK		SEPARATE GOVERNMENT DOCUMENTS COLLECTIONS (VOLS.)	MICROFORMS			ALL OTHER LIBRARY MATERIALS	BOOKSTOCK		
		VOLUMES	TITLES		BOOK TITLES	PERIODICAL TITLES	OTHER PHYSICAL UNITS		VOLUMES	TITLES	
(1)	(2)	(3)	(4)	(5)	(6)	(7)	(8)	(9)	(10)	(11)	(12)
MISSOURI	--CONTINUED										
STEPHENS COLLEGE	PRI-FN	117,819	106,037	0	0	0	7,178	1,649	3,718	3,346	530
TARKIO COLLEGE	PRI-FN	65,612	65,030	0	5	27	0	25	1,280	1,082	212
THREE RIVERS CMTY COLLEGE	PUB-T	20,340	19,515	150	0	85	2,485	0	2,640	1,825	381
TRENTON JUNIOR COLLEGE	PUB-T	12,271	11,150	43	38	29	991	900	711	604	108
U OF MO CEN ADMIN ALL CAM											
U OF MISSOURI-COLUMBIA	PUB-U	2,109,107	1,200,000	136,740	86,509	979	1,953,161	100,002	60,214	45,158	22,054
U OF MISSOURI-KANSAS CITY	PUB-FG	634,796	408,557	133,934	286,530	2,417	289,001	774	24,624	12,792	9,031
U OF MISSOURI-ROLLA	PUB-FG	284,892	A	41,089	288,900	243	1,390	0	13,153	A	1,718
U OF MISSOURI-SAINT LOUIS	PUB-FG	346,964	281,108	179,455	2,056	1,900	630,000	0	18,828	14,620	2,931
WASHINGTON UNIVERSITY	PRI-U	1,754,680	874,374	211,444	162,131	266	165,065	83,281	50,416	22,290	11,997
WEBSTER COLLEGE	PRI FG	SEE EDEN-WEBSTER JT LIB									
WENTWORTH MILITARY ACAD	PRI-T	16,085	14,750	0	0	17	0	3	100	100	116
WESTMINSTER COLLEGE	PRI-FN	53,026	50,770	7,166	5	29	5,268	0	1,864	1,770	321
WILLIAM JEWELL COLLEGE	PRI-FN	131,657	A	0	0	3,579	5,309	0	3,676	A	583
WILLIAM WOODS COLLEGE	PRI-FN	53,523	48,171	0	0	21	0	667	2,680	2,412	334
MONTANA											
CARROLL COLLEGE	PRI-FN	75,068	69,434	0	626	2,674	875	30	4,278	4,201	514
COLLEGE OF GREAT FALLS	PRI-FN	54,015	43,796	272	12,539	115	0	0	1,893	1,552	397
DAWSON COMMUNITY COLLEGE	PUB-T	17,666	15,776	0	0	37	15	17	315	275	191
FLATHEAD VLY CMTY COLLEGE	PUB-T	9,680	8,416	0	0	0	0	0	716	633	125
MILES COMMUNITY COLLEGE	PUB-T	11,233	10,494	0	0	139	0	133	748	742	189
MONTANA INST OF THE BIBLE	PRI-FN	17,186	17,073	0	0	0	0	97	649	536	66
MONTANA U SYSTEM ALL INST											
EASTERN MONTANA COLLEGE	PUB-FG	126,919	103,212	145,676	0	282	197,459	45,755	5,143	3,580	1,250
MONTANA C MINRL SCI-TECHN	PUB-FG	72,770	68,800	23,865	0	0	0	65,000	2,044	2,300	688
MONTANA STATE UNIVERSITY	PUB-U	395,180	178,920	44,203	0	0	412,583	0	15,670	6,602	4,381
NORTHERN MONTANA COLLEGE	PUB-FG	81,171	79,455	300	145,363	20	0	125	2,230	1,907	560
UNIVERSITY OF MONTANA	PUB-U	711,673	A	73,199	212,271	36,706	63,732	512	20,726	A	7,241
WESTERN MONTANA COLLEGE	PUB-FG	49,344	A	0	19,500	238	3,491	251	866	A	356
ROCKY MOUNTAIN COLLEGE	PRI-FN	58,300	52,800	0	10	6	500	1,600	1,884	1,599	315
NEBRASKA											
BELLEVUE COLLEGE	PRI-FN	43,150	37,932	580	6,078	56	0	28	4,042	3,572	275
CEN TECH CMTY-C AREA	PUB-T	43,375	26,806	0	0	30	824	0	1,555	774	735
CHADRON STATE COLLEGE	PUB-FG	138,122	135,618	0	15	3	43,628	630	6,494	6,292	970
COLLEGE OF SAINT MARY	PRI-FN	61,784	61,576	70	0	36	277	25	1,745	1,537	335
CONCORDIA TCHRS COLLEGE	PRI-FG	120,453	116,032	0	3,796	184	2,030	0	3,734	2,702	648
CREIGHTON UNIVERSITY	PRI-U	394,224	226,318	44,800	22,740	39,633	7,145	102	17,917	11,188	2,897
DANA COLLEGE	PRI-FN	84,753	78,000	16,956	0	1,469	0	1,526	2,178	2,000	496
DOANE COLLEGE	PRI-FN	62,181	61,559	37,643	0	48	2,852	11,590	1,723	1,706	308
GRACE C OF THE BIBLE	PRI-FN	46,878	A	0	121	15	0	0	790	A	292
HASTINGS COLLEGE	PRI-FN	95,786	62,000	0	39	678	12,531	3,526	2,776	2,450	497
KEARNEY STATE COLLEGE	PUB-FG	130,982	108,205	117,998	47,719	16,126	332,134	3,939	3,100	2,717	2,137
METROPOLITAN TECHNICAL CC	PUB-T	24,062	17,806	0	0	401	31,436	3	5,934	4,391	748
MIDLAND LUTHERAN COLLEGE	PRI-FN	75,588	64,800	15,000	200	85	0	514	1,992	1,680	601
MID PLAINS CC ALL CAM											
MCCOOK COMMUNITY COLLEGE	PUB-T	20,050	18,050	0	2	29	612	10	2,500	2,250	195
MID PLAINS CC	PUB-T	16,127	15,362	0	0	45	0	0	826	743	154
NEBR CHRISTIAN COLLEGE	PRI-FN	20,025	A	0	10	4	0	0	601	A	81
NEBR WESLEYAN UNIVERSITY	PRI-FN	180,931	120,620	0	0	2,693	0	0	5,773	3,848	727
NEBRASKA WESTERN COLLEGE	PUB-T	20,986	16,850	0	0	0	304	814	569	450	221
NORTHEAST TECHNICAL CC	PUB-T	22,966	22,822	0	0	13	294	30	1,125	984	470
PERU STATE COLLEGE	PUB-FN	81,907	48,340	0	7,225	23	0	10	5,820	2,724	541
PLATTE VLY BIBLE COLLEGE	PRI-FN	12,000	11,750	0	0	0	0	0	250	A	20
STHESTN NEBR TECH ALL CAM											
STHEST CC FAIRBY-BEATRICE	PUB-T	10,623	10,500	0	0	18	0	1,385	510	510	125
SOUTHEAST CC LINCOLN CAM	PUB-T	14,513	11,567	0	0	130	27	18	1,276	831	285
SOUTHEAST CC MILFORD CAM	PUB-T	5,608	4,888	135	0	78	556	1,500	593	585	380
UNION COLLEGE	PRI-FN	115,670	105,240	0	42	11	719	50	2,481	1,236	659
U NEBR CEN ADMIN ALL INST											

SEE FOOTNOTES AT END OF TABLE

Table 1. — Collections in College and University Libraries, by State or Other Area and Institution: Aggregate United States, 1978-79, and Fall 1979 — Continued

STATE OR OTHER AREA AND INSTITUTION	CONTROL AND TYPE OF INSTITUTION	HELD AT END OF YEAR							ADDED DURING YEAR		CURRENT PERIODICAL SUBSCRIPTION TITLES FALL 1979
		BOOKSTOCK		SEPARATE GOVERNMENT DOCUMENTS COLLECTIONS (VOLS.)	MICROFORMS			ALL OTHER LIBRARY MATERIALS	BOOKSTOCK		
		VOLUMES	TITLES		BOOK TITLES	PERIODICAL TITLES	OTHER PHYSICAL UNITS		VOLUMES	TITLES	
(1)	(2)	(3)	(4)	(5)	(6)	(7)	(8)	(9)	(10)	(11)	(12)
NEBRASKA --CONTINUED											
U OF NEBRASKA-LINCOLN	PUB-U	1,441,515	631,789	140,000	9,706	1,781	851,812	51,085	60,379	35,528	21,193
U NEBRASKA MEDICAL CTR	PUB-FG	173,702	50,106		0	366	698,432	0	8,163	2,770	3,212
U OF NEBRASKA AT OMAHA	PUB-FG	363,179	357,509	275,436	900	213	287,702	408	23,017	17,644	8,601
WAYNE STATE COLLEGE	PUB-FG	149,548	99,412	19,000	5,675	130	117	257	6,163	5,245	1,130
YORK COLLEGE	PRI-T	25,497	20,046	0	4,731			66	630	458	244
NEVADA											
SIERRA NEVADA COLLEGE	PRI-FN	11,308	A	11,308	0	0	0	1,200	2,190	A	111
U OF NEVADA SYS ALL INST				10,233	0	0	353,287	4,122	19,914	A	0
U OF NEVADA LAS VEGAS	PUB-FG	358,922	A			221	1,489	2,425	30,033	13,482	5,100
U OF NEVADA RENO	PUB-U	622,050	289,326	966,417	121,074	4,261	1,214,500	152,602	17,455	1,516	306
CLARK CO CMTY COLLEGE	PUB-T	23,169	19,294	0	0	56		4	485	450	284
NORTHERN NEV CMTY COLLEGE	PUB-T	23,846	22,942	0		69	4,097	268	4,790	4,497	342
WESTERN NEV CMTY COLLEGE	PUB-T	27,503	25,520	0	662						
NEW HAMPSHIRE											
CASTLE JUNIOR COLLEGE	PRI-T	4,447	4,427	0	0	0	0	0	0	0	56
COLBY-SAWYER COLLEGE	PRI-FN	A	A						A	A	A
DANIEL WEBSTER COLLEGE	PRI-FN	17,549	17,200	0	0	20	0	5	1,483	1,100	186
DARTMOUTH COLLEGE	PRI-FG	1,347,278	775,000	18,000	300,000	11,500	0	100,000	55,087	25,000	17,253
FRANKLIN PIERCE COLLEGE	PRI-FN	A	45,983	0	0	10	0	0	A	A	387
FRANKLIN PIERCE LAW CTR	PRI-FG	57,872	6,699	2,250	0	19	67,170	0	3,297	651	1,291
MCINTOSH COLLEGE	PRI-T	5,027	4,927	0	0	A	0	2	71	71	25
NATHANIEL HAWTHORNE C	PRI-FN	A	A	3,457	413	9,067	94	1,000	3,452	2,147	499
NEW ENGLAND COLLEGE	PRI-FN	81,739	63,204	11,027	2,167	118	33,944	330	3,188	2,587	810
NEW HAMPSHIRE COLLEGE	PRI-FG	53,838	35,335		7	32	7,500	5	1,028	785	269
NH TECHNICAL INSTITUTE	PUB-T	20,244	15,657	0	0	0	90	0	168	168	126
NH VOC-TECH C BERLIN	PUB-T	6,142	4,494	0	0	1	130	39	566	484	76
NH VOC-TECH C CLAREMONT	PUB-T	7,155	6,669	120	18	42	199	21	667	625	81
NH VOC-TECH C LACONIA	PUB-T	6,648	6,570	0	2	23	217	0	526	407	105
NH VOC-TECH C MANCHESTER	PUB-T	7,414	6,000	0	0	15	244	6	457	412	96
NH VOC-TECH C NASHUA	PUB-T	5,967	5,490	0	2	25		0	883	750	92
NH VOC-TECH C PORTSMOUTH	PUB-T	7,839	6,548	0	0	71	0	163			268
NOTRE DAME COLLEGE	PRI-FG	40,625	40,000	0	0	25	3,512	654	1,994	1,800	463
RIVIER COLLEGE	PRI-FG	90,523	80,400	0	8	428	30,819	155	8,022	6,321	1,287
SAINT ANSELM'S COLLEGE	PRI-FN	130,254	97,051	8,000	17,511						
U SYS OF NH ALL INST	PUB-U			183,000	257,500	832	478,577	0	29,364	13,236	6,350
U OF NEW HAMPSHIRE	PUB-FG	780,242	306,187	3,181	38,972	111	5,074	443	8,252	7,619	828
U OF NH KEENE ST COLLEGE	PUB-FG	149,596	112,316	0	0	0	251,822	14,126	10,089	6,299	1,415
U NH PLYMOUTH ST COLLEGE	PUB-FG	171,499	107,180	0	0	110	0	113	698	664	102
WHITE PINES COLLEGE	PRI-T	17,705	12,046								
NEW JERSEY											
ASSUMPTION C FOR SISTERS	PRI-T	19,848	19,814	0	0	0	0	0	404	370	148
ATLANTIC CMTY COLLEGE	PUB-T	78,449	67,126	0	0	112	89	1,769	3,750	3,199	312
BERGEN COMMUNITY COLLEGE	PUB-T	84,310	54,873	0	0	0	7,306	53	3,140	2,130	494
THE BERKELEY SCHOOL	PRI-T	28,473	28,240	0	A	0	0	0	579	346	100
BETH MEDRASH GOVOHA	PRI-FG	A			A	A	A	A	A	A	A
BLOOMFIELD COLLEGE	PRI-FN	115,013	72,793		0	142	3,152	0	2,236	2,069	760
BROOKDALE CMTY COLLEGE	PUB-T	64,780	40,000	8,644	30	130	6,286	713	6,746	3,500	755
BURLINGTON COUNTY COLLEGE	PUB-T	56,437	48,227	112	10	328	610	800	4,649	4,026	555
CALDWELL COLLEGE	PRI-FN	96,675	75,100	0	9	23	620	94	2,575	2,275	550
CAMDEN COUNTY COLLEGE	PUB-T	69,981	65,180	1,601	169	9	15,092	350	6,202	4,818	650
CENTENARY COLLEGE	PRI-FN	43,421	34,494	0	1	89	6,419	573	2,017	1,761	354
C MED & DENT OF NJ NEWARK	PUB-FG	100,000	45,000	0	0	0	14,076	6,775	4,000	4,783	937
COLLEGE OF SNT ELIZABETH	PRI-FN	145,839	93,140	24,604	21	93	387	2,857	5,179	5,010	709
COUNTY COLLEGE OF MORRIS	PUB-T	82,389	76,552	4,844	0	292	8,564	258	5,010	1,750	253
CUMBERLAND COUNTY COLLEGE	PUB-T	47,686	38,371	0	0	72	4,219	160			
DON BOSCO COLLEGE	PRI-FN	50,869	48,600			110	28	1,000	500	440	192
DREW UNIVERSITY	PRI-FG	389,777	292,332	124,265	7,418	291	16,445	126,709	9,239	6,628	1,851
ESSEX COUNTY COLLEGE	PUB-T	72,213	66,102	1,774	0	372	211,808	256	4,890	4,001	691

SEE FOOTNOTES AT END OF TABLE

Table 1. — Collections in College and University Libraries, by State or Other Area and Institution: Aggregate United States, 1978-79, and Fall 1979 — Continued

		HELD AT END OF YEAR							ADDED DURING YEAR		
		BOOKSTOCK		SEPARATE GOVERN- MENT DOCU- MENTS COLLEC- TIONS (VOLS.)	MICROFORMS			ALL OTHER LIBRARY MATE- RIALS	BOOKSTOCK		CURRENT PERIOD- ICAL SUB- SCRIPTION TITLES FALL 1979
STATE OR OTHER AREA AND INSTITUTION	CON- TROL· AND TYPE OF IN- STITU- TION	VOLUMES	TITLES		BOOK TITLES	PERI- ODICAL TITLES	OTHER PHYS- ICAL UNITS		VOLUMES	TITLES	
(1)	(2)	(3)	(4)	(5)	(6)	(7)	(8)	(9)	(10)	(11)	(12)
NEW JERSEY --CONTINUED											
FAIRLEIGH DCKSN U ALL CAM											
FARLGH DCKSN U EDW WMS·C	PRI-T	10,030	7,277	0	0	0	0	0	173	112	92
FARLGH DCKSN MADISON CAM	PRI-FG	146,310	A	0	80	136	10,935	420	4,412	4,079	1,416
FARLGH DCKSN U RUTHERFD	PRI-FG	161,177	134,314	60,779	209	342	0	0	2,527	2,105	1,566
FARLGH DCKSN TEANECK CAM	PRI-FG	233,456	134,727	38,044	0	0	214,241	18	5,260	4,312	2,668
FELICIAN COLLEGE	PRI-FN	66,925	56,965	0	831	154	0	2,528	5,700	5,248	504
GEORGIAN COURT COLLEGE	PRI-FG	70,221	52,754	0	0	270	111,356	0	2,949	2,356	583
GLASSBORO STATE COLLEGE	PUB-FG	260,227	238,180	106,778	56,100	9,567	19,270	14,132	20,621	14,438	2,017
GLOUCESTER COUNTY COLLEGE	PUB-T	48,927	45,991	0	3	244	14,104	349	1,871	1,821	361
HUDSON CO CC COMMISSION[2/]	PUB-T	NO LIBRARY FACILITIES									
IMMACULATE CONCEPTION SEM	PRI-FG	69,282	68,977	0	0	20	0	0	1,487	1,453	648
JERSEY CITY STATE COLLEGE	PUB-FG	224,795	168,453	51,199	185,391	1,105	192,540	16,288	9,773	9,517	1,235
KATHARINE GIBBS SCHOOL	PRI-T	3,189	1,967	0	0	0	0	0	11	9	32
KEAN C OF NEW JERSEY	PUB-FG	288,053	220,982	10,598	0	466	0	5,336	10,088	8,685	1,590
MERCER CO CMTY COLLEGE	PUB-T	62,185	60,000	529	0	142	9,338	50	3,379	3,200	898
MIDDLESEX COUNTY COLLEGE	PUB-T	71,140	66,459	0	6	122	85	805	2,454	2,292	975
MONMOUTH COLLEGE	PRI-FG	208,898	156,921	48,100	35	655	102,080	710	7,752	6,589	1,717
MONTCLAIR STATE COLLEGE	PUB-FG	311,306	217,350	35,416	0	0	461,368	0	20,951	16,570	2,464
NEW BRUNSWICK THEOL SEM	PRI-FG	133,577	73,200	0	73	19	0	0	1,061	1,000	341
NJ INSTITUTE TECHNOLOGY	PUB-FG	125,450	90,324	0	13	138	4,343	750·	6,146	4,425	1,500
NTHESTN BIBLE COLLEGE	PRI-FN	A	A	A	A	A	A	A	A	A	A
OCEAN COUNTY COLLEGE	PUB-T	66,544	63,310	16,954	5	207	0	504	4,023	4,402	430
PASSAIC CO CMTY COLLEGE	PUB-T	24,482	18,810	0	136	25	240	200	3,678	2,133	287
PRINCETON THEOLOGICAL SEM	PRI-FG	343,653	293,721	0	331	150	0	0	5,372	5,250	1,250
PRINCETON UNIVERSITY	PRI-U	3,172,238	A	0	0	0	1,210,189	312,361	82,632	A	31,361
RAB COLLEGE OF AMERICA	PRI-FN	6,000	1,150	0	0	0	0	0	50	12	30
RAMAPO C OF NEW JERSEY	PRI-FN	137,632	80,011	59,000	80	580	20,412	16	8,542	3,922	1,786
RIDER COLLEGE	PRI-FG	312,310	310,000	0	0	510	235,000	0	11,727	11,700	1,650
RUTGERS THE ST U ALL CAM											
RUTGERS U CAMDEN CAMPUS	PUB-FG	277,176	A	151,851	0	0	180,529	10,946	10,270	A	3,184
RUTGERS U NEWARK CAMPUS	PUB-FG	433,025	A	344,371	0	0	278,227	76,933	8,984	A	6,133
RUTGERS U NEW BRUNSWICK	PUB-U	1,455,999	A	1,956,023	0	0	875,540	2,601,741	67,745	A	15,122
SNT MICHAELS PASIONST.MON	PRI-FG	19,000	15,000	0	0	0	0	0	275	225	75
SAINT PETERS COLLEGE	PRI-FG	237,343	161,642	0	0	205	7,443	729	6,890	4,919	1,728
SALEM COMMUNITY COLLEGE	PUB-T	18,468	17,500	0	189	0	0	3	2,365	2,200	319
SETON HALL UNIVERSITY[2/]	PRI-U	319,687	205,422	98,856	0	145	219,772	697	14,325	10,625	2,141
SOMERSET COUNTY COLLEGE	PUB-T	63,598	63,000	0	4,434	203	4,237	665	2,482	2,400	445
STEVENS INST TECHNOLOGY	PRI-FG	95,792	52,026	0	0	710	0	0	3,950	1,218	850
STOCKTON STATE COLLEGE	PUB-FN	105,390	85,076	98,253	22,000	797	57,652	94	8,500	8,036	2,032
TALMUD INST OF CEN JERSEY	PRI-FG	A	A						A	A	A
THOMAS A EDISON COLLEGE	PUB-FN	NO LIBRARY FACILITIES									
TRENTON STATE COLLEGE	PUB-FG	380,654	285,319	25,931	0	687	69,984	20,500	24,981	20,105	1,748
UNION COLLEGE	PRI-T	82,081	74,170	0	0	70	98	109	4,649	3,102	608
UNION CO TECHNICAL INST	PUB-T	18,770	16,914	0	0	52	48	532	2,079	1,856	370
UPSALA COLLEGE	PRI-FG	147,192	92,466	4,500	450	1,072	9,954	3 ·	3,431	2,349	900
WESTMINSTER CHOIR COLLEGE	PRI-FG	31,500	28,600	0	200	35	0	0	670	632	117
WILLIAM PATERSON COLLEGE	PUB-FG	270,726	209,026	5,150	242	1,052	382,526	300	19,110	13,365	3,557
NEW MEXICO											
COLLEGE OF SANTA FE	PRI-FN	85,000	51,000	0	1	59	1,117	406	3,900	2,500	211
COLLEGE OF THE SOUTHWEST	PRI-FN	34,816	27,900	4,600	0	14	9,753	43	2,663	2,500	404
EASTERN NM U ALL CAMPUSES											
EASTERN NM U MAIN CAMPUS	PUB-FG	222,016	150,531	146,621	70,555	630	254,063	2,453	8,555	6,056	1,328
EASTERN NM U ROSWELL CAM	PUB-T	22,915	21,769	0	4	170	13,145	0	1,311	1,245	223
INST AMERICAN INDIAN ARTS	PUB-T	A	A		A	A	A	A	A	A	A
NEW MEXICO HIGHLANDS U	PUB-FG	166,720	149,511	82,104	2,677	655	167,258	0	9,059	7,204	1,395
NM INST OF MINING & TECHN	PUB-FG	51,665	A	6,718	3,641	3,230	2,408	8,500	2,943	A	984
NEW MEXICO JUNIOR COLLEGE	PUB-T	80,407	64,325	5,940	31	190	11,049	16,712	4,642	3,946	1,234
NEW MEXICO MILITARY INST	PUB-T	61,337	39,800	0	0	126	0	0	1,164	720	174
NM STATE U ALL CAMPUSES											

SEE FOOTNOTES AT·END OF TABLE

51

Table 1. — Collections in College and University Libraries, by State or Other Area and Institution: Aggregate United States, 1978-79, and Fall 1979 — Continued

STATE OR OTHER AREA AND INSTITUTION (1)	CONTROL AND TYPE OF INSTITUTION (2)	HELD AT END OF YEAR							ADDED DURING YEAR		CURRENT PERIODICAL SUBSCRIPTION TITLES FALL 1979 (12)
		BOOKSTOCK VOLUMES (3)	BOOKSTOCK TITLES (4)	SEPARATE GOVERNMENT DOCUMENTS COLLECTIONS (VOLS.) (5)	MICROFORMS BOOK TITLES (6)	MICROFORMS PERIODICAL TITLES (7)	MICROFORMS OTHER PHYSICAL UNITS (8)	ALL OTHER LIBRARY MATERIALS (9)	BOOKSTOCK VOLUMES (10)	BOOKSTOCK TITLES (11)	
NEW MEXICO — CONTINUED											
NM STATE U MAIN CAMPUS	PUB-U	611,922	346,772	253,916	222,846	1,492	204,458	35,250	54,493	37,328	6,079
NM STATE U ALAMOGORDO	PUB-T	27,468	27,203	0	0	1	5,121	1,725	1,672	1,400	195
NM STATE U CARLSBAD	PUB-T	17,345	14,631	0	0	0	1,429	89	1,274	1,043	88
NM STATE U GRANTS BRANCH	PUB-T	19,304	17,817	235	2	43	12,134	0	2,304	2,259	39
NM STATE U SAN JUAN	PUB-T	23,499	18,800	707	0	8	1,100	151	1,840	1,800	224
NTHN NM COMMUNITY COLLEGE	PUB-T	A	A		A	A	A		1,976	1,753	421
UNIVERSITY OF ALBUQUERQUE	PRI-FN	54,194	46,140	0	19,034	293	25,281	0			
U OF NM ALL CAMPUSES	PUB-U	1,143,247	641,446	240,026	32,282	50	1,299,702	71,554	72,972	42,488	16,749
U OF NM MAIN CAMPUS	PUB-U				17			2,910	1,124	944	88
U OF NM GALLUP BRANCH	PUB-T	14,745	13,190	0	17	0	0	0	3,917	3,447	726
WESTERN NM UNIVERSITY	PUB-FG	117,723	103,596	18,333	245,761	428	0	0			
NEW YORK											
ACADEMY OF AERONAUTICS	PRI-T	24,581	23,893	24,708	0	128	4,956	0	1,904	1,872	381
ADELPHI UNIVERSITY	PRI-U	350,761	215,363	72,804	412	312	280,906	200	20,023	11,306	3,377
ALBANY BUSINESS COLLEGE	PRI-T	4,073	4,000	0	0	0	0	0	90	90	48
ALBANY COLLEGE PHARMACY	PRI-FN	6,636	0	0	0	0	0	0	211	A	94
ALBANY LAW SCHOOL	PRI-FG	83,386	15,097	5,840	517	8	0	0	20,634	1,960	771
ALBANY MEDICAL COLLEGE	PRI-FG	82,955	61,800	0	0	0	0	0	4,171	1,941	1,220
ALFRED U ALL CAMPUSES											1,044
ALFRED UNIVERSITY	PRI-FG	162,845	138,418	455	79	211	18,349	30,566	6,693	5,689	854
NY ST C CERAMICS ALFRED U	PUB-FG	57,925	33,900	6,669	0	1	405	3,668	3,159	3,140	A
AMER ACAD DRAMATIC ARTS	PRI-T	A	A	A	A	A	A	A	A	A	A
ASSOCD BETH RIVKAH SCHS	PRI-FN	A	A						A	A	A
BAIS YAAKOV SEMINARY	PRI-FN	A	A					96	2,864	1,432	598
BANK STREET COLLEGE OF ED	PRI-FG	92,580	51,315	0	163,842	49	0	65	3,205	2,696	560
BARD COLLEGE	PRI-FN	145,999	93,000	3,350	2,016	115	1,400		A	A	A
BE'ER SHMUEL TALMUD ACAD	PRI-FG	A	A						A	A	A
BELZER YESH-MACHZIKEI SEM	PRI-FG	A	A	0	0	0	0	9	67	67	23
BERK-CLAREMONT HICRSVL	PRI-T	243	243	0	0	0	0	0	50	21	30
BERK-CLAREMONT NY CITY	PRI-T	375	300	0	0	A		A	A	A	A
THE BERKELEY SCHOOL	PRI-T	A	A						A	A	A
BETH HMDRSH SHAAREI TORAH	PRI-FG	A	A						A	A	A
BETH HATALMUD RAB C	PRI-FG	A	A						A	A	A
BETH JACOB HEBREW TCHRS C	PRI-FN	A	A						A	A	A
BETH JOSEPH RAB SEMINARY	PRI-FG	A	A						A	A	A
BETH MEDRASH EMEK HALACHA	PRI-FG	A	A						A	A	A
BETH MDRASH EYUN HATALMUD	PRI-FN	A	A						A	A	A
BORICUA COLLEGE	PRI-FN	A	A	0	0	0	0	0	500	450	31
BRAMSON ORT TRAINING CTR	PRI-T	3,000	2,850	0	0	0	0	0	8,750	6,200	9,873
BROOKLYN LAW SCHOOL	PRI-FG	145,979	30,917	0	1,390	0	0	0	176	181	35
BRYANT-STRATTON BUS INST	PRI-T	805	690	0	0	0	0	0	176	181	35
BRYANT-STRATTON BUS INST	PRI-T	805	690	0	0	0	0	0			
CANISIUS COLLEGE	PRI-FG	208,354	159,951	0	35	16	9,230	900	8,534	4,179	1,200
CTHDL C IMMAC CONCEPTION	PRI-FN	76,784	70,631	9,706		77	6,686	105	2,648	2,448	475
CAZENOVIA COLLEGE	PRI-T	35,158	30,000			6		0	682	600	185
CEN CITY BUSINESS INST	PRI-T	NO LIBRARY FACILITIES									
CEN YESH TOM TMIMIM LUBVZ	PRI-FG	A							A	A	A
CHRIST THE KING SEMINARY	PRI-FG	70,542	A	0	30	11	0	30	5,753	A	0
CITY U OF NY SYS ALL INST				0		18	0	176,933	10,779	6,915	1,550
CUNY BERNARD BARUCH C	PUB-FG	252,299	165,435	0	0	91	4,145	375	2,075	1,254	492
CUNY BORO OF MANHATTAN CC	PUB-T	50,732	37,746	0	0	70	0	0	2,443	1,966	378
CUNY BRONX CMTY COLLEGE	PUB-T	76,869	A	200,521	0	0	463,408	105,348	16,329	11,664	3,981
CUNY BROOKLYN COLLEGE	PUB-FG	580,500	423,154	253,746	106,337	2,843	388,971	78	14,315	10,573	3,423
CUNY CITY COLLEGE	PUB-FG	937,302	439,583	0	230,641	2,215	0	0	4,643	4,126	1,541
CUNY C OF STATEN ISLAND	PUB-FG	127,790	127,991	0	2,675	224	0	1,406	7,255	5,774	1,618
CUNY GRAD SCH & U CENTER	PUB-FG	141,603	111,078	0	1,065	88	4,084	0	2,475	2,129	151
CUNY HOSTOS CMTY COLLEGE	PUB-T	26,847	19,678								
CUNY HUNTER COLLEGE	PUB-FG	438,705	243,629	24,323	2,040	241	522,947	37,000	10,364	7,851	2,979
CUNY JOHN JAY C CRIM JUST	PUB-FG	119,165	83,397	0	7,256	276	29,312	0	6,383	3,325	918

SEE FOOTNOTES AT END OF TABLE

Table 1. — Collections in College and University Libraries, by State or Other Area and Institution: Aggregate United States, 1978-79, and Fall 1979 — Continued

STATE OR OTHER AREA AND INSTITUTION	CON-TROL AND TYPE OF IN-STITU-TION	HELD AT END OF YEAR							ADDED DURING YEAR		CURRENT PERIOD-ICAL SUB-SCRIPTION TITLES FALL 1979
		BOOKSTOCK		SEPARATE GOVERN-MENT DOCU-MENTS COLLEC-TIONS (VOLS.)	MICROFORMS			ALL OTHER LIBRARY MATE-RIALS	BOOKSTOCK		
		VOLUMES	TITLES		BOOK TITLES	PERI-ODICAL TITLES	OTHER PHYS-ICAL UNITS		VOLUMES	TITLES	
(1)	(2)	(3)	(4)	(5)	(6)	(7)	(8)	(9)	(10)	(11)	(12)
NEW YORK	--CONTINUED										
CUNY KINGSBOROUGH CC	PUB-T	91,877	66,567	0	0	108	0	430	2,463	1,513	398
CUNY LA GUARDIA CC	PUB-T	45,489	43,215	0	0	273	128,670	5,105	1,895	1,800	771
CUNY LEHMAN COLLEGE	PUB-FG	364,075	280,233	1,675	0	722	293,383	10,137	13,241	9,969	1,480
CUNY MEDGAR EVERS COLLEGE	PUB-FN	76,168	65,139	0	21,011	415	27,489	0	2,451	2,451	674
CUNY NEW YORK CITY CC	PUB-T	118,960	81,531	0	7	100	0	14,303	2,992	2,186	376
CUNY QUEENSBOROUGH CC	PUB-T	118,867	96,805	0	5	67	4,545	48,330	3,227	2,556	691
CUNY QUEENS COLLEGE	PUB-FG	511,384	321,816	287,539	161,500	2,323	247,966	150,000	19,830	11,434	4,142
CUNY YORK COLLEGE	PUB-FN	119,438	98,842	0	21,414	411	92,901	3,881	2,912	1,936	964
CLARKSON COLLEGE OF TECHN	PRI-FG	87,586	66,357	42,718	77,736	258	5,188	4,418	4,451	3,916	1,360
CCLG ROCH-BEXLEY-CROZER	PRI-FG	196,759	136,731	0	842	91	145	25	3,220	2,254	574
COLGATE UNIVERSITY	PRI-FG	325,383	312,368	47,018	92,541	114	35,437	647	8,896	8,540	2,024
COLLEGE FOR HUMAN SERVICE	PRI-FN	19,543	A	0	0	0	185	4	3,500	2,500	210
COLLEGE OF INSURANCE	PRI-FG	76,339	75,278	19,789	853	10	6	0	1,967	A	450
COLLEGE OF MT SNT VINCENT	PRI-FG	113,965	104,300	105	7,797	111	2,185	3,500	3,614	3,282	573
COLLEGE OF NEW ROCHELLE	PRI-FG	137,172	87,523	0	11,987	2,566	0	0	5,214	3,510	845
COLLEGE OF SAINT ROSE	PRI-FG	125,490	106,667	0	33,902	56	2,344	0	5,483	4,660	808
COLUMBIA U ALL CAMPUSES											
COLUMBIA U MAIN DIVISION	PRI-U	4,893,138	1,951,600	31,331	64,200	1,440	1,915,900	210,000	104,610	50,900	25,000
BARNARD COLLEGE	PRI-FN	146,829	A	0	6	65	0	0	3,490	A	649
COLUMBIA U TCHRS COLLEGE	PRI-FG	393,978	179,236	0	5,800	191	226,492	230	9,423	3,989	1,875
CONCORDIA COLLEGE	PRI-FN	40,846	37,468	0	18,234	224	2,291	0	1,810	1,752	475
COOPER UNION	PRI-FG	73,142	50,255	0	1	35	3,200	70,528	1,863	913	286
CORNELL U ALL CAMPUSES											
CORNEL U ENDOWED COLLEGES	PRI-U	3,544,853	A	0	0	0	1,771,503	0	93,298	A	37,123
CORNELL U MEDICAL CENTER	PRI-FG	101,944	38,807	0	0	8	295	0	6,068	2,897	1,969
CORNELL U STATUTORY C	PUB-FG	730,537	A	0	0	0	205,225	0	18,665	A	12,822
CULINARY INST OF AMERICA	PRI-T	15,904	11,968	0	0	0	0	10,373	2,265	1,345	170
CAEMEN COLLEGE	PRI-FN	99,564	69,242	0	362	29	424	0	3,672	2,724	498
DERECH AYSON RAB SEMINARY	PRI-FG	A	A						A	A	A
DOMINICAN C OF BLAUVELT	PRI-FN	76,259	70,583	0	0	447	5,897	0	2,498	2,265	650
DOWLING COLLEGE	PRI-FN	88,051	67,062	20,120	162,463	220	7,607	3,689	5,516	3,959	762
D'YOUVILLE COLLEGE	PRI-FN	90,693	55,819	0	52	218	7,632	3,410	4,016	2,214	604
EISENHOWER COLLEGE	PRI-FN	79,535	55,700	0	0	0	5,663	645	4,496	3,200	790
ELIZABETH SETON COLLEGE	PRI-T	40,611	31,049	0	0	91	795	25	1,737	792	224
ELMIRA COLLEGE	PRI-FG	134,345	129,000	156,522	20,050	164	35,307	138	4,855	3,400	635
FIVE TOWNS COLLEGE	PRI-T	8,300	8,203	0	0	26	0	0	2,100	2,003	180
FORDHAM UNIVERSITY	PRI-U	1,249,303	556,849	139,650	348,613	492	226,392	100	40,857	18,231	4,053
FRIENDS WORLD COLLEGE	PRI-FN	A	A						A	A	A
GENERAL THEOLOGICAL SEM	PRI-FG	192,253	146,295	0	1,220	0	0	38	2,734	2,131	325
GRUSS GIRLS SEMINARY	PRI-FN	A	A						A	A	A
HADAR HATORAH RAB SEM	PRI-FN	A		A				A	A	A	A
HAMILTON COLLEGE	PRI-FN	349,336	203,814	0	222	38	94,509	0	9,266	6,816	1,687
HARRIMAN COLLEGE	PRI-T	32,900	31,600	400	0	4	388	3,200	1,104	1,054	202
HARTWICK COLLEGE	PRI-FN	156,488	112,000	0	4,000	146	16,354	600	6,008	3,950	938
HILBERT COLLEGE	PRI-T	43,083	43,083	0	10	71	604	52	1,370	1,370	230
HOBART-WM SMITH COLLEGES	PRI-FN	A	A		A	A	A	A	A	A	A
HOFSTRA UNIVERSITY	PRI-FG	795,014	385,773	160,963	21,197	76	281,419	63,305	25,764	14,274	3,510
HOLY TRINITY ORTHODOX SEM	PRI-FN	A	A			A	A	A	A	A	A
HOUGHTON COLLEGE	PRI-FN	164,663	A	0	5	212	4,659	500	5,441	A	656
INST OF DESIGN AND CONSTR	PRI-T			NO LIBRARY FACILITIES							
INTERBORO INSTITUTE	PRI-T	3,542	3,014	0	0	0	0	0	500	450	10
IONA COLLEGE	PRI-FG	170,928	A	0	44,004	190	0	3,110	6,567	A	719
ITHACA COLLEGE	PRI-FG	259,731	155,685	0	23,153	0	83,695	208	5,954	4,425	2,198
JAMESTWN BUSINESS COLLEGE	PRI-T	A	A						A	A	A
JEWISH THEOL SEM AMERICA	PRI-FG	A	A		A	A	A	A	A	A	A
THE JUILLIARD SCHOOL	PRI-FG	14,644	A	0	0	0	0	0	776	A	86
KATHARINE GIBBS SCHOOL	PRI-T	1,500	1,400	0	0	0	0	0	50	A	16
KEHILATH YAKOV RAB SEM	PRI-FG	A	A						A	A	A
KEUKA COLLEGE	PRI-FN	92,382	72,589	0	0	3	5,076	88	1,941	1,311	542
KING'S COLLEGE	PRI-FN	73,500	72,100	0	0	260	7,758	0	2,248	2,178	550
LAB INST OF MERCHANDISING	PRI-T	3,000	2,500	0	0	0	0	50	100	100	50

SEE FOOTNOTES AT END OF TABLE

STATE OR OTHER AREA AND INSTITUTION	CON-TROL AND TYPE OF IN-STITU-TION	HELD AT END OF YEAR							ADDED DURING YEAR		CURRENT PERIOD-ICAL SUB-SCRIPTION TITLES FALL 1979
		BOOKSTOCK		SEPARATE GOVERN-MENT DOCU-MENTS COLLEC-TIONS (VOLS.)	MICROFORMS			ALL OTHER LIBRARY MATE-RIALS	BOOKSTOCK		
		VOLUMES	TITLES		BOOK TITLES	PERI-ODICAL TITLES	OTHER PHYS-ICAL UNITS		VOLUMES	TITLES	
(1)	(2)	(3)	(4)	(5)	(6)	(7)	(8)	(9)	(10)	(11)	(12)
NEW YORK	--CONTINUED										
LADYCLIFF COLLEGE	PRI-FN	76,960	62,222	289	0	106	5,258	360	1,587	1,099	500
LE MOYNE COLLEGE	PRI-FN	144,167	91,208	50	44	114	7,847	653	4,908	3,090	1,030
LONG IS C HOSP SCH NURS	PRI-T	15,070	5,370	0	0	0	0	0	1,370	1,070	370
LONG IS SEM JEWISH STDIES	PRI-FN	A	A						A	A	A
LONG IS U ALL CAMPUSES											
LONG IS U BROOKLYN CENTER	PRI-FG	219,089	218,964	24,657	26,892	18	26,910	475	9,725	9,600	1,828
LONG IS U C W POST CENTER	PRI-U	387,562	296,513	200,277	0	0	205,343	2,929	20,010	11,793	4,328
LONG IS U SOUTHAMPTON CTR	PRI-FG	104,000	87,000	12,900	3	37	1,100	150	3,500	2,500	660
MACHZIKEI HADATH RAB C	PRI-FG	A	A						A	A	A
MANHATTAN COLLEGE	PRI-FG	221,523	141,758	0	80	178	0	128	7,743	5,482	2,005
MANHATTAN SCHOOL OF MUSIC	PRI-FG	90,073	54,200	0	0	2	2,311	0	3,151	3,073	77
MANHATTANVILLE COLLEGE	PRI-FG	292,828	182,800	0	44	103	16,708	0	5,328	A	1,061
MANNES COLLEGE OF MUSIC	PRI-FN	22,315	A	0	0	0	0	0	1,040	481	48
MARIA COLLEGE OF ALBANY	PRI-T	42,725	42,725	300	0	525	0	0	1,400	4,039	260
MARIA REGINA COLLEGE	PRI-T	37,986	34,308	0	2,912	269	0	99	861	800	210
MARIST COLLEGE	PRI-FG	80,690	51,815	0	8	2,220	0	169	1,795	1,180	483
MARYKNOLL SCH OF THEOLOGY	PRI-FG	82,650	78,500	0	20	10	0	0	3,450	3,000	640
MARYMOUNT COLLEGE	PRI-FN	107,603	102,257	0	36	39	454	275	2,695	2,160	531
MARYMOUNT MANHATTAN C	PRI-FN	58,898	52,729	0	0	8	0	341	5,346	A	465
MATER DEI COLLEGE	PRI-T	46,879	30,469	0	1	42	514	326	978	916	310
MEDAILLE COLLEGE	PRI-FN	89,175	89,075	0	1,600	1,200	55,000	0	2,800	2,000	430
MERCY COLLEGE	PRI-FN	241,117	181,095	8,528	24,495	422	210,635	4,567	106,198	91,967	1,266
MESIVTA ESTN PKWY RAB SEM	PRI-FG	A	A					A	A	A	A
MES TORAH VODAATH SEM	PRI-FG	A	A					A	A	A	A
MESIVTHA TIFERETH JER AMR	PRI-FG	A	A					A	A	A	A
MIRRER YESHIVA CEN INST	PRI-FG	A	A					A	A	A	A
MOLLCY COLLEGE	PRI-FN	78,600	68,000	0	3,000	40	0	1,500	2,500	2,000	530
MONROE BUSINESS INSTITUTE	PRI-T	2,577	2,174	0	0	0	0	0	958	853	50
MOUNT SAINT ALPHONSUS SEM	PRI-FG	72,410	63,774	0	682	61	674	0	2,260	2,150	819
MOUNT SAINT MARY COLLEGE	PRI-FN	74,005	73,946	0	2	33	5,980	9,243	2,457	2,398	599
SINAI SCH OF MED CUNY	PRI-FG	32,817	A	0	0	2	0	0	2,519	1,925	1,775
NAZARETH C OF ROCHESTER	PRI-FG	179,240	133,615	0	36,000	121	0	0	6,947	4,391	1,005
NEW SCH FOR SOC RESEARCH	PRI-FG	109,236	97,775	0	463	224	63,410	0	3,255	2,914	895
N Y CHIROPRACTIC COLLEGE	PRI-FG	5,000	5,000	0	0	10	0	5	320	320	90
NY COLLEGE PODIATRIC MED	PRI-FG	5,847	3,090	217	0	12	94	0	557	482	200
NY INST TECHN ALL CAM											
NY INST TECHN MAIN CAMPUS	PRI-FG	84,850	55,320	0	0	725	223,700	55	6,600	A	1,045
NY INST TECHN NY CTY CAM	PRI-FG	38,000	30,000	0	0	350	9,900	15	1,900	A	550
NEW YORK LAW SCHOOL	PRI-FG	119,731	21,606	15,061	961	31	51,257	0	13,108	2,773	600
NEW YORK MEDICAL COLLEGE	PRI-FG	100,000	55,385	0	0	56	0	0	910	504	1,321
NY SCH OF INTERIOR DESIGN	PRI-FN	1,979	1,672	0	0	0	0	0	160	132	47
NEW YORK THEOL SEMINARY	PRI-FG	16,893	16,220	0	0	5	0	6	843	800	48
NEW YORK UNIVERSITY	PRI-U	2,700,201	A	343,074	0	0	1,366,699	757,340	104,658	A	23,686
NIAGARA UNIVERSITY	PRI-FG	164,592	121,620	0	14	88	32,560	3,510	8,336	7,086	1,459
NYACK COLLEGE	PRI-FG	63,932	50,395	0	5	56	535	0	2,259	1,870	579
OHEL SHMUEL YESHIVA	PRI-FG	A	A						A	A	A
OHR HAMEIR THEOL SEM	PRI-FG	A	A						A	A	A
OHR YISROEL RAB COLLEGE	PRI-FN	A	A						A	A	A
OLEAN BUSINESS INSTITUTE	PRI-T	1,638	1,590	0	0	0	0	0	65	65	17
PACE UNIVERSITY ALL CAM											
PACE U C OF WHITE PLAINS	PRI-FG	152,385	70,562	441	1	352	92,651	0	7,660	3,324	2,474
PACE UNIVERSITY NEW YORK	PRI-FG	261,100	189,967	0	0	860	388	36,200	15,871	12,292	1,195
PACE U PLSNTVL-BRCLF CAM	PRI-FG	193,897	157,112	0	0	649	0	0	5,389	4,068	971
PARSONS SCHOOL OF DESIGN	PRI-FG	32,400	29,000	0	0	0	0	30,000	1,524	1,200	133
PAUL SMITH'S C ARTS & SCI	PRI-T	33,120	32,206	0	12	2	182	28,000	1,322	1,258	327
POLYTECHNIC INST NEW YORK	PRI-FG	258,091	99,051	45,000	4,383	137	100,000	19,000	6,579	4,269	1,291
POWELSON BUSINESS INST	PRI-T	1,182	1,161	0	0	0	0	20	100	100	13
PRATT INSTITUTE	PRI-U	221,820	A	96,968	3,922	5,084	507	108,718	4,545	2,048	1,092
RABBI ISAAC ELCHANAN SEM	PRI-FG	6,402	A	0	0	0	0	548	10	A	102
RAB AC MES RAB CHAIM BRLN	PRI-FG	A	A					A	A	A	A
RAB COLLEGE BETH SHRAGA	PRI-FG	A	A						A	A	A

SEE FOOTNOTES AT END OF TABLE

Table 1. – Collections in College and University Libraries, by State or Other Area and Institution: Aggregate United States, 1978-79, and Fall 1979 – Continued

STATE OR OTHER AREA AND INSTITUTION (1)	CON-TROL AND TYPE OF IN-STITU-TION (2)	HELD AT END OF YEAR							ADDED DURING YEAR		CURRENT PERIOD-ICAL SUB-SCRIPTION TITLES FALL 1979 (12)
		BOOKSTOCK		SEPARATE GOVERN-MENT DOCU-MENTS COLLEC-TIONS (VOLS.) (5)	MICROFORMS			ALL OTHER LIBRARY MATE-RIALS (9)	BOOKSTOCK		
		VOLUMES (3)	TITLES (4)		BOOK TITLES (6)	PERI-ODICAL TITLES (7)	OTHER PHYS-ICAL UNITS (8)		VOLUMES (10)	TITLES (11)	
NEW YORK	--CONTINUED										
RAB C BOBOVER B'NEI ZION	PRI-FG	A	A					A	A	A	A
RAB C CH'SAN SOFER NY	PRI-FG	A	A						A	A	A
RAB C OF KAMENITZ YESHIVA	PRI-FN	A	A						A	..	A
RAB COLLEGE LONG ISLAND	PRI-FG	A	A						A	A	A
RAB COLLEGE OF SANZ	PRI-FG	A	A						A	A	
RABBINICAL C OF TASH	PRI-FG	A	A					A	A	A	A
RAB SEMINARY ADAS YEREIM	PRI-FN	A	A						A	A	A
RABBINICAL SEM OF AMERICA	PRI-FG	A	A						A	A	A
RAB SEM BETH YIT D'SPINKA	PRI-FG	A	A					A	A	A	A
RAB SEMINARY M'KOR CHAIM	PRI-FG	A	A								
RABBINICAL SEM OF MUNKACS	PRI-FG	A	A						A	A	A
RAB SEM OF NEW SQUARE	PRI-FG	A	A						A	A	A
RENSSELAER POLY INSTITUTE	PRI-U	284,600	214,640	0	50	50	305,370	42,640	8,430	5,660	3,090
RIKA BREUER TEACHERS SEM	PRI-FN	A	A						A	A	A
ROBERTS WESLEYAN COLLEGE	PRI-FN	78,196	57,095	0	0	108	614	0	2,750	1,996	442
ROCHESTER BUS INSTITUTE	PRI-T	2,279	1,679	0	0	0	0	0	10	10	25
ROCHESTER INST TECHNOLOGY	PRI-FG	181,807	136,169	0	1,330	1,123	0	0	7,709	6,667	3,917
ROCKEFELLER UNIVERSITY	PRI-FG	187,595	A	0	0	4	0	0	6,205	A	1,500
RUSSELL SAGE C ALL CAM											
RUSSELL SAGE C MAIN CAM	PRI-FG	182,949	93,884	0	0	0	6,589	0	8,595	4,821	1,359
RUSSELL SAGE JC OF ALBANY	PRI-T	74,407	49,101	0	0	0	1,427	0	3,888	2,755	819
SAINT BERNARD'S SEMINARY	PRI-FG	64,415	32,842	0	0	0	0	0	4,378	2,868	575
SAINT BONAVENTURE U	PRI-FG	245,762	245,538	23,015	26,244	108	4,812	180	8,814	8,590	1,652
SAINT FRANCIS COLLEGE	PRI-FN	122,119	122,183	0	0	400	1,200	0	3,436	3,500	650
SAINT JOHN FISHER COLLEGE	PRI-FN	120,410	77,680	2,340	1,120	38	1,810	740	5,480	3,162	725
SAINT JOHN'S UNIVERSITY	PRI-U	881,949	491,746	56,596	121,771	2,155	5,028	2,250	35,672	26,393	5,203
SNT JOSEPHS C ALL CAM											
SNT JOSEPH'S C MAIN CAM	PRI-FN	107,711	80,754	0	71	140	2,150	871	3,249	2,890	511
SNT JOSEPHS C SUFFOLK CAM	PRI-FN	45,424	34,132	0	0	1,843	0	5,000	1,623	1,538	350
SNT JOSEPHS SEM & COLLEGE	PRI-FG	92,642	48,000	0	440	270	300	0	1,566	1,200	420
SAINT LAWRENCE UNIVERSITY	PRI-FG	281,347	199,804	36,952	3,500	350	120,000	0	8,869	7,391	1,522
SAINT THOMAS AQUINAS C	PRI-FN	78,480	60,100	0	0	407	4,241	115	3,418	2,633	526
SNT VLADMR ORTH THEOL SEM	PRI-FG	37,000	32,000	0	160	31	0	0	1,000	900	293
SARAH LAWRENCE COLLEGE	PRI-FG	155,714	125,472	25,645	82	75	10,948	266	6,639	5,730	1,047
SARA SCHENIRER TCHRS SEM	PRI-FN	A	A						A	A	A
SCHOOL OF VISUAL ARTS	PRI-FN	20,000	16,000	0	0	0	0	28,000	1,500	1,200	178
SEM IMMAC CONCEPTION	PRI-FG	43,692	41,992	0	0	0	395	0	1,815	1,700	315
SH'CR YOSHUV RAB COLLEGE	PRI-FG	A	A						A	A	A
SIENA COLLEGE	PRI-FN	168,200	56,066	0	23,284	18	0	0	6,187	2,062	1,103
SKIDMORE COLLEGE	PRI-FN	218,635	188,026	45,487	310	91	26,272	4,269	9,413	8,754	1,334
STATE U NY SYS ALL INST											
SUNY AT ALBANY	PUB-U	878,569	503,001	263,873	3,947	2,467	1,547,159	0	46,652	26,067	7,241
SUNY AT BINGHAMTON	PUB-FG	820,000	595,831	270,714	440,857	0	0	59,404	45,975	42,967	13,774
SUNY AT BUFFALO ALL CAM											
SUNY AT BUFFALO MAIN CAM	PUB-U	1,697,624	1,018,574	630,221	0	91	0	0	70,918	45,089	12,291
SUNY HEALTH SCI CTR BFLO	PUB-FG	187,319	70,000	0	0	9	0	0	9,135	3,384	2,887
SUNY AT STONY BK ALL CAM											
SUNY AT STONY BK MAIN CAM	PUB-FG	1,018,864	499,425	27,500	0	0	1,499,014	60,234	42,779	22,472	9,325
SUNY HLTH SCI CTR STNY BK	PUB-FG	159,254	35,966	0	5	45	3,413	0	10,667	4,270	2,521
SUNY DOWNSTATE MEDL CTR	PUB-FG	237,715	40,000	0	0	0	0	0	6,571		1,680
SUNY UPSTATE MEDICAL CTR	PUB-FG	125,486	64,306	779	0	0	96	0	4,924	4,500	1,830
SUNY COLLEGE AT BROCKPORT	PUB-FG	356,529	255,980	72,451	0	0	945,501	220	23,365	17,038	3,800
SUNY COLLEGE AT BUFFALO	PUB-FG	408,415	340,345	0	0	0	362,079	1,299	19,059	11,713	5,526
SUNY COLLEGE AT CORTLAND	PUB-FG	245,860	169,643	199,721	220,105	98	0	12,043	11,964	8,288	1,515
SUNY COLLEGE AT FREDONIA	PUB-FG	313,613	261,344	2,683	6,124	396	572,243	314	9,687	8,072	2,038
SUNY COLLEGE AT GENESEO	PUB-FG	325,544	244,909	136,671	80,542	236	203,228	5,840	11,017	10,715	2,551
SUNY COLLEGE AT NEW PALTZ	PUB-FG	295,558	236,446	37,500	0	1	538,345	64	12,901	10,321	1,690
SUNY COLLEGE OLD WESTBURY	PUB-FN	105,921	87,586	0	1,588	511	125,144	0	9,791	7,932	1,323
SUNY COLLEGE AT ONEONTA	PUB-FG	366,097	247,718	42,079	0	0	158,096	83,932	20,807	13,940	2,996
SUNY COLLEGE AT OSWEGO	PUB-FG	296,130	196,485	132,631	35,418	315	769,115	6,823	18,240	11,006	3,070
SUNY COLLEGE PLATTSBURGH	PUB-FG	227,160	218,074	83,714	255,000	839	0	4,294	3,680	3,533	1,681

SEE FOOTNOTES AT END OF TABLE

55

Table 1. — Collections in College and University Libraries, by State or Other Area and Institution: Aggregate United States, 1978-79, and Fall 1979 — Continued

STATE OR OTHER AREA AND INSTITUTION (1)	CONTROL AND TYPE OF INSTITUTION (2)	HELD AT END OF YEAR							ADDED DURING YEAR		CURRENT PERIODICAL SUBSCRIPTION TITLES FALL 1979 (12)
		BOOKSTOCK		SEPARATE GOVERNMENT DOCUMENTS COLLECTIONS (VOLS.) (5)	MICROFORMS			ALL OTHER LIBRARY MATERIALS (9)	BOOKSTOCK		
		VOLUMES (3)	TITLES (4)		BOOK TITLES (6)	PERIODICAL TITLES (7)	OTHER PHYSICAL UNITS (8)		VOLUMES (10)	TITLES (11)	
NEW YORK	—CONTINUED										
SUNY COLLEGE AT POTSDAM	PUB-FG	297,131	222,848	0	1,856	614	227,325	4,080	12,554	9,415	1,830
SUNY COLLEGE AT PURCHASE	PUB-FN	147,942	111,743	40,985	8,792	301	33,000	10,707	9,485	7,186	1,295
SUNY C OF TECH UTICA-ROME	PUB-FG	91,480	A	11,661	0	0	191,753	114	9,818	A	2,200
SUNY EMPIRE STATE COLLEGE	PUB-FN	4,387	1,914	0	10,000	0	0	0	70	68	30
SUNY C ENVRNNTL SCI-FORS	PUB-FG	75,090	31,586	0	43	4	41,575	0	2,450	278	2,342
SUNY MARITIME COLLEGE	PUB-FG	65,469	50,872	33,439	3,986	76	0	81	2,134	1,396	529
SUNY STATE C OF OPTOMETRY	PUB-FG	17,827	9,715	0	171	40	1,857	1	1,616	909	367
SUNY AGRL & TECH C ALFRED	PUB-T	54,750	36,444	0	3	113	2,679	57,411	2,551	1,521	871
SUNY AGRL & TECH C CANTON	PUB-T	34,309	30,005	0	0	2,511	0	0	1,333	1,304	335
SUNY AGRL TECH C COBLESKL	PUB-T	62,920	48,656	20,000	107	21	5,010	300	3,351	2,573	540
SUNY AGRL & TECH C DELHI	PUB-T	44,737	33,047	11,481	0	394	410	202	1,595	1,328	549
SUNY AGRL TECH C FARMNGDL	PUB-T	86,876	75,800	58,324	0	0	11,709	36	5,520	4,460	1,030
SUNY AGRL TECH C MORRISVL	PUB-T	74,588	63,399	0	0	246	0	93	3,271	2,780	515
ADIRONDACK CNTY COLLEGE	PUB-T	44,442	44,442	0	0	37	2,578	0	800	800	321
BROOME COMMUNITY COLLEGE	PUB-T	52,066	46,860	0	0	40	149	10,034	2,960	2,664	623
CAYUGA CO CMTY COLLEGE	PUB-T	62,747	60,000	2,000	25	490	500	200	1,900	1,825	747
CLINTON COMMUNITY COLLEGE	PUB-T	33,511	28,724	0	1,140	42	158,308	20	2,846	2,548	295
COLUMBIA-GREENE CC	PUB-T	30,562	26,432	0	0	327	0	403	3,007	2,838	611
CMTY COLLEGE FINGER LAKES	PUB-T	40,635	27,707	0	0	177	9,750	116	1,717	1,409	565
CORNING COMMUNITY COLLEGE	PUB-T	66,224	53,914	34,047	222	79	1,479	2,146	2,368	2,170	462
DUTCHESS CNTY COLLEGE	PUB-T	76,945	63,870	6,219	0	189	104	0	5,270	4,527	479
ERIE COMMUNITY COLLEGE	PUB-T	109,626	86,768	554	12,539	313	10,873	11,154	7,985	6,363	956
FASHION INST TECHNOLOGY	PUB-FN	54,615	48,920	0	0	35	2,343	89,154	3,694	2,727	498
FULTON-MONTGOMERY CC	PUB-T	53,787	51,274	0	0	83	2,616	170	3,195	1,067	291
GENESEE COMMUNITY COLLEGE	PUB-T	46,569	43,569	0	0	159	6,000	188	1,449	200	480
HERKIMER CO CMTY COLLEGE	PUB-T	52,524	41,409	0	89	216	0	205	3,199	2,522	487
HUDSON VLY CMTY COLLEGE	PUB-T	92,121	89,430	0	16,116	180	9,060	2,123	5,752	5,752	803
JAMESTOWN CMTY COLLEGE	PUB-T	46,882	31,000	700	11	44	7,329	384	1,820	1,200	485
JEFFERSON CMTY COLLEGE	PUB-T	56,248	51,992	0	18	45	1,706	1,065	1,142	1,064	418
MOHAWK VLY CMTY COLLEGE	PUB-T	65,036	56,129	0	35	50	36	0	3,344	2,675	796
MONROE COMMUNITY COLLEGE	PUB-T	73,967	53,407	0	2	278	9,862	0	2,617	1,764	740
NASSAU COMMUNITY COLLEGE	PUB-T	137,921	99,778	0	1	394	15	6	5,021	3,284	792
NIAGARA CO CMTY COLLEGE	PUB-T	36,512	34,445	0	4	316	6,097	113	1,143	1,066	350
N COUNTRY CMTY COLLEGE	PUB-T	30,600	26,010	0	0	122	0	16	1,852	1,820	328
ONONDAGA CMTY COLLEGE	PUB-T	78,553	75,029	7,658	5	211	12,529	390	4,546	4,395	752
ORANGE CO CMTY COLLEGE	PUB-T	69,214	56,284	0	0	72	15,093	0	3,269	2,334	521
ROCKLAND CMTY COLLEGE	PUB-T	126,966	126,731	7,687	36,979	964	5,402	2,195	5,213	4,978	775
SCHENECTADY COUNTY CC	PUB-T	39,077	37,578	612	2	144	519	76	3,694	3,356	260
SUFFOLK CO CMTY COLLEGE	PUB-T	143,337	121,254	0	10,000	806	11,305	134	11,021	9,511	1,491
SULLIVAN CO CMTY COLLEGE	PUB-T	42,947	38,653	0	0	261	4,174	1,440	2,497	2,248	548
TOMPKINS-CORTLAND CC	PUB-T	28,751	24,283	0	387	104	21	216	1,842	1,525	406
ULSTER CO CMTY COLLEGE	PUB-T	68,938	59,654	0	0	52	4,023	0	4,793	4,369	451
WESTCHESTER CMTY COLLEGE	PUB-T	87,165	53,633	0	15,460	313	0	363	2,715	2,108	473
GENOTYPE INSTITUTE	PRI-T	200	100	0	0	0	0	0	10	10	2
SYRACUSE U ALL CAMPUSES											
SYRACUSE U MAIN CAMPUS	PRI-U	1,822,027	1,093,216	0	0	0	1,715,880	267,833	74,134	44,480	9,084
UTICA C OF SYRACUSE U	PRI-FN	116,574	76,508	0	400	116	50	0	4,216	2,471	1,208
TALMUDICAL INST UPST NY	PRI-FN	A	A						A	A	A
TALMUD SEM OHOLEI TORAH	PRI-FG	A	A					A	A	A	A
TAYLOR BUSINESS INSTITUTE	PRI-T	2,134	1,612	200	0	0	0	3,100	277	197	52
TECH CAREER INSTITUTES	PRI-T	2,051	1,910	0	0	0	0	44	49	17	46
TOBE-COBURN SCH FASH CARS	PRI-T	2,266	A	0	0	0	0	400	51	44	23
TOURO COLLEGE	PRI-FG	120,000	85,000	0	0	220	4,250	500	25,000	18,000	550
TROCAIRE COLLEGE	PRI-T	37,996	30,700	0	0	0	0	890	750	720	240
UNION COLLEGE	PRI-FG	383,430	193,819	29,229	200	338	160,232	48,927	14,088	9,959	2,993
UNION THEOLOGICAL SEM	PRI-FG	A	A						A	A	A
UNITED TALMUDICAL ACADEMY	PRI-FG	A	A						A	A	A
UNIVERSITY OF ROCHESTER	PRI-U	1,835,704	695,537	0	31,230	265	1,527,552	75,645	54,873	21,613	12,044
U ST NY REGENTS EXTNL DEG	PUB-FN	NO LIBRARY FACILITIES									
UTICA SCHOOL OF COMMERCE	PRI-T	1,479	A	0	0	0	0	0	344	A	33
VASSAR COLLEGE	PRI-FG	518,604	264,488	67,623	8,674	8,007	0	71,000	18,830	9,603	3,087

SEE FOOTNOTES AT END OF TABLE

Table 1. — Collections in College and University Libraries, by State or Other Area and Institution: Aggregate United States, 1978-79, and Fall 1979 — Continued

		HELD AT END OF YEAR							ADDED DURING YEAR		
		BOOKSTOCK		SEPARATE GOVERN-MENT DOCU-MENTS COLLEC-TIONS (VOLS.)	MICROFORMS			ALL OTHER LIBRARY MATE-RIALS	BOOKSTOCK		CURRENT PERIOD-ICAL SUB-SCRIPTION TITLES FALL 1979
STATE OR OTHER AREA AND INSTITUTION	CON-TROL AND TYPE OF IN-STITU-TION	VOLUMES	TITLES		BOOK TITLES	PERI-ODICAL TITLES	OTHER PHYS-ICAL UNITS		VOLUMES	TITLES	
(1)	(2)	(3)	(4)	(5)	(6)	(7)	(8)	(9)	(10)	(11)	(12)
NEW YORK --CONTINUED											
VILLA MARIA COLLEGE BFLO	PRI-T	46,035	40,895	0	0	7	1,959	73	1,319	1,295	285
WADHAMS HALL SEM-COLLEGE	PRI-FN	79,677	63,500	0	122	23	1,970	50	2,563	2,023	540
WAGNER COLLEGE	PRI-FG	251,169	175,291	5,260	32,420	288	373,057	675	4,655	3,425	1
WEBB INST OF NAVAL ARCH	PRI-FN	32,136	28,266	0	3	10	181	346	1,734	1,408	209
WELLS COLLEGE	PRI-FN	195,122	113,489	0	79	30	2,603	0	3,239	1,631	641
WESTCHESTER INSTITUTE	PRI-FG	A	A					A	A	A	A
THE WOOD SCHOOL	PRI-T	500	477	0	0	0	0	0	81	81	20
YESH BETH HILLEL KRASNA	PRI-FG	A	A						A	A	A
YESH BETH SHEARM RAB INST	PRI-FG	A	A					A	A	A	A
YESH CHOFETZ CHAIM RADUN	PRI-FG	A	A						A	A	A
YESH KARLIN STOLIN INST	PRI-FG	A	A						A	A	A
YESHIVA NACHLAS HALEVIYIM	PRI-FG	A	A						A	A	A
YESH OF NITRA RAB COLLEGE	PRI-FN	A	A						A	A	A
YESHIVA SHAAR HATORAH	PRI-FG	A	A						A	A	A
YESHIVA UNIVERSITY	PRI-U	770,826	431,503	18,825	3,797	650	256,258	351	29,400	18,009	4,850
YESH MIKDASH MELECH	PRI-FN	A	A					A	A	A	A
YESHIVATH VIZHITZ	PRI-FG	A	A					A	A	A	A
YESHIVATH ZICHRON MOSHE	PRI-FG	A	A					A	A	A	A
NORTH CAROLINA											
ANSON TECHNICAL COLLEGE	PUB-T	12,522	12,511	0	0	170	56	35	513	500	146
ASHEBORO COLLEGE	PRI-T	A	A						A	A	A
ASHEVL BUNCOMBE TECH C	PUB-T	24,775	23,933	0	0	252	1,005	23	938	930	286
ATLANTIC CHRISTIAN C	PRI-FN	93,130	A	2,762	0	140	0	86	3,580	A	562
BARBER-SCOTIA COLLEGE	PRI-FN	67,526	48,816	0	0	2,529	0	26	4,041	1,462	299
BEAUFORT CO CMTY COLLEGE	PUB-T	16,283	16,150	0	0	7	0	0	1,583	1,453	111
BELMONT ABBEY COLLEGE	PRI-FN	79,717	59,475	0	132	108	7,978	0	4,620	4,083	485
BENNETT COLLEGE	PRI-FN	78,930	39,672	0	0	2,288	0	150	1,086	643	332
BLADEN TECHNICAL INST	PUB-T	13,782	A	0	0	52	45	1	1,818	1,342	83
BLANTONS JUNIOR COLLEGE	PRI-T	5,266	4,987	0	0	0	0	0	213	197	50
BLUE RIDGE TECHNICAL C	PUB-T	14,552	14,344	0	115	538	0	354	1,208	1,000	181
BREVARD COLLEGE	PRI-T	37,820	23,026	0	6	11	139	210	359	300	191
CALDWELL CC AND TECH INST	PUB-T	21,816	21,741	0	0	111	1,631	0	1,432	1,432	202
CAMPBELL UNIVERSITY[1]	PRI-FG	153,889	110,680	83,751	3,061	76	63,481	12,450	5,833	10,330	877
CAPE FEAR TECHNICAL INST	PUB-T	18,731	15,027	0	1,302	224	3,896	380	1,899	1,481	347
CARTERET TECHNICAL INST	PUB-T	17,022	15,600	0	0	86	71	0	547	A	187
CATAWBA COLLEGE	PRI-FN	121,754	75,349	13,155	14,198	259	2,273	6,387	4,703	2,473	1,005
CATAWBA VALLEY TECH C	PUB-T	25,824	23,824	0	0	71	931	20	1,914	1,914	198
CECILS JUNIOR COLLEGE	PRI-T	6,423	5,859	0	0	0	0	0	219	213	53
CEN CAROLINA TECH C	PUB-T	18,970	16,644	0	0	99	877	56	1,080	637	251
CEN PIEDMONT CMTY COLLEGE	PUB-T	67,192	56,873	0	7,693	229	15,355	647	3,059	2,032	383
CHOWAN COLLEGE	PRI-T	62,500	46,177	29,115	84	302	0	1	3,175	2,782	348
CLEVELAND CO TECH INST	PUB-T	20,921	18,618	0	200	66	187	4	1,362	1,240	210
COASTAL CAROLINA CC	PUB-T	26,236	22,403	0	0	6,776	0	29	627	430	175
COLLEGE OF THE ALBEMARLE	PUB-T	33,925	26,563	0	0	56	377	40	1,311	850	233
CRAVEN COMMUNITY COLLEGE	PUB-T	17,928	17,601	0	1	105	2,410	2	1,247	1,209	188
DAVIDSON COLLEGE	PRI-FN	250,641	173,000	65,754	63	98	47,244	2,195	9,475	9,198	1,597
DAVIDSON CO CMTY COLLEGE	PUB-T	34,875	32,667	0	0	163	2,327	115	1,387	A	265
DUKE UNIVERSITY	PRI-U	3,022,916	A	521,720	0	0	354,223	111,975	74,536	A	31,838
DURHAM COLLEGE	PRI-T	A	A				A		A	A	A
DURHAM TECHNICAL INST	PUB-T	19,084	17,635	623	0	143	0	21	2,235	2,197	330
EDGECOMBE TECH INST	PUB-T	16,072	12,822	0	9	75	1,171	2	523	504	141
ELON COLLEGE	PRI-FN	122,105	74,150	24,991	111	84	4,092	2,137	3,593	2,254	893
FAYETTEVILLE TECH INST	PUB-T	29,642	22,842	100	198	59	1,452	32	3,069	2,386	261
FORSYTH TECHNICAL INST	PUB-T	26,583	25,894	0	0	952	468	21	1,417	1,379	295
GARDNER-WEBB COLLEGE	PRI-FN	105,415	101,801	8,293	1,971	298	5,472	491	8,227	7,798	835
GASTON COLLEGE	PUB-T	41,904	38,100	0	0	255	78	68	1,187	1,100	234
GREENSBORO COLLEGE	PRI-FN	73,681	67,500	0	1	57	0	0	2,316	1,800	412
GUILFORD COLLEGE	PRI-FN	143,572	141,572	0	8,710	80	0	14,779	5,682	5,183	0
GUILFORD TECHNICAL INST	PUB-T	36,694	36,079	0	112	139	2,106	29	3,241	3,175	437
HALIFAX CMTY COLLEGE	PUB-T	20,369	17,477	0	0	108	454	0	2,375	2,204	274

SEE FOOTNOTES AT END OF TABLE

Table 1. — Collections in College and University Libraries, by State or Other Area and Institution: Aggregate United States, 1978-79, and Fall 1979 — Continued

STATE OR OTHER AREA AND INSTITUTION	CONTROL AND TYPE OF INSTITUTION	HELD AT END OF YEAR							ADDED DURING YEAR		CURRENT PERIODICAL SUBSCRIPTION TITLES FALL 1979
		BOOKSTOCK		SEPARATE GOVERNMENT DOCUMENTS COLLECTIONS (VOLS.)	MICROFORMS			ALL OTHER LIBRARY MATERIALS	BOOKSTOCK		
		VOLUMES	TITLES		BOOK TITLES	PERIODICAL TITLES	OTHER PHYSICAL UNITS		VOLUMES	TITLES	
(1)	(2)	(3)	(4)	(5)	(6)	(7)	(8)	(9)	(10)	(11)	(12)
NORTH CAROLINA --CONTINUED											
HAMILTON COLLEGE	PRI-T	5,976	5,926	0	0	0	0	0	621	621	59
HARDBARGER JC BUSINESS	PRI-T	A	A						A	A	A
HAYWOOD TECHNICAL INST	PUB-T	20,490	19,928	0	0	105	0	0	1,299	1,248	255
HIGH POINT COLLEGE	PRI-FN	102,624	99,520	0	0	2	2,341	0	3,950	3,900	481
ISOTHERMAL CMTY COLLEGE	PUB-T	27,563	26,459	0	0	80	0	0	1,479	1,259	159
JAMES SPRUNT INSTITUTE	PUB-T	21,531	18,910	150	0	50	573	40	812	750	213
JEFFERSON COLLEGE	PRI-T	5,388	5,388	0	0	0	0	10	0	0	30
JOHNSN C SMITH UNIVERSITY	PRI-FN	92,903	56,472	3,427	0	18	5,451	128	3,427	2,357	465
JOHNSTON TECHNICAL INST	PUB-T	12,572	12,350	0	0	125	92	0	701	638	224
JOHN WESLEY COLLEGE	PRI-FN	16,196	15,433	0	0	0	0	0	863	763	120
KING'S C-CHARLOTTE	PRI-T	A	A					A	A	A	A
KING'S COLLEGE-RALEIGH	PRI-T	11,451	5,525	0	0	0	0	0	1,129	568	73
LAFAYETTE COLLEGE	PRI-T	5,435	A	0	0	0	0	0	518	A	86
LEES-MCRAE COLLEGE	PRI-T	A	56,350	0	0	0	3,726	250	A	1,650	309
LENOIR CMTY COLLEGE	PUB-T	41,067	A	0	0	5,850	2,015	0	2,452	A	358
LENOIR-RHYNE COLLEGE	PRI-FN	99,541	89,801	0	0	305	8,314	0	4,900	4,500	790
LIVINGSTONE COLLEGE	PRI-FN	69,285	69,176	0	2,612	2,360	1,527	8	2,613	2,504	257
LOUISBURG COLLEGE	PRI-T	46,825	43,168	0	0	16	275	0	1,241	1,166	172
MARS HILL COLLEGE	PRI-FN	62,872	59,728	3,368	174	335	13	735	3,553	3,528	725
MARTIN COMMUNITY COLLEGE	PUB-T	16,127	11,982	340	20	47	733	34	1,059	957	164
MAYLAND TECHNICAL INST	PUB-T	13,029	11,200	0	0	920	541	1	1,677	1,625	152
MCDOWELL TECHNICAL INST	PUB-T	14,164	13,878	0	0	1,107	0	12	867	850	130
MEREDITH COLLEGE	PRI-FN	88,527	A	2,126	0	0	49,221	14	4,025	A	526
METHODIST COLLEGE	PRI-FN	65,280	50,045	0	14	96	176	98	1,442	972	404
MITCHELL CMTY COLLEGE	PUB-T	28,705	26,700	0	87	365	21	150	1,478	1,460	146
MCNTGOMERY TECH INSTITUTE	PUB-T	8,786	8,004	0	0	37	0	13	730	700	121
MONTREAT-ANDERSON COLLEGE	PRI-T	44,353	35,650	0	0	4	14	0	1,611	1,500	270
MOUNT OLIVE COLLEGE	PRI-T	28,902	A	6,033	2	667	75	10	1,129	A	197
NASH TECHNICAL INSTITUTE	PUB-T	18,042	15,426	325	0	70	1,088	448	918	785	103
NC WESLEYAN COLLEGE	PRI-FN	55,882	42,801	0	1	110	0	123	2,564	1,022	855
PAMLICO TECHNICAL C	PUB-T	10,829	10,750	0	0	54	9	16	535	529	138
PEACE COLLEGE	PRI-T	31,850	30,850	0	0	12	561	5	1,551	1,520	165
PFEIFFER COLLEGE	PRI-FN	92,954	76,779	0	2,501	48	2,305	1	3,310	3,034	465
PIEDMONT BIBLE COLLEGE	PRI-FN	39,156	31,074	0	0	0	0	0	1,942	1,522	135
PIEDMONT TECHNICAL INST	PUB-T	15,078	15,078	0	231	67	574	330	1,748	1,748	264
PITT CMTY COLLEGE	PUB-T	28,097	26,692	0	0	130	2,624	144	3,077	2,923	387
QUEENS COLLEGE	PRI-FN	98,864	74,057	22,166	0	3	2,622	10	3,024	1,757	575
RANDOLPH TECHNICAL C	PUB-T	19,256	17,200	0	0	32	148	1	1,001	928	238
RICHMOND TECHNICAL INST	PUB-T	23,013	A	0	0	32	38	52	1,522	A	111
ROANOKE BIBLE COLLEGE	PRI-FN	19,848	18,394	0	50	1	0	458	2,082	1,764	122
ROANOKE-CHOWAN TECH INST	PUB-T	22,435	19,517	0	16	44	127	175	1,387	1,149	227
ROBESON TECHNICAL INST	PUB-T	29,224	28,285	0	0	75	572	70	2,954	2,800	186
ROCKINGHAM CMTY COLLEGE	PUB-T	28,823	23,058	0	0	123	2,121	110	1,300	1,040	211
ROWAN TECHNICAL INSTITUTE	PUB-T	20,982	20,810	25	0	49	0	0	615	172	298
SACRED HEART COLLEGE	PRI-FN	48,047	48,036	0	0	42	3,256	210	631	620	226
SNT ANDREWS PRESB COLLEGE	PRI-FN	91,893	71,801	7,049	45	121	8,808	0	2,238	1,765	476
SAINT AUGUSTINES COLLEGE	PRI-FN	99,658	A	0	0	50	0	100	4,300	A	460
SAINT MARY'S COLLEGE	PRI-T	30,243	23,809	0	0	18	0	0	1,591	1,298	224
SALEM COLLEGE	PRI-FN	106,031	85,783	0	2	5	7,001	0	2,146	2,033	410
SAMPSON TECHNICAL C	PUB-T	15,690	14,235	0	0	87	0	55	1,387	1,220	156
SANDHILLS CMTY COLLEGE	PUB-T	42,223	41,813	0	0	127	5,527	0	3,307	3,257	248
SHAW UNIVERSITY	PRI-FN	79,374	70,105	0	23	153	0	0	1,898	1,835	428
STHESTN BAPTIST THEOL SEM	PRI-FG	115,769	81,080	0	75,000	92	1,000	200	3,380	2,583	964
SOUTHEASTERN CMTY COLLEGE	PUB-T	39,679	36,457	455	419	176	41,179	74	2,481	2,239	278
SOUTHWESTERN TECH C	PUB-T	20,241	17,340	0	142	126	0	81	1,401	1,261	233
STANLY TECHNICAL C	PUB-T	16,011	15,956	0	49	16	92	735	1,196	1,141	150
SURRY COMMUNITY COLLEGE	PUB-T	27,803	23,400	0	0	123	3,902	30	1,740	1,461	290
TECH C OF ALAMANCE	PUB-T	22,000	18,950	0	0	94	1,564	398	825	825	133
TRI-COUNTY COMMUNITY C	PUB-T	15,387	15,300	0	0	94	1,503	0	2,612	2,600	295
U OF NC ALL CAMPUSES											
APPALACHIAN ST UNIVERSITY	PUB-FG	397,051	271,828	111,051	299,206	1,025	24,748	1,810	25,403	20,606	5,103

SEE FOOTNOTES AT END OF TABLE

58

Table 1. – Collections in College and University Libraries, by State or Other Area and Institution: Aggregate United States, 1978-79, and Fall 1979 – Continued

STATE OR OTHER AREA AND INSTITUTION (1)	CONTROL AND TYPE OF INSTITUTION (2)	HELD AT END OF YEAR — BOOKSTOCK VOLUMES (3)	BOOKSTOCK TITLES (4)	SEPARATE GOVERNMENT DOCUMENTS COLLECTIONS (VOLS.) (5)	MICROFORMS BOOK TITLES (6)	MICROFORMS PERIODICAL TITLES (7)	MICROFORMS OTHER PHYSICAL UNITS (8)	ALL OTHER LIBRARY MATERIALS (9)	ADDED DURING YEAR — BOOKSTOCK VOLUMES (10)	BOOKSTOCK TITLES (11)	CURRENT PERIODICAL SUBSCRIPTION TITLES FALL 1979 (12)
NORTH CAROLINA	--CONTINUED										
EAST CAROLINA UNIVERSITY	PUB-FG	577,578	448,266	283,000	237,304	3,197	137,773	3,921	29,059	23,058	7,740
ELIZABETH CITY STATE U	PUB-FN	88,164	75,124	0	15,000	212	800	55	2,704	2,34	1,260
FAYETTEVL ST UNIVERSITY	PUB-FN	112,858	112,658	0	1	0	97,201	969	8,723	8,513	1,346
NC AGRL & TECH STATE U	PUB-FG	288,694	169,991	116,720	56,482	174	83,752	1,026	12,160	7,092	1,448
NC CENTRAL UNIVERSITY	PUB-FG	434,650	299,360	62,245	130,242	350	297	34,503	21,660	10,939	3,508
NC SCHOOL OF THE ARTS	PUB-FN	76,209	57,150	0	17	3	0	92	5,392	4,100	336
NC STATE U RALEIGH	PUB-U	890,024	405,982	562,515	11,738	571	1,483,905	45,064	76,124	28,734	12,001
PEMBROKE STATE UNIVERSITY	PUB-FG	151,554	151,554	24,066	25,470	4	4,418	1	12,224	12,224	755
U OF NC AT ASHEVILLE	PUB-FN	107,871	75,190	30,455	43	438	14,365	370	5,027	3,609	1,323
U OF NC AT CHAPEL HILL	PUB-U	2,315,237	1,035,407	1,624,346	38,521	3,484	1,283,636	199,434	110,528	58,789	31,205
U OF NC AT CHARLOTTE	PUB-FG	284,710	189,508	133,592	267,810	11,822	0	19,435	22,913	15,635	4,864
U OF NC AT GREENSBORO	PUB-FG	551,700	338,732	208,010	190,830	1,259	832	3,413	30,006	20,286	6,823
U OF NC AT WILMINGTON	PUB-FG	178,597	126,253	121,827	151	674	219,180	849	15,089	11,486	2,732
WSTN CAROLINA UNIVERSITY	PUB-FG	295,152	231,430	49,404	109,387	2,005	457,924	36,569	20,697	17,365	2,385
WINSTON-SALEM STATE U	PUB-FN	144,238	106,108	0	50	142	4	12,872	7,009	6,108	1,157
VANCE-GRANVL CMTY COLLEGE	PUB-T	20,413	18,606	0	54	111	2,382	37	1,841	1,713	249
WAKE FOREST UNIVERSITY	PRI-U	678,242	325,150	67,750	143,411	4,050	128,502	147	35,515	19,270	9,286
WAKE TECHNICAL INSTITUTE	PUB-T	27,580	19,263	2,160	557	11	0	188	1,746	1,324	205
WARREN WILSON COLLEGE	PRI-FN	72,132	58,184	0	59	73	0	766	2,798	1,707	485
WAYNE COMMUNITY COLLEGE	PUB-T	33,550	33,000	0	200	245	0	3,138	1,070	1,060	222
WESTERN PIEDMONT CC	PUB-T	31,194	29,200	0	0	65	1,790	5,296	1,180	1,100	238
WILKES COMMUNITY COLLEGE	PUB-T	39,337	A	0	0	2,994	100	50	3,814	A	186
WILSON CO TECHNICAL INST	PUB-T	24,804	18,107	0	13	82	465	2,575	1,437	1,121	173
WINGATE COLLEGE	PRI-FN	76,444	60,540	0	0	86	0	8	2,693	2,570	321
WINSALM COLLEGE	PRI-T	5,600	5,500	0	0	0	0	50	90	90	45
NORTH DAKOTA											
BISMARCK JUNIOR COLLEGE	PUB-T	30,717	27,920	0	5	13	0	141	1,057	1,012	338
DICKINSON STATE COLLEGE	PUB-FN	62,386	60,000	7,000	400	610	0	6,000	2,996	2,937	540
JAMESTOWN COLLEGE	PRI-FN	66,027	64,180	3,248	9	129	0	42	1,329	1,309	425
LAKE REGION JR COLLEGE	PUB-T	19,582	19,367	0	2	5	3	33	295	253	248
MARY COLLEGE	PRI-FN	38,302	37,877	0	0	44	732	100	1,570	1,514	475
MAYVILLE STATE COLLEGE	PUB-FN	69,591	48,164	0	0	5	1,391	496	2,247	A	374
MINOT STATE COLLEGE	PUB-FG	120,229	88,872	71,538	1,558	156	28,847	1,083	3,577	1,892	1,075
ND STATE SCHOOL SCIENCE	PUB-T	56,381	49,876	0	11,966	1,954	0	13,993	3,999	3,519	585
ND STATE U ALL CAMPUSES											
ND STATE U MAIN CAMPUS	PUB-U	333,187	166,553	151,187	1,390	472	34,817	63,000	9,340	7,776	2,751
ND STATE U BOTTINEAU BR	PUB-T	25,224	26,000	0	0	56	0	48	933	21	273
NORTHWEST BIBLE COLLEGE	PRI-FN	26,770	18,546	0	400	5	0	0	1,720	6,504	85
STANDING ROCK CC	PRI-T	5,526	5,166	509	0	0	0	622	350	4,816	70
TRINITY BIBLE INSTITUTE	PRI-FN	44,231	31,954	0	1,001	2	4,782	3	3,038	2,274	358
U OF ND ALL CAMPUS 6/											
U OF ND MAIN CAMPUS 6/	PUB-U	524,452	298,808	337,063	0	1,740	359,599	150,000	27,455	17,375	6,290
U OF ND WILLISTON BRANCH	PUB-T	10,454	7,847	0	54	564	0	0	171	147	90
VALLEY CITY STATE COLLEGE	PUB-FN	70,971	60,999	17,636	0	0	2,165	1,228	4,383	3,768	381
OHIO											
ANTIOCH UNIVERSITY	PRI-FG	A	A	A	A	A	A	A	A	A	A
ART ACADEMY OF CINCINNATI	PRI-FN	42,802	41,436	0	0	0	0	354,210	823	793	98
ASHLAND COLLEGE	PRI-FG	172,308	113,948	25,891	4,435	143	46,004	9,824	6,139	4,454	960
ATHENAEUM OF OHIO	PRI-FG	105,500	91,567	0	700	30	0	0	2,500	2,400	353
BALDWIN-WALLACE COLLEGE	PRI-FG	173,419	121,660	0	0	0	90,000	0	5,319	4,300	1,009
BELMONT TECHNICAL COLLEGE	PUB-T	4,497	3,921	0	0	24	275	22	339	260	137
BLUFFTON COLLEGE	PRI-FN	89,075	68,029	2,600	62	141	299	3,830	2,985	2,275	1,168
BORROMEO COLLEGE OF OHIO	PRI-FN	61,597	57,504	0	0	0	1,148	222	4,769	4,769	193
BOWLING GRN ST U ALL CAM											
BOWLING GRN ST U MAIN CAM	PUB-U	635,484	319,662	340,728	0	0	1,170,107	17,308	20,859	16,072	4,535
BOWLING GRN ST U FIRELDS	PUB-T	30,367	26,346	6,162	0	20	0	7	1,303	1,142	268
CAPITAL UNIVERSITY	PRI-FG	245,315	146,303	7,745	22	501	15,815	25,497	15,352	9,125	1,973
CASE WESTERN RESERVE U	PRI-U	1,346,464	A	315,959	0	0	369,678	0	29,016	A	13,422
CEDARVILLE COLLEGE	PRI-FN	75,869	64,867	0	630	581	0	0	3,900	3,176	710

SEE FOOTNOTES AT END OF TABLE

Table 1. — Collections in College and University Libraries, by State or Other Area and Institution: Aggregate United States, 1978-79, and Fall 1979 — Continued

		HELD AT END OF YEAR							ADDED DURING YEAR		
		BOOKSTOCK			MICROFORMS				BOOKSTOCK		
STATE OR OTHER AREA AND INSTITUTION	CONTROL AND TYPE OF INSTITUTION	VOLUMES	TITLES	SEPARATE GOVERNMENT DOCUMENTS COLLECTIONS (VOLS.)	BOOK TITLES	PERIODICAL TITLES	OTHER PHYSICAL UNITS	ALL OTHER LIBRARY MATERIALS	VOLUMES	TITLES	CURRENT PERIODICAL SUBSCRIPTION TITLES FALL 1979
(1)	(2)	(3)	(4)	(5)	(6)	(7)	(8)	(9)	(10)	(11)	(12)
OHIO --CONTINUED											
CENTRAL OHIO TECHNICAL C [2/]	PUB-T	NO LIBRARY FACILITIES									
CENTRAL STATE UNIVERSITY	PUB-FN	138,165	119,473	0	8,137	177	315,270	0	4,837	3,170	545
CHATFIELD COLLEGE	PRI-T	17,198	15,320	0	0	0	0	18	390	370	74
CINCINNATI BIBLE SEMINARY	PRI-FG	A	A	A	A	A	A	A	A	A	A
CINCINNATI TECH COLLEGE	PUB-T	13,972	13,922	122	0	109	22,124	0	1,928	1,908	339
CIRCLEVILLE BIBLE COLLEGE	PRI-FN	18,139	18,000	0	141	2	0	0	754	725	173
CLARK TECHNICAL COLLEGE	PUB-T	23,720	22,900	0	0	27	515	0	870	800	497
CLEVELAND C JEWISH STDIES	PRI-FG	A	A	A	A	A	A	90,000	A	A	A
CLEVELAND INST OF ART	PRI-FN	33,528	25,146	0	120	106	9,104		2,000	1,600	214
CLEVELAND INST OF MUSIC	PRI-FG	42,145	A	0	0	150	0	0	1,700	A	152
CLEVELAND ST UNIVERSITY	PUB-FG	568,632	301,392	0	0	0	296,191	0	28,497	17,386	4,762
C MT SNT JOS-ON-THE-OHIO	PRI-FN	105,973	59,372	0	109	3	0	0	1,827	1,309	517
COLLEGE OF STEUBENVILLE	PRI-FN	173,829	150,000	0	1	77	0	0	12,003	10,000	600
COLLEGE OF WOOSTER	PRI-FN	270,591	236,498	132,570	0	0	20,411	0	7,104	4,550	1,100
COLUMBUS C ART AND DESIGN	PRI-FN	16,620	16,451	0	0	0	0	19,693	811	673	127
COLUMBUS TECHNICAL INST	PUB-T	17,173	13,596	0	0	110	0	0	738	354	411
CUYAHOGA CC DISTRICT	PUB-T	146,665	104,266	0	0	5,074	12,015	150	4,812	2,770	1,150
DAVIS JUNIOR COLLEGE	PRI-T	3,188	3,133	0	0	0	0	0	36	35	93
DEFIANCE COLLEGE	PRI-FN	83,108	59,256	1,027	420	159	4,555	365	2,085	1,227	481
DENISON UNIVERSITY	PRI-FN	237,889	190,131	246,079	290	13	0	1,017	6,177	4,068	1,030
DYKE COLLEGE	PRI-FN	10,101	9,500	0	0	1	0	0	446	400	82
EDGECLIFF COLLEGE	PRI-FN	71,703	69,997	0	9	18	0	53	3,585	3,470	414
EDISON STATE CMTY COLLEGE	PUB-T	16,840	16,800	250	0	13	102	12	2,137	2,117	102
FINDLAY COLLEGE	PRI-FN	103,660	68,123	39,107	59	226	10,506	350	2,836	2,035	631
FRANKLIN UNIVERSITY	PRI-FN	43,662	39,500	0	0	0	23,037	0	3,086	2,870	951
HEBREW UNION C ALL CAM											
HEBREW UNION C MAIN CAM	PRI-FG	294,820	A	0	0		19,816	0	10,346	A	2,017
HEBREW UNION C CAL BRANCH	PRI-FG	62,750	59,300	0	0	40	4,180	0	1,905	1,750	267
HEBREW UNION C NY BRANCH	PRI-FG	A	A		A	A			A	A	A
HEIDELBERG COLLEGE	PRI-FN	123,082	98,641	21,000	17	52	6,081	694	2,905	1,819	843
HIRAM COLLEGE	PRI-FN	151,899	150,718	128,192	60	120	18,995	0	2,727	2,467	627
HOCKING TECHNICAL COLLEGE	PUB-T	14,548	14,400	0	0	65	1,699	12	1,406	1,400	270
JEFFERSON TECHNICAL C	PUB-T	18,300	17,387	0	7	48	0	81	800	769	190
JOHN CARROLL UNIVERSITY	PRI-FG	349,758	172,742	800	6,600	130	65,663	250	7,403	4,329	1,046
KENT STATE U ALL CAMPUSES											
KENT STATE U MAIN CAMPUS	PUB-U	1,062,895	615,970	260,477	0	0	794,963	122,514	62,269	28,221	8,899
KENT ST ASHTABULA REG CAM	PUB-T	42,339	26,109	0	152	24	4,631	135	1,098	481	327
KENT ST E LIVERPL REG CAM	PUB-T	28,920	28,282	0	0	1	60	300	1,321	1,282	205
KENT ST U SALEM REG CAM	PUB-T	21,659	21,600	0	0	51	3,733	635	3,669	3,489	391
KENT ST STARK CO REG CAM	PUB-T	61,013	56,156	1,651	0	0			4,816	3,702	403
KENT ST TRUMBULL REG CAM	PUB-T	43,582	35,000	0	0	92	2,950	0	1,500	1,500	321
KENT ST TUSCARAWS REG CAM	PUB-T	36,873	35,873	0	0	36	1,617	249	7,988	5,240	965
KENYON COLLEGE	PRI-FN	195,455	130,492	87,238	47	71	12,174	0	3,722	A	867
KETTERING C MEDICAL ARTS	PRI-T	45,999	23,123	0	0	1	0	0	1,994	1,511	341
LAKE ERIE COLLEGE	PRI-FG	85,530	53,300	0	20	125	4,313	0			
LAKELAND CMTY COLLEGE	PUB-T	66,896	47,863	470	12,001	2,272	0	0	2,401	2,147	310
LIMA TECHNICAL COLLEGE [8/]	PUB-T	NO LIBRARY FACILITIES									
LORAIN CO CMTY COLLEGE	PUB-T	83,230	67,620	A	0	0	323	3	25	3,516	627
LOURDES COLLEGE	PRI-T	58,980	A		0	0	1,217	6	2,215	2,110	155
MALONE COLLEGE	PRI-FN	92,015	68,179	30,350	55	1	16,101	26	4,151	3,025	522
MARIETTA COLLEGE	PRI-FG	236,511	210,750	0	0	2,900	6,635	44,795	4,277	3,975	1,450
MARION TECHNICAL COLLEGE [9/]	PUB-T	NO LIBRARY FACILITIES									
MEDL COLLEGE OHIO-TOLEDO	PUB-FG	74,186	24,439	0	6	200	0	13	2,799	2,625	340
METHODIST THEOL SCH OHIO	PRI-FG	71,561	65,000		0	53	52	0	494	422	80
MIAMI-JACOBS JC BUSINESS	PRI-T	1,951	1,694		0	0	0	0			
MIAMI UNIVERSITY ALL CAM											
MIAMI U HAMILTON CAMPUS	PUB-T	55,705	49,786	0	16	370	16,634	71	2,834	2,580	418
MIAMI U MIDDLETOWN CAMPUS	PUB-T	65,017	55,870	37,591	1,660	273	10,443	898	2,206	1,633	537
MIAMI UNIV OXFORD CAM	PUB-U	925,179	584,384	101,000	0	0	1,248,533	80,000	31,230	19,474	5,172
MICHAEL J OWENS TECH C	PUB-T	35,646	33,575	0	0	21	357	61	1,605	1,121	394
MOUNT UNION COLLEGE	PRI-FN	185,062	113,645	75,000	453	673	0	5,148	5,037	3,753	947

SEE FOOTNOTES AT END OF TABLE

Table 1. — Collections in College and University Libraries, by State or Other Area and Institution: Aggregate United States, 1978-79, and Fall 1979 — Continued

| STATE OR OTHER AREA AND INSTITUTION (1) | CON-TROL AND TYPE OF IN-STITU-TION (2) | HELD AT END OF YEAR | | | | | | | ADDED DURING YEAR | | CURRENT PERIODICAL SUBSCRIPTION TITLES FALL 1979 (12) |
| | | BOOKSTOCK | | SEPARATE GOVERNMENT DOCUMENTS COLLECTIONS (VOLS.) (5) | MICROFORMS | | | ALL OTHER LIBRARY MATERIALS (9) | BOOKSTOCK | | |
		VOLUMES (3)	TITLES (4)		BOOK TITLES (6)	PERIODICAL TITLES (7)	OTHER PHYSICAL UNITS (8)		VOLUMES (10)	TITLES (11)	
OHIO	--CONTINUED										
MOUNT VERNON NAZARENE C	PRI-FN	54,071	48,809	0	1,921	43	0	1,662	2,568	2,547	471
MUSKINGUM AREA TECH C	PUB-T	A	A			3		A			A
MUSKINGUM COLLEGE	PRI-FN	A	A			A			A	A	A
NORTH CEN TECH COLLEGE10/	PUB-T	NO LIBRARY FACILITIES				A	A	A	A	A	A
NTHESTN OHIO U C MED	PUB-FG	19,748	8,479	0	0	0	10	0	7,202	3,631	633
NORTHWEST TECH COLLEGE	PUB-T	8,800	8,000	0	0	0	2	6	1,600	1,200	158
NOTRE DAME COLLEGE	PRI-FN	98,541	58,789	0	8	0	16	150	4,233	2,287	243
OBERLIN COLLEGE	PRI-FG	802,563	480,700	0	2,600	0	175,481	44,000	13,305	A	2,392
OHIO C PODIATRIC MEDICINE	PRI-FG	8,479	6,168	0	0	0	0	5	846	816	166
OHIO DOMINICAN COLLEGE	PRI-FN	91,655	80,468	0	0	4,706	0	111	3,299	2,513	565
OHIO INST OF TECHNOLOGY	PRI-FN	5,100	A	0	0	25	134	0	200	A	79
OHIO NORTHERN UNIVERSITY	PRI-FG	242,008	111,260	82,161	74	91	104,760	900	13,237	6,317	2,086
OHIO STATE U ALL CAMPUSES											
OHIO STATE U MAIN CAMPUS	PUB-U	3,315,029	1,479,541	385,627	0	0	1,296,153	253,858	103,210	50,823	23,303
OHIO ST U AGRL TECH INST	PUB-T	11,863	7,108	0	0	0	0	6,708	1,077	745	593
OHIO STATE U LIMA BR	PUB-T	51,000	29,597	0	0	0	0				
OHIO STATE U MANSFIELD BR	PUB-T	41,117	22,359	0	0	0	0	20,992	3,560	2,931	522
OHIO STATE U MARION BR	PUB-T	29,299	16,005	0	0	0	0	12,122	2,147	1,298	396
OHIO STATE U NEWARK BR	PUB-T	40,435	22,785	0	0	0	0	6,143	1,300	997	285
OHIO U ALL CAMPUSES	PUB-U							5,050	3,030	2,406	436
OHIO U MAIN CAMPUS	PUB-U	736,673	500,646	306,780	160,189	6,336	647,014	37,772	21,824	13,064	5,455
OHIO U BELMONT CO BRANCH	PUB-T	36,327	30,117	95	0	113	3,510	94	610	374	302
OHIO U CHILLICOTHE BR	PUB-T	45,940	37,193	0	0	68	4,239	212	1,183	669	326
OHIO U IRONTON BRANCH	PUB-T	9,689	A	0	0	0	0	54	0	0	38
OHIO U LANCASTER BRANCH	PUB-T	47,216	45,311	0	0	108	64,174	184	2,658	2,620	376
OHIO U ZANESVILLE BRANCH	PUB-T	54,104	47,987	0	5	100	0	0	1,441	1,324	452
OHIO WESLEYAN UNIVERSITY	PRI-FN	378,956	340,000	200,000	844	300	0	0	5,885	5,329	1,132
OTTERBEIN COLLEGE	PRI-FN	117,579	88,184	4,705	134	107	11,808	1,200	3,581	2,865	788
PAYNE THEOLOGICAL SEM	PRI-FG	16,976	10,000	0	49	1	0	477	27	A	53
PONTIFICAL C JOSEPHINUM	PRI-FG	92,227	60,471	0	0	2	0	0	2,771	2,337	331
RABBINICAL COLLEGE TELSHE	PRI-FG	NO LIBRARY FACILITIES									
RIO GRANDE COLLEGE	PRI-FN	58,706	42,613	23,200	9,042	9,003	0	0	2,099	1,913	498
SAINT MARY SEMINARY	PRI-FG	40,058	38,263	0	68	47	0	1,029	1,581	1,552	351
SHAWNEE ST CMTY COLLEGE	PUB-T	61,157	54,488	0	5,382	165	4,498	0	1,439	1,119	510
SINCLAIR CMTY COLLEGE	PUB-T	71,759	66,018	0	64	127	512	973	7,888	7,257	551
SOUTHERN OHIO COLLEGE	PRI-T	A	A	A	A	A	A	A	A	A	A
STHN ST GEN-TECH COLLEGE	PUB-T	18,000	15,000	22	27	18	1	30	3,000	1,800	352
STARK TECHNICAL COLLEGE11/	PUB-T	NO LIBRARY FACILITIES									
TERRA TECHNICAL COLLEGE	PUB-T	11,870	8,630	0	0	147	0	29	1,870	1,630	460
TIFFIN UNIVERSITY	PRI-FN	9,326	8,300	0	0	1,402	0	0	239	200	113
TRINITY LUTHERAN SEMINARY	PRI-FG	74,550	77,120	0	150	197	0	21	2,800	2,605	474
UNION EXPERIMENTING C & U	PRI-FG	NO LIBRARY FACILITIES									
UNITED THEOLOGICAL SEM	PRI-FG	90,840	A	0	0	0	1,211	0	2,097	1,665	363
U OF AKRON ALL CAMPUSES											
U OF AKRON MAIN CAMPUS	PUB-U	693,168	376,331	172,126	348,866	3	731,817	5,246	37,991	20,736	5,774
U AKRON WAYNE GEN-TECH C	PUB-T	18,920	14,851	0	0	60	0	128	1,000	794	329
U OF CINCINNATI ALL CAM											
U OF CINCINNATI MAIN CAM	PUB-U	1,174,705	417,735	111,054	0	28,774	938,031	35,862	41,376	15,322	8,514
U CINCIN CLERMNT GEN-TECH	PUB-T	12,643	11,297	2,123	0	351	6,157	21	1,273	1,100	218
U CINCIN RAYMND WALTERS C	PUB-T	30,237	25,000	1,043	1,240	190	2,964	128	2,637	2,500	641
UNIVERSITY OF DAYTON2/	PRI-FG	425,189	276,643	115,190	125,266	382	0	200	13,206	9,615	2,801
UNIVERSITY OF TOLEDO2/	PUB-U	513,036	303,304	546,590	0	282	726,416	223,176	32,464	25,619	4,423
URBANA COLLEGE	PRI-FN	52,916	46,695	0	0	197	0	4,542	2,065	1,365	326
URSULINE COLLEGE	PRI-FN	65,725	48,600	0	0	0	0	0	3,927	2,658	403
WALSH COLLEGE	PRI-FN	66,951	53,552	0	1	30	2,687	0	2,212	2,012	431
WASHINGTON TECH COLLEGE	PUB-T	10,450	10,067	0	0	0	0	0	2,000	2,000	148
WILBERFORCE UNIVERSITY	PRI-FN	37,963	A	0	0	40	1,766	0	1,450	1,190	375
WILMINGTON COLLEGE	PRI-FN	106,406	A	0	728	74	1,293	0	2,128	A	590
WITTENBERG UNIVERSITY	PRI-FG	288,618	174,772	26,875	226	152	53,221	0	6,618	4,772	1,227
WOOSTER BUSINESS COLLEGE	PRI-T	A	A	A	A	A	A	A	A	A	A
WRIGHT ST U ALL CAMPUSES											

SEE FOOTNOTES AT END OF TABLE

Table 1. — Collections in College and University Libraries, by State or Other Area and Institution: Aggregate United States, 1978-79, and Fall 1979 — Continued

STATE OR OTHER AREA AND INSTITUTION	CON-TROL AND TYPE OF IN-STITU-TION	HELD AT END OF YEAR							ADDED DURING YEAR		CURRENT PERIOD-ICAL SUB-SCRIPTION TITLES FALL 1979
		BOOKSTOCK		SEPARATE GOVERN-MENT DOCU-MENTS COLLEC-TIONS (VOLS.)	MICROFORMS			ALL OTHER LIBRARY MATE-RIALS	BOOKSTOCK		
		VOLUMES	TITLES		BOOK TITLES	PERI-ODICAL TITLES	OTHER PHYS-ICAL UNITS		VOLUMES	TITLES	
(1)	(2)	(3)	(4)	(5)	(6)	(7)	(8)	(9)	(10)	(11)	(12)
OHIO	--CONTINUED										
WRIGHT ST U MAIN CAMPUS	PUB-FG	419,868	A	0	0	23	584,502	0	21,591	A	8,003
WRIGHT ST U WSTN OHIO BR	PUB-T	20,962	20,908	0	0	0	49,000	27	611	557	347
XAVIER UNIVERSITY	PRI-FG	197,663	157,578	0	6,679	179	173,161	435	11,871	9,121	1,691
YOUNGSTOWN ST UNIVERSITY	PUB-FG	417,301	274,543	79,537	233,132	1,010	75	102	17,727	15,278	3,082
OKLAHOMA											
BACONE COLLEGE	PRI-T	25,651	25,450	250	0	64	1,087	832	1,976	1,775	250
BARTLESVILLE WESLEYAN C	PRI-FN	45,736	42,504	0	19,000	15	13,084	0	1,986	1,804	216
BETHANY NAZARENE COLLEGE	PRI-FG	94,716	71,449	16,675	2	29	26,637	0	2,177	1,793	648
CAMERON UNIVERSITY	PUB-FN	155,827	144,582	0	95	161	4,671	6,996	5,670	3,768	919
CARL ALBERT JR COLLEGE	PUB-T	12,303	5,905	0	0	32	7,529	429	2,100	1,111	188
CENTRAL STATE UNIVERSITY	PUB-FG	267,335	181,583	234,312	48,318	2,270	109,588	2,783	14,634	10,117	4,752
CLAREMORE JUNIOR COLLEGE	PUB-T	22,482	22,457	0	0	16	3,634	589	967	942	171
CONNORS STATE COLLEGE	PUB-T	30,200	22,600	0	0	98	16,759	0	1,824	1,824	290
EAST CENTRAL OKLA STATE U	PUB-FG	166,808	142,657	93,175	172,114	3	37,200	293	15,525	12,000	1,487
EASTERN OKLA ST COLLEGE	PUB-T	35,506	35,471	0	0	0	0	0	997	962	233
EL RENO JUNIOR COLLEGE	PUB-T	13,276	12,479	0	1	63	7,387	319	2,515	2,364	265
FLAMING RAINBOW U	PRI-FN	A	A						A	A	A
HILLSDL FREE WILL BAPT C	PRI-FN	10,293	10,000	120	7	1	0	60	429	329	125
LANGSTON UNIVERSITY	PUB-FN	131,029	104,885	51,000	160	255	9,620	0	3,418	2,796	346
MIDWEST CHRISTIAN COLLEGE	PRI-FN	18,189	17,799	0	0	37	0	1,865	1,147	1,107	81
MURRAY STATE COLLEGE	PUB-T	18,028	15,449	0	3	● 5	0	0	1,120	933	121
NTHESTN OKLA AGRL-MECH C	PUB-T	51,505	43,907	0	0	93	5,084	240	3,172	2,680	327
NORTHEASTERN OKLA STATE U	PUB-FG	180,567	111,746	210,647	140,211	920	17,503	1,078	7,391	4,471	2,107
NORTHERN OKLAHOMA COLLEGE	PUB-T	28,673	25,639	0	2	26	4,511	0	1,244	1,113	249
NTHWSTN OKLA STATE U	PUB-FG	114,532	96,174	96,923	0	8	258,030	1,000	3,020	2,873	1,128
OKLAHOMA BAPT UNIVERSITY	PRI-FN	122,310	93,500	38,000	12,000	12	41,000	25,000	3,928	3,500	625
OKLA CHRISTIAN COLLEGE	PRI-FN	87,177	81,190	0	3,925	126	0	713	2,500	2,455	449
OKLAHOMA CTY STHWSTN C	PRI-T	40,820	34,920	0	0	9	0	3	2,406	2,300	279
OKLAHOMA CITY UNIVERSITY	PRI-FG	212,109	119,778	53,653	743	213	7,729	0	7,068	3,973	1,667
OKLA C OSTEO MED AND SURG	PUB-FG	7,334	6,814	0	3	62	2	87	1,998	1,803	411
OKLA PANHANDLE STATE U	PUB-FN	75,336	75,100	0	0	325	1,357	0	3,491	3,450	397
OKLA SCH BUS ACCT LAW FIN	PRI-T	A	A						A	A	A
OKLA STATE U ALL CAMPUSES											
OKLA STATE U MAIN CAMPUS	PUB-U	1,287,101	A	0	0	0	465,000	95,997	30,670	A	9,022
OKLA STATE U TECH INST	PUB-T	11,954	10,520	0	0	18	4	0	585	576	151
ORAL ROBERTS UNIVERSITY	PRI-FG	493,910	243,120	0	229,660	1,670	0	1,097	54,850	31,620	3,640
OSCAR ROSE JUNIOR COLLEGE	PUB-T	57,146	50,418	0	0	445	66,500	0	5,345	4,987	744
PHILLIPS UNIVERSITY	PRI-FG	224,183	207,594	0	4,444	343	24,382	1,174	6,602	5,898	1,205
SAINT GREGORY'S COLLEGE	PRI-T	48,863	A	0	0	1,519	0	300	1,797	A	195
SAYRE JUNIOR COLLEGE	PUB-T	6,634	6,609	0	0	0	0	0	956	931	80
SEMINOLE JUNIOR COLLEGE	PUB-T	20,493	17,466	0	14,570	95	0	0	2,351	1,808	237
STHESTN OKLA STATE U	PUB-FG	123,488	79,800	40,388	471	13	566	110	2,596	2,332	659
SOUTH OKLA CTY JR COLLEGE	PUB-T	18,873	15,342	0	169	151	7	30	2,545	2,094	354
STHWSTN OKLA STATE U	PUB-FG	196,741	182,114	15,760	0	0	483,461	0	9,215	6,764	1,514
TULSA JUNIOR COLLEGE	PUB-T	48,970	44,073	100	574	96	12,099	375	6,153	3,000	452
U OF OKLAHOMA ALL CAM											
U OF OKLA HEALTH SCI CTR	PUB-FG	128,676	80,500	0	650	22	0	546	4,710	3,500	2,049
U OF OKLAHOMA NORMAN CAM	PUB-U	1,562,991	628,645	717,323	110,759	3,206	47,377	439,860	40,490	20,496	12,967
U OF SCI & ARTS OF OKLA	PUB-FN	81,427	48,774	0	0	215	0	3	3,488	2,744	651
UNIVERSITY OF TULSA	PRI-U	514,738	456,818	239,864	248,400	100	0	1,142	37,697	33,927	5,094
WESTERN OKLAHOMA STATE C	PUB-T	30,543	30,498	0	0	55	115	0	3,001	2,056	194
OREGON											
BASSIST INSTITUTE	PRI-T	3,825	A	0	0	0	0	0	402	383	79
BLUE MTN CMTY COLLEGE	PUB-T	35,479	34,493	200	0	1,836	0	651	1,675	1,471	459
CENTRAL OREG CMTY COLLEGE	PUB-T	36,000	35,500	0	0	5	0	1,168	873	785	317
CHEMEKETA CMTY COLLEGE	PUB-T	44,549	37,000	0	0	163	1,518	0	2,841	2,600	1,507
CLACKAMAS CMTY COLLEGE	PUB-T	41,213	34,390	0	4	203	15,514	3	2,777	1,403	483
CLATSOP COMMUNITY COLLEGE	PUB-T	32,739	25,079	172	12	85	5,337	69	1,732	1,498	573

SEE FOOTNOTES AT END OF TABLE

STATE OR OTHER AREA AND INSTITUTION	CON- TROL AND TYPE OF IN- STITU- TION	HELD AT END OF YEAR							ADDED DURING YEAR		CURRENT PERIOD- ICAL SUB- SCRIPTION TITLES FALL 1979
		BOOKSTOCK		SEPARATE GOVERN- MENT DOCU- MENTS COLLEC- TIONS (VOLS.)	MICROFORMS			ALL OTHER LIBRARY MATE- RIALS	BOOKSTOCK		
		VOLUMES	TITLES		BOOK TITLES	PERI- ODICAL TITLES	OTHER PHYS- ICAL UNITS		VOLUMES	TITLES	
(1)	(2)	(3)	(4)	(5)	(6)	(7)	(8)	(9)	(10)	(11)	(12)
OREGON	--CONTINUED										
COLEGIO CESAR CHAVEZ	PRI-FN		A		A				A	A	A
COLUMBIA CHRISTIAN C	PRI-FN	33,361	22,161	0	21,500	8	0	0	1,581	1,194	72
CONCORDIA COLLEGE	PRI-FN	40,102	39,392	693	0	1,353	0	5,965	2,334	135	565
GEORGE FOX COLLEGE	PRI-FN	65,869	49,791	375	28	73	1,059	352	3,111	3,027	575
JUDSON BAPTIST COLLEGE	PRI-T	25,361	21,896	0	0	36	225	48	645	580	107
LANE COMMUNITY COLLEGE	PUB-T	53,265	44,844	0	0	550	32,991	0	3,127	2,658	400
LEWIS AND CLARK COLLEGE	PRI-FN	239,115	131,263	30,867	248	149	46,239	0	15,096	7,928	1,682
LINFIELD COLLEGE	PRI-FG	97,521	71,787	47,816	19,952	231	729	2,100	2,355	1,893	743
LINN-BENTON CMTY COLLEGE	PUB-T	38,430	32,880	0	210	225	9,972	569	4,218	3,598	489
MARYLHURST ED CENTER	PRI-FN	107,800	74,954	1,700	399	15	554	13,508	2,850	2,534	200
MOUNT ANGEL SEMINARY	PRI-FG	104,000	79,000	0	1,051	22	29,633	728	3,653	3,470	540
MOUNT HOOD CMTY COLLEGE	PUB-T	54,008	51,756	0	0	119	0	239	1,339	1,251	363
MULTNOMAH SCHOOL OF BIBLE	PRI-FG	27,062	23,006	0	1	2	0	0	2,134	1,575	306
MUSEUM ART SCHOOL	PRI-FN	11,044	10,321	0	0	0	0	11,025	1,424	1,154	77
NTHWST CHRISTIAN COLLEGE	PRI-FN	44,977	32,775	0	0	12	329	723	1,310	1,056	259
OREGON GRADUATE CENTER	PRI-FG	8,664	5,900	0	0	59	3,887	0	1,068	720	289
OR ST HI ED SYS ALL INST											
EASTERN OREGON ST COLLEGE	PUB-FG	86,116	51,029	89,867	6,815	311	18,015	49,239	2,600	2,194	1,092
OREGON COLLEGE OF ED	PUB-FG	161,869	115,149	53,803	43,364	207	153,835	627	4,861	3,459	1,598
OREGON INST OF TECHNOLOGY	PUB-FN	52,225	27,401	5,324	0	0	9,290	208	2,993	2,007	1,246
OREGON STATE UNIVERSITY	PUB-U	844,143	388,984	358,345	0	0	671,079	1,380	23,889	13,210	17,888
PORTLAND STATE UNIVERSITY	PUB-FG	574,477	321,405	206,486	0	97	462,900	31,726	29,644	14,567	11,444
STHN OREGON ST COLLEGE	PUB-FG	180,834	134,864	149,476	124,785	947	64,699	36,199	8,547	5,745	4,941
U OF OREGON ALL CAM											
U OF OREGON MAIN CAMPUS	PUB-U	1,424,882	792,699	244,471	0	0	642,404	279,198	47,846	29,508	17,931
U OF OREGON HLTH SCI CTR	PUB-FG	160,579	52,762	0	23	40	52	0	5,288	1,606	2,896
PACIFIC UNIVERSITY	PRI-FG	122,208	A	144,252	0	0	6,073	5,266	4,733	A	855
PORTLAND CMTY COLLEGE	PUB-T	67,347	35,624	0	1	110	4,798	567	3,640	1,856	570
REED COLLEGE	PRI-FG	274,184	147,497	4,521	16,095	75	41	0	7,501	3,895	1,221
ROGUE COMMUNITY COLLEGE	PUB-T	29,019	27,000	0	0	0	458	639	4,700	4,500	169
STHWSTN OREG CMTY COLLEGE	PUB-T	47,625	39,504	0	147	23	2,488	109	1,872	1,339	484
TREASURE VLY CMTY COLLEGE	PUB-T	26,830	25,850	51	0	3	0	700	848	800	234
UMPQUA COMMUNITY COLLEGE	PUB-T	42,860	41,260	3,480	0	14	3	368	1,682	1,675	423
UNIVERSITY OF PORTLAND	PRI-U	179,399	163,097	1,987	50,261	826	8,409	0	6,619	5,500	1,307
WARNER PACIFIC COLLEGE	PRI-FG	50,000	45,729	0	0	0	0	0	2,062	1,778	231
WESTERN BAPTIST COLLEGE	PRI-FN	40,263	29,197	0	1,211	11	0	0	5,015	2,390	406
WESTERN CONS BAPTIST SEM	PRI-FG	35,922	28,522	15	156	57	0	76	1,547	1,428	427
WSTN EVANGELICAL SEM	PRI-FG	36,734	24,367	0	57	4	2	109	1,787	1,500	386
WSTN STATES CHIRPRCTC C	PRI-FG	6,992	6,142	0	0	0	0	0	1,313	1,272	12,309
WILLAMETTE UNIVERSITY 2/	PRI-FG	200,649	128,256	850	16,544	243	9,825	100	6,528	3,967	3,305
PENNSYLVANIA											
ACADEMY OF THE NEW CHURCH	PRI-FG	98,163	67,000	0	910	35	0	15,000	2,764	1,756	354
ALBRIGHT COLLEGE	PRI-FN	122,607	121,997	0	6,243	4,822	0	0	4,314	4,292	802
ALLEGHENY COLLEGE	PRI-FG	263,172	169,710	141,763	74	388	0	1,526	8,867	6,985	960
ALLNTWN C SNT FRAN DESALS	PRI-FN	92,774	56,500	0	3	105	0	655	4,574	2,300	701
ALLIANCE COLLEGE	PRI-FN	66,499	49,360	6,852	3	51	3,775	140	1,677	1,437	309
ALVERNIA COLLEGE	PRI-FG	52,477	47,967	0	3	96	156	0	1,934	1,874	420
AMERICAN COLLEGE	PRI-FG	12,600	8,600	0	10	6	600	10	1,307	577	550
BAPT BIBLE COLLEGE OF PA	PRI-FG	64,766	A	0	749	1,575	783	6,816	3,182	A	509
BEAVER COLLEGE	PRI-FG	118,576	106,718	0	800	79	5,811	0	3,847	3,462	490
BLOOMSBURG STATE COLLEGE	PUB-FG	292,020	241,302	0	0	0	996,183	6,637	12,430	7,930	2,033
BRYN MAWR COLLEGE	PRI-FG	548,203	362,910	46,595	0	0	17,036	0	19,773	13,090	2,160
BUCKNELL UNIVERSITY	PRI-FG	395,253	251,083	141,760	10,146	449	71,576	1,430	16,211	11,076	2,128
BUCKS COUNTY CMTY COLLEGE	PUB-T	103,054	102,000	0	0	258	166,264	10,008	8,026	7,500	804
BUTLER CO CMTY COLLEGE	PUB-T	38,277	31,264	0	20	33	5,947	37	1,917	1,641	315
CABRINI COLLEGE	PRI-FN	57,569	53,540	0	113	1	1,794	11	1,432	1,331	335
CALIFORNIA STATE COLLEGE	PUB-FG	226,734	199,012	1,035	226,392	0	665,606	3,864	3,784	3,509	1,154
CARLOW COLLEGE	PRI-FN	102,876	73,228	0	129	62	0	154	2,119	1,745	411
CARNEGIE-MELLON U	PRI-U	465,022	A	105,663	0	119	20,751	31,382	14,940	6,600	2,630
CEDAR CREST COLLEGE	PRI-FN	103,245	76,200	0	27	260	8,468	0	3,825	A	800

SEE FOOTNOTES AT END OF TABLE

Table 1. – Collections in College and University Libraries, by State or Other Area and Institution: Aggregate United States, 1978-79, and Fall 1979 – Continued

STATE OR OTHER AREA AND INSTITUTION	CONTROL AND TYPE OF INSTITUTION	HELD AT END OF YEAR							ADDED DURING YEAR		CURRENT PERIODICAL SUBSCRIPTION TITLES FALL 1979
		BOOKSTOCK		SEPARATE GOVERNMENT DOCUMENTS COLLECTIONS (VOLS.)	MICROFORMS			ALL OTHER LIBRARY MATERIALS	BOOKSTOCK		
		VOLUMES	TITLES		BOOK TITLES	PERIODICAL TITLES	OTHER PHYSICAL UNITS		VOLUMES	TITLES	
(1)	(2)	(3)	(4)	(5)	(6)	(7)	(8)	(9)	(10)	(11)	(12)
PENNSYLVANIA	--CONTINUED										
CENTER FOR DEGREE STUDIES	PRI-T	2,690	2,585	0	0	0	0	0	40	40	64
CEN PA BUSINESS SCHOOL	PRI-T	3,745	3,585	0	0	0	0	25	200	185	75
CHATHAM COLLEGE	PRI-FN	118,064	82,897	0	98	331	0	0	2,577	1,601	566
CHESTNUT HILL COLLEGE	PRI-FN	92,656	65,000	7,000	0	18	0	1,127	2,645	2,500	842
CHEYNEY STATE COLLEGE	PUB-FG	124,700	123,500	22,558	20,096	415	184,615	967	664	319	987
CLARION STATE C ALL CAM											
CLARION STATE C MAIN CAM	PUB-FG	299,551	211,644	0	0	0	746,678	2,866	14,999	12,698	1,944
CLARION ST C VENANGO CAM	PUB-T	23,438	A	0	0	71	3,138	122	1,107	960	202
COLLEGE MISERICORDIA	PRI-FN	102,383	76,377	0	143	168	1,813	20	4,383	3,600	749
COMBS COLLEGE OF MUSIC	PRI-FG	12,000	11,300	0	1,000	0	0	13,300	2,000	2,000	18
CC ALLEGHENY CO ALL CAM											
CC ALLEGHENY CO ALLEG CAM	PUB-T	72,812	72,812	0	479	262	0	93	2,957	2,957	435
CC ALLEGHENY CO BOYCE CAM	PUB-T	53,589	39,567	0	0	154	2,220	150	1,174	960	323
CC ALLEGHENY CO NORTH CAM	PUB-T	11,931	10,500	0	0	214	3,010	102	1,641	1,409	381
CC ALLEGHENY CO SOUTH CAM	PUB-T	42,375	36,368	0	112	226	0	1,266	1,743	1,700	282
CMTY COLLEGE OF BEAVER CO	PUB-T	35,371	A	0	0	17	966	141	1,998	A	329
CMTY COLLEGE DELAWARE CO	PUB-T	51,621	49,445	0	22,000	217	10,499	0	2,275	2,220	525
CMTY COLLEGE PHILADELPHIA	PUB-T	76,307	55,330	0	14,000	73	2,775	72	1,571	1,178	540
CURTIS INSTITUTE OF MUSIC	PRI-FG	38,300	34,300	0	0	0	63	0	1,831	1,587	27
DELAWARE VLY C SCI & AGR	PRI-FN	47,995	47,321	17,790	0	44	0	1,213	1,371	1,321	596
DICKINSON COLLEGE	PRI-FN	245,697	159,476	56,795	291	132	276,546	6,086	8,505	6,733	1,636
DICKINSON SCHOOL OF LAW	PRI-FG	92,630	11,760	0	10	131	0	0	13,733	1,800	3,600
DREXEL UNIVERSITY	PRI-FG	386,178	253,088	93,181	1,597	386	258,323	6	13,905	7,842	4,412
THE DROPSIE UNIVERSITY	PRI-FG	130,000	115,000	0	0	0	2,294	800	250	100	350
DUQUESNE UNIVERSITY	PRI-U	473,816	6,804	3,726	1,999	698	57,866	0	16,673	214	4,507
EASTERN BAPTIST THEOL SEM	PRI-FG	84,156	60,377	0	570	170	17	0	1,456	1,021	418
EASTERN COLLEGE	PRI-FN	64,456	64,456	0	1,213	22	6,500	0	1,608	1,608	281
EAST STROUDSBG ST COLLEGE	PUB-FG	304,790	195,669	36,864	659,140	1,216	9,485	7,656	13,941	8,707	1,358
EDINBORO STATE COLLEGE	PUB-FG	337,265	180,445	24,024	47,046	1,103	805,451	19,655	8,714	5,238	2,080
ELIZABETHTOWN COLLEGE	PRI-FN	127,408	86,384	0	84	135	8,328	575	3,669	2,342	801
FAITH THEOLOGICAL SEM	PRI-FG	22,455	22,323	0	0	0	0	0	151	96	42
FRANKLIN AND MARSHALL C	PRI-FN	254,709	0	239,548	103	1,006	0	0	7,352	6,943	1,631
GANNON COLLEGE	PRI-FG	154,635	98,612	0	70,425	427	215,574	2,305	7,619	6,856	1,064
GENEVA COLLEGE	PRI-FN	119,204	82,495	0	56,643	132	0	0	4,071	2,724	656
GETTYSBURG COLLEGE	PRI-FN	246,687	209,680	30,240	1,950	1,650	31,400	274	7,694	6,540	1,128
GRATZ COLLEGE	PRI-FG	28,000	25,000	0	0	0	0	0	1,000	900	110
GROVE CITY COLLEGE	PRI-FN	127,148	A	0	0	34	2,094	0	4,310	A	520
GWYNEDD-MERCY COLLEGE	PRI-FN	58,100	58,000	200	0	44	7,913	40	3,000	3,000	445
HAHNEMANN MEDL C AND HOSP	PRI-FG	68,305	25,194	0	0	34	5	0	2,530	2,214	1,003
HARCUM JUNIOR COLLEGE	PRI-T	30,380	29,800	0	0	2	18	346	1,975	1,450	168
HARRISBURG AREA CC	PUB-T	86,739	A	0	0	192	12,659	257	3,903	A	579
HAVERFORD COLLEGE	PRI-FN	414,000	356,450	86,000	2,500	28	0	224,300	7,900	6,800	1,102
HOLY FAMILY COLLEGE	PRI-FN	88,443	69,716	0	37	84	2	0	4,327	3,396	371
IMMACULATA COLLEGE	PRI-FN	115,400	100,323	0	152	18	3,248	3	3,267	3,000	575
INDIANA U OF PENNSYLVANIA	PUB-FG	481,303	316,766	147,795	10,880	30	1,052,181	19,861	22,105	20,000	4,544
JUNIATA COLLEGE	PRI-FN	128,928	103,100	43,850	23	205	12,725	0	3,524	2,822	551
KEYSTONE JUNIOR COLLEGE	PRI-T	33,444	31,923	0	0	27	0	209	850	775	288
KING'S COLLEGE	PRI-FN	150,515	120,000	327,896	8,754	290	163,898	0	4,988	4,160	1,020
KUTZTOWN STATE COLLEGE	PUB-FG	267,470	108,650	13,598	0	0	711,359	7,394	13,947	11,757	1,950
LACKAWANNA JUNIOR COLLEGE	PRI-T	24,000	16,891	0	0	10	0	3	620	470	134
LAFAYETTE COLLEGE	PRI-FN	353,314	337,023	0	72	607	6,808	145	11,309	6,508	1,535
LANCASTER BIBLE COLLEGE	PRI-FN	26,199	A	0	1	0	15	0	2,027	A	363
LANCASTER THEOLOGICAL SEM	PRI-FG	122,401	121,000	0	732	460	2,884	2,442	3,071	3,071	475
LA ROCHE COLLEGE	PRI-FN	50,000	37,500	30,700	0	58	2,998	0	2,600	2,100	460
LA SALLE COLLEGE	PRI-FG	250,963	179,754	0	193	338	4,430	0	10,538	7,758	1,109
LEBANON VALLEY COLLEGE	PRI-FN	110,539	95,639	0	0	11,281	0	0	3,702	2,617	622
LEHIGH CO CMTY COLLEGE	PUB-T	41,870	33,976	0	13	160	17,215	9,674	1,872	1,340	432
LEHIGH UNIVERSITY	PRI-FG	699,492	280,753	39,655	0	0	421,941	0	25,890	6,165	5,616
LINCOLN UNIVERSITY	PUB-FG	136,018	113,273	14,022	211	114	17,257	41	3,600	3,116	581
LOCK HAVEN STATE COLLEGE	PUB-FN	284,579	161,503	0	12,000	258	213,955	1,310	5,288	3,596	1,234
LUTH THEOL SEM GETTYSBURG	PRI-FG	118,284	85,223	0	153	5	0	0	2,920	2,103	602

SEE FOOTNOTES AT END OF TABLE

Table 1. — Collections in College and University Libraries, by State or Other Area and Institution: Aggregate United States, 1978-79, and Fall 1979 — Continued

STATE OR OTHER AREA AND INSTITUTION	CON-TROL AND TYPE OF IN-STITU-TION	HELD AT END OF YEAR							ADDED DURING YEAR		CURRENT PERIOD-ICAL SUB-SCRIPTION TITLES FALL 1979
		BOOKSTOCK		SEPARATE GOVERN-MENT DOCU-MENTS COLLEC-TIONS (VOLS.)	MICROFORMS			ALL OTHER LIBRARY MATE-RIALS	BOOKSTOCK		
		VOLUMES	TITLES		BOOK TITLES	PERI-ODICAL TITLES	OTHER PHYS-ICAL UNITS		VOLUMES	TITLES	
(1)	(2)	(3)	(4)	(5)	(6)	(7)	(8)	(9)	(10)	(11)	(12)

PENNSYLVANIA	--CONTINUED										
LUTHERAN THEOL SEM PHILA	PRI-FG	127,230	101,784	0	84	30	240	3,253	3,442	2,754	590
LUZERNE CO CMTY COLLEGE	PUB-T	52,027	48,385	0	0	252	5,062	2,345	1,776	1,651	508
LYCOMING COLLEGE	PRI-FN	132,221	54,007	10,435	786	240	11,570	66	3,528	2,081	902
MANOR JUNIOR COLLEGE	PRI-T	21,635	2,187	0	0	14	51	62	320	31	185
MANSFIELD STATE COLLEGE	PUB-FG	175,718	123,520	8,300	0	0	547,288	377	3,759	1,994	2,540

MARY IMMACULATE SEMINARY	PRI-FG	56,650	35,871	0	112	42	0	0	1,650	1,105	366
MARYWOOD COLLEGE	PRI-FG	152,771	110,088	0	101	659	1,313	250	6,128	5,700	1,204
THE MEDL COLLEGE OF PA	PRI-FG	30,960	A	0	0	11	1,255	0	1,911	A	935
MERCYHURST COLLEGE	PRI-FG	75,835	66,950	0	9,035	93	4,956	0	2,663	2,060	587
MESSIAH COLLEGE	PRI-FN	95,954	84,000	0	97	190	3,223	0	6,874	5,667	496

MILLERSVILLE ST COLLEGE	PUB-FG	306,972	219,156	64,983	283	1,675	96,517	22,930	13,628	10,449	2,277
MONTGOMERY CO COMMUNITY C	PUB-T	76,618	71,745	6,600	0	110	17,770	456	3,143	3,068	492
MOORE COLLEGE OF ART	PRI-FN	31,000	23,000	0	0	4	1,757	10,000	1,087	1,051	245
MORAVIAN COLLEGE	PRI-FN	161,189	126,564	0	600	78	6,892	0	4,401	3,803	946
MOUNT ALOYSIUS JR COLLEGE	PRI-T	30,222	27,555	0	0	72	7	15	1,176	993	238

MUHLENBERG COLLEGE	PRI-FN	176,669	120,000	147,264	26	69	15,455	0	5,283	A	815
NEW SCHOOL OF MUSIC	PRI-FN	1,531	1,261	0	0	0	0	4,490	108	100	14
NORTHAMPTON CO AREA CC	PUB-T	51,504	41,097	0	0	117	2,040	130	3,991	3,743	558
NORTHEASTERN CHRISTIAN JC	PRI-T	25,250	21,896	0	0	4	282	85	1,318	1,270	167
OUR LADY ANGELS COLLEGE	PRI-FN	65,099	50,600	0	0	61	21	0	2,534	1,900	593

PEIRCE JUNIOR COLLEGE	PRI-T	34,906	34,208	0	0	50	0	164	1,873	1,858	240
PA COLLEGE OF OPTOMETRY	PRI-FG	14,300	4,501	82	11	0	0	0	443	430	230
PA COLLEGE PODIATRIC MED	PRI-FG	11,802	7,055	670	0	21	0	0	732	628	166
PA STATE U ALL CAMPUSES											
PA STATE U MAIN CAMPUS	PUB-U	1,556,981	902,669	1,004,651	310,000	1,700	804,200	1,896,672	50,320	37,337	17,642

PA STATE U ALLENTOWN CAM	PUB-T	23,124	19,655	197	0	0	2,615	1,423	7,267	3,447	167
PA STATE U ALTOONA CAM	PUB-T	40,336	34,286	437	0	0	11,189	961	2,608	2,217	285
PA STATE U BEAVER CAMPUS	PUB-T	28,891	24,557	0	0	0	3,626	506	1,073	912	230
PA ST U BEHREND COLLEGE	PUB-FG	50,772	43,156	350	0	0	33,760	353	1,964	1,669	612
PA STATE U BERKS CAMPUS	PUB-T	30,037	25,531	0	0	0	1,602	558	1,689	1,436	375

PA STATE U CAPITOL CAMPUS	PUB-FG	139,651	122,250	4,142	9,600	162	551,378	235	5,400	3,877	1,340
PA STATE U DELAWARE CAM	PUB-T	27,034	22,979	37	0	0	3,513	792	1,209	1,028	411
PA STATE U DU BOIS CAMPUS	PUB-T	28,115	23,898	165	0	0	1,187	295	1,048	891	169
PA STATE U FAYETTE CAMPUS	PUB-T	32,392	27,533	1	0	0	5,972	1,642	1,273	1,082	228
PA STATE U HAZLETON CAM	PUB-T	32,428	27,564	1,178	0	0	5,412	1,794	1,070	910	210

PA ST U HERSHEY MEDL CTR	PUB-FG	83,486	15,736	0	0	0	0	0	2,470	657	1,664
PA STATE U MCKEESPORT CAM	PUB-T	27,415	23,303	202	0	0	3,392	20	790	672	458
PA STATE U MONT ALTO CAM	PUB-T	28,083	23,871	1,061	0	0	1,532	772	1,413	1,201	259
PA ST U NEW KENSINGTN CAM	PUB-T	25,039	21,283	0	0	0	5,165	463	857	728	291
PA STATE U OGONTZ CAMPUS	PUB-T	44,211	37,579	2,236	0	0	4,902	498	1,556	1,323	341

PA ST U RADNOR CENTER	PUB-FG	10,216	8,684	1,408	0	0	1,675	3,505	823	700	201
PA STATE U SCHUYLKILL CAM	PUB-T	26,399	22,439	39	0	0	1,810	935	1,176	1,000	228
PA ST U SHENANGO VLY CAM	PUB-T	17,143	13,572	243	0	0	3,061	333	671	570	151
PA ST U WILKES-BARRE CAM	PUB-T	15,083	12,821	0	0	0	1,251	0	455	387	149
PA ST U WRTHGTN SCRTN CAM	PUB-T	29,678	25,226	1,118	0	0	2,614	3,110	1,976	1,680	208

PA STATE U YORK CAMPUS	PUB-T	18,762	15,948	21	0	0	2,764	1,322	995	846	162
PHILA COLLEGE OF ART	PRI-FG	44,966	34,314	0	16	48	171	414	1,693	1,204	181
PHILA COLLEGE OF BIBLE	PRI-FN	44,200	34,000	8,888	2,776	49	0	924	1,187	846	485
PHILA COLLEGE OSTEO MED	PRI-FG	40,000	15,333	0	1	0	0	0	2,279	1,333	420
PHILA C PERFORMING ARTS	PRI-FG	13,981	12,729	0	8	2	0	0	640	591	172

PHILA COLLEGE PHAR & SCI	PRI-FG	72,462	25,636	0	48	433	20,400	0	1,569	1,154	926
PHILA C TEXTILES AND SCI	PRI-FG	64,626	64,626	0	0	731	4,115	0	3,269	3,250	1,210
PINEBROOK JUNIOR COLLEGE	PRI-T	28,284	22,000	0	0	1	181	10	11,000	8,500	75
PITTSBURGH THEOL SEMINARY	PRI-FG	186,721	A	0	1,277	83	0	0	2,873	1,875	946
POINT PARK COLLEGE	PRI-FN	98,837	63,283	0	7,890	421	14,208	6,518	2,692	1,754	506

READING AREA CMTY COLLEGE	PUB-T	14,554	12,893	0	0	39	633	396	1,207	1,052	293
REFORMED PRESB THEOL SEM	PRI-FG	20,455	16,300	0	13	8	0	205	617	571	144
ROBERT MORRIS COLLEGE	PRI-FG	84,760	62,645	2,592	500	103	46,209	0	6,495	4,902	802
ROSEMONT COLLEGE	PRI-FN	129,220	77,690	0	1,718	612	15,683	738	3,775	2,547	640
SNT CHARLES BORROMEO SEM	PRI-FG	174,994	166,460	0	15	20	1,137	0	5,059	3,249	565

| SAINT FRANCIS COLLEGE | PRI-FG | 143,794 | 99,379 | 0 | 3 | 96 | 1,416 | 2,028 | 4,122 | 1,809 | 384 |

SEE FOOTNOTES AT END OF TABLE

Table 1. — Collections in College and University Libraries, by State or Other Area and Institution: Aggregate United States, 1978-79, and Fall 1979 — Continued

STATE OR OTHER AREA AND INSTITUTION (1)	CONTROL AND TYPE OF INSTITUTION (2)	HELD AT END OF YEAR — BOOKSTOCK: VOLUMES (3)	TITLES (4)	SEPARATE GOVERNMENT DOCUMENTS COLLECTIONS (VOLS.) (5)	MICROFORMS: BOOK TITLES (6)	PERIODICAL TITLES (7)	OTHER PHYSICAL UNITS (8)	ALL OTHER LIBRARY MATERIALS (9)	ADDED DURING YEAR — BOOKSTOCK: VOLUMES (10)	TITLES (11)	CURRENT PERIODICAL SUBSCRIPTION TITLES FALL 1979 (12)
PENNSYLVANIA --CONTINUED											
SAINT JOSEPH'S UNIVERSITY	PRI-FG	181,144	140,701	30,101	2,881	408	249,646	4,100	8,125	6,609	1,560
SAINT VINCENT COLLEGE	PRI FN	SEE SNT VINCENT C-SEM JT LIB									
SNT VINCENT C-SEM JT LIB	PRI-FN	207,732	200,628	0	76,590	101	54,181	0	4,765	4,715	775
SAINT VINCENT SEMINARY	PRI FG	SEE SNT VINCENT C-SEM JT LIB									
SETON HILL COLLEGE	PRI-FN	67,592	57,061	0	16	85	0	77	1,043	1,004	394
SHIPPENSBURG ST COLLEGE	PUB-FG	343,341	277,307	30,870	55,751	2,343	738,444	451	7,853	5,559	1,552
SLIPPERY ROCK ST COLLEGE	PUB-FG	408,166	346,941	91,879	10,946	654	514,963	12,143	11,908	10,122	2,323
SPRING GARDEN COLLEGE	PRI-FN	18,145	17,165	0	0	0	0	0	742	500	464
SUSQUEHANNA UNIVERSITY	PRI-FN	108,088	84,500		1,283	341	25	4,300	6,511	3,809	1,052
SWARTHMORE COLLEGE	PRI-FG	448,806	299,204	118,250	17,375	238	183,950	14,142	13,456	8,970	2,450
TALMUD YESHIVA OF PHILA	PRI-FG	A							A	A	A
TEMPLE UNIVERSITY	PUB-U	1,637,641	771,924	73,951	280,254	2,584	294,319	69,789	58,419	28,049	13,448
THEOL SEM REFORMD EPIS CH	PRI-FG	20,164	18,068	0	0	0	0	20	611	556	50
THIEL COLLEGE	PRI-FN	107,644	82,992	204,623	33	93	0	0	3,654	3,254	774
THOMAS JEFF UNIVERSITY	PRI-FG	117,642	50,658	1,785	0	104	3,383	0	5,927	3,594	1,715
UNITED WESLEYAN COLLEGE	PRI-FN	28,076	24,614	0	0	0	559	155	624	364	108
U OF PENNSYLVANIA	PRI-U	3,043,428	1,712,661	0	0	0	1,372,445	67,577	86,471	43,754	29,739
U OF PITTSBG ALL CAMPUSES				262,892	236,084	4,028	1,115,241	1,329,561	65,913	45,061	18,184
U OF PITTSBG MAIN CAMPUS	PUB-U	1,914,422	1,107,700	210	5	22	1,730	150	3,898	3,598	344
U OF PITTSBG BRADFORD CAM	PUB-FN	46,945	43,200								
U OF PITTSBG GREENSBG CAM	PUB-T	46,552	45,552	0	0	145	4,247	0	3,138	3,088	207
U OF PITTSBG JOHNSTWN CAM	PUB-FN	74,197	60,359	0	132	96	6,344	1,712	2,819	2,283	627
U OF PITTSBG TITUSVL CAM	PUB-T	27,585	21,384	0	0	1	841	1,250	1,200	1,175	186
UNIVERSITY OF SCRANTON	PRI-FG	189,484	116,677	0	0	0	18,996	0	7,068	6,036	1,172
URSINUS COLLEGE	PRI-FN	137,787	102,170	0	0	0	105,584	208	4,702	3,476	707
VALLEY FORGE CHRISTIAN C	PRI-FN	29,327	25,245	0	0	6	33	0	1,676	1,420	267
VALLEY FORGE MILITARY JC	PRI-T	59,214	58,840	0	0	48	0	0	2,100	2,090	95
VILLA MARIA COLLEGE	PRI-FN	42,680	42,657	0	0	0	0	0	2,182	2,160	300
VILLANOVA UNIVERSITY	PRI-U	637,218	356,350	10,956	30,857	1,586	182,824	14	20,076	8,388	4,294
WASHINGTON JEFF COLLEGE	PRI-FG	167,578	137,000	44,000	34	390	0	0	4,568	3,800	739
WAYNESBURG COLLEGE	PRI-FN	112,775	100,972	5,434	0	69	0	79	2,678	2,663	650
WEST CHESTER ST COLLEGE	PUB-FG	370,428	259,958	134,620	57,655	302	213,486	36,637	13,187	6,341	2,600
WESTMINSTER COLLEGE	PRI-FG	186,782	125,144	0	461	168	6,004	215	6,955	4,660	1,220
WESTMINSTER THEOL SEM	PRI-FG	83,500	80,000	0	550	10	0	0	3,500	3,000	632
WESTMORELAND COUNTY CC	PUB-T	26,816	25,475	27,620	1,149	1,574	0	155	2,320	2,302	711
WIDENER C OF WIDENER U	PRI-FG	153,830	83,049	0	31	91	11,013	0	7,188	4,433	1,385
WILKES COLLEGE	PRI-FG	165,307	112,887	0	53,403	1,029	238,459	4,456	5,213	4,238	1,700
WILLIAMSPORT AREA CC	PUB-T	42,000	33,070	1,283	0	1,177	6,074	0	499	397	324
WILSON COLLEGE	PRI-FN	151,610	105,000	0	5	71	7,658	0	1,289	1,092	627
YESHIVATH BETH MOSHE	PRI-FG	A	A						A	A	
YORK COLLEGE PENNSYLVANIA	PRI-FG	100,942	89,700	99,573	342	142	19,000	320	4,082	3,253	998
RHODE ISLAND											
BARRINGTON COLLEGE	PRI-FN	65,501	61,619	0	15	42	665	261	1,330	1,082	267
BROWN UNIVERSITY	PRI-FG	1,636,206	A	158,650	0	0	580,106	581,142	42,632	32,758	14,511
BRYANT C BUSINESS ADMIN	PRI-FG	89,023	63,250	2,144	0	128	8,625	0	3,108	2,860	814
JOHNSON & WALES COLLEGE	PRI-FN	14,500	13,250	0	0	0	0	0	217	180	134
NEW ENG INST TECHNOLOGY	PRI-T	11,110	8,072	0	0	0	0	0	203	165	40
PROVIDENCE COLLEGE	PRI-FG	227,508	136,505	36,016	0	227	12,318	0	10,358	7,251	1,846
RHODE ISLAND COLLEGE	PUB-FG	239,868	156,719	55,877	50,080	1,213	350,680	8,984	13,744	9,893	2,092
RHODE ISLAND JR COLLEGE	PUB-T	72,224	61,478	0	1,152	693	10,780	0	5,185	4,489	1,055
RI SCHOOL OF DESIGN	PRI-FG	57,004	32,211	0	0	0	0	226,151	1,279	776	250
ROGER WILLIAMS C ALL CAM				0	7	280	0	212	4,927	4,286	782
ROGER WILLIAMS C MAIN CAM	PRI-FN	71,120	61,874	NO LIBRARY FACILITIES							
ROGER WILLIAMS C PROV BR	PRI-FN			0	1	360	4,051	4,643	3,203	2,443	629
SALVE REGINA-NEWPORT C	PRI-FG	66,896	48,931					10,532	22,488	17,990	6,843
U OF RHODE ISLAND	PUB-U	669,689	535,751	300,000	125,519	2,558	498,538				
SOUTH CAROLINA											
AIKEN TECHNICAL COLLEGE	PUB-T	14,150	12,340	3,287	0	0	0	0	1,572	1,414	179

SEE FOOTNOTES AT END OF TABLE

Table 1. — Collections in College and University Libraries, by State or Other Area and Institution: Aggregate United States, 1978-79, and Fall 1979 — Continued

STATE OR OTHER AREA AND INSTITUTION (1)	CONTROL AND TYPE OF INSTITUTION (2)	HELD AT END OF YEAR — BOOKSTOCK VOLUMES (3)	BOOKSTOCK TITLES (4)	SEPARATE GOVERNMENT DOCUMENTS COLLECTIONS (VOLS.) (5)	MICROFORMS BOOK TITLES (6)	MICROFORMS PERIODICAL TITLES (7)	MICROFORMS OTHER PHYSICAL UNITS (8)	ALL OTHER LIBRARY MATERIALS (9)	ADDED DURING YEAR — BOOKSTOCK VOLUMES (10)	BOOKSTOCK TITLES (11)	CURRENT PERIODICAL SUBSCRIPTION TITLES FALL 1979 (12)
SOUTH CAROLINA	**--CONTINUED**										
ALLEN UNIVERSITY	PRI-FN	38,710	30,200	545	0	2	333	0	2,929	2,620	252
ANDERSON COLLEGE	PRI-T	27,254	25,000	0	0	9	184	0	2,149	2,000	218
BAPT COLLEGE AT CHASTN	PRI-FN	94,385	86,000	60,017	0	11	7,910	4,000	4,409	3,386	957
BEAUFORT TECH COLLEGE	PUB-T	12,751	11,864	0	0	170	17,100	18	2,150	2,036	161
BENEDICT COLLEGE	PRI-FN	119,733	109,795	450	3,440	582	26	823	86	1	616
BCB JONES UNIVERSITY	PRI-FG	163,451	118,002	0	6,150	65	2,618	0	5,577	3,517	600
CENTRAL WESLEYAN COLLEGE	PRI-FN	47,596	46,202	0	3	22	280	2,213	2,456	2,440	373
CHESTERFLO-MARLBORO TECH	PUB-T	15,335	14,234	0	0	51	365	1	681	611	162
CITADEL MILITARY C OF SC	PUB-FG	165,206	151,071	34,867	58,366	798	0	0	4,585	4,401	1,362
CLAFLIN COLLEGE	PRI-FN	116,625	92,243	656	19,239	332	1,454	0	5,457	5,312	657
CLEMSON UNIVERSITY	PUB-U	497,793	289,335	249,485	526	427	393,255	27,556	23,700	13,529	13,058
CLINTON JUNIOR COLLEGE	PRI-T	3,000	2,600	15	0	0	0	0	0	0	15
COKER COLLEGE	PRI-FN	60,645	49,692	0	1	43	4,131	0	1,235	836	256
COLLEGE OF CHARLESTON	PUB-FG	197,254	A	0	26,451	711	195,270	0	5,949	A	1,909
COLUMBIA BIBLE COLLEGE	PRI-FG	49,215	37,895	0	186	12	140	7,297	3,460	2,664	507
COLUMBIA COLLEGE	PRI-FN	101,948	69,237	0	353	92	7,093	25	5,493	3,834	852
COLUMBIA JUNIOR C	PRI-T	4,194	2,349	0	0	0	0	0	288	184	25
CONVERSE COLLEGE	PRI-FG	113,026	105,000	0	36	20	0	47	3,816	3,750	500
DENMARK TECHNICAL COLLEGE	PUB-T	13,554	8,217	0	0	114	0	36	905	710	217
ERSKINE C AND SEMINARY	PRI-FG	110,814	A	0	0	2,817	0	42	5,849	A	800
FLORENCE DARLINGTON TECH	PUB-T	25,770	24,190	0	0	88	1,429	0	1,164	1,060	356
FRANCIS MARION COLLEGE	PUB-FG	160,487	152,463	0	20,830	28,476	0	226	12,035	11,433	1,359
FRIENDSHIP COLLEGE	PRI-T	9,437	9,251	0	0	50	0	15	863	764	112
FURMAN UNIVERSITY	PRI-FG	247,502	149,956	14,617	17,346	113	44,567	0	14,048	12,722	1,452
GREENVILLE TECH COLLEGE	PUB-T	32,664	28,027	2,156	0	63	5,382	0	1,999	1,839	356
HORRY-GEORGETOWN TECH C	PUB-T	17,476	14,934	87	15	127	23	0	965	781	349
LANDER COLLEGE	PUB-FN	87,248	73,272	0	14,015	584	10,844	2	6,247	A	1,180
LIMESTONE COLLEGE	PRI-FN	52,925	42,528	0	0	74	699	0	1,525	1,525	385
LUTHERAN THEOL STHN SEM	PRI-FG	68,423	A	0	3,612	30	0	0	3,170	A	440
MEDICAL UNIVERSITY OF SC	PUB-FG	128,117	100,000	0	0	0	100	0	6,602	5,000	2,243
MIDLANDS TECH COLLEGE	PUB-T	47,914	46,072	283	0	123	0	0	3,510	3,273	586
MORRIS COLLEGE	PRI-FN	61,395	25,513	0	20,000	165	9,263	32	4,296	911	576
NEWBERRY COLLEGE	PRI-FN	63,782	46,131	0	0	0	7,260	0	5,205	4,551	660
NORTH GREENVILLE COLLEGE	PRI-T	33,806	28,453	0	222	44	552	315	876	653	185
ORANGEBURG CALHOUN TECH C	PUB-T	24,524	24,499	0	141	82	4,295	13,338	1,570	1,562	463
PIEDMONT TECH COLLEGE	PUB-T	17,559	16,803	0	156	62	0	1	847	782	280
PRESBYTERIAN COLLEGE	PRI-FN	109,259	102,000	0	5	110	1,955	38	8,697	7,500	629
RICE COLLEGE	PRI-T	A	A						A	A	A
RUTLEDGE COLLEGE	PRI-T	A	A					A	A	A	A
SC STATE COLLEGE	PUB-FG	214,267	144,683	38,104	35,412	651	130,083	0	8,958	6,502	999
SPARTANBURG METH COLLEGE	PRI-T	26,944	20,129	0	0	89	779	0	500	500	164
SPARTANBURG TECH COLLEGE	PUB-T	21,616	20,000	0	72	0	0	0	1,385	1,380	339
SUMTER AREA TECH COLLEGE	PUB-T	18,414	18,398	372	0	54	0	0	987	971	233
TRI-COUNTY TECH COLLEGE	PUB-T	30,078	30,078	0	0	45	270	0	3,054	3,054	343
TRIDENT TECHNICAL COLLEGE	PUB-T	45,464	A	0	0	109	5,527	314	3,832	A	501
U OF SC ALL CAMPUSES											
U OF SC AT AIKEN	PUB-FN	56,805	48,960	200	0	314	884	922	7,917	6,916	904
U OF SC AT BEAUFORT	PUB-T	29,338	A	0	0	153	1,859	0	1,567	A	277
U OF SC COASTAL CAROLINA	PUB-FN	57,165	A	0	0	0	10,935	0	5,514	A	875
U OF SC AT COLUMBIA	PUB-U	1,321,971	649,080	430,433	1,493	4	1,275,675	158,178	79,960	36,760	13,892
U OF SC AT LANCASTER	PUB-T	32,308	26,213	0	0	131	200	0	679	640	361
U OF SC AT SALKEHATCHIE	PUB-T	25,504	19,215	0	0	78	930	0	1,391	1,300	288
U OF SC AT SPARTANBURG	PUB-FN	51,725	47,430	0	1,300	482	20,921	6	4,492	4,200	1,120
U OF SC AT SUMTER	PUB-T	A	A	1,000	6,469	275	0	0	A	A	366
U OF SC AT UNION	PUB-T	24,730	20,501	0	0	0	1,051	0	808	539	187
VOORHEES COLLEGE	PRI-FN	76,873	50,798	0	22,000	2,745	0	12	2,280	2,061	402
WILLIAMSBURG TECH C	PUB-T	9,666	8,551	0	0	23	0	0	1,262	1,110	277
WINTHROP COLLEGE	PUB-FG	271,500	196,024	146,058	0	0	441,979	4,088	9,760	6,362	2,303
WOFFORD COLLEGE	PRI-FN	124,819	97,740	0	49	329	15,041	1,500	6,761	5,808	651
YORK TECHNICAL COLLEGE	PUB-T	16,745	16,245	0	148	54	1,390	0	715	685	250
SOUTH DAKOTA											
AUGUSTANA COLLEGE	PRI-FG	150,391	124,600	58,861	574	320	6,830	5	5,230	4,968	766

SEE FOOTNOTES AT END OF TABLE

Table 1. – Collections in College and University Libraries, by State or Other Area and Institution: Aggregate United States, 1978-79, and Fall 1979 – Continued

STATE OR OTHER AREA AND INSTITUTION	CON-TROL AND TYPE OF IN-STITU-TION	HELD AT END OF YEAR							ADDED DURING YEAR		CURRENT PERIOD-ICAL SUB-SCRIPTION TITLES FALL 1979
		BOOKSTOCK		SEPARATE GOVERN-MENT DOCU-MENTS COLLEC-TIONS (VOLS.)	MICROFORMS			ALL OTHER LIBRARY MATE-RIALS	BOOKSTOCK		
		VOLUMES	TITLES		BOOK TITLES	PERI-ODICAL TITLES	OTHER PHYS-ICAL UNITS		VOLUMES	TITLES	
(1)	(2)	(3)	(4)	(5)	(6)	(7)	(8)	(9)	(10)	(11)	(12)
SOUTH DAKOTA	--CONTINUED										
BLACK HILLS STATE COLLEGE	PUB-FG	102,784	83,364	40,341	13,865	68	10,570	0	3,438	3,120	682
DAKOTA STATE COLLEGE	PUB-FN	76,775	74,106	0	17	15	3,824	1,032	3,261	3,165	558
DAKOTA WESLEYAN U	PRI-FN	68,000	65,000	0	0	15	0	2,000	1,400	1,300	326
FREEMAN JUNIOR COLLEGE	PRI-T	14,532	12,932	950	1	5	157	206	543	510	160
HURON COLLEGE	PRI-FN	59,941	59,811	0	1	44	3,000	18	683	658	205
MOUNT MARTY COLLEGE	PRI-FN	69,078	57,200	0	18	14	0	785	2,060	1,985	535
NATIONAL COLLEGE	PRI-FN	20,414	18,000	0	0	18	0	75	1,721	1,710	246
NORTH AMERICAN BAPT SEM	PRI-FG	52,796	A	0	202	160	0	788	2,004	A	309
NORTHERN STATE COLLEGE	PUB-FG	120,997	88,000	17,810	34,190	90	0	0	5,198	4,500	674
OGLALA SIOUX CC	PUB-T	11,000	10,500	0	250	0	500	55	0	0	80
PRESENTATION COLLEGE	PRI-T	32,093	27,491	0	0	11	0	0	1,080	894	225
SINTE GLESKA COLLEGE	PRI-FN	17,000	15,500	0	1,500	0	0	100	2,300	100	110
SIOUX FALLS COLLEGE	PRI-FN	76,327	67,483	0	522	70	1,181	23	2,120	1,898	445
SD SCH MINES & TECHNOLOGY	PUB-FG	85,825	50,620	63,125	51	427	108,315	18,404	2,230	2,180	947
SD STATE UNIVERSITY	PUB-U	308,870	177,068	266,693	0	0	91,998	69,650	10,248	5,223	2,914
U OF SD ALL CAMPUSES											
U OF SD MAIN CAMPUS	PUB-U	447,201	215,303	129,100	6,481	5	225,348	8,479	19,179	7,413	5,297
U OF SD AT SPRINGFIELD	PUB-FN	79,725	75,648	0	0	570	71,300	1,010	0	0	660
YANKTON COLLEGE	PRI-FN	64,655	39,475	36,500	0	18	378	2	1,810	1,630	390
TENNESSEE											
AMER BAPT THEOL SEM	PRI-FN	16,113	A	0	0	0	0	800	863	A	155
AQUINAS JUNIOR COLLEGE	PRI-T	21,295	21,190	1,160	0	12	140	2,936	525	512	175
BELMONT COLLEGE	PRI-FN	75,386	63,293	0	0	237	1,598	0	2,127	2,127	590
BETHEL COLLEGE	PRI-FN	67,154	48,198	0	0	743	0	5	1,136	1,056	287
BRISTOL COLLEGE	PRI-T	2,028	A	0	0	0	0	10	350	A	55
BRYAN COLLEGE	PRI-FN	60,511	50,000	0	4	31	2,016	75	2,353	2,250	392
CARSON-NEWMAN COLLEGE	PRI-FN	137,031	107,706	51,027	42	231	3,390	694	4,401	3,380	1,023
CHRISTIAN BROS COLLEGE	PRI-FN	79,577	67,470	0	0	128	2,600	137	2,803	2,500	581
CUMBERLAND COLLEGE TENN	PRI-T	28,547	28,447	0	0	15	0	25	559	559	125
DAVID LIPSCOMB COLLEGE	PRI-FN	106,034	A	0	101	51	677	171	3,713	A	847
DRAUGHON'S JR COLLEGE	PRI-T	1,448	1,432	0	0	0	0	100	113	113	46
DRAUGHON'S JC BUSINESS	PRI-T	A	A	A					A	A	A
DRAUGHONS JC BUSINESS	PRI-T	2,268	1,938	0	0	0	0	0	224	206	14
EDMONDSON JR COLLEGE	PRI-T	1,005	959	0	0	0	0	0	111	103	28
EMMANUEL SCH OF RELIGION	PRI-FG	44,090	25,100	3	1,943	13	0	594	4,001	2,364	457
FISK UNIVERSITY	PRI-FG	A	A	A	A	A		A	A	A	A
FREED-HARDEMAN COLLEGE	PRI-FN	84,256	70,215	0	2,064	68	5,415	1,215	8,607	7,046	*58
FREE WILL BAPTIST BIBLE C	PRI-FN	30,104	A	0	0	490	0	0	1,571	1,560	196
HIWASSEE COLLEGE	PRI-T	34,992	34,642	0	0	142	0	0	493	493	315
JOHN A GUPTON COLLEGE	PRI-T	4,755	4,633	102	1	1	122	535	76	75	36
JOHNSON BIBLE COLLEGE	PRI-FN	36,349	18,543	0	5,485	89	0	0	2,680	2,072	229
KING COLLEGE	PRI-FN	74,051	A	55,901	11	77	2,778	10	1,389	1,046	500
KNOXVILLE BUSINESS C	PRI-T	3,071	2,938	29	0	0	0	0	A	387	36
KNOXVILLE COLLEGE	PRI-FN	78,455	A	0	0	105	0	400	2,383	A	0
LAMBUTH COLLEGE	PRI-FN	78,826	48,311	24,149	8	51	2,131	0	2,369	1,943	417
LANE COLLEGE	PRI-FN	80,536	57,293	0	2	1,359	3,273	170	1,581	1,020	488
LEE COLLEGE	PRI-FN	83,428	72,528	0	10	247	0	3	5,167	4,443	700
LE MOYNE-OWEN COLLEGE	PRI-FN	79,104	69,782	0	0	2	0	0	1,375	1,275	257
LINCOLN MEM UNIVERSITY	PRI-FN	55,412	55,337	0	0	0	36	0	1,175	1,100	350
MARTIN COLLEGE	PRI-T	20,579	18,500	0	0	0	51	574	1,392	1,250	155
MARYVILLE COLLEGE	PRI-FN	109,761	105,561	0	188	35	12,628	9,600	1,819	1,496	504
MCKENZIE COLLEGE	PRI-T	201	A	0	0	0	0	0	110	110	91
MEHARRY MEDICAL COLLEGE	PRI-FG	40,243	A	0	0	0	0	110	892	A	988
MEMPHIS ACADEMY OF ARTS	PRI-FN	16,832	12,500	0	0	0	0	0	488	480	112
MEMPHIS THEOLOGICAL SEM	PRI-FG	67,778	44,000	0	0	0	305	0	2,910	2,000	650
MID AMERICA BAPT SEMINARY	PRI-FG	A	A	A	A	A	A	A	A	A	A
MID-SOUTH BIBLE COLLEGE	PRI-FN	19,172	13,930	0	0	3	0	36	704	448	135
MILLIGAN COLLEGE	PRI-FN	84,776	75,000	500	18,813	70	5,400	1,250	2,675	2,530	382
MORRISTOWN COLLEGE	PRI-T	22,719	19,487	0	0	0	0	349	430	371	82
NASHVILLE STATE TECH INST	PUB-T	19,659	17,211	0	13	13	5,290	810	1,846	1,650	252

SEE FOOTNOTES AT END OF TABLE

Table 1. — Collections in College and University Libraries, by State or Other Area and Institution: Aggregate United States, 1978-79, and Fall 1979 — Continued

STATE OR OTHER AREA AND INSTITUTION (1)	CON-TROL AND TYPE OF IN-STITU-TION (2)	HELD AT END OF YEAR — BOOKSTOCK VOLUMES (3)	BOOKSTOCK TITLES (4)	SEPARATE GOVERN-MENT DOCU-MENTS COLLEC-TIONS (VOLS.) (5)	MICROFORMS BOOK TITLES (6)	PERI-ODICAL TITLES (7)	OTHER PHYS-ICAL UNITS (8)	ALL OTHER LIBRARY MATE-RIALS (9)	ADDED DURING YEAR — BOOKSTOCK VOLUMES (10)	BOOKSTOCK TITLES (11)	CURRENT PERIOD-ICAL SUB-SCRIPTION TITLES FALL 1979 (12)
TENNESSEE	--CONTINUED										
O'MORE SCH INTRIOR DESIGN	PRI-T	A	A	A	A		A	A	A	A	A
SCARRITT COLLEGE	PRI-FG	52,633	38,364	0	4	119	552	47	2,248	1,637	134
STHN COLLEGE OF OPTOMETRY	PRI-FG	14,710	12,310	15	412	7	0	0	469	450	202
STHN MISSIONARY COLLEGE	PRI-FN	112,268	108,339	2,024	500	125	21,609	0	4,345	4,203	1,409
SOUTHWESTERN AT MEMPHIS	PRI-FN	172,831	115,616	0	0	8	1,060	0	5,122	A	942
STATE TECH INST KNOXVILLE	PUB-T	5,286	5,078	0	0	106	0	0	1,147	1,132	181
STATE TECH INST MEMPHIS	PUB-T	29,994	16,845	0	8,131	90	5	1,501	1,712	1,544	345
ST U-CC SYS TENN ALL INST											
AUSTIN PEAY ST UNIVERSITY	PUB-FG	183,942	147,154	15,278	0	0	144,102	546	8,128	7,693	1,473
EAST TENN ST UNIVERSITY	PUB-FG	559,090	450,925	136,432	150,604	2,793	184,542	1,376	21,935	18,519	4,050
MEMPHIS STATE UNIVERSITY	PUB-FG	867,718	564,614	185,449	0	0	1,621,683	118	31,636	20,542	6,809
MIDDLE TENN ST UNIVERSITY	PUB-FG	403,795	271,695	3,750	3,555	437	427,540	5,974	20,993	13,177	2,883
TENNESSEE ST UNIVERSITY	PUB-FG	348,582	200,486	8,494	167,203	235	276,670	130	14,732	10,435	2,453
TENNESSEE TECHNOLOGICAL U	PUB-FG	337,349	226,023	90,502	394,297	19,448	0	12,479	12,697	8,507	1,980
CHATTANOOGA ST TECH CC	PUB-T	28,671	28,500	0	2,020	0	0	56	3,492	3,482	425
CLEVELAND ST CMTY COLLEGE	PUB-T	46,876	40,413	6,773	14	305	9,779	2,095	2,437	2,084	415
COLUMBIA ST CMTY COLLEGE	PUB-T	43,480	38,885	2,759	2	33	2,682	0	1,195	703	155
DYERSBURG ST CMTY COLLEGE	PUB-T	27,267	22,121	1,299	0	154	1,959	45	1,650	1,521	301
JACKSON ST CMTY COLLEGE	PUB-T	47,264	38,707	1,525	2	178	5,141	8	1,696	1,284	346
MOTLOW STATE CMTY COLLEGE	PUB-T	30,977	28,887	0	0	141	0	15	1,642	1,471	310
ROANE STATE CMTY COLLEGE	PUB-T	28,664	27,476	0	0	4,479	0	0	3,725	3,636	416
SHELBY STATE CMTY COLLEGE	PUB-T	43,842	40,000	0	0	142	1,622	4,225	4,524	3,500	454
VOLUNTEER ST CMTY COLLEGE	PUB-T	31,333	27,625	0	9	133	1,037	34	2,234	1,928	255
WALTERS ST CMTY COLLEGE	PUB-T	36,416	33,005	0	0	213	1,987	15	875	806	388
STEED COLLEGE	PRI-FN	7,327	7,101	0	0	0	0	104	380	368	40
TENNESSEE TEMPLE U	PRI-FN	71,345	68,112	0	4,258	27	9	1,194	6,169	5,969	804
TENN WESLEYAN COLLEGE	PRI-FN	64,501	59,797	0	0	75	3,049	3,150	2,507	1,838	318
TOMLINSON COLLEGE	PRI-T	25,489	18,481	0	0	0	0	64	1,276	1,018	197
TREVECCA NAZARENE COLLEGE	PRI-FN	73,103	72,100	0	14,570	2,000	0	56,088	2,661	2,510	448
TUSCULUM COLLEGE	PRI-FN	55,323	44,258	0	0	264	0	259	1,156	925	403
UNION UNIVERSITY	PRI-FN	72,909	72,347	0	11	117	1,570	0	1,577	1,552	575
UNIVERSITY OF THE SOUTH	PRI-FG	329,017	215,000	98,600	6,900	2	19,900	18	13,869	12,000	1,850
U OF TENNESSEE ALL CAM											
U OF TENN CTR HEALTH SCI	PUB-FG	137,892	35,007	0	0	9	115	0	21,347	1,592	2,655
U OF TENN AT CHATTANOOGA	PUB-FG	272,177	196,322	0	0	9,088	371,732	0	12,651	10,000	2,980
U OF TENNESSEE KNOXVILLE	PUB-U	1,457,351	A	56,048	0	0	1,368,667	494	55,900	A	22,464
U OF TENNESSEE AT MARTIN	PUB-FG	206,967	175,922	82,962	55,671	1,029	30,214	3	10,536	8,956	1,616
VANDERBILT UNIVERSITY	PRI-U	1,560,147	959,205	927,416	8	3	970,142	89,426	53,769	33,344	16,863
TEXAS											
ABILENE CHRSTN UNIVERSITY	PRI-FG	235,633	167,493	2,188	65,377	1,431	108,017	554	9,090	6,247	1,356
ALVIN COMMUNITY COLLEGE	PUB-T	34,120	31,588	0	1	138	0	1,724	2,123	2,008	203
AMARILLO COLLEGE	PUB-T	64,976	64,476	2,317	8,693	117	0	0	2,942	2,692	469
AMERICAN TECHNOLOGICAL U	PRI-FG	13,845	11,466	0	3,000	52	453	0	3,065	2,813	156
ANGELINA COLLEGE	PUB-T	28,780	24,168	0	0	110	10,227	24	1,483	1,331	0
ANGELO STATE UNIVERSITY	PUB-FG	168,975	113,080	107,025	177,836	326	4,670	66	9,768	7,000	1,940
AUSTIN COLLEGE	PRI-FG	127,194	99,049	23,124	14,002	350	70,000	0	5,335	4,555	638
AUSTIN COMMUNITY COLLEGE	PUB-T	26,635	19,948	0	0	78	5,500	4	5,993	3,763	528
AUSTIN PRESB THEOL SEM	PRI-FG	109,232	84,000	0	762	738	330	0	1,855	1,390	347
BAYLOR COLLEGE DENTISTRY	PRI-FG	51,060	44,167	0	1	9	0	0	4,505	3,900	522
BAYLOR COLLEGE MEDICINE[12/]	PRI FG	SEE TEXAS MEDL CTR JOINT LIB									
BAYLOR UNIVERSITY	PRI-U	833,305	557,500	215,159	33,600	26	22,508	0	29,597	22,500	7,185
BEE COUNTY COLLEGE	PUB-T	34,516	30,616	0	0	74	3,850	0	2,222	1,906	391
BISHOP COLLEGE	PRI-FN	167,500	A	15,206	700	27	0	0	1,500	1,311	0
BLINN COLLEGE	PUB-T	64,347	62,000	0	0	117	3,500	156	5,241	5,000	517
BRAZOSPORT COLLEGE	PUB-T	42,877	38,225	8,640	18	293	29,455	421	2,155	2,004	468
CENTRAL TEXAS COLLEGE	PUB-T	46,016	39,662	0	52,897	168	5,431	0	3,765	3,480	454
CISCO JUNIOR COLLEGE	PUB-T	26,931	26,879	0	2	9	0	0	786	734	174
CLARENDON COLLEGE	PUB-T	20,282	16,613	0	0	22	311	9	1,518	1,437	125
COLLEGE OF THE MAINLAND	PUB-T	40,306	33,588	0	0	228	13,665	197	2,369	1,564	340
CONCORDIA LUTH COLLEGE	PRI-T	22,156	A	0	0	70	2,653	0	1,804	1,580	162

SEE FOOTNOTES AT END OF TABLE

Table 1. — Collections in College and University Libraries, by State or Other Area and Institution: Aggregate United States, 1978-79, and Fall 1979 — Continued

		HELD AT END OF YEAR							ADDED DURING YEAR		
STATE OR OTHER AREA AND INSTITUTION	CONTROL AND TYPE OF INSTITUTION	BOOKSTOCK		SEPARATE GOVERNMENT DOCUMENTS COLLECTIONS (VOLS.)	MICROFORMS			ALL OTHER LIBRARY MATERIALS	BOOKSTOCK		CURRENT PERIODICAL SUBSCRIPTION TITLES FALL 1979
		VOLUMES	TITLES		BOOK TITLES	PERIODICAL TITLES	OTHER PHYSICAL UNITS		VOLUMES	TITLES	
(1)	(2)	(3)	(4)	(5)	(6)	(7)	(8)	(9)	(10)	(11)	(12)
TEXAS	--CONTINUED										
COOKE COUNTY COLLEGE	PUB-T	34,256	25,605	0	0	0	0	0	1,786	1,641	422
DALLAS BAPTIST COLLEGE	PRI-FN	137,296	133,296	35,936	27,301	133	209,510	1,228	2,269	2,103	481
DALLAS BIBLE COLLEGE	PRI-FN	28,869	25,000	0	0	0	0	0	2,772	2,395	89
DALLAS CHRISTIAN COLLEGE	PRI-FN	24,135	18,406	0	0	0	0	0	2,503	1,929	122
DALLAS CO CC DIST ALLINST											
BROOKHAVEN COLLEGE	PUB-T	9,308	9,284	0	16	57	0	0	4,839	4,815	265
CEDAR VALLEY COLLEGE	PUB-T	13,023	A	0	0	159	4,439	2,112	4,290	A	314
EASTFIELD COLLEGE	PUB-T	43,845	36,373	0	0	2,486	1,625	36	2,576	2,465	440
EL CENTRO COLLEGE	PUB-T	58,022	58,021	0	0	248	6,696	25	3,535	3,534	330
MOUNTAIN VIEW COLLEGE	PUB-T	36,194	32,334	0	3	247	3,351	428	1,194	900	510
NORTH LAKE COLLEGE	PUB-T	15,250	15,075	795	0	310	773	125	5,100	5,000	365
RICHLAND COLLEGE	PUB-T	50,137	A	0	0	243	2	24	5,280	A	374
DALLAS THEOL SEMINARY	PRI-FG	A	A		A	A	A	A	A	A	A
DEL MAR COLLEGE	PUB-T	109,944	98,714	0	18	41	2,788	506	5,653	5,195	679
DEVRY INST OF TECHNOLOGY	PRI-FN	A									A
EAST TEXAS BAPT COLLEGE	PRI-FN	88,824	67,248	0	2,002	167	3,765	1,959	2,393	2,345	584
EAST TEXAS ST UNIVERSITY	PUB-FG	518,926	317,912	199,151	223,817	343	0	354	23,571	16,314	2,768
EL PASO CO CMTY COLLEGE	PUB-T	41,300	41,000	0	0	205	14,612	7	6,295	5,996	771
EPIS THEOL SEM SOUTHWEST	PRI-FG	79,823	60,687	0	80	49	646	0	18,930	968	239
FRANK PHILLIPS COLLEGE	PUB-T	28,918	21,240	1,000	19	123	2,044	2,000	1,672	1,353	220
GALVESTON COLLEGE	PUB-T	34,197	31,218	1,120	1	163	2	255	2,100	1,827	543
GRAYSON CO JUNIOR COLLEGE	PUB-T	48,579	A	0	50	2,566	0	0	3,577	A	515
GULF COAST BIBLE COLLEGE	PRI-FN	35,044	33,078	0	9,499	4,218	1,568	1,480	4,979	3,983	205
HARDIN-SIMMONS UNIVERSITY	PRI-FG	154,276	128,249	118,360	2,500	60	15,204	5	4,979	3,983	998
HAROLD R. YEARY JT LIB	PUB-FG	121,874	95,932	63,868	181,161	670	0	221	9,770	7,947	1,212
HENDERSON CO JR COLLEGE	PUB-T	28,000	7,500	0	0	175	2,160	38,835	1,000	450	240
HILL JUNIOR COLLEGE	PUB-T	24,891	A	0	799	210	0	0	1,077	A	253
HOUSTON BAPT UNIVERSITY	PRI-FG	94,063	70,276	0	3,535	60	0	0	5,609	4,493	515
HOUSTON COMMUNITY COLLEGE	PUB-T	41,217	28,407	0	0	126	32,000	0	7,012	4,935	488
HOWARD C AT BIG SPRING	PUB-T	31,023	29,139	0	0	59	2,259	0	1,165	1,082	136
HOWARD PAYNE UNIVERSITY	PRI-FN	119,779	A	9,989	0	0	7,741	0	3,400	A	730
HUSTON-TILLOTSON COLLEGE	PRI-FN	60,867	50,032	0	25	61	11,135	71	1,941	1,669	399
INCARNATE WORD COLLEGE	PRI-FG	119,593	76,250	0	9,577	81	2,510	6,008	3,968	3,350	611
JACKSONVILLE COLLEGE	PRI-T	18,797	12,475	0	0	57	517	1	526	424	127
JARVIS CHRISTIAN COLLEGE	PRI-FN	55,376	49,376	0	0	94	979	245	3,887	3,822	429
KILGORE COLLEGE	PUB-T	59,067	49,098	0	0	185	0	345	1,752	876	377
LAMAR UNIVERSITY	PUB-FG	377,490	244,777	36,798	0	235	686,912	0	17,674	11,020	3,143
LAREDO JUNIOR COLLEGE	PUB T			SEE HAROLD R. YEARY JT LIB							
LEE COLLEGE	PUB-T	90,641	56,044	17,450	0	7	13,983	700	2,576	1,874	783
LETOURNEAU COLLEGE	PRI-FN	96,742	76,380	0	28,144	31	0	206	5,450	5,000	547
LON MORRIS COLLEGE	PRI-T	21,136	15,196	0	0	68	3,318	200	814	671	95
LUBBOCK CHRISTIAN COLLEGE	PRI-FN	67,194	46,821	2,587	2,390	194	0	24	2,729	2,246	609
MCLENNAN CMTY COLLEGE	PUB-T	66,913	51,747	0	0	33	770	0	3,373	2,865	576
MCMURRY COLLEGE	PRI-FN	136,056	97,678	0	0	113	0	0	3,613	2,408	470
MIDLAND COLLEGE	PUB-T	20,995	18,636	0	76	0	0	0	2,810	2,441	230
MIDWESTERN ST UNIVERSITY	PUB-FG	215,690	A	61,531	73,399	0	0	300	11,213	A	1,229
NAVARRO COLLEGE	PUB-T	33,248	31,562	0	0	1	6,280	750	1,015	1,010	131
NORTH HARRIS CO COLLEGE	PUB-T	23,003	22,500	5,525	0	294	24,710	0	2,643	2,550	569
NORTH TEXAS ST UNIVERSITY	PUB-U	818,918	335,280	164,151	205,315	41,386	33,561	8,675	33,323	18,981	4,881
OBLATE COLLEGE OF STHWST	PRI-FG	37,241	25,312	0	0	1	0	8	534	534	291
ODESSA COLLEGE	PUB-T	60,452	54,221	0	32	164	10	19	2,439	1,880	432
OUR LADY OF LAKE U	PRI-FG	102,883	82,098	0	92	32	223,154	895	3,975	2,490	780
PAN AMERICAN UNIVERSITY	PUB-FG	186,818	128,510	136,285	2,955	64,361	401,987	787	17,928	15,178	3,451
PANOLA JUNIOR COLLEGE	PUB-T	25,073	19,924	0	0	33	605	223	1,069	936	153
PARIS JUNIOR COLLEGE	PUB-T	26,174	25,650	0	3,522	2,688	0	117	1,830	1,793	420
PAUL QUINN COLLEGE	PRI-FN	88,883	A	635	32,500	6	0	18	3,463	3,397	426
RANGER JUNIOR COLLEGE	PUB-T	20,958	19,091	0	1,420	1,420	0	0	620	610	120
RICE UNIVERSITY	PRI-U	901,953	456,226	118,226	0	0	1,115,251	18,849	21,276	12,195	8,655
SAINT EDWARD'S UNIVERSITY	PRI-FG	83,795	A	0	1	121	1,961	500	6,422	5,474	660
SNT MARY'S U SAN ANTONIO	PRI-FG	279,161	147,480	125,678	297	194	20,326	0	8,639	4,690	2,052
SAM HOUSTON ST UNIVERSITY	PUB-FG	590,953	A	83,952	0	0	341,454	393	34,106	18,375	4,950

SEE FOOTNOTES AT END OF TABLE

70

Table 1. – Collections in College and University Libraries, by State or Other Area and Institution: Aggregate United States, 1978-79, and Fall 1979 – Continued

STATE OR OTHER AREA AND INSTITUTION	CON-TROL AND TYPE OF IN-STITU-TION	BOOKSTOCK VOLUMES	BOOKSTOCK TITLES	SEPARATE GOVERN-MENT DOCU-MENTS COLLEC-TIONS (VOLS.)	MICROFORMS BOOK TITLES	MICROFORMS PERI-ODICAL TITLES	MICROFORMS OTHER PHYS-ICAL UNITS	ALL OTHER LIBRARY MATE-RIALS	BOOKSTOCK VOLUMES (ADDED)	BOOKSTOCK TITLES (ADDED)	CURRENT PERIOD-ICAL SUB-SCRIPTION TITLES FALL 1979
(1)	(2)	(3)	(4)	(5)	(6)	(7)	(8)	(9)	(10)	(11)	(12)
TEXAS	—CONTINUED										
SN ANTO DIST JC ALL CAM											
SAINT PHILIP'S COLLEGE	PUB-T	55,614	55,096	948	4,371	2,119	0	32	4,790	4,277	455
SAN ANTONIO COLLEGE	PUB-T	203,289	172,795	15,601	11,311	1,800	25,552	0	18,023	15,319	2,703
SAN JACINTO C ALL CAM											
SAN JACINTO C CENTRAL CAM	PUB-T	103,074	75,816	0	0	800	12,835	0	5,655	A	856
SAN JACINTO C NORTH CAM	PUB-T	29,703	24,300	0	0	200	4,717	0	6,473	0	434
SCHREINER COLLEGE	PRI-T	15,787	14,567	0	150	11	5,082	694	979	791	140
SOUTHERN BIBLE COLLEGE	PRI-FN	18,076	17,575	0	0	0	0	0	1,036	1,036	0
SOUTHERN METH UNIVERSITY	PRI-U	1,103,300	658,640	423,301	43,609	506	347,262	166,695	38,045	17,661	4,906
SOUTH PLAINS COLLEGE	PUB-T	47,571	47,111	503	232	71	2,189	568	2,226	A	294
SOUTH TEXAS COLLEGE LAW	PRI-FG	80,960	10,556	0	14,712	28,075	0	0	7,712	1,116	1,943
STHWSTN ADVENTIST COLLEGE	PRI-FN	95,889	95,749	0	15,408	673	16,462	6,192	3,589	A	591
SOUTHWESTERN ASSEMB GOD C	PRI-FN	56,309	38,432	879	4	144	1	13,897	2,091	1,578	429
STHWSTN BAPT THEOL SEM	PRI-FG	A	A	A	A	A	A	A	A	A	A
STHWSTN CHRISTIAN COLLEGE	PRI-T	19,581	19,449	55	0	0	0	6	1,574	1,442	202
SOUTHWESTERN UNIVERSITY	PRI-FN	131,710	98,783	3,322	0	114	801	267	4,980	3,735	413
SOUTHWEST TEX JR COLLEGE	PUB-T	32,705	32,705	0	0	141	0	0	1,760	1,760	195
STHWST TEX ST UNIVERSITY	PUB-FG	365,108	A	162,697	193,639	371	0	99	17,963	A	4,564
STEPHEN F AUSTIN STATE U	PUB-FG	333,986	215,870	415,138	64,959	578	177,632	9,126	17,500	12,017	2,908
SUL ROSS STATE UNIVERSITY	PUB-FG	192,225	123,772	142	4,114	25,303	0	349	12,704	8,769	1,336
TARRANT CO JUNIOR COLLEGE	PUB-T	128,725	113,986	0	0	1,510	46,851	202	7,885	6,942	1,614
TEMPLE JUNIOR COLLEGE	PUB-T	29,935	28,000	0	0	31	1,544	0	1,465	1,400	271
TEXARKANA CMTY COLLEGE	PUB-T	30,333	27,530	7,200	161	225	10,182	0	789	774	282
TEXAS A&M U SYS ALL INST											
PRAIRIE VIEW A&M U 12/	PUB-FG	A	A	A	A	A	A	A	A	A	A
TARLETON STATE UNIVERSITY	PUB-FG	144,325	97,156	8,881	90,847	108	10,614	50,943	8,218	6,420	1,875
TEXAS A&M U ALL CAMPUSES											
TEXAS A&M U MAIN CAMPUS	PUB-U	1,222,740	917,055	138,678	0	0	1,183,871	61,979	55,951	41,963	10,966
TEX A&M U AT GALVESTON	PUB-FN	22,102	17,029	0	85	18	11,408	176	5,102	1,571	466
TEXAS CHIROPRACTIC C	PRI-FG	3,000	2,000	0	0	35	2,278	300	288	157	172
TEXAS CHRISTIAN U	PRI-U	849,129	A	0	91,288	0	0	2,220	35,722	A	5,031
TEXAS COLLEGE	PRI-FN	100,246	A	0	23,087	186	974	0	1,332	A	495
TEXAS COLLEGE OSTEO MED	PRI-FG	36,556	12,281	0	31	1	0	35	12,496	5,830	2,370
TEXAS LUTHERAN COLLEGE	PRI-FN	89,635	76,000	0	45	18	1,959	11,557	3,054	2,600	586
TEXAS MEDL CTR JOINT LIB 12/	PUB-FG	147,153	62,000	0	0	79	0	0	8,806	4,349	4,267
TEXAS SOUTHERN UNIVERSITY	PUB-FG	336,616	304,233	7,373	175,000	96	27,212	6,889	20,116	18,912	3,165
TEXAS SOUTHMOST COLLEGE	PUB-T	109,868	80,000	4,369	12	42	39,035	0	12,874	A	824
TEX ST TECH INST ALL CAM											
TEX ST TECH AMARILLO CAM	PUB-T	11,115	9,502	0	0	600	68	35	1,242	1,023	305
TEX ST TECH-HARLINGEN CAM	PUB-T	13,650	10,181	0	163	52	6,094	0	1,195	902	452
TEX ST TECH INST WACO CAM	PUB-T	51,263	41,630	0	0	103	213,369	863	3,865	3,454	717
TEXAS TECH UNIVERSITY	PUB-U	1,151,944	906,027	428,858	72	12	605,413	92,046	59,046	42,420	12,310
TEXAS WESLEYAN COLLEGE	PRI-FN	126,030	95,000	0	11,508	115	7,351	15,817	4,726	3,587	854
TEXAS WOMAN'S UNIVERSITY 12/	PUB-U	522,091	281,341	112,750	180,362	1,040	0	1	19,485	14,622	2,400
TRINITY UNIVERSITY	PRI-FG	287,219	203,242	164,888	58,067	316	333,541	2,591	13,109	9,011	2,713
TYLER JUNIOR COLLEGE	PUB-T	60,051	A	0	4	183	66	0	2,795	2,351	332
UNIVERSITY OF DALLAS	PRI-T	131,846	130,846	0	27,982	66	40,000	3,650	6,555	6,055	809
U OF HOUSTON ALL CAMPUSES											
U OF HOUSTON CEN CAMPUS 12/	PUB-U	1,196,071	477,886	205,565	33,023	385	934,523	30,364	56,527	26,748	13,329
U HOUSTON CLEAR LAKE CITY	PUB-FG	218,046	163,534	0	0	0	803,384	0	11,168	6,571	1,600
U OF HOUSTON DOWNTOWN C	PUB-FN	91,360	88,346	0	0	0	0	450	16,360	14,540	515
U HOUSTON VICTORIA CAMPUS	PUB FG	SEE VC UHVC JOINT LIB									
U OF MARY HARDIN-BAYLOR	PRI-FN	84,191	79,139	0	19,223	106	0	174	844	795	712
UNIVERSITY OF SNT THOMAS	PRI-FG	120,925	99,421	0	87	179	6,299	178	5,077	2,178	881
U SYS S TEXAS ALL INST											
CORPUS CHRISTI STATE U	PUB-FG	158,680	150,000	22,401	250,000	282	149,513	595	11,301	10,000	1,791
LAREDO STATE UNIVERSITY	PUB FG	SEE HAROLD R. YEARY JT LIB									
TEXAS A&I UNIVERSITY	PUB-FG	386,310	378,583	110,915	0	0	162,153	1,188	15,195	14,891	2,142
U OF TEXAS SYS ALL INST											
U OF TEXAS AT AUSTIN	PUB-U	3,972,303	1,950,790	433,890	0	0	1,982,117	281,841	214,645	118,916	60,000
U OF TEXAS AT ARLINGTON	PUB-FG	439,954	260,405	181,949	42,302	27,082	56,637	13,375	31,279	18,579	3,258

SEE FOOTNOTES AT END OF TABLE

STATE OR OTHER AREA AND INSTITUTION (1)	CON-TROL AND TYPE OF IN-STI-TU-TION (2)	HELD AT END OF YEAR							ADDED DURING YEAR		CURRENT PERIOD-ICAL SUB-SCRIPTION TITLES FALL 1979 (12)
		BOOKSTOCK		SEPARATE GOVERN-MENT DOCU-MENTS COLLEC-TIONS (VOLS.) (5)	MICROFORMS			ALL OTHER LIBRARY MATE-RIALS (9)	BOOKSTOCK		
		VOLUMES (3)	TITLES (4)		BOOK TITLES (6)	PERI-ODICAL TITLES (7)	OTHER PHYS-ICAL UNITS (8)		VOLUMES (10)	TITLES (11)	
TEXAS --CONTINUED											
U OF TEXAS AT DALLAS	PUB-FG	193,749	175,169	79,907	179,656	14,348	93,901	9,342	32,513	29,395	3,067
U OF TEXAS AT EL PASO	PUB-FG	475,639	292,335	117,393	131,765	1,365	1	66,671	33,138	20,605	3,800
U TEX HLTH SCI CTR DALLAS	PUB-FG	156,792	45,000	8,300	0	0	22,546	0	6,639	A	3,128
U TEX HLTH SCI CTR HOUSTN12/	PUB FG	SEE TEXAS MEDL CTR JOINT LIB									
U TEX HLTH SCI SN ANTO	PUB-FG	112,929	A		0	0	25	850	0	6,486	3,271	2,207
U TEX MEDL BR GALVESTON	PUB-FG	234,728	56,469	0	13,812	0	0	5,112	14,861	6,657	4,206
U OF TEXAS PERMIAN BASIN	PUB-FG	161,324	115,230	0	36,558	1,119	402,576	0	4,169	4,169	1,146
U' OF TEXAS SAN ANTONIO	PUB-FG	255,767	213,139	73,216	58,899	3,123	706,131	4,424	38,050	30,412	2,964
U OF TEXAS AT TYLER	PUB-FG	134,630	117,838	4,003	29,429	643	183,320	1,6..	11,190	10,019	1,191
VERNON REG JUNIOR COLLEGE	PUB-T	20,153	20,019	396	23	19	21	70	1,103	1,080	155
VICTORIA COLLEGE	PUB T	SEE VC UHVC JOINT LIB									
VC UHVC JOINT LIBRARY	PUB-T	144,178	115,401	34,855	0	0	318,300	2,200	5,179	4,606	1,652
WAYLAND BAPTIST COLLEGE	PRI-FN	77,883	52,866	7,500	205	48	7,117	0	2,479	1,675	525
WEATHERFORD COLLEGE	PUB-T	46,550	42,500	0	0	21	8,500	12	2,171	1,950	403
WESTERN TEXAS COLLEGE	PUB-T	33,034	32,051	0	0	110	1,740	4,500	2,855	2,743	270
WEST TEXAS ST UNIVERSITY	PUB-FG	247,261	161,672	543,507	24,630	235	414,003	0	10,944	7,914	2,325
WHARTON CO JR COLLEGE	PUB-T	51,478	44,692	4,281	190	92	3,953	96	1,834	1,399	408
WILEY COLLEGE	PRI-FN	57,825	25,274	4,849	18,673	2,055	0	91	152	64	53
UTAH											
BRIGHAM YOUNG U ALL CAM											
BRIGHAM YOUNG U MAIN CAM	PRI-U	1,437,439	A	101,673	0	0	719,040	245	60,672	36,235	17,000
BRIGHAM YOUNG U-HAWA CAM	PRI-FN	96,249	A	10,750	225,000	364	0	765	5,318	A	929
LATTER-DAY SAINTS BUS C	PRI-T	3,820	3,600	0	0	0	0	25	0	0	51
STEVENS HENAGER COLLEGE	PRI-T	2,243	2,073	0	0	0	0	30	69	65	30
UTAH HI ED SYS ALL INST											
UNIVERSITY OF UTAH	PUB-U	2,119,959	A	242,182	0	0	1,548,240	0	127,824	A	24,665
UTAH STATE UNIVERSITY	PUB-U	312,144	255,317	406,747	0	0	527,465	33,283	12,570	10,200	6,230
SOUTHERN UTAH ST COLLEGE	PUB-FN	137,146	88,293	42,284	41,300	40	0	2,500	11,660	9,250	875
WEBER STATE COLLEGE	PUB-FG	233,595	213,739	124,384	95	130	177,456	3,006	17,611	16,026	2,160
COLLEGE OF EASTERN UTAH	PUB-T	24,793	20,214	0	0	18	0	0	552	507	183
DIXIE COLLEGE	PUB-T	48,005	34,295	0	12,540	8	0	864	1,946	1,619	216
SNOW COLLEGE	PUB-T	28,762	26,835	3,000	0	40	3,168	85	323	302	148
UTAH TECH COLLEGE PROVO	PUB-T	A	18,000	0	20	0	20	20	2,705	A	296
UTAH TECH COLLEGE SALT LK	PUB-T	17,100	15,500	0	0	10	0	1,500	2,176	2,060	369
WESTMINSTER COLLEGE	PRI-FG	56,302	46,750	3,000	2	78	0	226	1,947	1,763	410
VERMONT											
BENNINGTON COLLEGE	PRI-FG	80,811	67,881	0	33	79	4,681	16,592	2,396	1,917	683
BURLINGTON COLLEGE2/	PRI-FN	NO LIBRARY FACILITIES									
CHAMPLAIN COLLEGE	PRI-T	26,700	21,021	0	0	0	1,471	229	1,925	1,575	267
C SNT JOSEPH THE PROVIDER	PRI-FG	20,204	20,194	0	1	19	182	0	386	376	99
GODDARD COLLEGE	PRI-FG	70,680	65,533	0	0	93	58,890	880	2,637	2,297	476
GREEN MOUNTAIN COLLEGE	PRI-FN	63,721	51,000	0	24,000	56	2,484	416	3,236	3,086	194
MARLBORO COLLEGE	PRI-FN	42,586	38,747	0	0	89	11,774	400	1,500	1,412	239
MIDDLEBURY COLLEGE	PRI-FG	275,869	192,684	120,256	123	520	25,606	0	13,731	9,300	1,604
NORWICH U ALL CAM											
NORWICH U MAIN CAM	PRI-FG	120,000	115,000	27,306	16,700	6,000	0	75	4,693	4,000	913
VERMONT COLLEGE	PRI-FG	27,988	26,345	700	19	10	1,795	0	1,071	649	235
SAINT MICHAEL'S COLLEGE	PRI-FG	102,897	65,854	0	22,786	104	19,755	10,472	3,983	2,549	992
SCH FOR INTRNATL TRAINING	PRI-FG	23,447	17,500	0	1,968	79	240	57	1,064	1,050	290
SOUTHERN VERMONT COLLEGE	PRI-FN	15,000	15,000	0	0	0	0	0	1,612	1,567	157
TRINITY COLLEGE	PRI-FN	52,438	35,960	0	18,283	71	0	2,491	2,591	1,928	352
U VT & STATE AGRL COLLEGE	PUB-U	699,690	483,882	220,803	170,777	1,205	56,224	135,919	36,997	22,123	8,299
VERMONT LAW SCHOOL	PRI-FG	55,769	5,773	7,317	1,364	43	51,388	147	7,178	1,178	915
VERMONT ST C ALL INST											
CASTLETON STATE COLLEGE	PUB-FG	64,869	47,752	23,164	13,220	142	3,620	587	1,340	1,118	384
CMTY COLLEGE OF VERMONT1/	PUB-T	NO LIBRARY FACILITIES									
JOHNSON STATE COLLEGE	PUB-FG	82,170	A	14,980	20,000	491	0	362	2,085	A	500
LYNDON STATE COLLEGE	PUB-FG	54,447	44,646	3,768	2	186	3,454	132	2,360	1,944	557

SEE FOOTNOTES AT END OF TABLE

Table 1. — Collections in College and University Libraries, by State or Other Area and Institution: Aggregate United States, 1978-79, and Fall 1979 — Continued

STATE OR OTHER AREA AND INSTITUTION	CON-TROL AND TYPE OF IN-STITU-TION	HELD AT END OF YEAR BOOKSTOCK VOLUMES	BOOKSTOCK TITLES	SEPARATE GOVERN-MENT DOCU-MENTS COLLEC-TIONS (VOLS.)	MICROFORMS BOOK TITLES	PERI-ODICAL TITLES	OTHER PHYS-ICAL UNITS	ALL OTHER LIBRARY MATE-RIALS	ADDED DURING YEAR BOOKSTOCK VOLUMES	TITLES	CURRENT PERIOD-ICAL SUB-SCRIPTION TITLES FALL 1979
(1)	(2)	(3)	(4)	(5)	(6)	(7)	(8)	(9)	(10)	(11)	(12)
VERMONT --CONTINUED											
VERMONT TECHNICAL COLLEGE	PUB-T	41,998	38,874	0	0	282	12,755	243	1,411	1,335	472
VIRGINIA											
AVERETT COLLEGE	PRI-FG	59,289	50,076	418	28	248	3,479	455	4,954	3,132	427
BLUEFIELD COLLEGE	PRI-FN	47,982	42,290	0	0	63	0	140	1,582	1,490	195
BRIDGEWATER COLLEGE	PRI-FN	106,382	90,772	47,897	34	40	9,206	3,256	4,650	4,101	731
C WILLIAM & MARY ALL CAM											
C OF WILLIAM AND MARY	PUB-FG	820,778	489,411	237,912	686	18	673,841	15,673	38,181	21,197	8,652
CHRISTOPHER NEWPORT C	PUB-FN	129,620	45,758	0	21,500	18	0	11	5,589	3,575	638
RICHARD BLAND C WM & MARY	PUB-T	46,954	42,578	0	2	2	2,071	665	1,735	996	290
ESTN MENNONITE C AND SEM	PRI-FG	92,169	88,000	0	205	26	3,776	4,547	4,284	3,480	1,009
EASTERN VA MEDL SCHOOL	PRI-FG	28,011	A	715	2	5	621	0	3,540	A	995
EMORY AND HENRY COLLEGE	PRI-FN	94,242	83,781	48,807	4,654	39	0	0	4,301	4,076	684
FERRUM COLLEGE	PRI-FN	64,117	50,000	0	410	27	3,655	150	5,023	4,200	544
GEORGE MASON UNIVERSITY	PUB-FN	177,854	163,449	0	20,620	654	220,603	3,766	18,480	11,372	3,012
HAMPDEN-SYDNEY COLLEGE	PRI-FN	118,511	78,252	5,471	9	25	6,269	1,186	4,267	2,845	564
HAMPTON INSTITUTE	PRI-FG	244,030	213,493	7,267	31,615	8	228,930	2,760	5,847	5,132	1,256
HOLLINS COLLEGE	PRI-FG	144,489	106,082	42,085	124	81	6,629	290	4,292	2,687	1,152
INST TEXTILE TECHNOLOGY	PRI-FG	A	A	A	A	A	A	A	A	A	A
JAMES MADISON UNIVERSITY	PUB-FG	273,857	182,475	51,162	15,737	165	290,000	10,100	11,856	6,757	3,259
LIBERTY BAPTIST COLLEGE	PRI-FN	80,285	79,521	0	1	272	6,201	9,944	4,901	3,951	443
LONGWOOD COLLEGE	PUB-FG	179,313	150,843	0	179	66	5,381	17,178	8,854	6,243	1,278
LYNCHBURG COLLEGE	PRI-FG	108,918	94,738	0	59	142	33,827	441	5,470	4,290	512
MARY BALDWIN COLLEGE	PRI-FN	120,533	75,626	0	770	41	0	2,393	3,326	2,302	600
MARYMOUNT COLLEGE OF VA	PRI-FG	52,677	37,532	0	0	37	1,863	9,651	4,130	3,070	360
MARY WASHINGTON COLLEGE	PUB-FN	254,756	195,907	28,056	1,059	33	9,473	36	7,028	5,405	1,127
NATIONAL BUSINESS COLLEGE	PRI-T	5,600	4,000	35	0	0	0	10	433	406	40
NORFOLK STATE UNIVERSITY	PUB-FG	241,924	193,539	0	139	254	17,580	2,000	13,542	8,471	2,465
OLD DOMINION UNIVERSITY	PUB-FG	443,467	283,284	115,065	14,274	2,284	346,166	3,019	26,585	12,145	5,329
PRESB SCH OF CHRISTIAN ED	PRI FG	SEE UNION THEOL SEM JOINT LIB									
PROT EPIS THEOL SEM IN VA	PRI-FG	100,000	A	0	1,400	0	0	0	3,328	A	418
RADFORD UNIVERSITY	PUB-FG	189,404	131,102	0	0	0	0	0	11,942	8,256	1,498
RANDOLPH-MACON COLLEGE	PRI-FN	109,221	90,889	3,829	997	69	227	0	3,213	2,409	515
RANDOLPH-MACON WOMAN'S C	PRI-FN	138,243	A	0	0	81	2,135	0	3,462	2,635	679
ROANOKE COLLEGE	PRI-FN	129,226	90,000	0	11	40	7,821	8	5,573	4,800	644
SAINT PAUL'S COLLEGE	PRI-FN	38,785	33,413	2,205	100	100	8,737	2	704	675	205
SHENANDOAH C-CONSV MUSIC	PRI-FN	56,050	45,310	0	36	151	2,449	0	5,900	5,000	454
SOUTHERN SEM JR COLLEGE	PRI-T	33,496	32,496	0	0	0	0	43	2,790	2,600	90
SWEET BRIAR COLLEGE	PRI-FN	174,545	A	1,600	0	51	7,570	0	3,444	2,461	817
UNION THEOL SEM IN VA	PRI FG	SEE UNION THEOL SEM JOINT LIB									
UNION THEOL SEM JOINT LIB	PRI-FG	207,155	A	0	0	22,079	0	0	6,366	A	1,247
UNIVERSITY OF RICHMOND	PRI-FG	282,428	257,000	113,490	0	0	16,238	0	13,940	12,685	2,803
U OF VIRGINIA ALL CAM											
U OF VIRGINIA MAIN CAMPUS	PUB-U	2,313,336	1,041,262	189,729	0	0	453,741	323,777	106,416	52,063	20,349
U VA CLINCH VLY COLLEGE	PUB-FN	82,052	55,969	0	2,381	56	0	32	5,172	3,309	819
VIRGINIA COLLEGE	PRI-T	A	A					A	A	A	A
VIRGINIA COMMONWEALTH U	PUB-U	540,586	365,246	47,604	27,372	960	591,549	1,657	45,603	31,327	7,489
VA INTERMONT COLLEGE	PRI-FN	55,979	44,381	0	0	43	13,773	0	2,763	2,230	439
VIRGINIA MILITARY INST	PUB-FN	244,666	172,299	58,882	137	178	6,065	1,014	6,343	4,845	914
VA POLY INST AND STATE U	PUB-U	1,157,590	663,821	131,822	44,392	11,533	1,575,973	97,410	83,150	44,668	12,356
VIRGINIA STATE UNIV	PUB-FG	197,357	139,363	55,517	3,725	264	283,047	0	6,189	3,882	1,269
VA STATE CC SYS ALL INST											
BLUE RIDGE CMTY COLLEGE	PUB-T	36,362	35,100	169	0	104	0	0	2,275	500	453
CENTRAL VA CMTY COLLEGE	PUB-T	37,590	35,593	0	2,230	183	5,617	110	1,645	1,342	266
DABNEY S LANCASTER CC	PUB-T	32,150	30,302	0	0	165	926	0	998	827	453
DANVILLE CMTY COLLEGE	PUB-T	36,607	32,850	11,255	0	93	205	602	1,623	1,393	388
ESTN SHORE CMTY COLLEGE	PUB-T	18,795	17,930	0	0	78	102	320	1,902	1,450	129
GERMANNA CMTY COLLEGE	PUB-T	20,096	A	0	0	11	848	0	1,668	A	181
J SARGEANT REYNOLDS CC	PUB-T	42,834	31,882	0	0	191	182	0	8,375	5,986	718
JOHN TYLER CMTY COLLEGE	PUB-T	27,375	A	0	0	0	20,752	0	1,009	A	230

SEE FOOTNOTES AT END OF TABLE

Table 1. — Collections in College and University Libraries, by State or Other Area and Institution: Aggregate United States, 1978-79, and Fall 1979 — Continued

STATE OR OTHER AREA AND INSTITUTION (1)	CONTROL AND TYPE OF INSTITUTION (2)	HELD AT END OF YEAR — BOOKSTOCK — VOLUMES (3)	TITLES (4)	SEPARATE GOVERNMENT DOCUMENTS COLLECTIONS (VOLS.) (5)	MICROFORMS — BOOK TITLES (6)	PERIODICAL TITLES (7)	OTHER PHYSICAL UNITS (8)	ALL OTHER LIBRARY MATERIALS (9)	ADDED DURING YEAR — BOOKSTOCK — VOLUMES (10)	TITLES (11)	CURRENT PERIODICAL SUBSCRIPTION TITLES FALL 1979 (12)
VIRGINIA — CONTINUED											
LORD FAIRFAX CMTY COLLEGE	PUB-T	29,351	26,773	0	12,222	124	4,302	233	2,211	1,877	402
MTN EMPIRE CMTY COLLEGE	PUB-T	19,934	15,758	0	0	106	4,133	0	1,245	913	243
NEW RIVER CMTY COLLEGE	PUB-T	23,266	18,811	0	77	121	2,272	4,354	1,803	1,681	255
NORTHERN VA CMTY COLLEGE	PUB-T	199,517	A	0	3,033	1,888	16,384	3,987	12,602	A	2,060
PATRICK HENRY CC	PUB-T	28,413	21,778	22,322	32	251	4,929	5	996	834	364
PAUL D CAMP CMTY COLLEGE	PUB-T	19,708	16,082	0	15	68	534	0	1,341	1,075	312
PIEDMONT VA CMTY COLLEGE	PUB-T	18,889	16,594	0	0	80	14,248	0	1,459	1,287	368
RAPPAHANNOCK CMTY COLLEGE	PUB-T	39,800	38,633	1,800	0	168	1	429	2,573	1,332	315
SOUTHSIDE VA CMTY COLLEGE	PUB-T	27,001	25,170	0	0	98	11	66	977	929	443
SOUTHWEST VA CMTY COLLEGE	PUB-T	33,551	28,528	0	14,850	437	1,600	0	2,126	1,807	365
THOMAS NELSN CMTY COLLEGE	PUB-T	46,340	34,440	0	13	189	11,907	0	3,184	2,177	648
TIDEWATER CMTY COLLEGE	PUB-T	105,758	96,717	0	1	465	14,600	1,434	5,478	5,283	741
VA HIGHLANDS CMTY COLLEGE	PUB-T	23,599	19,842	0	1	112	2,737	407	968	719	242
VA-WESTERN CMTY COLLEGE	PUB-T	42,415	36,952	0	0	215	11,143	0	2,066	1,999	625
WYTHEVILLE CMTY COLLEGE	PUB-T	29,375	25,595	0	5	65	319	300	996	725	267
VIRGINIA UNION UNIVERSITY	PRI-FG	123,267	69,262	0	25	434	10,078	0	1,853	1,700	665
VIRGINIA WESLEYAN COLLEGE	PRI-FN	65,697	52,558	420	247	28	1,099	78	2,853	2,049	597
WASHINGTON AND LEE U [1]	PRI-FG	256,768	200,000	56,652	55	36	8,939	65,441	9,436	8,500	2,480
WASHINGTON											
BELLEVUE CMTY COLLEGE	PUB-T	38,264	29,117	0	128	142	21,743	456	1,475	1,136	520
BIG BEND CMTY COLLEGE	PUB-T	36,137	36,108	76	10	332	0	14	1,537	1,508	328
CENTRALIA COLLEGE	PUB-T	30,255	24,762	0	1	105	3,106	14	1,069	0	249
CENTRAL WASH UNIVERSITY	PUB-FG	302,380	250,000	296,584	527,671	385	9,425	54,000	14,060	11,500	2,394
CITY COLLEGE [1]	PRI-FG	NO LIBRARY FACILITIES									
CLARK COLLEGE	PUB-T	A	A	40	0	54	1,847	9	1,403	1,292	401
COLUMBIA BASIN CC	PUB-T	36,436	30,875	5,200	14	130	11,284	2,200	1,718	1,551	507
CORNISH INSTITUTE	PRI-FN	3,630	3,600	0	0	0	0	0	630	600	80
EASTERN WASH UNIVERSITY	PUB-FG	313,848	190,755	130,696	344,125	0	0	0	15,433	8,130	4,683
EVERGREEN STATE COLLEGE	PUB-FN	135,496	112,913	38,016	46,809	1,165	64,512	742	8,455	7,045	2,385
FORT STEILACOOM CC	PUB-T	31,148	26,491	0	763	40	0	75	2,857	2,593	417
FORT WRIGHT C HOLY NAMES	PRI-FG	70,810	69,644	0	0	43	65	20	1,797	1,166	312
GONZAGA UNIVERSITY	PRI-FG	316,688	139,107	9,318	11,350	206	21,027	560	9,259	4,899	2,282
GRAYS HARBOR COLLEGE	PUB-T	40,598	36,613	127	0	10	633	11	790	661	332
GREEN RIVER CMTY COLLEGE	PUB-T	35,000	30,500	0	0	0	0	0	1,809	1,468	480
GRIFFIN COLLEGE	PRI-FN	A	A	A	A	55	2,584	300	2,624	1,418	567
HIGHLINE CMTY COLLEGE	PUB-T	64,562	36,877	0	0	35	966	10	1,415	1,353	356
LOWEF COLUMBIA COLLEGE	PUB-T	25,800	23,200	0	0	0	0	75	1,500	1,000	82
LUTH BIBLE INST SEATTLE	PRI-FN	20,000	16,000	0	550	0	0	236	1,220	A	257
NTHWST C ASSEMBLIES GOD	PRI-FN	47,853	47,778	0	25	65	4,607	169	1,642	1,374	166
OLYMPIA TECH CMTY COLLEGE	PUB-T	6,888	5,695	0	0	29	317	148	1,922	1,825	373
OLYMPIC COLLEGE	PUB-T	48,363	45,116	0	21	135	2,912	264	1,495	1,335	329
PACIFIC LUTH UNIVERSITY	PRI-FG	206,032	130,932	0	0	248	25,263	3,651	10,680	7,032	1,254
PENINSULA COLLEGE	PUB-T	32,264	30,868	0	0	65	468	264	1,495	1,335	329
PUGET SOUND C OF BIBLE	PRI-FN	21,501	19,350	0	809	5	2,427	175	2,399	2,159	203
SAINT MARTIN'S COLLEGE	PRI-FN	88,956	88,825	0	0	43	2,522	0	1,363	1,254	355
SEATTLE CC DIST ALL CAM											
NORTH SEATTLE CC	PUB-T	33,091	27,037	0	0	124	1,968	27	2,896	2,366	392
SEATTLE CC CENTRAL CAMPUS	PUB-T	55,000	50,000	0	982	233	12,399	900	1,598	726	553
SEATTLE CC SOUTH CAMPUS	PUB-T	16,164	12,457	3,000	3	29	0	0	910	722	375
SEATTLE PACIFIC U	PRI-FG	115,735	104,162	0	153	160	155,928	130	4,208	3,788	794
SEATTLE UNIVERSITY	PRI-FG	182,513	124,062	0	3	222	8,173	672	4,490	2,782	1,505
SHORELINE CMTY COLLEGE	PUB-T	68,086	57,197	0	1,200	206	0	463	2,924	2,604	675
SKAGIT VALLEY COLLEGE	PUB-T	58,724	42,973	0	0	113	2	0	2,791	2,239	359
TACOMA COMMUNITY COLLEGE	PUB-T	68,932	57,536	0	1	4,391	80	500	2,162	1,649	406
UNIVERSITY OF PUGET SOUND	PRI-FG	326,341	182,472	78,076	32,234	2,584	134,387	20	16,764	A	2,077
UNIVERSITY OF WASHINGTON	PUB-U	2,903,685	A	945,274	2,070	16	2,445,096	1,040,450	122,449	A	33,169
WALLA WALLA COLLEGE	PRI-FG	138,157	105,256	3,222	2,536	32	2,281	14,204	4,152	3,711	100
WALLA WALLA CMTY COLLEGE	PUB-T	32,207	26,958	0	3,125	43	301	253	1,483	1,383	387
WASH ST CC DIST 5 ALLINST											
EDMONDS COMMUNITY COLLEGE	PUB-T	30,086	20,973	0	0	13	0	211	1,994	1,760	497

SEE FOOTNOTES AT END OF TABLE

Table 1. — Collections in College and University Libraries, by State or Other Area and Institution: Aggregate United States, 1978-79, and Fall 1979 — Continued

		HELD AT END OF YEAR							ADDED DURING YEAR		
STATE OR OTHER AREA AND INSTITUTION	CON-TROL AND TYPE OF IN-STITU-TION	BOOKSTOCK		SEPARATE GOVERN-MENT DOCU-MENTS COLLEC-TIONS (VOLS.)	MICROFORMS			ALL OTHER LIBRARY MATE-RIALS	BOOKSTOCK		CURRENT PERIOD-ICAL SUB-SCRIPTION TITLES FALL 1979
		VOLUMES	TITLES		BOOK TITLES	PERI-ODICAL TITLES	OTHER PHYS-ICAL UNITS		VOLUMES	TITLES	
(1)	(2)	(3)	(4)	(5)	(6)	(7)	(8)	(9)	(10)	(11)	(12)
WASHINGTON	--CONTINUED										
EVERETT CMTY COLLEGE WASH ST CC DIST 17 ALL	PUB-T	46,417	32,219	0	30	86	0	200	2,234	1,964	539
SPOKANE COMMUNITY COLLEGE	PUB-T	26,525	25,666	0	0	782	0	25	4,083	437	490
SPOKANE FLS CMTY COLLEGE	PUB-T	38,606	31,766	0	0	218	0	0	2,809	2,562	825
WASHINGTON ST UNIVERSITY	PUB-U	1,189,899	A	0	0	0	1,565,203	0	48,477	A	25,990
WENATCHEE VALLEY COLLEGE	PUB-T	25,585	A	2,000	1,451	56	199	393	1,193	A	320
WESTERN WASH UNIVERSITY	PUB-FG	374,111	305,275	237,854	0	0	421,055	0	21,347	15,636	4,638
WHATCOM CMTY COLLEGE	PUB-T	9,756	8,781	0	1	43	0	205	768	718	175
WHITMAN COLLEGE	PRI-FN	158,614	124,980	97,085	9,128	137	0	0	5,719	4,286	1,950
WHITWORTH COLLEGE	PRI-FG	73,784	59,027	0	0	0	41,686	31	2,730	2,436	726
YAKIMA VALLEY CC	PUB-T	37,782	36,782	0	0	84	1,019	0	1,161	1,141	143
WEST VIRGINIA											
ALDERSON BROADDUS COLLEGE	PRI-FN	77,946	77,946	0	0	27	2,030	230	3,293	3,293	469
APPALACHIAN BIBLE COLLEGE	PRI-FN	26,923	A	0	0	0	0	0	1,673	A	218
BECKLEY COLLEGE	PRI-T	11,633	8,749	0	0	0	0	30	390	326	96
BETHANY COLLEGE	PRI-FN	132,940	126,143	533	8	315	0	125	1,895	1,781	644
BLUEFIELD STATE COLLEGE	PUB-FN	109,369	A	19,366	12,474	73	172,241	150	3,450	A	540
CONCORD COLLEGE	PUB-FN	121,185	106,643	31,438	20	362	14,990	1,500	4,701	4,622	643
DAVIS AND ELKINS COLLEGE	PRI-FN	81,529	64,000	0	0	19	4,553	112	5,345	5,200	581
FAIRMONT STATE COLLEGE	PUB-FN	156,822	A	10,899	0	0	25,560	0	4,661	A	728
GLENVILLE STATE COLLEGE	PUB-FN	96,480	90,423	30,107	12,900	7,973	174,712	692	2,364	2,103	663
MARSHALL UNIVERSITY	PUB-FG	334,780	A	431,746	91	855	211,516	31,764	8,924	A	2,725
OHIO VALLEY COLLEGE	PRI-T	18,985	18,500	290	0	455	0	0	665	590	80
PARKERSBURG CMTY COLLEGE	PUB-T	39,693	34,350	0	4,985	315	0	0	2,240	1,907	306
POTOMAC STATE COLLEGE	PUB-T	38,054	34,695	0	0	39	4,829	62	946	878	166
SALEM COLLEGE ALL CAM SALEM COLLEGE MAIN CAMPUS	PRI-FG	96,000	A	0	0	400	21,000	0	6,000	A	600
SALEM COLLEGE CLARKSBURG	PRI-T	19,000	A	0	0	0	0	0	400	A	12
SHEPHERD COLLEGE SOUTHERN W VA CC ALL CAM	PUB-FN	123,380	115,934	2,691	23,201	310	5,745	438	4,670	4,403	614
STHN W VA CC-LOGAN CAM	PUB-T	25,344	19,943	0	0	284	0	50	1,395	985	368
STHN W VA CC-WILLIAMSON	PUB-T	22,918	20,000	0	0	134	0	0	1,015	A	0
U OF CHARLESTON	PRI-FG	85,389	60,485	1,100	0	0	626	1,488	2,078	1,769	444
WEST LIBERTY ST COLLEGE	PUB-FN	171,913	100,000	8,000	16,007	5,710	0	150	0	0	1,100
W VA COLLEGE GRAD STUDIES	PUB-FG	47,759	38,088	6,696	12	578	159,552	0	2,231	1,558	663
WEST VA INST TECHNOLOGY	PUB-FG	130,982	98,974	1,424	23,966	220	201,048	152	5,168	3,721	869
WEST VIRGINIA NORTHERN CC	PUB-T	28,112	19,907	1,180	1	120	0	0	3,286	3,209	214
W VA SCH OSTEOPATHIC MED	PUB-FG	8,000	6,000	0	0	1	0	0	1,500	890	350
W VA STATE COLLEGE	PUB-FN	161,982	144,951	13,825	152	211	3,515	892	4,760	4,065	1,110
WEST VIRGINIA UNIVERSITY	PUB-U	778,176	480,000	0	0	0	723,126	0	29,436	17,500	7,210
WEST VA WESLEYAN COLLEGE	PRI-FG	123,228	A	0	0	10	2,770	511	4,339	3,066	661
WHEELING COLLEGE	PRI-FG	104,105	91,100	0	0	125	13,217	125	3,755	2,281	750
WISCONSIN											
ALVERNO COLLEGE	PRI-FN	73,109	A	5,031	14	17	87,450	3,190	3,093	A	734
BELOIT COLLEGE	PRI-FG	225,000	A	85,000	0	0	0	0	4,250	A	930
BLACKHAWK TECHNICAL INST	PUB-T	13,000	12,000	0	0	0	310	10	600	500	380
CARDINAL STRITCH COLLEGE	PRI-FG	69,509	69,470	0	0	4	7,222	0	3,298	3,239	398
CARROLL COLLEGE	PRI-FN	155,955	114,399	0	4	11	7,836	0	4,610	3,563	575
CARTHAGE COLLEGE	PRI-FG	110,816	78,957	0	3,980	279	38,436	6,356	3,690	2,423	869
CONCORDIA COLLEGE	PRI-FN	41,846	37,661	0	110	7	2,000	130	1,272	1,145	133
DISTRICT ONE TECH INST	PUB-T	39,650	38,500	0	0	0	107	0	2,800	80	741
EDGEWOOD COLLEGE	PRI-FN	59,728	40,828	0	10,464	52	13,027	0	1,173	1,073	408
FOX VALLEY TECH INST	PUB-T	27,173	23,172	0	91	92	0	5,835	3,500	3,200	834
GATEWAY TECH INST ALL CAM GATEWAY TECH INST-KENOSHA	PUB-T	28,471	28,135	0	25	112	2,263	0	1,037	995	318
GATEWAY TECH INST-RACINE	PUB-T	13,261	13,068	0	87	52	597	0	654	598	214
HOLY REDEEMER COLLEGE	PRI-FN	31,929	21,822	0	1	17	0	0	1,612	1,530	262
INSTITUTE PAPER CHEMISTRY	PRI-FG	39,000	A	0	2,505	18	0	0	801	A	825
LAKELAND COLLEGE	PRI-FN	48,110	38,130	0	20,000	45	1,770	0	3,137	2,726	218

SEE FOOTNOTES AT END OF TABLE

Table 1. — Collections in College and University Libraries, by State or Other Area and Institution: Aggregate United States, 1978-79, and Fall 1979 — Continued

STATE OR OTHER AREA AND INSTITUTION	CONTROL AND TYPE OF INSTITUTION	HELD AT END OF YEAR							ADDED DURING YEAR		CURRENT PERIODICAL SUBSCRIPTION TITLES FALL 1979
		BOOKSTOCK		SEPARATE GOVERN- MENT DOCU- MENTS COLLEC- TIONS (VOLS.)	MICROFORMS			ALL OTHER LIBRARY MATE- RIALS	BOOKSTOCK		
		VOLUMES	TITLES		BOOK TITLES	PERI- ODICAL TITLES	OTHER PHYS- ICAL UNITS		VOLUMES	TITLES	
(1)	(2)	(3)	(4)	(5)	(6)	(7)	(8)	(9)	(10)	(11)	(12)
WISCONSIN --CONTINUED											
LAKESHORE TECHNICAL INST	PUB-T	22,375	21,571	0	187	21	150	74	2,560	804	669
LAWRENCE UNIVERSITY	PRI-FN	224,218	A	170,929	0	0	108,514	U	6,627	A	1,106
MADISON AREA TECH COLLEGE	PUB-T	52,000	36,140	0	0	130	2,570	4	3,700	3,465	544
MADISON BUSINESS COLLEGE	PRI-T	7,446	A	0	104	81	0	7,631	352	305	41
MARIAN C OF FOND DU LAC	PRI-FN	72,000	71,975	0	450	0	77,000	1,000	4,500	4,475	475
MARQUETTE UNIVERSITY	PRI-U	639,325	341,607	0	7,984	1,751	223,041	2	24,741	11,571	7,753
MEDICAL COLLEGE OF WIS	PRI-FG	95,702	92,000	1,000	25	54	0	12	5,754	5,000	1,507
MID-STATE TECHNICAL INST	PUB-T	26,992	24,880	10	0	55	1	95	2,112	2,066	621
MILTON COLLEGE	PRI-FN	62,595	62,595	0	0	2	0	0	0	0	289
MILWAUKEE AREA TECH C	PUB-T	49,455	42,588	0	356	0	0	0	4,734	4,322	646
MILWAUKEE SCH OF THE ARTS	PRI-FN	A	A				A		A	A	A
MILWAUKEE SCH ENGINEERING	PRI-FG	29,150	29,150	0	0	11	0	0	1,801	1,801	369
MILWAUKEE STRATTON C	PRI-T	A	A						A	A	A
MORAINE PARK TECH INST	PUB-T	24,000	16,000	0	0	21	0	140	6,000	3,000	500
MOUNT MARY COLLEGE	PRI-FN	106,541	71,284	12,113	3	76	2,575	86	2,969	2,667	694
MOUNT SENARIO COLLEGE	PRI-FN	39,140	32,738	0	50	75	6,729	0	1,849	340	277
NASHOTAH HOUSE	PRI-FG	57,769	A	0	28	7	0	0	2,609	2,385	518
NICOLET COLLEGE-TECH INST	PUB-T	29,738	23,200	6,500	500	45	2,500	3,500	2,200	2,125	560
NORTH CENTRAL TECH INST	PUB-T	27,677	25,672	0	189	69	0	0	2,816	2,556	350
NORTHEAST WIS TECH INST	PUB-T	12,982	9,537	0	409	290	2,160	45	1,032	735	550
NORTHLAND COLLEGE	PRI-FN	67,051	60,346	0	7	11	0	0	2,774	2,497	396
NORTHWESTERN COLLEGE	PRI-FN	A	A	A				A	A	A	A
RIPON COLLEGE	PRI-FN	109,341	74,352	0	20	23	0	0	3,626	2,466	462
SACRED HEART SCH THEOLOGY	PRI-FG	48,554	A	0	3,100	4	313	200	1,573	A	180
SNT FRANCIS DE SALES C	PRI-FN	28,015	A	0	0	22	547	0	782	A	200
SNT FRAN SEM PSTL MINSTRY	PRI-FG	57,504	57,460	0	0	0	164	0	2,294	2,250	369
SAINT NORBERT COLLEGE	PRI-FN	125,717	103,675	0	25	16,097	380	1,023	5,068	2,976	699
SILVER LAKE COLLEGE	PRI-FN	60,071	58,269	0	10	10	125	1,283	1,740	1,679	260
STHWST WIS VOC TECH INST	PUB-T	A	A		A		A	A	A	A	A
U OF WIS SYS ALL INST											
U OF WISCONSIN EAU CLAIRE	PUB-FG	405,753	324,603	201,070	0	0	662,131	8,887	21,491	17,631	3,702
U OF WISCONSIN GREEN BAY	PUB-FG	281,800	225,000	225,676	51,925	1,000	368,396	76,489	20,000	17,500	2,400
U OF WISCONSIN LA CROSSE	PUB-FG	318,055	226,311	105,671	5,585	1,491	359,219	24,212	14,004	7,780	2,969
U OF WISCONSIN MADISON	PUB-U	3,501,402	1,440,227	247,002	155,883	2,387	1,487,739	60,923	129,271	61,454	50,198
U OF WISCONSIN MILWAUKEE	PUB-FG	1,169,444	712,108	123,830	0	0	765,960	905	56,509	34,149	12,000
U OF WISCONSIN OSHKOSH	PUB-FG	306,063	235,915	241,958	188,570	190	88,989	24,190	15,669	12,148	1,791
U OF WISCONSIN PARKSIDE	PUB-FG	284,456	199,121	0	0	0	483,625	9,596	9,977	7,046	1,887
U OF WISCONSIN PLATTEVL	PUB-FG	188,810	157,342	128,999	852	752	0	33,493	9,022	7,518	2,976
U OF WISCONSIN RIVER FLS	PUB-FG	187,844	155,371	119,669	248,482	13,468	8,525	37,833	9,244	6,646	1,540
U OF WISCONSIN STEVNS PNT	PUB-FG	260,392	162,109	236,148	12	205	90,575	498	14,183	5,765	2,366
U OF WISCONSIN STOUT	PUB-FG	172,012	162,453	0	0	20,285	435,198	318	13,036	12,764	2,290
U OF WISCONSIN SUPERIOR	PUB-FG	211,200	172,699	172,000	239,156	342	32,448	0	5,682	5,563	1,100
U OF WISCONSIN WHITEWATER	PUB-FG	304,453	201,965	210,930	1,065	363	422,430	0	11,109	7,776	1,569
U OF WISCONSIN CTR SYS	PUB-T	408,283	365,661	12,609	950	899	3,516	8,299	11,359	10,067	2,951
VITERBO COLLEGE	PRI-FN	66,937	50,807	0	3	447	0	0	2,034	1,745	555
WAUKESHA COUNTY TECH INST	PUB-T	19,750	12,944	0	4	32	158,000	5	2,011	1,911	443
WESTERN WIS TECH INST	PUB-T	24,315	20,000	0	0	105	105	0	2,352	A	450
WISCONSIN CONSV OF MUSIC	PRI-FG	A	A						A	A	A
WISCONSIN LUTHERAN C	PRI-T	7,500	7,400	0	0	0	0	250	4,000	4,000	77
WYOMING											
CASPER COLLEGE	PUB-T	54,083	40,382	0	0	35	1,611	15,553	4,006	3,646	515
CENTRAL WYOMING COLLEGE	PUB-T	23,322	19,169	4,101	0	123	34	1,152	1,493	1,238	300
EASTERN WYOMING COLLEGE	PUB-T	20,421	19,002	0	0	70	3,640	15	483	451	183
LARAMIE CO CMTY COLLEGE	PUB-T	19,752	17,119	0	1	94	1,816	3	1,364	1,107	359
NORTHWEST CMTY COLLEGE	PUB-T	32,379	32,179	900	0	1	956	800	593	590	328
SHERIDAN COLLEGE	PUB-T	35,994	21,360	19,382	31	51	0	500	818	558	346
UNIVERSITY OF WYOMING[2]/	PUB-U	654,586	394,539	1,443,075	0	0	106,075	5,708	31,020	17,179	5,961
WESTERN WYO CMTY COLLEGE	PUB-T	18,943	17,768	8,900	0	86	0	2,010	1,175	1,133	257
U.S. SERVICE SCHOOLS											
AIR FORCE INST TECHNOLOGY	PUB-FG	76,284	33,334	3,779	4	48	0	0	2,631	788	1,074

SEE FOOTNOTES AT END OF TABLE

Table 1. – Collections in College and University Libraries, by State or Other Area and Institution: Aggregate United States, 1978-79, and Fall 1979 – Continued

STATE OR OTHER AREA AND INSTITUTION	CON-TROL AND TYPE OF INSTITUTION	HELD AT END OF YEAR							ADDED DURING YEAR		CURRENT PERIODICAL SUBSCRIPTION TITLES FALL 1979
		BOOKSTOCK		SEPARATE GOVERNMENT DOCUMENTS COLLECTIONS (VOLS.)	MICROFORMS			ALL OTHER LIBRARY MATERIALS	BOOKSTOCK		
		VOLUMES	TITLES		BOOK TITLES	PERIODICAL TITLES	OTHER PHYSICAL UNITS		VOLUMES	TITLES	
(1)	(2)	(3)	(4)	(5)	(6)	(7)	(8)	(9)	(10)	(11)	(12)
U.S. SERVICE SCHOOLS --CONTINUED											
CC OF THE AIR FORCE	PUB-T	A	A		A			A		A	A	A
NAVAL POSTGRADUATE SCHOOL	PUB-FG	184,718	115,776	6,700	259	112	247,795	166,246	8,287	4,444	1,792
UNIFORMED SERV U HLTH SCI	PUB-FG	A	A		A	A	A	A	A	A	A
US AIR FORCE ACADEMY	PUB-FN	363,305	216,765	96,596	350	236	303,004	2,500	12,169	9,142	1,767
US ARMY CMND-GEN STAFF C	PUB-FG	A	A		A	A	A	A	A	A	A
US COAST GUARD ACADEMY	PUB-FN	120,000	109,000	0	23,000	2,000	0	200	4,500	4,000	650
US MERCHANT MARINE ACAD	PUB-FN	88,890	68,952	5,000	1	18	23,000	200	4,165	2,650	1,000
US MILITARY ACADEMY	PUB-FN	382,024	359,582	163,542	160,872	1,987	122,149	16,120	9,479	8,909	1,65.
US NAVAL ACADEMY	PUB-FN	359,147	199,397	74,455	3,118	444	18,636	9,076	16,603	9,575	1,914
AMERICAN SAMOA											
AMER SAMOA CMTY COLLEGE	PUB-T	18,000	16,500	0	0	1	17,000	0	1,050	1,050	188
CANAL ZONE											
PANAMA CANAL COLLEGE	PUB-FN	34,082	33,368	2,400	3	85	3,542	2,000	A	1,077	126
GUAM											
UNIVERSITY OF GUAM	PUB-FG	90,000	81,000	0	0	1,900	250,000	1,500	5,763	A	1,148
PUERTO RICO											
AMERICAN C PUERTO RICO	PRI-FN	11,000	8,570	0	0	0	0	0	1,000	A	200
ANTILLIAN COLLEGE	PRI-FN	29,445	23,556	0	1,000	43	319	60	4,493	3,594	318
BAYAMON CEN UNIVERSITY	PRI-FN	34,458	30,320	2,487	53	190	6,839	118	8,544	7,178	601
CAGUAS CITY COLLEGE	PRI-T	4,210	3,280	60	0	0	0	13	1,803	1,344	65
CARIBBEAN CTR ADV STUDIES	PRI-FN	A	A						A	A	A
CARIBBEAN U COLLEGE	PRI-FN	10,500	7,723	170	0	0	0	30	3,850	3,200	150
CATHOLIC U PUERTO RICO	PRI-FG	294,707	201,485	0	54,101	187	5,806	5,652	14,278	9,040	3,877
CONSERVATORY OF MUSIC PR	PUB-FN	14,826	13,890	0	10	0	0	0	2,436	1,837	40
EDP C OF PUERTO RICO	PRI-T	1,980	A	30	0	0	0	356	959	A	9
FUNDACION EDUCATIVA ALL											
COLEGIO U DEL TURABO	PRI-FN	34,827	29,815	630	2	0	0	0	1,741	1,125	226
PUERTO RICO JR COLLEGE	PRI-T	35,276	23,451	0	0	3	0	101	1,215	631	505
INST COMERCIAL DE PR JC	PRI-T	6,200	6,200	0	0	0	0	28	600	600	45
INST TECNICO COMERCIAL JC	PRI-T	2,725	100	0	0	0	20	0	725	A	40
INTER AMER U PR ALL CAM											
INTER AMER U METRO CAM	PRI-FG	89,877	58,382	6,682	7	115	157,694	50	10,235	A	1,137
INTER AMER U ARECIBO BR	PRI-T	28,517	22,986	0	27	0	5,550	0	2,245	2,073	214
INTER AMER U BARNQUITS BR	PRI-T	19,548	14,866	0	0	5	1,758	0	382	232	203
INTER AMER U SAN GERMAN CAM	PRI-FG	90,916	60,547	0	111	139	0	0	1,761	855	1,072
INTER AMER U AGUADILLA BR	PRI-T	33,154	27,973	0	0	1,700	5,546	0	4,665	2,134	435
INTER AMER U FAJARDO BR	PRI-T	18,848	16,163	0	0	0	0	0	3,797	3,121	245
INTER AMER U GUAYAMA BR	PRI-T	17,415	15,798	0	0	76	14,200	0	2,897	1,842	196
INTER AMER U PONCE BR	PRI-T	15,802	13,879	0	0	152	14,200	0	1,419	1,317	248
INTRATL INST WORLD U	PRI-FG	70,795	61,242	0	0	253	0	0	6,447	5,708	279
RAMIREZ C BUS AND TECHN	PRI-T	2,891	2,364	50	0	0	0	53	157	110	26
SAN JUAN TECHNOLOGICAL CC	PUB-T	3,310	A	0	0	0	0	0	432	A	101
UNIV POLITECNICA DE PR	PRI-FN	1,500	1,350	0	0	0	0	0	200	150	40
UNIVERSIDAD DE PONCE	PRI-T	5,299	5,501	0	0	0	0	1	455	202	43
U OF PUERTO RICO ALL CAM											
U OF PR RIO PIEDRAS	PUB-U	1,076,005	650,162	1,240,392	17,693	3,352	1,001	243	32,157	21,439	5,711
U OF PR MAYAGUEZ	PUB-FG	200,031	94,550	299,574	7,141	350	36,132	1,220	3,489	1,460	1,436
U OF PR MEDICAL SCIENCES	PUB-FG	43,592	42,577	0	0	0	0	0	2,404	1,015	1,208
U PR CAYEY UNIVERSITY C	PUB-FN	76,158	62,292	4,500	0	20	2,607	55	3,135	2,586	1,151
U PR HUMACAO U COLLEGE	PUB-FN	48,640	A	0	0	2	1,064	1,700	3,082	A	789
U PR REG COLLEGES ADMIN	PUB-T	124,291	95,464	0	0	1,821	4,693	1,168	7,410	5,506	1,948
U OF THE SACRED HEART	PRI-FN	70,929	45,977	0	30	146	0	536	3,631	3,203	488
TRUST TERRITORY											
CMTY COLLEGE MICRONESIA	PUB-T	9,000	7,050	0	60	0	0	120	540	339	139

SEE FOOTNOTES AT END OF TABLE

Table 1. — Collections in College and University Libraries, by State or Other Area and Institution: Aggregate United States, 1978-79, and Fall 1979 — Continued

STATE OR OTHER AREA AND INSTITUTION	CON-TROL AND TYPE OF IN-STITU-TION	HELD AT END OF YEAR							ADDED DURING YEAR		CURRENT PERIOD-ICAL SUB-SCRIPTION TITLES FALL 1979
		BOOKSTOCK		SEPARATE GOVERN-MENT DOCU-MENTS COLLEC-TIONS (VOLS.)	MICROFORMS			ALL OTHER LIBRARY MATE-RIALS	BOOKSTOCK		
		VOLUMES	TITLES		BOOK TITLES	PERI-ODICAL TITLES	OTHER PHYS-ICAL UNITS		VOLUMES	TITLES	
(1)	(2)	(3)	(4)	(5)	(6)	(7)	(8)	(9)	(10)	(11)	(12)
VIRGIN ISLANDS											
COLLEGE OF VIRGIN ISLANDS	PUB-FG	71,009	64,611	11,300	1	218	305,158	475	6,622	5,118	945

A - DATA NOT PROVIDED
1/ - USES LOCAL LIBRARIES
2/ - EXCLUDES THE LAW LIBRARY
3/ - USES FACILITIES OF EMMANUEL COLLEGE
4/ - JESUIT SCHOOL OF THEOLOGY AT CHICAGO IS ALSO A MEMBER OF THE JKM JOINT LIBRARY
5/ - CONTRACTS FOR USE OF LIBRARY FACILITIES
6/ - EXCLUDES THE MEDICAL LIBRARY
7/ - SHARES FACILITIES OF OHIO STATE UNIVERSITY NEWARK BRANCH
8/ - SHARES FACILITIES OF OHIO STATE UNIVERSITY LIMA BRANCH
9/ - SHARES FACILITIES OF OHIO STATE UNIVERSITY MARION BRANCH
10/ - SHARES FACILITIES OF OHIO STATE UNIVERSITY MANSFIELD BRANCH
11/ - SHARES FACILITIES OF KENT STATE UNIVERSITY STARK COUNTY REGIONAL CAMPUS
12/ - THE TEXAS MEDICAL CENTER LIBRARY OF THE HOUSTON ACADEMY OF MEDICINE HOUSES COLLECTIONS AND PROVIDES LIBRARY SERVICES FOR:
         BAYLOR COLLEGE OF MEDICINE
         PRAIRIE VIEW A&M UNIVERSITY SCHOOL OF NURSING
         TEXAS WOMEN'S UNIVERSITY SCHOOL OF NURSING AND HEALTH SCIENCES
         UNIVERSITY OF HOUSTON COLLEGE OF PHARMACY
         UNIVERSITY OF TEXAS HEALTH SCIENCE CENTER AT HOUSTON MEDICAL SCHOOL, GRADUATE SCHOOL OF BIOMEDICAL SCIENCES,
            SCHOOL OF ALLIED HEALTH, SPEECH AND HEARING INSTITUTE, AND SCHOOL OF NURSING

Table 2. — Library Operating Expenditures (in Dollars) of College and University Libraries, by Category of Expenditure and by State or Other Area and Institution: Aggregate United States, 1978-79

STATE OR OTHER AREA AND INSTITUTION (1)	CONTROL AND TYPE OF INSTITUTION (2)	TOTAL (3)	SALARIES AND WAGES			BOOKSTOCK (7)	PERIODICALS (8)	MICROFORMS (9)	AUDIOVISUAL (10)	BINDING AND REBINDING (11)	ALL OTHER OPERATING EXPENDITURES (12)
			LIBRARY STAFF (4)	FRINGE BENEFITS (5)	STUDENTS ON HOURLY BASIS (6)						
ALABAMA											
ALABAMA A & M UNIVERSITY	PUB-FG	592,076	380,000	0	63,672	44,400	45,220	15,000	2,450	9,592	31,742
ALABAMA CHRISTIAN COLLEGE	PRI-T	56,312	B	B	5,018	12,181	2,351	211	17	1,132	B
ALA LUTH ACAD AND COLLEGE	PRI-T	38,305	B	B	2,518	5,690	1,830	0	1,268	124	B
ALABAMA STATE UNIVERSITY	PUB-FG	729,718	361,460	0	19,781	243,723	49,419	0	0	1,423	45,912
ALEXANDER CITY STATE JC	PUB-T	140,208	109,506	1,215	3,142	7,852	8,082	1,355	2,100	2,325	4,631
ATHENS STATE COLLEGE	PUB-FN	98,496	64,505	12,805	0	8,777	6,702	0	884	3,300	1,523
AUBURN U ALL CAMPUSES											
AUBURN U MAIN CAMPUS	PUB-U	2,569,229	1,042,032	22,200	81,287	445,155	632,540	67,661	2,829	64,642	210,883
AUBURN U AT MONTGOMERY	PUB-FG	340,695	136,026	1,982	19,648	121,341	25,374	2,550	5,254	12,394	15,526
BIRMINGHAM STHN COLLEGE	PRI-FN	171,235	68,759	0	361	47,297	38,248	2,662	0	3,496	10,412
BOOKER T WASHINGTON BUS C	PRI-T	A	A	A	A	A	A	A	A	A	A
BREWER STATE JR COLLEGE	PUB-T	95,628	60,081	989	0	14,340	4,615	842	3,377	0	11,384
CHATTAHOOCHEE VALLEY CC	PUB-T	295,198	97,670	1,513	0	80,406	12,778	7,363	45,250	338	49,880
ENTERPRISE ST JR COLLEGE	PUB-T	206,881	102,584	11,756	2,263	12,946	6,486	2,177	5,391	298	62,980
FAULKNER STATE JR COLLEGE	PUB-T	114,279	59,337	1,424	10,884	18,207	5,000	1,698	6,357	600	10,772
GADSDEN STATE JR COLLEGE	PUB-T	222,506	142,560	20,343	0	21,861	9,364	5,867	845	1,381	20,285
GEO C WALLACE ST CC-DOTHN	PUB-T	165,570	94,867	0	1,821	15,674	8,870	345	5,473	2,694	35,826
GEO C WALLACE ST CC-HNCV	PUB-T	67,215	41,206	0	0	11,457	4,066	0	4,732	42	5,712
GEO C WALLACE ST CC-SELMA	PUB-T	116,636	64,626	742	8,134	18,000	5,000	1,316	6,755	233	11,830
HUNTINGDON COLLEGE	PRI-FN	105,601	54,113	5,178	10,399	18,778	7,718	1,089	769	864	6,693
JACKSONVL ST UNIVERSITY	PUB-FG	999,995	451,265	37,137	70,916	326,360	43,372	38,808	9,980	9,251	12,906
JEFFERSON DAVIS STATE JC	PUB-T	59,531	B	B	0	6,086	5,762	0	509	278	B
JEFFERSON ST JR COLLEGE	PUB-T	269,122	210,773	12,324	7,374	19,282	5,809	0	2,379	986	10,195
JOHN C CALHOUN ST CC	PUB-T	130,443	83,121	0	3,454	21,669	6,737	528	4,840	1,705	8,389
JUDSON COLLEGE	PRI-FN	51,269	28,354	900	1,700	11,737	4,197	782	0	1,364	2,235
LAWSON STATE CMTY COLLEGE	PUB-T	86,357	76,259	608	0	1,160	4,823	0	166	0	3,341
LIVINGSTON UNIVERSITY	PUB-FG	201,916	90,829	18,165	26,726	25,880	20,768	2,746	1,405	4,054	11,343
LOMAX-HANNON JC	PRI-T	12,357	B	B	1,600	2,500	2,500	0	0	0	B
LURLEEN B WALLACE ST JC	PUB-T	92,750	52,978	1,241	13,557	12,065	2,713	704	5,080	0	4,412
MARION MILITARY INSTITUTE	PRI-T	44,826	B	B	509	5,026	1,650	0	11,976	692	B
MILES COLLEGE	PRI-FN	174,055	126,589	10,224	12,490	10,140	2,070	6,620	90	810	5,022
MOBILE COLLEGE	PRI-FN	87,269	45,663	7,763	0	20,704	4,700	601	750	1,879	5,209
NTHEST ALA ST JR COLLEGE	PUB-T	83,775	B	B	0	15,000	6,500	0	0	3,300	B
NTHWST ALA ST JR COLLEGE	PUB-T	71,912	54,888	460	2,726	7,452	3,688	796	0	0	1,902
OAKWOOD COLLEGE	PRI-FN	203,398	106,019	20,470	33,980	23,434	5,253	50	5,548	1,552	7,092
PATRICK HENRY STATE JC	PUB-T	46,403	B	0	700	4,068	1,491	0	0	214	B
S D BISHOP ST JR COLLEGE	PUB-T	133,270	85,513	1,483	13,118	14,492	5,481	1,391	5,049	1,728	5,015
SAMFORD UNIVERSITY	PRI-FG	898,043	359,924	57,029	98,480	116,196	197,027	29,201	13,592	10,972	15,622
SELMA UNIVERSITY	PRI-FN	11,862	0	0	0	3,906	1,824	0	0	356	5,776
SNEAD STATE JR COLLEGE	PUB-T	129,997	81,730	0	1,715	18,684	7,210	0	6,885	2,758	11,015
S THESTN BIBLE COLLEGE	PRI-FG	38,420	23,545	0	4,350	4,402	2,086	0	836	842	2,359
SOUTHERN JC OF BUSINESS	PRI-T	A	A	A	A	A	A	A	A	A	A
STHN UNION ST JR COLLEGE	PUB-T	107,392	61,219	605	4,173	13,361	12,322	0	4,118	4,053	7,541
STHN VOCATIONAL COLLEGE	PRI-T	A	A	A	A	A	A	A	A	A	A
SPRING HILL COLLEGE	PRI-FN	161,347	84,081	9,342	11,172	22,265	13,785	0	1,676	4,895	14,131
STILLMAN COLLEGE	PRI-FN	96,781	55,690	9,307	10,033	12,997	7,367	1,375	0	526	3,486
TALLADEGA COLLEGE	PRI-FN	93,063	44,900	2,752	1,642	22,872	10,819	891	157	2,541	6,489
TROY STATE U ALL CAM											
TROY STATE U MAIN CAMPUS	PUB-FG	467,376	256,491	10,103	15,029	71,398	52,704	14,587	10,490	5,198	51,380
TROY ST U DOTHN-FT RUCKER	PUB-FG	109,121	41,504	665	0	30,178	13,515	5,281	6,622	587	6,769
TROY STATE U MONTGOMERY	PUB-FG	60,230	B	B	574	18,798	6,846	2,381	6,004	845	B
TUSKEGEE INSTITUTE	PRI-FG	444,559	214,481	21,832	88,158	33,639	60,977	2,442	300	5,286	17,444
U OF ALABAMA ALL INST											
UNIVERSITY OF ALABAMA	PUB-U	2,296,112	957,539	68,599	152,959	314,240	539,369	41,260	3,710	36,780	181,656
U ALABAMA IN BIRMINGHAM	PUB-FG	2,216,162	879,117	149,690	122,261	424,975	316,522	0	5,000	53,537	265,060
U ALABAMA IN HUNTSVILLE	PUB-FG	704,833	278,554	62,396	39,208	107,460	152,028	0	0	27,500	37,687
UNIVERSITY OF MONTEVALLO	PUB-FG	241,012	127,432	0	25,933	38,654	33,633	5,049	250	2,529	7,532
U OF NORTH ALABAMA	PUB-FG	519,196	246,043	61,511	40,455	86,174	40,641	6,999	0	9,053	28,320
U OF SOUTH ALABAMA	PUB-FG	1,543,687	552,942	131,052	30,622	275,430	405,548	7,634	32,954	37,578	69,927
WALKER COLLEGE	PRI-T	50,779	B	B	5,303	7,602	5,340	0	0	337	B
ALASKA											
ALASKA BIBLE COLLEGE	PRI-FN	A	A	A	A	A	A	A	A	A	A
ALASKA PACIFIC UNIVERSITY	PRI-FG			SEE U ALASKA ANCHORAGE JT LIB							
INUPIAT U OF THE ARCTIC	PRI-FN			NO LIBRARY FACILITIES							

SEE FOOTNOTES AT END OF TABLE

Table 2. – Library Operating Expenditures (in Dollars) of College and University Libraries, by Category of Expenditure and by State or Other Area and Institution: Aggregate United States, 1978-79 – Continued

STATE OR OTHER AREA AND INSTITUTION	CONTROL AND TYPE OF INSTITUTION	TOTAL	SALARIES AND WAGES			BOOK-STOCK	PERIODICALS	MICRO-FORMS	AUDIO-VISUAL	BINDING AND RE-BINDING	ALL OTHER OPERATING EXPENDITURES
			LIBRARY STAFF	FRINGE BENEFITS	STUDENTS ON HOURLY BASIS						
(1)	(2)	(3)	(4)	(5)	(6)	(7)	(8)	(9)	(10)	(11)	(12)
ALASKA	--CONTINUED										
SHELDON JACKSON COLLEGE	PRI FN			SEE STRATTON JOINT LIBRARY							
STRATTON JOINT LIBRARY	PUB-T	104,250	66,200	9,925	3,500	10,000	4,300	2,000	3,800	200	4,325
U ALASKA ALL INSTITUTION											
U ALAS FAIRBANKS ALL CAM											
U ALASKA FAIRBANKS CAMPUS	PUB-U	2,218,207	1,177,283	237,750	171,163	338,983	146,690	24,463	17,445	16,043	88,387
U OF ALASKA TANANA VLY CC	PUB-T			NO LIBRARY FACILITIES							
U ALAS ANCHORAGE ALL CAM											
U ALAS ANCHORAGE CAMPUS	PUB FG			SEE U ALASKA ANCHORAGE JT LIB							
U OF ALASKA ANCHORAGE CC	PUB T			SEE U ALASKA ANCHORAGE JT LIB							
U OF ALASKA KENAI CC	PUB-T	82,582	B	B	0	33,870	6,322	440	0	0	B
U OF ALASKA KODIAK CC	PUB-T	65,243	B	B	0	16,000	643	0	0	0	B
U OF ALASKA KUSKOKWIM CC	PUB-T	109,000	B	B	6,658	15,873	6,079	3,735	1,156	177	B
U ALAS MATANUSKA-SUSITNA	PUB-T	77,516	B	B	272	17,156	1,000	760	1,000	291	B
U ALASKA STHESTN ALL CAM											
U ALAS STHESTN SENIOR C	PUB FG			SEE U ALASKA JUNEAU JT LIB							
U OF ALAS JUNEAU-DGLS CC	PUB T			SEE U ALASKA JUNEAU JT LIB							
U OF ALASKA KETCHIKAN CC	PUB-T	72,423	B	B	0	10,400	912	202	0	0	B
U OF ALASKA SITKA CC	PUB T			SEE STRATTON JOINT LIBRARY							
U ALASKA ANCHORAGE JT LIB	PUB-FG	1,194,853	535,035	96,515	66,507	294,810	68,374	24,135	68	6,520	102,889
U OF ALASKA JUNEAU JT LIB	PUB-FG	266,735	152,200	29,100	485	39,000	14,900	15,300	800	350	14,600
ARIZONA											
AMER GRAD SCH OF MGMT	PRI-FG	A	73,690	0	16,065	48,227	24,669	0	0	683	0
ARIZONA C OF THE BIBLE	PRI-FN	A	B	0	5,719	1,634	405	0	0	0	B
ARIZONA STATE UNIVERSITY	PUB-U	4,600,952	1,763,440	202,374	349,589	937,149	819,236	130,937	0	102,402	295,825
ARIZONA WESTERN COLLEGE	PUB-T	136,499	68,549	15,442	0	17,200	6,000	3,900	12,600	100	12,708
CENTRAL ARIZONA COLLEGE	PUB-T	294,791	141,583	22,747	7,832	37,983	10,651	2,963	18,278	4,928	47,826
COCHISE COLLEGE	PUB-T	188,810	113,939	21,887	9,648	14,419	5,784	1,186	9,024	973	11,950
COLLEGE OF GANADO	PRI-T	37,297	B	B	0	9,124	4,545	0	0	0	B
DEVRY INST OF TECHNOLOGY	PRI-FN	A	A			A	A	A	A		A
EASTERN ARIZONA COLLEGE	PUB-T	131,053	79,841	14,165	0	21,392	3,651	402	4,765	229	6,608
GRAND CANYON COLLEGE	PRI-FN	89,696	44,033	5,450	8,713	17,300	11,100	500	500	30	2,070
MRICPA CO CC SYS ALL INST											
GLENDALE CMTY COLLEGE	PUB-T	470,706	256,127	45,875	43,039	13,246	16,616	7,402	17,588	2,091	68,722
MARICOPA TECH CC	PUB-T	161,168	81,721	19,260	4,162	21,000	10,000	2,440	14,160	800	7,625
MESA COMMUNITY COLLEGE	PUB-T	423,099	280,886	42,896	16,960	15,082	15,366	7,789	6,855	2,196	35,069
PHOENIX COLLEGE	PUB-T	479,606	299,225	65,829	24,722	23,924	15,952	2,088	2,000	949	44,917
SCOTTSDALE CMTY COLLEGE	PUB-T	249,088	141,586	23,401	14,460	20,000	12,291	5,848	424	600	30,478
MOHAVE COMMUNITY COLLEGE	PUB-T	157,643	62,352	11,223	8,281	44,761	10,146	1,540	7,502	161	11,677
NAVAJO COMMUNITY COLLEGE	PUB-T	A	A	A	A	A	A	A	A	A	A
NORTHERN ARIZ UNIVERSITY	PUB-FG	1,436,305	444,108	82,914	76,840	317,240	173,399	44,325	50,375	49,400	197,704
NORTHLAND PIONEER COLLEGE	PUB-T	197,098	83,199	17,554	886	32,105	3,276	3,000	17,993	752	38,333
PIMA COMMUNITY COLLEGE	PUB-T	727,782	389,846	69,808	12,683	113,712	37,914	10,526	33,786	4,403	55,104
PRESCOTT CENTER COLLEGE	PRI-FN	9,477	B	B	573	775	0	0	0	0	B
STHWSTN BAPT BIBLE C	PRI-FN	25,725	B	0	5,300	2,237	210	0	150	493	B
UNIVERSITY OF ARIZONA	PUB-U	6,086,306	2,209,997	376,243	267,867	1,934,457	662,384	53,115	19,301	168,346	394,596
UNIVERSITY OF PHOENIX	PRI-FG	A	A	A	A	A	A	A	A	A	A
YAVAPAI COLLEGE	PUB-T	241,093	101,873	17,543	15,043	40,259	8,762	3,971	13,523	3,151	36,968
ARKANSAS											
AMERICAN C OF COMMERCE	PRI-T	A	A	A	A	A	A	A	A	A	A
ARKANSAS BAPTIST COLLEGE	PRI-FN	A	A	A	A	A	A	A	A	A	A
ARKANSAS COLLEGE	PRI-FN	110,226	B	B	0	12,478	7,271	0	0	2,000	B
ARKANSAS STATE U ALL CAM											
ARKANSAS STATE U MAIN CAM	PUB-FG	905,235	285,381	56,790	93,475	208,186	133,564	8,684	18,000	23,237	77,918
ARKANSAS STATE U BEEBE BR	PUB-T	68,151	B	B	4,033	22,486	4,057	342	204	1,024	B
ARKANSAS TECH UNIVERSITY	PUB-FG	281,595	113,026	20,910	17,794	48,820	26,584	18,378	0	1,646	34,437
CAPITAL CITY BUS COLLEGE	PRI-T	23,186	B	B	986	6,000	2,000	0	1,500	0	B
CENTRAL BAPTIST COLLEGE	PRI-FN	17,910	B	B	0	5,963	1,582	164	0	356	B
COLLEGE OF THE OZARKS	PRI-FN	60,196	B	B	8,871	15,297	5,045	345	0	1,583	B
CROWLEY'S RIDGE COLLEGE	PRI-T	9,816	B	B	0	671	728	0	10	0	B
EAST ARK CMTY COLLEGE	PUB-T	106,957	48,872	11,496	8,966	16,508	6,591	906	7,300	0	6,218
GARLAND CO CMTY COLLEGE	PUB-T	112,015	36,831	5,863	0	29,574	6,743	5,634	1,212	0	26,158
HARDING U ALL CAM											
HARDING U MAIN CAM	PRI-FG	277,238	112,398	10,587	32,281	54,832	21,561	8,128	408	6,905	30,138

SEE FOOTNOTES AT END OF TABLE

Table 2. – Library Operating Expenditures (in Dollars) of College and University Libraries, by Category of Expenditure and by State or Other Area and Institution: Aggregate United States, 1978-79 – Continued

STATE OR OTHER AREA AND INSTITUTION	CONTROL AND TYPE OF INSTITUTION	TOTAL	SALARIES AND WAGES			BOOK-STOCK	PERIODICALS	MICRO-FORMS	AUDIO-VISUAL	BINDING AND RE-BINDING	ALL OTHER OPERATING EXPENDITURES
			LIBRARY STAFF	FRINGE BENEFITS	STUDENTS ON HOURLY BASIS						
(1)	(2)	(3)	(4)	(5)	(6)	(7)	(8)	(9)	(10)	(11)	(12)
ARKANSAS	--CONTINUED										
HARDING GRAD SCH RELIGION	PRI-FG	90,649	41,614	4,443	4,494	19,105	6,978	1,126	262	5,888	6,739
HENDERSON ST UNIVERSITY	PUB-FG	411,245	169,328	34,204	11,859	58,124	56,006	17,154	14,261	83	50,226
HENDRIX COLLEGE	PRI-FN	204,790	87,193	14,800	19,003	44,465	17,697	4,660	472	5,037	11,463
JOHN BROWN UNIVERSITY	PRI-FN	109,006	B	B	8,627	29,877	3,221	1,251	5,374	1,015	B
MISS CO CMTY COLLEGE	PUB-T	93,017	48,831	9,767	5,419	18,000	3,000	1,000	1,000	0	6,000
NORTH ARKANSAS CC	PUB-T	86,531	B	B	7,415	27,174	2,500	1,590	2,542	0	B
OUACHITA BAPT UNIVERSITY	PRI-FG	210,346	75,929	11,589	40,607	28,619	17,910	5,288	406	3,168	26,830
PHILANDER SMITH COLLEGE	PRI-FN	27,778	0	0	0	21,973	5,805	0	0	0	0
PHILLIPS CO CMTY COLLEGE	PUB-T	110,925	55,792	10,154	2,842	26,124	3,805	1,721	4,020	1,219	5,248
SHORTER COLLEGE	PRI-T	A	A	A	A	A	A	A	A	A	A
STHN ARK U ALL CAMPUSES											
STHN ARK U MAIN CAMPUS	PUB-FG	248,889	78,007	8,843	44,287	67,108	23,505	7,475	503	796	18,365
STHN ARK U EL DORADO BR	PUB-T	75,109	B	B	7,469	23,775	4,095	1,103	1,160	44	B
STHN ARK U STHWST TECH	PUB-T	53,837	B	B	4,983	14,518	2,883	0	10,105	354	B
SOUTHERN BAPTIST COLLEGE	PRI-T	57,769	33,515	3,473	2,802	8,839	1,188	0	3,715	1,875	2,362
U OF ARKANSAS ALL CAM											
U OF ARKANSAS MAIN CAMPUS	PUB-U	1,973,147	799,255	144,505	79,386	427,954	395,727	27,684	897	36,052	61,687
U OF ARK AT LITTLE ROCK	PUB-FG	1,293,280	415,667	62,351	113,236	199,365	302,718	17,749	943	23,981	157,270
U OF ARK MEDL SCI CAMPUS	PUB-FG	737,273	389,769	38,977	2,350	50,641	162,049	0	23,800	16,513	53,174
U OF ARKANSAS-MONTICELLO	PUB-FN	216,018	84,237	7,753	18,485	67,885	21,893	2,669	228	3,159	9,709
U OF ARKANSAS PINE BLUFF	PUB-FN	466,334	218,288	34,926	0	57,325	35,226	38,337	40	0	82,192
U OF CENTRAL ARKANSAS	PUB-FG	642,054	174,082	27,853	74,110	208,357	73,125	30,451	0	14,274	39,802
WESTARK COMMUNITY COLLEGE	PUB-T	160,674	88,561	16,914	13,545	13,124	10,818	982	4,432	1,037	11,261
CALIFORNIA											
ALLAN HANCOCK COLLEGE	PUB-T	308,403	146,193	36,428	23,372	15,488	6,394	38	6,015	0	74,475
AMER ACAD DRAMATIC ARTS-W	PRI-T	2,674	0	0	0	1,008	300	0	811	0	555
AMER BAPT SEM OF WEST	PRI FG			SEE GRAD THEOL UN JT LIB							
AMERICAN CONSV THEATRE	PRI-FG	A	A	A	A	A	A	A	A	A	A
ANTELOPE VALLEY COLLEGE	PUB-T	173,168	97,350	22,729	4,543	16,003	5,348	752	4,971	249	21,223
ARMSTRONG COLLEGE	PRI-FG	23,230	B	0	2,000	7,480	2,300	220	0	0	B
ART CTR COLLEGE OF DESIGN	PRI-FG	90,282	52,097	7,176	4,346	11,283	9,715	0	1,073	598	3,994
AZUSA PACIFIC COLLEGE	PRI-FG	270,786	138,614	26,569	18,394	54,696	8,397	2,914	4,450	0	16,752
BAKERSFIELD COLLEGE	PUB-T	346,880	305,474	0	14,193	15,221	6,850	1,001	3,340	261	540
BARSTOW COLLEGE	PUB-T	119,035	69,454	15,977	5,460	12,639	6,069	540	886	0	8,010
BETHANY BIBLE COLLEGE	PRI-FN	103,960	40,404	16,252	12,307	15,798	8,765	118	606	736	8,974
BIOLA COLLEGE	PRI-FG	311,226	113,035	15,269	48,727	70,000	28,508	0	4,827	30,860	
BROOKS COLLEGE	PRI-T	16,300	B	0	0	5,000	500	0	150	800	B
BROOKS INSTITUTE	PRI-FG	37,950	B	B	0	6,500	1,500	0	100	50	B
BUTTE COLLEGE	PUB-T	290,912	189,476	15,955	17,900	15,900	9,964	3,146	21,140	0	17,431
CABRILLO COLLEGE	PUB-T	453,385	319,303	60,032	4,800	20,000	9,500	1,950	15,000	550	22,250
CAL BAPTIST COLLEGE	PRI-FN	116,440	57,590	0	18,850	25,000	15,000	0	0	0	0
CALIFORNIA CHRISTIAN C	PRI-FN	2,606	B	B	0	73	87	0	0	0	B
CAL COLLEGE ARTS & CRAFTS	PRI-FG	A	A	A	A	A	A	A	A	A	A
CAL COLLEGE PODIATRIC MED	PRI-FG	93,000	62,700	500	0	7,000	13,000	0	0	5,000	4,300
CALIFORNIA INST OF ARTS	PRI-FG	293,838	161,846	21,959	21,686	39,291	12,074	2,530	7,822	6,084	20,546
CAL INST OF ASIAN STUDIES	PRI-FG	16,952	B	0	2,304	0	0	9,248	0	0	B
CAL INST OF TECHNOLOGY	PRI-FG	1,267,278	555,200	131,002	8,131	108,309	312,514	0	0	29,055	123,067
CAL LUTHERAN COLLEGE	PRI-FG	195,141	95,239	16,175	18,145	35,512	13,462	3,034	0	808	12,766
CALIFORNIA MARITIME ACAD	PUB-FN	93,720	B	B	0	16,335	7,945	7,525	0	1,120	B
CAL SCH PROF PSYC ALL CAM											
CAL SCH PSYC BERKELEY	PRI-FG	55,932	B	B	0	18,010	6,251	0	0	2,200	B
CAL SCH PROF PSYC FRESNO	PRI-FG	44,264	B	B	0	6,585	4,880	227	192	359	B
CAL SCH PROF PSYC LOS ANG	PRI-FG	53,068	B	B	3,384	12,506	4,600	300	350	825	B
CAL SCH PROF PSYC SN DEGO	PRI-FG	46,121	B	B	970	17,636	4,734	1,112	1,694	500	B
CAL ST U & C SYS ALL INST											
CAL ST COLLEGE-BAKERSFLD	PUB-FG	756,273	285,335	71,062	59,040	167,889	100,909	0	0	4,702	67,336
CAL STATE C-SN BERNARDINO	PUB-FG	964,625	451,134	117,418	28,444	219,333	65,009	12,765	855	23,685	45,982
CAL ST COLLEGE-STANISLAUS	PUB-FG	799,206	326,187	83,181	33,384	158,150	81,623	37,602	504	1,063	77,512
CAL POLY ST U-SN LUIS OB	PUB-FG	2,178,336	965,657	257,841	171,962	360,970	199,509	34,108	12,169	18,106	158,014
CAL STATE POLY U-POMONA	PUB-FG	1,879,862	808,618	202,500	106,601	382,707	109,058	46,287	446	17,865	205,780
CAL STATE U-CHICO	PUB-FG	1,998,007	956,503	260,603	107,358	307,250	180,181	13,046	31,054	58,926	83,086
CAL STATE U-DOMINGUEZ HLS	PUB-FG	1,351,900	596,300	156,200	137,900	245,600	85,300	12,800	22,300	18,800	76,700
CAL STATE U-FRESNO	PUB-FG	2,272,301	1,065,247	283,501	135,701	418,532	161,036	25,231	8,015	48,259	126,779
CAL STATE U-FULLERTON	PUB-FG	2,443,060	1,157,023	310,709	230,326	295,661	237,552	26,893	3,800	34,895	146,201

SEE FOOTNOTES AT END OF TABLE

Table 2. — Library Operating Expenditures (in Dollars) of College and University Libraries, by Category of Expenditure and by State or Other Area and Institution: Aggregate United States, 1978-79 — Continued

STATE OR OTHER AREA AND INSTITUTION	CONTROL AND TYPE OF INSTITUTION	TOTAL	SALARIES AND WAGES			BOOK-STOCK	PERIODICALS	MICROFORMS	AUDIO-VISUAL	BINDING AND RE-BINDING	ALL OTHER OPERATING EXPENDITURES
			LIBRARY STAFF	FRINGE BENEFITS	STUDENTS ON HOURLY BASIS						
(1)	(2)	(3)	(4)	(5)	(6)	(7)	(8)	(9)	(10)	(11)	(12)
CALIFORNIA	--CONTINUED										
CAL STATE U-HAYWARD	PUB-FG	1,625,516	763,301	202,292	92,313	322,661	79,470	0	0	14,328	151,151
CAL STATE U-LONG BEACH	PUB-FG	3,087,191	1,406,220	370,061	203,810	428,600	304,000	41,000	10,500	10,900	312,100
CAL STATE U-LOS ANGELES	PUB-FG	2,608,782	1,283,520	324,444	242,047	359,140	238,750	10,542	14,369	34,593	101,377
CAL STATE U-NORTHRIDGE	PUB-FG	2,699,792	1,265,777	253,155	292,793	347,305	289,769	36,640	12,246	42,000	160,107
CAL STATE U-SACRAMENTO	PUB-FG	2,543,678	1,111,735	280,824	252,881	454,649	144,827	34,588	16,430	76,903	170,841
HUMBOLDT STATE U	PUB-FG	1,379,578	586,349	155,561	128,687	226,967	96,425	37,845	2,521	20,115	125,108
SAN DIEGO STATE U	PUB-FG	3,517,344	1,585,233	413,936	371,013	301,828	480,007	60,654	5,449	104,329	194,895
SAN FRANCISCO STATE U	PUB-FG	2,772,247	1,350,972	266,009	336,782	429,054	156,386	43,105	8,654	50,973	126,817
SAN JOSE STATE U	PUB-FG	2,803,299	1,384,434	356,891	122,767	430,120	220,734	43,361	0	54,468	184,019
SONOMA STATE UNIVERSITY	PUB-FG	1,159,902	507,851	130,509	96,832	210,011	104,758	12,958	2,924	22,073	71,986
CAL WESTERN SCHOOL OF LAW	PRI-FG	301,086	90,700	13,890	46,500	41,807	77,955	17,133	0	4,279	8,822
CENTER FOR EARLY ED	PRI-FG	28,966	B	B	2,381	9,734	1,727	0	141	443	13,719
CERRITOS COLLEGE	PUB-T	606,585	403,572	64,427	31,046	31,445	8,500	1,500	52,376	0	13,719
CERRO COSO CMTY COLLEGE	PUB-T	171,405	115,423	23,084	0	8,906	3,000	720	8,480	750	11,042
CHABOT COLLEGE	PUB-T	938,828	535,321	121,562	73,213	58,622	0	32,051	0	4,578	113,481
CHAFFEY COLLEGE	PUB-T	245,876	171,611	17,787	2,389	33,955	6,429	2,061	399	4,677	6,568
CHAPMAN COLLEGE	PRI-FG	267,483	123,810	18,436	24,002	56,011	26,253	2,005	4,001	5,061	7,904
CHRIST COLLEGE IRVINE	PRI-FN	64,237	B	B	25,509	7,374	2,023	185	836	550	B
CHRISTIAN HERITAGE C	PRI-FN	86,009	41,771	8,510	13,738	16,041	2,135	0	0	1,285	2,529
CHURCH DIV SCH OF PACIFIC	PRI FG	SEE GRAD THEOL UN JT LIB									
CITRUS COLLEGE	PUB-T	283,302	216,915	0	6,000	15,389	7,052	450	11,000	1,373	25,033
CLAREMONT U SYS ALL INST											
CLAREMONT GRADUATE SCHOOL	PRI FG	SEE HONNOLD JOINT LIBRARY									
CLAREMONT MEN'S COLLEGE	PRI FN	SEE HONNOLD JOINT LIBRARY									
HARVEY MUDD COLLEGE	PRI FG	SEE HONNOLD JOINT LIBRARY									
PITZER COLLEGE	PRI FN	SEE HONNOLD JOINT LIBRARY									
POMONA COLLEGE	PRI FN	SEE HONNOLD JOINT LIBRARY									
SCRIPPS COLLEGE	PRI FN	SEE HONNOLD JOINT LIBRARY									
COAST CC SYS ALL INST											
COASTLINE CMTY COLLEGE[1]	PUB-T	NO LIBRARY FACILITIES									
GOLDEN WEST COLLEGE	PUB-T	547,353	337,664	82,003	29,658	32,996	15,825	2,675	17,424	297	28,811
ORANGE COAST COLLEGE	PUB-T	546,009	390,208	25,200	27,397	45,056	13,042	3,317	1,602	876	39,311
COGSWELL COLLEGE	PRI-FN	33,287	B	B	B	10,778	3,388	422	91	0	B
COLEMAN COLLEGE	PRI-FN	29,576	B	B	3,000	1,336	592	0	2,800	100	B
COLLEGE OF THE CANYONS	PUB-T	238,409	134,080	37,578	6,914	24,423	3,040	1,665	4,355	0	26,354
COLLEGE OF THE DESERT	PUB-T	66,233	36,680	10,996	2,978	12,303	255	770	223	0	2,028
COLLEGE OF MARIN	PUB-T	312,934	230,247	13,300	11,537	23,406	11,300	1,700	11,200	1,269	8,975
COLLEGE OF NOTRE DAME	PRI-FG	112,380	52,647	0	6,518	32,615	15,603	770	237	532	3,458
COLLEGE OSTEO MED PACIFIC	PRI-FG	53,937	B	B	5,197	12,000	10,000	0	2,000	0	B
COLLEGE OF THE REDWOODS	PUB-T	141,929	73,649	20,016	9,000	29,441	5,596	1,149	1,386	395	1,297
COLLEGE OF THE SEQUOIAS	PUB-T	193,218	111,549	21,984	19,716	26,063	8,685	1,295	0	1,364	2,562
COLLEGE OF THE SISKIYOUS	PUB-T	106,998	62,634	14,406	0	15,158	4,300	270	8,923	842	465
COLUMBIA COLLEGE	PUB-T	132,321	98,673	15,400	0	8,870	5,920	1,190	20	736	1,512
COMPTON CMTY COLLEGE	PUB-T	A	A	A	A	A	A	A	A	A	A
CNTR CSTA CC ALL INST											
CONTRA COSTA COLLEGE	PUB-T	304,363	173,618	34,167	17,820	35,632	12,000	0	23,926	0	7,200
DIABLO VALLEY COLLEGE	PUB-T	776,427	405,470	86,053	58,143	55,531	11,036	1,846	38,281	606	119,461
LOS MEDANOS COLLEGE	PUB-T	384,898	265,785	55,161	20,726	16,000	6,570	2,900	7,956	300	9,500
CRAFTON HILLS COLLEGE	PUB-T	151,461	72,511	7,000	11,000	33,500	12,243	3,182	750	4,998	6,277
CUESTA COLLEGE	PUB-T	285,860	196,981	46,640	11,653	5,770	5,021	1,057	1,035	226	17,477
CYPRESS COLLEGE	PUB-T	256,439	193,464	23,475	4,000	15,126	12,900	1,974	500	1,500	3,500
D-Q UNIVERSITY	PRI-T	A	A	A	A	A	A	A	A	A	A
DEEP SPRINGS COLLEGE	PRI-T	1,500	0	0	0	1,200	300	0	0	0	0
DOMINICAN C OF SAN RAFAEL	PRI-FG	102,978	56,817	6,818	6,397	18,137	10,859	482	0	1,300	2,168
DOMINICAN SCH PHIL & THEO	PRI FG	SEE GRAD THEOL UN JT LIB									
DON BOSCO TECHNICAL INST	PRI-T	43,288	B	B	0	4,332	966	0	3,016	0	B
EL CAMINO COLLEGE	PUB-T	417,054	275,114	53,438	11,658	35,965	18,477	6,000	0	4,312	12,090
FASH INST DESIGN & MERCH	PRI-T	A	A	A	A	A	A	A	A	A	A
FIELDING INSTITUTE	PRI-FG	NO LIBRARY FACILITIES									
FOOTHL-DEANZA CC ALL INST											
DE ANZA COLLEGE	PUB-T	740,083	512,434	97,362	19,910	34,967	11,950	5,332	16,468	815	40,845
FOOTHILL COLLEGE	PUB-T	527,695	315,500	50,200	22,880	38,740	12,560	3,125	7,930	1,000	75,760
FRANCISCAN SCH THEOLOGY	PRI FG	SEE GRAD THEOL UN JT LIB									
FRESNO PACIFIC COLLEGE	PRI FG	SEE MENNONITE-PACIFIC JT LIB									
FULLER THEOLOGICAL SEM	PRI-FG	265,045	104,081	22,005	40,139	50,000	20,500	2,000	0	6,300	20,020

SEE FOOTNOTES AT END OF TABLE

Table 2. — Library Operating Expenditures (in Dollars) of College and University Libraries, by Category of Expenditure and by State or Other Area and Institution: Aggregate United States, 1978-79 — Continued

STATE OR OTHER AREA AND INSTITUTION	CONTROL AND TYPE OF IN- STITU- TION	TOTAL	SALARIES AND WAGES			BOOK- STOCK	PERIOD- ICALS	MICRO- FORMS	AUDIO- VISUAL	BINDING AND RE- BINDING	ALL OTHER OPER- ATING EXPEND- ITURES
			LIBRARY STAFF	FRINGE BENEFITS	STUDENTS ON HOURLY BASIS						
(1)	(2)	(3)	(4)	(5)	(6)	(7)	(8)	(9)	(10)	(11)	(12)
CALIFORNIA	--CONTINUED										
FULLERTON COLLEGE	PUB-T	665,755	468,046	153,963	14,627	13,821	10,217	965	347	169	3,600
GAVILAN COLLEGE	PUB-T	120,122	79,170	7,632	0	20,000	5,800	1,200	1,175	500	4,645
GLENDALE CMTY COLLEGE	PUB-T	336,862	212,661	42,555	17,636	31,407	7,600	0	1,925	474	22,604
GOLDEN GATE BAPT SEMINARY	PRI-FG	A	A	A	A	A	A	A	A	A	A
GOLDEN GATE UNIVERSITY2/	PRI-FG	425,854	172,998	22,749	35,090	79,697	30,006	29,736	1,402	522	53,654
GRADUATE THEOL UNION	PRI FG		SEE GRAD THEOL UN JT LIB								
GRAD THEOL UN JT LIBRARY	PRI-FG	501,356	183,753	34,433	45,814	87,179	36,116	4,711	4,447	6,896	98,007
GROSSMONT COLLEGE	PUB-T	877,098	511,872	127,322	31,746	45,145	17,650	2,639	68,195	1,269	71,260
HARTNELL COLLEGE	PUB-T	385,064	200,801	51,603	18,484	30,272	7,273	3,131	10,672	342	62,96
HEALD ENGR COLLEGE	PRI-FN	A	A	A	A	A	A				A
HOLY FAMILY COLLEGE	PRI-FN	33,305	B	B	0	2,596	1,846	150	346	0	B
HOLY NAMES COLLEGE	PRI-FG	84,951	41,458	1,716	9,973	19,769	6,949	1,968	309	891	1,918
HONNOLD JOINT LIBRARY	PRI-FG	2,069,871	763,921	160,092	100,630	212,732	406,257	0	0	35,804	390,435
HUMANISTIC PSYC INST	PRI-FG	A	A	A	A	A	A	A	A	A	A
HUMPHREYS COLLEGE	PRI-T	21,565	B	B	0	7,840	883	0	573	12	B
IMMACULATE HEART COLLEGE	PRI-FG	76,312	46,743	8,881	0	6,040	11,627	863	789	0	1,369
IMPERIAL VALLEY COLLEGE	PUB-T	204,725	130,665	30,522	19,544	7,680	7,019	4,447	29	0	4,819
INDIAN VALLEY COLLEGES	PUB-T	157,948	95,439	21,950	2,391	24,850	6,535	4,221	0	590	1,972
INTERNATIONAL COLLEGE	PRI-FG		NO LIBRARY FACILITIES								
JESUIT SCHOOL OF THEOLOGY	PRI FG		SEE GRAD THEOL UN JT LIB								
JOHN F KENNEDY UNIVERSITY	PRI-FG	102,616	42,304	0	9,154	35,420	5,988	75	0	1,057	8,618
LAKE TAHOE CMTY COLLEGE	PUB-T	170,985	53,126	13,418	0	70,630	5,520	2,611	14,384	0	11,296
LASSEN COLLEGE	PUB-T	143,298	69,108	15,028	0	8,362	4,500	1,400	32,000	0	12,900
LIFE BIBLE COLLEGE	PRI-FN	69,978	32,432	3,589	15,240	10,881	1,931	0	0	710	5,195
LINCOLN UNIVERSITY	PRI-FG	125,044	48,000	6,500	14,000	43,000	6,000	1,044	0	0	6,500
LOMA LINDA UNIVERSITY	PRI-FG	1,155,907	530,435	102,092	72,695	139,596	140,748	5,151	0	25,023	140,167
LONG BEACH CITY COLLEGE	PUB-T	496,177	268,162	42,150	22,140	68,159	27,891	0	37,113	962	29,600
LOS ANGELES BAPT COLLEGE	PRI-FN	47,131	B	0	2,319	9,370	6,725	2,400	1,960	0	B
LOS ANG C OF CHIROPRACTIC	PRI-FG	69,030	B	B	4,130	12,000	5,000	0	12,000	3,000	B
LOS ANG CC SYS ALL INST											
EAST LOS ANGELES COLLEGE	PUB-T	336,920	276,378	0	12,096	22,413	11,113	0	12,222	0	2,698
LOS ANGELES CITY COLLEGE	PUB-T	300,656	236,700	0	10,962	37,251	10,000	700	0	5,043	0
LOS ANG HARBOR COLLEGE	PUB-T	257,567	158,747	36,226	13,900	30,867	15,606	0	0	0	2,221
LOS ANGELES MISSION C	PUB-T	279,369	155,000	34,894	14,200	36,150	5,250	1,800	8,850	0	23,225
LOS ANG PIERCE COLLEGE	PUB-T	438,720	272,081	48,014	11,880	49,500	12,045	1,700	25,000	0	18,500
LOS ANG SOUTHWEST COLLEGE	PUB-T	245,544	186,554	0	809	28,553	12,000	0	6,000	0	11,628
LOS ANG TR TECH COLLEGE	PUB-T	315,818	233,889	0	2,688	25,566	16,502	5,000	15,873	300	16,000
LOS ANG VALLEY COLLEGE	PUB-T	316,926	188,269	47,067	7,117	45,989	14,308	3,906	0	470	9,800
WEST LOS ANGELES COLLEGE	PUB-T	412,203	269,000	69,978	5,400	23,892	10,760	2,000	4,000	409	26,764
LOS RIOS CC SYS ALL INST											
AMERICAN RIVER COLLEGE	PUB-T	357,756	253,947	43,321	6,200	18,783	14,350	5,400	4,735	100	10,920
COSUMNES RIVER COLLEGE	PUB-T	332,741	220,000	44,000	40,626	16,659	6,000	1,600	3,510	193	153
SACRAMENTO CITY COLLEGE	PUB-T	497,768	356,900	0	92,568	7,000	6,000	720	29,000	1,200	4,380
LOYOLA MARYMOUNT U	PRI-FG	1,243,208	563,883	111,931	78,290	139,253	237,946	15,826	6,601	36,659	52,819
MARYMOUNT PALOS VERDES C	PRI-T	58,403	B	B	0	9,653	3,648	2,977	0	0	B
MELODYLAND SCH THEOLOGY	PRI-FG	44,763	B	B	6,246	4,766	3,669	350	426	239	B
MENDOCINO COLLEGE	PUB-T	100,940	56,533	8,180	633	19,038	5,903	4,466	0	289	5,898
MENLO COLLEGE	PRI-FN	69,342	41,400	5,574	3,651	10,669	4,852	0	0	1,011	2,185
MENNONITE BRTHREN BIB SEM	PRI FG		SEE MENNONITE-PACIFIC JT LIB								
MENNONITE-PACIFIC JT LIB	PRI-FG	121,238	44,603	5,993	22,461	18,195	12,029	780	1,250	0	15,927
MERCED COLLEGE	PUB-T	280,961	175,035	27,005	9,230	21,796	9,694	3,610	12,498	328	21,765
MILLS COLLEGE	PRI-FG	296,185	141,205	22,000	18,550	82,151	18,409	2,522	689	3,775	6,884
MIRA COSTA COLLEGE	PUB-T	223,107	114,982	23,374	12,442	22,962	8,252	1,946	6,687	98	32,364
MODESTO JUNIOR COLLEGE	PUB-T	319,447	219,982	51,712	1,000	14,106	15,000	2,000	1,000	1,000	13,647
MONTEREY INTRNATL STDIES	PRI-FG	131,123	79,212	12,723	12,600	9,350	13,100	0	0	990	3,148
MONTEREY PEN COLLEGE	PUB-T	158,800	97,639	28,542	584	12,719	5,687	5,272	3,855	0	4,502
MOUNT SNT MARY'S COLLEGE	PRI-FG	236,002	123,173	10,252	14,890	14,918	15,441	70	39,470	267	17,521
MOUNT SAN ANTONIO COLLEGE	PUB-T	1,123,168	801,880	193,500	17,150	23,349	14,247	3,810	11,285	847	57,100
MT SAN JACINTO COLLEGE	PUB-T	105,908	46,040	11,167	0	13,882	7,172	2,919	8,778	0	15,950
NAPA COLLEGE	PUB-T	322,872	100,909	25,243	15,276	4,905	5,468	730	0	8,905	161,436
NATIONAL UNIVERSITY	PRI-FG	201,579	45,965	18,158	3,600	66,883	12,274	1,791	40,718	0	12,190
NEW COLLEGE OF CALIFORNIA	PRI-FG	30,400	B	B	1,600	15,000	1,750	700	0	0	B
NORTHROP UNIVERSITY	PRI-FG	112,513	54,620	7,957	23,064	10,073	11,121	565	181	2,534	2,398
NYINGMA INSTITUTE	PRI-FG	A	A	A	A	A	A	A	A	A	A
OCCIDENTAL COLLEGE	PRI-FG	628,390	261,609	46,927	52,112	138,149	75,514	0	0	21,879	32,200

SEE FOOTNOTES AT END OF TABLE

Table 2. – Library Operating Expenditures (in Dollars) of College and University Libraries, by Category of Expenditure and by State or Other Area and Institution: Aggregate United States, 1978-79 – Continued

STATE OR OTHER AREA AND INSTITUTION	CONTROL AND TYPE OF INSTITUTION	TOTAL	SALARIES AND WAGES			BOOK-STOCK	PERIOD-ICALS	MICRO-FORMS	AUDIO-VISUAL	BINDING AND RE-BINDING	ALL OTHER OPER-ATING EXPEND-ITURES
			LIBRARY STAFF	FRINGE BENEFITS	STUDENTS ON HOURLY BASIS						
(1)	(2)	(3)	(4)	(5)	(6)	(7)	(8)	(9)	(10)	(11)	(12)
CALIFORNIA	--CONTINUED										
OHLONE COLLEGE	PUB-T	493,328	327,000	50,000	12,000	37,828	11,000	3,000	19,000	500	33,000
OTIS ART INST PARSON SCH	PRI-FG	62,112	B	0	11,388	7,780	7,658	0	5,498	600	B
PACIFIC CHRISTIAN COLLEGE	PRI-FG	77,417	B	B	3,960	7,129	4,630	0	150	100	B
PACIFIC LUTH THEOL SEM	PRI FG				SEE GRAD THEOL UN JT LIB						
PACIFIC OAKS COLLEGE	PRI-FG	47,753	B	B	0	5,273	3,473	0	169	860	B
PACIFIC SCH OF RELIGION	PRI FG				SEE GRAD THEOL UN JT LIB						
PACIFIC UNION COLLEGE	PRI-FG	325,261	127,866	25,525	29,515	77,542	21,908	4,257	6,938	3,656	28,054
PALOMAR COLLEGE	PUB-T	685,229	464,225	71,300	8,448	52,827	16,977	4,382	5,000	150	61,920
PALO VERDE COLLEGE	PUB-T	53,548	B	B	0	3,157	4,948	1,676	1,438	88	B
PASADENA CITY COLLEGE	PUB-T	507,737	358,631	67,411	21,915	31,740	9,656	4,226	948	914	12,296
PASADENA COLLEGE CHIRO	PRI-FG	17,908	B	0	2,880	2,450	925	0	1,028	0	B
PATTEN COLLEGE	PRI-FN	24,336	B	B	0	3,977	3,013	399	0	0	B
PEPPERDINE UNIVERSITY2/	PRI-FG	685,107	236,020	36,736	46,571	195,237	62,710	28,828	3,045	12,430	63,530
PERALTA CC SYS ALL INST COLLEGE OF ALAMEDA	PUB-T	335,053	208,528	53,436	14,401	19,254	11,357	2,888	0	686	24,503
FEATHER RIVER COLLEGE	PUB-T	29,162	B	0	0	3,400	1,451	186	0	17	B
LANEY COLLEGE	PUB-T	418,948	281,082	46,200	21,632	29,245	8,006	3,054	9,491	1,000	19,238
MERRITT COLLEGE	PUB-T	311,287	212,449	62,873	9,757	13,067	6,478	0	0	369	6,294
VISTA COLLEGE	PUB-T	A	A	A	A	A	A	A	A	A	A
POINT LOMA COLLEGE	PRI-FG	582,157	162,420	24,693	28,735	23,081	20,375	1,626	0	8,084	313,143
PORTERVILLE COLLEGE	PUB-T	75,747	53,591	3,575	0	5,153	3,692	1,800	3,500	200	4,236
RAND GRAD INST POL STDIES	PRI-FG	776,325	375,210	115,940	0	53,407	107,820	0	0	5,427	118,521
RIO HONDO COLLEGE	PUB-T	422,274	223,952	52,206	22,419	44,782	13,640	4,809	28,925	312	31,229
RIVERSIDE CITY COLLEGE	PUB-T	395,461	264,685	56,487	15,803	38,225	7,282	1,553	0	0	11,426
SADDLEBACK CMTY COLLEGE	PUB-T	435,322	316,789	9,678	19,579	40,531	10,116	3,000	24,734	500	10,395
SAINT JOHN'S COLLEGE	PRI-FG	26,528	6,214	0	0	13,551	3,471	0	502	1,003	473
SNT MARY'S COLLEGE OF CAL	PRI-FG	168,678	76,055	0	10,681	37,023	15,921	1,655	277	3,439	23,627
SAINT PATRICK'S COLLEGE	PRI-FN	34,750	B	0	0	11,630	2,690	0	1,070	0	B
SAINT PATRICK'S SEMINARY	PRI-FG	42,607	B	B	1,601	8,409	5,456	151	305	1,219	B
SN BERNARDINO VLY COLLEGE	PUB-T	374,414	238,128	57,060	8,332	28,310	17,932	0	7,154	3,821	13,677
SAN DIEGO CC ALL CAMPUSES											
SAN DIEGO CITY COLLEGE	PUB-T	470,629	280,797	61,350	0	39,240	8,004	3,005	15,367	3,280	59,586
SAN DIEGO EVENING C	PUB-T				NO LIBRARY FACILITIES						
SAN DIEGO MESA COLLEGE	PUB-T	393,156	226,975	51,346	4,767	42,654	26,992	5,000	5,500	851	29,071
SAN DIEGO MIRAMAR COLLEGE	PUB-T	64,457	B	0	0	5,184	3,601	0	9,823	0	B
SAN FERNANDO VALLEY C LAW	PRI-FG	178,399	B	B	23,756	13,412	69,939	6,134	0	1,425	B
SAN FRANCISCO ART INST	PRI-FG	103,606	72,275	385	8,160	9,503	4,697	0	3,700	3,180	1,706
SN FRISCO CC DISTRICT	PUB-T	616,581	464,279	81,580	21,108	17,218	12,293	3,412	4,876	694	11,121
SAN FRANCISCO CONSV MUSIC	PRI-FG	47,107	31,310	4,250	4,510	4,234	993	0	589	383	838
SAN FRANCISCO THEOL SEM	PRI-FG				SEE GRAD THEOL UN JT LIB						
SAN JOAQUIN DELTA COLLEGE	PUB-T	442,653	279,624	69,049	12,116	35,576	11,597	7,615	4,872	1,229	20,975
SAN JOSE BIBLE COLLEGE	PRI-FN	34,604	B	0	750	3,468	1,311	142	238	131	B
SAN JOSE CC ALL INST											
EVERGREEN VALLEY COLLEGE	PUB-T	447,406	149,174	54,495	12,607	37,382	8,793	2,926	1,720	0	180,309
SAN JOSE CITY COLLEGE	PUB-T	368,513	231,182	54,735	12,397	40,391	10,435	2,076	1,223	995	15,079
SAN MATEO CC SYS ALL INST											
CANADA COLLEGE	PUB-T	240,350	152,786	26,731	3,021	12,593	7,478	1,146	33,402	0	3,193
COLLEGE OF SAN MATEO	PUB-T	227,234	154,912	29,250	8,859	9,958	12,514	2,656	0	320	8,765
SKYLINE COLLEGE	PUB-T	226,138	113,880	21,595	7,439	38,374	10,515	10,316	6,000	449	17,570
SANTA ANA COLLEGE	PUB-T	310,051	217,752	15,765	15,642	36,402	15,500	0	3,906	329	4,755
SANTA BARBARA CTY COLLEGE	PUB-T	281,423	207,243	11,352	8,400	34,605	8,444	1,072	0	55	10,252
SANTA MONICA COLLEGE	PUB-T	328,492	195,753	42,017	7,309	58,768	14,485	1,000	980	987	7,193
SANTA ROSA JUNIOR COLLEGE	PUB-T	290,791	181,848	2,012	23,348	40,200	14,304	3,897	8,520	2,498	14,164
SCH OF THEO AT CLAREMONT	PRI-FG	149,945	81,778	13,556	0	37,179	5,826	100	0	5,516	5,990
SHASTA COLLEGE	PUB-T	281,723	230,753	0	21,402	10,000	6,095	3,910	4,000	400	5,163
SIERRA COLLEGE	PUB-T	249,297	168,138	36,253	5,258	12,693	6,000	1,153	7,764	100	11,938
SIMPSON COLLEGE	PRI-FG	44,166	B	B	7,614	2,337	2,930	0	187	0	B
SOLANO COMMUNITY COLLEGE	PUB-T	117,804	79,368	19,482	5,474	8,941	2,050	0	0	350	2,139
SOUTHERN CAL COLLEGE	PRI-FN	79,143	38,875	6,185	8,559	15,125	6,805	0	0	50	3,544
STHN CAL C OF OPTOMETRY	PRI-FG	72,851	37,265	4,844	4,159	9,334	6,981	9	5,000	1,300	3,959
STHN CAL INSTITUTE ARCH	PRI-FG	30,111	B	B	0	6,593	0	0	8,604	0	B
SOUTHWESTERN COLLEGE	PUB-T	474,362	278,073	60,484	32,454	44,877	17,939	4,385	11,508	1,584	23,058
STHWSTN U SCHOOL OF LAW	PRI-FG	554,529	267,436	20,058	42,140	18,107	146,040	9,198	2,230	5,849	43,471
STANFORD UNIVERSITY	PRI-U	12,701,692	5,974,730	1,251,551	443,484	2,202,035	1,479,727	0	0	241,677	1,108,488
STARR KNG SCH FOR MINSTRY	PRI FG				SEE GRAD THEOL UN JT LIB						

SEE FOOTNOTES AT END OF TABLE

84

Table 2. – Library Operating Expenditures (in Dollars) of College and University Libraries, by Category of Expenditure and by State or Other Area and Institution: Aggregate United States, 1978-79 – Continued

STATE OR OTHER AREA AND INSTITUTION	CON-TROL AND TYPE OF IN-STITU-TION	TOTAL	SALARIES AND WAGES			BOOK-STOCK	PERIOD-ICALS	MICRO-FORMS	AUDIO-VISUAL	BIND-ING AND RE-BIND-ING	ALL OTHER OPER-ATING EXPENDO-ITURES
			LIBRARY STAFF	FRINGE BENEFITS	STUDENTS ON HOURLY BASIS						
(1)	(2)	(3)	(4)	(5)	(6)	(7)	(8)	(9)	(10)	(11)	(12)

CALIFORNIA --CONTINUED

STATE CTR CC SYS ALL INST											
FRESNO CITY COLLEGE	PUB-T	412,280	266,870	59,134	23,146	33,588	11,358	0	2,013	688	15,483
REEDLEY COLLEGE	PUB-T	187,337	125,886	28,417	6,186	10,851	3,608	2,074	1,378	544	8,393
TAFT COLLEGE	PUB-T	68,116	46,326	0	1,190	9,500	3,300	0	3,000	500	4,300
US INTERNATIONAL U	PRI-FG	278,215	141,243	24,220	17,282	52,469	26,312	0	12,367	1,096	3,226

U CAL SYSW ADMIN ALL CAM											
U OF CAL-BERKELEY	PUB-U	14,520,865	6,777,351	1,389,586	1,301,771	1,708,893	1,403,981	45,810	3,263	316,647	1,573,563
U OF CAL-DAVIS	PUB-FG	7,518,862	2,669,908	707,419	1,035,160	1,073,546	1,184,279	53,072	2,305	191,401	601,772
U OF CAL HASTINGS C LAW	PUB-FG	595,763	208,256	77,055	43,205	30,265	206,719	0	0	11,146	19,117
U OF CAL-IRVINE	PUB-FG	5,084,900	2,436,163	456,402	37,384	701,611	580,751	22,000	6,500	151,300	692,789

U OF CAL-LOS ANGELES	PUB-U	13,242,868	5,982,253	1,309,248	1,339,655	1,365,300	1,326,404	189,283	12,183	432,022	1,286,520
U OF CAL-RIVERSIDE	PUB-FG	4,642,141	2,047,042	362,293	206,025	969,507	459,992	44,025	14,663	99,400	439,194
U OF CAL-SAN DIEGO	PUB-FG	6,421,148	2,849,367	567,416	348,027	803,440	760,831	129,075	11,535	175,724	775,733
U OF CAL-SAN FRANCISCO	PUB-FG	1,699,784	950,308	217,019	0	93,256	252,140	0	0	41,900	145,161
U OF CAL-SANTA BARBARA	PUB-FG	5,920,974	2,572,068	580,173	537,089	761,229	778,269	10,000	61,181	121,559	499,406

U OF CAL-SANTA CRUZ	PUB-FG	2,710,962	1,218,877	272,669	181,942	270,273	510,664	0	8,300	85,285	162,952
UNIVERSITY OF JUDAISM	PRI-FG	103,500	66,000	0	2,500	21,000	4,500	0	0	3,500	6,000
UNIVERSITY OF LA VERNE	PRI-FG	717,798	150,714	19,000	22,771	73,768	84,549	78,463	2,604	2,092	283,837
UNIVERSITY OF THE PACIFIC	PRI-U	834,661	445,604	80,209	43,698	182,806	12,000	14,500	1,000	12,000	42,844
UNIVERSITY OF REDLANDS	PRI-FG	372,117	146,215	21,932	29,536	87,889	47,776	0	0	0	38,769

UNIVERSITY OF SAN DIEGO2/	PRI-FG	932,002	329,107	57,100	92,756	183,465	169,561	20,697	6,458	12,955	59,903
U OF SAN FRANCISCO	PRI-FG	1,063,568	441,741	94,921	48,892	166,728	192,261	25,838	600	38,380	54,207
UNIVERSITY OF SANTA CLARA	PRI-U	1,277,753	531,380	96,071	93,264	192,777	140,484	35,915	616	33,575	153,671
U OF SOUTHERN CALIFORNIA	PRI-U	5,959,189	2,759,095	345,324	330,183	854,531	948,513	44,060	43,812	109,755	523,916
U OF WEST LOS ANGELES	PRI-FG	53,586	B	B	0	6,621	7,165	0	0	5,500	B

VENTURA CO CC SYS INST											
MOORPARK COLLEGE	PUB-T	146,209	100,905	9,022	1,625	12,217	3,713	2,100	0	400	16,227
OXNARD COLLEGE	PUB-T	137,332	80,872	17,057	3,500	9,000	6,000	0	8,000	0	12,903
VENTURA COLLEGE	PUB-T	329,620	191,880	47,488	18,352	27,529	12,257	3,794	15,142	1,550	11,628
VICTOR VALLEY COLLEGE	PUB-T	139,866	97,018	5,500	0	9,683	9,128	0	11,068	1,971	5,498

WEST COAST BIBLE COLLEGE	PRI-FN	19,403	B	B	3,915	1,400	700	0	0	0	B
WEST COAST U ALL CAMPUSES											
WEST COAST U MAIN CAMPUS	PRI-FG	58,816	0	0	0	57,136	1,680	0	0	0	0
W COAST U ORANGE CO CTR	PRI-FG	A	A	A	A	A	A				A
WSTN STATES COLLEGE ENGR	PRI-FN	5,160	B	B	0	680	0	0	280	0	B

WSTN ST U C LAW ALL CAM											
WSTN ST U C LAW ORANGE CO	PRI-FG	A	A		A	A	A		A	A	A
WSTN ST U C LAW SAN DIEGO	PRI-FG	A	A		A	A	A		A	A	A
WEST HILLS COLLEGE	PUB-T	109,127	42,009	4,280	15,088	18,500	12,850	3,000	800	300	12,300
WESTMONT COLLEGE	PRI-FN	224,796	93,728	14,996	27,756	37,830	25,953	9,700	901	1,279	12,653

MISSION COLLEGE	PUB-T	369,162	247,629	13,573	6,100	0	26,750	0	16,700	0	58,410
WEST VALLEY COLLEGE	PUB-T	540,638	354,064	0	23,514	44,000	20,000	0	37,000	0	62,060
WHITTIER COLLEGE	PRI-FG	579,853	217,669	35,446	41,353	143,498	93,927	11,871	7,500	7,112	21,477
WOODBURY UNIVERSITY	PRI-FG	174,854	62,826	10,052	20,000	53,193	11,537	7,382	715	3,342	5,807
WORLD COLLEGE WEST	PRI-FN	9,436	B	B	250	5,499	1,227	0	300	0	B

THE WRIGHT INSTITUTE	PRI-FG	21,589	B	B	415	6,546	610	0	85	0	B
YESHIVA U OF LOS ANGELES	PRI-FG	A	A	A	A	A	A				A
YUBA COLLEGE	PUB-T	253,947	171,870	5,200	10,634	20,960	5,000	315	22,968	0	17,000

COLORADO

ADAMS STATE COLLEGE	PUB-FG	220,650	125,198	16,855	20,752	12,396	24,427	469	5,282	3,825	11,446
AIMS COMMUNITY COLLEGE	PUB-T	88,907	39,788	7,905	7,011	19,367	8,569	1,574	1,916	0	2,777
ARAPAHOE CMTY COLLEGE	PUB-T	171,934	94,585	12,274	9,696	18,373	8,735	2,100	16,235	615	9,321
AURARIA JOINT LIBRARY	PUB-FN	1,651,925	845,230	104,808	65,040	337,844	107,870	58,976	24,010	10,293	97,494
BAPT BIBLE C OF DENVER	PRI-FG	10,308	B	0	2,018	250	1,200	0	0	340	B

COLORADO COLLEGE	PRI-FG	434,011	185,820	28,105	25,832	83,184	61,022	0	2,607	15,662	31,779
COLO MTN COLLEGE ALL CAM											
COLO MTN COLLEGE EAST CAM	PUB-T	74,035	40,678	6,144	685	12,506	4,227	1,243	3,718	0	4,834
COLO MTN COLLEGE WEST CAM	PUB-T	78,340	45,300	8,620	0	7,520	4,500	1,000	2,500	0	8,900
COLORADO NORTHWESTERN CC	PUB-T	64,753	31,470	5,193	0	16,164	3,995	978	2,323	6	4,624

COLORADO SCHOOL OF MINES	PUB-FG	557,309	258,372	32,100	3,115	74,892	158,577	3,047	0	10,505	16,701
COLORADO STATE UNIVERSITY	PUB-U	2,792,103	1,336,813	141,218	110,941	271,856	493,415	4,061	355	76,953	356,491
COLO TECHNICAL COLLEGE	PRI-FN	5,773	B	0	0	1,800	193	0	0	0	B
COLORADO WOMEN'S COLLEGE	PRI-FN	119,244	66,678	6,001	16,709	9,253	8,167	468	297	4,227	7,444
CC OF DENVER ALL CAM											

SEE FOOTNOTES AT END OF TABLE

Table 2. — Library Operating Expenditures (in Dollars) of College and University Libraries, by Category of Expenditure and by State or Other Area and Institution: Aggregate United States, 1978-79 — Continued

STATE OR OTHER AREA AND INSTITUTION	CON-TROL AND TYPE OF IN-STITU-TION	TOTAL	SALARIES AND WAGES			BOOK-STOCK	PERIOD-ICALS	MICRO-FORMS	AUDIO-VISUAL	BIND-ING AND RE-BIND-ING	ALL OTHER OPER-ATING EXPEND-ITURES
			LIBRARY STAFF	FRINGE BENEFITS	STUDENTS ON HOURLY BASIS						
(1)	(2)	(3)	(4)	(5)	(6)	(7)	(8)	(9)	(10)	(11)	(12)
COLORADO	--CONTINUED										
CC OF DENVER AURARIA CAM	PUB T				SEE AURARIA JOINT LIBRARY						
CC OF DENVER NORTH CAMPUS	PUB-T	385,762	205,875	26,121	12,936	35,137	13,817	11,823	56,688	0	23,365
CC DENVER RED ROCKS CAM	PUB-T	340,749	173,537	22,145	9,068	39,362	14,988	7,261	46,603	684	27,101
CONS BAPTIST THEOL SEM	PRI-FG	90,408	34,333	3,826	10,237	26,743	4,015	0	0	4,255	6,999
FORT LEWIS COLLEGE	PUB-FN	354,358	190,838	24,977	9,219	64,253	39,973	395	11,219	489	12,995
ILIFF SCHOOL OF THEOLOGY	PRI-FG	164,437	74,743	9,405	7,140	23,920	15,830	10,305	408	1,861	20,825
INTERMOUNTAIN BIBLE C	PRI-FN	8,284	B	0	1,884	3,598	193	0	197	0	B
LAMAR COMMUNITY COLLEGE	PUB-T	33,001	B	B	170	3,362	1,956	916	116	0	B
LORETTO HEIGHTS COLLEGE	PRI-FN	125,417	53,542	10,308	19,464	10,716	10,904	537	4,137	2,096	13,713
MESA COLLEGE	PUB-FN	230,570	107,751	14,381	18,590	47,935	22,923	1,873	9,443	3,414	4,260
METROPOLITAN ST COLLEGE	PUB FN				SEE AURARIA JOINT LIBRARY						
MORGAN COMMUNITY COLLEGE	PUB-T	30,315	B	B	3,744	8,960	1,365	0	2,777	0	B
NAZARENE BIBLE COLLEGE	PRI-T	58,113	28,505	3,945	6,227	7,715	3,154	5,448	454	0	2,665
NORTHEASTERN JR COLLEGE	PUB-T	82,198	47,100	6,400	0	13,685	7,374	2,391	702	1,032	3,514
OTERO JUNIOR COLLEGE	PUB-T	A	A	A	A	A	A	A	A	A	A
PARKS COLLEGE	PRI-T	A	A							A	
PIKES-PEAK CMTY COLLEGE	PUB-T	351,340	166,976	21,199	0	29,864	18,016	3,444	49,981	447	61,413
PUEBLO VOCATIONAL CC	PUB-T	A	A	A	A	A	A	A	A	A	A
REGIS COLLEGE	PRI-FG	164,966	69,500	8,356	21,181	20,151	16,743	481	2,244	6,558	19,752
ROCKMONT COLLEGE	PRI-FN	27,069	B	0	0	13,517	945	480	207	0	B
SAINT THOMAS SEMINARY	PRI-FG	79,702	B	B	8,472	16,613	8,460	200	0	1,698	B
TRINIDAD STATE JR COLLEGE	PUB-T	95,461	46,660	5,991	0	22,806	4,874	425	1,510	1,541	11,654
U OF COLORADO ALL INST											
U OF COLORADO AT BOULDER	PUB-U	4,117,433	2,178,775	226,934	309,301	513,554	553,243	0	0	72,013	263,613
U OF COLO COLO SPRINGS	PUB-FG	441,036	154,788	18,404	30,253	121,205	57,156	11,220	0	8,610	39,400
U OF COLO AT DENVER	PUB FG				SEE AURARIA JOINT LIBRARY						
U OF COLO HLTH SCI CENTER	PUB-FG	763,434	407,360	51,103	688	54,052	140,840	0	0	18,000	91,391
UNIVERSITY OF DENVER	PRI-U	1,763,774	655,560	114,341	59,806	295,770	404,899	18,957	14,000	35,000	165,441
U OF NORTHERN COLORADO	PUB-FG	1,568,690	885,260	113,070	22,527	225,800	167,261	29,152	25,203	21,622	78,795
U OF SOUTHERN COLORADO	PUB-FG	448,124	251,962	33,396	0	54,544	46,827	6,236	28,363	10,000	16,796
WESTERN BIBLE COLLEGE	PRI-FN	23,794	B	B	0	10,000	2,500	0	0	0	B
WESTERN ST COLLEGE COLO	PUB-FG	316,116	148,054	18,638	20,822	55,316	40,020	8,388	6,761	3,000	15,117
YESH TORAS CHAIM TALMUD	PRI-FG	A	A			A				A	
CONNECTICUT											
ALBERTUS MAGNUS COLLEGE	PRI-FN	74,361	36,313	1,750	5,898	14,926	5,726	1,044	510	1,205	6,989
ANNHURST COLLEGE	PRI-FN	42,946	B	0	9,338	5,569	2,180	167	297	0	B
ASNUNTUCK CMTY COLLEGE	PUB-T	72,018	B	B	0	4,553	2,775	2,053	1,028	0	B
BAIS BINYOMIN ACADEMY	PRI-FG	A				A				A	A
BOARD STATE ACAD AWARDS	PUB-T				NO LIBRARY FACILITIES						
BRIDGEPORT ENGR INSTITUTE	PRI-FN	5,700	0	0	0	1,500	100	0	0	0	4,100
CENTRAL CONN ST COLLEGE	PUB-FG	706,519	415,647	8,346	15,806	175,000	55,000	0	1,500	12,000	23,220
CONNECTICUT COLLEGE	PRI-FG	578,375	244,340	48,868	35,025	105,861	58,043	4,771	4,669	14,788	62,010
EASTERN CONN ST COLLEGE	PUB-FG	337,492	188,829	44,790	3,758	72,309	17,761	0	0	798	9,727
FAIRFIELD UNIVERSITY	PRI-FG	448,545	195,183	25,837	13,710	96,091	56,319	7,264	1,382	6,562	46,197
GREATER HARTFORD CC	PUB-T	136,114	71,553	16,972	21,377	10,645	7,560	2,216	3,180	483	2,128
GREATER NEW HAVEN TECH c/	PUB-T				NO LIBRARY FACILITIES						
HARTFORD COLLEGE WOMEN	PRI-T	39,505	B	B	8,489	8,691	2,266	0	558	0	B
HARTFORD GRADUATE CENTER	PRI-FG	65,420	B	B	0	6,094	14,048	180	0	0	B
HARTFORD SEM FOUNDATION	PRI-FG	A	A	A	A	A					A
HARTFORD ST TECH COLLEGE	PUB-T	32,613	B	B	0	300	2,500	0	0	0	B
HOLY APOSTLES COLLEGE	PRI-FG	64,385	55,260	0	0	4,750	875	0	0	0	3,500
HOUSATONIC REGIONAL CC	PUB-T	185,057	90,253	19,789	2,585	12,465	4,711	713	12,017	807	41,717
MANCHESTER CMTY COLLEGE	PUB-T	179,180	117,623	29,535	0	12,618	8,535	1,015	2,366	0	7,488
MATTATUCK CMTY COLLEGE	PUB-T	171,551	95,073	24,243	12,720	13,770	3,593	3,825	8,814	0	9,513
MIDDLESEX CMTY COLLEGE	PUB-T	94,321	69,299	0	0	9,198	5,945	3,479	161	237	6,002
MITCHELL COLLEGE	PRI-T	61,581	37,150	5,247	3,369	10,200	1,605	680	1,530	0	1,800
MOHEGAN COMMUNITY COLLEGE	PUB-T	94,711	62,534	14,833	0	8,978	3,141	0	209	0	5,016
MT SACRED HEART COLLEGE	PRI-T	4,972	B	0	0	1,500	1,000	0	300	0	B
NTHWSTN CONN CMTY COLLEGE	PUB-T	102,029	B	B	6,829	5,427	4,466	764	0	128	B
NORWALK COMMUNITY COLLEGE	PUB-T	133,056	109,127	0	0	5,467	3,820	3,541	6,240	1,706	3,155
NORWALK ST TECH COLLEGE	PUB-T	55,269	B	B	0	10,654	4,103	0	8,803	0	B
POST COLLEGE	PRI-FN	61,777	B	0	0	24,000	6,000	2,810	0	0	B
QUINEBAUG VALLEY CC	PUB-T	158,405	54,195	13,608	0	4,875	4,635	836	0	2,430	80,256
QUINNIPIAC COLLEGE	PRI-FG	393,864	216,535	32,897	1,599	45,436	37,110	5,081	27,239		25,537

SEE FOOTNOTES AT END OF TABLE

Table 2. — Library Operating Expenditures (in Dollars) of College and University Libraries, by Category of Expenditure and by State or Other Area and Institution: Aggregate United States, 1978-79 — Continued

STATE OR OTHER AREA AND INSTITUTION	CON-TROL AND TYPE OF IN-STITU-TION	TOTAL	SALARIES AND WAGES			BOOK-STOCK	PERIOD-ICALS	MICRO-FORMS	AUDIO-VISUAL	BIND-ING AND RE-BIND-ING	ALL OTHER OPER-ATING EXPEND-ITURES
			LIBRARY STAFF	FRINGE BENEFITS	STUDENTS ON HOURLY BASIS						
(1)	(2)	(3)	(4)	(5)	(6)	(7)	(8)	(9)	(10)	(11)	(12)
CONNECTICUT	--CONTINUED										
SACRED HEART UNIVERSITY	PRI-FG	209,576	105,000	0	20,300	42,237	20,878	4,186	496	1,526	14,953
SAINT ALPHONSUS COLLEGE	PRI-FN	12,844	0	0	0	3,157	4,112	31	300	1,492	2,000
SAINT BASIL'S COLLEGE	PRI-FN	20,784	B	B	0	1,492	1,074	0	0	0	B
SAINT JOSEPH COLLEGE	PRI-FG	128,737	92,003	4,834	0	12,520	11,800	1,294	1,206	2,000	3,080
SAINT THOMAS SEMINARY	PRI-T	20,774	B	0	1,170	3,164	1,637	19	0	1,419	B
SOUTH CEN CMTY COLLEGE	PUB-T	153,713	109,686	0	0	21,690	5,453	1,470	7,673	0	7,738
SOUTHERN CONN ST COLLEGE	PUB-FG	721,375	462,200	105,525	0	80,500	48,200	9,500	4,500	7,300	3,650
THAMES VLY STATE TECH C	PUB-T	36,011	B	B	0	400	2,000	0	0	0	B
TRINITY COLLEGE	PRI-FG	660,177	292,320	50,405	40,665	117,291	83,509	7,501	0	13,953	54,533
TUNXIS COMMUNITY COLLEGE	PUB-T	108,815	57,616	11,802	0	16,278	8,302	1,899	2,337	0	10,581
UNIVERSITY OF BRIDGEPORT2/	PRI-FG	654,231	331,688	54,261	36,326	82,000	86,980	10,000	400	8,500	44,076
U OF CONN ALL CAMPUSES											
UNIVERSITY OF CONNECTICUT	PUB-U	3,739,540	1,741,961	0	292,375	766,464	548,171	88,256	10,893	52,711	238,709
U OF CONN HEALTH CENTER	PUB-FG	892,303	368,718	79,274	38,493	50,337	201,887	380	42,630	15,078	95,506
UNIVERSITY OF HARTFORD	PRI-FG	541,500	233,000	0	58,600	122,900	83,800	2,000	0	9,100	32,100
UNIVERSITY OF NEW HAVEN	PRI-FG	485,102	237,136	39,936	5,583	110,517	30,806	14,797	8,072	4,490	33,765
WATERBURY ST TECH COLLEGE	PUB-T	41,982	B	B	0	6,500	2,000	30	1,500	0	B
WESLEYAN UNIVERSITY	PRI-FG	1,155,213	490,365	96,317	52,592	192,154	234,250	0	0	27,442	62,093
WESTERN CONN ST COLLEGE	PUB-FG	408,078	213,584	50,662	34,020	71,370	19,212	9,799	1,976	1,491	5,964
YALE UNIVERSITY	PRI-U	12,397,438	6,402,670	1,033,110	299,310	1,454,842	1,163,418	161,726	26,990	264,646	1,590,726
DELAWARE											
BRANDYWINE C OF WIDENER U	PRI-T	69,989	B	B	8,034	9,009	3,479	3,568	725	902	B
DELAWARE STATE COLLEGE	PUB-FN	348,411	188,149	40,841	33,645	53,599	17,963	1,595	753	2,584	9,282
DEL TECH & CC ALL CAM											
DEL TECH & CC STHN CAM	PUB-T	121,565	86,865	18,242	0	4,800	6,500	1,200	1,000	0	2,958
DEL TECH & CC STANTON CAM	PUB-T	147,718	B	0	0	9,755	4,960	542	1,440	0	B
DEL TECH & CC TERRY CAM	PUB-T	107,417	56,212	11,367	0	20,794	4,426	12	14,411	0	195
DEL TECH & CC WILMINGTON	PUB-T	151,029	84,345	18,555	0	35,381	5,533	1,286	2,909	0	3,020
GOLDEY BEACOM COLLEGE	PRI-FN	54,104	B	B	590	7,689	2,999	2,005	852	28	B
UNIVERSITY OF DELAWARE	PUB-U	2,606,660	915,647	163,900	118,750	667,492	440,055	50,430	0	85,287	165,099
WESLEY COLLEGE	PRI-FN	118,111	72,382	13,029	977	16,669	6,976	2,305	2,852	825	2,096
WILMINGTON COLLEGE	PRI-FG	54,022	B	B	786	11,571	6,389	523	3,772	124	B
DISTRICT OF COLUMBIA											
AMERICAN UNIVERSITY	PRI-U	1,560,957	626,399	74,004	106,067	250,975	346,903	22,279	5,586	27,776	100,968
BEACON COLLEGE	PRI-FG		NO LIBRARY FACILITIES								
CATHOLIC U OF AMERICA	PRI-U	1,609,253	792,591	76,307	136,816	192,355	212,254	32,394	2,078	19,703	144,755
CORCORAN SCHOOL OF ART	PRI-FG	3,346	0	0	0	1,860	586	0	0	500	400
DOMINICAN HOUSE STUDIES	PRI-FG	61,481	B	B	0	11,857	3,490	0	0	2,129	B
GALLAUDET COLLEGE	PRI-FG	765,220	402,811	41,916	43,606	78,725	16,187	60,817	20,013	3,000	98,145
GEORGETOWN UNIVERSITY	PRI-U	3,897,029	1,678,554	365,973	277,962	476,730	552,535	89,833	33,491	87,725	334,226
GEORGE WASH UNIVERSITY	PRI-U	3,131,146	1,277,947	194,790	268,188	416,513	378,110	0	10,339	51,269	533,990
HOWARD UNIVERSITY	PRI-U	5,168,802	2,771,587	554,317	124,700	827,896	462,603	0	0	38,008	389,691
MOUNT VERNON COLLEGE	PRI-FN	124,567	63,780	11,997	435	19,771	6,110	5,640	3,993	0	12,641
OBLATE COLLEGE	PRI-FG	A	A	A	A	A	A	A		A	A
SOUTHEASTERN UNIVERSITY	PRI-FG	99,542	B	B	3,500	7,477	9,544	0	13,893	0	B
STRAYER COLLEGE	PRI-FN	58,830	B	B	4,572	6,141	3,954	0	532	88	B
TRINITY COLLEGE	PRI-FG	117,766	53,006	6,100	11,145	26,160	13,940	2,250	1,150	1,913	2,102
UNIVERSITY OF DC	PUB-FG	2,279,224	1,488,185	320,039	0	182,690	94,575	47,444	40,000	3,002	103,289
WASH INTRNATL COLLEGE1/	PRI-FN		NO LIBRARY FACILITIES								
WESLEY THEOLOGICAL SEM	PRI-FG	136,750	64,217	0	12,614	33,640	8,902	0	1,665	4,541	10,171
FLORIDA											
BARRY COLLEGE	PRI-FG	257,235	164,773	13,446	0	42,633	18,576	1,142	1,138	2,257	13,270
BAUDER FASHION COLLEGE	PRI-T	A	A	A		A	A	A	A	A	A
BETHUNE COOKMAN COLLEGE	PRI-FN	244,200	125,943	17,488	15,004	66,522	4,240	2,111	0	5,035	7,857
BISCAYNE COLLEGE	PRI-FG	117,194	57,729	3,294	6,113	25,608	11,202	1,453	1,833	37	9,925
BREVARD CMTY COLLEGE	PUB-T	711,868	403,245	65,240	0	64,803	28,584	6,500	42,176	1,331	99,989
BROWARD CMTY COLLEGE	PUB-T	1,055,205	630,406	121,779	0	142,769	28,102	21,565	27,040	3,640	79,904
CENTRAL FLA CMTY COLLEGE	PUB-T	236,909	128,948	18,377	0	31,805	8,847	4,285	29,870	983	13,794
CHIPOLA JUNIOR COLLEGE	PUB-T	189,306	117,829	16,452	0	21,190	10,070	0	10,640	3,221	9,904
CLEARWATER CHRISTIAN C	PRI-FN	14,467	B	B	2,093	550	764	0	0	0	B
COLLEGE OF BOCA RATON	PRI-T	24,519	B	B	0	6,451	3,726	0	2,619	764	B
DAYTONA BCH CMTY COLLEGE	PUB-T	581,744	325,041	65,082	0	36,177	8,937	1,094	57,294	0	88,119

SEE FOOTNOTES AT END OF TABLE

Table 2. — Library Operating Expenditures (in Dollars) of College and University Libraries, by Category of Expenditure and by State or Other Area and Institution: Aggregate United States, 1978-79 — Continued

STATE OR OTHER AREA AND INSTITUTION	CONTROL AND TYPE OF INSTITUTION	TOTAL	SALARIES AND WAGES			BOOK-STOCK	PERIODICALS	MICRO-FORMS	AUDIO-VISUAL	BINDING AND RE-BINDING	ALL OTHER OPERATING EXPENDITURES
			LIBRARY STAFF	FRINGE BENEFITS	STUDENTS ON HOURLY BASIS						
(1)	(2)	(3)	(4)	(5)	(6)	(7)	(8)	(9)	(10)	(11)	(12)
FLORIDA --CONTINUED											
ECKERD COLLEGE	PRI-FN	205,456	88,597	19,491	0	24,644	49,845	3,143	73	6,291	13,372
EDISON COMMUNITY COLLEGE	PUB-T	361,857	182,248	33,219	29,073	39,534	6,620	3,000	10,148	0	58,015
EDWARD WATERS COLLEGE	PRI-FN	145,967	74,450	4,963	0	30,000	3,000	4,000	4,000	1,000	24,554
EMBRY-RIDDLE AERON U	PRI-FG	307,485	99,000	14,850	24,000	40,000	23,800	1,200	15,000	1,000	88,635
FLAGLER COLLEGE	PRI-FN	123,969	48,308	1,646	8,138	39,434	8,340	3,369	298	0	14,436
FLORIDA BEACON COLLEGE	PRI-FG	A	A			A	A		A	A	A
FLORIDA COLLEGE	PRI-T	54,095	28,218	3,892	9,572	6,408	3,458	0	50	378	2,119
FLORIDA INST TECHNOLOGY	PRI-FG	316,305	142,575	14,257	0	51,400	76,000	500	187	9,400	21,986
FLA JR COLLEGE JACKSONVL	PUB-T	1,490,349	870,951	126,260	0	180,121	51,655	20,826	78,028	1,349	161,159
FLORIDA KEYS CMTY COLLEGE	PUB-T	110,827	74,684	13,204	0	9,486	4,811	1,630	1,790	0	5,222
FLORIDA MEMORIAL COLLEGE	PRI-FN	85,363	58,400	5,000	0	8,506	6,000	0	0	0	7,457
FLORIDA SOUTHERN COLLEGE	PRI-FN	232,345	87,573	8,701	10,744	47,699	35,490	4,767	0	8,682	28,689
FORT LAUDERDALE COLLEGE	PRI-FN	A	A	A	A	A	A		A	A	A
GULF COAST CMTY COLLEGE	PUB-T	301,087	177,735	28,021	6,000	24,546	8,802	5,358	12,585	4,748	33,292
HEED UNIVERSITY	PRI-FG	A	A	A	A	A	A				A
HILLSBOROUGH CMTY COLLEGE	PUB-T	307,034	168,207	23,705	4,169	80,469	10,725	880	10,223	0	8,656
HOREB SEMINARY	PRI-FN	A	A			A					
INDIAN RIVER CMTY COLLEGE	PUB-T	216,491	100,726	18,355	0	40,342	6,064	2,000	44,744	589	3,671
INTERNATIONAL FINE ARTS C	PRI-T	A	A			A	A		A	A	A
JACKSONVILLE UNIVERSITY	PRI-FG	267,537	140,813	16,898	15,134	46,597	14,211	0	3,335	3,677	26,872
JONES COLLEGE ALL CAM											
JONES COLLEGE JACKSONVL	PRI-FN	22,609	B	0	0	5,889	1,701	0	1,590	0	B
JONES COLLEGE ORLANDO	PRI-FN	18,748	B	0	0	7,420	2,226	0	0	0	B
LAKE CITY CMTY COLLEGE	PUB-T	221,807	98,888	17,079	8,086	11,818	6,433	7,118	42,615	169	29,601
LAKE-SUMTER CMTY COLLEGE	PUB-T	152,902	92,320	15,167	0	15,265	6,707	1,522	6,062	1,650	14,209
LAKELAND C BUS AND FASH	PRI-T	A	A	A	A	A	A		A		A
LUTHER RICE SEMINARY	PRI-FG	32,375	B	B	700	5,875	350	150	0	0	B
MANATEE JUNIOR COLLEGE	PUB-T	245,603	157,384	26,009	17,010	250	8,280	1,894	24,129	965	9,682
MIAMI CHRISTIAN COLLEGE	PRI-FN	80,844	30,667	3,657	6,912	17,925	1,812	50	3,790	2,995	13,036
MIAMI-DADE CMTY COLLEGE	PUB-T	1,899,708	1,174,011	225,559	0	251,760	104,706	43,755	0	12,692	87,225
MORRIS C OF BUSINESS	PRI-T	6,206	B	0	0	281	483	0	0	0	B
NORTH FLORIDA JR COLLEGE	PUB-T	104,434	59,778	7,373	0	16,760	3,411	5,463	10,461	296	892
NOVA UNIVERSITY	PRI-FG	596,167	183,499	25,500	22,556	118,832	155,944	15,000	30,000	7,788	37,048
OKALOOSA-WALTON JUNIOR C	PUB-T	296,300	185,705	30,590	0	39,809	11,360	3,380	5,427	0	20,029
PALM BCH ATLANTIC COLLEGE	PRI-FN	86,431	40,325	5,242	7,920	18,500	7,500	833	0	1,000	4,108
PALM BEACH JUNIOR COLLEGE	PUB-T	554,962	349,161	50,940	3,327	53,592	16,399	6,200	20,690	6,300	48,353
PASCO-HERNANDO CC	PUB-T	265,543	104,042	18,207	0	113,321	7,642	2,901	4,121	0	15,309
PENSACOLA JUNIOR COLLEGE	PUB-T	662,091	346,152	59,634	72	101,230	41,459	6,551	71,640	6,216	29,137
POLK COMMUNITY COLLEGE	PUB-T	333,770	190,284	37,807	0	51,181	7,795	6,661	16,195	1,826	22,021
RINGLING SCHOOL OF ART	PRI-FN	71,130	30,200	3,200	980	13,000	2,000	0	18,000	1,000	2,750
ROLLINS COLLEGE	PRI-FG	364,254	194,508	22,480	0	88,593	37,370	3,748	189	5,515	11,851
SAINT JOHNS RIVER CC	PUB-T	117,900	68,166	10,770	0	17,796	2,774	45	1,403	1,342	15,604
SNT JOHN VIANNEY C SEM	PRI-FN	35,734	B	B	0	8,021	1,820	0	1,020	1,025	B
SAINT LEO COLLEGE	PRI-FN	142,470	92,094	10,632	74	17,117	10,326	2,290	1,235	1,030	7,672
SAINT PETERSBG JR COLLEGE	PUB-T	844,160	550,459	90,922	36,583	39,853	21,427	721	19,535	3,453	81,207
SANTA FE CMTY COLLEGE	PUB-T	252,820	125,711	21,371	8,809	53,840	8,509	1,402	22,390	2,312	8,476
SEM SAINT VINCENT DE PAUL	PRI-FG	53,471	B	0	0	15,627	4,058	200	0	1,840	B
SEMINOLE CMTY COLLEGE	PUB-T	430,467	203,896	30,344	1,265	58,136	21,201	10,271	42,223	2,403	60,728
STHESTN C ASSEMBLIES GOD	PRI-FN	84,781	40,500	10,000	16,820	14,996	2,465	0	0	0	B
SOUTH FLORIDA JR COLLEGE	PUB-T	85,934	47,234	7,131	0	12,363	3,558	0	4,857	304	10,487
ST U SYS OF FLA ALL INST											
FLA AGRICULTURAL & MECH U	PUB-U	1,336,938	352,022	105,150	15,049	102,122	154,444	324	3,476	5,586	598,765
FLA ATLANTIC UNIVERSITY	PUB-FG	1,426,204	478,155	87,104	35,638	328,909	347,671	66,147	26,829	13,478	42,273
FLORIDA INTERNATIONAL U	PUB-FG	2,913,628	831,463	133,557	208,820	901,107	351,704	95,647	256,679	37,757	96,894
FLORIDA STATE UNIVERSITY	PUB-U	5,829,581	1,770,079	265,878	208,732	1,291,660	940,190	549,755	208,114	164,963	430,210
U OF CENTRAL FLORIDA	PUB-FG	1,908,880	586,062	87,330	79,062	427,508	346,087	142,413	57,873	44,821	137,724
UNIVERSITY OF FLORIDA	PUB-U	7,521,173	2,444,932	409,671	512,511	3,266,474	0	0	72,095	381,967	433,523
U OF NORTH FLORIDA	PUB-FG	1,419,604	394,949	61,727	56,112	270,160	166,591	96,381	66,640	26,097	280,947
U OF SOUTH FLORIDA	PUB-FG	4,299,803	1,497,697	209,203	93,850	1,036,832	903,881	9,497	106,563	120,271	322,009
U OF WEST FLORIDA	PUB-FG	1,480,185	422,523	125,170	45,517	331,918	231,755	189,667	6,758	37,619	89,258
STETSON UNIVERSITY	PRI-FG	317,968	139,087	26,858	23,203	70,682	25,497	0	606	9,681	22,354
TALLAHASSEE CMTY COLLEGE	PUB-T	273,247	137,834	22,637	26,703	29,850	13,456	5,417	19,513	413	17,424
TALMUDIC C OF FLORIDA	PRI-FG	A				A				A	A
TAMPA COLLEGE	PRI-FN	33,614	B	B	3,600	14,670	3,000	0	0	10	B
UNIVERSITY OF MIAMI	PRI-U	3,413,215	1,575,550	304,379	102,570	510,305	655,292	3,000	500	72,679	188,940

SEE FOOTNOTES AT END OF TABLE

Table 2. — Library Operating Expenditures (in Dollars) of College and University Libraries, by Category of Expenditure and by State or Other Area and Institution: Aggregate United States, 1978-79 — Continued

STATE OR OTHER AREA AND INSTITUTION	CON- TROL AND TYPE OF IN- STITU- TION	TOTAL	SALARIES AND WAGES			BOOK- STOCK	PERIOD- ICALS	MICRO- FORMS	AUDIO- VISUAL	BIND- ING AND RE- BIND- ING	ALL OTHER OPER- ATING EXPEND- ITURES
			LIBRARY STAFF	FRINGE BENEFITS	STUDENTS ON HOURLY BASIS						
(1)	(2)	(3)	(4)	(5)	(6)	(7)	(8)	(9)	(10)	(11)	(12)
FLORIDA	--CONTINUED										
UNIVERSITY OF SARASOTA	PRI-FG	23,308	B	B	0	2,567	1,832	1,800	0	0	B
UNIVERSITY OF TAMPA	PRI-FG	310,930	128,099	19,215	20,302	25,574	18,184	31,167	116	4,554	63,819
VALENCIA CMTY COLLEGE	PUB-T	554,945	345,367	57,016	12,929	54,381	20,368	13,613	14,214	1,155	35,902
WARNER SOUTHERN COLLEGE	PRI-FN	76,506	B	B	9,910	11,771	5,768	0	3,146	2,981	B
WEBBER COLLEGE	PRI-FN	35,201	B	B	0	7,065	2,173	111	1,281	B	B
GEORGIA											
ABRAHAM BALDWIN AGRL C	PUB-T	167,494	80,293	16,862	6,905	38,609	11,101	2,492	721	982	9,529
AGNES SCOTT COLLEGE	PRI-FN	232,262	102,019	16,185	8,500	56,594	26,289	0	532	3,803	18,340
ALBANY JUNIOR COLLEGE	PUB-T	232,426	123,725	24,071	2,082	30,399	21,410	2,728	3,906	3,034	21,071
ALBANY STATE COLLEGE	PUB-FN	230,407	134,611	0	4,862	31,442	42,268	30	0	5,629	11,565
ANDREW COLLEGE	PRI-T	30,416	1,800	0	0	6,487	1,639	0	1,792	281	1,161
ARMSTRONG STATE COLLEGE	PUB-FG	317,013	168,675	38,795	7,957	19,420	37,015	9,108	5,038	6,000	25,005
ATLANTA CHRISTIAN COLLEGE	PRI-FN	27,103	B	B	4,731	3,544	1,667	449	0	614	B
ATLANTA COLLEGE OF ART	PRI-FN	56,100	B	B	0	12,000	4,400	0	3,000	1,600	B
ATLANTA JUNIOR COLLEGE	PUB-T	187,462	62,693	12,410	0	23,591	10,788	28,958	11,558	0	37,464
ATLANTA UNIVERSITY	PRI-FG	370,091	192,516	19,958	34,800	41,834	55,848	1,810	2,300	5,736	15,289
AUGUSTA COLLEGE	PUB-FG	479,101	245,980	45,155	1,753	71,819	32,590	3,588	1,965	8,950	67,301
BAINBRIDGE JUNIOR COLLEGE	PUB-T	93,010	38,695	2,920	0	23,733	5,185	610	2,521	663	18,683
BERRY COLLEGE	PRI-FG	253,227	95,261	12,433	32,267	49,556	18,375	10,984	3,803	1,523	29,025
BRENAU COLLEGE	PRI-FG	63,087	35,693	0	11,762	9,448	2,833	1,234	100	1,047	970
BREWTON-PARKER COLLEGE	PRI-T	38,947	B	B	0	7,085	3,380	604	1,468	1,131	B
BRUNSWICK JUNIOR COLLEGE	PUB-T	197,128	93,923	18,463	1,263	20,947	11,229	8,857	3,494	1,406	37,546
CLARK COLLEGE	PRI-FN	158,509	68,167	8,400	38,642	22,945	4,643	0	0	16	15,696
CLAYTON JUNIOR COLLEGE	PUB-T	224,155	101,683	9,242	10,851	29,216	13,702	1,894	10,803	2,280	44,484
COLUMBIA THEOLOGICAL SEM	PRI-FG	90,296	51,406	12,644	0	18,008	3,332	200	500	1,631	2,575
COLUMBUS COLLEGE	PUB-FG	614,484	243,274	53,520	27,238	147,199	49,017	28,382	6,956	7,364	51,534
COVENANT COLLEGE	PRI-FN	103,599	B	B	7,069	15,723	8,984	3,228	5,533	0	B
CRANDALL COLLEGE	PRI-T	15,913	B	B	2,640	750	183	0	40	0	B
DALTON JUNIOR COLLEGE	PUB-T	192,027	87,195	0	0	45,418	9,070	14,733	16,263	903	18,445
DEKALB COMMUNITY COLLEGE	PUB-T	A	A	A	A	A	A	A	A	A	A
DRAUGHON'S JC BUSINESS	PRI-T	14,210	B	B	0	2,122	406	0	0	0	B
EMANUEL CO JUNIOR COLLEGE	PUB-T	85,405	35,380	8,285	2,800	18,800	8,000	2,056	2,675	809	6,600
EMMANUEL COLLEGE	PRI-T	41,945	B	B	5,282	7,074	2,118	0	421	562	B
EMMANUEL SCH MINISTRIES3/	PRI-FN	NO LIBRARY FACILITIES									
EMORY UNIVERSITY	PRI-U	3,765,138	1,516,060	193,225	175,566	804,365	718,644	0	0	95,097	262,181
FLOYD JUNIOR COLLEGE	PUB-T	192,764	107,650	23,683	1,890	37,102	5,812	2,603	4,522	1,263	8,239
FORT VALLEY STATE COLLEGE	PUB-FG	366,675	181,383	36,276	6,754	70,082	45,323	1,530	2,764	6,076	16,487
GAINESVILLE JR COLLEGE	PUB-T	118,562	59,209	12,300	1,325	20,738	7,534	2,871	2,709	1,114	10,762
GEORGIA COLLEGE	PUB-FG	414,072	187,700	30,434	25,757	44,571	60,207	8,831	3,418	4,600	48,554
GA INST TECHN ALL CAM											
GA INST OF TECHN MAIN CAM	PUB-FG	2,549,363	964,923	191,574	113,996	108,847	671,363	106,935	0	114,199	277,526
GA INST TECHN-STHN TECH	PUB-FN	188,512	74,072	13,870	9,576	15,190	36,575	2,356	861	8,500	27,512
GEORGIA MILITARY COLLEGE	PRI-T	35,085	B	0	1,900	8,534	184	700	0	0	55,438
GEORGIA SOUTHERN COLLEGE	PUB-FG	786,803	408,694	0	38,586	284,085	0	0	0	0	55,438
GA SOUTHWESTERN COLLEGE	PUB-FG	338,457	144,613	13,286	6,831	80,576	51,370	5,488	141	13,700	22,452
GEORGIA STATE UNIVERSITY	PUB-FG	2,630,041	1,008,465	193,593	184,752	522,780	486,540	0	0	59,568	174,343
GORDON JUNIOR COLLEGE	PUB-T	218,255	79,047	10,000	1,551	58,108	8,013	8,908	21,358	1,387	29,883
INTRDENOMINATL THEOL CTR	PRI-FG	66,851	40,750	5,561	0	14,763	440	0	0	1,211	4,126
KENNESAW COLLEGE	PUB-FN	356,439	145,571	30,396	16,767	65,548	28,054	5,753	17,400	524	46,426
LA GRANGE COLLEGE	PRI-FG	103,075	55,770	6,853	0	25,026	7,336	2,643	912	2,683	1,852
LIFE CHIROPRACTIC COLLEGE	PRI-FG	44,642	24,987	3,748	0	12,166	0	0	0	0	3,741
MACON JUNIOR COLLEGE	PUB-T	158,000	79,276	0	0	29,794	13,618	4,320	6,931	1,615	22,446
MEDICAL COLLEGE OF GA	PUB-FG	655,589	282,620	71,762	12,896	30,000	132,000	0	14,000	20,500	91,811
MERCER U ALL CAMPUSES											
MERCER U MAIN CAMPUS	PRI-FG	586,862	231,309	38,486	20,508	99,246	134,376	11,181	4,077	10,267	37,412
MERCER U IN ATLANTA	PRI-FG	168,230	70,793	12,540	838	44,208	15,384	6,324	1,480	1,470	15,193
MERCER U STHN SCHOOL PHAR	PRI-FG	79,818	B	0	5,810	9,000	6,000	0	0	1,650	B
MIDDLE GEORGIA COLLEGE	PUB-T	203,829	100,422	34,529	159	30,135	13,097	3,292	5,790	1,794	14,611
MOREHOUSE COLLEGE	PRI-FG	A	A	A	A	A	A	A	A	A	A
MORRIS BROWN COLLEGE	PRI-FN	147,062	66,821	6,147	5,633	37,554	9,761	0	2,847	2,027	16,272
NORTH GEORGIA COLLEGE	PUB-FG	242,013	115,241	18,481	10,865	31,280	25,208	11,370	2,950	4,895	21,723
OGLETHORPE UNIVERSITY	PRI-FG	103,908	64,385	10,689	0	9,428	14,484	0	819	1,951	2,152
PAINE COLLEGE	PRI-FN	103,700	36,613	6,679	0	45,014	8,925	3,314	588	1,556	1,011
PHILLIPS COLLEGE	PRI-T	A	A		A	A					

SEE FOOTNOTES AT END OF TABLE

Table 2. – Library Operating Expenditures (in Dollars) of College and University Libraries, by Category of Expenditure and by State or Other Area and Institution: Aggregate United States, 1978-79

STATE OR OTHER AREA AND INSTITUTION	CON-TROL AND TYPE OF IN-STITU-TION	TOTAL	SALARIES AND WAGES			BOOK-STOCK	PERIOD-ICALS	MICRO-FORMS	AUDIO-VISUAL	BIND-ING AND RE-BIND-ING	ALL OTHER OPER-ATING EXPEND-ITURES
			LIBRARY STAFF	FRINGE BENEFITS	STUDENTS ON HOURLY BASIS						
(1)	(2)	(3)	(4)	(5)	(6)	(7)	(8)	(9)	(10)	(11)	(12)
GEORGIA	**--CONTINUED**										
PHILLIPS COLLEGE	PRI-T	A	A	A	A	A	A		A	A	A
PIEDMONT COLLEGE	PRI-FN	64,917	B	B	7,000	26,312	5,000	0	4,712	3,500	B
REINHARDT COLLEGE	PRI-T	71,150	42,610	4,097	5,374	10,992	2,230	86	1,970	393	3,398
SAVANNAH STATE COLLEGE	PUB-FG	261,086	142,195	0	0	56,839	39,836	0	2,911	4,861	14,444
SHORTER COLLEGE	PRI-FN	98,228	43,535	0	5,234	27,097	8,026	500	2,500	2,140	9,196
SOUTH GEORGIA COLLEGE	PUB-T	147,682	90,875	16,525	0	18,486	9,803	579	838	0	10,576
SPELMAN COLLEGE	PRI-FN	99,607	42,997	5,056	17,124	25,548	1,867	0	0	266	6,749
THOMAS COUNTY CC	PRI-T	19,264	B	B	0	2,708	900	0	0	0	84
TIFT COLLEGE	PRI-FN	74,623	B	B	13,380	15,534	1,486	2,148	462	1,929	B
TOCCOA FALLS COLLEGE	PRI-FN	57,442	B	B	8,710	12,695	2,848	730	404	1,394	B
TRUETT MCCONNELL COLLEGE	PRI-T	46,275	B	B	8,800	8,200	1,605	0	535	100	B
UNIVERSITY OF GEORGIA	PUB-U	5,376,965	2,146,171	364,849	228,713	968,793	1,110,638	0	0	161,267	396,534
VALDOSTA STATE COLLEGE	PUB-FG	739,695	338,319	67,102	7,898	113,249	82,918	16,669	26,301	15,178	72,061
WAYCROSS JUNIOR COLLEGE	PUB-T	106,593	44,624	0	0	36,058	3,686	3,718	3,435	819	14,253
WESLEYAN COLLEGE	PRI-FN	220,616	55,669	9,089	15,250	47,903	19,604	1,475	1,089	5,298	65,239
WEST GEORGIA COLLEGE	PUB-FG	605,610	293,272	57,714	29,786	90,078	69,525	6,839	0	3,941	54,455
YOUNG HARRIS COLLEGE	PRI-T	58,324	B	B	9,708	7,653	3,917	5,821	1,798	449	B
HAWAII											
CHAMINADE U OF HONOLULU	PRI-FG	124,666	69,369	6,943	8,110	20,274	6,758	757	9,791	500	2,164
HAWAII LOA COLLEGE	PRI-FN	76,999	B	B	15,555	10,400	9,000	1,500	800	0	B
HAWAII PACIFIC COLLEGE	PRI-FN	85,371	B	B	16,839	5,139	7,852	0	0	0	B
U OF HAWAII SYS ALL INST U OF HAWAII AT MANOA	PUB-U	5,393,978	2,377,657	524,560	240,372	660,041	745,430	37,708	2,443	121,025	684,742
U OF HAWAII AT HILO	PUB-FN	609,396	249,396	54,000	0	195,000	47,000	10,000	15,000	14,000	25,000
U OF HAWAII WEST OAHU C	PUB-FN	62,285	B	B	5,423	23,560	2,613	0	0	0	B
U OF HAWAII HONOLULU CC	PUB-T	354,971	209,300	52,325	0	26,962	5,359	8,131	27,201	0	25,693
U OF HAWAII KAPIOLANI CC	PUB-T	138,933	87,564	18,388	2,243	18,127	5,913	712	1,820	0	4,166
U OF HAWAII KAUAI CC	PUB-T	230,835	111,713	25,375	1,571	29,997	6,456	6,236	2,509	22	46,956
U OF HAWAII LEEWARD CC	PUB-T	295,152	212,880	36,190	0	24,823	5,042	3,208	178	78	12,753
U OF HAWAII MAUI CC	PUB-T	123,942	73,512	18,378	4,392	11,861	6,326	1,440	719	0	7,314
U OF HAWAII WINDWARD CC	PUB-T	121,070	54,885	12,075	950	28,041	4,128	1,892	9,366	206	9,527
IDAHO											
BOISE STATE UNIVERSITY	PUB-FG	1,234,293	603,587	117,296	23,645	203,225	98,948	2,730	49,859	20,088	114,915
COLLEGE OF IDAHO	PRI-FG	146,776	68,402	7,956	16,836	30,271	14,937	3,610	500	2,333	1,931
COLLEGE OF SOUTHERN IDAHO	PUB-T	167,299	108,333	20,583	0	12,703	5,792	1,500	203	1,226	16,959
IDAHO STATE UNIVERSITY	PUB-FG	1,387,471	518,715	108,415	70,040	324,935	180,928	25,658	21,630	1,451	135,699
LEWIS-CLARK ST COLLEGE	PUB-FN	209,134	111,358	25,481	16,916	26,577	10,269	4,153	723	1,402	12,255
NORTH IDAHO COLLEGE	PUB-T	120,270	57,180	10,353	0	19,686	10,390	0	13,404	1,035	8,222
NTHWST NAZARENE COLLEGE	PRI-FG	171,368	60,167	3,008	36,321	39,056	9,359	480	69	920	21,988
RICKS COLLEGE	PRI-T	745,809	406,070	0	61,483	157,660	17,463	29,217	5,576	3,493	64,847
UNIVERSITY OF IDAHO	PUB-U	1,774,090	784,302	142,707	70,942	335,556	291,941	18,140	5,574	24,903	100,025
ILLINOIS											
AERO-SPACE INSTITUTE	PRI-FN	15,200	B	0	0	500	700	0	0	0	B
ALFRED ADLER INST CHICAGO	PRI-FG	8,547	B	0	0	1,389	370	0	62	0	B
AMERICAN ACADEMY OF ART	PRI-T	NO LIBRARY FACILITIES									
AMERICAN CONSV OF MUSIC	PRI-FG	39,986	B	B	11,020	4,310	725	535	391	2,772	B
AUGUSTANA COLLEGE	PRI-FG	349,596	149,519	20,454	28,241	74,400	28,466	9,498	544	4,526	33,948
AURORA COLLEGE	PRI-FN	123,377	73,227	7,323	9,554	19,045	5,445	0	0	1,342	7,441
BARAT COLLEGE	PRI-FN	117,475	53,643	8,046	20,359	14,800	8,600	0	766	2,000	9,261
BELLEVILLE AREA COLLEGE	PUB-T	195,990	132,656	3,310	5,818	29,169	7,347	2,525	1,409	1,471	12,285
BETHANY-NTHN BAPT JT LIB	PRI-FG	141,307	54,959	14,078	14,552	19,419	10,058	0	774	2,532	24,935
BETHANY THEOLOGICAL SEM	PRI FG	SEE BETHANY-NTHN BAPT JT LIB									
BLACKBURN COLLEGE	PRI-FN	96,471	46,396	7,183	1,117	15,106	11,910	1,366	3,168	1,692	8,533
BLACK HAWK C ALL CAMPUSES											
BLACK HAWK C EAST CAMPUS	PUB-T	62,916	36,454	1,798	2,691	8,420	5,411	1,137	3,862	0	3,143
BLACK HAWK C QUAD-CITIES	PUB-T	205,739	131,311	12,862	13,137	24,797	7,553	3,019	4,877	1,322	6,861
BRADLEY UNIVERSITY	PRI-U	557,067	239,700	0	46,219	116,364	94,201	0	0	11,051	49,532
BRISK RABBINICAL COLLEGE	PRI-FG	A			A	A				A	
CARL SANDBURG COLLEGE	PUB-T	158,694	88,705	11,938	270	13,039	15,474	3,135	6,286	0	19,847
CATHOLIC THEOL UNION	PRI-FG	93,251	48,603	5,004	5,670	20,000	7,600	0	0	1,200	5,174
CENTRAL YMCA CMTY COLLEGE	PRI-T	123,715	87,466	10,870	0	12,562	6,807	837	2,503	0	2,670
CHGO C OSTEOPATHIC MED	PRI-FG	674,002	148,685	22,303	225	44,915	85,408	0	6,724	5,745	359,997

SEE FOOTNOTES AT END OF TABLE

Table 2. — Library Operating Expenditures (in Dollars) of College and University Libraries, by Category of Expenditure and by State or Other Area and Institution: Aggregate United States, 1978-79 — Continued

STATE OR OTHER AREA AND INSTITUTION	CONTROL AND TYPE OF INSTITUTION	TOTAL	SALARIES AND WAGES LIBRARY STAFF	FRINGE BENEFITS	STUDENTS ON HOURLY BASIS	BOOK-STOCK	PERIOD-ICALS	MICRO-FORMS	AUDIO-VISUAL	BINDING AND RE-BINDING	ALL OTHER OPERATING EXPENDITURES
(1)	(2)	(3)	(4)	(5)	(6)	(7)	(8)	(9)	(10)	(11)	(12)
ILLINOIS	--CONTINUED										
CHGO CONSERVATORY COLLEGE	PRI-FG	A	A	A	A	A	A				
CHICAGO STATE UNIVERSITY	PUB-FG	1,063,692	607,585	0	11,547	120,959	45,868	11,272	13,838	8,002	244,621
CHICAGO THEOLOGICAL SEM	PRI-FG	83,204	B	B	1,500	16,947	4,180	163	0	1,317	B
CITY COLLEGES CHGO ALL CAM											
CITY C CHGO CITY-WIDE C1/	PUB-T	NO LIBRARY FACILITIES									
CITY C CHGO KENNEDY-KING	PUB-T	A	A	A	A	A	A	A	A		A
CITY C CHICAGO LOOP C	PUB-T	364,731	229,621	30,000	27,000	34,366	5,624	2,011	10,563	62	25,484
CITY C CHGO MALCOLM X C	PUB-T	181,377	137,480	15,500	0	14,654	6,938	770	2,918	383	2,734
CITY C CHGO OLIVE-HARVEY	PUB-T	233,180	198,180	0	0	18,726	6,022	3,046	6,646	305	255
CITY C CHICAGO DALEY C	PUB-T	260,824	199,488	23,021	0	20,099	4,536	2,429	9,600	0	1,651
CITY'C CHGO TRUMAN C	PUB-T	250,413	153,839	0	9,616	27,819	5,643	859	7,043	1,783	43,811
CITY C CHICAGO WRIGHT C	PUB-T	328,484	252,688	22,996	0	22,996	10,994	3,643	6,045	700	8,422
COLLEGE OF DUPAGE	PUB-T	1,367,385	769,680	44,776	61,680	92,180	20,747	8,071	44,267	2,437	323,547
COLLEGE OF LAKE COUNTY	PUB-T	486,308	287,001	0	12,619	62,184	24,085	0	43,085	0	57,334
COLLEGE OF SAINT FRANCIS	PRI-FN	154,632	79,668	6,606	6,808	24,879	8,544	0	4,722	2,063	21,342
COLUMBIA COLLEGE	PRI-FN	193,019	69,445	5,505	9,840	65,640	5,942	0	4,000	0	32,647
CONCORDIA COLLEGE	PRI-FG	192,301	92,701	11,118	28,851	16,592	12,598	2,783	190	3,992	23,476
DANIEL HALE WILLIAMS U	PRI-FN	NO LIBRARY FACILITIES									
DANVILLE AREA CMTY C	PUB-T	158,917	106,992	0	0	8,000	9,000	3,000	4,800	0	27,125
DELOURDES COLLEGE	PRI-FN	37,012	28,000	0	0	2,265	3,305	0	1,400	217	322
DEPAUL UNIVERSITY	PRI-U	1,732,179	870,380	122,594	74,674	171,901	264,697	41,289	2,558	25,894	158,192
DEVRY INST OF TECHNOLOGY	PRI-FN	20,922	B	0	0	5,695	1,131	0	145	0	B
EASTERN ILL UNIVERSITY	PUB-FG	1,323,747	687,505	110,998	67,681	162,750	185,816	14,072	6,727	24,432	63,766
ELGIN COMMUNITY COLLEGE	PUB-T	240,443	170,285	0	0	22,852	8,500	0	1,000	900	36,906
ELMHURST COLLEGE	PRI-FN	407,410	186,290	27,900	14,200	86,000	40,000	0	4,000	6,000	43,020
EUREKA COLLEGE	PRI-FN	75,921	38,595	6,080	8,204	9,835	8,066	1,187	60	1,006	2,888
FELICIAN COLLEGE	PRI-T	57,295	36,589	4,731		4,701	2,911	0	613	0	7,750
GARRETT-EVANGELCL THEOL	PRI-FG	196,599	92,027	14,979	17,397	43,267	8,173	0	461	3,902	16,393
GEORGE WILLIAMS COLLEGE	PRI-FG	179,671	107,336	14,392	3,808	19,087	13,165	300	3,000	2,788	15,795
GOVERNORS ST UNIVERSITY	PUB-FG	876,460	533,255	85,365	11,580	141,780	85,486	0	0	7,463	11,531
GREENVILLE COLLEGE	PRI-FN	132,825	65,810	7,450	20,962	15,225	8,510	764	2,134	256	11,714
HARRINGTON INSTITUTE	PRI-T	A	A			A	A		A		
HEBREW THEOL COLLEGE	PRI-FG	A	A	A	A	A					
HIGHLAND CMTY COLLEGE	PUB-T	67,995	B	B	0	17,473	6,049	1,728	3,719	A	B
ILL BENEDICTINE COLLEGE	PRI-FG	270,001	163,978	14,220	18,515	35,760	15,000	1,650	5,118	5,000	10,760
ILLINOIS CENTRAL COLLEGE	PUB-T	471,035	258,499	11,823	53,329	43,462	12,873	3,116	65,093	97	22,743
ILLINOIS COLLEGE	PRI-FN	134,926	57,800	4,624	14,500	29,205	11,500	1,000	0	5,500	10,797
ILL COLLEGE OF OPTOMETRY	PRI-FG	83,725	45,007	6,276	7,546	11,845	7,456	891	38	1,308	3,358
ILL COLLEGE PODIATRIC MED	PRI-FG	76,775	40,625	5,785	3,000	15,060	10,305	0	0	2,000	0
ILL ESTN CC SYS ALL INST											
ILL ESTN CC FRONTIER CC	PUB-T	19,088	8,700	0	0	4,500	1,200	0	2,400	400	1,888
ILL ESTN CC LINCOLN TRAIL C	PUB-T	50,975	B	0	0	10,237	3,120	370	2,968	150	B
ILL ESTN CC OLNEY CEN C	PUB-T	69,966	42,654	1,000	0	9,946	4,792	6,062	2,189	0	3,323
ILL ESTN CC WABASH VLY C	PUB-T	121,722	71,000	0	3,000	11,269	5,401	2,982	12,124	1,093	14,853
ILLINOIS INST TECHNOLOGY	PRI-FG	965,850	307,898	25,751	22,723	149,238	226,781	13,819	325	11,165	208,150
ILLINOIS STATE UNIVERSITY	PUB-FG	2,776,699	1,369,591	223,243	169,694	479,960	318,011	32,346	1,799	46,380	135,675
ILLINOIS VLY CMTY COLLEGE	PUB-T	213,818	124,166	3,051	16,654	10,782	10,899	1,275	4,885	3,807	38,299
ILL WESLEYAN UNIVERSITY	PRI-FN	340,948	145,050	24,490	59,700	45,135	32,450	2,000	4,500	6,258	21,365
JKM JOINT LIBRARY4/	PRI-FG	370,896	204,261	31,645	17,640	84,675	0	0	600	8,000	24,055
JOHN A LOGAN COLLEGE	PUB-T	171,948	88,909	9,420	12,497	12,684	4,988	894	12,700	0	29,856
JOHN MARSHALL LAW SCHOOL	PRI-FG	620,197	161,646	23,154	50,981	40,395	216,540	55,629	1,157	1,642	69,053
JOHN WOOD CMTY COLLEGE5/	PUB-T	44,918	11,035	1,406	12,065	7,812	1,500	0	11,100	0	0
JOLIET JUNIOR COLLEGE	PUB-T	344,092	194,842	18,815	14,740	23,225	14,500	2,600	37,070	800	37,500
JUDSON COLLEGE	PRI-FN	105,272	38,042	6,456	22,083	8,501	9,526	384	0	0	20,280
KANKAKEE CMTY COLLEGE	PUB-T	156,238	78,102	5,981	5,823	37,773	9,726	1,761	6,205	450	10,417
KASKASKIA COLLEGE	PUB-T	150,504	63,923	4,453	26,521	8,556	9,956	4,815	7,261	0	25,019
KELLER GRAD SCHOOL MGMT	PRI-FG	2,100	0	0	0	1,200	900	0	0	0	0
KENDALL COLLEGE	PRI-FN	34,357	B	B	960	5,000	4,000	500	0	0	B
KISHWAUKEE COLLEGE	PUB-T	85,748	51,634	1,579	2,085	15,603	4,419	1,847	241	0	8,340
KNOX COLLEGE	PRI-FN	302,893	116,725	17,508	25,397	71,144	26,366	0	6,264	1,103	38,386
LAKE FOREST COLLEGE	PRI-FG	300,350	128,640	0	43,000	58,000	28,000	4,800	1,600	1,400	34,910
LAKE LAND COLLEGE	PUB-T	80,347	43,074	1,361	0	20,787	6,899	1,497	1,690	0	5,039
LEWIS AND CLARK CC	PUB-T	189,110	109,096	6,616	0	15,863	9,595	2,744	5,416	634	39,146
LEWIS UNIVERSITY	PRI-FG	229,210	103,054	13,146	32,000	40,000	15,000	4,500	0	1,970	19,540
LINCOLN CHRISTIAN COLLEGE	PRI-FG	66,850	B	B	14,727	7,284	5,143	0	499	1,035	B

SEE FOOTNOTES AT END OF TABLE

Table 2. – Library Operating Expenditures (in Dollars) of College and University Libraries, by Category of Expenditure and by State or Other Area and Institution: Aggregate United States, 1978-79 – Continued

STATE OR OTHER AREA AND INSTITUTION	CONTROL AND TYPE OF INSTITUTION	TOTAL	SALARIES AND WAGES			BOOK-STOCK	PERIODICALS	MICRO-FORMS	AUDIO-VISUAL	BINDING AND RE-BINDING	ALL OTHER OPERATING EXPENDITURES
			LIBRARY STAFF	FRINGE BENEFITS	STUDENTS ON HOURLY BASIS						
(1)	(2)	(3)	(4)	(5)	(6)	(7)	(8)	(9)	(10)	(11)	(12)
ILLINOIS	--CONTINUED										
LINCOLN COLLEGE	PRI-T	77,222	42,866	0	500	13,846	7,000	2,000	2,000	200	8,810
LINCOLN LAND CMTY COLLEGE	PUB-T	405,726	245,015	7,264	21,667	30,915	12,436	1,084	16,382	770	70,193
LOYOLA U OF CHICAGO	PRI-U	1,992,509	822,213	129,134	149,105	405,215	281,660	2,942	3,832	60,272	138,136
LUTH SCH THEOLOGY CHICAGO	PRI FG	SEE JKM JOINT LIBRARY									
MACCORMAC COLLEGE	PRI-T	A	A			A	A		A		A
MACMURRAY COLLEGE	PRI-FN	139,917	70,503	7,205	14,148	19,886	14,813	3,908	79	1,492	7,878
MALLINCKRODT COLLEGE	PRI-T	39,852	B	B	0	11,148	1,993	0	314	778	B
MCCORMICK THEOLOGICAL SEM	PRI FG	SEE JKM JOINT LIBRARY									
MCHENRY COUNTY COLLEGE	PUB-T	292,759	136,541	6,044	9,816	19,832	11,156	5,255	7,620	1,098	95,397
MCKENDREE COLLEGE	PRI-FN	118,225	50,383	4,355	11,598	27,488	9,806	1,985	2,017	1,773	8,820
MEADVL-LOMBARD THEOL SCH	PRI-FG	23,900	B	B	6,200	7,000	0	0	0	0	B
MIDSTATE COLLEGE	PRI-T	10,012	7,509	0	0	-810	419	0	1,274	0	0
MIDWEST COLLEGE OF ENGR	PRI-FG					A					
MILLIKIN UNIVERSITY	PRI-FN	225,967	107,221	21,506	11,583	44,990	21,754	1,110	0	3,582	14,221
MONMOUTH COLLEGE	PRI-FN	119,615	47,026	6,078	14,136	17,206	22,151	900	0	1,879	10,239
MOODY BIBLE INSTITUTE	PRI-FN	110,173	44,000	13,200	23,535	10,700	4,100	200	50	4,238	10,150
MORAINE VLY CMTY COLLEGE	PUB-T	335,774	182,458	9,741	40,668	44,308	18,173	1,849	20,681	884	17,012
MORRISON INST OF TECHN	PRI-T	400	0	0	0	300	100	0	0	0	0
MORTON COLLEGE	PUB-T	141,895	66,924	0	22,225	14,011	12,261	3,099	1,920	946	20,509
MUNDELEIN COLLEGE	PRI-FG	230,308	124,318	6,243	37,596	21,853	7,692	0	0	5,768	26,838
NATL COLLEGE CHIROPRACTIC	PRI-FG	161,115	47,230	15,585	3,500	32,000	22,000	0	3,000	3,114	34,686
NATL COLLEGE ED ALL CAM											
NATL COLLEGE ED MAIN CAM	PRI-FG	218,576	146,071	23,618	17,802	7,600	9,680	2,020	3,000	300	8,485
NATL COLLEGE ED URBAN CAM	PRI-FG	70,658	41,519	6,500	5,025	7,895	3,710	970	990	480	3,569
NATIVE AMERICAN EDUC SERV	PRI-FN	13,436	10,000	800	1,300	1,001	85	0	0	0	250
NORTH CENTRAL COLLEGE	PRI-FN	118,376	55,247	6,501	9,619	21,500	11,500	0	1,745	2,700	9,564
NTHESTN ILL UNIVERSITY	PUB-FG	1,319,569	697,270	105,174	65,551	213,087	104,695	6,756	9,934	14,125	102,977
NORTHERN BAPT THEOL SEM	PRI FG	SEE BETHANY-NTHN BAPT JT LIB									
NORTHERN ILL UNIVERSITY	PUB-U	3,302,131	1,773,105	18,000	228,067	558,108	440,865	40,896	1,261	42,636	199,193
NORTH PARK C & THEOL SEM.	PRI-FG	262,102	109,465	20,500	20,807	55,023	17,786	2,216	0	6,093	30,212
NORTHWESTERN UNIVERSITY	PRI-U	7,348,867	3,244,029	463,896	603,393	690,510	935,211	33,410	0	123,707	1,254,711
OAKTON COMMUNITY COLLEGE	PUB-T	465,278	242,647	15,700	42,808	28,054	17,585	9,000	19,911	0	89,573
OLIVET NAZARENE COLLEGE	PRI-FG	220,896	94,307	24,032	26,906	39,573	14,861	582	2,609	4,407	13,619
PARKLAND COLLEGE	PUB-T	656,146	316,050	15,821	49,600	55,000	17,500	6,000	14,000	6,000	176,175
PRAIRIE STATE COLLEGE	PUB-T	166,788	122,949	0	12,839	21,400	3,000	0	1,250	600	4,750
PRINCIPIA COLLEGE	PRI-FN	266,262	120,278	0	38,333	40,265	31,324	3,115	1,874	2,000	29,073
QUINCY COLLEGE	PRI-FN	176,986	75,014	5,974	13,307	36,548	28,038	350	250	5,147	12,358
REND LAKE COLLEGE	PUB-T	105,523	67,179	1,940	0	3,702	5,487	2,008	2,620	885	21,702
RICHLAND CMTY COLLEGE	PUB-T	158,167	99,910	2,650	5,000	8,000	8,800	1,200	16,000	0	16,607
ROCKFORD COLLEGE	PRI-FG	A	A	A	A	A	A	A	A	A	A
ROCK VALLEY COLLEGE	PUB-T	173,479	99,792	7,615	21,360	10,961	14,464	2,513	6,461	160	10,153
ROOSEVELT UNIVERSITY	PRI-FG	A	A	A	A	A	A	A	A	A	A
ROSARY COLLEGE	PRI-FG	289,973	123,214	9,767	31,094	70,329	20,747	3,247	4,403	2,546	24,626
RUSH UNIVERSITY	PRI-FG	618,905	302,443	42,299	10,593	81,754	100,000	0	35,920	15,311	30,585
SNT MARY OF THE LAKE SEM	PRI-FG	60,671	35,412	3,386	0	12,151	6,701	0	185	1,192	1,644
SAINT XAVIER COLLEGE	PRI-FG	189,885	94,080	4,600	10,200	55,098	10,367	4,260	0	1,065	10,215
SANGAMON STATE UNIVERSITY	PUB-FG	1,195,312	628,868	0	72,703	161,827	125,133	38,425	9,095	14,775	144,486
SAUK VALLEY COLLEGE	PUB-T	126,093	67,075	6,176	9,369	27,238	4,024	601	7,168	107	4,335
SCH ART INSTITUTE CHICAGO	PRI-FG	648,440	311,100	124,440	21,800	92,900	11,800	5,000	21,600	15,000	44,800
SEABURY-WESTERN THEOL SEM	PRI-FG	69,988	B	B	5,188	25,400	3,740	118	0	1,989	B
SHAWNEE COLLEGE	PUB-T	63,513	B	0	6,524	9,434	5,749	564	3,134	802	B
SHERWOOD MUSIC SCHOOL	PRI-FN	A	A			A	A		A		A
SHIMER COLLEGE	PRI-FN	A	A	A	A	A	A	A	A	A	A
SOUTHEASTERN ILL COLLEGE	PUB-T	68,762	44,881	993	367	15,025	1,346	770	881	63	4,436
STHN ILLINOIS U ALL INST											
STHN ILLINOIS U CARBONDL	PUB-U	5,408,919	2,336,057	376,349	499,822	416,703	1,063,478	29,828	59,447	102,654	524,581
STHN ILLINOIS U EDWARDSVL	PUB-FG	1,973,482	903,169	132,766	236,787	270,517	151,929	20,337	10,608	30,000	217,369
SPERTUS COLLEGE JUDAICA	PRI-FG	108,037	70,184	15,115	756	12,608	7,830	43	0	0	1,501
SPOON-RIVER COLLEGE	PUB-T	146,832	59,445	2,063	4,140	31,995	4,366	7,565	5,613	0	31,645
SPRINGFLD COLLEGE IN ILL	PRI-T	41,431	B	B	1,862	8,747	2,898	0	1,093	511	B
STATE COMMUNITY COLLEGE	PUB-T	88,145	57,687	10,051	0	12,456	1,800	0	4,208	0	1,943
TELSHE YESHIVA-CHICAGO	PRI-FG	A	A	A	A	A	A	A	A	A	A
THORNTON CMTY COLLEGE	PUB-T	258,679	137,105	6,513	21,472	26,560	6,855	1,637	35,737	1,400	21,400
TRINITY CHRISTIAN COLLEGE	PRI-FN	58,756	B	B	5,591	14,991	5,452	0	547	202	B
TRINITY COLLEGE	PRI-FN	135,555	73,908	0	3,840	26,312	14,643	0	0	985	15,867

SEE FOOTNOTES AT END OF TABLE

Table 2. – Library Operating Expenditures (in Dollars) of College and University Libraries, by Category of Expenditure and by State or Other Area and Institution: Aggregate United States, 1978-79 – Continued

STATE OR OTHER AREA AND INSTITUTION	CONTROL AND TYPE OF INSTITUTION	TOTAL	SALARIES AND WAGES			BOOK-STOCK	PERIODICALS	MICRO-FORMS	AUDIO-VISUAL	BINDING AND RE-BINDING	ALL OTHER OPERATING EXPENDITURES
			LIBRARY STAFF	FRINGE BENEFITS	STUDENTS ON HOURLY BASIS						
(1)	(2)	(3)	(4)	(5)	(6)	(7)	(8)	(9)	(10)	(11)	(12)
ILLINOIS	**--CONTINUED**										
TRINITY EVANGELCL DIV SCH	PRI-FG	187,701	85,154	9,851	17,615	45,101	13,360	438	468	0	15,714
TRITON COLLEGE	PUB-T	437,881	201,673	18,864	34,125	70,000	31,400	0	51,250	0	30,569
UNIVERSITY OF CHICAGO	PRI-U	6,895,348	3,527,697	442,917	74,395	411,771	1,090,112	4,247	0	215,909	1,128,300
U HLTH SCI-CHGO MEDL SCH	PRI-FG	282,712	110,362	15,000	250	42,000	100,000	0	0	8,300	6,800
U OF ILLINOIS ALL CAM											
U OF ILL CHICAGO CIRCLE	PUB-FG	3,073,681	1,334,565	199,517	141,631	756,192	306,900	0	0	41,500	293,376
U OF ILL MEDL CTR CHGO	PUB-FG	2,244,101	1,196,175	201,555	57,907	231,470	291,023	0	46,175	31,194	188,602
U OF ILL URBANA CAMPUS	PUB-U	9,993,030	4,523,166	768,938	655,872	1,377,745	1,421,500	0	0	183,094	1,062,715
VANDERCOOK C OF MUSIC	PRI-FG	23,463	B	B	2,209	5,144	1,000	0	0	0	B
WAUBONSEE CMTY COLLEGE	PUB-T	233,799	139,461	4,930	2,211	22,489	6,919	3,603	5,072	615	48,499
WESTERN ILL UNIVERSITY	PUB-U	1,655,147	812,016	121,802	75,750	326,899	175,499	4,967	1,300	29,999	106,915
WHEATON COLLEGE	PRI-FG	403,205	202,029	40,000	20,000	71,720	37,036	4,000	0	6,000	22,420
WM RAINEY HARPER COLLEGE	PUB-T	687,450	456,066	25,011	36,977	44,040	17,443	2,222	42,014	2,578	61,099
INDIANA											
ANCILLA DOMINI COLLEGE	PRI-T	28,136	B	B	0	462	1,870	0	24	0	B
ANDERSON COLLEGE	PRI-FG	349,072	162,485	15,454	55,478	52,676	16,778	1,098	3,070	4,119	37,914
BALL STATE UNIVERSITY	PUB-U	3,026,865	1,513,669	0	294,655	502,655	291,817	0	77,014	72,984	274,071
BETHEL COLLEGE	PRI-FN	54,842	B	B	8,172	10,736	10,018	0	0	1,290	B
BUTLER UNIVERSITY	PRI-U	320,609	161,379	3,281	52,899	44,995	42,688	1,493	1,657	8,888	3,329
CALUMET COLLEGE	PRI-FN	115,817	62,718	0	12,502	16,604	10,819	1,051	0	3,471	8,652
CHRISTIAN THEOLOGICAL SEM	PRI-FG	96,717	48,457	9,165	2,924	21,585	5,401	0	1,152	2,664	5,369
CLARK COLLEGE	PRI-T	A	A			A	A				
CONCORDIA THEOLOGICAL SEM	PRI-FG	150,837	59,314	9,861	14,980	38,941	10,917	2,052	5,357	1,909	7,506
DEPAUW UNIVERSITY	PRI-FG	345,141	177,126	25,702	23,486	43,357	43,482	2,972	1,327	6,057	21,632
EARLHAM COLLEGE	PRI-FG	314,315	112,257	42,475	21,295	62,783	43,611	6,000	1,000	7,032	17,862
FORT WAYNE BIBLE COLLEGE	PRI-FN	62,392	33,048	3,862	8,466	8,173	4,321	1,068	1,189	533	1,732
FRANKLIN COLLEGE INDIANA	PRI-FG	130,652	58,984	8,645	11,128	21,066	9,951	770	411	631	19,066
GOSHEN BIBLICAL SEMINARY	PRI FG	SEE MENNONITE BIB SEM JT LIB									
GOSHEN COLLEGE	PRI-FN	120,968	42,014	11,625	19,383	22,408	12,942	2,350	825	1,173	8,248
GRACE COLLEGE	PRI-FN	148,723	66,521	10,223	6,334	33,088	12,874	0	800	6,396	12,487
HANOVER COLLEGE	PRI-FN	A	A	A	A	A	A	A	A	A	A
HOLY CROSS JUNIOR COLLEGE	PRI-T	20,470	12,680	0	531	3,258	2,048	0	0	162	B
HUNTINGTON COLLEGE	PRI-FG	103,149	34,431	0	24,041	32,500	8,736	2,541	0	900	0
INDIANA CEN UNIVERSITY	PRI-FG	241,273	102,047	10,143	16,289	61,141	17,602	480	1,791	5,952	25,828
INDIANA C MORTUARY SCI	PRI-T	430	0	0	0	55	375	0	0	0	0
INDIANA INST TECHNOLOGY	PRI-FN	32,216	B	B	6,000	3,469	4,521	0	0	301	B
IND NTHN GRAD SCH MGMT	PRI-FG	4,120	B	0	0	150	250	0	0	0	B
INDIANA STATE U ALL CAM											
INDIANA STATE U MAIN CAM	PUB-U	1,709,169	835,762	125,364	120,166	222,324	172,218	32,138	7,978	48,058	145,161
INDIANA ST U EVANSVL CAM	PUB-FN	296,921	139,974	11,200	14,086	55,157	35,073	4,935	4,797	5,846	25,853
INDIANA U ALL CAMPUSES											
INDIANA U BLOOMINGTON2/	PUB-U	7,918,031	3,690,805	450,486	724,973	1,092,056	856,716	62,430	45,942	142,468	852,155
INDIANA UNIVERSITY EAST	PUB-T	100,248	37,427	4,421	2,796	16,954	22,529	4,796	4,363	238	6,724
INDIANA U AT KOKOMO	PUB-FN	195,584	74,705	2,166	28,459	27,552	39,375	2,942	1,500	2,763	16,122
INDIANA U NORTHWEST	PUB-FG	268,920	113,357	14,687	8,807	40,032	78,650	750	0	5,992	6,645
IND-PURDUE U INDIANAPOLIS	PUB-FG	2,122,737	985,746	140,530	85,021	166,941	464,730	23,522	345	30,559	225,343
INDIANA U AT SOUTH BEND	PUB-FG	406,700	187,183	24,714	50,899	23,500	77,522	3,781	0	10,907	28,194
INDIANA U SOUTHEAST	PUB-FG	255,678	121,102	13,195	24,088	24,744	51,883	0	0	6,573	14,093
IND-PURDUE U FORT WAYNE	PUB-FG	572,694	203,881	22,426	39,124	173,546	94,350	3,400	1,000	12,000	22,967
IND VOC TECH C ALL CAM											
IND VOC TECH C-CEN IND	PUB-T	69,059	35,197	3,697	0	2,485	3,574	0	6,855	0	17,251
IND VOC TECH C-COLUMBUS	PUB-T	32,404	B	B	0	695	1,720	15	0	0	B
IND VOC TECH C-KOKOMO	PUB-T	49,245	31,131	4,223	4,314	5,341	148	180	1,280	0	2,628
IND VOC TECH C-LAFAYETTE	PUB-T	65,364	46,893	9,006	0	2,129	2,010	24	4,280	228	794
IND VOC TECH C-NTH CEN	PUB-T	33,750	B	B	0	4,724	2,700	0	6,160	0	B
IND VOC TECH C NORTHEAST	PUB-T	30,128	B	B	674	1,141	2,820	300	3,221	0	B
IND VOC TECH C-STHCEN	PUB-T	65,935	B	B	0	1,698	1,291	0	2,271	0	B
IND VOC TECH C-SOUTHWEST	PUB-T	24,948	B	B	2,496	3,906	2,350	0	570	0	B
IND VOC TECH-WABASH VLY	PUB-T	53,640	B	0	0	2,000	2,000	0	0	0	B
INTERNATIONAL BUSINESS C	PRI-T	10,300	B	0	400	1,000	500	0	3,000	0	0
LOCKYEAR COLLEGE	PRI-T	26,372	B	0	608	1,150	575	0	0	0	0
MANCHESTER COLLEGE	PRI-FG	171,427	78,346	11,491	11,790	40,770	14,199	1,260	1,341	2,755	9,475
MARIAN COLLEGE	PRI-FN	85,447	42,300	763	8,007	16,362	5,945	0	1,240	2,609	8,221
MARION COLLEGE	PRI-FG	98,660	42,858	6,972	15,225	16,403	7,200	1,002	475	398	8,127

SEE FOOTNOTES AT END OF TABLE.

STATE OR OTHER AREA AND INSTITUTION	CON-TROL AND TYPE OF IN-STITU-TION	TOTAL	SALARIES AND WAGES			BOOK-STOCK	PERIOD-ICALS	MICRO-FORMS	AUDIO-VISUAL	BIND-ING AND RE-BINDING	ALL OTHER OPER-ATING EXPEND-ITURES
			LIBRARY STAFF	FRINGE BENEFITS	STUDENTS ON HOURLY BASIS						
(1)	(2)	(3)	(4)	(5)	(6)	(7)	(8)	(9)	(10)	(11)	(12)
INDIANA	--CONTINUED										
MENNONITE BIBLICAL SEM	PRI FG			SEE MENNONITE BIB SEM JT LIB							
MENNONITE BIB SEM JT LIB	PRI-FG	76,537	40,722	6,067	1,407	14,481	3,381	5,256	30	770	4,423
OAKLAND CITY COLLEGE	PRI-FN	49,487	B	B	5,120	14,935	7,653	0	1,377	1,614	B
PURDUE U ALL CAMPUSES											
PURDUE U MAIN CAMPUS	PUB-U	4,493,936	2,288,061	243,458	248,427	415,248	860,365	32,476	17,911	76,978	311,012
PURDUE U CALUMET CAMPUS	PUB-FG	421,463	195,675	26,359	12,678	56,482	66,514	2,573	0	7,263	53,919
PURDUE U NORTH CEN CAMPUS	PUB-T	106,866	61,894	7,952	0	19,130	12,843	0	303	2,071	2,673
ROSE-HULMAN INST OF TECHN	PRI-FG	91,535	37,560	7,182	3,393	17,500	18,500	0	0	5,000	2,400
SAINT FRANCIS COLLEGE	PRI-FG	73,390	38,351	2,858	0	13,461	12,203	2,466	0	1,529	2,522
SAINT JOSEPH'S COLLEGE	PRI-FG	176,027	84,493	16,963	15,453	20,805	17,648	1,779	1,154	2,998	14,734
SAINT MARY'S COLLEGE	PRI-FN	245,542	111,015	18,189	28,878	51,106	20,660	0	676	4,403	10,615
SAINT MARY-OF-THE-WOODS C	PRI-FN	85,648	58,061	2,000	2,778	14,568	4,520	0	0	1,450	2,271
SAINT MEINRAD COLLEGE	PRI FN			SEE SNT MEINRAD C JT LIBRARY							
SNT MEINRAD C JT LIBRARY	PRI-FN	129,644	51,599	890	1,287	30,956	12,685	0	1,000	3,881	27,346
SNT MEINRAD SCH THEOLOGY	PRI FG			SEE SNT MEINRAD C JT LIBRARY							
TAYLOR UNIVERSITY	PRI-FN	179,727	80,382	13,945	23,257	41,863	13,565	1,237	1,197	2,500	1,781
TRI-STATE UNIVERSITY	PRI-FN	119,438	55,715	9,470	3,877	22,117	19,641	2,178	0	3,572	2,868
UNIVERSITY OF EVANSVILLE	PRI-FG	523,225	236,470	41,399	16,529	79,088	49,000	0	912	2,795	97,032
UNIVERSITY OF NOTRE DAME	PRI-U	2,742,715	1,234,021	134,322	67,489	481,089	585,001	0	0	58,457	182,336
VALPARAISO UNIVERSITY	PRI-FG	544,717	213,400	20,872	42,070	166,806	39,623	17,214	2,856	17,436	24,440
VINCENNES UNIVERSITY	PUB-T	254,168	153,412	0	7,200	33,976	8,760	2,356	3,876	5,410	39,178
WABASH COLLEGE	PRI-FN	215,684	67,153	18,064	17,558	46,730	41,561	2,439	1,494	7,346	13,339
IOWA											
AMERICAN INSTITUTE BUS	PRI-T	A	A	A	A	A	A	A	A	A	A
AQUINAS INST OF THEOLOGY	PRI-FG	69,331	31,013	5,066	5,611	15,440	3,465	0	1,539	1,474	5,723
BRIAR CLIFF COLLEGE	PRI-FN	83,591	B	B	12,687	12,580	8,510	1,787	95	1,484	B
BUENA VISTA COLLEGE	PRI-FN	120,385	52,388	6,359	12,349	29,213	14,375	1,344	1,418	398	2,541
CENTRAL U OF IOWA	PRI-FN	196,980	65,282	8,150	27,730	43,822	18,308	3,869	4,998	2,767	22,054
CLARKE COLLEGE	PRI-FG	89,569	40,056	4,806	547	18,102	8,580	0	0	2,198	15,280
COE COLLEGE	PRI-FN	262,111	102,988	11,143	37,197	41,264	30,960	1,100	1,400	3,103	32,956
COLLEGE OSTEO MED-SURGERY	PRI-FG	80,548	35,146	3,998	0	9,884	23,126	0	0	4,234	4,160
CORNELL COLLEGE	PRI-FN	176,961	81,450	9,271	29,322	24,872	18,430	2,235	78	993	10,310
DES MOINES AREA CC	PUB-T	294,572	134,296	28,202	12,295	44,428	15,584	0	17,856	0	41,911
DIVINE WORD COLLEGE	PRI-FN	70,350	41,300	0	0	16,000	6,000	500	2,500	1,500	2,550
DORDT COLLEGE	PRI-FN	139,304	66,632	6,794	6,513	33,926	12,406	3,105	0	149	9,779
DRAKE UNIVERSITY	PRI-U	1,108,884	417,049	74,168	112,980	264,671	143,522	20,410	3,794	23,894	48,396
ESTN IOWA CC DIST ALL CAM											
CLINTON COMMUNITY COLLEGE	PUB-T	60,997	B	B	0	6,917	4,285	1,000	2,000	200	B
MUSCATINE CMTY COLLEGE	PUB-T	105,444	B	B	0	11,118	3,877	0	2,889	0	B
SCOTT COMMUNITY COLLEGE	PUB-T	106,062	72,750	3,495	3,528	14,765	4,888	95	2,503	0	4,038
ELLSWORTH CMTY COLLEGE	PUB-T	114,676	60,009	9,039	10,378	11,937	8,774	850	2,408	0	11,281
FAITH BAPT BIBLE COLLEGE	PRI-FN	57,734	21,388	5,806	7,687	10,504	2,745	0	0	2,187	7,417
GRACELAND COLLEGE	PRI-FN	151,533	73,919	11,753	20,073	19,900	10,177	279	0	1,241	14,191
GRAND VIEW COLLEGE	PRI-FN	121,835	47,074	10,000	4,277	33,346	11,983	823	820	949	12,563
GRINNELL COLLEGE	PRI-FN	397,406	147,045	22,194	24,193	107,454	53,548	0	1,376	10,781	30,815
HAWKEYE INST TECHNOLOGY	PUB-T	118,362	51,024	10,204	0	13,572	7,620	2,649	0	0	33,293
INDIAN HILLS CC	PUB-T	137,182	47,368	8,283	1,348	16,563	3,547	720	7,046	166	52,141
IOWA CENTRAL CC	PUB-T	183,908	102,062	17,111	9,679	13,161	18,380	2,187	1,741	418	19,169
IOWA LAKES CC ALL CAM											
IOWA LAKES CC NORTH CTR	PUB-T	99,026	56,990	9,668	2,475	9,859	4,831	566	1,369	827	12,441
IOWA LAKES CC SOUTH CTR	PUB-T	72,786	B	B	2,475	7,118	3,660	0	3,542	0	B
IOWA STATE U SCI & TECHN	PUB-U	4,337,786	1,823,912	468,528	213,804	553,219	849,504	51,467	7,437	100,199	269,716
IOWA WESLEYAN COLLEGE	PRI-FN	122,568	60,247	9,314	16,200	11,765	12,154	838	3,000	900	8,150
IOWA WESTERN CMTY COLLEGE	PUB-T	199,097	104,465	15,438	6,368	24,970	7,657	1,934	7,057	304	30,904
KIRKWOOD CMTY COLLEGE	PUB-T	158,182	108,693	17,010	267	19,043	2,711	1,125	2,058	334	6,941
LORAS COLLEGE	PRI-FG	184,033	76,986	14,652	19,154	46,502	20,475	624	0	4,781	859
LUTHER COLLEGE	PRI-FN	340,764	149,144	33,957	41,996	51,660	24,557	11,639	606	6,161	21,650
MAHARISHI INTRNATL U	PRI-FG	62,495	0	0	0	28,250	9,820	4,809	2,535	1,735	14,740
MARSHALLTWN CMTY COLLEGE	PUB-T	103,247	59,068	8,384	8,058	12,874	5,646	2,316	1,352	118	5,431
MARYCREST COLLEGE	PRI-FG	116,654	59,254	0	12,000	17,000	9,500	2,000	4,000	500	12,400
MORNINGSIDE COLLEGE	PRI-FN	179,746	85,236	10,741	9,874	27,245	11,526	1,200	1,904	353	31,667
MOUNT MERCY COLLEGE	PRI-FN	136,294	72,092	6,285	14,478	24,389	8,638	693	2,094	2,001	5,624
MOUNT SAINT CLARE COLLEGE	PRI-FN	31,023	B	0	936	8,639	2,761	29	335	0	B
NTHEST IA TECH INSTITUTE	PUB-T	109,699	47,778	8,219	0	12,618	8,035	200	12,742	138	19,969

SEE FOOTNOTES AT END OF TABLE

Table 2. — Library Operating Expenditures (in Dollars) of College and University Libraries, by Category of Expenditure and by State or Other Area and Institution: Aggregate United States, 1978-79 — Continued

STATE OR OTHER AREA AND INSTITUTION (1)	CONTROL AND TYPE OF INSTITUTION (2)	TOTAL (3)	SALARIES AND WAGES			BOOK-STOCK (7)	PERIODICALS (8)	MICRO-FORMS (9)	AUDIO-VISUAL (10)	BINDING AND RE-BINDING (11)	ALL OTHER OPERATING EXPENDITURES (12)
			LIBRARY STAFF (4)	FRINGE BENEFITS (5)	STUDENTS ON HOURLY BASIS (6)						
IOWA	--CONTINUED										
N IOWA AREA CMTY COLLEGE	PUB-T	223,040	98,629	16,743	14,655	15,400	7,581	270	27,397	482	41,883
NTHWST IOWA TECH C	PUB-T	29,948	B	B	0	11,798	3,146	0	0	0	B
NORTHWESTERN COLLEGE	PRI-FN	148,526	57,581	6,969	16,042	33,465	14,275	3,870	647	768	14,909
OPEN BIBLE COLLEGE	PRI-FN	11,028	B	0	1,500	3,112	663	0	59	0	B
PALMER C OF CHIROPRACTIC	PRI-FG	177,481	100,295	10,029	0	10,584	20,047	5,782	10,965	1,210	18,569
SAINT AMBROSE COLLEGE	PRI-FN	164,500	73,000	4,500	15,000	25,000	23,000	3,000	2,500	1,000	17,500
SIMPSON COLLEGE	PRI-FN	119,416	50,977	8,560	12,697	22,188	11,805	585	524	242	11,838
SIOUX EMPIRE COLLEGE	PRI-T	19,797	B	0	0	4,020	656	0	1,411	582	B
SOUTHEASTERN CMTY COLLEGE	PUB-T	188,374	104,622	14,615	6,927	10,352	5,098	0	16,190	695	29,875
SOUTHWESTERN CMTY COLLEGE	PUB-T	124,111	90,529	0	1,839	9,118	2,352	619	3,394	7	16,260
UNIVERSITY OF DUBUQUE	PRI-FG	156,031	73,513	9,361	6,512	25,991	16,897	1,441	2,361	4,187	15,768
UNIVERSITY OF IOWA	PUB-U	5,658,460	2,459,304	403,289	304,088	863,370	1,146,182	84,983	24,624	178,368	194,252
U OF NORTHERN IOWA	PUB-FG	1,707,508	796,454	161,502	110,836	322,704	122,996	19,755	2,611	45,000	125,650
UPPER IOWA UNIVERSITY	PRI-FN	72,676	44,514	3,541	0	7,479	9,851	975	276	2,276	3,764
VENNARD COLLEGE	PRI-FN	30,927	B	0	5,915	3,700	1,961	157	641	B	B
WALDORF COLLEGE	PRI-T	50,853	B	B	3,098	7,913	3,239	4,179	1,053	130	B
WARTBURG COLLEGE	PRI-FN	189,205	74,077	15,445	16,343	34,723	22,891	2,085	378	3,377	19,886
WARTBURG THEOLOGICAL SEM	PRI-FG	69,332	31,012	5,067	5,611	15,440	3,465	0	1,540	1,475	5,722
WESTERN IOWA TECH	PUB-T	175,735	76,123	12,166	863	22,958	11,461	6,293	21,418	0	24,453
WESTMAR COLLEGE	PRI-FN	76,668	42,470	4,990	6,922	10,396	7,790	0	0	217	3,883
WILLIAM PENN COLLEGE	PRI-FN	62,945	B	B	994	14,096	4,575	425	1,606	1,291	B
KANSAS											
ALLEN CO CMTY JR COLLEGE	PUB-T	45,086	B	B	3,239	12,318	4,634	48	1,594	912	B
BAKER UNIVERSITY	PRI-FG	109,676	46,194	5,013	16,458	33,987	3,392	481	519	1,009	2,623
BARTON CO CMTY JR COLLEGE	PUB-T	85,809	58,654	0	2,691	7,691	7,279	0	5,754	0	3,740
BENEDICTINE COLLEGE	PRI-FN	177,619	98,108	4,389	4,522	9,608	11,564	211	557	2,273	46,387
BETHANY COLLEGE	PRI-FN	116,208	40,137	5,225	14,882	26,360	5,914	1,041	5,707	3,943	12,999
BETHEL COLLEGE	PRI-FN	103,472	52,533	7,338	17,118	13,075	5,658	997	50	1,987	4,716
BUTLER CO CMTY JR COLLEGE	PUB-T	76,102	39,335	3,360	0	12,089	5,557	2,686	2,150	286	10,639
CENTRAL BAPTIST THEOL SEM	PRI-FG	42,082	B	B	3,912	11,535	4,176	0	395	1,012	B
CENTRAL COLLEGE	PRI-T	27,034	B	0	3,528	4,418	1,844	482	928	0	B
CLOUD CO CMTY JR COLLEGE	PUB-T	63,695	33,801	2,074	0	7,852	3,099	686	8,722	0	7,461
COFFEYVL CMTY JR COLLEGE	PUB-T	92,370	54,327	8,234	0	4,051	5,507	0	12,891	1,395	5,965
COLBY COMMUNITY COLLEGE	PUB-T	90,280	62,015	1,635	0	10,656	5,475	681	1,566	701	7,551
COWLEY CO CMTY JR COLLEGE	PUB-T	78,448	B	B	0	18,608	4,301	0	18,015	209	B
DODGE CTY CMTY JR COLLEGE	PUB-T	134,273	62,146	12,429	19,998	12,000	4,800	1,800	10,000	100	11,000
DONNELLY COLLEGE	PRI-T	46,676	35,280	2,457	0	2,634	3,034	0	877	0	2,394
EMPORIA STATE UNIVERSITY	PUB-FG	938,063	332,227	51,931	115,791	170,739	83,894	10,122	37,911	16,738	118,710
FORT HAYS ST UNIVERSITY	PUB-FG	603,586	256,678	25,064	71,724	113,000	61,250	2,400	0	18,957	54,513
FT SCOTT CMTY JR COLLEGE	PUB-T	57,355	B	0	0	4,387	4,907	0	5,252	0	B
FRIENDS BIBLE COLLEGE	PRI-FN	36,589	B	B	11,100	2,515	827	0	99	148	B
FRIENDS UNIVERSITY	PRI-FN	105,147	47,707	0	12,174	15,377	12,405	1,961	2,527	1,999	10,997
GARDEN CITY COMMUNITY JC	PUB-T	66,793	B	B	0	11,340	7,081	808	390	1,455	B
HASKELL INDIAN JR COLLEGE	PUB-T	225,906	147,662	14,529	5,040	16,812	7,698	8,525	10,280	0	15,360
HESSTON COLLEGE	PRI-T	48,383	B	B	9,223	5,513	4,727	0	0	245	B
HIGHLAND CMTY JR COLLEGE	PUB-T	41,481	B	B	3,420	2,493	4,063	207	1,699	615	B
HUTCHINSN CMTY JR COLLEGE	PUB-T	107,161	70,284	6,542	6,770	12,308	5,216	475	2,124	67	3,375
INDEPENDENCE COMMUNITY JC	PUB-T	46,780	B	B	0	12,412	3,624	0	963	0	B
JOHNSN CO CMTY JR COLLEGE	PUB-T	237,993	125,583	9,585	18,666	45,795	11,398	2,406	11,254	0	13,266
KANSAS CITY KANS CMTY JC	PUB-T	134,083	89,734	5,266	0	20,882	7,603	629	3,444	3,668	2,857
KANSAS NEWMAN COLLEGE	PRI-EN	88,805	43,271	2,024	5,297	18,137	9,879	36	2,927	526	6,708
KANSAS ST U AGR & APP SCI	PUB-U	2,343,035	883,827	137,948	88,847	269,158	707,670	12,120	986	31,715	210,764
KANSAS TECHNICAL INST	PUB-T	67,409	B	B	866	15,435	3,905	0	6,431	0	B
KANSAS WESLEYAN	PRI-FN	94,887	43,914	4,718	9,818	16,975	10,437	278	1,064	3,947	3,736
LABETTE CMTY COLLEGE	PUB-T	56,292	B	B	1,402	7,038	3,706	23	11,191	0	B
MANHATTAN CHRSTN COLLEGE	PRI-FN	21,335	B	0	791	3,558	1,288	0	454	0	B
MARYHOUNT COLLEGE KANSAS	PRI-FN	99,109	43,519	4,500	7,296	18,902	8,084	679	2,228	566	13,335
MCPHERSON COLLEGE	PRI-FN	87,493	B	B	0	9,173	10,001	0	2,767	1,708	B
MID-AMERICA NAZARENE C	PRI-FN	105,046	44,700	11,174	9,089	15,242	9,022	818	555	1,606	12,840
NEOSHO CO CMTY JR COLLEGE	PUB-T	60,965	B	B	0	11,637	3,213	0	7,211	0	B
OTTAWA UNIVERSITY	PRI-FN	72,706	B	B	11,714	9,680	12,034	634	0	0	B
PITTSBURG ST UNIVERSITY	PUB-FG	685,784	378,607	41,239	58,571	96,050	60,128	5,344	0	340	41,269
PRATT CMTY JUNIOR COLLEGE	PUB-T	49,019	B	B	0	11,942	3,596	574	3,699	0	B

SEE FOOTNOTES AT END OF TABLE

Table 2. – Library Operating Expenditures (in Dollars) of College and University Libraries, by Category of Expenditure and by State or Other Area and Institution: Aggregate United States, 1978-79 – Continued

STATE OR OTHER AREA AND INSTITUTION	CONTROL AND TYPE OF INSTITUTION	TOTAL	SALARIES AND WAGES			BOOK-STOCK	PERIOD-ICALS	MICRO-FORMS	AUDIO-VISUAL	BINDING AND RE-BINDING	ALL OTHER OPERATING EXPENDITURES
			LIBRARY STAFF	FRINGE BENEFITS	STUDENTS ON HOURLY BASIS						
(1)	(2)	(3)	(4)	(5)	(6)	(7)	(8)	(9)	(10)	(11)	(12)
KANSAS	--CONTINUED										
SAINT JOHN'S COLLEGE	PRI-T	52,100	32,793	6,343	570	6,931	1,699	940	1,293	156	1,375
SAINT MARY COLLEGE	PRI-FN	87,224	60,850	370	4,782	9,291	5,573	103	829	2,500	3,126
SAINT MARY PLAINS COLLEGE	PRI-FN	87,916	59,147	1,600	7,392	7,136	6,757	293	1,387	275	3,929
SEWARD CO CMTY JR COLLEGE	PUB-T	58,974	B	B	4,560	9,244	3,461	0	0	179	B
SOUTHWESTERN COLLEGE	PRI-FN	80,549	29,500	3,067	6,298	14,752	8,777	3,639	38	1,420	13,058
STERLING COLLEGE	PRI-FN	81,528	32,825	5,326	9,433	14,158	10,630	838	703	1,417	6,198
TABOR COLLEGE	PRI-FN	68,343	29,990	5,098	6,580	11,000	6,500	0	0	0	9,175
U KANSAS ALL CAMPUSES											
U OF KANSAS MAIN CAMPUS	PUB-U	4,634,266	1,910,525	305,000	333,404	833,348	678,302	25,000	1,000	94,059	453,628
U OF KANS MEDICAL CENTER	PUB-FG	701,854	341,988	54,020	10,606	40,161	123,928	15,656	0	11,575	103,920
WASHBURN U OF TOPEKA	PUB-FG	649,011	191,655	22,056	40,309	139,219	157,919	22,913	11,819	9,173	53,948
WICHITA STATE UNIVERSITY	PUB-U	1,785,180	654,162	97,567	104,128	405,812	220,664	7,404	3,181	27,150	265,112
KENTUCKY											
ALICE LLOYD COLLEGE	PRI-T	56,957	32,058	3,792	7,885	4,051	3,254	152	2,661	7	3,097
ASBURY COLLEGE	PRI-FN	224,381	100,036	700	15,744	47,723	12,492	6,246	11,769	1,613	28,058
ASBURY THEOLOGICAL SEM	PRI-FG	240,395	155,901	12,443	16,671	33,261	6,530	520	1,100	2,288	11,681
BELLARMINE COLLEGE	PRI-FG	166,409	90,573	11,291	4,054	23,379	10,676	3,542	1,053	393	21,448
BEREA COLLEGE	PRI-FN	339,453	167,860	20,949	38,185	60,980	27,740	2,822	451	6,620	13,846
BRESCIA COLLEGE	PRI-FN	123,821	73,869	790	10,373	19,704	9,075	2,562	165	1,742	5,541
CAMPBELLSVILLE COLLEGE	PRI-FN	100,511	50,564	5,480	18,761	13,717	7,278	0	1,012	1,649	2,050
CENTRE COLLEGE OF KY	PRI-FN	221,305	85,170	13,887	24,743	34,321	29,875	0	2,745	5,540	25,024
CUMBERLAND COLLEGE	PRI-FN	162,135	78,986	8,900	24,660	25,290	7,388	2,379	1,383	690	12,459
DRAUGHON'S COLLEGE	PRI-T	10,000	B	0	2,000	2,000	0	0	0	0	B
EASTERN KY UNIVERSITY	PUB-FG	1,602,474	765,070	90,959	91,786	433,312	85,000	10,020	0	38,357	87,970
GEORGETOWN COLLEGE	PRI-FG	126,022	49,232	9,262	10,526	28,416	14,760	2,966	252	4,480	6,128
KENTUCKY BUSINESS COLLEGE	PRI-T	10,806	B	B	0	0	3,491	0	661	0	B
KY CHRISTIAN COLLEGE	PRI-FN	11,322	B	0	0	3,588	1,214	586	204	314	B
KENTUCKY STATE UNIVERSITY	PUB-FG	397,359	220,429	35,269	0	49,209	40,103	3,593	1,449	6,005	41,302
KENTUCKY WESLEYAN COLLEGE	PRI-FN	118,643	65,201	12,532	8,670	5,977	6,943	1,616	3,906	466	13,332
LEES JUNIOR COLLEGE	PRI-T	43,970	B	B	4,643	9,533	4,169	0	351	0	B
LEXINGTON THEOL SEMINARY	PRI-FG	99,000	B	B	5,000	30,000	0	0	0	5,000	B
LINDSEY WILSON COLLEGE	PRI-T	28,319	B	B	825	3,390	1,300	0	540	200	B
LOUISVL PRESB THEOL SEM	PRI-FG	147,040	90,572	0	7,345	24,379	7,108	0	4,391	5,337	7,908
LOUISVILLE SCHOOL OF ART	PRI-FN	18,497	B	0	2,523	3,597	1,246	0	150	502	B
MIDWAY COLLEGE	PRI-T	34,527	B	0	3,230	12,304	3,824	660	0	0	B
MOREHEAD STATE UNIVERSITY	PUB-FG	943,678	469,302	107,560	70,296	201,550	63,100	0	0	8,000	23,870
MURRAY STATE UNIVERSITY	PUB-FG	1,003,611	392,740	76,930	42,429	238,862	145,527	9,096	9,406	18,024	70,597
NORTHERN KY UNIVERSITY	PUB-FG	1,387,245	389,553	57,164	79,185	448,407	257,560	64,880	1,274	8,458	80,764
OWENSBORO BUSINESS C	PRI-T	23,550	B	B	3,750	2,100	350	0	150	0	B
PIKEVILLE COLLEGE	PRI-FN	109,841	55,353	4,639	6,651	13,583	4,722	8,325	770	0	15,798
SAINT CATHARINE COLLEGE	PRI-T	25,890	B	0	0	4,389	705	389	1,241	252	B
SEMINARY OF SAINT PIUS X	PRI-FN	74,950	44,910	0	2,322	16,277	3,107	80	845	537	6,872
SOUTHERN BAPT THEOL SEM	PRI-FG	416,319	179,726	30,389	66,862	64,319	17,140	500	7,899	13,807	35,677
SPALDING COLLEGE	PRI-FG	113,783	77,896	5,823	0	10,255	9,677	0	0	2,162	7,970
SUE BENNETT COLLEGE	PRI-T	23,389	B	B	982	6,786	1,011	0	99	186	B
SULLIVAN JC BUSINESS	PRI-T	25,927	B	B	0	8,422	902	83	-15	0	B
THOMAS MORE COLLEGE	PRI-FN	85,248	37,358	3,909	0	16,979	15,933	1,172	0	1,522	8,375
TRANSYLVANIA UNIVERSITY	PRI-FN	126,372	80,314	11,558	0	17,772	8,500	528	750	0	6,950
UNION COLLEGE	PRI-FG	116,965	59,370	5,254	6,311	14,641	5,367	1,401	6,219	2,547	15,855
U KENTUCKY ALL CAMPUSES											
UNIVERSITY OF KENTUCKY	PUB-U	4,666,538	2,154,004	149,557	243,823	496,805	887,288	0	8,937	97,829	628,295
U OF KENTUCKY CC SYSTEM	PUB-T	1,173,443	722,451	91,951	33,373	149,100	47,261	20,187	44,338	1,374	63,408
UNIVERSITY OF LOUISVILLE	PUB-U	2,774,261	1,326,199	198,238	139,520	450,001	342,395	12,377	6,540	57,339	241,652
WATTERSON COLLEGE	PRI-T	A	A	A	A	A	A				A
WESTERN KY UNIVERSITY	PUB-FG	1,799,671	855,781	160,888	176,528	218,059	233,919	37,062	10,152	31,309	75,973
LOUISIANA											
BOSSIER PARISH CC	PUB-T	45,870	28,040	0	0	14,607	878	0	1,260	928	157
CENTENARY C OF LOUISIANA	PRI-FG	170,981	65,504	8,040	13,238	48,231	21,464	715	220	5,999	7,570
DELGADO COLLEGE	PUB-T	331,886	216,356	21,229	0	38,358	4,229	4,200	26,168	0	21,346
DILLARD UNIVERSITY	PRI-FN	205,708	106,351	13,801	28,014	28,349	16,110	447	319	4,366	7,951
GRAMBLING STATE U	PUB-FG	498,536	223,183	25,181	0	100,939	73,835	11,073	7,736	6,000	50,589
LOUISIANA COLLEGE	PRI-FN	141,750	69,775	9,717	17,159	20,600	15,000	1,200	800	4,359	3,140

SEE FOOTNOTES AT END OF TABLE

Table 2. – Library Operating Expenditures (in Dollars) of College and University Libraries, by Category of Expenditure and by State or Other Area and Institution: Aggregate United States, 1978-79 – Continued

STATE OR OTHER AREA AND INSTITUTION	CON-TROL AND TYPE OF IN-STITU-TION	TOTAL	SALARIES AND WAGES			BOOK-STOCK	PERIOD-ICALS	MICRO-FORMS	AUDIO-VISUAL	BIND-ING AND RE-BIND-ING	ALL OTHER OPER-ATING EXPEND-ITURES
			LIBRARY STAFF	FRINGE BENEFITS	STUDENTS ON HOURLY BASIS						
(1)	(2)	(3)	(4)	(5)	(6)	(7)	(8)	(9)	(10)	(11)	(12)
LOUISIANA	--CONTINUED										
LOUISIANA ST U ALL CAM											
LA STATE U AND A&M C	PUB-U	4,075,531	1,625,493	253,396	202,664	714,628	763,619	1,708	2,103	93,207	418,713
LA STATE U ALEXANDRIA	PUB-T	313,488	136,809	14,900	9,275	86,519	31,648	8,465	1,008	10,014	14,850
LA STATE U EUNICE	PUB-T	179,694	97,328	9,897	7,986	25,765	13,000	500	484	6,947	17,787
LA ST U MEDICAL CENTER	PUB-FG	620,219	304,122	32,409	9,700	183,298	0	0	0	12,750	77,940
LA STATE U SHREVEPORT	PUB-FG	436,046	219,644	17,155	4,022	86,944	78,996	3,000	0	15,000	11,285
UNIVERSITY OF NEW ORLEANS	PUB-FG	1,353,305	584,200	68,351	73,432	220,158	254,726	28,818	1,089	40,025	82,506
LOUISIANA TECH UNIVERSITY	PUB-FG	821,602	435,757	52,291	14,588	59,552	114,485	1,780	1,725	16,178	125,246
LOYOLA U IN NEW ORLEANS	PRI-U	841,039	335,486	47,288	25,850	140,298	150,728	18,615	1,254	9,262	112,258
MCNEESE STATE UNIVERSITY	PUB-FG	646,642	364,368	33,986	8,218	107,045	68,179	6,440	0	13,843	44,563
NEW ORLS BAPT THEOL SEM	PRI-FG	140,694	64,191	7,131	17,349	25,531	8,619	80	1,856	5,305	10,632
NICHOLLS STATE UNIVERSITY	PUB-FG	637,015	390,173	38,887	12,415	79,895	61,842	8,133	0	12,554	33,016
NORTHEAST LOUISIANA U	PUB-FG	979,021	429,017	36,466	88,925	114,549	178,659	27,161	0	8,828	95,416
NTHWSTN ST U OF LA	PUB-FG	606,114	390,124	37,751	15,058	35,575	82,328	8,900	706	12,684	22,988
NOTRE DAME SEM SCH THEO	PRI-FG	53,577	15,700	0	0	17,516	0	0	746	1,406	0
OUR LADY OF HOLY CROSS C	PRI-FN	A	A	A	A	A	A	A	A	A	A
PHILLIPS C NEW ORLEANS	PRI-T	A	A	A	A	A	A	A	A	A	A
SAINT BERNARD PARISH CC	PUB-T	60,290	52,280	1,448	0	2,891	2,727	0	0	200	744
SAINT JOSEPH SEM COLLEGE	PRI-FN	23,363	B	B	0	6,514	3,112	0	0	1,091	B
SAINT MARY'S DOMINICAN C	PRI-FN	88,189	53,697	2,717	3,157	5,760	6,569	450	944	2,284	12,611
STHESTN LA UNIVERSITY	PUB-FG	633,808	268,158	28,961	25,870	131,969	62,808	18,051	54,434	5,482	38,075
SOUTHERN U A&M ALL CAM											
SOUTHERN U A&M C MAIN CAM	PUB-FG	689,669	405,362	41,120	802	141,169	50,738	13,268	0	5,912	31,298
STHN U IN NEW ORLEANS	PUB-FN	298,829	205,424	19,529	0	38,116	20,069	931	0	5,000	9,760
STHN U SHREVEPORT-BOSSIER	PUB-T	135,092	63,275	5,502	0	35,903	1,501	13,419	6,524	345	8,623
TULANE U OF LOUISIANA	PRI-U	2,750,856	1,316,950	122,048	90,723	776,652	94,150	32,433	1,169	83,446	233,285
U OF STHWSTN LOUISIANA	PUB-FG	1,101,448	564,119	56,412	0	214,434	219,178	12,245	280	30,609	4,171
XAVIER UNIVERSITY OF LA	PRI-FG	402,256	180,111	17,132	88,498	55,564	25,896	13,040	3,300	2,813	15,902
MAINE											
ANDOVER COLLEGE	PRI-T	6,858	B	0	0	150	537	0	0	0	B
BANGOR THEOLOGICAL SEM	PRI-FG	44,421	B	0	3,519	9,684	5,307	0	0	891	B
BATES COLLEGE	PRI-FN	546,082	206,613	29,534	35,002	120,407	67,829	2,803	1,941	12,916	69,037
BEAL COLLEGE	PRI-T	12,510	B	0	0	4,700	0	0	350	0	B
BOWDOIN COLLEGE	PRI-FN	666,576	257,686	30,922	34,064	166,859	113,343	0	300	20,676	42,726
CASCO BAY COLLEGE	PRI-T	A	A	A	0	0	A				A
COLBY COLLEGE	PRI-FN	709,985	266,270	34,175	61,305	163,380	78,500	0	1,000	0	105,355
COLLEGE OF THE ATLANTIC	PRI-FN	60,999	B	B	6,346	11,963	6,707	500	0	0	B
EASTERN ME VOC-TECH INST	PUB-T	23,387	B	B	0	4,449	1,956	0	131	64	B
HUSSON COLLEGE	PRI-FG	46,583	B	B	0	6,400	3,851	36	0	0	B
MAINE MARITIME ACADEMY	PUB-FN	206,575	81,764	21,258	8,596	32,720	28,566	5,217	0	1,433	27,021
NASSON COLLEGE	PRI-FN	109,412	48,852	6,405	11,960	9,760	27,306	0	0	2,251	2,878
NTHN ME VOC TECH INST	PUB-T	44,600	B	B	0	7,500	2,400	0	0	0	B
PORTLAND SCHOOL OF ART	PRI-FN	27,637	B	B	0	7,723	677	0	0	0	B
SAINT JOSEPH'S COLLEGE	PRI-FN	73,725	B	B	515	15,250	12,300	7,000	4,000	4,000	B
SOUTHERN ME VOC TECH INST	PUB-T	12,088	B	0	0	4,567	3,931	0	0	0	B
THOMAS COLLEGE	PRI-FG	36,728	B	B	3,023	8,017	6,817	355	0	0	B
UNITY COLLEGE	PRI-FN	78,381	B	B	29,723	9,283	9,374	480	745	274	B
U OF MAINE ALL CAMPUSES											
U OF MAINE AT AUGUSTA	PUB-T	109,526	45,746	7,205	0	31,024	9,172	2,133	1,716	0	12,530
U OF MAINE AT FARMINGTON	PUB-FN	155,067	83,493	17,310	0	23,443	17,895	4,065	868	516	7,477
U OF MAINE AT FORT KENT	PUB-FN	82,673	46,023	7,870	0	15,747	4,295	3,537	0	0	5,201
U OF MAINE AT MACHIAS	PUB-FN	100,939	56,185	9,791	0	19,725	9,877	1,112	400	1,338	2,511
U OF MAINE AT ORONO	PUB-U	1,542,169	688,905	121,154	78,397	217,995	251,007	0	0	25,553	159,158
U OF ME AT PRESQUE ISLE	PUB-FN	118,838	53,113	9,082	0	23,189	12,280	11,879	17	200	9,078
U OF SOUTHERN MAINE	PUB-FG	570,499	290,730	45,063	18,114	99,087	71,521	6,641	870	5,614	32,859
UNIVERSITY OF NEW ENGLAND	PRI-FG	103,578	65,395	7,847	0	15,239	10,184	1,635	91	0	3,187
WESTBROOK COLLEGE	PRI-FN	69,701	38,125	5,719	3,700	11,067	6,152	1,500	0	0	3,438
MARYLAND											
ALLEGANY CMTY COLLEGE	PUB-T	112,533	84,450	4,570	0	12,456	5,671	1,947	0	481	2,958
ANNE ARUNDEL CMTY COLLEGE	PUB-T	251,273	165,150	10,217	4,872	31,900	10,000	0	5,875	7,000	16,259
BALTIMORE HEBREW COLLEGE	PRI-FG	A	A	A	A	A	A	A	0	2,200	A
BOWIE STATE COLLEGE	PUB-FG.	435,393	271,181	0	29,522	20,733	48,488	15,749	4,585	9,900	35,235
CAPITOL INST TECHNOLOGY	PRI-FN	24,644	B	B	4,791	4,690	1,471	0	13	0	B

SEE FOOTNOTES AT END OF TABLE

Table 2. — Library Operating Expenditures (in Dollars) of College and University Libraries, by Category of Expenditure and by State or Other Area and Institution: Aggregate United States, 1978-79 — Continued

STATE OR OTHER AREA AND INSTITUTION	CONTROL AND TYPE OF INSTITUTION	TOTAL	SALARIES AND WAGES			BOOKSTOCK	PERIODICALS	MICROFORMS	AUDIOVISUAL	BINDING AND REBINDING	ALL OTHER OPERATING EXPENDITURES
			LIBRARY STAFF	FRINGE BENEFITS	STUDENTS ON HOURLY BASIS						
(1)	(2)	(3)	(4)	(5)	(6)	(7)	(8)	(9)	(10)	(11)	(12)
MARYLAND	--CONTINUED										
CATONSVILLE CMTY COLLEGE	PUB-T	707,923	508,128	62,000	20,559	29,642	28,023	2,591	192	4,000	52,788
CECIL COMMUNITY COLLEGE	PUB-T	95,197	58,304	8,783	0	13,284	4,619	0	2,511	0	7,696
CHARLES CO CMTY COLLEGE	PUB-T	283,825	144,844	21,726	10,547	36,729	6,218	3,700	8,896	1,165	50,000
CHESAPEAKE COLLEGE	PUB-T	79,622	49,900	0	0	11,163	3,500	1,000	1,200	200	12,659
COLLEGE OF NOTRE DAME MD	PRI FN		SEE LOYOLA-NOTRE DAME JT LIB								
COLUMBIA UNION COLLEGE	PRI-FN	188,023	73,776	4,285	30,828	35,636	12,232	826	5,224	5,939	19,277
CMTY COLLEGE OF BALTIMORE	PUB-T	454,484	307,911	17,843	0	60,593	17,382	4,784	17,809	248	27,914
COPPIN STATE COLLEGE	PUB-FG	361,302	214,736	3,235	0	67,028	21,905	13,335	6,218	4,520	27,325
DE SALES HALL SCH THEO	PRI-FG	19,743	B	B	0	3,700	1,800	0	150	450	B
DUNDALK CMTY COLLEGE	PUB-T	229,466	126,550	10,123	0	40,131	1,314	1,901	24,331	0	25,116
ESSEX COMMUNITY COLLEGE	PUB-T	351,502	250,110	21,723	4,260	16,030	25,957	3,740	0	1,735	27,947
FREDERICK CMTY COLLEGE	PUB-T	180,155	131,164	4,864	10,100	10,927	11,593	0	3,435	0	8,032
FROSTBURG STATE COLLEGE	PUB-FG	551,939	384,260	57,740	6,245	28,535	23,398	14,500	2,713	8,422	25,423
GARRETT COMMUNITY COLLEGE	PUB-T	117,097	40,604	4,182	0	41,121	14,075	0	11,585	0	5,530
GOUCHER COLLEGE	PRI-FG	262,463	137,432	32,262	7,802	38,860	26,397	2,255	669	2,514	14,272
HAGERSTOWN JUNIOR COLLEGE	PUB-T	176,923	111,685	16,753	0	17,961	10,585	2,000	6,382	500	11,057
HARFORD COMMUNITY COLLEGE	PUB-T	174,445	128,795	11,025	0	10,559	10,464	4,065	4,004	65	5,437
HOOD COLLEGE	PRI-FG	226,564	106,399	15,960	5,264	45,816	22,519	4,463	626	5,550	19,967
HOWARD COMMUNITY COLLEGE	PUB-T	216,039	172,629	5,239	0	9,258	6,382	1,067	3,300	1,089	16,975
JOHNS HOPKINS UNIVERSITY	PRI-U	4,526,119	2,139,050	285,535	92,535	251,012	818,179	17,027	13,210	55,800	740,618
LOYOLA COLLEGE	PRI FG		SEE LOYOLA-NOTRE DAME JT LIB								
LOYOLA-NOTRE DAME JT LIB	PRI-FG	382,648	206,368	21,271	3,993	54,867	52,291	4,702	3,718	7,224	28,214
MARYLAND C ART AND DESIGN	PRI-T	14,723	B	0	466	4,437	245	0	679	0	B
MD INST COLLEGE OF ART	PRI-FG	123,301	82,343	12,351	219	12,895	4,465	0	0	1,776	9,252
MONTGOMERY C ALL CAMPUSES											
MONTGOMERY C GERMANTOWN	PUB-T	94,535	66,608	6,522	11,394	0	10,011	0	0	0	0
MONTGOMERY C ROCKVILLE	PUB-T	654,829	448,146	39,456	21,050	66,046	21,650	5,564	0	3,969	48,948
MONTGOMERY C TAKOMA PARK	PUB-T	274,151	190,802	16,369	8,979	28,200	9,744	2,672	0	1,500	15,885
MORGAN STATE UNIVERSITY	PUB-FG	960,130	546,666	0	16,319	194,097	73,448	51,843	3,455	2,436	71,866
MOUNT SNT MARY'S COLLEGE	PRI-FG	191,000	86,400	0	11,100	49,100	18,000	4,000	0	5,000	17,400
NER ISRAEL RAB COLLEGE	PRI-FG	14,983	7,500	0	120	0	415	0	300	240	158
PEABODY INST OF JHU	PRI-FG	79,646	32,430	5,604	0	19,434	0	150	2,746	8,963	10,319
PRINCE GEORGES CC	PUB-T	714,081	381,908	72,613	54,224	61,946	11,946	6,516	44,054	1,734	79,140
SAINT JOHN'S C ALL CAM											
SAINT JOHN'S C MAIN CAM	PRI-FG	77,120	B	B	13,154	10,391	3,536	120	763	600	B
SNT JOHN'S C SANTA FE NM	PRI-FG	95,479	43,231	6,317	26,747	5,056	4,006	395	224	661	8,842
SNT MARY'S COLLEGE OF MD	PUB-FN	318,448	150,268	26,187	6,011	44,954	45,904	6,862	788	3,170	34,304
SAINT MARY'S SEMINARY & U	PRI-FG	81,321	35,215	2,805	4,682	22,598	9,148	300	0	3,896	2,677
SALISBURY STATE COLLEGE	PUB-FG	476,405	262,094	0	25,456	94,944	53,644	7,841	2,250	6,556	23,620
TOWSON STATE UNIVERSITY	PUB-FG	1,217,641	575,096	115,019	41,756	291,460	93,164	12,000	5,000	16,678	67,468
UNIVERSITY OF BALTIMORE	PUB-FG	856,216	388,838	64,578	38,830	98,357	137,976	24,020	812	7,603	95,202
U MARYLAND SYS ALL INST											
U OF MARYLAND ALL CAM											
U OF MD COLLEGE PARK CAM	PUB-U	6,292,444	3,020,892	489,448	459,529	740,713	895,359	0	22,571	149,601	514,331
U OF MD BALTIMORE CO CAM	PUB-FG	1,251,315	555,403	101,147	43,003	122,226	249,881	1,856	68,255	14,434	95,110
U OF MD BALT PROF SCHOOLS	PUB-FG	1,595,118	829,376	130,405	11,820	255,246	229,166	10,182	1,594	29,927	97,402
U MD UNIVERSITY COLLEGE	PUB-FG		NO LIBRARY FACILITIES								
U OF MD-EASTERN SHORE	PUB-FG	291,155	179,957	33,372	6,680	16,000	33,000	2,000	3,900	1,900	14,338
VILLA JULIE COLLEGE	PRI-T	37,839	B	B	0	10,700	2,000	0	0	500	B
WASHINGTON BIBLE COLLEGE	PRI-FG	73,527	B	B	21,341	17,784	4,025	1,276	1,678	541	B
WASHINGTON COLLEGE	PRI-FG	195,090	88,336	10,864	12,122	35,495	28,673	6,230	249	3,367	9,754
WASHINGTON THEOL UNION	PRI-FG	A	A	A	A	A	A	A	A	A	A
WESTERN MARYLAND COLLEGE	PRI-FG	255,074	105,652	19,485	16,455	44,535	29,647	10,939	227	3,631	24,503
WOR-WIC TECH CMTY COLLEGE	PUB-T		NO LIBRARY FACILITIES								
MASSACHUSETTS											
AMERICAN INTRNATL COLLEGE	PRI-FG	109,474	53,000	0	4,040	26,545	20,372	148	1,014	265	4,090
AMHERST COLLEGE	PRI-FN	844,063	423,630	49,950	23,059	144,913	119,551	0	4,693	12,833	65,234
ANDOVER NEWTON THEOL SCH	PRI-FG	141,436	72,938	11,302	1,516	33,422	7,936	2,102	0	4,403	7,817
ANNA MARIA COLLEGE	PRI-FG	51,803	25,437	2,088	1,037	9,938	3,934	1,900	696	308	6,465
AQUINAS JC ALL CAMPUSES											
AQUINAS JC AT MILTON	PRI-T	19,105	B	B	578	3,521	2,633	185	607	404	B
AQUINAS JC AT NEWTON	PRI-T	26,310	15,000	0	0	3,716	2,476	0	1,339	294	455
ADL MGMT ED INSTITUTE	PRI-FG	683,300	224,000	50,000	0	96,800	145,200	10,000	0	2,000	155,300
ASSUMPTION COLLEGE	PRI-FG	160,472	67,109	7,346	13,731	31,465	18,866	1,100	0	7,148	13,707

SEE FOOTNOTES AT END OF TABLE

STATE OR OTHER AREA AND INSTITUTION	CONTROL AND TYPE OF INSTITUTION	TOTAL	SALARIES AND WAGES			BOOK-STOCK	PERIODICALS	MICRO-FORMS	AUDIO-VISUAL	BINDING AND RE-BINDING	ALL OTHER OPERATING EXPENDITURES
			LIBRARY STAFF	FRINGE BENEFITS	STUDENTS ON HOURLY BASIS						
(1)	(2)	(3)	(4)	(5)	(6)	(7)	(8)	(9)	(10)	(11)	(12)
MASSACHUSETTS	--CONTINUED										
ATLANTIC UNION COLLEGE	PRI-FN	117,370	47,635	8,162	24,330	15,038	9,428	1,985	0	3,133	7,659
BABSON COLLEGE	PRI-FG	371,808	170,644	23,158	40,989	57,529	17,651	13,298	4,000	627	43,912
BAY PATH JUNIOR COLLEGE	PRI-T	53,073	B	B	2,935	10,350	6,143	0	0	0	B
BAY STATE JC OF BUS	PRI-T	17,492	B	B	946	1,119	2,093	0	1,734	0	B
BECKER JC ALL INSTITUTION											
BECKER JC-LEICESTER	PRI-T	39,439	B	B	0	12,054	2,826	0	2,537	0	B
BECKER JC-WORCESTER	PRI-T	68,453	B	B	0	19,122	3,546	1,080	2,928	99	B
BENTLEY COLLEGE	PRI-FG	484,201	198,199	31,660	41,924	92,585	9,334	47,156	5,189	1,153	57,001
BERKLEE COLLEGE OF MUSIC	PRI-FN	82,735	B	B	23,446	9,223	1,250	0	2,127	0	B
BERKSHIRE CHRISTIAN C	PRI-FN	35,225	B	B	3,189	6,399	1,951	542	252	1,136	B
BLUE HILLS REG TECH INST	PUB-T	28,987	B	0	0	3,996	1,436	0	3,557	0	B
BOSTON COLLEGE	PRI-U	2,313,596	1,130,033	199,073	41,667	456,399	223,717	68,480	1,635	44,533	148,059
BOSTON CONSV OF MUSIC	PRI-FG	A	A	A	A	A	A	A	A	A	A
BOSTON UNIVERSITY	PRI-U	3,976,617	2,010,105	323,862	110,413	429,879	665,607	55,000	3,715	69,463	308,573
BRADFORD COLLEGE	PRI-FN	67,875	39,275	0	0	14,000	5,000	3,000	2,000	300	4,300
BRANDEIS UNIVERSITY	PRI-U	1,752,132	743,888	100,891	148,346	375,301	224,754	17,880	942	44,825	95,305
CEN NEW ENG COLLEGE TECHN	PRI FN			SEE WORCESTER JOINT LIBRARY							
CHAMBERLAYNE JR COLLEGE	PRI-T	14,959	B	B	3,300	503	877	0	209	0	B
CLARK UNIVERSITY	PRI-FG	615,320	251,373	37,705	30,680	67,582	141,218	3,726	2,500	22,223	58,313
COLLEGE OF THE HOLY CROSS	PRI-FG	452,750	231,000	0	20,000	112,000	45,000	4,000	0	10,000	30,750
COLLEGE OUR LADY OF ELMS	PRI-FN	113,616	74,426	129	0	14,563	9,527	935	3,142	2,295	8,599
CURRY COLLEGE	PRI-FN	139,940	72,407	7,815	11,782	18,655	12,284	3,362	654	404	12,577
DEAN JUNIOR COLLEGE	PRI-T	129,833	60,321	10,449	4,746	20,637	11,978	10,885	0	1,563	9,254
EASTERN NAZARENE COLLEGE	PRI-FG	105,868	36,458	6,622	18,536	19,719	17,654	3,328	0	0	3,551
EMERSON COLLEGE	PRI-FG	225,063	122,971	15,101	7,379	29,542	10,847	3,370	6,596	800	28,457
EMMANUEL COLLEGE	PRI-FG	130,775	56,328	5,731	7,093	32,297	20,969	531	104	557	7,165
ENDICOTT COLLEGE	PRI-T	89,772	58,302	10,016	6,490	6,775	3,395	640	303	342	3,509
EPISCOPAL DIVINITY SCHOOL	PRI-FG	103,978	64,846	5,201	1,229	17,810	3,765	1,541	0	2,243	7,343
ESSEX AGRL-TECH INST	PUB-T	68,954	B	B	0	14,233	8,057	1,138	4,980	635	B
FISHER JUNIOR COLLEGE	PRI-T	39,309	B	B	1,810	11,623	982	0	0	0	B
FORSYTH SCH DENTL HYGNSTS	PRI-T	42,552	B	B	1,260	3,500	12,000	400	0	1,200	B
FRANKLIN INST OF BOSTON	PRI-T	15,818	B	B	0	2,177	1,780	0	0	0	B
GORDON COLLEGE	PRI-FN	158,400	81,601	12,241	1,717	29,193	21,702	599	975	791	9,581
GORDON-CONWELL THEOL SEM	PRI-FG	153,394	70,178	10,055	10,392	34,958	6,807	803	1,047	1,763	17,391
HAMPSHIRE COLLEGE	PRI-FN	450,216	248,566	42,429	24,411	28,241	31,375	2,618	5,237	1,884	65,455
HARVARD UNIVERSITY	PRI-U	18,105,671	9,050,694	1,481,688	650,000	1,717,652	2,195,122	250,000	0	482,059	2,278,456
HEBREW COLLEGE	PRI-FG	60,567	B	B	1,250	6,337	1,856	800	108	1,800	B
HELLENIC C-HOLY CROSS SCH	PRI-FG	87,648	43,317	3,977	6,248	20,574	8,112	1,205	0	1,785	2,430
KATHARINE GIBBS SCHOOL	PRI-T	3,775	0	0	2,575	500	300	0	400	0	0
LABOURE JUNIOR COLLEGE	PRI-T	55,299	B	B	1,900	7,280	3,229	0	3,313	118	B
LASELL JUNIOR COLLEGE	PRI-T	67,787	37,695	3,343	0	14,466	5,300	931	2,402	0	3,650
LESLEY COLLEGE	PRI-FG	262,495	131,043	18,038	8,802	31,045	10,341	8,894	11,113	700	42,519
MASS BOARD CC ALL INST											
BERKSHIRE CMTY COLLEGE	PUB-T	105,429	61,099	4,040	0	26,995	6,329	2,724	1,317	0	2,925
BRISTOL COMMUNITY COLLEGE	PUB-T	379,283	192,975	47,279	57,935	20,438	7,044	3,787	23,950	900	24,975
BUNKER HILL CMTY COLLEGE	PUB-T	234,972	113,040	27,129	23,771	48,732	11,039	1,856	8,500	0	905
CAPE COD CMTY COLLEGE	PUB-T	217,837	117,356	16,507	28,440	26,310	7,028	5,005	12,930	150	4,111
GREENFIELD CMTY COLLEGE	PUB-T	215,129	129,880	31,262	0	20,209	9,164	2,082	6,419	3,250	12,863
HOLYOKE COMMUNITY COLLEGE	PUB-T	209,940	130,820	0	11,307	28,372	13,057	2,858	12,505	1,327	9,694
MASS BAY CMTY COLLEGE	PUB-T	218,420	141,754	3,473	914	13,604	14,962	9,635	9,134	600	24,344
MASSASOIT CMTY COLLEGE	PUB-T	183,197	125,592	0	0	27,000	7,745	4,475	17,500	0	885
MIDDLESEX CMTY COLLEGE	PUB-T	146,967	95,400	0	0	35,457	5,010	300	6,000	100	4,700
MT WACHUSETT CMTY COLLEGE	PUB-T	96,719	60,780	3,195	0	22,759	5,759	1,317	257	144	2,508
NTHN ESSEX CMTY COLLEGE	PUB-T	199,272	85,559	21,389	10,706	43,000	4,570	2,150	14,692	0	17,206
NORTH SHORE CMTY COLLEGE	PUB-T	A	A	A	A	A	A	A	A	A	A
QUINSIGAMOND CMTY COLLEGE	PUB-T	95,356	47,758	11,462	0	15,000	8,000	2,511	6,057	60	4,508
ROXBURY COMMUNITY COLLEGE	PUB-T	119,275	77,425	0	0	25,000	5,100	6,000	3,900	0	1,850
SPRINGFIELD TECHNICAL CC	PUB-T	182,241	97,190	21,294	0	28,021	5,447	1,876	16,701	393	11,319
MASS C. PHAR-HLTH SCI	PRI-FG	218,158	116,136	14,869	8,369	29,470	35,646	2,068	1,147	3,309	7,144
MASS INST OF TECHNOLOGY	PRI-U	4,332,702	2,177,978	458,617	199,682	331,031	665,273	30,000	19,220	71,137	379,764
MASS STATE C SYS ALL INST											
BOSTON STATE COLLEGE	PUB-FG	532,925	299,668	0	6,550	130,561	35,000	10,000	500	5,000	45,646
BRIDGEWATER STATE COLLEGE	PUB-FG	670,723	389,574	16,227	14,679	119,553	65,990	2,600	452	11,426	50,222
FITCHBURG STATE COLLEGE	PUB-FG	359,532	188,356	0	12,000	66,000	55,976	17,000	2,000	3,000	15,200
FRAMINGHAM STATE COLLEGE	PUB-FG	337,791	214,568	8,000	4,877	53,764	36,591	6,479	1,500	2,763	9,249

SEE FOOTNOTES AT END OF TABLE

Table 2. — Library Operating Expenditures (in Dollars) of College and University Libraries, by Category of Expenditure and by State or Other Area and Institution: Aggregate United States, 1978-79 — Continued

| STATE OR OTHER AREA AND INSTITUTION (1) | CONTROL AND TYPE OF INSTITUTION (2) | TOTAL (3) | SALARIES AND WAGES | | | BOOK-STOCK (7) | PERIOD-ICALS (8) | MICRO-FORMS (9) | AUDIO-VISUAL (10) | BINDING AND RE-BINDING (11) | ALL OTHER OPER-ATING EXPEND-ITURES (12) |
			LIBRARY STAFF (4)	FRINGE BENEFITS (5)	STUDENTS ON HOURLY BASIS (6)						
MASSACHUSETTS --CONTINUED											
MASS COLLEGE OF ART	PUB-FG	164,346	69,951	16,837	8,896	35,000	10,000	200	20,000	2,000	1,462
MASS MARITIME ACADEMY	PUB-FN	116,682	59,000	5,482	0	16,300	7,400	19,000	7,500	0	2,000
NORTH ADAMS STATE COLLEGE	PUB-FG	274,001	135,077	7,381	16,061	54,912	22,281	7,369	6,396	296	24,228
SALEM STATE COLLEGE	PUB-FG	455,933	285,869	0	6,024	74,000	33,000	9,500	10,000	8,540	29,000
WESTFIELD STATE COLLEGE	PUB-FG	268,044	144,800	5,000	6,376	89,582	18,059	3,464	0	763	0
WORCESTER STATE COLLEGE	PUB-FG	479,577	331,737	6,635	18,471	30,288	26,690	8,752	8,867	1,347	46,790
MERRIMACK COLLEGE	PRI-FN	191,600	79,250	8,350	22,000	32,000	33,000	1,000	1,000	1,000	14,000
MOUNT HOLYOKE COLLEGE	PRI-FG	723,003	333,758	45,713	34,426	113,134	112,828	984	100	26,316	55,744
MOUNT IDA JUNIOR COLLEGE	PRI-T	50,925	B	B	9,466	7,697	4,061	1,564	477	336	B
NEWBURY JUNIOR COLLEGE	PRI-T	74,688	B	B	5,244	6,224	3,345	311	39,100	0	B
NEW ENGLAND C OPTOMETRY	PRI-FG	82,860	46,502	6,045	3,583	7,998	6,328	142	3,002	1,494	7,766
NEW ENG CONSV OF MUSIC	PRI-FG	174,639	64,281	11,344	41,023	24,721	1,966	0	6,604	5,698	19,002
NEW ENG INST APP ARTS-SCI	PRI-T	19,838	B	B	0	1,934	1,357	0	3,783	0	B
NEW ENGLAND SCHOOL OF LAW	PRI-FG	320,320	105,629	16,604	27,585	52,049	90,674	7,758	500	4,054	15,467
NICHOLS COLLEGE	PRI-FG	A	A	A	A	A	A	A	A	A	A
NORTHEASTERN UNIVERSITY2/	PRI-U	2,397,337	1,340,012	136,165	133,100	442,770	130,000	15,000	21,000	38,400	140,890
PINE MANOR COLLEGE	PRI-FN	84,154	51,584	0	0	23,845	1,524	1,666	642	223	4,670
POPE JOHN XXIII NATL SEM	PRI-FG	A	B	A	A	A	A	A	A	A	B
QUINCY JUNIOR COLLEGE	PUB-T	89,549	B	0	9,766	5,242	4,375	7,584	2,528	0	B
RADCLIFFE COLLEGE	PRI-FN	301,818	189,641	39,009	2,685	12,743	0	6,375	1,000	928	49,437
REGIS COLLEGE	PRI-FG	154,767	89,626	5,200	1,931	31,532	14,036	1,248	796	2,397	8,001
SNT HYACINTH COLLEGE-SEM	PRI-FN	27,079	B	0	0	4,615	2,349	0	0	884	B
SAINT JOHN'S SEMINARY	PRI-FG	81,142	B	B	1,014	30,339	7,188	285	0	2,224	B
SCH OF MUSEUM FINE ARTS	PRI-FG	29,682	B	B	7,395	7,214	1,189	0	902	0	B
SCH WORCESTER ART MUSEUM	PRI-T	40,796	B	B	0	6,256	3,416	267	0	423	B
SIMMONS COLLEGE	PRI-FG	471,698	184,026	21,565	77,989	90,777	47,582	2,872	1,094	6,161	39,632
SIMON'S ROCK EARLY C.	PRI-FN	105,842	54,595	8,189	1,421	21,079	9,887	2,388	1,200	0	7,083
SMITH COLLEGE	PRI-FG	1,438,538	754,666	123,075	55,444	175,862	145,067	18,601	14,506	40,000	111,317
STHESTN MASS UNIVERSITY	PUB-FG	1,673,136	417,028	95,805	18,143	513,420	148,243	84,805	211,442	11,500	172,745
SPRINGFIELD COLLEGE	PRI-FG	228,303	126,784	19,018	17,972	21,236	24,249	6,929	800	2,800	8,515
STONEHILL COLLEGE	PRI-FN	249,422	134,393	17,400	16,373	39,320	28,587	4,002	116	1,422	7,809
SUFFOLK UNIVERSITY	PRI-FG	929,173	304,569	39,437	25,000	373,604	67,757	50,688	4,486	17,023	46,609
SWAIN SCHOOL OF DESIGN	PRI-FN	19,195	B	B	0	4,008	1,319	0	804	862	B
TUFTS UNIVERSITY	PRI-U	1,819,250	828,101	126,524	91,527	253,688	327,125	22,169	4,692	48,121	117,303
UNIVERSITY OF LOWELL	PUB-FG	1,462,985	593,386	0	4,200	268,280	133,029	22,343	109,303	68,775	263,669
U OF MASS ALL CAMPUSES											
U OF MASS AMHERST CAMPUS	PUB-U	3,618,858	2,097,926	0	148,697	233,947	682,846	0	0	57,204	398,238
U OF MASS BOSTON CAMPUS	PUB-FG	1,115,448	589,685	40,000	21,220	177,406	248,500	2,200	2,000	23,800	10,637
U MASS MEDL SCH-WORCESTER	PUB-FG	572,333	205,574	0	4,312	98,490	158,435	40,190	24,296	15,000	26,036
WELLESLEY COLLEGE	PRI-FN	962,986	470,260	94,515	12,864	153,548	162,655	6,288	0	18,292	44,564
WENTWORTH INST OF TECH	PRI-FN	135,590	57,780	14,445	13,986	34,640	4,006	1,667	5,666	0	3,400
WESTERN NEW ENG COLLEGE	PRI-FG	688,337	190,015	21,917	46,144	227,728	118,856	24,675	300	4,731	53,971
WHEATON COLLEGE	PRI-FN	531,165	217,200	43,440	56,564	84,460	65,133	5,554	477	2,304	56,033
WHEELOCK COLLEGE	PRI-FG	145,221	84,724	9,807	14,964	14,105	11,147	1,116	689	524	8,145
WILLIAMS COLLEGE	PRI-FG	713,448	283,789	60,090	52,226	108,372	146,550	11,130	3,284	18,006	30,001
WORCESTER JUNIOR COLLEGE	PRI T	SEE WORCESTER JOINT LIBRARY									
WORCESTER JOINT LIBRARY	PRI-FN	66,689	B	B	1,000	9,500	16,000	0	1,200	1,200	B
WORCESTER POLY INSTITUTE	PRI-FG	504,042	190,911	28,636	34,923	103,463	88,778	8,424	3,000	9,352	36,555
MICHIGAN											
ADRIAN COLLEGE	PRI-FN	204,900	88,774	18,776	22,552	30,423	23,335	1,565	913	3,592	15,070
ALBION COLLEGE	PRI-FN	326,050	138,658	22,174	27,007	60,159	28,700	7,452	0	7,644	34,256
ALMA COLLEGE	PRI-FN	319,619	134,407	24,957	23,155	63,489	31,698	0	0	4,945	36,968
ALPENA COMMUNITY COLLEGE	PUB-T	110,333	53,049	12,339	0	6,136	2,233	1,146	5,877	26	29,527
ANDREWS UNIVERSITY	PRI-FG	866,876	327,222	50,506	92,928	185,064	105,226	7,439	10,200	11,673	76,618
AQUINAS COLLEGE	PRI-FG	257,247	102,837	11,749	17,688	40,765	15,719	10,103	13,237	1,000	44,149
BAKER JUNIOR COLLEGE BUS	PRI-T	34,946	B	B	7,500	2,700	460	0	516	0	B
BAY DE NOC CMTY COLLEGE	PUB-T	120,235	53,635	14,416	12,184	9,729	4,942	0	12,618	1,656	11,055
CALVIN COLLEGE	PRI FG	SEE CALVIN COLLEGE JOINT LIB									
CALVIN COLLEGE JOINT LIB	PRI-FG	473,280	171,718	30,583	40,996	111,122	72,473	320	0	19,645	26,423
CALVIN THEOLOGICAL SEM	PRI FG	SEE CALVIN COLLEGE JOINT LIB									
CTR FOR CREATIVE STUDIES	PRI-FN	34,846	B	B	784	9,771	1,325	0	268	1,542	B
CENTRAL MICH UNIVERSITY	PUB-FG	2,367,739	962,604	221,107	198,150	321,209	351,058	74,684	32,496	40,238	166,128
CHAS S MOTT CMTY COLLEGE	PUB-T	301,802	189,817	49,984	8,701	25,307	11,628	1,271	2,557	1,491	11,046
CLEARY COLLEGE	PRI-FN	19,548	B	0	824	4,104	1,786	0	0	104	B

SEE FOOTNOTES AT END OF TABLE

Table 2. — Library Operating Expenditures (in Dollars) of College and University Libraries, by Category of Expenditure and by State or Other Area and Institution: Aggregate United States, 1978-79 — Continued

STATE OR OTHER AREA AND INSTITUTION	CONTROL AND TYPE OF INSTITUTION	TOTAL	SALARIES AND WAGES			BOOK-STOCK	PERIOD-ICALS	MICRO-FORMS	AUDIO-VISUAL	BINDING AND RE-BINDING	ALL OTHER OPERATING EXPENDITURES
			LIBRARY STAFF	FRINGE BENEFITS	STUDENTS ON HOURLY BASIS						
(1)	(2)	(3)	(4)	(5)	(6)	(7)	(8)	(9)	(10)	(11)	(12)
MICHIGAN	--CONTINUED										
CONCORDIA COLLEGE	PRI-FN	137,509	B	B	10,414	27,776	7,961	549	0	5	B
CRANBROOK ACADEMY OF ART	PRI-FG	23,500	B	B	0	5,800	2,000	0	400	0	B
DAVENPORT COLLEGE OF BUS	PRI-T	47,922	B	B	6,264	9,200	3,316	0	1,621	0	B
DELTA COLLEGE	PUB-T	373,974	180,672	37,869	67,521	41,846	14,617	1,947	11,163	1,342	16,997
DETROIT BIBLE COLLEGE	PRI-FN	68,217	29,449	2,732	2,608	9,652	2,683	62	3	660	20,368
DETROIT C OF BUS ADMIN	PRI-FN	69,144	B	B	782	12,014	5,091	454	820	0	B
DETROIT COLLEGE OF LAW	PRI-FG	280,746	94,250	13,046	14,100	14,249	99,932	32,350	0	2,761	10,058
DETROIT INST TECHNOLOGY	PRI-FN	61,854	37,805	0	5,348	6,229	7,691	1,207	1,063	0	2,511
EASTERN MICH UNIVERSITY	PUB-FG	1,729,923	956,238	209,231	78,651	168,866	193,518	14,695	7,817	21,826	72,981
FERRIS STATE COLLEGE	PUB-FG	1,100,978	595,182	130,941	54,497	103,603	78,800	22,801	27,707	2,287	85,160
GENERAL MOTORS INSTITUTE	PRI-FN	102,190	0	0	0	35,500	33,260	5,550	300	2,200	25,380
GLEN OAKS CMTY COLLEGE	PUB-T	60,432	B	B	0	10,308	3,441	403	8,107	84	B
GOGEBIC COMMUNITY COLLEGE	PUB-T	95,344	38,520	9,058	6,679	10,481	3,068	4,220	4,158	96	19,064
GRACE BIBLE COLLEGE	PRI-FN	9,545	0	0	1,307	7,238	800	0	0	0	200
GRAND RAPIDS BAPT C & SEM	PRI-FG	108,978	21,860	5,853	265	16,500	13,500	3,000	1,000	3,800	43,200
GRAND RAPIDS JR COLLEGE	PUB-T	253,500	140,700	37,500	32,000	13,000	4,700	300	12,000	0	13,300
GRAND RAPIDS SCH BIBLE		24,606	B	B	8,100	2,000	500	0	300	337	B
GRAND VALLEY ST COLLEGES	PUB-FG	534,331	227,269	51,250	21,487	101,743	90,265	9,000	1,000	3,357	28,960
GREAT LAKES BIBLE COLLEGE	PRI-FN	33,707	B	B	7,220	5,636	2,179	291	219	558	B
HENRY FORD CMTY COLLEGE	PUB-T	515,356	318,181	69,723	25,303	38,280	17,461	3,420	28,658	7,509	6,821
HIGHLAND PK CMTY COLLEGE	PUB-T	98,008	64,009	12,802	0	14,137	1,699	1,170	191	0	4,000
HILLSDALE COLLEGE	PRI-FN	208,438	74,257	10,340	18,016	69,126	20,707	2,114	521	1,473	11,884
HOPE COLLEGE	PRI-FN	402,837	141,557	21,598	49,615	78,854	78,586	0	0	10,870	21,757
JACKSON COMMUNITY COLLEGE	PUB-T	151,603	71,875	17,627	0	28,963	12,757	3,128	5,155	213	11,885
JOHN WESLEY COLLEGE	PRI-FN	47,117	B	B	6,997	192	28	789	918	1,200	B
JORDAN COLLEGE	PRI-FN	10,656	B	0	0	549	1,031	0	0	0	B
KALAMAZOO COLLEGE	PRI-FN	296,725	102,855	18,182	44,400	68,737	32,837	591	164	5,000	23,959
KALAMAZOO VALLEY CC	PUB-T	346,512	186,837	39,597	1,701	32,371	9,027	409	10,609	2,252	63,709
KELLOGG COMMUNITY COLLEGE	PUB-T	375,254	193,591	45,910	43,724	22,404	12,479	998	22,503	276	33,369
KENDALL SCH OF DESIGN	PRI-FN	52,933	B	B	3,000	7,863	1,305	0	5,508	1,460	B
KIRTLAND CMTY COLLEGE	PUB-T	96,546	B	B	175	23,574	4,424	1,862	10,268	0	B
LAKE MICHIGAN COLLEGE	PUB-T	170,156	71,144	18,498	30,790	17,461	10,757	0	1,873	3,571	16,062
LAKE SUPERIOR ST COLLEGE	PUB-FN	307,649	143,632	31,754	11,146	50,983	23,762	192	13,890	3,691	28,599
LANSING COMMUNITY COLLEGE	PUB-T	1,024,706	526,157	116,786	127,266	72,338	22,564	3,650	31,526	163	124,256
LAWRENCE INST TECHNOLOGY	PRI-FN	157,550	76,891	13,065	21,984	19,573	15,353	2,326	251	1,763	6,344
LEWIS C BUSINESS	PRI-T	7,599	B	0	0	4,008	283	0	15	0	B
MACOMB CO CC ALL CAM											
MACOMB CO CC-CENTER CAM	PUB-T	441,764	250,644	64,871	43,141	47,670	15,069	3,052	5,750	133	11,434
MACOMB CO CC-SOUTH CAMPUS	PUB-T	907,404	474,820	133,346	112,540	43,361	29,354	18,999	49,265	982	44,737
MADONNA COLLEGE	PRI-FN	158,950	86,640	2,638	6,060	19,933	8,188	1,425	6,179	1,924	25,963
MARYGROVE COLLEGE	PRI-FG	139,640	87,165	0	7,853	20,431	13,989	1,553	84	3,547	5,018
MERCY COLLEGE OF DETROIT	PRI-FN	237,717	120,644	12,370	13,763	31,520	21,803	2,540	2,862	2,168	30,047
MERRILL-PALMER INSTITUTE	PRI-FG	A	A	A	A	A	A	A	A	A	A
MICH CHRISTIAN COLLEGE	PRI-T	52,833	B	B	9,015	19,322	4,554	0	49	0	B
MICHIGAN STATE UNIVERSITY	PUB-U	5,602,027	2,473,218	445,179	366,882	655,721	879,682	126,279	400	117,227	537,439
MICHIGAN TECHNOLOGICAL U	PUB-FG	846,301	304,708	111,724	46,571	126,315	185,909	4,869	128	17,029	49,048
MID MICHIGAN CMTY COLLEGE	PUB-T	87,169	47,497	12,360	0	8,634	6,233	2,026	4,198	788	5,433
MONROE CO CMTY COLLEGE	PUB-T	206,955	141,230	24,009	6,868	12,028	6,001	1,902	10,937	120	3,860
MONTCALM CMTY COLLEGE	PUB-T	71,818	B	B	2,939	9,074	3,767	774	0	110	B
MUSKEGON BUSINESS COLLEGE	PRI-T	28,882	B	B	1,856	6,882	696	0	0	294	B
MUSKEGON CMTY COLLEGE	PUB-T	182,777	88,388	18,249	25,725	23,171	8,039	3,053	5,000	526	10,627
NAZARETH COLLEGE	PRI-FN	91,143	58,774	2,318	0	7,250	9,571	761	3,277	2,704	6,488
NORTH CEN MICH COLLEGE	PUB-T	50,422	B	B	2,030	9,279	2,607	1,697	0	168	B
NORTHERN MICH UNIVERSITY	PUB-FG	732,479	250,522	71,561	51,525	179,218	111,064	5,661	21,490	21,732	19,706
NORTHWESTERN MICH COLLEGE	PUB-T	228,681	129,913	0	21,205	12,548	12,003	2,750	16,032	1,024	33,206
NORTHWOOD INSTITUTE	PRI-FN	101,877	67,900	10,805	3,702	9,500	7,600	0	0	800	1,570
OAKLAND COMMUNITY COLLEGE	PUB-T	739,678	453,879	130,625	20,099	39,200	17,126	6,153	21,454	2,957	48,185
OAKLAND UNIVERSITY	PUB-FG	1,284,441	634,061	121,626	61,365	157,867	134,493	28,337	0	15,917	130,775
OLIVET COLLEGE	PRI-FG	136,835	55,801	8,370	19,590	13,030	19,470	133	3,852	2,902	13,687
REFORMED BIBLE COLLEGE	PRI-FN	42,640	B	B	2,200	7,222	1,137	0	432	293	B
SACRED HEART SEMINARY C	PRI-FN	47,535	B	B	0	7,605	2,831	138	1,904	1,586	B
SAGINAW VLY STATE COLLEGE	PUB-FG	354,745	122,485	27,766	12,034	113,605	34,000	17,433	2,615	1,061	23,746
SNT CLAIR CO CMTY COLLEGE	PUB-T	249,681	143,960	35,387	0	18,843	13,420	5,751	16,900	0	15,420
SNT JOHN PROVINCIAL SEM	PRI-FG.	A	A	A	A	A	A	A	A	A	A
SAINT MARY'S COLLEGE	PRI-FN	62,405	35,643	0	2,942	12,000	5,500	0	2,000	1,100	3,220

SEE FOOTNOTES AT END OF TABLE

Table 2. – Library Operating Expenditures (in Dollars) of College and University Libraries, by Category of Expenditure and by State or Other Area and Institution: Aggregate United States, 1978-79 – Continued

STATE OR OTHER AREA AND INSTITUTION	CONTROL AND TYPE OF INSTITUTION	TOTAL	SALARIES AND WAGES			BOOK-STOCK	PERIODICALS	MICRO-FORMS	AUDIO-VISUAL	BINDING AND RE-BINDING	ALL OTHER OPERATING EXPENDITURES
			LIBRARY STAFF	FRINGE BENEFITS	STUDENTS ON HOURLY BASIS						
(1)	(2)	(3)	(4)	(5)	(6)	(7)	(8)	(9)	(10)	(11)	(12)
MICHIGAN	--CONTINUED										
SCHOOLCRAFT COLLEGE	PUB-T	339,279	206,527	54,866	17,482	23,918	13,627	1,031	6,956	2,700	12,172
SHAW COLLEGE AT DETROIT	PRI-FN	99,265	69,331	9,706	0	9,843	2,374	0	8,011	0	0
SIENA HEIGHTS COLLEGE	PRI-FG	124,746	53,142	5,314	6,240	19,000	6,000	1,000	2,000	2,500	29,550
SOUTHWESTERN MICH COLLEGE	PUB-T	88,783	39,076	10,428	2,171	22,972	3,944	1,171	1,757	649	6,615
SPRING ARBOR COLLEGE	PRI-FN	147,722	70,446	11,272	19,091	24,863	7,892	158	0	2,284	11,716
SUOMI COLLEGE	PRI-T	55,245	B	B	0	12,524	6,401	1,544	5,366	0	B
THOMAS M COOLEY LAW SCH	PRI-FG	A	A	A	A	A	A	A	A	A	A
UNIVERSITY OF DETROIT	PRI-U	1,157,388	611,328	105,087	52,800	77,549	215,635	7,158	7,567	15,821	64,443
U OF MICHIGAN ALL CAM											
U MICHIGAN-ANN ARBOR	PUB-U	10,246,781	5,320,811	803,442	702,018	1,159,964	1,075,001	154,993	9,997	199,157	821,398
U OF MICHIGAN-DEARBORN	PUB-FG	594,639	205,675	45,087	51,208	163,680	93,954	0	0	11,145	23,890
U OF MICHIGAN-FLINT	PUB-FG	575,925	212,433	44,422	26,464	190,937	43,350	3,167	3,007	4,906	47,239
WALSH C ACCTY & BUS ADMIN	PRI-FG	47,466	B	B	2,900	8,220	11,815	29	357	112	45,018
WASHTENAW CMTY COLLEGE	PUB-T	374,360	203,825	55,240	0	45,166	15,803	5,443	3,670	195	22,847
WAYNE COUNTY CMTY COLLEGE	PUB-T	601,360	308,116	102,018	7,523	96,851	8,597	500	54,908	0	22,847
WAYNE STATE UNIVERSITY	PUB-U	4,934,989	2,355,165	360,832	348,096	696,886	598,958	0	0	80,000	495,052
WESTERN MICH UNIVERSITY	PUB-FG	2,362,481	961,944	218,065	212,134	306,878	333,299	24,056	0	36,672	269,433
WESTERN THEOLOGICAL SEM	PRI-FG	81,147	30,575	8,292	0	24,661	4,167	1,102	279	3,668	8,403
WEST SHORE CMTY COLLEGE	PUB-T	70,222	37,475	8,007	4,256	3,900	6,850	284	4,000	0	5,450
MINNESOTA											
AUGSBURG COLLEGE	PRI-FN	234,179	82,729	16,811	45,846	42,194	18,631	933	2,145	3,232	21,658
BETHANY LUTHERAN COLLEGE	PRI-T	39,913	B	B	7,882	809	2,401	0	873	417	B
BETHEL C & SEM ALL CAM											
BETHEL COLLEGE	PRI-FN	267,266	111,530	20,046	26,632	57,417	14,132	0	0	2,378	35,131
BETHEL THEOL SEMINARY	PRI-FG	113,930	44,200	10,200	12,000	24,800	7,100	1,145	2,600	1,930	9,955
CARLETON COLLEGE	PRI-FN	608,029	194,470	26,252	49,946	173,817	80,102	0	0	38,076	45,366
COLLEGE OF SAINT BENEDICT	PRI-FN	337,752	101,533	15,610	60,464	101,401	12,000	3,500	9,851	1,895	31,498
COLLEGE OF SNT CATHERINE	PRI-FN	450,240	218,359	32,753	38,637	71,072	25,811	1,047	11,310	2,881	48,370
COLLEGE SAINT SCHOLASTICA	PRI-FG	164,923	77,031	9,055	15,480	29,865	12,550	500	8,566	3,290	8,586
COLLEGE OF SAINT TERESA	PRI-FN	180,790	90,761	5,880	26,000	21,621	18,508	499	1,148	3,070	13,303
COLLEGE OF SAINT THOMAS	PRI-FG	549,532	266,475	37,337	55,388	67,882	30,588	6,892	15,350	6,773	62,847
CONCORDIA C AT MOORHEAD	PRI-FN	452,720	183,225	29,109	42,452	81,423	42,369	4,672	20,079	6,156	43,235
CONCORDIA C-SAINT PAUL	PRI-FN	144,770	59,560	10,125	27,800	21,500	6,500	985	7,500	770	10,030
CROSIER SEMINARY	PRI-T	39,862	B	0	0	5,000	2,000	600	1,300	0	B
DR MARTIN LUTHER COLLEGE	PRI-FN	108,768	51,679	2,677	6,609	32,302	5,008	65	2,798	1,750	5,880
GOLDEN VLY LUTH COLLEGE	PRI-T	66,590	35,534	5,793	6,554	10,813	3,752	0	1,256	526	2,362
GUSTAVUS ADOLPHUS COLLEGE	PRI-FN	380,451	150,114	31,040	43,772	98,542	23,900	2,999	1,152	5,212	23,720
HAMLINE UNIVERSITY	PRI-FG	469,616	205,316	30,000	30,300	89,000	54,000	22,000	0	9,000	30,000
LUTHER NTHWSTN SEM JT LIB	PRI-FG	183,006	99,470	9,500	16,000	31,874	11,759	700	283	3,641	9,779
LUTHER THEOLOGICAL SEM	PRI FG	SEE LUTHER NTHWSTN SEM JT LIB									
MACALESTER COLLEGE	PRI-FN	286,634	98,301	18,675	44,750	66,537	26,642	0	2,014	1,246	28,469
MAYO MEDICAL SCHOOL	PRI-FG	44,520	B	B	6,084	5,300	327	0	1,500	0	B
MINNEAPOLIS C-ART DESIGN	PRI-FN	131,087	81,634	9,796	0	9,208	3,599	0	4,045	1,452	21,353
MINNESOTA BIBLE COLLEGE	PRI-FN	29,057	B	B	1,827	4,793	1,249	179	452	350	B
MINN CC SYSTEM ALL INST											
ANOKA-RAMSEY CMTY COLLEGE	PUB-T	141,364	86,576	22,888	0	8,533	6,214	2,250	0	0	14,903
AUSTIN COMMUNITY COLLEGE	PUB-T	98,548	50,846	11,295	0	6,344	4,148	2,614	4,119	0	19,182
BRAINERD CMTY COLLEGE	PUB-T	64,311	B	B	10,970	9,810	1,431	0	5,647	115	B
FERGUS FALLS CMTY COLLEGE	PUB-T	76,453	B	B	9,115	10,465	3,647	2,280	473	60	B
HIBBING COMMUNITY COLLEGE	PUB-T	75,245	41,346	5,262	9,847	5,185	4,306	2,922	2,899	396	3,082
INVER HILLS CMTY COLLEGE	PUB-T	156,894	91,163	13,674	0	14,963	7,753	1,211	6,904	239	20,987
ITASCA COMMUNITY COLLEGE	PUB-T	75,017	B	B	5,734	10,114	3,730	888	3,332	286	B
LAKEWOOD CMTY COLLEGE	PUB-T	181,212	108,906	16,336	13,976	13,848	7,006	2,003	300	273	18,564
MESABI COMMUNITY COLLEGE	PUB-T	51,767	B	B	0	8,227	2,583	494	10,734	38	B
METROPOLITAN CMTY COLLEGE	PUB-T	128,212	82,224	16,445	6,138	12,250	1,300	500	4,300	1,200	3,855
NORMANDALE CMTY COLLEGE	PUB-T	365,076	173,190	33,653	26,189	34,529	10,747	2,861	23,371	265	60,271
N HENNEPIN CMTY COLLEGE	PUB-T	285,670	147,152	29,430	39,339	20,180	7,033	100	16,590	474	25,372
NORTHLAND CMTY COLLEGE	PUB-T	46,035	B	B	7,047	7,500	3,000	0	1,500	0	B
RAINY RIVER CMTY COLLEGE	PUB-T	47,357	B	B	2,068	8,231	2,435	869	840	34	B
ROCHESTER CMTY COLLEGE	PUB-T	140,111	102,773	15,354	0	9,597	7,525	335	0	200	4,327
VERMILION CMTY COLLEGE	PUB-T	56,042	B	B	11,106	11,892	4,198	1,421	1,162	0	B
WILLMAR CMTY COLLEGE	PUB-T	56,695	B	B	3,087	7,824	4,622	1,907	4,693	17	B
WORTHINGTON CMTY COLLEGE	PUB-T	48,729	B	B	9,474	7,480	2,619	1,019	2,672	497	B
NORTH CEN BIBLE COLLEGE	PRI-FN	28,271	B	0	8,416	5,830	1,347	0	0	0	B

SEE FOOTNOTES AT END OF TABLE

| STATE OR OTHER AREA AND INSTITUTION (1) | CONTROL AND TYPE OF INSTITUTION (2) | TOTAL (3) | SALARIES AND WAGES | | | BOOK-STOCK (7) | PERIODICALS (8) | MICRO-FORMS (9) | AUDIO-VISUAL (10) | BINDING AND RE-BINDING (11) | ALL OTHER OPER-ATING EXPENDITURES (12) |
			LIBRARY STAFF (4)	FRINGE BENEFITS (5)	STUDENTS ON HOURLY BASIS (6)						
MINNESOTA	--CONTINUED										
NORTHWESTERN COLLEGE	PRI-FN	81,638	52,816	0	9,450	11,907	4,145	30	146	1,480	1,664
NTHWSTN C CHIROPRACTIC	PRI-FG	62,190	40,504	0	2,000	7,242	3,400	200	2,000	2,100	4,744
NTHWSTN LUTH THEOL SEM	PRI FG	SEE LUTHER NTHWSTN SEM JT LIB									
SAINT JOHN'S UNIVERSITY	PRI-FG	428,260	170,072	30,013	32,295	100,884	32,059	6,517	12,141	4,027	40,263
SAINT MARY'S COLLEGE	PRI-FG	200,677	85,330	11,757	26,938	44,802	12,995	0	2,889	4,823	11,143
SAINT MARY'S JR COLLEGE	PRI-T	58,180	B	B	5,228	9,746	3,338	0	2,619	330	B
SAINT OLAF COLLEGE	PRI-FN	422,686	193,804	24,092	40,003	82,694	48,029	2,259	0	2,753	29,052
SAINT PAUL BIBLE COLLEGE	PRI-FN	82,677	36,592	8,526	12,798	14,692	2,786	2,243	510	121	4,409
SAINT PAUL SEMINARY	PRI-FG	69,840	28,500	1,500	13,200	10,340	6,500	0	0	2,500	7,300
STATE U SYS MINN ALL INST											
BEMIDJI STATE U	PUB-FG	539,576	285,516	35,310	59,442	86,274	36,147	3,829	3,118	5,500	24,440
MANKATO STATE UNIVERSITY	PUB-FG	1,419,445	827,462	95,731	81,451	199,036	91,832	8,634	65,624	5,481	44,194
METROPOLITAN STATE U1/	PUB-FN	NO LIBRARY FACILITIES									
MOORHEAD STATE UNIVERSITY	PUB-FG	542,984	341,471	41,994	7,053	80,341	44,734	1,884	0	5,383	20,124
SAINT CLOUD ST UNIVERSITY	PUB-FG	1,415,222	773,435	97,099	81,685	224,000	52,600	0	0	15,000	171,403
STHWST STATE UNIVERSITY	PUB-FN	346,476	204,723	25,738	24,701	34,412	25,000	3,156	9,634	975	18,137
WINONA STATE UNIVERSITY	PUB-FG	517,484	264,508	50,465	44,073	83,170	38,398	12,313	8,309	5,996	10,252
UNITED THEOLOGICAL SEM	PRI-FG	64,124	B	B	5,280	10,593	4,787	345	1,045	642	B
U OF MINNESOTA ALL CAM											
U OF MINNESOTA DULUTH	PUB-FG	1,016,764	447,272	80,563	100,745	103,410	172,169	0	15,534	23,136	73,935
U MINN MAYO GRAD SCH MED	PRI-FG	840,976	388,498	84,472	32,760	45,679	176,000	0	0	21,000	92,567
U OF MINN MNPLS SNT PAUL	PUB-U	9,080,504	4,484,155	837,145	899,295	667,684	1,184,730	0	0	179,604	827,891
U OF MINNESOTA MORRIS	PUB-FN	311,094	132,927	24,591	10,160	62,566	43,427	2,206	290	2,597	32,330
U MINN TECH COL CROOKSTON	PUB-T	200,845	115,167	22,760	0	17,950	16,760	180	3,491	46	24,491
U OF MINN TECH C-WASECA	PUB-T	145,193	71,272	14,967	0	22,942	14,297	2,536	5,758	25	13,396
WM MITCHELL COLLEGE LAW	PRI-FG	352,701	138,575	19,658	29,624	27,536	111,953	10,430	350	5,018	9,557
MISSISSIPPI											
ALCORN STATE UNIVERSITY	PUB-FG	444,030	164,238	29,703	0	120,310	39,263	10,723	6,635	16,288	56,870
BELHAVEN COLLEGE	PRI-FN	85,161	44,443	5,333	4,629	18,669	6,207	0	200	1,527	4,153
BLUE MOUNTAIN COLLEGE	PRI-FN	52,610	B	B	14,876	11,507	2,484	350	623	43	B
CLARKE COLLEGE	PRI-T	20,053	B	B	5,000	1,502	2,689	13	0	0	B
COAHOMA JUNIOR COLLEGE	PUB-T	166,585	101,825	15,242	14,000	21,000	3,363	425	10,000	520	210
COPIAH-LINCOLN JR COLLEGE	PUB-T	112,073	48,936	8,979	9,593	24,986	5,565	0	665	1,277	12,072
DELTA STATE UNIVERSITY	PUB-FG	564,359	191,000	31,500	3,000	244,524	31,500	15,000	20,000	7,000	20,835
EAST CENTRAL JR COLLEGE	PUB-T	76,001	B	B	5,730	11,897	1,779	0	6,701	537	B
EAST MISS JUNIOR COLLEGE	PUB-T	55,604	B	B	0	12,253	3,408	523	3,213	1,812	B
HINDS JUNIOR COLLEGE	PUB-T	573,771	217,477	38,907	20,228	71,455	12,829	19,140	32,383	2,729	158,623
HOLMES JUNIOR COLLEGE	PUB-T	53,847	B	B	7,098	5,200	7,355	0	1,101	1,335	B
ITAWAMBA JUNIOR COLLEGE	PUB-T	182,171	92,806	14,755	0	17,534	7,530	3,420	16,108	384	29,634
JACKSON STATE UNIVERSITY	PUB-FG	916,909	359,704	61,445	0	328,772	88,845	30,822	9,899	15,266	22,156
JONES CO JUNIOR COLLEGE	PUB-T	275,254	100,538	15,978	24,700	40,165	6,758	14,525	21,303	956	50,331
MARY HOLMES COLLEGE	PRI-T	77,673	33,560	4,953	0	32,476	1,921	529	0	0	4,234
MERIDIAN JUNIOR COLLEGE	PUB-T	198,043	121,074	18,161	0	21,355	7,036	2,323	6,460	1,350	20,284
MILLSAPS COLLEGE	PRI-FN	174,171	84,171	10,000	9,000	29,500	20,000	1,000	0	4,500	16,000
MINISTERIAL INST AND C	PRI-T	12,888	B	B	0	1,450	980	0	47	0	B
MISSISSIPPI COLLEGE	PRI-FG	384,581	149,691	19,875	33,159	39,686	86,072	11,840	8,150	7,376	28,732
MISS DELTA JUNIOR COLLEGE	PUB-T	146,886	72,643	11,485	12,014	9,820	2,683	2,410	6,772	544	28,515
MISS GULF CST JC ALL CAM											
MISS GULF CST JC JACKSON	PUB-T	173,302	114,000	2,070	8,500	18,068	6,882	1,500	7,006	1,048	14,228
MISS GULF CST JC JEFF DAVIS	PUB-T	154,021	97,889	0	11,802	18,205	6,503	7,741	10,329	1,257	295
MISS GULF CST JC PERKNSTN	PUB-T	157,002	90,904	15,162	6,888	21,622	3,081	1,465	16,149	86	1,645
MISS INDUSTRIAL COLLEGE	PRI-FN	8,394	0	B	B	3,866	689	0	0	0	B
MISSISSIPPI ST UNIVERSITY	PUB-U	1,933,362	790,765	107,947	94,848	209,970	508,776	68,307	8,667	63,056	81,026
MISS UNIVERSITY FOR WOMEN	PUB-FG	397,193	140,095	25,005	25,050	98,000	63,000	14,000	0	8,671	23,372
MISS VLY ST UNIVERSITY	PUB-FG	461,067	270,379	50,205	0	46,662	0.	0	0	0	140,483
NORTHEAST MISS JR COLLEGE	PUB-T	110,136	54,478	8,996	0			0			0
NORTHWEST MISS JR COLLEGE	PUB-T	125,781	86,151	12,660	7,055	7,488	4,582	0	4,627	1,136	2,082
PEARL RIVER JR COLLEGE	PUB-T	A	A	A	A	A	A	A	A	A	A
PHILLIPS COLLEGE	PRI-T	16,489	B	B	0	6,519	396	0	312	0	B
PRENTISS NORM-INDUS INST	PRI-T	25,408	B	B	1,566	5,778	2,000	0	700	0	B
REFORMED THEOLOGICAL SEM	PRI-FG	128,909	52,707	1,853	7,082	39,000	12,000	3,000	1,500	7,000	4,767
RUST COLLEGE	PRI-FN	152,276	43,499	5,587	25,000	45,000	9,300	5,000	350	1,350	17,190
SOUTHEASTERN BAPT COLLEGE	PRI-FN	10,937	B	0	0	2,700	501	432	365	729	B

SEE FOOTNOTES AT END OF TABLE

Table 2. — Library Operating Expenditures (in Dollars) of College and University Libraries, by Category of Expenditure and by State or Other Area and Institution: Aggregate United States, 1978-79 — Continued

STATE OR OTHER AREA AND INSTITUTION	CONTROL AND TYPE OF INSTITUTION	TOTAL	SALARIES AND WAGES			BOOK-STOCK	PERIODICALS	MICRO-FORMS	AUDIO-VISUAL	BINDING AND RE-BINDING	ALL OTHER OPERATING EXPENDITURES
			LIBRARY STAFF	FRINGE BENEFITS	STUDENTS ON HOURLY BASIS						
(1)	(2)	(3)	(4)	(5)	(6)	(7)	(8)	(9)	(10)	(11)	(12)
MISSISSIPPI	--CONTINUED										
SOUTHWEST MISS JR COLLEGE	PUB-T	89,556	52,9,77	7,802	1,001	11,025	3,263	1,105	2,859	153	9,371
TOUGALOO COLLEGE	PRI-FN	112,969	73,290	7,767	0	11,648	3,890	4,770	0	3,246	8,358
U OF MISSISSIPPI ALL CAM											
U OF MISSISSIPPI MAIN CAM	PUB-U	1,558,607	608,202	125,280	112,866	246,290	269,979	0	0	13,025	182,965
U OF MISSISSIPPI MEDL CTR	PUB-FG	516,104	206,994	43,786	9,588	20,693	178,791	1,000	0	12,551	42,701
U OF SOUTHERN MISSISSIPPI	PUB-FG	1,616,231	559,129	102,765	173,860	330,619	232,411	92,002	16,884	28,940	79,621
UTICA JUNIOR COLLEGE	PUB-T	117,572	78,702	11,960	0	8,402	7,573	0	4,282	3,000	3,653
WESLEY COLLEGE	PRI-FN	31,388	B	0	3,600	10,477	509	0	0	255	B
WHITWORTH BIBLE COLLEGE	PRI-FN	6,140	B	0	800	150	35	0	40	0	B
WILLIAM CAREY COLLEGE	PRI-FG	174,699	85,576	7,727	28,723	13,117	23,500	0	124	5,530	10,402
WOOD JUNIOR COLLEGE	PRI-T	34,951	B	B	3,061	3,808	1,437	1,837	938	323	B
MISSOURI											
ASSEMBLIES GOD GRAD SCH	PRI-FG	117,938	55,810	2,840	873	33,975	8,650	2,550	500	900	11,840
AVILA COLLEGE	PRI-FG	91,364	50,111	6,731	656	8,618	8,799	295	1,410	1,942	12,802
BAPTIST BIBLE COLLEGE	PRI-FN	101,109	53,916	2,321	13,522	19,000	1,200	500	500	1,700	8,450
CALVARY BIBLE COLLEGE	PRI-FG	32,915	1,800	0	3,024	2,633	1,645	0	1,800	635	853
CARDINAL GLENNON COLLEGE	PRI-FN	37,485	B	B	3,414	13,971	0	0	0	43	B
CARDINAL NEWMAN COLLEGE	PRI-FN	40,200	B	B	3,672	3,946	1,719	0	0	0	B
CENTRAL BIBLE COLLEGE	PRI-FN	142,120	34,000	6,980	43,900	23,400	4,900	2,800	3,100	2,400	20,640
CEN CHRSTN C OF THE BIBLE	PRI-FN	16,413	B	B	1,740	3,459	831	76	196	269	B
CENTRAL METHODIST COLLEGE	PRI-FN	81,380	35,936	10,203	10,173	6,120	9,737	1,500	868	2,518	4,325
CENTRAL MO ST UNIVERSITY	PUB-FG	1,194,344	469,794	125,436	96,688	200,662	115,895	28,270	25,270	29,708	102,620
CHRIST SEMINARY-SEMINEX	PRI-FG	129,966	67,288	8,550	6,470	19,806	1,642	500	0	860	24,850
CLEVELAND CHIROPRACTIC C	PRI-FG	37,191	B	B	0	13,200	2,655	0	5,100	760	B
COLUMBIA COLLEGE	PRI-FN	119,098	46,600	4,450	0	29,537	7,751	16,976	1,597	27	12,160
CONCEPTION SEM COLLEGE	PRI-FN	41,558	22,935	195	0	11,001	4,035	30	479	167	2,716
CONCORDIA SEMINARY	PRI-FG	262,304	80,994	15,094	28,939	83,992	18,875	5,127	8,734	6,855	13,694
COTTEY COLLEGE	PRI-T	A	A	A	A	A	A	A	A	A	A
COVENANT THEOLOGICAL SEM	PRI-FG	68,240	40,781	5,014	2,443	10,915	3,710	100	400	1,264	3,613
CROWDER COLLEGE	PUB-T	64,045	21,788	3,422	15,679	10,285	3,359	1,035	1,074	30	7,373
CULVER-STOCKTON COLLEGE	PRI-FN	56,933	24,208	1,100	11,100	12,000	5,700	425	200	900	1,300
DRURY COLLEGE	PRI-FG	157,907	62,543	9,726	17,853	29,220	17,518	350	808	4,386	15,503
EAST CENTRAL MO DIST JC	PUB-T	70,287	32,102	4,234	2,369	14,874	4,952	1,388	0	0	10,368
EDEN THEOLOGICAL SEMINARY	PRI FG	SEE EDEN-WEBSTER JT LIB									
EDEN-WEBSTER JT LIBRARIES	PRI-FN	355,474	169,948	24,810	2,000	41,195	25,491	5,830	1,651	5,927	78,622
EVANGEL COLLEGE	PRI-FN	122,753	55,415	13,576	0	21,919	13,000	0		4,583	14,260
FONTBONNE COLLEGE	PRI-FN	103,274	57,825	9,236	4,455	10,707	6,560	137	6,179	1,151	7,024
HANNIBAL-LAGRANGE COLLEGE	PRI-FN	28,746	B	0	3,257	11,727	0	700	842	805	B
HARRIS-STOWE STATE C	PUB-FN	79,278	50,610	4,554	0	10,401	8,043	3,463	95	280	1,832
JEFFERSON COLLEGE	PUB-T	118,019	60,349	7,450	5,933	16,059	1,520	0	12,925	420	13,363
KANSAS CITY ART INSTITUTE	PRI-FN	60,932	34,672	4,160	1,092	15,481	2,033	0	0	900	2,594
KANSAS CITY C OSTEO MED	PRI-FG	187,100	67,400	10,500	0	60,000	30,000	0	9,000	4,200	6,000
KEMPER MILITARY SCH AND C	PRI-T	11,387	B	0	0	1,126	801	178	0	0	B
KENRICK SEMINARY	PRI-FG	56,789	B	B	5,693	11,618	7,289	410	613	1,746	B
KIRKSVL COLLEGE OSTEO MED	PRI-FG	147,721	35,555	5,685	14,094	20,067	50,732	0	990	7,137	13,461
LINCOLN UNIVERSITY	PUB-FG	276,878	117,919	17,400	9,938	79,453	17,785	7,702	12,208	1,383	13,090
THE LINDENWOOD COLLEGES	PRI-FG	108,689	54,697	7,214	0	23,047	10,572	2,604	377	742	9,436
LOGAN C OF CHIROPRACTIC	PRI-FG	62,025	32,250	859	2,517	12,517	6,576	0	1,444	0	5,862
MARYVILLE C-SAINT LOUIS	PRI-FG	160,436	86,312	8,709	17,632	15,459	6,453	1,462	957	253	23,199
METRO CC ADMINV ALL INST											
LONGVIEW CMTY COLLEGE	PUB-T	114,851	71,772	4,840	4,418	10,203	3,500	1,000	2,000	75	17,043
MAPLE WOODS CMTY COLLEGE	PUB-T	92,335	66,546	9,401	563	10,000	3,000	0	250	0	2,575
PENN VALLEY CMTY COLLEGE	PUB-T	160,090	133,090	0	0	21,800	4,400	0	0	800	0
PIONEER COMMUNITY COLLEGE	PUB-T	15,844	B	B	0	2,000	1,000	0	0	0	B
MIDWESTERN BAPT THEOL SEM	PRI-FG	A	A	A	A	A	A	A	A	A	A
MINERAL AREA COLLEGE	PUB-T	80,664	48,048	5,330	0	13,313	4,823	1,555	3,750	466	3,379
MISSOURI BAPTIST COLLEGE	PRI-FN	53,761	B	B	4,075	8,440	4,435	138	25	102	B
MISSOURI INST TECHNOLOGY	PRI-FN	A	A	A	A	A	A	A	A	A	A
MISSOURI STHN ST COLLEGE	PUB-FN	592,128	165,464	17,300	40,568	235,324	39,014	36,379	8,000	5,208	44,871
MISSOURI VALLEY COLLEGE	PRI-FN	44,690	B	0	5,649	6,599	7,126	770	410	2,015	B
MISSOURI WSTN ST COLLEGE	PUB-FN	357,698	117,588	17,057	12,979	112,817	32,063	1,058	16,125	5,456	42,555
MOBERLY JUNIOR COLLEGE	PUB-T	45,119	B	B	0	5,470	3,682	0	4,297	0	B
NAZARENE THEOLOGICAL SEM	PRI-FG	75,092	B	0	23,199	14,098	6,430	510	520	0	B

SEE FOOTNOTES AT END OF TABLE

Table 2. — Library Operating Expenditures (in Dollars) of College and University Libraries, by Category of Expenditure and by State or Other Area and Institution: Aggregate United States, 1978-79 — Continued

STATE OR OTHER AREA AND INSTITUTION	CONTROL AND TYPE OF INSTITUTION	TOTAL	SALARIES AND WAGES			BOOK-STOCK	PERIODICALS	MICRO-FORMS	AUDIO-VISUAL	BINDING AND RE-BINDING	ALL OTHER OPERATING EXPENDITURES
			LIBRARY STAFF	FRINGE BENEFITS	STUDENTS ON HOURLY BASIS						
(1)	(2)	(3)	(4)	(5)	(6)	(7)	(8)	(9)	(10)	(11)	(12)

MISSOURI --CONTINUED

NTHEST MO ST UNIVERSITY	PUB-FG	747,548	230,557	30,723	30,931	219,207	53,676	54,585	40,505	14,953	72,311
NTHWST MO ST UNIVERSITY	PUB-FG	455,861	181,534	28,473	23,060	99,681	54,448	42,396	752	10,783	14,734
PARK COLLEGE	PRI-FN	A	A	A	A	A	A	A	A	A	A
ROCKHURST COLLEGE	PRI-FG	135,508	66,920	6,136	9,025	27,462	14,240	0	0	5,506	5,219
SNT LOUIS CHRISTIAN C	PRI-FN	34,645	B	B	1,200	469	1,130	8,250	0	0	B
SNT LOUIS COLLEGE OF PHAR	PRI-FN	88,815	43,584	5,689	9,079	12,280	9,730	1,200	325	1,465	5,463
SNT LU CC CENTER ALL CAM											
SNT LU CC-FLORISSANT VLY	PUB-T	583,776	430,082	39,342	10,200	43,394	8,592	1,305	2,866	0	47,995
SNT LU CC-FOREST PARK	PUB-T	487,284	308,705	30,809	56,387	38,380	9,378	8,022	5,900	0	29,703
SAINT LOUIS CC-MERAMEC	PUB-T	514,853	329,106	29,575	40,356	35,926	9,952	3,889	6,609	0	59,440
SNT LOUIS CONSV OF MUSIC	PRI-FG	34,933	B	B	0	5,114	613	0	1,216	70	B
SAINT LOUIS RAB COLLEGE	PRI-FG	A	A		A	A				A	A
SAINT LOUIS U ALL CAM											
SAINT LOUIS U MAIN CAMPUS	PRI-U	1,323,016	689,849	56,445	68,591	104,261	245,827	20,275	200	30,523	107,045
SAINT LOUIS U-PARKS C	PRI-FN	58,252	B	B	3,434	9,696	10,420	1,145	0	1,749	B
SAINT MARY'S C O'FALLON	PRI-T	67,654	45,000	0	6,726	6,916	4,025	0	3,022	620	1,345
SAINT MARY'S SEM-COLLEGE	PRI-FN	34,560	B	B	0	8,430	2,517	0	491	958	B
SNT PAUL SCH OF THEOLOGY	PRI-FG	77,492	41,232	0	1,889	17,541	6,886	0	0	4,653	5,291
SAINT PAUL'S COLLEGE	PRI-T	57,064	B	B	2,976	6,691	2,636	0	2,938	307	B
SCHOOL OF THE OZARKS	PRI-FN	180,945	67,468	10,795	46,478	26,248	11,500	1,645	1,000	5,773	10,038
STHEST MO ST UNIVERSITY	PUB-FG	1,036,815	427,355	69,524	72,159	231,776	126,432	20,014	30,911	14,672	43,972
SOUTHWEST BAPTIST COLLEGE	PRI-FN	104,349	54,826	7,323	2,531	11,931	13,377	2,464	786	1,571	9,540
STHWST MO ST UNIVERSITY	PUB-FG	1,079,492	436,514	69,714	84,706	187,326	180,165	12,000	34,193	13,743	61,131
STATE FAIR CMTY COLLEGE	PUB-T	113,723	52,677	7,791	0	16,000	5,200	800	10,900	500	19,855
STEPHENS COLLEGE	PRI-FN	294,362	161,504	21,840	22,629	54,585	11,343	2,899	692	2,443	16,427
TARKIO COLLEGE	PRI-FN	40,483	B	0	5,607	6,428	4,249	0	150	723	B
THREE RIVERS CMTY COLLEGE	PUB-T	64,244	B	B	5,760	20,000	4,000	2,500	5,500	500	B
TRENTON JUNIOR COLLEGE	PUB-T	36,038	B	B	239	7,765	1,819	1,002	694	0	B
U OF MO CEN ADMIN ALL CAM											
U OF MISSOURI-COLUMBIA	PUB-U	4,494,596	2,020,894	253,755	228,166	402,292	1,099,769	78,160	1,500	100,870	309,190
U OF MISSOURI-KANSAS CITY	PUB-FG	1,716,810	834,415	136,143	110,949	137,088	259,140	77,416	3,694	22,155	135,810
U OF MISSOURI-ROLLA	PUB-FG	601,881	241,661	38,595	13,597	116,400	173,376	0	2,238	14,369	1,645
U OF MISSOURI-SAINT LOUIS	PUB-FG	1,239,733	431,248	57,260	126,216	194,693	304,340	0	0	22,392	103,584
WASHINGTON UNIVERSITY	PRI-U	4,143,595	1,843,042	184,622	163,820	494,323	872,351	45,543	7,500	100,790	431,604
WEBSTER COLLEGE	PRI FG	SEE EDEN-WEBSTER JT LIB									
WENTWORTH MILITARY ACAD	PRI-T	10,146	B	B	0	260	1,236	238	0	250	B
WESTMINSTER COLLEGE	PRI-FN	111,135	54,404	7,352	583	16,371	12,194	0	0	2,605	17,626
WILLIAM JEWELL COLLEGE	PRI-FN	189,100	81,265	11,598	12,286	40,448	18,345	800	4,917	2,627	16,814
WILLIAM WOODS COLLEGE	PRI-FN	110,894	54,404	7,265	6,827	17,639	5,434	0	4,754	5,200	9,371

MONTANA

CARROLL COLLEGE	PRI-FN	132,685	52,036	0	35,459	13,580	13,896	0	510	1,698	15,506
COLLEGE OF GREAT FALLS	PRI-FN	121,430	74,619	9,763	7,048	15,000	12,500	0	0	0	2,500
DAWSON COMMUNITY COLLEGE	PUB-T	44,339	B	B	0	3,750	3,319	6,049	931	67	B
FLATHEAD VLY CMTY COLLEGE	PUB-T	64,583	B	B	929	9,500	2,500	0	0	0	B
MILES COMMUNITY COLLEGE	PUB-T	61,946	B	B	785	11,549	4,251	0	3,309	0	B
MONTANA INST OF THE BIBLE	PRI-FN	24,923	B	B	2,371	1,800	565	0	95	0	B
MONTANA U SYSTEM ALL INST											
EASTERN MONTANA COLLEGE	PUB-FG	294,218	151,640	29,378	14,000	18,200	49,500	2,000	0	6,000	23,500
MONTANA C MINRL SCI-TECHN	PUB-FG	132,308	65,640	0	6,551	18,501	32,469	0	238	4,166	4,743
MONTANA STATE UNIVERSITY	PUB-U	1,121,785	605,402	74,247	35,738	89,869	261,015	1,040	8,543	17,000	28,931
NORTHERN MONTANA COLLEGE	PUB-FG	139,768	63,026	10,863	17,848	17,874	16,224	978	911	700	11,344
UNIVERSITY OF MONTANA	PUB-U	1,671,082	687,245	101,025	114,070	190,601	353,049	18,991	32,250	24,734	149,117
WESTERN MONTANA COLLEGE	PUB-FG	120,450	B	B	62,205	15,844	6,100	2,760	30	117	B
ROCKY MOUNTAIN COLLEGE	PRI-FN	76,054	B	B	12,373	13,691	6,550	480	490	1,200	B

NEBRASKA

BELLEVUE COLLEGE	PRI-FN	100,639	B	B	0	42,730	5,773	0	2,193	1,302	B
CEN TECH CMTY C AREA	PUB-T	279,046	154,706	23,533	0	11,801	15,954	546	19,695	311	52,500
CHADRON STATE COLLEGE	PUB-FG	314,714	136,165	18,333	18,626	72,512	23,901	2,329	16,430	5,726	20,692
COLLEGE OF SAINT MARY	PRI-FN	68,164	B	B	10,334	15,241	6,910	59	5,472	1,417	B
CONCORDIA TCHRS COLLEGE	PRI-FG	211,452	88,355	11,780	34,687	57,867	0	0	0	4,357	14,406
CREIGHTON UNIVERSITY	PRI-U	1,168,980	504,014	35,082	58,848	311,523	134,708	10,500	12,382	15,376	86,547
DANA COLLEGE	PRI-FN	67,149	28,250	3,275	6,333	12,875	9,266	0	0	2,498	4,652
DOANE COLLEGE	PRI-FN	81,077	40,815	3,689	4,687	15,797	5,588	1,174	0	3,030	6,297

SEE FOOTNOTES AT END OF TABLE

105

Table 2. – Library Operating Expenditures (in Dollars) of College and University Libraries, by Category of Expenditure and by State or Other Area and Institution: Aggregate United States, 1978-79 – Continued

STATE OR OTHER AREA AND INSTITUTION (1)	CONTROL AND TYPE OF INSTITUTION (2)	TOTAL (3)	SALARIES AND WAGES — LIBRARY STAFF (4)	SALARIES AND WAGES — FRINGE BENEFITS (5)	SALARIES AND WAGES — STUDENTS ON HOURLY BASIS (6)	BOOK-STOCK (7)	PERIODICALS (8)	MICRO-FORMS (9)	AUDIO-VISUAL (10)	BINDING AND RE-BINDING (11)	ALL OTHER OPERATING EXPENDITURES (12)
NEBRASKA — CONTINUED											
GRACE C OF THE BIBLE	PRI-FN	38,359	B	0	3,681	4,000	1,440	39	57	550	B
HASTINGS COLLEGE	PRI-FN	103,655	46,338	11,186	8,469	18,437	13,645	2,400	225	1,488	1,467
KEARNEY STATE COLLEGE	PUB-FG	658,941	289,885	47,596	23,571	56,226	100,643	15,395	28,000	7,118	90,507
METROPOLITAN TECHNICAL CC	PUB-T	404,902	157,396	22,412	0	141,321	34,654	0	0	0	49,119
MIDLAND LUTHERAN COLLEGE	PRI-FN	108,730	47,689	150	14,350	21,393	9,272	1,850	7,041	783	6,202
MID PLAINS CC ALL CAM											
MCCOOK COMMUNITY COLLEGE	PUB-T	70,231	39,701	5,868	2,471	12,559	2,729	691	1,815	0	4,397
MID PLAINS CC	PUB-T	48,606	B	B		9,193	2,911	812	2,768	110	B
NEBR CHRISTIAN COLLEGE	PRI-FN	9,848	4,246	0	3,022	1,945	71	0	363	198	3
NEBR WESLEYAN UNIVERSITY	PRI-FN	165,013	67,770	0	11,282	55,268	17,329	0	0	4,374	8,990
NEBRASKA WESTERN COLLEGE	PUB-T	89,687	55,988	8,803	1,180	7,686	3,277	73	7,850	373	4,457
NORTHEAST TECHNICAL CC	PUB-T	86,449	33,003	9,477	0	27,818	6,800	230	6,339	632	2,150
PERU STATE COLLEGE	PUB-FN	211,887	85,520	10,951	0	37,885	17,512	0	31,904	3,504	24,611
PLATTE VLY BIBLE COLLEGE	PRI-FN	2,860	0	0	2,160	500	150	0	0	0	50
STHESTN NEBR TECH ALL CAM											
STHEST CC FAIRBY-BEATRICE	PUB-T	53,273	30,500	5,011	0	5,660	3,950	300	1,800	274	5,778
SOUTHEAST CC LINCOLN CAM	PUB-T	97,638	42,650	5,791	0	15,322	5,220	1,535	8,604	0	18,516
SOUTHEAST CC MILFORD CAM	PUB-T	89,485	30,353	3,324	1,224	9,797	8,471	1,061	1,495	50	33,710
UNION COLLEGE	PRI-FN	145,046	50,061	8,010	25,564	13,777	9,930	0	1,043	5,912	30,749
U NEBR CEN ADMIN ALL INST											
U OF NEBRASKA-LINCOLN	PUB-U	3,957,885	1,654,513	212,456	234,841	563,305	818,415	40,404	1,207	83,153	349,591
U NEBRASKA MEDICAL CTR	PUB-FG	1,023,842	381,319	48,229	35,484	63,061	189,036			27,589	71,552
U OF NEBRASKA AT OMAHA	PUB-FG	1,492,467	571,566	69,872	66,600	462,982	222,306				
WAYNE STATE COLLEGE	PUB-FG	368,731	197,690	25,700	8,523	44,556	22,345	7,404	14,849	3,424	44,240
YORK COLLEGE	PRI-T	66,867	35,311	4,269	7,434	7,478	5,146	2,921	418	680	3,210
NEVADA											
SIERRA NEVADA COLLEGE	PRI-FN	30,418	B	0	9,312	11,060	4,646	0	0	0	B
U OF NEVADA SYS ALL INST											
U OF NEVADA LAS VEGAS	PUB-FG	1,377,160	633,034	78,283	43,294	263,763	241,716	37,806	15,971	29,548	33,745
U OF NEVADA RENO	PUB-U	2,382,518	1,206,223	151,498	111,596	401,149	352,942	0	0	59,999	99,111
CLARK CO CMTY COLLEGE	PUB-T	287,844	191,688	22,974	15,000	25,379	588	0	0	159	32,056
NORTHERN NEV CMTY COLLEGE	PUB-T	95,376	B	B	6,652	6,635	4,265	300	13,500	225	B
WESTERN NEV CMTY COLLEGE	PUB-T	281,988	160,753	18,350	4,519	18,400	3,985	3,742	16,713	4,848	50,678
NEW HAMPSHIRE											
CASTLE JUNIOR COLLEGE	PRI-T	14,374	B	B	0	460	416	0	115	0	B
COLBY-SAWYER COLLEGE	PRI-FN	A	A	A	A	A	A	A	A	A	A
DANIEL WEBSTER COLLEGE	PRI-FN	36,412	B	B	4,363	6,607	5,245	443	552	0	B
DARTMOUTH COLLEGE	PRI-FG	3,101,812	1,291,635	229,881	83,636	357,034	620,815	85,124	3,695	33,238	396,754
FRANKLIN PIERCE COLLEGE	PRI-FN	93,369	40,651	5,007	7,435	14,000	13,319	0	0	4,582	8,375
FRANKLIN PIERCE LAW CTR	PRI-FG	187,789	69,841	10,162	16,420	16,535	54,291	13,258	0	5,200	2,082
MCINTOSH COLLEGE	PRI-T	A	A	A	A	A	A	A	A	A	A
NATHANIEL HAWTHORNE C	PRI-FN	A	A	A	A	A	A	A	A	A	A
NEW ENGLAND COLLEGE	PRI-FN	225,919	115,016	17,252	1,764	32,237	18,233	3,383	2,103	2,767	33,164
NEW HAMPSHIRE COLLEGE	PRI-FG	269,019	93,264	23,316	51,457	62,457	8,551	11,268	5,067	7	13,632
NH TECHNICAL INSTITUTE	PUB-T	54,423	B	B	0	5,398	1,590	400	1,175	253	B
NH VOC-TECH C BERLIN	PUB-T	25,345	B	B	0	4,200	2,057	0	2,103	0	B
NH VOC-TECH C CLAREMONT	PUB-T	22,153	B	B	0	4,265	1,357	0	650	0	B
NH VOC-TECH C LACONIA	PUB-T	26,436	B	B	0	6,960	778	307	465	0	B
NH VOC-TECH C MANCHESTER	PUB-T	22,537	B	B	0	4,500	2,500	371	1,165	0	B
NH VOC-TECH C NASHUA	PUB-T	26,812	B	B	0	6,788	2,017	359	1,485	0	B
NH VOC-TECH C PORTSMOUTH	PUB-T	24,077	B	0		6,778	1,733	593	202	0	B
NOTRE DAME COLLEGE	PRI-FG	67,989	42,420	1,305	3,580	11,126	3,517	675	3,390	40	1,936
RIVIER COLLEGE	PRI-FG	99,078	59,370	531	4,358	11,631	5,891	896	994	2,094	13,313
SAINT ANSELM'S COLLEGE	PRI-FN	350,855	157,973	15,172	1,448	85,498	38,789	15,462	1,160	4,499	30,854
U SYS OF NH ALL INST											
U OF NEW HAMPSHIRE	PUB-U	2,070,278	858,280	158,781	111,739	252,026	364,959	20,632	27,073	25,233	251,555
U OF NH KEENE ST COLLEGE	PUB-FG	287,372	116,975	20,765	11,358	71,754	29,458	2,363	608	8,913	25,178
U OF NH PLYMOUTH ST COLLEGE	PUB-FG	485,280	207,306	37,514	20,347	114,669	27,728	10,807	10,738	1,161	55,010
WHITE PINES COLLEGE	PRI-T	16,000	B	B	0	5,982	564	392	274	0	B
NEW JERSEY											
ASSUMPTION C FOR SISTERS	PRI-T	32,078	B	0	0	1,843	1,661	0	1,711	0	B
ATLANTIC CMTY COLLEGE	PUB-T	192,440	118,230	23,646	0	28,077	4,464	2,380	9,692	84	5,867

SEE FOOTNOTES AT END OF TABLE

Table 2. — Library Operating Expenditures (in Dollars) of College and University Libraries, by Category of Expenditure and by State or Other Area and Institution: Aggregate United States, 1978-79 — Continued

STATE OR OTHER AREA AND INSTITUTION	CON-TROL AND TYPE OF IN-STITU-TION	TOTAL	SALARIES AND WAGES			BOOK-STOCK	PERIOD-ICALS	MICRO-FORMS	AUDIO-VISUAL	BIND-ING AND RE-BIND-ING	ALL OTHER OPER-ATING EXPEND-ITURES
			LIBRARY STAFF	FRINGE BENEFITS	STUDENTS ON HOURLY BASIS						
(1)	(2)	(3)	(4)	(5)	(6)	(7)	(8)	(9)	(10)	(11)	(12)
NEW JERSEY --CONTINUED											
BERGEN COMMUNITY COLLEGE	PUB-T	1,050,061	674,576	141,750	0	56,842	13,701	3,175	6,276	900	152,841
THE BERKELEY SCHOOL	PRI-T	57,570	B	B	2,460	7,907	1,137	0	7,876	0	B
BETH MEDRASH GOVOHA	PRI-FG	A	A	A		A	A	A		A	A
BLOOMFIELD COLLEGE	PRI-FN	175,460	114,398	15,657	0	15,274	16,218	1,101	3,340	2,173	7,299
BROOKDALE CMTY COLLEGE	PUB-T	1,228,375	753,009	125,455	6,077	70,793	30,249	0	79,561	375	162,856
BURLINGTON COUNTY COLLEGE	PUB-T	219,484	86,305	17,261	0	55,900	5,900	4,250	0	1,360	48,508
CALDWELL COLLEGE	PRI-FN	95,439	48,630	3,272	9,741	19,786	5,146	970	7??	268	6,840
CAMDEN COUNTY COLLEGE	PUB-T	364,285	222,988	40,137	0	27,437	17,362	1,845	49,4?.	2,031	3,000
CENTENARY COLLEGE	PRI-FN	74,471	49,412	7,757	2,551	4,913	4,187	2,152	801	188	2,510
C MED & DENT OF NJ NEWARK	PUB-FG	831,261	491,600	98,321	0	33,875	129,598	0	10,727	8,500	58,640
COLLEGE OF SNT ELIZABETH	PRI-FN	160,506	85,139	5,428	9,160	26,497	15,025	653	1,186	3,050	14,368
COUNTY COLLEGE OF MORRIS	PUB-T	570,283	371,614	0	37,751	67,699	20,068	9,448	21,903	2,324	39,476
CUMBERLAND COUNTY COLLEGE	PUB-T	130,537	90,467	13,570	0	15,250	4,500	1,500	2,000	400	2,850
DON BOSCO COLLEGE	PRI-FN	21,883	6,580	B	0	3,094	2,200	886	0	269	1,073
DREW UNIVERSITY	PRI-FG	711,329	349,696	78,409	58,100	131,026	42,687	11,159	300	9,843	30,109
ESSEX COUNTY COLLEGE	PUB-T	562,426	337,047	43,810	2,500	56,231	22,490	5,673	67,431	0	27,244
FAIRLEIGH DCKSN U ALL CAM											
FARLGH DCKSN U EDW WMS C	PRI-T	19,558	B	B	0	2,749	733	0	0	0	B
FARLGH DCKSN MADISON CAM	PRI-FG	434,078	231,311	48,849	17,025	58,888	52,578	0	4,033	1,560	19,834
FARLGH DCKSN U RUTHERFO	PRI-FG	561,439	328,318	72,230	26,622	64,970	45,339	0	3,705	2,931	17,324
FARLGH DCKSN TEANECK CAM	PRI-FG	822,488	421,636	84,328	22,309	166,377	83,005	5,881	8,242	4,223	26,487
FELICIAN COLLEGE	PRI-FN	119,251	53,817	2,997	545	39,801	9,440	3,985	1,059	5,644	1,963
GEORGIAN COURT COLLEGE	PRI-FG	141,668	74,503	5,693	8,883	24,934	13,015	5,569	430	2,074	6,567
GLASSBORO STATE COLLEGE	PUB-FG	750,393	408,475	89,665	0	134,831	81,842	8,948	1,500	13,787	11,345
GLOUCESTER COUNTY COLLEGE	PUB-T	217,756	104,952	29,601	6,908	22,925	11,949	3,479	18,115	0	19,827
HUDSON CO CC COMMISSION2/	PUB-T	NO LIBRARY FACILITIES									
IMMACULATE CONCEPTION SEM	PRI-FG	92,200	B	0	0	20,000	8,000	0	0	1,000	B
JERSEY CITY STATE COLLEGE	PUB-FG	661,148	407,413	0	0	125,688	45,627	55,243	13,395	715	13,067
KATHARINE GIBBS SCHOOL	PRI-T	3,875	0	0	0	169	564	0	1,251	0	1,891
KEAN C OF NEW JERSEY	PUB-FG	858,792	517,247	100,863	0	106,164	85,098	31,355	1,007	3,605	13,453
MERCER CO CMTY COLLEGE	PUB-T	352,745	205,063	34,861	35,184	27,000	15,910	3,000	21,667	2,000	8,060
MIDDLESEX COUNTY COLLEGE	PUB-T	382,489	274,936	13,746	8,642	23,334	19,745	0	11,100	4,915	26,071
MONMOUTH COLLEGE	PRI-FG	462,925	223,840	32,556	19,413	93,642	69,374	5,210	725	16,027	2,138
MONTCLAIR STATE COLLEGE	PUB-FG	1,212,351	680,482	0	1,261	244,197	111,149	61,481	24,149	19,274	70,358
NEW BRUNSWICK THEOL SEM	PRI-FG	57,110	32,404	6,755	0	10,655	4,153	0	91	2,405	647
NJ INSTITUTE TECHNOLOGY	PUB-FG	541,050	254,130	43,682	29,317	47,762	112,982	1,800	122	4,500	46,755
NTHESTN BIBLE COLLEGE	PRI-FN	A	A	A	A	A	A	A	A	A	A
OCEAN COUNTY COLLEGE	PUB-T	395,495	222,778	37,872	18,416	50,000	7,616	1,769	11,984	600	44,460
PASSAIC CO CMTY COLLEGE	PUB-T	218,157	119,007	16,480	1,821	42,834	8,034	0	6,287	0	23,694
PRINCETON THEOLOGICAL SEM	PRI-FG	357,030	167,687	28,700	12,416	73,334	30,000	1,000	0	7,782	36,111
PRINCETON UNIVERSITY	PRI-U	7,263,907	3,491,061	625,329	279,754	1,112,294	1,087,581	0	0	112,832	555,056
RAB COLLEGE OF AMERICA	PRI-FN	19,470	B	0	700	500	220	0	0	450	B
RAMAPO C OF NEW JERSEY	PUB-FN	615,156	415,199	0	0	72,800	55,525	7,100	10,000	700	53,832
RIDER COLLEGE	PRI-FG	592,848	291,877	54,695	31,633	100,274	60,130	4,000	0	12,740	37,499
RUTGERS THE ST U ALL CAM											
RUTGERS U CAMDEN CAMPUS	PUB-FG	1,094,144	519,774	121,938	38,432	378,000	0	0	0	15,000	21,000
RUTGERS U NEWARK CAMPUS	PUB-FG	1,401,038	694,194	162,857	49,987	431,000	0	0	0	29,000	34,000
RUTGERS U NEW BRUNSWICK	PUB-U	6,682,420	3,199,085	750,505	418,830	1,902,000	0	0	0	156,000	256,000
SNT MICHAELS PASIONST MON	PRI-FG	15,550	B	0	0	1,500	1,200	0	200	0	B
SAINT PETERS COLLEGE	PRI-FG	499,191	263,756	57,955	20,796	77,167	52,097	5,788	320	5,235	16,077
SALEM COMMUNITY COLLEGE	PUB-T	77,041	32,033	3,524	0	32,869	5,399	0	0	0	3,217
SETON HALL UNIVERSITY2/	PRI-U	1,018,734	564,200	0	24,000	187,000	160,000	0	0	30,000	53,534
SOMERSET COUNTY COLLEGE	PUB-T	304,391	186,394	32,830	20,958	21,911	13,553	2,028	10,927	3,861	11,929
STEVENS INST TECHNOLOGY	PRI-FG	303,594	111,111	7,539	9,400	42,800	92,200	700	1,500	13,400	24,944
STOCKTON STATE COLLEGE	PUB-FN	1,046,408	484,423	82,351	16,694	167,512	115,433	28,626	20,000	0	131,369
TALMUD INST OF CEN JERSEY	PRI-FG	A	A	A	A	A				A	A
THOMAS A EDISON COLLEGE	PUB-FN	NO LIBRARY FACILITIES									
TRENTON STATE COLLEGE	PUB-FG	1,206,235	636,938	118,742	60,830	266,034	64,666	8,279	3,493	22,331	24,922
UNION COLLEGE	PRI-T	322,689	185,662	34,199	10,923	31,715	21,727	2,277	4,942	303	30,941
UNION CO TECHNICAL INST	PUB-T	102,182	B	B	2,457	42,300	0	0	5,800	0	B
UPSALA COLLEGE	PRI-FN	215,610	121,582	21,344	6,736	32,340	18,533	1,085	3,906	3,000	7,087
WESTMINSTER CHOIR COLLEGE	PRI-FG	138,054	71,359	10,704	16,860	17,916	2,003	15	160	1,018	18,019
WILLIAM PATERSON COLLEGE	PUB-FG	1,164,650	684,290	0	0	268,756	122,581	22,537	3,189	8,674	54,623
NEW MEXICO											
COLLEGE OF SANTA FE	PRI-FN	60,965	35,277	108	0	9,881	5,091	635	1,068	2,632	6,273

SEE FOOTNOTES AT END OF TABLE

STATE OR OTHER AREA AND INSTITUTION (1)	CON-TROL AND TYPE OF IN-STITU-TION (2)	TOTAL (3)	SALARIES AND WAGES			BOOK-STOCK (7)	PERIOD-ICALS (8)	MICRO-FORMS (9)	AUDIO-VISUAL (10)	BIND-ING AND RE-BINDING (11)	ALL OTHER OPER-ATING EXPEND-ITURES (12)
			LIBRARY STAFF (4)	FRINGE BENEFITS (5)	STUDENTS ON HOURLY BASIS (6)						
NEW MEXICO	--CONTINUED										
						18,179	6,910	1,427	547	3,825	9,184
COLLEGE OF THE SOUTHWEST	PRI-FN	97,920	46,382	5,153	6,313						
EASTERN NM U ALL CAMPUSES	PUB-FG					144,368	56,000	21,632	37,626	10,914	103,527
EASTERN NM U MAIN CAMPUS	PUB-FG	763,098	293,918	49,383	45,730					430	B
EASTERN NM U ROSWELL CAM	PUB-T	58,634	B	B	1,127	10,331	4,996	4,386	153		A
INST AMERICAN INDIAN ARTS	PUB-T	A	A			A			A		
						128,482	61,535	0	1,861	6,774	65,445
NEW MEXICO HIGHLANDS U	PUB-FG	471,730	162,906	24,085	20,642	13,299	69,692	0	0		24,467
NM INST OF MINING & TECHN	PUB-FG	210,617	71,077	11,101	20,981	20,358	7,804	2,763	10,803	424	36,387
NEW MEXICO JUNIOR COLLEGE	PUB-T	211,467	114,758	11,475	6,695	11,717	4,263	2,413	3,396	419	15,800
NEW MEXICO MILITARY INST	PUB-T	114,273	65,728	9,413	1,124						
NM STATE U ALL CAMPUSES						316,624	271,806	38,308	0	49,053	104,421
						6,880	2,869	770	1,386	1,532	8,723
NM STATE U MAIN CAMPUS	PUB-U	1,826,805	810,541	137,792	98,260	4,103	1,473	768	612	39	B
NM STATE U ALAMOGORDO	PUB-T	87,047	54,762	8,110	2,015	4,711	201	298	1,117	0	
NM STATE U CARLSBAD	PUB-T	36,401	B	B	814	6,579	1,079	50	1,611	150	13,951
NM STATE U GRANTS BRANCH	PUB-T	37,525	B	B	664	A	A	A	A		A
NM STATE U SAN JUAN	PUB-T	92,483	58,316	8,747	2,000						
		A	A	A	A	A	8,710	1,744	204	240	4,233
NTHN NM COMMUNITY COLLEGE	PUB-T					17,160					
UNIVERSITY OF ALBUQUERQUE	PRI-FN	160,281	116,866	7,110	4,014	709,854	755,068	27,000	0	91,794	297,966
U OF NM ALL CAMPUSES						8,416	3,015	0	77	488	B
U OF NM MAIN CAMPUS	PUB-U	4,613,464	2,185,326	366,928	179,928						
U OF NM GALLUP BRANCH	PUB-T	50,985	B	B	1,190	30,000	16,500	4,200	3,950	1,800	17,770
WESTERN NM UNIVERSITY	PUB-FG	198,383	94,630	17,033	12,500						
NEW YORK						0	0	22,810	0	0	0
						265,550	217,160	21,130	32,917	35,265	86,997
ACADEMY OF AERONAUTICS	PRI-T	91,898	51,581	10,290	7,217	366	1,362	0	25	0	B
ADELPHI UNIVERSITY	PRI-U	1,759,472	868,219	173,644	58,590	0	0	0	6,461	0	B
ALBANY BUSINESS COLLEGE	PRI-T	10,541	B	B	2,033	71,392	124,726	34,660	0	3,200	81,234
ALBANY COLLEGE PHARMACY	PRI-FN	23,773	B	B	29,250						
ALBANY LAW SCHOOL	PRI-FG	444,302	80,300	19,540		105,442	0		5,868	9,196	59,041
					0						
ALBANY MEDICAL COLLEGE	PRI-FG	465,101	259,594	25,960		64,500	34,250	2,750	0	5,000	28,980
ALFRED U ALL CAMPUSES					12,166	24,638	49,109	1,905	0	5,377	35,975
ALFRED UNIVERSITY	PRI-FG	340,719	172,104	20,969	11,720	A	A	A	A	A	A
NY ST C CERAMICS ALFRED U	PUB-FG	313,057	142,156	42,177	A	A					
AMER ACAD DRAMATIC ARTS	PRI-T	A	A		A	A					
					A	A					
ASSOCD BETH RIVKAH SCHS	PRI-FN	A	A		A	A	13,495	1,997	0	1,619	20,087
BAIS YAAKOV SEMINARY	PRI-FN	A	A	20,644	1,529	35,155	28,392	1,115	450	2,670	5,679
BANK STREET COLLEGE OF ED	PRI-FG	208,169	113,643	16,280	7,410	23,231	A			A	A
BARD COLLEGE	PRI-FN	166,623	81,396	A	A						
BE'ER SHMUEL TALMUD ACAD	PRI-FG	A	A		A	A	200	0	800	0	125
					0	1,000	2,000	0	1,000	250	B
BELZER YESH-MACHZIKEI SEM	PRI-FG	A	A	0	0	4,000	A		A		
BERK-CLAREMONT HICKSVL	PRI-T	2,125	0	B	0	A					
BERK-CLAREMONT NY CITY	PRI-T	25,530	B	A	A						
THE BERKELEY SCHOOL	PRI-T	A	A		A	A					
BETH HMDRSH SHAAREI YOSH	PRI-FG	A	A		A	A	A				A
					A	A	A				
BETH HATALMUD RAB C	PRI-FG	A	A		A	A	A				
BETH JACOB HEBREW TCHRS C	PRI-FN	A	A		A	A	A				
BETH JOSEPH RAB SEMINARY	PRI-FG	A	A		A	A	A				
BETH MEDRASH EMEK HALACHA	PRI-FG	A	A		A	A	2,000	0	1,100	0	A
BETH MDRASH EYUN HATALMUD	PRI-FN				A	A					B
BORICUA COLLEGE	PRI-FN	A	A	B	1,325	10,495	122,848	26,219	884	10,995	11,826
BRAMSON ORT TRAINING CTR	PRI-T	36,863	B	15,138	14,905	32,847	1,194	0	0	0	2,732
BROOKLYN LAW SCHOOL	PRI-FG	373,282	137,620	80	769	0	1,194	0	0	0	2,732
BRYANT-STRATTON BUS INST	PRI-T	5,464	689	80	769	0					
BRYANT-STRATTON BUS INST	PRI-T	5,464	689			74,634	46,994	1,536	105	2,989	20,537
				17,000	9,413	21,658	6,768	902	559	0	3,841
CANISIUS COLLEGE	PRI-FG	333,215	160,007	4,752	11,122	19,500	0	0	0		645
CTHOL C IMMAC CONCEPTION	PRI-FN	99,142	49,540	0							
CAZENOVIA COLLEGE	PRI-T	54,217	34,072								A
CEN CITY BUSINESS INST	PRI-T		NO LIBRARY FACILITIES								
CEN YESH TOM TMIMIM LUBVZ	PRI-FG	A	A	A	A	A	7,670	210	360	3,621	7,886
					0	32,922					
CHRIST THE KING SEMINARY	PRI-FG	82,503	24,053	5,781			41,037	7,000	8,200	6,940	29,663
CITY U OF NY SYS ALL INST				102,917	40,830	151,462	7,000	2,000	2,000	0	9,000
CUNY BERNARD BARUCH C	PUB-FG	902,634	514,585	0	0	39,000	14,253	3,031	18,197	832	11,204
CUNY BORO OF MANHATTAN CC	PUB-T	344,902	285,902	0	0	29,349					203,587
CUNY BRONX CMTY COLLEGE	PUB-T	537,283	460,417			101,787	186,627	12,733	0	18,266	
CUNY BROOKLYN COLLEGE	PUB-FG	1,992,368	1,223,666	224,634	21,068						

SEE FOOTNOTES AT END OF TABLE

Table 2. — Library Operating Expenditures (in Dollars) of College and University Libraries, by Category of Expenditure and by State or Other Area and Institution: Aggregate United States, 1978-79 — Continued

STATE OR OTHER AREA AND INSTITUTION	CON-TROL AND TYPE OF IN-STITU-TION	TOTAL	SALARIES AND WAGES			BOOK-STOCK	PERIOD-ICALS	MICRO-FORMS	AUDIO-VISUAL	BIND-ING AND RE-BIND-ING	ALL OTHER OPER-ATING EXPENDI-TURES
			LIBRARY STAFF	FRINGE BENEFITS	STUDENTS ON HOURLY BASIS						
(1)	(2)	(3)	(4)	(5)	(6)	(7)	(8)	(9)	(10)	(11)	(12)

NEW YORK --CONTINUED

CUNY CITY COLLEGE	PUB-FG	1,974,729	1,243,369	241,002	21,463	144,888	240,001	9,980	6,834	19,759	47,433
CUNY C OF STATEN ISLAND	PUB-FG	775,788	519,289	116,623	0	35,089	79,024	10,961	204	240	14,358
CUNY GRAD SCH & U CENTER	PUB-FG	674,860	377,608	86,850	15,250	52,256	88,462	15,016	0	12,060	27,318
CUNY HOSTOS CMTY COLLEGE	PUB-T	257,893	153,078	30,615	0	58,000	4,200	2,000	5,700	0	4,300
CUNY HUNTER COLLEGE	PUB-FG	1,616,510	1,029,744	221,916	69,312	77,877	145,483	10,257	0	12,900	49,021
CUNY JOHN JAY C CRIM JUST	PUB-FG	493,067	297,332	59,460	4,275	52,677	37,173	8,857	0	7,188	26,105
CUNY KINGSBOROUGH CC	PUB-T	320,525	220,417	59,513	0	19,844	13,395	679	0	3,550	3,127
CUNY LA GUARDIA CC	PUB-T	431,700	296,962	78,888	0	9,757	22,565	4,005	8,858	0	10,665
CUNY LEHMAN COLLEGE	PUB-FG	921,449	563,571	135,257	16,170	75,757	81,673	5,358	263	5,800	37,600
CUNY MEDGAR EVERS COLLEGE	PUB-FN	345,293	229,609	57,402	2,582	7,846	20,427	8,414	5,610	994	12,409
CUNY NEW YORK CITY CC	PUB-T	480,936	349,616	69,923	0	40,901	8,870	7,336	0	287	4,003
CUNY QUEENSBOROUGH CC	PUB-T	687,990	484,611	127,330	0	28,252	27,088	3,065	2,564	1,728	13,352
CUNY QUEENS COLLEGE	PUB-FG	2,155,807	1,234,113	297,216	33,572	219,115	201,873	5,748	4,121	37,932	122,117
CUNY YORK COLLEGE	PUB-FN	317,350	194,065	59,772	1,721	10,526	28,824	8,791	120	0	13,531
CLARKSON COLLEGE OF TECHN	PRI-FG	471,280	182,369	28,127	28,952	71,200	113,493	10,827	0	1,473	34,839
COLG ROCH-BEXLEY-CROZER	PRI-FG	129,079	58,697	7,993	3,046	39,516	7,216	1,461	250	3,726	7,180
COLGATE UNIVERSITY	PRI-FG	704,044	306,383	65,087	50,140	138,538	97,298	9,120	267	12,817	24,394
COLLEGE FOR HUMAN SERVICE	PRI-FN	34,160	B	B	0	3,724	2,871	0	0	0	B
COLLEGE OF INSURANCE	PRI-FG	172,862	103,893	25,974	0	37,529	0	0	0	5,466	0
COLLEGE OF MT SNT VINCENT	PRI-FN	245,700	138,647	16,246	8,559	20,377	21,183	1,923	5,169	1,119	32,477
COLLEGE OF NEW ROCHELLE	PRI-FG	277,965	141,779	20,912	17,020	46,128	24,161	2,247	911	2,728	22,079
COLLEGE OF SAINT ROSE	PRI-FG	224,813	99,346	14,000	15,076	57,200	20,364	812	647	3,725	13,643
COLUMBIA U ALL CAMPUSES											
COLUMBIA U MAIN DIVISION	PRI-U	9,760,440	4,948,827	1,222,155	606,424	966,358	1,196,863	0	0	210,454	609,359
BARNARD COLLEGE	PRI-FN	773,824	218,585	59,261	37,950	38,987	20,001	1,102	918	4,026	392,994
COLUMBIA U TCHRS COLLEGE	PRI-FG	1,084,905	661,792	183,041	85,000	65,770	31,996	5,260	4,790	5,030	42,226
CONCORDIA COLLEGE	PRI-FN	90,933	32,604	5,754	11,564	18,996	12,506	2,117	2,159	999	4,234
COOPER UNION	PRI-FG	239,598	104,191	18,333	14,421	23,173	25,500	0	2,333	5,592	46,055
CORNELL U ALL CAMPUSES											
CORNEL U ENDOWED COLLEGES	PRI-U	7,263,357	3,428,283	622,162	280,388	2,038,878	0	0	0	143,179	750,467
CORNELL U MEDICAL CENTER	PRI-FG	788,798	396,768	79,354	0	67,511	132,655	365	1,785	14,296	96,264
CORNELL U STATUTORY C	PUB-FG	1,755,908	1,023,611	0	83,760	655,854	0	0	0	45,700	146,983
CULINARY INST OF AMERICA	PRI-T	82,312	41,031	9,109	8,901	12,387	2,357	0	0	665	7,862
DAEMEN COLLEGE	PRI-FN	138,140	68,188	11,038	9,757	21,834	14,641	0	703	4,011	7,968
DERECH AYSON RAB SEMINARY	PRI-FG	A	A	A	A						
DOMINICAN C OF BLAUVELT	PRI-FN	127,161	62,263	5,060	0	29,925	9,173	13,696	656	610	5,778
DOWLING COLLEGE	PRI-FG	291,595	159,837	31,767	4,843	47,336	24,537	2,175	989	3,209	16,902
D'YOUVILLE COLLEGE	PRI-FN	241,660	117,050	11,957	13,689	42,457	16,299	3,056	3,068	5,395	28,629
EISENHOWER COLLEGE	PRI-FN	158,996	71,856	0	11,089	41,102	21,305	2,660	0	5,201	5,783
ELIZABETH SETON COLLEGE	PRI-T	70,592	44,296	1,472	654	8,505	5,171	662	4,332	301	5,199
ELMIRA COLLEGE	PRI-FG	332,348	145,971	27,939	23,338	64,879	15,000	4,000	3,000	4,021	44,200
FIVE TOWNS COLLEGE	PRI-T	23,622	B	0	43	4,635	-1,991	1,201	550	252	B
FORDHAM UNIVERSITY	PRI-U	2,136,060	1,012,226	177,520	1,000	573,010	186,634	14,515	0	54,618	116,537
FRIENDS WORLD COLLEGE	PRI-FN	A	A	A	A	A					
GENERAL THEOLOGICAL SEM	PRI-FG	151,944	59,205	17,697	0	41,028	12,069	0	0	4,833	17,112
GRUSS GIRLS SEMINARY	PRI-FN	A	A		A	A					
HADAR HATORAH RAB SEM	PRI-FN	A			A	A					
HAMILTON COLLEGE	PRI-FN	615,358	263,764	36,572	8,465	121,565	110,614	0	15,911	8,809	49,658
HARRIMAN COLLEGE	PRI-T	39,220	B	0	0	3,980	3,170	496	169	0	B
HARTWICK COLLEGE	PRI-FN	305,990	126,486	25,218	1,664	85,712	38,557	0	0	9,025	19,328
HILBERT COLLEGE	PRI-T	84,893	48,358	3,810	257	18,318	3,237	0	1,521	1,580	7,812
HOBART-WM SMITH COLLEGES	PRI-FG	A	A	A	A	A	A	A	A	A	A
HOFSTRA UNIVERSITY	PRI-FG	1,859,211	968,228	148,906	69,812	285,869	238,759	16,495	0	32,882	98,260
HOLY TRINITY ORTHODOX SEM	PRI-FN	A	A	A	A	A	A	A	A	A	A
HOUGHTON COLLEGE	PRI-FN	198,426	81,859	14,466	10,381	57,397	13,431	1,292	117	1,592	17,891
INST OF DESIGN AND CONSTR	PRI-T	NO LIBRARY FACILITIES									
INTERBORO INSTITUTE	PRI-T	12,100	B	0	0	1,600	900	0	0	0	B
IONA COLLEGE	PRI-FG	441,894	256,500	25,650	36,000	85,864	23,426	0	10,250	6,204	0
ITHACA COLLEGE	PRI-FG	680,548	364,194	61,304	22,021	67,952	120,812	7,626	2,065	8,187	26,387
JAMESTWN BUSINESS COLLEGE	PRI-T	A	A	A	A	A	A				A
JEWISH THEOL SEM AMERICA	PRI-FG	A	A	A	A	A	A	A	A	A	A
THE JUILLIARD SCHOOL	PRI-FG	89,157	50,270	10,150	0	13,989	720	0	1,458	12,570	0
KATHARINE GIBBS SCHOOL	PRI-T	6,638	B	0	1,008	400	250	0	1,880	0	B
KEHILATH YAKOV RAB SEM	PRI-FG	A	A	A	A	A	A	A	A	A	A
KEUKA COLLEGE	PRI-FN	160,236	76,761	9,288	15,774	28,764	15,731	1,683	1,608	2,504	8,123

SEE FOOTNOTES AT END OF TABLE

Table 2. – Library Operating Expenditures (in Dollars) of College and University Libraries, by Category of Expenditure and by State or Other Area and Institution: Aggregate United States, 1978-79 – Continued

STATE OR OTHER AREA AND INSTITUTION	CONTROL AND TYPE OF INSTITUTION	TOTAL	SALARIES AND WAGES — LIBRARY STAFF	FRINGE BENEFITS	STUDENTS ON HOURLY BASIS	BOOK-STOCK	PERIOD-ICALS	MICRO-FORMS	AUDIO-VISUAL	BINDING AND RE-BINDING	ALL OTHER OPERATING EXPENDITURES
(1)	(2)	(3)	(4)	(5)	(6)	(7)	(8)	(9)	(10)	(11)	(12)
NEW YORK	--CONTINUED										
KING'S COLLEGE	PRI-FN	135,802	63,870	11,497	10,375	25,091	10,121	3,829	0	1,740	9,279
LAB INST OF MERCHANDISING	PRI-T	14,675	B	B	600	900	500	0	25	0	B
LADYCLIFF COLLEGE	PRI-FN	108,419	82,921	2,950	5,142	8,245	6,996	971	166	24	1,004
LE MOYNE COLLEGE	PRI-FN	240,296	118,440	18,456	22,137	40,576	20,875	568	1,344	4,003	13,897
LONG IS C HOSP SCH NURS	PRI-T	161,168	88,274	17,654	0	16,000	17,000	0	300	5,000	16,940
LONG IS SEM JEWISH STDIES	PRI-FN	A	A		A						
LONG IS U ALL CAMPUSES											
LONG IS U BROOKLYN CENTER	PRI-FG	554,705	326,163	0	100,000	32,896	58,505	450	4,085	16,479	16,127
LONG IS U C W POST CENTER	PRI-U	1,719,669	951,528	176,032	106,200	151,594	117,283	58,764	5,700	28,455	124,113
LONG IS U SOUTHAMPTON CTR	PRI-FG	215,618	120,447	22,885	2,100	26,368	30,268	1,369	39	4,700	7,442
MACHZIKEI HADATH RAB C	PRI-FG	A	A	A	A	A	A			A	A
MANHATTAN COLLEGE	PRI-FG	598,781	273,395	47,373	0	109,698	59,741	1,934	2,035	10,000	94,605
MANHATTAN SCHOOL OF MUSIC	PRI-FG	102,349	76,300	10,376	0	8,517	1,942	0	262	3,668	1,284
MANHATTANVILLE COLLEGE	PRI-FG	355,244	148,841	22,000	24,161	73,530	43,912	0	0	5,086	37,714
MANNES COLLEGE OF MUSIC	PRI-FN	44,036	B	B	1,674	5,877	1,070	0	0	651	1,255
MARIA COLLEGE OF ALBANY	PRI-T	37,526	24,564	1,705	2,968	2,932	3,489	313	0	300	1,255
MARIA REGINA COLLEGE	PRI-T	37,617	23,086	1,311	4,136	4,956	2,943	0	438	208	539
MARIST COLLEGE	PRI-FG	191,244	107,635	26,909	17,225	5,739	23,765	1,384	451	1,753	6,383
MARYKNOLL SCH OF THEOLOGY	PRI-FN	94,069	46,145	0	0	30,712	5,000	0	0	2,000	10,212
MARYMOUNT COLLEGE	PRI-FN	142,605	93,626	13,107	0	13,150	13,597	2,025	0	2,271	4,829
MARYMOUNT MANHATTAN C	PRI-FN	182,686	80,631	9,762	9,946	48,703	17,610	954	633	6,176	8,271
MATER DEI COLLEGE	PRI-T	57,861	B	B	684	7,401	3,792	495	2,181	0	B
MEDAILLE COLLEGE	PRI-FN	59,462	31,835	4,457	2,765	14,000	5,000	650	300	0	455
MERCY COLLEGE	PRI-FN	732,948	288,080	51,840	55,400	297,790	33,617	3,200	649	81	2,291
MESIVTA ESTN PKWY RAB SEM	PRI-FG	A	A	A	A	A	A				A
MES TORAH VODAATH SEM	PRI-FG	A	A	A	A	A	A				A
MESIVTHA TIFERETH JER AMR	PRI-FG	A	A	A	A	A	A				A
MIRRER YESHIVA CEN INST	PRI-FG	A	A	A	A	A	A				A
MOLLOY COLLEGE	PRI-FN	153,152	89,884	9,488	10,197	15,233	9,939	0	4,944	0	13,467
MONROE BUSINESS INSTITUTE	PRI-T	19,271	B	0	270	5,543	374	0	0	0	B
MOUNT SAINT ALPHONSUS SEM	PRI-FG	62,530	32,724	2,000	0	12,680	9,167	430	18	2,315	3,196
MOUNT SAINT MARY COLLEGE	PRI-FN	168,958	92,182	8,515	16,638	32,005	7,441	726	6,643	2,072	2,736
SINAI SCH OF MED CUNY	PRI-FG	799,450	522,301	9,457	0	33,456	138,841	410	24,730	13,934	56,321
NAZARETH C OF ROCHESTER	PRI-FG	330,467	160,348	24,052	3,219	58,844	26,664	14,952	19,031	6,692	16,665
NEW SCH FOR SOC RESEARCH	PRI-FG	513,869	195,677	46,174	0	60,856	48,724	1,856	0	2,604	157,978
N Y CHIROPRACTIC COLLEGE	PRI-FG	23,621	B	B	0	5,337	1,720	200	500	1,700	B
NY COLLEGE PODIATRIC MED	PRI-FG	51,882	B	B	2,387	3,998	6,021	370	1,220	1,296	B
NY INST TECHN ALL CAM											
NY INST TECHN MAIN CAMPUS	PRI-FG	641,654	298,976	50,618	41,505	88,570	46,425	11,960	69,000	4,600	30,000
NY INST TECHN NY CTY CAM	PRI-FG	153,750	71,601	12,172	10,440	23,100	17,800	3,590	0	947	14,100
NEW YORK LAW SCHOOL	PRI-FG	404,929	111,235	14,892	16,812	28,412	155,753	32,682	140	3,653	41,350
NEW YORK MEDICAL COLLEGE	PRI-FG	369,468	182,818	31,650	0	21,000	100,000	0	2,000	9,000	23,000
NY SCH OF INTERIOR DESIGN	PRI-FN	14,000	B	B	0	2,500	1,000	0	500	0	B
NEW YORK THEOL SEMINARY	PRI-FG	35,654	B	B	0	3,266	411	25	277	0	B
NEW YORK UNIVERSITY	PRI-U	6,689,683	3,383,243	676,649	295,378	709,940	804,290	160,259	9,555	129,426	520,943
NIAGARA UNIVERSITY	PRI-FG	493,283	213,450	34,772	34,922	115,211	45,470	2,460	0	7,117	39,881
NYACK COLLEGE	PRI-FG	119,301	55,070	7,963	7,645	24,662	10,250	1,002	352	1,955	10,402
OHEL SHMUEL YESHIVA	PRI-FG	A	A	A	A	A	A				A
OHR HAMEIR THEOL SEM	PRI-FG	A	A	A	A	A	A				A
OHR YISROEL RAB COLLEGE	PRI-FN	A	A	A	A	A	A				A
OLEAN BUSINESS INSTITUTE	PRI-T	8,750	B	0	500	1,000	600	0	0	0	B
PACE UNIVERSITY ALL CAM											
PACE U C OF WHITE PLAINS	PRI-FG	542,086	207,445	29,075	18,346	124,488	94,348	24,975	206	7,413	35,790
PACE UNIVERSITY NEW YORK	PRI-FG	542,520	286,763	39,759	11,387	108,362	31,736	8,153	0	2,311	54,049
PACE U PLSNTVL-BRCLF CAM	PRI-FG	330,997	167,240	23,412	18,260	63,098	19,735	5,886	550	3,828	28,988
PARSONS SCHOOL OF DESIGN	PRI-FG	130,741	82,374	17,985	0	18,125	3,624	84	0	2,790	5,759
PAUL SMITH'S C ARTS & SCI	PRI-T	89,370	54,239	9,953	1,916	9,922	10,000	0	350	595	2,395
POLYTECHNIC INST NEW YORK	PRI-FG	554,868	287,622	48,895	12,000	44,719	127,991	0	0	13,920	19,721
POWELSON BUSINESS INST	PRI-T	8,696	B	B	5,952	500	200	0	100	0	B
PRATT INSTITUTE	PRI-U	510,610	326,280	57,966	12,067	63,696	23,649	2,089	1,430	6,897	16,536
RABBI ISAAC ELCHANAN SEM	PRI-FG	14,640	B	B	1,125	165	0	0	0	0	A
RAB AC MES RAB CHAIM BRLN	PRI-FG	A	A	A	A	A	A				A
RAB COLLEGE BETH SHRAGA	PRI-FG	A	A	A	A	A	A				A
RAB C BOBOVER B'NEI ZION	PRI-FG	A	A	A	A	A	A			A	A
RAB C CH'SAN SOFER NY	PRI-FG	A	A	A	A	A	A				

SEE FOOTNOTES AT END OF TABLE

Table 2. — Library Operating Expenditures (in Dollars) of College and University Libraries, by Category of Expenditure and by State or Other Area and Institution: Aggregate United States, 1978-79 — Continued

STATE OR OTHER AREA AND INSTITUTION	CONTROL AND TYPE OF INSTITUTION	TOTAL	SALARIES AND WAGES			BOOK-STOCK	PERIODICALS	MICRO-FORMS	AUDIO-VISUAL	BINDING AND RE-BINDING	ALL OTHER OPERATING EXPENDITURES
			LIBRARY STAFF	FRINGE BENEFITS	STUDENTS ON HOURLY BASIS						
(1)	(2)	(3)	(4)	(5)	(6)	(7)	(8)	(9)	(10)	(11)	(12)

NEW YORK	--CONTINUED										
RAB C OF KAMENITZ YESHIVA	PRI-FN	A	A			A	A			A	A
RAB COLLEGE LONG ISLAND	PRI-FG	A	A		A	A	A			A	A
RAB COLLEGE OF SANZ	PRI-FG	A	A		A	A					A
RABBINICAL C OF TASH	PRI-FG	A	A	A	A	A					
RAB SEMINARY ADAS YEREIM	PRI-FN	A	A		A	A					
RABBINICAL SEM OF AMERICA	PRI-FG	A	A		A	A	A		A	A	A
RAB SEM BETH YIT D'SPINKA	PRI-FG	A	A		A	A	A			A	A
RAB SEMINARY M'KOR CHAIM	PRI-FG	A	A		A	A	A				
RABBINICAL SEM OF MUNKACS	PRI-FG	A	A		A	A	A				
RAB SEM OF NEW SQUARE	PRI-FG	A	A			A					
RENSSELAER POLY INSTITUTE	PRI-U	937,970	386,800	71,560	34,050	79,540	305,440	4,960	0	18,320	37,300
RIKA BREUER TEACHERS SEM	PRI-FN	A	A		A	A					
ROBERTS WESLEYAN COLLEGE	PRI-T	125,305	67,164	5,561	10,600	21,307	11,100	568	665	1,972	6,368
ROCHESTER BUS INSTITUTE	PRI-T	1,613	B	B	0	75	130	0	102	0	B
ROCHESTER INST TECHNOLOGY	PRI-FN	1,035,500	417,767	83,939	74,361	126,491	156,235	14,756	4,013	9,851	148,087
ROCKEFELLER UNIVERSITY	PRI-FG	587,900	240,277	46,387	0	68,354	160,651	430	0	20,421	51,380
RUSSELL SAGE C ALL CAM											
RUSSELL SAGE C MAIN CAM	PRI-FG	405,262	173,272	37,067	23,158	73,339	47,748	0	8,000	837	41,841
RUSSELL SAGE JC OF ALBANY	PRI-T	227,892	90,325	14,707	20,444	49,299	22,047	0	8,000	303	22,767
SAINT BERNARD'S SEMINARY	PRI-FG	72,075	39,183	4,826	0	13,400	6,631	0	1,228	3,405	3,402
SAINT BONAVENTURE U	PRI-FG	393,766	189,818	18,657	27,643	68,051	33,771	1,944	273	10,000	43,609
SAINT FRANCIS COLLEGE	PRI-FN	231,443	99,511	15,330	17,800	51,000	17,500	4,000	2,500	5,000	18,802
SAINT JOHN FISHER COLLEGE	PRI-FN	321,833	187,500	24,433	0	55,000	34,500	1,500	5,900	10,500	2,500
SAINT JOHN'S UNIVERSITY	PRI-U	1,718,856	702,325	160,816	92,727	303,841	362,983	1,349	15,877	15,412	63,526
SNT JOSEPHS C ALL CAM											
SNT JOSEPH'S C MAIN CAM	PRI-FN	94,161	54,164	0	3,438	17,570	9,026	1,194	376	1,618	6,775
SNT JOSEPHS C SUFFOLK CAM	PRI-FN	110,957	31,568	0	299	13,931	3,327	2,910	1,353	312	57,257
SNT JOSEPHS SEM & COLLEGE	PRI-FG	86,186	B	B	5,571	22,252	9,096	0	0	2,882	B
SAINT LAWRENCE UNIVERSITY	PRI-FG	491,861	210,785	39,417	21,271	87,386	70,290	0	1,787	13,513	47,412
SAINT THOMAS AQUINAS C	PRI-FN	137,102	73,877	6,156	733	25,910	8,456	2,573	8,330	200	10,867
SNT VLADMR ORTH THEOL SEM	PRI-FG	39,958	B	B	0	7,480	2,819	1,990	0	203	B
SARAH LAWRENCE COLLEGE	PRI-FG	306,199	156,214	34,367	28,326	35,251	19,437	1,508	4,882	5,912	20,302
SARA SCHENIRER TCHRS SEM	PRI-FN	A	A		A	A					
SCHOOL OF VISUAL ARTS	PRI-FN	110,769	59,001	1,989	11,994	24,000	2,469	0	7,514	1,000	2,802
SEM IMMAC CONCEPTION	PRI-FG	53,173	B	B	0	7,364	5,233	0	0	1,195	B
SH'OR YOSHUV RAB COLLEGE	PRI-FG	A	A		A						
SIENA COLLEGE	PRI-FN	336,226	144,038	20,390	23,720	59,917	60,150	0	0	11,048	16,963
SKIDMORE COLLEGE	PRI-FN	501,552	234,187	39,812	27,006	100,117	48,245	0	3,226	8,258	40,701
STATE U NY SYS ALL INST[13]/											
SUNY AT ALBANY	PUB-U	3,653,909	1,701,556	504,852	115,000	269,207	737,267	26,804	3,342	40,963	254,918
SUNY AT BINGHAMTON	PUB-FG	2,940,826	1,349,600	400,426	113,000	564,944	457,856	0	0	55,000	0
SUNY AT BUFFALO ALL CAM											
SUNY AT BUFFALO MAIN CAM	PUB-U	4,858,693	2,256,068	734,125	198,220	697,237	383,533	168,000	0	116,796	304,714
SUNY HEALTH SCI CTR BFLD	PUB-FG	806,572	384,916	12,525	29,943	111,363	190,485	450	0	27,000	49,890
SUNY AT STONY BK ALL CAM											
SUNY AT STONY BK MAIN CAM	PUB-FG	3,480,618	1,668,916	495,167	112,700	384,677	458,511	42,416	14,418	58,000	245,813
SUNY HLTH SCI CTR STNY BK	PUB-FG	758,803	257,575	76,423	26,000	60,610	233,976	1,224	70	16,500	86,425
SUNY DOWNSTATE MEDL CTR	PUB-FG	863,056	431,679	133,093	16,905	33,600	130,000	0	5,000	16,468	96,309
SUNY UPSTATE MEDICAL CTR	PUB-FG	669,547	271,074	80,427	16,613	51,019	129,330	0	16,254	13,090	91,740
SUNY COLLEGE AT BROCKPORT	PUB-FG	1,318,097	521,443	154,712	64,166	228,557	229,310	24,154	9,034	28,000	58,721
SUNY COLLEGE AT BUFFALO	PUB-FG	1,356,579	699,287	207,478	31,659	175,540	130,494	16,350	11,404	16,911	67,456
SUNY COLLEGE AT CORTLAND	PUB-FG	828,871	441,849	143,778	20,338	79,400	77,400	3,340	5,450	12,238	45,078
SUNY COLLEGE AT FREDONIA	PUB-FG	790,998	382,400	124,432	29,000	75,531	94,287	26,868	5,290	15,363	37,827
SUNY COLLEGE AT GENESEO	PUB-FG	857,282	409,623	121,535	25,824	139,704	121,098	198	1,000	13,000	25,300
SUNY COLLEGE AT NEW PALTZ	PUB-FG	881,182	427,600	126,869	38,200	146,395	91,508	5,412	0	9,763	35,435
SUNY COLLEGE OLD WESTBURY	PUB-FN	602,853	259,700	77,053	7,883	131,232	41,722	10,836	12,000	3,000	59,427
SUNY COLLEGE AT ONEONTA	PUB-FG	1,032,499	530,734	157,469	31,650	156,630	66,752	11,445	4,619	12,562	60,638
SUNY COLLEGE AT OSWEGO	PUB-FG	1,132,373	582,739	172,879	20,752	106,838	143,839	22,730	3,645	11,920	67,032
SUNY COLLEGE PLATTSBURGH	PUB-FG	885,935	435,974	129,353	47,964	24,304	145,222	30,089	1,428	11,919	59,682
SUNY COLLEGE AT POTSDAM	PUB-FG	772,724	402,332	119,369	39,211	72,840	75,252	11,833	1,949	9,643	40,295
SUNY COLLEGE AT PURCHASE	PUB-FN	678,326	278,919	102,061	25,730	130,031	70,285	5,907	7,724	22,217	35,452
SUNY C OF TECH UTICA-ROME	PUB-FG	422,935	132,465	45,060	5,057	97,510	46,301	19,139	15,057	4,055	58,291
SUNY EMPIRE STATE COLLEGE	PUB-FN	34,520	11,729	3,480	0	8,011	3,052	0	0	0	8,248
SUNY C ENVRNMTL SCI-FORS	PUB-FG	366,913	178,000	52,813	7,000	5,500	96,000	4,000	1,500	7,000	15,100
SUNY MARITIME COLLEGE	PUB-FG	303,355	175,061	56,965	4,300	39,788	13,403	4,517	871	822	7,628

SEE FOOTNOTES AT END OF TABLE

Table 2. – Library Operating Expenditures (in Dollars) of College and University Libraries, by Category of Expenditure and by State or Other Area and Institution: Aggregate United States, 1978-79 – Continued

STATE OR OTHER AREA AND INSTITUTION	CON-TROL AND TYPE OF IN-STITU-TION	TOTAL	SALARIES AND WAGES			BOOK-STOCK	PERIOD-ICALS	MICRO-FORMS	AUDIO-VISUAL	BIND-ING AND RE-BIND-ING	ALL OTHER OPER-ATING EXPEND-ITURES
			LIBRARY STAFF	FRINGE BENEFITS	STUDENTS ON HOURLY BASIS						
(1)	(2)	(3)	(4)	(5)	(6)	(7)	(8)	(9)	(10)	(11)	(12)

NEW YORK   --CONTINUED

SUNY STATE C OF OPTOMETRY	PUB-FG	129,421	58,636	17,397	0	14,103	17,525	504	2,740	1,355	17,161
SUNY AGRL & TECH C ALFRED	PUB-T	251,634	152,000	45,098	0	16,635	15,921	1,586	1,101	1,801	17,492
SUNY AGRL & TECH C CANTON	PUB-T	160,013	84,783	25,155	9,645	20,167	13,310	2,201	0	648	4,104
SUNY AGRL TECH C COBLESKL	PUB-T	331,000	189,600	56,300	0	29,400	7,000	2,700	8,000	1,165	36,835
SUNY AGRL & TECH C DELHI	PUB-T	211,811	106,464	33,611	10,037	29,230	13,207	7,303	10,013	1,625	321
SUNY AGRL TECH C FARMNGDL	PUB-T	581,019	338,571	100,453	1,504	56,517	35,043	3,906	6,976	1,984	36,065
SUNY AGRL TECH C MORRISVL	PUB-T	215,623	124,780	37,002	1,620	37,602	7,565	4,791	85	1,297	881
ADIRONDACK CMTY COLLEGE	PUB-T	131,648	75,460	17,331	410	14,161	6,888	770	10,306	0	6,322
BROOME COMMUNITY COLLEGE	PUB-T	297,986	186,784	53,233	0	37,007	9,860	728	4,172	1,127	5,075
CAYUGA CO CMTY COLLEGE	PUB-T	140,711	54,427	16,328	0	20,872	18,618	7,207	16,972	1,410	4,877
CLINTON COMMUNITY COLLEGE	PUB-T	202,227	58,025	17,216	0	39,760	10,597	4,614	23,290	580	48,145
COLUMBIA-GREENE CC	PUB-T	154,026	51,666	12,916	10,520	40,206	14,500	10,500	150	0	13,570
CMTY COLLEGE FINGER LAKES	PUB-T	177,469	99,776	25,148	0	19,500	12,302	1,619	7,407	2,333	9,384
CORNING COMMUNITY COLLEGE	PUB-T	336,190	209,400	50,721	0	20,178	14,715	1,230	1,245	2,797	35,904
DUTCHESS CMTY COLLEGE	PUB-T	290,162	157,338	39,334	20,302	40,571	9,998	4,995	0	1,108	16,516
ERIE COMMUNITY COLLEGE	PUB-T	602,616	305,682	95,093	8,412	116,796	22,547	3,792	30,224	1,217	18,853
FASHION INST TECHNOLOGY	PUB-FN	718,754	437,047	167,389	45,540	21,105	11,786	1,110	9,138	5,883	19,756
FULTON-MONTGOMERY CC	PUB-T	140,547	90,255	30,000	0	11,262	5,376	1,112	0	1,000	1,542
GENESEE COMMUNITY COLLEGE	PUB-T	169,084	95,703	27,395	1,055	26,224	9,000	2,300	1,763	0	5,644
HERKIMER CO CMTY COLLEGE	PUB-T	219,831	86,695	19,272	0	34,711	13,817	1,740	6,719	3,333	53,544
HUDSON VLY CMTY COLLEGE	PUB-T	692,684	375,081	112,524	2,195	54,215	16,890	4,282	27,589	5,101	94,807
JAMESTOWN CMTY COLLEGE	PUB-T	226,785	100,585	25,146	13,781	35,755	21,027	3,779	1,057	473	25,182
JEFFERSON CMTY COLLEGE	PUB-T	138,837	86,243	25,873	1,276	15,000	5,150	1,500	0	500	3,295
MOHAWK VLY CMTY COLLEGE	PUB-T	304,106	187,461	0	7,837	44,505	15,384	1,460	7,510	3,240	36,709
MONROE COMMUNITY COLLEGE	PUB-T	359,772	224,373	61,000	10,033	25,000	20,868	0	0	2,114	16,384
NASSAU COMMUNITY COLLEGE	PUB-T	1,065,507	644,661	226,469	51,109	51,015	28,519	5,282	31,907	714	25,831
NIAGARA CO CMTY COLLEGE	PUB-T	380,051	249,836	62,459	2,573	13,770	16,057	2,662	8,000	0	24,694
N COUNTRY CMTY COLLEGE	PUB-T	106,235	42,017	10,504	0	16,539	7,484	2,802	9,285	0	17,604
ONONDAGA CMTY COLLEGE	PUB-T	526,764	326,737	63,751	3,780	56,400	15,700	5,500	25,025	4,960	24,911
ORANGE CO CMTY COLLEGE	PUB-T	274,665	154,500	46,350	1,700	40,000	19,169	0	0	3,031	9,915
ROCKLAND CMTY COLLEGE	PUB-T	481,590	242,691	57,718	16,712	58,046	24,730	6,076	2,718	2,190	70,709
SCHENECTADY COUNTY CC	PUB-T	279,767	142,999	41,683	0	56,259	7,385	2,920	10,761	203	17,557
SUFFOLK CO CMTY COLLEGE	PUB-T	1,044,116	626,206	179,178	1,396	97,908	29,842	9,843	20,509	1,859	77,375
SULLIVAN CO CMTY COLLEGE	PUB-T	185,778	104,157	27,080	0	25,101	16,854	4,168	0	250	8,168
TOMPKINS-CORTLAND CC	PUB-T	219,668	129,433	28,475	2,116	19,003	8,068	2,689	7,465	283	22,136
ULSTER CO CMTY COLLEGE	PUB-T	259,425	139,987	41,966	10,500	44,483	9,288	2,303	2,221	3,900	4,777
WESTCHESTER CMTY COLLEGE	PUB-T	561,847	374,729	93,683	12,437	40,590	20,774	2,226	6,000	0	11,408
STENOTYPE INSTITUTE	PRI-T	125	0	0	0	100	25	0	0	0	0
SYRACUSE U ALL CAMPUSES											
SYRACUSE U MAIN CAMPUS	PRI-U	3,852,231	1,717,327	472,264	117,283	806,348	342,203	72,695	0	69,343	254,768
UTICA C OF SYRACUSE U	PRI-FN	301,902	160,561	37,907	3,389	23,610	54,414	3,197	89	4,757	13,978
TALMUDICAL INST UPST NY	PRI-FN	A	A	A	A	A					A
TALMUD SEM OHOLEI TORAH	PRI-FG	A	A	A	A	A	A	A	A	A	A
TAYLOR BUSINESS INSTITUTE	PRI-T	24,791	B	B	0	737	913	0	448	0	B
TECH CAREER INSTITUTES	PRI-T	14,787	B	B	1,972	1,831	0	0	0	0	B
TOBE-COBURN SCH FASH CARS	PRI-T	9,769	B	0	0	194	738	0	0	72	B
TOURO COLLEGE	PRI-FG	176,600	74,500	0	10,500	78,000	2,300	5,800	0	1,000	4,500
TROCAIRE COLLEGE	PRI-T	129,147	96,748	9,016	3,863	4,243	3,782	0	7,268	490	3,737
UNION COLLEGE	PRI-FG	723,912	294,003	47,459	29,047	138,189	127,211	4,398	0	7,326	76,279
UNION THEOLOGICAL SEM	PRI-FG	A	A	A	A	A	A	A	A	A	A
UNITED TALMUDICAL ACADEMY	PRI-FG	A	A	A	A	A	A	A	A	A	A
UNIVERSITY OF ROCHESTER	PRI-U	3,838,189	1,844,088	356,581	152,582	290,819	748,747	0	8,817	87,098	349,457
U ST NY REGENTS EXTNL DEG	PUB-FN			NO LIBRARY FACILITIES							
UTICA SCHOOL OF COMMERCE	PRI-T	7,486	B	B	0	296	438	0	0	0	B
VASSAR COLLEGE	PRI-FG	1,064,767	477,103	72,949	15,819	192,024	184,327	21,194	5,267	51,287	44,797
VILLA MARIA COLLEGE BFLO	PRI-T	79,488	57,207	1,102	845	6,652	3,561	922	916	1,176	7,107
WADHAMS HALL SEM-COLLEGE	PRI-FN	56,756	B	B	371	11,102	7,138	61	414	503	B
WAGNER COLLEGE	PRI-FN	310,479	157,550	22,750	13,022	61,888	37,014	0	886	6,103	11,266
WEBB INST OF NAVAL ARCH	PRI-FN	54,359	B	B	0	12,103	5,204	426	367	1,472	B
WELLS COLLEGE	PRI-FN	183,631	82,000	16,400	18,171	30,571	24,630	685	181	4,533	6,460
WESTCHESTER INSTITUTE	PRI-FG	A	A	A	A	A					A
THE WOOD SCHOOL	PRI-T	5,359	B	0	1,950	528	398	0	683	0	B
YESH BETH HILLEL KRASNA	PRI-FG	A	A	A	A	A					A
YESH BETH SHEARM RAB INST	PRI-FG	A	A	A	A	A					A
YESH CHOFETZ CHAIM RADUN	PRI-FG	A	A	A	A	A					A

SEE FOOTNOTES AT END OF TABLE

Table 2. — Library Operating Expenditures (in Dollars) of College and University Libraries, by Category of Expenditure and by State or Other Area and Institution: Aggregate United States, 1978-79 — Continued

STATE OR OTHER AREA AND INSTITUTION	CON-TROL AND TYPE OF IN-STITU-TION	TOTAL	SALARIES AND WAGES			BOOK-STOCK	PERIOD-ICALS	MICRO-FORMS	AUDIO-VISUAL	BIND-ING AND RE-BIND-ING	ALL OTHER OPER-ATING EXPEND-ITURES
			LIBRARY STAFF	FRINGE BENEFITS	STUDENTS ON HOURLY BASIS						
(1)	(2)	(3)	(4)	(5)	(6)	(7)	(8)	(9)	(10)	(11)	(12)
NEW YORK	--CONTINUED										
YESH KARLIN STOLIN INST	PRI-FG	A	A			A	A			A	A
YESHIVA NACHLAS HALEVIYIM	PRI-FG	A	A		A	A	A			A	A
YESH OF NITRA RAB COLLEGE	PRI-FN	A	A		A	A					
YESHIVA SHAAR HATORAH	PRI-FG	A	A	A	A	A					
YESHIVA UNIVERSITY	PRI-U	1,907,544	987,203	157,734	52,127	315,190	228,999	39,260	4,695	22,088	90,248
YESH MIKDASH MELECH	PRI-FN	A	A		A	A					A
YESHIVATH VIZHITZ	PRI-FG	A	A	A	A	A					A
YESHIVATH ZICHRON MOSHE	PRI-FG	A	A		A	A					
NORTH CAROLINA											
ANSON TECHNICAL COLLEGE	PUB-T	102,775	52,618	9,637	9,055	6,244	5,079	0	17,545	0	2,597
ASHEBORO COLLEGE	PRI-T	A	A		A	A	A				
ASHEVL BUNCOMBE TECH C	PUB-T	110,937	61,284	10,337	0	23,046	5,060	3,500	5,334	0	2,376
ATLANTIC CHRISTIAN C	PRI-FN	133,403	72,595	0	10,730	28,663	10,184	1,386	1,647	3,980	4,218
BARBER-SCOTIA COLLEGE	PRI-FN	64,710	B	B	6,285	5,518	3,700	0	0	0	B
BEAUFORT CO CMTY COLLEGE	PUB-T	61,603	42,255	6,144	0	6,668	1,401	0	3,741	0	1,394
BELMONT ABBEY COLLEGE	PRI-FN	99,759	63,952	7,007	0	14,643	5,635	4,773	273	970	2,506
BENNETT COLLEGE	PRI-FN	160,660	61,670	5,620	2,500	16,000	6,000	750	500	1,000	66,620
BLADEN TECHNICAL INST	PUB-T	58,228	37,693	4,823	0	13,112	1,500	0	0	0	1,100
BLANTONS JUNIOR COLLEGE	PRI-T	8,983	5,280	55	0	3,001	647	0	0	0	0
BLUE RIDGE TECHNICAL C	PUB-T	67,673	B	B	4,677	8,592	3,859	1,000	6,485	215	B
BREVARD COLLEGE	PRI-T	64,546	37,676	4,175	6,413	8,725	3,369	0	395	600	3,193
CALDWELL CC AND TECH INST	PUB-T	124,127	74,072	11,974	0	13,445	3,959	1,436	8,805	145	10,291
CAMPBELL UNIVERSITY2/	PRI-FG	271,314	133,169	12,035	21,457	43,105	17,592	9,297	0	5,699	28,960
CAPE FEAR TECHNICAL INST	PUB-T	197,156	120,758	17,460	4,140	35,378	6,000	2,000	5,264	600	5,556
CARTERET TECHNICAL INST	PUB-T	140,763	93,161	15,695	0	9,938	2,413	725	3,906	0	14,925
CATAWBA COLLEGE	PRI-FN	155,452	86,600	10,525	8,686	18,122	16,516	2,150	1,427	1,352	10,074
CATAWBA VALLEY TECH C	PUB-T	140,118	82,603	14,808	0	20,150	3,002	1,188	10,372	314	7,681
CECILS JUNIOR COLLEGE	PRI-T	16,480	B	B	780	2,550	600	0	1,500	0	B
CEN CAROLINA TECH C	PUB-T	244,175	181,363	18,220	1,236	14,445	3,775	669	17,342	231	6,894
CEN PIEDMONT CMTY COLLEGE	PUB-T	400,036	215,478	36,057	8,817	40,723	7,298	4,937	76,531	980	9,215
CHOWAN COLLEGE	PRI-T	131,059	55,350	8,377	10,926	31,606	8,726	10,336	211	730	4,797
CLEVELAND CO TECH INST	PUB-T	135,719	57,489	10,236	0	16,513	4,967	783	32,774	92	12,865
COASTAL CAROLINA CC	PUB-T	132,861	66,418	11,418	0	7,849	2,874	14,327	28,108	85	1,782
COLLEGE OF THE ALBEMARLE	PUB-T	79,191	48,223	7,276	0	13,528	3,902	1,418	3,160	56	1,628
CRAVEN COMMUNITY COLLEGE	PUB-T	83,912	50,558	3,992	0	17,114	2,275	0	7,080	443	2,450
DAVIDSON COLLEGE	PRI-FN	476,698	177,201	26,720	19,699	146,099	59,027	0	0	16,307	31,645
DAVIDSON CO CMTY COLLEGE	PUB-T	171,030	79,020	13,807	11,710	20,683	3,998	2,770	15,485	403	23,154
DUKE UNIVERSITY	PRI-U	5,867,176	2,792,190	449,292	231,499	685,784	1,089,111	0	0	117,904	501,396
DURHAM COLLEGE	PRI-T	A	A	A	A	A	A	A	A	A	A
DURHAM TECHNICAL INST	PUB-T	141,649	81,912	12,770	0	32,633	4,253	116	8,000	146	1,819
EDGECOMBE TECH INST	PUB-T	162,767	122,795	21,339	0	9,137	3,562	1,228	2,994	207	1,505
ELON COLLEGE	PRI-FN	171,583	63,303	9,307	14,713	35,330	16,467	662	0	2,054	29,747
FAYETTEVILLE TECH INST	PUB-T	283,783	165,948	38,259	7,212	37,422	3,871	1,038	23,425	0	6,608
FORSYTH TECHNICAL INST	PUB-T	151,159	72,800	12,859	8,000	16,973	5,550	1,920	13,107	350	19,600
GARDNER-WEBB COLLEGE	PRI-FN	243,330	80,026	10,403	44,645	55,997	14,137	4,000	6,559	5,060	22,503
GASTON COLLEGE	PUB-T	126,833	68,230	12,727	0	16,132	5,697	1,656	15,759	1,036	5,596
GREENSBORO COLLEGE	PRI-FN	76,626	37,495	7,364	0	14,692	11,198	518	400	1,289	3,670
GUILFORD COLLEGE	PRI-FN	211,603	94,702	15,478	7,805	48,456	24,291	1,216	3,411	3,229	13,015
GUILFORD TECHNICAL INST	PUB-T	364,897	248,152	34,312	0	33,451	10,455	1,788	12,755	422	23,562
HALIFAX CMTY COLLEGE	PUB-T	90,030	48,800	8,784	0	21,549	3,839	0	3,518	0	3,540
HAMILTON COLLEGE	PRI-T	15,348	B	B	0	6,000	800	0	200	0	B
HARDBARGER JC BUSINESS	PRI-T	A				A	A		A		
HAYWOOD TECHNICAL INST	PUB-T	133,343	75,098	10,504	1,697	13,669	1,200	856	9,600	250	21,469
HIGH POINT COLLEGE	PRI-FN	130,608	56,454	6,005	14,879	21,037	19,192	0	0	8,145	4,896
ISOTHERMAL CMTY COLLEGE	PUB-T	90,190	48,312	8,631	0	22,891	4,441	0	3,732	0	2,183
JAMES SPRUNT INSTITUTE	PUB-T	87,617	47,955	8,152	0	17,146	3,600	900	6,150	0	3,714
JEFFERSON COLLEGE	PRI-T	13,927	8,400	857	0	869	1,492	0	331	0	1,978
JOHNSN C SMITH UNIVERSITY	PRI-FN	187,773	102,935	11,796	28,342	23,000	12,500	1,000	1,000	1,600	5,600
JOHNSTON TECHNICAL INST	PUB-T	84,990	48,502	8,334	0	18,062	5,085	0	1,574	0	3,433
JOHN WESLEY COLLEGE	PRI-FN	10,941	B	B	0	1,204	379	0	0	0	B
KING'S C-CHARLOTTE	PRI-T	A			A	A	A		A		A
KING'S COLLEGE-RALEIGH	PRI-T	48,592	B	B	3,158	15,158	2,625	0	965	0	B
LAFAYETTE COLLEGE	PRI-T	36,600	0	0	0	6,000	1,200	0	1,200	0	B
LEES-MCRAE COLLEGE	PRI-T	74,126	46,107	0	0	15,724	4,259	1,322	2,622	959	3,133

SEE FOOTNOTES AT END OF TABLE

113

Table 2. – Library Operating Expenditures (in Dollars) of College and University Libraries, by Category of Expenditure and by State or Other Area and Institution: Aggregate United States, 1978-79 – Continued

| STATE OR OTHER AREA AND INSTITUTION (1) | CONTROL AND TYPE OF INSTITUTION (2) | TOTAL (3) | SALARIES AND WAGES | | | BOOK-STOCK (7) | PERIOD-ICALS (8) | MICRO-FORMS (9) | AUDIO-VISUAL (10) | BINDING AND RE-BINDING (11) | ALL OTHER OPERATING EXPENDITURES (12) |
			LIBRARY STAFF (4)	FRINGE BENEFITS (5)	STUDENTS ON HOURLY BASIS (6)						
NORTH CAROLINA	--CONTINUED										
LENOIR CMTY COLLEGE	PUB-T	175,360	92,257	14,030	7,296	36,210	6,687	1,584	9,102	415	7,779
LENOIR-RHYNE COLLEGE	PRI-FN	212,826	85,090	12,571	26,390	33,644	24,590	3,650	4,884	1,367	20,640
LIVINGSTONE COLLEGE	PRI-FN	100,624	61,545	9,231	10,600	9,143	5,755	392	0	1,062	2,896
LOUISBURG COLLEGE	PRI-T	65,134	42,283	7,611	834	7,001	2,596	254	0	523	4,032
MARS HILL COLLEGE	PRI-FN	161,730	76,544	9,185	4,972	27,099	18,659	1,000	4,681	1,446	18,144
MARTIN COMMUNITY COLLEGE	PUB-T	78,332	B	B	0	9,850	2,785	0	7,683	112	B
MAYLAND TECHNICAL INST	PUB-T	62,376	38,177	6,412	0	8,462	3,302	86	3,897	1,109	931
MCDOWELL TECHNICAL INST	PUB-T	44,710	B	B	0	8,479	2,425	1,674	4,794	244	B
MEREDITH COLLEGE	PRI-FN	246,377	94,951	14,242	30,699	52,465	11,145	6,727	12,319	2,843	20,986
METHODIST COLLEGE	PRI-FN	98,629	36,854	6,281	23,646	13,446	11,792	1,394	470	656	4,090
MITCHELL CMTY COLLEGE	PUB-T	96,735	55,155	9,937	0	15,097	2,781	306	5,022	425	8,012
MONTGOMERY TECH INSTITUTE	PUB-T	46,070	B	B	0	10,785	2,000	702	1,953	0	B
MONTREAT-ANDERSON COLLEGE	PRI-T	88,569	47,127	6,692	10,300	10,305	5,280	0	2,472	1,087	5,306
MOUNT OLIVE COLLEGE	PRI-T	50,824	B	B	0	10,056	2,343	869	1,777	205	B
NASH TECHNICAL INSTITUTE	PUB-T	125,332	88,588	13,506	0	12,419	1,856	567	2,443	82	5,871
NC WESLEYAN COLLEGE	PRI-FN	91,060	36,400	4,004	5,092	14,450	12,483	1,500	1,000	3,412	12,719
PAMLICO TECHNICAL C	PUB-T	74,558	52,919	8,831	0	5,679	1,976	867	2,011	0	2,275
PEACE COLLEGE	PRI-T	44,744	B	B	5,400	11,040	1,621	80	180	400	B
PFEIFFER COLLEGE	PRI-FN	153,330	69,318	17,330	10,565	30,994	13,885	3,396	0	4,277	3,565
PIEDMONT BIBLE COLLEGE	PRI-FN	23,762	6,211	258	9,208	5,230	1,514	0	755	398	188
PIEDMONT TECHNICAL INST	PUB-T	139,460	77,567	13,186	0	20,444	6,564	5,586	8,233	0	7,880
PITT CMTY COLLEGE	PUB-T	205,426	97,951	16,521	3,630	28,167	6,691	1,270	17,419	209	33,568
QUEENS COLLEGE	PRI-FN	111,277	66,150	0	491	20,986	14,969	469	436	5,139	2,637
RANDOLPH TECHNICAL C	PUB-T	83,988	38,235	7,023	0	14,092	4,977	543	8,368	1,669	9,081
RICHMOND TECHNICAL INST	PUB-T	109,330	56,502	9,074	2,750	19,273	2,583	0	14,579	0	4,569
ROANOKE BIBLE COLLEGE	PRI-FN	23,130	9,163	354	3,045	5,118	894	0	0	0	4,556
ROANOKE-CHOWAN TECH INST	PUB-T	149,819	92,868	19,502	5,105	10,571	4,047	0	295	728	16,703
ROBESON TECHNICAL INST	PUB-T	90,332	51,095	9,213	0	17,000	2,688	100	6,416	517	3,303
ROCKINGHAM CMTY COLLEGE	PUB-T	132,852	74,627	12,686	0	14,360	4,313	8,685	8,598	360	9,223
ROWAN TECHNICAL INSTITUTE	PUB-T	114,307	72,868	11,357	0	13,606	3,150	336	8,640	350	4,000
SACRED HEART COLLEGE	PRI-FN	50,769	33,506	3,686	1,798	4,581	3,174	827	0	595	2,602
SNT ANDREWS PRESB COLLEGE	PRI-FN	147,494	65,842	12,022	12,399	15,758	28,115	999	0	2,392	9,967
SAINT AUGUSTINES COLLEGE	PRI-FN	205,928	90,000	13,500	16,000	65,000	8,000	1,500	0	1,500	10,428
SAINT MARY'S COLLEGE	PRI-T	82,354	44,383	4,628	7,566	16,485	4,544	797	0	1,361	2,590
SALEM COLLEGE	PRI-FN	145,007	65,248	9,787	909	33,829	19,462	1,127	0	1,886	12,759
SAMPSON TECHNICAL C	PUB-T	91,499	53,786	12,569	0	11,873	2,980	2,957	3,593	41	3,700
SANDHILLS CMTY COLLEGE	PUB-T	118,704	66,320	11,454	0	28,546	3,799	5,147	0	612	2,826
SHAW UNIVERSITY	PRI-FN	103,474	51,167	3,138	30,884	2,070	12,729	0	0	0	3,486
STHESTN BAPTIST THEOL SEM	PRI-FG	240,161	114,335	17,401	33,923	25,732	14,367	2,518	3,385	2,731	25,769
SOUTHEASTERN CMTY COLLEGE	PUB-T	241,338	157,854	20,839	0	19,534	4,492	14,127	5,662	788	18,042
SOUTHWESTERN TECH C	PUB-T	56,280	B	B	3,454	9,216	3,506	1,041	5,884	0	B
STANLY TECHNICAL C	PUB-T	87,364	47,094	9,419	1,750	9,286	2,641	0	11,795	200	5,179
SURRY COMMUNITY COLLEGE	PUB-T	106,825	51,917	9,999	0	21,371	6,368	3,906	6,897	1,062	5,305
TECH C OF ALAMANCE	PUB-T	95,462	53,430	8,813	0	10,485	2,206	15,268	1,894	399	2,967
TRI-COUNTY COMMUNITY C	PUB-T	90,378	B	B	1,288	13,031	6,516	3,899	20,695	480	B
U OF NC ALL CAMPUSES APPALACHIAN ST UNIVERSITY	PUB-FG	1,680,622	592,691	99,633	112,964	418,739	220,455	45,600	52,500	41,112	96,928
EAST CAROLINA UNIVERSITY	PUB-FG	2,751,644	1,211,467	212,805	150,264	811,497	153,686	5,755	11,112	4,986	190,072
ELIZABETH CITY STATE U	PUB-FN	324,354	114,289	27,386	1,773	89,146	22,000	4,500	4,325	4,200	56,735
FAYETTEVL ST UNIVERSITY	PUB-FN	423,297	194,642	35,989	2,545	89,530	42,561	28,375	1,472	5,389	22,794
NC AGRL & TECH STATE U	PUB-FG	1,086,513	505,211	84,415	0	272,544	82,075	14,000	27,404	11,820	89,044
NC CENTRAL UNIVERSITY	PUB-FG	1,249,064	566,017	85,372	12,537	291,770	127,698	44,143	18,883	14,071	88,573
NC SCHOOL OF THE ARTS	PUB-FN	249,460	113,905	19,196	1,938	69,342	8,227	469	13,775	10,328	12,280
NC STATE U RALEIGH	PUB-U	3,640,408	1,415,530	242,119	258,686	479,278	703,668	85,072	14,746	66,192	375,117
PEMBROKE STATE UNIVERSITY	PUB-FG	464,718	189,188	32,591	3,966	160,177	41,804	3,002	2,362	13,000	18,628
U OF NC AT ASHEVILLE	PUB-FN	327,726	149,032	26,161	11,805	53,821	37,503	3,990	0	5,507	39,907
U OF NC AT CHAPEL HILL	PUB-U	6,384,514	2,938,764	475,053	283,277	1,369,417	539,382	206,885	8,750	112,295	450,691
U OF NC AT CHARLOTTE	PUB-FG	1,961,473	681,012	113,673	40,210	634,345	250,000	45,000	40,000	35,000	122,233
U OF NC AT GREENSBORO	PUB-FG	1,910,591	827,046	139,465	51,975	285,957	374,066	9,757	11,819	31,115	179,391
U OF NC AT WILMINGTON	PUB-FG	744,213	257,188	40,936	24,974	169,748	101,100	44,997	12,811	16,846	75,613
WSTN CAROLINA UNIVERSITY	PUB-FG	1,299,772	427,025	70,531	32,288	324,701	166,108	88,934	366	29,415	160,332
WINSTON-SALEM STATE U	PUB-FN	356,409	189,238	32,985	B	8,050	65,438	26,675	1,380	1,040	3,275	28,328
VANCE-GRANVL CMTY COLLEGE	PUB-T	82,868	B	B	2,736	17,574	4,330	0	0	44	B
WAKE FOREST UNIVERSITY	PRI-U	2,073,018	745,732	115,484	115,707	450,184	395,950	49,989	20,699	53,251	126,022
WAKE TECHNICAL INSTITUTE	PUB-T	132,950	91,599	15,858	148	17,904	2,550	0	3,278	106	1,507

SEE FOOTNOTES AT END OF TABLE

Table 2. – Library Operating Expenditures (in Dollars) of College and University Libraries, by Category of Expenditure and by State or Other Area and Institution: Aggregate United States, 1978-79 – Continued

STATE OR OTHER AREA AND INSTITUTION	CON- TROL AND TYPE OF IN- STITU- TION	TOTAL	SALARIES AND WAGES			BOOK- STOCK	PERIOD- ICALS	MICRO- FORMS	AUDIO- VISUAL	BIND- ING AND RE- BIND- ING	ALL OTHER OPER- ATING EXPEND- ITURES
			LIBRARY STAFF	FRINGE BENEFITS	STUDENTS ON HOURLY BASIS						
(1)	(2)	(3)	(4)	(5)	(6)	(7)	(8)	(9)	(10)	(11)	(12)
NORTH CAROLINA	--CONTINUED										
WARREN WILSON COLLEGE	PRI-FN	123,819	52,392	10,591	21,797	15,557	9,494	2,748	0	805	10,435
WAYNE COMMUNITY COLLEGE	PUB-T	284,256	143,969	25,423	19,841	34,489	5,272	1,672	11,671	164	41,755
WESTERN PIEDMONT CC	PUB-T	186,336	119,696	20,947	0	14,240	5,489	930	17,417	0	7,617
WILKES COMMUNITY COLLEGE	PUB-T	201,179	156,438	0	3,862	22,591	2,335	2,243	9,033	121	4,556
WILSON CO TECHNICAL INST	PUB-T	169,432	116,025	19,437	0	14,330	2,797	1,428	5,603	347	9,465
WINGATE COLLEGE	PRI-FN	140,868	55,604	8,628	16,765	22,921	6,968	5,198	1,622	1,427	21,735
WINSALM COLLEGE	PRI-T	9,654	B	8	452	284	1,116	0	293	0	B
NORTH DAKOTA											
BISMARCK JUNIOR COLLEGE	PUB-T	112,495	73,563	6,068	0	13,313	7,194	1,310	4,750	241	6,056
DICKINSON STATE COLLEGE	PUB-FN	144,660	72,873	9,793	8,345	29,488	13,087	2,339	0	75	8,660
JAMESTOWN COLLEGE	PRI-FN	62,478	37,800	1,885	890	1,908	8,455	422	2,430	270	8,418
LAKE REGION JR COLLEGE	PUB-T	31,192	17,800	2,462	0	6,690	3,192	133	518	0	397
MARY COLLEGE	PRI-FN	74,210	B	B	9,417	14,269	8,286	0	3,558	57	B
MAYVILLE STATE COLLEGE	PUB-FN	116,316	53,195	6,089	14,011	27,963	10,000	0	0	550	4,508
MINOT STATE COLLEGE	PUB-FG	249,032	139,642	19,347	12,135	36,042	18,431	2,980	4,092	945	15,418
ND STATE SCHOOL SCIENCE	PUB-T	227,180	111,745	13,062	7,408	56,545	17,426	0	7,198	660	13,136
ND STATE U ALL CAMPUSES											
ND STATE U MAIN CAMPUS	PUB-U	1,202,054	450,079	60,752	42,222	218,754	213,490	0	0	37,430	179,327
ND STATE U BOTTINEAU BR	PUB-T	73,239	B	B	2,667	16,263	6,000	2,000	0	700	B
NORTHWEST BIBLE COLLEGE	PRI-FN	33,676	B	B	7,869	7,108	1,097	117	264	0	B
STANDING ROCK CC	PRI-T	30,150	11,400	0	0	3,000	675	0	0	0	15,075
TRINITY BIBLE INSTITUTE	PRI-FN	47,539	22,946	2,638	2,282	12,439	2,042	0	1,549	178	3,465
U OF ND ALL CAMPUSES											
U OF ND MAIN CAMPUS5/	PUB-U	1,323,491	487,564	10,493	40,343	396,282	280,679	10,000	0	16,186	81,944
U OF ND WILLISTON BRANCH	PUB-T	24,688	B	B	836	4,426	2,769	243	256	0	B
VALLEY CITY STATE COLLEGE	PUB-FN	143,084	59,879	8,215	4,326	43,761	8,650	0	7,239	664	10,350
OHIO											
ANTIOCH UNIVERSITY	PRI-FG	A	A	A	A	A	A	A	A	A	A
ART ACADEMY OF CINCINNATI	PRI-FN	72,278	48,149	5,747	0	12,791	2,040	0	0	334	3,217
ASHLAND COLLEGE	PRI-FG	236,349	118,934	15,137	4,607	36,839	16,234	3,820	7,281	1,870	31,627
ATHENAEUM OF OHIO	PRI-FG	105,378	B	B	7,392	17,386	7,624	400	700	3,237	B
BALDWIN-WALLACE COLLEGE	PRI-FG	364,780	192,984	33,033	22,370	65,000	23,328	1,200	2,455	7,500	16,910
BELMONT TECHNICAL COLLEGE	PUB-T	25,186	B	B	0	3,384	3,593	1,228	854	0	B
BLUFFTON COLLEGE	PRI-FN	127,255	54,823	8,306	20,319	17,035	8,775	2,173	1,004	2,078	12,742
BORROMEO COLLEGE OF OHIO	PRI-FN	25,780	B	B	0	4,830	3,300	145	1,047	690	B
BOWLING GRN ST U ALL CAM											
BOWLING GRN ST U MAIN CAM	PUB-U	2,637,102	919,047	179,924	113,203	378,610	197,610	556,220	0	33,093	259,395
BOWLING GRN ST U FIRELDS	PUB-T	91,685	53,380	9,040	2,770	10,490	5,760	795	430	0	9,020
CAPITAL UNIVERSITY	PRI-FG	503,663	201,689	21,516	28,052	98,687	116,921	3,670	2,800	8,225	22,103
CASE WESTERN RESERVE U	PRI-U	3,271,403	1,679,710	293,949	77,272	171,007	723,346	0	0	67,456	258,663
CEDARVILLE COLLEGE	PRI-FN	167,086	81,603	0	4,495	31,728	21,079	0	2,138	2,699	23,344
CENTRAL OHIO TECHNICAL c2/	PUB-T	NO LIBRARY FACILITIES									
CENTRAL STATE UNIVERSITY	PUB-FN	384,979	213,704	47,496	3,902	32,323	36,021	4,407	1,707	6,952	38,467
CHATFIELD COLLEGE	PRI-T	10,752	B	0	0	1,295	843	0	410	0	B
CINCINNATI BIBLE SEMINARY	PRI-FG	A	A	A	A	A	A	A	A	A	A
CINCINNATI TECH COLLEGE	PUB-T	149,237	77,829	12,881	0	28,441	8,081	13,164	1,284	495	7,062
CIRCLEVILLE BIBLE COLLEGE	PRI-FN	21,572	B	B	3,052	6,331	2,126	0	0	416	B
CLARK TECHNICAL COLLEGE	PUB-T	173,818	81,868	14,916	12,644	17,744	9,274	381	2,053	290	34,648
CLEVELAND C JEWISH STOIES	PRI-FG	A	A								
CLEVELAND INST OF ART	PRI-FG	88,916	33,735	7,363	11,406	19,821	4,356	2,640	3,097	1,573	4,925
CLEVELAND INST OF MUSIC	PRI-FG	79,617	41,592	6,028	5,162	12,715	3,990	0	1,846	2,654	5,630
CLEVELAND ST UNIVERSITY	PUB-FG	2,544,044	912,486	183,973	228,171	323,267	400,263	132,262	0	43,412	320,210
C HT SNT JOS-ON-THE-OHIO	PRI-FN	114,692	44,030	4,893	16,765	22,257	12,511	0	8,128	2,151	3,957
COLLEGE OF STEUBENVILLE	PRI-FN	94,708	41,566	5,650	4,379	14,169	16,966	0	0	749	11,229
COLLEGE OF WOOSTER	PRI-FN	445,200	149,098	30,425	58,730	75,179	65,381	5,000	23,084	10,617	27,686
COLUMBUS C ART AND DESIGN	PRI-FN	72,200	42,750	7,094	2,685	7,825	4,232	0	1,186	1,315	5,113
COLUMBUS TECHNICAL INST	PUB-T	525,109	222,342	35,040	6,750	34,502	9,822	1,275	19,417	1,435	194,526
CUYAHOGA CC DISTRICT	PUB-T	747,780	478,970	103,187	26,503	55,222	36,874	6,601	4,990	500	34,933
DAVIS JUNIOR COLLEGE	PRI-T	7,955	6,000	0	0	575	1,380	0	0	0	0
DEFIANCE COLLEGE	PRI-FN	154,233	72,035	12,245	11,476	22,358	16,203	1,830	4,556	1,678	11,852
DENISON UNIVERSITY	PRI-FN	402,874	179,994	39,123	25,912	79,578	44,199	829	3,816	5,070	24,353
DYKE COLLEGE	PRI-FN	66,098	36,734	7,710	2,783	8,953	1,946	165	4,072	0	3,735
EDGECLIFF COLLEGE	PRI-FN	92,119	38,507	4,879	12,852	21,500	7,157	995	776	729	4,724

SEE FOOTNOTES AT END OF TABLE

115

Table 2. — Library Operating Expenditures (in Dollars) of College and University Libraries, by Category of Expenditure and by State or Other Area and Institution: Aggregate United States, 1978-79 — Continued

STATE OR OTHER AREA AND INSTITUTION	CONTROL AND TYPE OF INSTITUTION	TOTAL	SALARIES AND WAGES			BOOK-STOCK	PERIOD-ICALS	MICRO-FORMS	AUDIO-VISUAL	BIND-ING AND RE-BIND-ING	ALL OTHER OPER-ATING EXPEND-ITURES
			LIBRARY STAFF	FRINGE BENEFITS	STUDENTS ON HOURLY BASIS						
(1)	(2)	(3)	(4)	(5)	(6)	(7)	(8)	(9)	(10)	(11)	(12)
OHIO	--CONTINUED										
EDISON STATE CMTY COLLEGE	PUB-T	44,751	B	B	700	0	2,000	2,420	3,906	0	B
FINDLAY COLLEGE	PRI-FN	163,411	65,602	11,616	9,217	44,159	12,630	687	2,500	3,112	13,888
FRANKLIN UNIVERSITY	PRI-FN	251,633	80,623	7,402	0	27,395	17,068	24,266	443	13,385	81,051
HEBREW UNION C ALL CAM											
HEBREW UNION C MAIN CAM	PRI-FG	484,287	272,687	91,159	13,380	72,950	0	0	0	4,723	29,388
HEBREW UNION C CAL BRANCH	PRI-FG	83,677	46,217	12,940	3,200	10,250	3,000	0	250	2,100	5,720
HEBREW UNION C NY BRANCH	PRI-FG	A	A	A	A	A	A	A	A	A	A
HEIDELBERG COLLEGE	PRI-FN	161,964	67,631	9,614	16,031	29,288	21,565	2,274	395	3,635	11,531
HIRAM COLLEGE	PRI-FN	203,723	88,745	13,506	8,928	57,349	19,001	2,695	329	2,316	10,854
HOCKING TECHNICAL COLLEGE	PUB-T	108,168	47,817	7,461	13,704	15,623	3,719	323	6,057	1,015	12,449
JEFFERSON TECHNICAL C	PUB-T	103,300	38,100	8,800	5,830	17,000	2,200	665	21,800	400	8,505
JOHN CARROLL UNIVERSITY	PRI-FG	309,737	119,250	20,000	24,312	65,397	52,526	1,892	87	8,944	17,329
KENT STATE U ALL CAMPUSES											
KENT STATE U MAIN CAMPUS	PUB-U	2,453,156	1,310,090	263,205	43,694	281,875	353,909	0	0	55,184	145,199
KENT ST ASHTABULA REG CAM	PUB-T	103,621	50,363	9,864	1,265	15,637	6,933	957	4,903	3,133	10,566
KENT ST E LIVERPL REG CAM	PUB-T	37,548	B	B	5,240	1,917	4,502	0	0	237	B
KENT ST U SALEM REG CAM	PUB-T	32,122	B	0	7,920	3,609	3,679	770	122	0	B
KENT ST STARK CO REG CAM	PUB-T	158,046	98,223	18,214	15,965	0	6,617	821	0	4,774	13,432
KENT ST TRUMBULL REG CAM	PUB-T	142,482	63,838	11,810	11,011	11,196	9,964	770	400	2,900	30,593
KENT ST TUSCARAWS REG CAM	PUB-T	73,436	B	B	11,600	10,157	9,360	963	528	2,681	B
KENYON COLLEGE	PRI-FN	325,667	121,781	17,967	24,326	83,341	37,123	962	20	8,530	31,617
KETTERING C MEDICAL ARTS	PRI-T	203,643	111,893	17,048	2,652	21,794	30,812	0	2,000	6,358	11,086
LAKE ERIE COLLEGE	PRI-FG	96,393	50,473	4,802	0	6,010	10,756	1,889	2,264	722	19,477
LAKELAND CMTY COLLEGE	PUB-T	164,246	89,108	16,905	4,000	39,053	5,152	435	106	0	9,487
LIMA TECHNICAL COLLEGE8/	PUB-T	NO LIBRARY FACILITIES									
LORAIN CO CMTY COLLEGE	PUB-T	248,604	144,253	28,599	6,708	25,316	15,680	5,145	0	3,921	18,982
LOURDES COLLEGE	PRI-T	31,549	22,500	0	0	3,986	1,605	770	1,802	32	17
MALONE COLLEGE	PRI-FN	151,884	60,924	16,000	8,358	36,906	10,697	693	0	3,215	15,091
MARIETTA COLLEGE	PRI-FG	250,175	96,341	10,598	13,756	41,832	52,878	8,500	1,630	8,761	15,879
MARION TECHNICAL COLLEGE9/	PUB-T	NO LIBRARY FACILITIES									
MEDL COLLEGE OHIO-TOLEDO	PUB-FG	488,517	196,502	40,324	0	60,000	146,646	0	563	15,000	29,482
METHODIST THEOL SCH OHIO	PRI-FG	128,417	64,653	12,630	2,937	30,880	4,808	0	2,790	2,122	7,597
MIAMI-JACOBS JC BUSINESS	PRI-T	10,342	B	B	300	875	616	0	250	0	B
MIAMI UNIVERSITY ALL CAM											
MIAMI U HAMILTON CAMPUS	PUB-T	189,425	89,900	19,040	13,580	40,370	9,790	3,420	1,590	5	11,730
MIAMI U MIDDLETOWN CAMPUS	PUB-T	154,220	75,361	13,256	7,914	34,225	11,120	4,909	1,740	653	5,042
MIAMI UNIV OXFORD CAM	PUB-U	2,412,536	1,145,414	220,000	119,573	359,500	300,000	30,000	10,000	47,928	180,121
MICHAEL J OWENS TECH C	PUB-T	252,037	83,933	19,304	39,150	70,000	10,000	0	10,000	450	19,200
MOUNT UNION COLLEGE	PRI-FN	188,831	71,627	12,717	14,039	49,774	28,850	4,364	0	1,954	5,506
MOUNT VERNON NAZARENE C	PRI-FN	128,077	58,157	8,727	18,276	19,548	8,246	205	2,425	1,182	11,311
MUSKINGUM AREA TECH C	PUB-T	A	A	A	A	A	A	A	A	A	A
MUSKINGUM COLLEGE	PRI-FN	A	A	A	A	A	A	A	A	A	A
NORTH CEN TECH COLLEGE10/	PUB-T	NO LIBRARY FACILITIES									
NTHESTN OHIO U C MED	PUB-FG	323,820	119,224	25,390	6,394	67,936	65,366	0	5,997	4,945	28,568
NORTHWEST TECH COLLEGE	PUB-T	35,721	B	B	1,170	8,304	4,699	1,196	3,356	160	B
NOTRE DAME COLLEGE	PRI-FN	81,897	58,116	3,930	1,584	7,270	4,689	0	1,609	519	4,180
OBERLIN COLLEGE	PRI-FG	1,127,364	565,172	90,877	68,620	112,146	80,821	4,407	9,395	23,593	172,333
OHIO C PODIATRIC MEDICINE	PRI-FG	104,808	65,058	0	11,000	13,000	5,000	0	500	2,500	7,750
OHIO DOMINICAN COLLEGE	PRI-FN	190,147	91,027	8,003	23,969	26,770	10,365	2,161	1,520	3,230	23,102
OHIO INST OF TECHNOLOGY	PRI-FN	30,270	B	0	6,670	5,500	1,400	500	0	400	B
OHIO NORTHERN UNIVERSITY	PRI-FG	636,692	239,828	38,372	38,360	91,886	157,324	2,828	1,544	15,289	51,261
OHIO STATE U ALL CAMPUSES											
OHIO STATE U MAIN CAMPUS	PUB-U	8,013,334	3,805,990	771,061	728,702	724,151	952,842	0	0	29,026	1,001,562
OHIO ST U AGRL TECH INST	PUB-T	96,544	49,450	10,410	10,111	5,567	7,864	644	489	223	11,786
OHIO STATE U LIMA BR	PUB-T	171,658	68,385	12,337	16,572	33,237	9,580	1,040	1,289	2	29,216
OHIO STATE U MANSFIELD BR	PUB-T	139,037	51,518	10,153	21,034	20,012	7,082	707	1,402	631	26,498
OHIO STATE U MARION BR	PUB-T	83,209	B	B	9,793	12,338	9,241	2,145	152	0	B
OHIO STATE U NEWARK BR	PUB-T	133,963	63,576	12,261	5,868	15,329	9,230	1,089	1,320	1,484	23,806
OHIO U ALL CAMPUSES											
OHIO U MAIN CAMPUS	PUB-U	2,082,789	937,389	186,477	99,589	321,578	271,973	36,516	12,657	24,000	192,610
OHIO U BELMONT CO BRANCH	PUB-T	49,837	B	B	2,245	2,560	6,041	948	331	568	B
OHIO U CHILLICOTHE BR	PUB-T	74,425	B	B	7,553	13,936	7,953	1,120	499	1,200	B
OHIO U IRONTON BRANCH	PUB-T	3,047	900	0	1,300	30	787	0	0	0	30
OHIO U LANCASTER BRANCH	PUB-T	145,418	64,807	12,518	9,034	29,991	8,543	1,684	800	238	17,803
OHIO U ZANESVILLE BRANCH	PUB-T	116,566	B	B	8,885	14,433	9,055	3,415	5,962	0	B

SEE FOOTNOTES AT END OF TABLE

Table 2. — Library Operating Expenditures (in Dollars) of College and University Libraries, by Category of Expenditure and by State or Other Area and Institution: Aggregate United States, 1978-79 — Continued

STATE OR OTHER AREA AND INSTITUTION	CONTROL AND TYPE OF INSTITUTION	TOTAL	SALARIES AND WAGES			BOOK-STOCK	PERIOD-ICALS	MICRO-FORMS	AUDIO-VISUAL	BINDING AND RE-BINDING	ALL OTHER OPERATING EXPENDITURES
			LIBRARY STAFF	FRINGE BENEFITS	STUDENTS ON HOURLY BASIS						
(1)	(2)	(3)	(4)	(5)	(6)	(7)	(8)	(9)	(10)	(11)	(12)
OHIO	--CONTINUED										
OHIO WESLEYAN UNIVERSITY	PRI-FN	412,808	188,2A2	37,117	39,624	66,179	48,015	4,270	5,198	4,119	20,044
OTTERBEIN COLLEGE	PRI-FN	206,310	84,539	12,281	23,261	33,999	20,640	1,377	10,322	5,773	14,118
PAYNE THEOLOGICAL SEM	PRI-FG	14,226	B	0	0	0	0	0	226	0	B
PONTIFICAL C JOSEPHINUM	PRI-FG	79,135	B	B	2,931	23,029	8,477	0	311	5,222	B
RABBINICAL COLLEGE TELSHE	PRI-FG	NO LIBRARY FACILITIES									
RIO GRANDE COLLEGE	PRI-FN	115,814	55,991	9,300	10,697	15,745	10,325	1,361	952	2,135	9,308
SAINT MARY SEMINARY	PRI-FG	33,442	B	B	0	11,594	4,584	18	315	3,373	B
SHAWNEE ST CMTY COLLEGE	PUB-T	109,294	53,857	9,637	2,700	17,500	11,000	5,800	0	300	8,500
SINCLAIR CMTY COLLEGE	PUB-T	520,389	185,698	35,433	111,636	78,109	13,322	2,347	19,532	26	7?,?96
SOUTHERN OHIO COLLEGE	PRI-T	A	A		A	A	A				A
STHN ST GEN-TECH COLLEGE	PUB-T	119,415	68,540	14,375	500	20,000	8,000	1,000	1,000	0	6,000
STARK TECHNICAL COLLEGE[11]	PUB-T	NO LIBRARY FACILITIES									
TERRA TECHNICAL COLLEGE	PUB-T	171,832	46,500	10,400	5,000	14,750	17,410	3,642	24,385	0	49,745
TIFFIN UNIVERSITY	PRI-FN	39,580	B	B	2,023	8,744	2,238	0	656	0	B
TRINITY LUTHERAN SEMINARY	PRI-FG	135,940	70,690	9,887	9,038	22,994	6,400	969	425	2,690	12,847
UNION EXPERIMENTING C & U	PRI-FG	NO LIBRARY FACILITIES									
UNITED THEOLOGICAL SEM	PRI-FG	124,687	69,750	12,326	2,300	20,195	5,949	0	1,715	1,725	10,727
U OF AKRON ALL CAMPUSES											
U OF AKRON MAIN CAMPUS	PUB-U	2,654,193	1,021,078	210,214	161,477	428,421	393,840	52,000	11,500	59,392	316,271
U AKRON WAYNE GEN-TECH C	PUB-T	37,830	B	B	854	11,955	0	0	0	0	B
U OF CINCINNATI ALL CAM											
U OF CINCINNATI MAIN CAM	PUB-U	4,736,645	2,480,444	463,374	222,458	525,712	539,091	67,145	30,455	59,818	348,148
U CINCIN CLERMNT GEN-TECH	PUB-T	97,943	B	B	6,244	27,324	4,655	8,813	2,586	0	B
U CINCIN RAYMND WALTERS C	PUB-T	268,816	123,795	23,414	12,617	32,028	23,477	19,122	2,244	0	32,119
UNIVERSITY OF DAYTON[2/]	PRI-FG	858,339	411,896	59,733	32,991	106,219	128,111	0	0	19,836	99,553
UNIVERSITY OF TOLEDO[2/]	PUB-U	2,283,490	1,062,584	213,825	142,937	326,439	306,710	0	26,089	30,750	174,156
URBANA COLLEGE	PRI-FN	91,962	40,600	5,381	0	11,979	4,752	1,015	1,888	4	26,343
URSULINE COLLEGE	PRI-FN	75,082	39,504	4,726	1,800	16,000	9,000	0	0	1,200	2,852
WALSH COLLEGE	PRI-FN	71,190	40,820	0	0	16,059	6,484	0	0	2,961	4,866
WASHINGTON TECH COLLEGE	PUB-T	34,613	B	0	0	13,635	3,829	0	0	0	B
WILBERFORCE UNIVERSITY	PRI-FN	122,007	79,704	12,925	1,080	9,963	7,000	2,850	0	1,000	7,485
WILMINGTON COLLEGE	PRI-FN	135,115	65,930	9,009	8,765	10,034	14,003	998	0	1,928	24,448
WITTENBERG UNIVERSITY	PRI-FG	455,150	200,193	40,038	28,739	72,749	66,357	0	3,987	6,991	36,096
WOOSTER BUSINESS COLLEGE	PRI-T	A	A			A	A				A
WRIGHT ST U ALL CAMPUSES											
WRIGHT ST U MAIN CAMPUS	PUB-FG	2,717,457	1,096,210	207,007	126,824	316,444	490,701	1,030	38,242	28,853	412,146
WRIGHT ST U WSTN OHIO BR	PUB-T	63,217	B	B	689	6,952	14,454	2,000	2,453	900	B
XAVIER UNIVERSITY	PRI-FG	394,933	136,516	25,255	17,721	88,286	62,993	7,003	1,798	12,000	43,361
YOUNGSTOWN ST UNIVERSITY	PUB-FG	1,276,569	521,705	119,129	97,830	212,637	213,000	35,000	0	30,000	47,268
OKLAHOMA											
BACONE COLLEGE	PRI-T	52,864	B	B	0	5,650	5,790	778	1,061	591	B
BARTLESVILLE WESLEYAN C	PRI-FN	69,461	B	B	13,445	14,767	2,899	4,186	3,248	0	B
BETHANY NAZARENE COLLEGE	PRI-FN	136,248	75,683	4,933	12,421	19,403	11,000	4,161	0	2,000	6,647
CAMERON UNIVERSITY	PUB-FN	319,500	167,332	15,842	7,725	69,501	34,098	11,322	407	4,496	8,777
CARL ALBERT JR COLLEGE	PUB-T	60,994	B	B	986	21,610	0	0	0	17	B
CENTRAL STATE UNIVERSITY	PUB-FG	1,106,511	463,470	40,550	98,291	205,000	120,700	87,000	10,000	1,700	79,800
CLAREMORE JUNIOR COLLEGE	PUB-T	69,249	33,648	4,620	1,389	5,671	2,873	651	5,891	998	13,508
CONNORS STATE COLLEGE	PUB-T	114,722	B	B	6,499	20,344	4,567	8,311	24,729	0	B
EAST CENTRAL OKLA STATE U	PUB-FG	314,545	155,191	14,819	16,433	37,804	27,624	12,023	3,313	14,047	33,291
EASTERN OKLA ST COLLEGE	PUB-T	82,584	B	B	10,383	9,948	2,000	0	5,380	645	B
EL RENO JUNIOR COLLEGE	PUB-T	54,382	B	B	5,545	14,840	0	0	0	232	B
FLAMING RAINBOW U	PRI-FN	A	A		A	A	A	A		A	B
HILLSDL FREE WILL BAPT C	PRI-FN	9,852	B	B	0	589	1,286	215	50	0	B
LANGSTON UNIVERSITY	PUB-FN	108,331	75,275	7,528		8,901	0	0	0	901	15,726
MIDWEST CHRISTIAN COLLEGE	PRI-FN	22,996	10,000	429	8,757	2,084	561	0	396	0	769
MURRAY STATE COLLEGE	PUB-T	95,290	66,410	7,305	6,000	7,319	2,046	0	1,100	350	4,760
NTHESTN OKLA AGRL-MECH C	PUB-T	210,474	110,318	11,984	11,525	52,499	0	0	0	1,571	22,577
NORTHEASTERN OKLA STATE U	PUB-FG	608,235	234,680	23,882	117,957	56,258	70,266	12,619	26,839	9,327	56,357
NORTHERN OKLAHOMA COLLEGE	PUB-T	91,711	53,389	5,119	5,682	12,040	4,247	0	200	971	10,063
NTHWSTN OKLA STATE U	PUB-FG	115,760	57,857	5,374	3,432	28,664	11,439	3,772	0	2,303	2,919
OKLAHOMA BAPT UNIVERSITY	PRI-FN	196,198	78,840	11,333	29,000	39,676	16,847	1,753	750	4,196	13,803
OKLA CHRISTIAN COLLEGE	PRI-FN	92,736	48,600	0	13,000	14,585	6,612	2,200	1,200	650	5,889
OKLAHOMA CTY STHWSTN C	PRI-T	41,333	B	B	3,421	6,706	3,424	141	76	150	B
OKLAHOMA CITY UNIVERSITY	PRI-FG	351,657	156,423	16,917	0	33,837	120,412	910	3,498	7,302	12,358

SEE FOOTNOTES AT END OF TABLE

Table 2. — Library Operating Expenditures (in Dollars) of College and University Libraries, by Category of Expenditure and by State or Other Area and Institution: Aggregate United States, 1978-79 — Continued

STATE OR OTHER AREA AND INSTITUTION	CON-TROL AND TYPE OF IN-STITU-TION	TOTAL	SALARIES AND WAGES			BOOK-STOCK	PERIOD-ICALS	MICRO-FORMS	AUDIO-VISUAL	BIND-ING AND RE-BIND-ING	ALL OTHER OPER-ATING EXPEND-ITURES
			LIBRARY STAFF	FRINGE BENEFITS	STUDENTS ON HOURLY BASIS						
(1)	(2)	(3)	(4)	(5)	(6)	(7)	(8)	(9)	(10)	(11)	(12)
OKLAHOMA	--CONTINUED										
OKLA C OSTEO MED AND SURG	PUB-FG	201,461	95,564	9,986	1,466	43,575	26,350	2,831	18,259	265	3,165
OKLA PANHANDLE STATE U	PUB-FN	116,352	B	B	16,651	29,651	7,754	3,023	269	1,487	B
OKLA SCH BUS ACCT LAW FIN	PRI-T	A	A			A	A			A	A
OKLA STATE U ALL CAMPUSES											
OKLA STATE U MAIN CAMPUS	PUB-U	2,048,535	816,067	97,928	236,079	129,439	469,592	26,117	0	49,228	224,085
OKLA STATE U TECH INST	PUB-T	69,560	42,060	7,000	3,000	7,963	2,667	795	575	0	5,500
ORAL ROBERTS UNIVERSITY	PRI-FG	2,065,295	458,683	59,251	114,874	459,668	418,283	315,124	31,877	17,771	189,764
OSCAR ROSE JUNIOR COLLEGE	PUB-T	497,851	240,188	21,890	0	85,527	20,525	17,428	22,818	193	89,282
PHILLIPS UNIVERSITY	PRI-FG	268,925	113,017	15,097	29,154	44,622	23,721	0	5,685	5,059	32,570
SAINT GREGORY'S COLLEGE	PRI-T	31,992	3,000	0	0	8,662	1,842	1,290	0	165	B
SAYRE JUNIOR COLLEGE	PUB-T	24,246	B	B	1,122	8,199	933	82	1,245	0	B
SEMINOLE JUNIOR COLLEGE	PUB-T	76,881	40,509	4,800	0	12,707	4,478	1,597	4,638	398	7,754
STHESTN OKLA STATE U	PUB-FG	151,207	65,520	6,234	30,125	25,026	7,908	601	3,541	2,014	10,238
SOUTH OKLA CTY JR COLLEGE	PUR-T	240,804	102,063	9,918	2,856	34,000	6,500	5,000	50,000	0	30,467
STHWSTN OKLA STATE U	PUB-FG	413,192	144,443	10,180	35,098	79,299	103,000	0	0	8,608	22,564
TULSA JUNIOR COLLEGE	PUB-T	506,055	312,171	30,982	0	72,959	12,301	2,586	24,495	379	50,182
U OF OKLAHOMA ALL CAM											
U OF OKLA HEALTH SCI CTR	PUB-FG	652,114	300,325	39,230	26,082	19,233	164,000	1,000	7,000	22,876	72,368
U OF OKLAHOMA NORMAN CAM	PUB-U	2,548,588	993,847	138,315	229,256	301,082	488,835	110,955	0	33,276	253,022
U OF SCI & ARTS OF OKLA	PUB-FN	134,967	65,271	6,782	6,933	21,816	11,298	1,128	3,454	2,149	16,136
UNIVERSITY OF TULSA	PRI-U	1,697,630	496,212	69,190	94,112	744,135	141,150	12,000	5,000	27,855	107,976
WESTERN OKLAHOMA STATE C	PUB-T	93,197	50,989	5,490	1,067	14,925	3,000	4,000	2,364	674	10,688
OREGON											
BASSIST INSTITUTE	PRI-T	19,161	B	B	0	5,450	540	0	1,250	0	B
BLUE MTN CMTY COLLEGE	PUB-T	189,738	90,270	23,470	3,917	19,779	10,613	3,074	5,412	0	33,203
CENTRAL OREG CMTY COLLEGE	PUB-T	81,160	43,487	7,610	0	13,275	9,649	725	2,168	173	4,073
CHEMEKETA CMTY COLLEGE	PUB-T	229,472	141,595	0	0	41,377	16,026	0	22,000	0	8,474
CLACKAMAS CMTY COLLEGE	PUB-T	194,799	113,490	26,107	3,458	26,180	5,597	5,955	1,046	600	12,366
CLATSOP COMMUNITY COLLEGE	PUB-T	135,040	77,001	16,245	2,307	15,257	5,081	2,493	3,109	20	13,527
COLEGIO CESAR CHAVEZ	PRI-FN	A	A	A	A	A	A	A	A	A	A
COLUMBIA CHRISTIAN C	PRI-FN	32,145	B	B	5,454	5,736	1,382	0	0	0	B
CONCORDIA COLLEGE	PRI-FN	65,454	B	B	9,700	15,777	5,561	1,236	2,891	746	B
GEORGE FOX COLLEGE	PRI-FN	106,811	45,702	6,400	18,740	25,152	7,812	55	0	1,166	1,784
JUDSON BAPTIST COLLEGE	PRI-T	33,624	B	B	12,739	4,800	2,811	0	1,009	48	B
LANE COMMUNITY COLLEGE	PUB-T	309,517	163,517	42,220	1,152	42,553	10,408	11,357	12,926	1,765	23,619
LEWIS AND CLARK COLLEGE	PRI-FG	844,727	276,159	41,318	89,941	182,042	122,579	25,822	2,728	22,972	81,166
LINFIELD COLLEGE	PRI-FG	162,953	69,363	13,899	34,632	24,068	13,325	2,100	325	600	4,641
LINN-BENTON CMTY COLLEGE	PUB-T	314,430	186,798	34,028	0	30,134	8,276	3,587	20,004	467	31,136
MARYLHURST ED CENTER	PRI-FN	87,437	65,400	3,200	0	12,982	3,350	300	500	100	1,605
MOUNT ANGEL SEMINARY	PRI-FG	109,963	72,150	0	1,100	15,130	8,583	0	0	0	13,000
MOUNT HOOD CMTY COLLEGE	PUB-T	209,056	133,935	26,519	8,544	11,543	8,337	2,056	7,986	193	9,943
MULTNOMAH SCHOOL OF BIBLE	PRI-FG	85,245	39,837	5,947	9,386	13,549	2,975	559	814	720	11,458
MUSEUM ART SCHOOL	PRI-FN	35,625	B	B	0	10,378	1,891	0	585	1,811	B
NTHWST CHRISTIAN COLLEGE	PRI-FN	72,515	40,414	6,687	2,040	14,257	2,523	100	1,153	572	4,769
OREGON GRADUATE CENTER	PRI-FG	89,392	B	B	0	19,153	38,108	1,327	0	1,192	B
OR ST HI ED SYS ALL INST											
EASTERN OREGON ST COLLEGE	PUB-FG	377,731	179,223	33,250	8,600	29,993	29,825	1,676	11,835	2,197	81,132
OREGON COLLEGE OF ED	PUB-FG	382,069	196,367	31,470	14,146	70,027	41,234	12,335	0	4,130	12,360
OREGON INST OF TECHNOLOGY	PUB-FN	209,274	101,972	17,898	7,053	22,374	29,284	217	18,051	7,565	4,860
OREGON STATE UNIVERSITY	PUB-U	2,706,315	1,028,640	180,768	150,578	383,814	619,325	9,485	0	52,365	281,340
PORTLAND STATE UNIVERSITY	PUB-FG	2,447,142	1,333,561	229,144	91,392	130,516	428,313	16,782	21,954	44,856	150,624
STHN OREGON ST COLLEGE	PUB-FG	602,184	343,881	60,761	13,950	63,268	64,082	10,342	6,340	11,270	28,290
U OF OREGON ALL CAM											
U OF OREGON MAIN CAMPUS	PUB-U	3,824,645	1,670,858	302,030	157,978	367,952	635,937	82,216	22,287	60,141	525,246
U OF OREGON HLTH SCI CTR	PUB-FG	763,344	397,483	66,624	36,990	29,760	136,630	3,310	2,802	17,517	72,228
PACIFIC UNIVERSITY	PRI-FG	272,273	125,146	20,952	32,220	39,938	21,813	1,748	410	3,911	26,135
PORTLAND CMTY COLLEGE	PUB-T	570,105	369,023	92,883	0	43,677	27,420	9,371	27,037	0	694
REED COLLEGE	PRI-FG	336,900	120,570	0	25,845	77,731	84,475	0	0	13,803	14,476
ROGUE COMMUNITY COLLEGE	PUB-T	90,078	50,212	10,161	1,931	15,510	2,716	300	500	498	8,250
STHWSTN OREG CMTY COLLEGE	PUB-T	258,106	136,754	28,382	28,990	22,150	7,139	0	0	0	34,691
TREASURE VLY CMTY COLLEGE	PUB-T	58,701	26,980	5,828	0	14,020	2,900	100	0	0	8,873
UMPQUA COMMUNITY COLLEGE	PUB-T	130,228	73,182	19,444	6,188	10,350	7,000	655	5,865	250	7,294
UNIVERSITY OF PORTLAND	PRI-U	258,099	104,174	16,318	31,436	50,793	30,081	6,758	356	358	17,825
WARNER PACIFIC COLLEGE	PRI-FG	88,019	B	B	15,968	7,507	3,332	0	1,137	1,090	B

SEE FOOTNOTES AT END OF TABLE

Table 2. — Library Operating Expenditures (in Dollars) of College and University Libraries, by Category of Expenditure and by State or Other Area and Institution: Aggregate United States, 1978-79 — Continued

STATE OR OTHER AREA AND INSTITUTION	CONTROL AND TYPE OF INSTITUTION	TOTAL	SALARIES AND WAGES			BOOK-STOCK	PERIODICALS	MICRO-FORMS	AUDIO-VISUAL	BINDING AND RE-BINDING	ALL OTHER OPERATING EXPENDITURES
			LIBRARY STAFF	FRINGE BENEFITS	STUDENTS ON HOURLY BASIS						
(1)	(2)	(3)	(4)	(5)	(6)	(7)	(8)	(9)	(10)	(11)	(12)
OREGON	--CONTINUED										
WESTERN BAPTIST COLLEGE	PRI-FN	67,374	36,841	3,641	4,868	8,941	5,340	300	100	900	6,443
WESTERN CONS BAPTIST SEM	PRI-FG	94,700	59,783	7,174	5,052	10,801	3,087	293	1,392	956	6,162
WSTN EVANGELICAL SEM	PRI-FG	58,560	29,061	1,722	4,646	10,530	3,552	0	0	0	9,049
WSTN STATES CHIRPRCTC C	PRI-FG	64,088	46,272	109	5,228	4,761	3,500	0	250	0	3,968
WILLAMETTE UNIVERSITY2/	PRI-FG	546,147	226,120	38,010	9,322	82,649	135,409	10,368	0	4,650	29,619
PENNSYLVANIA											
ACADEMY OF THE NEW CHURCH	PRI-FG	88,720	54,470	9,006	2,740	10,746	5,661	870	90	1,082	4,055
ALBRIGHT COLLEGE	PRI-FN	237,783	112,226	11,950	5,885	53,274	27,608	3,321	2,058	6,201	15,260
ALLEGHENY COLLEGE	PRI-FG	306,760	112,028	16,772	14,163	81,133	54,095	3,756	0	6,789	18,024
ALLNTWN C SNT FRAN DESALS	PRI-FN	131,866	41,077	6,408	8,348	32,400	12,244	690	4,539	5,745	20,⎯
ALLIANCE COLLEGE	PRI-FN	51,278	32,934	5,000	0	5,392	5,159	520	0	1,773	500
ALVERNIA COLLEGE	PRI-FN	64,325	42,034	1,646	0	9,068	4,089	104	1,626	1,406	4,352
AMERICAN COLLEGE	PRI-FG	44,690	0	0	0	12,520	20,250	100	325	880	10,615
BAPT BIBLE COLLEGE OF PA	PRI-FG	139,717	84,148	12,178	10,520	10,833	6,610	695	2,719	1,706	10,308
BEAVER COLLEGE	PRI-FG	197,813	109,661	21,803	15,532	9,753	21,456	2,182	0	1,748	15,678
BLOOMSBURG STATE COLLEGE	PUB-FG	1,012,821	407,274	113,942	43,962	151,726	152,225	60,890	9,734	7,035	66,033
BRYN MAWR COLLEGE	PRI-FG	1,170,031	442,270	77,840	67,419	284,671	144,120	4,828	0	67,606	81,277
BUCKNELL UNIVERSITY	PRI-FG	908,630	421,180	67,390	50,160	201,000	115,000	3,000	200	5,000	45,700
BUCKS COUNTY CMTY COLLEGE	PUB-T	437,726	274,792	49,588	0	41,492	4,937	5,209	31,361	1,323	29,024
BUTLER CO CMTY COLLEGE	PUB-T	132,750	80,990	12,149	6,494	13,760	5,777	1,026	7,112	1,802	3,640
CABRINI COLLEGE	PRI-FN	74,061	43,881	5,950	0	10,045	8,506	1,099	0	589	3,991
CALIFORNIA STATE COLLEGE	PUB-FG	649,200	403,700	110,100	30,100	31,000	40,000	6,000	0	4,400	23,900
CARLOW COLLEGE	PRI-FN	108,412	61,978	6,668	0	23,100	6,444	697	1,268	1,287	6,970
CARNEGIE-MELLON U	PRI-U	912,695	424,754	67,933	36,099	128,283	198,825	2,656	2,398	9,661	42,086
CEDAR CREST COLLEGE	PRI-FN	176,709	78,602	14,420	8,396	32,244	24,630	1,789	426	2,881	13,321
CENTER FOR DEGREE STUDIES	PRI-T	4,590	8	0	0	400	90	0	0	0	8
CEN PA BUSINESS SCHOOL	PRI-T	10,797	0	0	1,309	4,988	1,560	0	2,522	0	418
CHATHAM COLLEGE	PRI-FN	120,424	48,200	8,758	0	26,809	24,131	318	761	3,465	7,982
CHESTNUT HILL COLLEGE	PRI-FN	122,625	67,425	4,971	5,912	23,841	9,036	770	291	3,163	7,216
CHEYNEY STATE COLLEGE	PUB-FG	410,222	276,922	70,753	9,505	4,407	40,796	0	0	0	7,839
CLARION STATE C ALL CAM											
CLARION STATE C MAIN CAM	PUB-FG	946,385	495,255	118,861	76,552	87,240	69,911	29,488	3,770	12,326	52,982
CLARION ST C VENANGO CAM	PUB-T	91,244	51,876	12,450	3,801	11,240	6,974	494	0	211	4,198
COLLEGE MISERICORDIA	PRI-FN	189,933	91,084	14,518	16,383	36,860	15,382	3,050	3,817	0	8,839
COMBS COLLEGE OF MUSIC	PRI-FG	40,665	8	0	0	23,500	250	100	2,500	150	8
CC ALLEGHENY CO ALL CAM											
CC ALLEGHENY CO ALLEG CAM	PUB-T	311,544	195,140	40,703	1,988	24,716	8,790	2,191	14,000	3,638	20,378
CC ALLEGHENY CO BOYCE CAM	PUB-T	136,761	97,253	21,400	862	6,891	5,574	2,118	671	365	1,627
CC ALLEGHENY CO NORTH CAM	PUB-T	167,138	72,676	17,442	0	35,600		0	25,000	0	16,420
CC ALLEGHENY CO SOUTH CAM	PUB-T	195,290	123,000	24,600	1,000	17,000	8,000	2,000	3,000	1,000	15,690
CMTY COLLEGE OF BEAVER CO	PUB-T	85,795	48,952	5,195	0	20,495	7,883	0	0	0	3,270
CMTY COLLEGE DELAWARE CO	PUB-T	203,069	112,707	21,174	0	34,565	12,695	12,338	0	0	9,590
CMTY COLLEGE PHILADELPHIA	PUB-T	720,103	463,844	69,577	10,590	47,476	15,760	1,259	43,362	881	67,354
CURTIS INSTITUTE OF MUSIC	PRI-FG	79,840	47,955	8,468	1,547	11,465	420	0	5,470	0	4,515
DELAWARE VLY C SCI & AGR	PRI-FN	129,060	55,636	6,676	435	24,108	26,156	1,000	100	2,133	12,816
DICKINSON COLLEGE	PRI-FN	512,042	205,321	40,926	38,149	120,812	58,473	0	0	8,506	39,855
DICKINSON SCHOOL OF LAW	PRI-FG	263,900	52,400	7,700	0	43,800	122,400	14,400	4,900	2,800	15,500
DREXEL UNIVERSITY	PRI-FG	1,203,978	534,051	68,650	43,294	158,581	267,943	19,542	8,972	23,539	79,406
THE DROPSIE UNIVERSITY	PRI-FG	74,108	8	8	4,095	7,293	2,034	4,512	0	196	8
DUQUESNE UNIVERSITY	PRI-U	822,321	299,693	47,547	41,071	218,338	127,379	9,896	0	17,505	60,892
EASTERN BAPTIST THEOL SEM	PRI-FG	75,222	42,726	5,529	5,000	12,268	4,836	0	7	1,026	3,830
EASTERN COLLEGE	PRI-FN	86,219	50,531	7,000	0	14,603	6,802	628	0	1,355	5,300
EAST STROUDSBG ST COLLEGE	PUB-FG	777,182	368,947	101,460	53,545	105,246	52,004	31,143	1,000	15,000	48,837
EDINBORO STATE COLLEGE	PUB-FG	1,098,785	564,225	167,121	36,224	61,797	120,340	42,666	3,920	18,700	83,792
ELIZABETHTOWN COLLEGE	PRI-FN	237,755	110,334	15,400	8,002	52,081	27,971	3,484	878	2,580	17,025
FAITH THEOLOGICAL SEM	PRI-FG	1,968	0	0	0	1,580	205	0	0	0	183
FRANKLIN AND MARSHALL C	PRI-FG	442,853	172,822	40,711	0	100,685	72,328	5,300	0	12,800	38,207
GANNON COLLEGE	PRI-FG	387,651	151,633	26,000	49,069	88,854	40,780	4,106	123	13,891	13,195
GENEVA COLLEGE	PRI-FN	218,941	88,887	26,061	27,218	34,275	20,952	770	3,553	3,283	13,942
GETTYSBURG COLLEGE	PRI-FN	423,082	198,981	29,847	6,495	92,292	44,129	10,540	6,135	8,905	25,758
GRATZ COLLEGE	PRI-FG	48,200	36,000	4,000	0	5,000	1,400	0	0	800	1,000
GROVE CITY COLLEGE	PRI-FN	73,133	0	0	0	35,279	23,462	8,143	0	4,973	1,276
GWYNEDO-MERCY COLLEGE	PRI-FN	122,010	46,550	1,007	6,147	30,350	4,164	1,589	5,371	992	25,840
HAHNEMANN MEDL C AND HOSP	PRI-FG	361,839	184,010	28,283	14,619	38,339	78,902	102	720	1,380	15,484

SEE FOOTNOTES AT END OF TABLE

119

Table 2. — Library Operating Expenditures (in Dollars) of College and University Libraries, by Category of Expenditure and by State or Other Area and Institution: Aggregate United States, 1978-79 — Continued

STATE OR OTHER AREA AND INSTITUTION	CONTROL AND TYPE OF INSTITUTION	TOTAL	SALARIES AND WAGES			BOOKSTOCK	PERIODICALS	MICROFORMS	AUDIOVISUAL	BINDING AND REBINDING	ALL OTHER OPERATING EXPENDITURES
			LIBRARY STAFF	FRINGE BENEFITS	STUDENTS ON HOURLY BASIS						
(1)	(2)	(3)	(4)	(5)	(6)	(7)	(8)	(9)	(10)	(11)	(12)
PENNSYLVANIA	--CONTINUED										
HARCUM JUNIOR COLLEGE	PRI-T	57,233	38,040	3,972	0	4,030	3,704	222	6,436	0	829
HARRISBURG AREA CC	PUB-T	373,899	211,099	35,464	24,500	40,450	15,600	4,320	13,000	416	29,050
HAVERFORD COLLEGE	PRI-FN	521,560	239,505	34,615	35,325	83,095	83,030	2,665	650	6,050	36,625
HOLY FAMILY COLLEGE	PRI-FN	92,887	58,865	3,840	3,032	8,060	6,590	324	1,681	727	9,768
IMMACULATA COLLEGE	PRI-FN	140,501	81,011	1,547	15,515	19,424	8,159	680	2,046	3,127	8,992
INDIANA U OF PENNSYLVANIA	PUB-FG	1,574,124	682,952	157,166	134,305	214,927	158,720	103,500	27,210	15,000	80,344
JUNIATA COLLEGE	PRI-FN	209,209	80,977	14,283	18,200	37,090	34,267	2,002	0	1,800	20,590
KEYSTONE JUNIOR COLLEGE	PRI-T	77,718	44,455	7,113	7,629	6,615	4,708	0	2,835	0	4,363
KING'S COLLEGE	PRI-FN	317,589	176,066	26,410	8,165	58,490	29,907	1,609	3,416	4,339	9,187
KUTZTOWN STATE COLLEGE	PUB-FG	777,471	374,581	95,541	44,946	118,480	72,102	24,489	3,369	12,937	31,026
LACKAWANNA JUNIOR COLLEGE	PRI-T	73,255	38,905	3,500	0	10,000	5,000	3,000	3,850	400	8,600
LAFAYETTE COLLEGE	PRI-FN	599,977	264,117	49,658	34,866	112,098	111,217	1,633	2,499	21,999	1,890
LANCASTER BIBLE COLLEGE	PRI-FN	57,775	30,000	6,700	0	9,000	3,000	0	5,000	0	4,075
LANCASTER THEOLOGICAL SEM	PRI-FG	105,192	38,834	18,863	7,323	23,884	6,157	0	0	1,349	8,782
LA ROCHE COLLEGE	PRI-FN	140,052	56,310	3,800	10,576	24,305	10,622	4,735	4,541	4,401	20,762
LA SALLE COLLEGE	PRI-FG	553,781	251,032	30,123	32,012	136,509	52,343	1,802	0	12,469	37,491
LEBANON VALLEY COLLEGE	PRI-FN	176,051	63,141	10,766	8,648	39,076	25,873	4,482	0	4,512	19,553
LEHIGH CO CMTY COLLEGE	PUB-T	125,732	63,705	11,467	5,175	11,227	8,466	3,158	4,809	250	17,475
LEHIGH UNIVERSITY	PRI-FG	1,207,544	482,062	115,000	58,730	155,879	260,966	9,976	2,484	19,405	103,042
LINCOLN UNIVERSITY	PUB-FG	283,696	163,463	20,433	21,995	15,799	33,084	2,627	12	1,446	24,837
LOCK HAVEN STATE COLLEGE	PUB-FN	481,569	240,107	72,120	46,638	38,908	51,101	4,754	0	7,370	20,571
LUTH THEOL SEM GETTYSBURG	PRI-FG	127,316	69,757	9,795	743	27,355	7,653	0	0	3,692	18,399
LUTHERAN THEOL SEM PHILA	PRI-FG	126,549	60,762	13,572	3,968	22,578	6,003	802	801	5,407	12,656
LUZERNE CO CMTY COLLEGE	PUB-T	162,668	80,339	16,068	0	27,600	11,601	6,461	7,787	1,297	11,515
LYCOMING COLLEGE	PRI-FN	223,410	93,390	9,152	10,664	39,942	31,700	3,000	225	6,677	28,660
MANOR JUNIOR COLLEGE	PRI-T	29,804	B	B	1,624	4,684	1,360	0	962	675	B
MANSFIELD STATE COLLEGE	PUB-FG	666,246	402,806	106,350	39,861	15,610	59,500	15,379	372	4,583	21,785
MARY IMMACULATE SEMINARY	PRI-FG	49,763	21,300	0	0	16,575	6,834	0	0	1,859	520
MARYWOOD COLLEGE	PRI-FG	368,309	199,037	37,749	19,387	57,748	29,081	5,052	4,052	3,831	12,372
THE MEDL COLLEGE OF PA	PRI-FG	252,899	144,478	7,389	3,900	3,500	71,000	0	0	6,700	15,932
MERCYHURST COLLEGE	PRI-FG	101,580	65,623	0	0	16,306	12,145	1,582	0	569	5,355
MESSIAH COLLEGE	PRI-FN	198,069	72,947	10,950	6,204	50,573	14,774	1,050	7,511	2,000	32,060
MILLERSVILLE ST COLLEGE	PUB-FG	930,066	511,108	136,822	73,545	66,138	48,881	12,276	6,028	6,440	68,828
MONTGOMERY CO COMMUNITY C	PUB-T	383,198	269,253	51,600	1,642	26,516	9,497	1,665	7,111	1,988	13,926
MOORE COLLEGE OF ART	PRI-FN	104,785	52,339	8,100	5,500	14,894	7,864	690	7,293	1,890	6,215
MORAVIAN COLLEGE	PRI-FN	239,246	80,268	16,500	13,833	54,032	38,534	7,000	0	7,638	21,441
MOUNT ALOYSIUS JR COLLEGE	PRI-T	102,357	72,566	5,320	5,502	9,220	3,500	2,860	918	1,166	1,305
MUHLENBERG COLLEGE	PRI-FN	295,751	123,135	18,766	10,110	56,545	43,700	5,190	400	8,600	29,305
NEW SCHOOL OF MUSIC	PRI-FN	15,645	B	B	0	627	230	0	723	0	B
NORTHAMPTON CO AREA CC	PUB-T	258,930	132,808	29,217	17,095	35,515	12,251	1,510	7,405	984	22,145
NORTHEASTERN CHRISTIAN JC	PRI-T	55,262	B	B	18,440	5,200	2,500	0	2,024	0	B
OUR LADY ANGELS COLLEGE	PRI-FN	148,730	83,405	1,018	3,000	19,000	9,000	0	10,000	10,222	13,085
PEIRCE JUNIOR COLLEGE	PRI-T	130,421	78,689	17,266	8,172	10,327	1,566	650	4,828	0	8,923
PA COLLEGE OF OPTOMETRY	PRI-FG	59,367	B	B	6,023	6,155	7,315	0	105	1,500	B
PA COLLEGE PODIATRIC MED	PRI-FG	92,946	46,483	7,437	0	11,994	12,557	5,603	1,876	2,149	4,847
PA STATE U ALL CAMPUSES											
PA STATE U MAIN CAMPUS	PUB-U	6,332,745	3,561,986	655,405	109,791	509,653	806,459	53,792	0	134,901	500,758
PA STATE U ALLENTOWN CAM	PUB-T	66,497	B	B	6,594	8,725	5,647	2,154	324	104	B
PA STATE U ALTOONA CAM	PUB-T	114,652	70,234	12,923	0	15,107	10,713	1,646	10	0	4,019
PA STATE U BEAVER CAMPUS	PUB-T	82,075	B	B	0	12,870	7,457	2,478	1,178	240	B
PA ST U BEHREND COLLEGE	PUB-FG	139,138	51,351	9,449	8,026	23,922	33,530	2,494	179	1,009	9,178
PA STATE U BERKS CAMPUS	PUB-T	100,317	57,503	10,581	3,625	11,195	10,003	1,822	200	757	4,631
PA STATE U CAPITOL CAMPUS	PUB-FG	401,338	B	B	34,375	54,557	39,044	5,000	290	6,890	B
PA STATE U DELAWARE CAM	PUB-T	75,133	B	B	954	9,688	11,804	1,706	0	0	B
PA STATE U DU BOIS CAMPUS	PUB-T	49,951	B	B	3,433	5,259	4,968	1,792	22	968	B
PA STATE U FAYETTE CAMPUS	PUB-T	86,130	49,766	9,157	356	11,134	6,533	1,987	3,035	75	4,087
PA STATE U HAZLETON CAM	PUB-T	88,631	52,980	9,748	286	11,963	6,895	2,300	342	39	4,078
PA ST U HERSHEY MEDL CTR	PUB-FG	367,211	157,937	29,060	8,393	15,442	131,899	0	0	9,546	14,934
PA STATE U MCKEESPORT CAM	PUB-T	69,361	B	B	3,336	8,025	8,731	1,788	1,155	685	B
PA STATE U MONT ALTO CAM	PUB-T	71,952	B	B	1,156	9,914	5,413	1,942	29	83	B
PA ST U NEW KENSINGTN CAM	PUB-T	78,780	B	B	0	10,288	7,539	3,214	1,827	191	B
PA STATE U OGONTZ CAMPUS	PUB-T	120,649	72,650	13,368	3,090	15,824	10,515	2,014	0	347	2,841
PA ST U RADNOR CENTER	PUB-FG	59,192	B	B	0	10,082	8,403	1,107	158	527	B
PA STATE U SCHUYLKILL CAM	PUB-T	58,220	B	B	3,778	5,509	7,529	1,576	267	8	B
PA ST U SHENANGO VLY CAM	PUB-T	58,099	B	B	987	8,198	5,400	3,255	177	0	B

SEE FOOTNOTES AT END OF TABLE

Table 2. — Library Operating Expenditures (in Dollars) of College and University Libraries, by Category of Expenditure and by State or Other Area and Institution: Aggregate United States, 1978-79 — Continued

STATE OR OTHER AREA AND INSTITUTION	CONTROL AND TYPE OF INSTITUTION	TOTAL	SALARIES AND WAGES			BOOK-STOCK	PERIOD-ICALS	MICRO-FORMS	AUDIO-VISUAL	BINDING AND RE-BINDING	ALL OTHER OPERATING EXPENDITURES
			LIBRARY STAFF	FRINGE BENEFITS	STUDENTS ON HOURLY BASIS						
(1)	(2)	(3)	(4)	(5)	(6)	(7)	(8)	(9)	(10)	(11)	(12)
PENNSYLVANIA --CONTINUED											
PA ST U WILKES-BARRE CAM	PUB-T	40,540	B	B	0	6,031	6,583	1,703	0	0	B
PA ST U WRTHGTN SCRTN CAM	PUB-T	76,945	B	B	289	11,039	6,690	1,998	340	416	B
PA STATE U YORK CAMPUS	PUB-T	57,542	B	B	525	7,821	6,204	1,827	715	60	B
PHILA COLLEGE OF ART	PRI-FG	130,321	91,440	9,144	0	13,307	6,311	0	0	2,495	7,624
PHILA COLLEGE OF BIBLE	PRI-FN	86,606	42,619	2,600	9,761	15,653	7,829	0	152	0	7,992
PHILA COLLEGE OSTEO MED	PRI-FG	294,691	145,841	21,900	15,000	25,000	43,500	10,000	6,500	7,000	19,950
PHILA C PERFORMING ARTS	PRI-FG	93,158	52,918	5,196	6,224	12,059	2,579	0	5,351	0	8,831
PHILA COLLEGE PHAR & SCI	PRI-FG	377,045	155,994	31,199	31,721	45,164	40,966	11,096	22,036	4,700	34,169
PHILA C TEXTILES AND SCI	PRI-FG	201,450	107,000	0	2,500	36,000	35,000	4,000	0	3,100	13,850
PINEBROOK JUNIOR COLLEGE	PRI-T	42,951	B	B	1,100	31,626	1,055	0	0	0	B
PITTSBURGH THEOL SEMINARY	PRI-FG	157,255	74,270	12,260	725	43,000	17,000	0	0	9,000	1,000
POINT PARK COLLEGE	PRI-FG	131,128	69,767	11,860	0	21,138	11,274	4,249	1,481	2,935	8,424
READING AREA CMTY COLLEGE	PUB-T	107,044	70,595	13,060	0	5,359	8,698	1,000	3,000	0	5,332
REFORMED PRESB THEOL SEM	PRI-FG	15,459	B	B	0	2,954	963	0	54	52	B
ROBERT MORRIS COLLEGE	PRI-FG	477,437	244,935	36,005	33,962	64,034	15,563	14,823	15,815	1,441	50,859
ROSEMONT COLLEGE	PRI-FN	127,286	71,589	7,741	600	17,048	10,460	3,446	600	2,007	13,795
SNT CHARLES BORROMEO SEM	PRI-FG	182,333	118,691	11,780	0	21,943	7,902	0	1,396	4,797	15,824
SAINT FRANCIS COLLEGE	PRI-FG	191,485	107,553	16,163	5,567	17,716	32,882	0	0	6,391	5,213
SAINT JOSEPH'S UNIVERSITY	PRI-FG	465,380	208,974	22,768	26,358	93,643	65,354	4,259	2,817	8,900	32,307
SAINT VINCENT COLLEGE	PRI FN	SEE SNT VINCENT C-SEM JT LIB									
SNT VINCENT C-SEM JT LIB	PRI-FN	246,160	106,296	23,149	12,957	65,353	14,145	2,517	24	9,469	12,250
SAINT VINCENT SEMINARY	PRI FG	SEE SAINT VINCENT C-SEM JT LIB									
SETON HILL COLLEGE	PRI-FN	110,441	48,920	7,322	16,650	12,186	6,614	5,998	391	3,677	8,683
SHIPPENSBURG ST COLLEGE	PUB-FG	883,738	514,674	137,005	45,850	95,862	51,610	11,133	1,188	1,639	24,777
SLIPPERY ROCK ST COLLEGE	PUB-FG	1,058,085	474,524	120,437	119,243	144,477	105,958	29,676	9,629	14,848	39,293
SPRING GARDEN COLLEGE	PRI-FN	65,037	B	B	6,437	15,300	4,200	0	0	0	B
SUSQUEHANNA UNIVERSITY	PRI-FN	296,675	103,572	16,572	36,805	67,698	38,144	4,407	186	1,424	27,867
SWARTHMORE COLLEGE	PRI-FG	846,487	384,153	83,154	37,080	176,374	107,300	4,700	300	21,000	32,426
TALMUD YESHIVA OF PHILA	PRI-FG	A	A	A	A	A	A	A	A	A	A
TEMPLE UNIVERSITY	PUB-U	4,940,085	2,633,695	419,300	237,750	473,924	787,765	37,191	1,780	95,683	252,997
THEOL SEM REFORMD EPIS CH	PRI-FG	10,922	B	0	0	1,500	150	0	250	75	B
THIEL COLLEGE	PRI-FN	178,152	74,463	17,221	26,697	30,000	16,000	1,200	500	7,500	4,571
THOMAS JEFF UNIVERSITY	PRI-FG	709,353	360,458	72,672	5,466	52,516	105,011	3,564	11,891	11,861	85,914
UNITED WESLEYAN COLLEGE	PRI-FN	14,186	B	B	383	1,062	624	0	64	76	B
U OF PENNSYLVANIA	PRI-U	7,678,626	3,807,905	1,002,254	328,199	673,357	994,972	0	12,093	258,742	601,104
U OF PITTSBG ALL CAMPUSES											
U OF PITTSBG MAIN CAMPUS	PUB-U	5,521,684	2,721,437	560,668	406,104	534,851	790,013	53,450	3,731	93,312	358,118
U OF PITTSBG BRADFORD CAM	PUB-FN	97,170	46,044	9,126	0	12,000	11,000	4,600	300	2,500	11,600
U OF PITTSBG GREENSBG CAM	PUB-T	92,300	B	B	4,961	30,912	4,371	2,253	216	159	B
U OF PITTSBG JOHNSTWN CAM	PUB-FN	316,005	179,140	32,279	0	27,735	26,661	2,472	1,360	3,101	43,257
U OF PITTSBG TITUSVL CAM	PUB-T	49,746	B	B	1,175	7,597	5,675	469	0	309	B
UNIVERSITY OF SCRANTON	PRI-FG	361,107	172,954	24,114	6,883	70,179	56,866	909	0	7,701	21,501
URSINUS COLLEGE	PRI-FN	211,519	89,152	13,373	27,123	38,280	24,931	3,890	1,106	2,004	11,660
VALLEY FORGE CHRISTIAN C	PRI-FN	40,731	B	0	3,822	15,262	3,185	0	452	306	B
VALLEY FORGE MILITARY JC	PRI-T	57,295	B	B	0	616	1,241	0	242	0	B
VILLA MARIA COLLEGE	PRI-FN	53,052	B	B	5,500	9,880	5,104	0	301	1,051	B
VILLANOVA UNIVERSITY	PRI-U	1,286,110	531,799	63,717	38,821	203,229	278,258	41,840	36,974	23,252	68,220
WASHINGTON JEFF COLLEGE	PRI-FG	192,916	100,090	11,859	5,329	29,410	26,085	4,647	4,335	3,023	8,138
WAYNESBURG COLLEGE	PRI-FN	135,780	51,311	11,640	10,358	23,744	22,703	1,134	439	1,543	12,908
WEST CHESTER ST COLLEGE	PUB-FG	1,246,648	545,242	153,786	109,759	150,741	162,801	23,705	11,597	32,017	57,000
WESTMINSTER COLLEGE	PRI-FG	325,406	117,486	21,147	14,029	84,297	53,151	1,200	500	6,291	27,305
WESTMINSTER THEOL SEM	PRI-FG	135,990	53,900	5,390	7,600	48,000	10,000	1,000	500	2,000	7,600
WESTMORELAND COUNTY CC	PUB-T	167,305	76,315	15,141	0	32,788	13,986	3,714	13,738	0	11,623
WIDENER C OF WIDENER U	PRI-FG	398,882	209,016	22,978	16,315	55,547	52,672	4,069	729	8,877	28,679
WILKES COLLEGE	PRI-FG	371,665	157,241	23,373	8,734	89,095	62,482	10,703	5,014	6,456	8,567
WILLIAMSPORT AREA CC	PUB-T	162,612	106,121	20,163	0	10,392	5,150	125	8,500	253	11,908
WILSON COLLEGE	PRI-FN	109,941	33,859	3,657	17,016	20,261	11,935	804	0	513	21,896
YESHIVATH BETH MOSHE	PRI-FG	A	A	A	A	A	A	A	A	A	A
YORK COLLEGE PENNSYLVANIA	PRI-FG	264,983	124,887	22,635	10,448	39,345	31,000	0	9,609	4,380	22,679
RHODE ISLAND											
BARRINGTON COLLEGE	PRI-FN	52,503	B	B	18	10,549	5,401	192	521	493	B
BROWN UNIVERSITY	PRI-FG	3,450,640	1,549,067	282,157	158,836	518,688	510,928	0	0	110,249	320,715
BRYANT C BUSINESS ADMIN	PRI-FG	275,370	113,222	22,644	25,253	49,908	31,623	4,574	3,391	0	24,755
JOHNSON & WALES COLLEGE	PRI-FN	74,095	B	B	0	19,408	1,000	0	18,986	0	B

SEE FOOTNOTES AT END OF TABLE

121

Table 2. – Library Operating Expenditures (in Dollars) of College and University Libraries, by Category of Expenditure and by State or Other Area and Institution: Aggregate United States, 1978-79 – Continued

STATE OR OTHER AREA AND INSTITUTION	CONTROL AND TYPE OF INSTITUTION	TOTAL	SALARIES AND WAGES			BOOK-STOCK	PERIOD-ICALS	MICRO-FORMS	AUDIO-VISUAL	BINDING AND RE-BINDING	ALL OTHER OPERATING EXPENDITURES
			LIBRARY STAFF	FRINGE BENEFITS	STUDENTS ON HOURLY BASIS						
(1)	(2)	(3)	(4)	(5)	(6)	(7)	(8)	(9)	(10)	(11)	(12)

RHODE ISLAND	--CONTINUED										
NEW ENG INST TECHNOLOGY	PRI-T	20,575	,B	B	0	861	539	0	2,860	0	B
PROVIDENCE COLLEGE	PRI-FG	547,870	219,096	52,297	36,799	135,662	69,144	2,216	389	8,785	23,482
RHODE ISLAND COLLEGE	PUB-FG	865,127	367,898	73,580	80,250	145,071	65,794	24,552	650	13,536	93,796
RHODE ISLAND JR COLLEGE	PUB-T	517,967	275,717	52,642	33,532	72,749	29,221	11,835	18,764	422	23,085
RI SCHOOL OF DESIGN	PRI-FG	181,826	105,253	16,741	21,875	19,878	6,748	0	1,844	2,097	7,390
ROGER WILLIAMS C ALL CAM	PRI-FN										
ROGER WILLIAMS C MAIN CAM	PRI-FN	270,121	138,965	28,437	0	44,430	21,169	5,177	2,737	214	28,992
ROGER WILLIAMS C PROV BR	PRI-FN			NO LIBRARY FACILITIES							
SALVE REGINA-NEWPORT C	PRI-FG	115,132	58,118	5,343	10,920	18,735	11,680	2,454	504	2,262	5,116
U OF RHODE ISLAND	PUB-U	1,898,260	884,021	152,650	92,395	248,064	349,449	32,000	0	34,555	105,126

SOUTH CAROLINA											
AIKEN TECHNICAL COLLEGE	PUB-T	79,676	47,142	0	50	26,696	0	0	3,593	0	2,195
ALLEN UNIVERSITY	PRI-FN	57,450	B	B	0	22,000	2,000	0	0	0	B
ANDERSON COLLEGE	PRI-T	78,861	41,261	5,466	4,488	21,742	3,420	0	0	543	1,941
BAPT COLLEGE AT CHASTN	PRI-FN	364,374	193,440	25,736	0	47,797	33,170	1,433	13,662	3,540	45,596
BEAUFORT TECH COLLEGE	PUB-T	93,712	60,021	8,619	0	13,064	2,000	0	6,341	0	3,667
BENEDICT COLLEGE	PRI-FN	290,067	143,235	25,782	0	67,360	16,840	700	0	2,500	33,650
BOB JONES UNIVERSITY	PRI-FG	154,912	89,913	0	0	44,954	12,201	469	0	5,507	1,868
CENTRAL WESLEYAN COLLEGE	PRI-FG	79,840	36,029	3,881	4,085	17,876	6,842	2,178	764	1,591	6,594
CHESTERFLD-MARLBORO TECH	PUB-T	40,591	B	B	0	6,691	3,049	0	5,266	0	B
CITADEL MILITARY C OF SC	PUB-FG	423,974	183,233	24,974	4,500	118,384	31,062	9,486	0	4,508	47,827
CLAFLIN COLLEGE	PRI-FN	235,257	116,004	5,254	0	92,304	16,077	31	0	947	4,640
CLEMSON UNIVERSITY	PUB-U	1,978,888	777,918	123,501	38,893	246,679	546,705	14,701	933	50,627	178,931
CLINTON JUNIOR COLLEGE	PRI-T	9,650	B	0	0	200	.150	0	0	0	B
COKER COLLEGE	PRI-FN	67,771	32,701	4,511	0	12,080	9,977	964	294	230	7,014
COLLEGE OF CHARLESTON	PUB-FG	618,614	287,882	54,835	14,060	56,447	82,900	59,631	80	7,128	55,651
COLUMBIA BIBLE COLLEGE	PRI-FG	129,582	65,924	10,547	7,460	24,154	8,350	1,946	1,882	3,170	6,149
COLUMBIA COLLEGE	PRI-FN	195,562	92,431	11,131	10,956	41,836	19,060	1,940	5,119	4,000	9,069
COLUMBIA JUNIOR C	PRI-T	13,671	B	0	2,117	2,691	126	0	160	0	B
CONVERSE COLLEGE	PRI-FG	187,178	90,714	6,284	10,500	43,150	16,000	4,000	2,000	4,660	9,870
DENMARK TECHNICAL COLLEGE	PUB-T	77,300	46,458	7,898	0	13,514	4,655	1,395	1,842	0	1,538
ERSKINE C AND SEMINARY	PRI-FG	118,145	50,826	4,968	7,261	31,693	17,172	0	0	0	6,225
FLORENCE DARLINGTON TECH	PUB-T	80,826	44,055	6,093	0	21,652	2,835	0	0	0	6,191
FRANCIS MARION COLLEGE	PUB-FG	554,312	237,176	36,347	5,134	172,164	50,111	8,747	0	11,448	33,185
FRIENDSHIP COLLEGE	PRI-T	68,688	34,116	3,704	22,272	3,279	2,283	0	1,335	0	1,699
FURMAN UNIVERSITY	PRI-FG	439,354	165,697	15,377	25,327	125,681	74,248	0	0	9,004	24,020
GREENVILLE TECH COLLEGE	PUB-T	196,851	119,350	20,290	0	26,675	9,610	1,387	11,137	111	8,291
HORRY-GEORGETOWN TECH C	PUB-T	73,958	B	B	5,606	15,213	5,755	1,454	2,688	0	B
LANDER COLLEGE	PUB-FN	354,611	150,716	27,129	16,461	68,416	44,747	5,521	6,000	3,636	31,985
LIMESTONE COLLEGE	PRI-FN	54,417	34,385	0	0	12,443	5,322	1,162	0	0	1,105
LUTHERAN THEOL STHN SEM	PRI-FG	89,079	B	B	3,651	31,707	0	0	0	3,496	B
MEDICAL UNIVERSITY OF SC	PUB-FG	903,399	418,830	70,489	23,396	64,145	210,000	0	8,000	24,625	83,914
MIDLANDS TECH COLLEGE	PUB-T	219,913	159,650	0	0	35,152	12,789	2,217	31	0	10,074
MORRIS COLLEGE	PRI-FN	126,646	42,815	6,850	28,506	24,216	16,015	3,810	103	402	3,929
NEWBERRY COLLEGE	PRI-FN	162,127	66,162	10,980	9,000	50,000	9,300	6,000	0	2,800	7,885
NORTH GREENVILLE COLLEGE	PRI-T	56,502	30,970	3,304	2,893	6,218	3,399	107	2,680	2,456	4,476
ORANGEBURG CALHOUN TECH C	PUB-T	156,444	95,710	15,587	10,549	11,712	4,554	721	6,181	26	11,404
PIEDMONT TECH COLLEGE	PUB-T	117,446	56,184	5,970	0	19,065	3,747	5,508	7,356	284	19,332
PRESBYTERIAN COLLEGE	PRI-FN	161,942	73,597	11,040	5,200	34,055	21,942	3,287	2,409	2,282	8,130
RICE COLLEGE	PRI-T	A	A	A	A	A	A	A	A	A	A
RUTLEDGE COLLEGE	PRI-T	A	A	A	A	A	A	A	A	A	A
SC STATE COLLEGE	PUB-FG	426,494	184,014	28,283	0	162,321	0	1,974	0	4,837	45,065
SPARTANBURG METH COLLEGE	PRI-T	57,921	34,577	648	4,321	10,606	2,235	425	2,498	0	2,611
SPARTANBURG TECH COLLEGE	PUB-T	76,573	44,615	8,159	0	18,925	2,758	75	575	0	1,466
SUMTER AREA TECH COLLEGE	PUB-T	75,802	B	B	0	10,987	4,758	1,230	1,073	456	B
TRI-COUNTY TECH COLLEGE	PUB-T	130,038	78,067	13,271	0	18,550	6,500	0	2,950	1,500	9,200
TRIDENT TECHNICAL COLLEGE	PUB-T	270,631	144,983	21,747	0	42,500	12,000	3,221	12,206	50	33,924
U OF SC ALL CAMPUSES											
U OF SC AT AIKEN	PUB-FN	352,523	87,004	13,313	2,424	129,281	36,837	49,667	0	7,983	26,014
U OF SC AT BEAUFORT	PUB-T	85,118	B	B	3,936	27,606	6,324	2,487	0	1,379	B
U OF SC COASTAL CAROLINA	PUB-FN	221,010	72,904	13,406	5,625	58,701	0	38,505	0	3,217	28,652
U OF SC AT COLUMBIA	PUB-U	4,035,911	1,776,451	265,391	172,877	575,899	764,233	124,321	26,365	98,921	231,453
U OF SC AT LANCASTER	PUB-T	60,261	32,025	4,420	630	10,041	8,577	1,159	1,880	880	649
U OF SC AT SALKEHATCHIE	PUB-T	48,203	B	B	3,950	14,693	5,837	1,390	791	804	B

SEE FOOTNOTES AT END OF TABLE

122

Table 2. — Library Operating Expenditures (in Dollars) of College and University Libraries, by Category of Expenditure and by State or Other Area and Institution: Aggregate United States, 1978-79 — Continued

STATE OR OTHER AREA AND INSTITUTION	CON-TROL AND TYPE OF IN-STITU-TION	TOTAL	SALARIES AND WAGES			BOOK-STOCK	PERIOD-ICALS	MICRO-FORMS	AUDIO-VISUAL	BIND-ING AND RE-BIND-ING	ALL OTHER OPER-ATING EXPEND-ITURES
			LIBRARY STAFF	FRINGE BENEFITS	STUDENTS ON HOURLY BASIS						
(1)	(2)	(3)	(4)	(5)	(6)	(7)	(8)	(9)	(10)	(11)	(12)
SOUTH CAROLINA	--CONTINUED										
U OF SC AT SPARTANBURG	PUB-FN	276,676	40,216	0	10,741	110,623	38,636	21,922	14,116	7,425	32,997
U OF SC AT SUMTER	PUB-T	100,130	41,990	7,065	2,267	19,572	10,000	3,276	1,000	778	14,182
U OF SC AT UNION	PUB-T	48,077	B	B	858	11,389	4,692	1,344	0	481	B
VOORHEES COLLEGE	PRI-FN	118,682	57,789	35,424	0	9,872	7,087	1,500	0	5,582	1,428
WILLIAMSBURG TECH C	PUB-T	67,245	22,172	3,271	2,656	12,149	8,571	0	4,502	3	13,924
WINTHROP COLLEGE	PUB-FG	741,640	375,694	66,292	53,426	75,691	101,796	18,758	0	8,466	41,517
WOFFORD COLLEGE	PRI-FN	205,167	97,716	15,096	12,648	39,866	20,217	2,849	174	5,030	11,571
YORK TECHNICAL COLLEGE	PUB-T	59,012	B	B	8,493	9,000	6,500	2,000	4,500	0	B
SOUTH DAKOTA											
AUGUSTANA COLLEGE	PRI-FG	333,414	131,577	27,387	53,570	41,754	27,083	6,876	5,351	3,527	36,284
BLACK HILLS STATE COLLEGE	PUB-FG	187,155	117,793	14,170	0	18,426	11,995	4,719	0	1,741	18,311
DAKOTA STATE COLLEGE	PUB-FN	114,792	54,349	11,132	2,024	24,361	13,088	1,700	2,318	2,457	3,363
DAKOTA WESLEYAN U	PRI-FN	69,610	B	B	14,080	7,000	5,000	800	2,000	1,600	B
FREEMAN JUNIOR COLLEGE	PRI-T	27,011	B	B	452	4,749	1,800	100	1,900	0	95
HURON COLLEGE	PRI-FN	26,287	B	B	B	3,442	2,671	27	147	195	B
MOUNT MARTY COLLEGE	PRI-FN	112,499	50,068	4,667	22,947	17,492	6,699	480	2,404	201	7,541
NATIONAL COLLEGE	PRI-FN	104,007	44,192	3,637	1,946	12,101	8,417	400	4,583	0	28,731
NORTH AMERICAN BAPT SEM	PRI-FG	56,222	B	B	2,997	14,756	5,665	16	598	940	B
NORTHERN STATE COLLEGE	PUB-FG	256,952	114,388	15,442	5,573	78,530	19,716	2,796	1,548	4,596	14,363
OGLALA SIOUX CC	PUB-T	36,900	B	B	0	0	400	250	0	0	B
PRESENTATION COLLEGE	PRI-T	50,994	B	B	3,647	9,124	3,378	0	957	736	B
SINTE GLESKA COLLEGE	PRI-FN	103,771	55,700	5,570	0	3,658	1,008	50	1,559	150	36,076
SIOUX FALLS COLLEGE	PRI-FN	84,430	37,857	7,360	6,138	12,889	9,477	1,107	327	1,041	8,234
SD SCH MINES & TECHNOLOGY	PUB-FG	227,602	104,537	15,106	1,382	20,460	65,058	2,345	0	1,645	17,069
SD STATE UNIVERSITY	PUB-U	784,436	272,682	27,248	59,132	132,522	198,309	2,000	0	16,635	76,108
U OF SD ALL CAMPUSES											
U OF SD MAIN CAMPUS	PUB-U	1,239,316	532,876	81,540	35,601	187,352	269,533	4,300	2,000	34,346	91,768
U OF SD AT SPRINGFIELD	PUB-FN	173,193	50,833	0	0	32,432	8,600	800	14,228	1,100	65,180
YANKTON COLLEGE	PRI-FN	50,526	B	B	0	6,888	6,650	0	0	0	B
TENNESSEE											
AMER BAPT THEOL SEM	PRI-FN	13,553	B	B	0	516	485	0	0	B	B
AQUINAS JUNIOR COLLEGE	PRI-T	51,124	B	B	6,483	4,351	2,062	0	1,554	206	B
BELMONT COLLEGE	PRI-FN	133,766	71,733	10,701	10,876	19,573	8,266	0	373	1,459	10,785
BETHEL COLLEGE	PRI-FN	61,495	27,116	3,340	5,579	10,478	10,116	294	890	2,112	1,570
BRISTOL COLLEGE	PRI-T	• A	A	A	A	A	A				A
BRYAN COLLEGE	PRI-FN	79,881	32,929	3,576	6,663	23,577	6,377	1,234	1,847	2,307	1,371
CARSON-NEWMAN COLLEGE	PRI-FN	162,224	71,833	15,213	14,391	26,657	15,018	2,682	0	6,348	10,082
CHRISTIAN BROS COLLEGE	PRI-FN	92,412	35,720	5,358	17,188	19,679	11,684	0	0	780	2,003
CUMBERLAND COLLEGE TENN	PRI-T	42,610	B	B	2,500	4,950	1,750	0	650	500	B
DAVID LIPSCOMB COLLEGE	PRI-FN	242,850	106,478	14,706	17,135	48,569	32,334	0	0	7,457	16,171
DRAUGHON'S JR COLLEGE	PRI-T	10,264	B	0	700	795	500	0	89	0	B
DRAUGHON'S JC BUSINESS	PRI-T	A	A			A	A				
DRAUGHONS JC BUSINESS	PRI-T	9,030	6,000	500	750	500	280	0	500	0	500
EDMONDSON JR COLLEGE	PRI-T	11,095	2,000	0	795	300	0	0	0	0	
EMMANUEL SCH OF RELIGION	PRI-FG	62,021	24,237	0	7,078	9,029	5,660	1,925	2,420	2,568	9,104
FISK UNIVERSITY	PRI-FG	A	A	A	A	A	A	A	A	A	A
FREED-HARDEMAN COLLEGE	PRI-FN	195,826	79,023	9,180	21,907	51,120	9,126	2,125	6,119	1,560	15,666
FREE WILL BAPTIST BIBLE C	PRI-FN	55,029	19,622	3,106	13,211	12,018	917	0	0	506	5,149
HIWASSEE COLLEGE	PRI-T	61,830	33,523	0	6,941	6,959	3,925	6,930	0	216	3,740
JOHN A GUPTON COLLEGE	PRI-T	7,408	B	B	0	748	83	0	30	32	B
JOHNSON BIBLE COLLEGE	PRI-FN	68,916	23,460	0	11,172	14,284	2,571	165	1,980	0	15,284
KING COLLEGE	PRI-FN	61,715	B	0	12,685	3,278	14,178	847	0	0	B
KNOXVILLE BUSINESS C	PRI-T	10,354	B	0	1,440	400	0	0	0	0	B
KNOXVILLE COLLEGE	PRI-FN	87,306	53,000	A	A	A	A	A	A	A	A
LAMBUTH COLLEGE	PRI-FN	100,762	55,770	5,935	7,907	14,356	6,877	368	1,105	2,908	5,536
LANE COLLEGE	PRI-FN	115,657	86,764	8,539	0	7,199	7,406	1,054	1,077	1,194	2,424
LEE COLLEGE	PRI-FN	169,635	105,602	6,335	3,330	23,734	11,407	4,329	977	2,527	11,394
LE MOYNE-OWEN COLLEGE	PRI-FN	83,152	42,577	6,387	0	26,062	5,062	0	0	169	2,895
LINCOLN MEM UNIVERSITY	PRI-FN	71,263	30,285	5,249	9,952	15,655	6,173	0	0	752	3,197
MARTIN COLLEGE	PRI-T	41,141	B	B	747	8,904	2,726	1,325	553	452	B
MARYVILLE COLLEGE	PRI-FN	101,801	52,995	7,275	11,964	14,255	10,069	1,117	200	1,538	2,388
MCKENZIE COLLEGE	PRI-T	37,590	B	0	6,000	1,224	2,543	0	5,349	0	B
MEHARRY MEDICAL COLLEGE	PRI-FG	516,381	168,730	8,323	0	40,000	132,000	0	101,500	8,000	57,828

SEE FOOTNOTES AT END OF TABLE

Table 2. – Library Operating Expenditures (in Dollars) of College and University Libraries, by Category of Expenditure and by State or Other Area and Institution: Aggregate United States, 1978-79 – Continued

STATE OR OTHER AREA AND INSTITUTION	CONTROL AND TYPE OF INSTITUTION	TOTAL	SALARIES AND WAGES			BOOK-STOCK	PERIODICALS	MICRO-FORMS	AUDIO-VISUAL	BINDING AND RE-BINDING	ALL OTHER OPERATING EXPENDITURES
			LIBRARY STAFF	FRINGE BENEFITS	STUDENTS ON HOURLY BASIS						
(1)	(2)	(3)	(4)	(5)	(6)	(7)	(8)	(9)	(10)	(11)	(12)
TENNESSEE	--CONTINUED										
MEMPHIS ACADEMY OF ARTS	PRI-FN	36,378	.B	B	0	7,178	2,000	0	1,000	360	B
MEMPHIS THEOLOGICAL SEM	PRI-FG	76,831	B	B	452	13,678	4,238	0	152	16,837	B
MID AMERICA BAPT SEMINARY	PRI-FG	A	A	A		A	A			A	A
MID-SOUTH BIBLE COLLEGE	PRI-FN	39,511	B	B	6,700	3,560	1,827	0	232	1,017	B
MILLIGAN COLLEGE	PRI-FN	75,707	36,610	4,793	9,606	14,012	6,011	75	363	574	3,663
MORRISTOWN COLLEGE	PRI-T	121,804	49,342	3,051	6,305	7,765	800	0	5,277	700	48,564
NASHVILLE STATE TECH INST	PUB-T	181,290	116,721	22,096	0	19,742	5,215	901	4,600	575	11,440
O'MORE SCH INTRIOR DESIGN	PRI-T	A	A	A	A	A	A	A		A	A
SCARRITT COLLEGE	PRI-FG	72,600	B	B	7,700	11,140	1,555	0	400	700	A
STHN COLLEGE OF OPTOMETRY	PRI-FG	94,401	29,423	5,085	9,124	12,810	7,140	150	1,460	1,320	27,909
STHN MISSIONARY COLLEGE	PRI-FN	272,496	131,074	22,943	30,706	52,119	17,869	0	0	4,749	13,060
SOUTHWESTERN AT MEMPHIS	PRI-FN	266,953	108,765	19,725	9,928	56,663	40,894	0	0	9,749	21,229
STATE TECH INST KNOXVILLE	PUB-T	67,971	B	B	0	18,083	1,369	1,371	3,904	0	B
STATE TECH INST MEMPHIS	PUB-T	164,462	111,490	5,479	1,662	25,355	10,750	3,840	0	1,129	4,787
ST U-CC SYS TENN ALL INST											
AUSTIN PEAY ST UNIVERSITY	PUB-FG	612,457	276,792	4,571	27,522	101,153	67,212	3,267	1,751	4,419	125,770
EAST TENN ST UNIVERSITY	PUB-FG	1,182,818	542,572	11,561	86,417	244,021	130,144	21,691	21,691	27,113	97,608
MEMPHIS STATE UNIVERSITY	PUB-FG	2,247,966	1,153,910	17,411	87,149	382,266	369,388	71,984	10,134	40,462	115,262
MIDDLE TENN ST UNIVERSITY	PUB-FG	1,101,136	416,469	82,179	103,188	264,663	124,893	18,810	0	26,000	64,934
TENNESSEE ST UNIVERSITY	PUB-FG	925,312	529,006	37,646	11,092	179,701	67,666	12,370	8,620	29,959	49,252
TENNESSEE TECHNOLOGICAL U	PUB-FG	742,202	352,385	7,091	44,405	83,550	121,761	16,937	52,798	15,217	48,058
CHATTANOOGA ST TECH CC	PUB-T	148,286	65,958	9,894	3,503	27,407	0	0	20,826	90	20,608
CLEVELAND ST CMTY COLLEGE	PUB-T	229,714	131,156	24,823	1,653	28,882	7,996	3,525	0	1,043	30,636
COLUMBIA ST CMTY COLLEGE	PUB-T	172,115	88,073	15,775	0	18,295	3,656	1,422	17,864	1,105	25,925
DYERSBURG ST CMTY COLLEGE	PUB-T	78,708	37,600	512	526	13,547	9,258	2,705	7,164	190	7,206
JACKSON ST CMTY COLLEGE	PUB-T	162,470	93,778	17,655	3,619	19,318	5,988	2,487	7,417	1,294	10,914
MOTLOW STATE CMTY COLLEGE	PUB-T	160,983	72,640	16,418	840	17,397	5,269	3,421	8,739	243	36,016
ROANE STATE CMTY COLLEGE	PUB-T	182,471	89,924	13,062	1,749	34,384	8,495	7,683	9,463	0	17,711
SHELBY STATE CMTY COLLEGE	PUB-T	265,074	108,984	18,154	7,286	36,784	11,048	803	52,209	58	29,748
VOLUNTEER ST CMTY COLLEGE	PUB-T	143,619	81,099	2,044	0	19,133	7,226	5,457	6,344	1,090	21,226
WALTERS ST CMTY COLLEGE	PUB-T	173,984	108,532	2,227	998	12,957	7,376	3,691	29,607	84	8,512
STEED COLLEGE	PRI-FN	25,515	B	0	0	172	922	0	4,868	0	B
TENNESSEE TEMPLE U	PRI-FG	224,507	84,333	9,161	89,657	0	19,779	2,544	0	3,353	15,680
TENN WESLEYAN COLLEGE	PRI-FN	91,627	37,609	6,241	6,660	20,702	8,520	2,019	2,982	2,416	4,478
TOMLINSON COLLEGE	PRI-T	36,662	B	B	302	2,200	500	0	300	500	B
TREVECCA NAZARENE COLLEGE	PRI-FN	102,350	36,681	5,802	18,399	14,671	4,993	0	3,883	1,757	16,164
TUSCULUM COLLEGE	PRI-FN	74,647	25,885	3,030	20,688	9,606	7,000	4,200	800	300	3,138
UNION UNIVERSITY	PRI-FN	130,256	67,730	4,306	11,154	24,559	10,023	683	1,967	4,549	5,285
UNIVERSITY OF THE SOUTH	PRI-FG	468,810	213,121	38,143	6,219	101,245	43,457	0	390	10,892	55,343
U OF TENNESSEE ALL CAM											
U OF TENN CTR HEALTH SCI	PUB-FG	758,624	368,714	37,344	12,474	42,041	187,200	100	150	20,922	89,679
U OF TENN AT CHATTANOOGA	PUB-FG	780,950	354,954	49,656	20,150	99,000	167,000	20,000	3,000	28,000	39,190
U OF TENNESSEE KNOXVILLE	PUB-U	4,253,505	1,952,158	284,396	173,239	338,573	931,653	129,442	40,047	94,874	309,123
U OF TENNESSEE AT MARTIN	PUB-FG	576,985	260,157	36,903	23,433	111,460	71,883	8,064	8,613	8,886	47,586
VANDERBILT UNIVERSITY	PRI-U	3,910,346	1,494,286	206,153	275,268	453,624	743,255	0	526	81,096	656,138
TEXAS											
ABILENE CHRSTN UNIVERSITY	PRI-FG	462,885	226,195	43,369	27,365	82,188	46,043	6,064	4,603	11,235	15,623
ALVIN COMMUNITY COLLEGE	PUB-T	110,029	72,459	3,646	3,745	16,603	3,208	2,264	60	721	7,323
AMARILLO COLLEGE	PUB-T	357,881	220,887	14,474	10,329	41,200	9,720	3,152	13,583	3,719	40,817
AMERICAN TECHNOLOGICAL U	PRI-FG	56,804	B	B	0	17,880	8,002	7,114	0	197	B
ANGELINA COLLEGE	PUB-T	104,445	58,644	11,703	0	7,501	15,740	6,440	1,920	306	2,191
ANGELO STATE UNIVERSITY	PUB-FG	468,750	179,863	15,349	23,241	98,899	80,878	13,854	28,459	12,998	17,209
AUSTIN COLLEGE	PRI-FG	209,281	79,489	11,669	3,941	65,234	25,432	4,329	430	4,320	14,437
AUSTIN COMMUNITY COLLEGE	PUB-T	563,243	369,175	4,200	5,538	55,516	15,318	13,165	21,533	200	78,598
AUSTIN PRESB THEOL SEM	PRI-FG	92,520	46,862	8,757	316	24,466	6,604	924	217	1,159	3,215
BAYLOR COLLEGE DENTISTRY	PRI-FG	130,920	41,950	4,195	3,000	24,000	32,400	600	0	15,000	9,775
BAYLOR COLLEGE MEDICINE12/	PRI-FG	SEE TEXAS MEDL CTR JOINT LIB									
BAYLOR UNIVERSITY	PRI-U	1,659,246	543,280	84,476	194,794	308,182	197,454	133,934	18,966	33,182	144,978
BEE COUNTY COLLEGE	PUB-T	137,261	74,919	7,801	0	20,423	7,409	2,350	9,331	1,600	13,428
BISHOP COLLEGE	PRI-FN	134,887	103,995	16,888	6,704	7,300	0	0	0	0	0
BLINN COLLEGE	PUB-T	211,285	61,041	7,794	12,900	62,252	8,621	12,833	15,942	5,954	23,948
BRAZOSPORT COLLEGE	PUB-T	162,340	82,943	7,138	3,511	32,239	4,634	6,229	0	2,132	23,514
CENTRAL TEXAS COLLEGE	PUB-T	235,781	87,493	7,874	6,408	66,889	13,647	11,428	2,400	1,404	38,238
CISCO JUNIOR COLLEGE	PUB-T	61,920	33,676	1,797	0	15,812	0	0	0	1,875	8,760

SEE FOOTNOTES AT END OF TABLE

124

Table 2. — Library Operating Expenditures (in Dollars) of College and University Libraries, by Category of Expenditure and by State or Other Area and Institution: Aggregate United States, 1978-79 — Continued

STATE OR OTHER AREA AND INSTITUTION	CON- TROL AND TYPE OF IN- STITU- TION	TOTAL	SALARIES AND WAGES			BOOK- STOCK	PERIOD- ICALS	MICRO- FORMS	AUDIO- VISUAL	BIND- ING AND RE- BIND- ING	ALL OTHER OPER- ATING EXPEND- ITURES
			LIBRARY STAFF	FRINGE BENEFITS	STUDENTS ON HOURLY BASIS						
(1)	(2)	(3)	(4)	(5)	(6)	(7)	(8)	(9)	(10)	(11)	(12)
TEXAS	**--CONTINUED**										
CLARENDON COLLEGE	PUB-T	39,350	B	B	1,379	8,874	1,777	323	1,978	62	B
COLLEGE OF THE MAINLAND	PUB-T	358,336	244,525	19,562	8,365	27,706	7,700	4,041	1,200	1,600	43,637
CONCORDIA LUTH COLLEGE	PRI-T	51,394	B	0	4,536	18,949	3,154	1,502	2,459	0	B
COOKE COUNTY COLLEGE	PUB-T	111,408	61,064	6,355	1,487	22,241	7,338	2,097	7,113	279	3,434
DALLAS BAPTIST COLLEGE	PRI-FN	204,831	90,419	13,502	31,856	9,315	13,875	6,771	310	1,798	36,985
DALLAS BIBLE COLLEGE	PRI-FN	28,383	B	0	5,111	4,390	716	293	429	791	B
DALLAS CHRISTIAN COLLEGE	PRI-FN	33,052	17,615	1,939	3,008	3,378	1,318	0	236	535	5,023
DALLAS CO CC DIST ALLINST											
BROOKHAVEN COLLEGE	PUB-T	421,855	171,807	0	14,694	50,000	6,500	685	22,000	810	155,359
CEDAR VALLEY COLLEGE	PUB-T	254,253	128,710	22,678	7,000	45,000	6,000	10,000	34,358	507	0
EASTFIELD COLLEGE	PUB-T	667,067	365,971	77,123	20,726	25,322	5,248	2,135	22,146	1,796	146,600
EL CENTRO COLLEGE	PUB-T	424,905	297,014	35,608	22,737	29,000	7,500	6,161	10,254	1,755	14,876
MOUNTAIN VIEW COLLEGE	PUB-T	482,367	268,570	29,463	23,540	23,323	7,375	3,398	17,753	426	108,519
NORTH LAKE COLLEGE	PUB-T	238,423	72,776	0	8,676	50,000	7,000	0	20,170	1,500	78,301
RICHLAND COLLEGE	PUB-T	1,163,567	431,653	0	30,005	56,223	5,649	4,135	33,309	2,307	600,286
DALLAS THEOL SEMINARY	PRI-FG	A	A			A	A		A		A
DEL MAR COLLEGE	PUB-T	487,560	299,339	0	36,657	61,204	19,335	515	27,072	3,815	39,623
DEVRY INST OF TECHNOLOGY	PRI-FN	A	A		A				A		
EAST TEXAS BAPT COLLEGE	PRI-FN	146,303	65,519	8,567	12,921	24,662	23,574	0	3,084	2,832	5,144
EAST TEXAS ST UNIVERSITY	PUB-FG	1,194,944	473,386	92,902	51,921	251,030	154,678	37,544	7,609	35,998	89,876
EL PASO CO CMTY COLLEGE	PUB-T	383,387	222,022	33,303	9,749	71,000	19,000	5,000	4,000	0	19,313
EPIS THEOL SEM SOUTHWEST	PRI-FG	77,006	41,690	17,916	0	9,114	4,839	0	200	1,354	1,893
FRANK PHILLIPS COLLEGE	PUB-T	61,540	24,356	930	5,978	12,837	4,978	1,845	1,646	674	8,296
GALVESTON COLLEGE	PUB-T	250,790	139,928	12,594	0	33,096	10,241	2,667	11,986	552	39,726
GRAYSON CO JUNIOR COLLEGE	PUB-T	197,215	77,963	5,499	0	33,361	8,334	3,410	9,500	549	58,599
GULF COAST BIBLE COLLEGE	PRI-FN	73,510	19,796	0	10,177	10,949	3,257	25,579	344	435	2,973
HARDIN-SIMMONS UNIVERSITY	PRI-FG	252,315	105,525	5,284	48,000	42,750	20,296	0	4,047	9,464	16,949
HAROLD R. YEARY JT LIB	PUB-FG	564,992	319,213	42,980	4,360	78,687	33,896	14,756	10,000	2,385	58,715
HENDERSON CO JR COLLEGE	PUB-T	98,098	B	0	0	8,000	3,500	10,000	3,000	0	B
HILL JUNIOR COLLEGE	PUB-T	51,000	B	0	0	12,000	2,500	2,500	350	650	B
HOUSTON BAPT UNIVERSITY	PRI-FG	186,367	112,367	0	9,000	30,000	12,000	2,000	2,000	7,000	12,000
HOUSTON COMMUNITY COLLEGE	PUB-T	890,578	515,519	0	0	103,000	24,000	5,000	100,000	750	142,309
HOWARD C AT BIG SPRING	PUB-T	59,490	44,103	4,091	1,149	3,252	2,533	366	1,818	165	2,013
HOWARD PAYNE UNIVERSITY	PRI-FN	150,626	65,126	0	20,000	30,000	25,000	0	0	4,500	6,000
HUSTON-TILLOTSON COLLEGE	PRI-FN	124,814	63,766	8,942	16,615	14,169	12,438	1,085	0	693	7,106
INCARNATE WORD COLLEGE	PRI-FG	249,019	119,533	11,924	23,832	36,293	21,258	469	3,485	7,321	24,904
JACKSONVILLE COLLEGE	PRI-T	32,334	B	B	0	6,365	1,987	1,196	2,625	611	B
JARVIS CHRISTIAN COLLEGE	PRI-FN	123,010	66,510	9,976	0	22,825	11,288	0	1,342	764	10,305
KILGORE COLLEGE	PUB-T	316,794	163,253	4,032	0	20,000	13,865	28,401	61,025	2,192	24,026
LAMAR UNIVERSITY	PUB-FG	1,174,367	447,943	36,654	22,575	267,477	262,277	31,627	0	25,005	80,809
LAREDO JUNIOR COLLEGE	PUB T	SEE HAROLD R. YEARY JT LIB									
LEE COLLEGE	PUB-T	365,545	189,518	4,800	19,822	40,562	43,200	2,712	10,000	1,500	83,431
LETOURNEAU COLLEGE	PRI-FN	153,245	82,801	8,133	4,137	35,277	11,800	0	0	2,579	8,518
LON MORRIS COLLEGE	PRI-T	62,073	B	B	7,856	6,073	2,164	196	834	71	B
LUBBOCK CHRISTIAN COLLEGE	PRI-FN	102,492	42,783	1,440	7,046	31,181	14,000	4,840	0	200	1,002
MCLENNAN CMTY COLLEGE	PUB-T	169,061	101,442	3,950	8,761	37,861	9,978	684	0	2,460	3,925
MCMURRY COLLEGE	PRI-FN	138,407	61,844	8,040	2,700	35,799	10,500	1,600	1,000	4,500	12,424
MIDLAND COLLEGE	PUB-T	153,731	99,257	10,675	946	22,229	3,640	1,660	3,906	385	11,033
MIDWESTERN ST UNIVERSITY	PUB-FG	459,745	138,738	0	34,618	115,600	71,376	8,578	6,330	10,000	74,505
NAVARRO COLLEGE	PUB-T	84,861	44,232	18,135	2,289	8,956	3,094	0	0	525	7,630
NORTH HARRIS CO COLLEGE	PUB-T	279,457	125,623	7,709	5,499	61,100	9,208	9,711	19,016	207	41,384
NORTH TEXAS ST UNIVERSITY	PUB-U	2,380,174	998,566	239,041	218,040	367,929	224,295	22,963	25,361	88,589	195,390
OBLATE COLLEGE OF STHWST	PRI-FG	32,954	B	B	0	8,476	4,148	0	654	563	B
ODESSA COLLEGE	PUB-T	296,375	166,636	20,830	0	21,000	12,000	2,800	30,000	1,500	41,609
OUR LADY OF LAKE U	PRI-FG	462,223	198,573	26,106	88,249	30,917	15,759	3,651	4,599	6,136	88,233
PAN AMERICAN UNIVERSITY	PUB-FG	807,724	378,619	71,133	82,654	82,588	133,471	17,270	0	16,742	25,247
PANOLA JUNIOR COLLEGE	PUB-T	49,191	B	B	2,820	6,492	3,578	397	2,986	697	B
PARIS JUNIOR COLLEGE	PUB-T	182,000	83,772	8,166	9,874	18,391	6,706	3,079	5,053	0	46,959
PAUL QUINN COLLEGE	PRI-FN	47,361	27,412	3,524	0	13,804	0	0	329	0	2,292
RANGER JUNIOR COLLEGE	PUB-T	41,794	B	B	0	8,449	548	0	308	389	B
RICE UNIVERSITY	PRI-U	2,167,484	856,550	85,625	73,463	384,134	466,936	0	0	43,577	257,199
SAINT EDWARD'S UNIVERSITY	PRI-FG	132,245	69,045	0	6,845	38,847	9,582	0	0	1,682	6,244
SNT MARY'S U SAN ANTONIO	PRI-FG	508,220	237,839	27,621	6,821	66,642	108,252	3,689	3,000	10,712	43,644
SAM HOUSTON ST UNIVERSITY	PUB-FG	1,050,434	385,756	0	107,356	307,099	152,960	0	3,280	24,173	69,810
SN ANTO DIST JC ALL CAM											

SEE FOOTNOTES AT END OF TABLE

Table 2. – Library Operating Expenditures (in Dollars) of College and University Libraries, by Category of Expenditure and by State or Other Area and Institution: Aggregate United States, 1978-79 – Continued

STATE OR OTHER AREA AND INSTITUTION	CON-TROL AND TYPE OF IN-STITU-TION	TOTAL	SALARIES AND WAGES			BOOK-STOCK	PERIOD-ICALS	MICRO-FORMS	AUDIO-VISUAL	BIND-ING AND RE-BIND-ING	ALL OTHER OPER-ATING EXPEND-ITURES
			LIBRARY STAFF	FRINGE BENEFITS	STUDENTS ON HOURLY BASIS						
(1)	(2)	(3)	(4)	(5)	(6)	(7)	(8)	(9)	(10)	(11)	(12)
TEXAS	--CONTINUED										
SAINT PHILIP'S COLLEGE	PUB-T	360,067	169,439	15,462	17,994	50,638	10,975	1,630	0	380	93,549
SAN ANTONIO COLLEGE	PUB-T	1,790,139	784,375	62,750	259,031	198,583	37,138	16,116	56,225	5,635	370,286
SAN JACINTO C ALL CAM											
SAN JACINTO C CENTRAL CAM	PUB-T	236,733	134,299	4,536	20,608	55,439	4,142	7,083	0	2,244	8,382
SAN JACINTO C NORTH CAM	PUB-T	100,484	28,178	1,008	2,940	49,367	2,113	12,797	0	1,501	2,580
SCHREINER COLLEGE	PRI-T	42,766	B	B	2,216	10,014	3,857	241	3,224	375	B
SOUTHERN BIBLE COLLEGE	PRI-FN	8,961	B	0	0	0	0	0	0	0	B
SOUTHERN METH UNIVERSITY	PRI-U	2,296,825	769,576	97,154	125,100	979,796	176,205	0	16,097	40,896	92,001
SOUTH PLAINS COLLEGE	PUB-T	131,367	63,417	1,000	4,000	25,240	6,661	3,500	10,243	2,640	14,666
SOUTH TEXAS COLLEGE LAW	PRI-FG	303,001	77,640	7,764	21,574	84,444	77,721	18,084	0	7,904	7,870
STHWSTN ADVENTIST COLLEGE	PRI-FN	140,257	53,459	9,212	25,228	30,184	8,016	4,959	2,029	1,810	5,360
SOUTHWESTERN ASSEMB GOD C	PRI-FN	52,418	25,586	2,540	172	11,240	2,247	4,741	1,155	1,163	3,574
STHWSTN BAPT THEOL SEM	PRI-FG	A	A	A	A	A	A	A	A	A	A
STHWSTN CHRISTIAN COLLEGE	PRI-T	53,892	B	B	11,293	10,223	4,567	0	5,846	568	B
SOUTHWESTERN UNIVERSITY	PRI-FN	195,288	96,896	17,557	12,332	31,090	15,370	3,220	32	2,295	16,496
SOUTHWEST TEX JR COLLEGE	PUB-T	127,707	79,725	7,973	1,108	7,863	4,977	0	12,918	400	12,743
STHWST TEX ST UNIVERSITY	PUB-FG	1,516,015	590,978	115,137	83,918	302,302	202,755	6,521	79,066	16,720	118,618
STEPHEN F AUSTIN STATE U	PUB-FG	1,212,139	480,941	99,703	99,403	140,905	221,978	24,325	11,430	28,345	105,109
SUL ROSS STATE UNIVERSITY	PUB-FG	478,499	164,362	11,775	38,386	118,505	33,382	17,593	5,286	4,801	84,409
TARRANT CO JUNIOR COLLEGE	PUB-T	1,714,275	1,030,150	163,881	84,950	99,498	50,762	27,166	50,000	8,231	199,637
TEMPLE JUNIOR COLLEGE	PUB-T	84,123	B	B	3,647	20,892	4,586	1,103	7,918	320	B
TEXARKANA CMTY COLLEGE	PUB-T	122,537	76,678	6,860	2,687	13,413	6,260	5,100	0	502	11,037
TEXAS A&M U SYS ALL INST											
PRAIRIE VIEW A&M U 12/	PUB-FG	A	A	A	A	A	A	A	A	A	A
TARLETON STATE UNIVERSITY	PUB-FG	415,869	139,950	0	22,831	151,352	52,142	29,656	4,489	1,353	14,096
TEXAS A&M U ALL CAMPUSES											
TEXAS A&M U MAIN CAMPUS	PUB-U	3,640,445	1,448,336	0	218,340	649,517	863,498	0	26,615	92,000	342,139
TEX A&M U AT GALVESTON	PUB-FN	237,780	79,963	8,930	5,126	63,008	29,190	3,869	12,354	5,025	27,315
TEXAS CHIROPRACTIC C	PRI-FG	39,596	B	B	1,260	4,705	3,151	3,338	1,905	0	B
TEXAS CHRISTIAN U	PRI-U	1,291,472	464,057	88,171	103,996	240,570	175,831	1,000	6,056	34,748	177,043
TEXAS COLLEGE	PRI-FN	71,762	43,439	3,616	14,122	5,083	1,309	0	0	2,135	2,058
TEXAS COLLEGE OSTEO MED	PUB-FG	1,191,912	226,719	51,012	24,252	125,520	203,640	0	106,042	20,892	433,835
TEXAS LUTHERAN COLLEGE	PRI-FN	129,034	69,178	11,985	6,237	25,876	9,004	919	607	509	4,719
TEXAS MEDL CTR JOINT LIB 12	PUB-FG	1,717,992	524,376	73,418	44,506	71,390	242,069	300	18,964	22,148	720,821
TEXAS SOUTHERN UNIVERSITY	PUB-FG	1,041,572	509,476	65,040	35,221	226,175	130,000	3,072	20,000	8,200	44,388
TEXAS SOUTHMOST COLLEGE	PUB-T	310,978	168,753	17,478	6,238	64,866	7,007	6,994	0	2,500	37,142
TEX ST TECH INST ALL CAM											
TEX ST TECH AMARILLO CAM	PUB-T	85,715	42,182	0	618	8,870	6,850	0	7,675	0	19,520
TEX ST TECH-HARLINGEN CAM	PUB-T	105,976	55,175	9,315	0	18,870	9,745	1,800	2,120	857	8,094
TEX ST TECH INST WACO CAM	PUB-T	338,536	173,539	28,349	4,461	46,921	17,361	5,525	17,386	5,062	39,932
TEXAS TECH UNIVERSITY	PUB-U	3,484,723	1,374,057	188,249	311,269	541,775	583,863	53,615	31,674	72,936	327,285
TEXAS WESLEYAN COLLEGE	PRI-FG	236,597	116,046	2,000	13,349	47,841	23,127	492	0	13,066	20,676
TEXAS WOMAN'S UNIVERSITY 12	PUB-U	965,069	388,325	0	43,000	184,190	128,193	24,272	3,827	9,580	183,682
TRINITY UNIVERSITY	PRI-FG	971,398	491,947	70,124	28,497	125,072	156,387	22,824	14,052	18,859	43,636
TYLER JUNIOR COLLEGE	PUB-T	246,884	124,226	16,200	6,779	46,828	16,509	0	15,911	1,305	19,126
UNIVERSITY OF DALLAS	PRI-FG	211,606	87,500	1,400	36,000	20,429	34,808	5,166	0	4,673	21,630
U OF HOUSTON ALL CAMPUSES											
U OF HOUSTON CEN CAMPUS 12	PUB-U	3,731,808	1,684,538	170,365	103,142	582,835	751,437	0	0	85,633	353,858
U HOUSTON CLEAR LAKE CITY	PUB-FG	507,702	256,443	58,101	13,000	31,524	77,386	31,145	0	10,000	30,103
U OF HOUSTON DOWNTOWN C	PUB-FN	472,231	215,212	0	5,661	77,749	30,000	2,000	10,000	4,000	127,609
U HOUSTON VICTORIA CAMPUS	PUB FG			SEE VC UHVC JOINT LIB							
U OF MARY HARDIN-BAYLOR	PRI-FN	94,952	54,702	7,414	0	9,898	15,164	0	0	3,139	4,635
UNIVERSITY OF SNT THOMAS	PRI-FG	258,098	128,059	10,870	6,767	61,897	21,160	524	6,804	7,990	14,027
U SYS S TEXAS ALL INST											
CORPUS CHRISTI STATE U	PUB-FG	453,421	162,054	16,730	42,611	84,766	64,000	0	35,000	11,677	36,583
LAREDO STATE UNIVERSITY	PUB FG			SEE HAROLD R. YEARY JT LIB							
TEXAS A&I UNIVERSITY	PUB-FG	639,110	237,096	40,306	68,113	119,889	104,622	4,500	13,322	10,824	40,438
U OF TEXAS SYS ALL INST											
U OF TEXAS AT AUSTIN	PUB-U	9,321,709	4,702,126	757,043	470,916	976,830	1,456,399	123,093	36,423	117,132	681,748
U OF TEXAS AT ARLINGTON	PUB-FG	1,511,904	717,681	0	55,996	254,243	307,420	18,401	4,244	36,103	117,816
U OF TEXAS AT DALLAS	PUB-FG	2,009,616	543,722	1,120	89,362	720,127	218,640	225,192	50,798	10,967	149,688
U OF TEXAS AT EL PASO	PUB-FG	1,703,409	656,002	108,202	227,775	250,526	230,129	24,137	616	60,515	145,504
U TEX HLTH SCI CTR DALLAS	PUB-FG	931,947	432,067	112,337	17,966	68,876	178,732	0	15,945	16,995	89,029
U TEX HLTH SCI CTR HOUS 12	PUB FG			SEE TEXAS MEDL CTR JOINT LIB							
U TEX HLTH SCI SN ANTO	PUB-FG	895,360	469,647	0	0	78,050	183,641	0	12,203	17,538	134,281

SEE FOOTNOTES AT END OF TABLE

Table 2. — Library Operating Expenditures (in Dollars) of College and University Libraries, by Category of Expenditure and by State or Other Area and Institution: Aggregate United States, 1978-79 — Continued

STATE OR OTHER AREA AND INSTITUTION	CONTROL AND TYPE OF INSTITUTION	TOTAL	SALARIES AND WAGES			BOOK-STOCK	PERIOD-ICALS	MICRO-FORMS	AUDIO-VISUAL	BINDING AND RE-BINDING	ALL OTHER OPER-ATING EXPENDITURES
			LIBRARY STAFF	FRINGE BENEFITS	STUDENTS ON HOURLY BASIS						
(1)	(2)	(3)	(4)	(5)	(6)	(7)	(8)	(9)	(10)	(11)	(12)
TEXAS	--CONTINUED										
U TEX MEDL BR GALVESTON	PUB-FG	A	A	A	A	A	A	A	A	A	A
U OF TEXAS PERMIAN BASIN	PUB-FG	298,640	95,251	9,525	15,638	48,545	61,917	23,722	2,084	8,198	33,760
U OF TEXAS SAN ANTONIO	PUB-FG	821,073	350,487	55,390	13,570	130,564	217,931	0	1,875	13,343	37,913
U OF TEXAS AT TYLER	PUB-FG	524,064	172,276	15,766	14,265	165,750	45,000	15,000	22,000	6,250	67,757
VERNON REG JUNIOR COLLEGE	PUB-T	84,841	37,675	1,147	925	7,126	2,130	686	10,354	200	24,598
VICTORIA COLLEGE	PUB T	SEE VC UHVC JOINT LIB									
VC UHVC JOINT LIBRARY	PUB-T	577,397	230,737	45,000	26,328	129,302	56,506	16,973	12,138	2,969	57,444
WAYLAND BAPTIST COLLEGE	PRI-FN	107,300	46,780	6,004	5,242	24,545	11,744	3,373	3,698	1,256	4,658
WEATHERFORD COLLEGE	PUB-T	97,371	42,278	2,068	5,426	17,588	5,472	3,537	7,581	1,121	12,300
WESTERN TEXAS COLLEGE	PUB-T	101,341	68,681	6,000	0	16,170	7,500	0	0	0	2,990
WEST TEXAS ST UNIVERSITY	PUB-FG	643,067	329,116	46,076	29,424	77,958	74,519	11,638	0	8,039	66,297
WHARTON CO JR COLLEGE	PUB-T	218,068	122,733	12,128	20,728	12,424	7,919	2,509	2,589	1,809	35,229
WILEY COLLEGE	PRI-FN	95,511	74,386	13,386	0	1,364	1,225	480	0	0	4,670
UTAH											
BRIGHAM YOUNG U ALL CAM											
BRIGHAM YOUNG U MAIN CAM	PRI-U	A	A	A	A	A	A	A	A	A	A
BRIGHAM YOUNG U-HAWA CAM	PRI-FN	612,075	263,000	51,500	136,500	93,000	27,500	15,300	22,000	2,200	1,075
LATTER-DAY SAINTS BUS C	PRI-T	19,232	B	0	2,132	2,000	1,575	0	992	0	B
STEVENS HENAGER COLLEGE	PRI-T	1,343	B	0	0	302	178	0	0	0	B
UTAH HI ED SYS ALL INST											
UNIVERSITY OF UTAH	PUB-U	4,724,848	2,071,407	0	548,984	726,590	742,536	0	0	94,197	541,134
UTAH STATE UNIVERSITY	PUB-U	1,502,685	581,034	150,711	111,062	227,129	253,728	6,062	26,246	31,948	114,765
SOUTHERN UTAH ST COLLEGE	PUB-FN	374,803	110,233	25,811	15,659	160,660	24,481	7,000	10,498	739	19,722
WEBER STATE COLLEGE	PUB-FG	1,218,736	400,048	106,066	89,545	250,396	163,934	0	25,498	12,376	170,873
COLLEGE OF EASTERN UTAH	PUB-T	86,648	B	B	3,650	10,200	6,683	0	2,709	863	B
DIXIE COLLEGE	PUB-T	79,307	46,388	11,709	2,058	11,485	3,361	52	460	1,256	2,538
SNOW COLLEGE	PUB-T	69,087	37,144	7,741	9,803	8,300	3,741	229	0	0	2,129
UTAH TECH COLLEGE PROVO	PUB-T	167,326	113,241	28,427	4,784	10,966	5,738	45	1,114	0	3,011
UTAH TECH COLLEGE SALT LK	PUB-T	156,312	81,650	21,868	0	21,054	7,460	0	17,223	0	7,057
WESTMINSTER COLLEGE	PRI-FG	76,409	36,602	2,849	4,549	5,372	17,925	1,284	0	2,161	5,667
VERMONT											
BENNINGTON COLLEGE	PRI-FG	163,775	83,166	0	12,838	34,084	23,019	1,435	922	1,699	6,612
BURLINGTON COLLEGE5/	PRI-FN	NO LIBRARY FACILITIES									
CHAMPLAIN COLLEGE	PRI-T	56,573	B	B	0	19,068	4,806	808	0	0	B
C SNT JOSEPH THE PROVIDER	PRI-FN	30,171	B	B	0	4,775	1,105	792	674	0	B
GODDARD COLLEGE	PRI-FG	150,667	98,749	13,825	0	17,843	4,488	1,856	742	411	12,753
GREEN MOUNTAIN COLLEGE	PRI-FN	106,512	72,742	10,276	4,703	9,555	3,112	1,327	2,878	0	1,919
MARLBORO COLLEGE	PRI-FN	52,004	B	B	600	17,798	5,820	1,819	0	2,144	B
MIDDLEBURY COLLEGE	PRI-FG	669,992	249,667	0	36,179	190,289	108,956	6,837	2,192	15,254	60,618
NORWICH U ALL CAM											
NORWICH U MAIN CAM	PRI-FG	247,656	98,820	15,620	13,000	35,000	20,500	1,000	500	1,200	62,016
VERMONT COLLEGE	PRI-FG	58,678	24,894	4,310	10,863	9,877	3,274	1,094	966	73	3,327
SAINT MICHAEL'S COLLEGE	PRI-FG	250,280	131,407	18,301	0	33,850	26,375	5,573	0	2,637	32,137
SCH FOR INTRNATL TRAINING	PRI-FG	46,374	B	B	5,417	5,941	5,421	2,596	0	103	B
SOUTHERN VERMONT COLLEGE	PRI-FN	34,450	B	B	0	6,877	3,749	0	2,932	0	B
TRINITY COLLEGE	PRI-FN	99,398	54,439	3,543	0	15,607	6,459	4,547	82	731	13,990
U VT & STATE AGRL COLLEGE	PUB-U	2,159,964	814,618	192,483	101,963	421,071	380,430	5,169	13,107	61,135	169,988
VERMONT LAW SCHOOL	PRI-FG	214,012	71,572	11,447	15,592	40,320	53,741	6,713	0	3,344	11,283
VERMONT ST C ALL INST											
CASTLETON STATE COLLEGE	PUB-FG	183,693	73,677	12,958	39,278	15,200	24,250	3,000	1,700	3,000	10,630
CMTY COLLEGE OF VERMONT1/	PUB-T	NO LIBRARY FACILITIES									
JOHNSON STATE COLLEGE	PUB-FG	173,295	75,309	14,332	25,096	28,349	11,318	3,930	3,590	100	11,271
LYNDON STATE COLLEGE	PUB-FG	134,221	66,526	13,849	0	28,848	8,933	1,043	309	1,011	13,702
VERMONT TECHNICAL COLLEGE	PUB-T	110,227	53,153	11,211	4,909	16,496	7,641	4,534	94	79	12,110
VIRGINIA											
AVERETT COLLEGE	PRI-FG	138,494	62,400	7,176	19,321	28,495	6,423	3,449	0	1,300	9,930
BLUEFIELD COLLEGE	PRI-FN	45,287	19,410	4,333	477	13,207	4,781	65	1,926	487	601
BRIDGEWATER COLLEGE	PRI-FN	159,883	61,870	7,259	23,164	22,193	14,401	5,931	1,388	1,185	22,492
C WILLIAM & MARY ALL CAM											
C OF WILLIAM AND MARY	PUB-FG	1,786,087	738,056	104,844	126,007	251,598	398,372	30,635	1,749	20,000	116,826
CHRISTOPHER NEWPORT C	PUB-FN	427,144	190,770	23,102	61,496	74,119	26,533	1,103	3,348	8,239	38,434

SEE FOOTNOTES AT END OF TABLE

Table 2. — Library Operating Expenditures (in Dollars) of College and University Libraries, by Category of Expenditure and by State or Other Area and Institution: Aggregate United States, 1978-79 — Continued

STATE OR OTHER AREA AND INSTITUTION	CONTROL AND TYPE OF IN-STITU-TION	TOTAL	SALARIES AND WAGES			BOOK-STOCK	PERIOD-ICALS	MICRO-FORMS	AUDIO-VISUAL	BIND-ING AND RE-BIND-ING	ALL OTHER OPER-ATING EXPEND-ITURES
			LIBRARY STAFF	FRINGE BENEFITS	STUDENTS ON HOURLY BASIS						
(1)	(2)	(3)	(4)	(5)	(6)	(7)	(8)	(9)	(10)	(11)	(12)
VIRGINIA	--CONTINUED										
RICHARD BLAND C WM & MARY	PUB-T	87,315	55,764	6,434	1,003	8,836	4,670	770	3,565	1,702	4,571
ESTN MENNONITE C AND SEM	PRI-FG	232,790	117,017	16,793	10,351	43,413	10,364	1,162	3,382	640	29,668
EASTERN VA MEDL SCHOOL	PRI-FG	333,658	150,617	15,973	6,300	18,909	80,637	0	1,054	7,559	52,609
EMORY AND HENRY COLLEGE	PRI-FN	169,112	66,477	19,558	5,423	33,689	19,046	1,145	2,399	3,450	17,925
FERRUM COLLEGE	PRI-FN	208,377	94,067	11,626	7,889	45,663	9,726	5,997	8,568	4,783	20,058
GEORGE MASON UNIVERSITY	PUB-FG	1,079,073	501,782	65,232	62,940	168,801	137,123	3,515	0	23,171	116,509
HAMPDEN-SYDNEY COLLEGE	PRI-FN	163,496	76,460	6,760	7,896	32,989	20,289	9,049	0	2,020	8,033
HAMPTON INSTITUTE	PRI-FG	405,740	214,514	21,451	53,967	20,585	58,436	5,458	0	12,049	19,280
HOLLINS COLLEGE	PRI-FG	295,292	144,143	20,000	22,418	45,368	28,075	525	4,450	6,043	24,270
INST TEXTILE TECHNOLOGY	PRI-FG	A	A	A	A	A	A	A	A	A	A
JAMES MADISON UNIVERSITY	PUB-FG	837,575	415,884	49,795	45,392	141,634	124,334	15,876	1,232	15,000	28,428
LIBERTY BAPTIST COLLEGE	PRI-FN	308,552	138,917	13,895	11,986	126,237	8,098	3,104	637	446	5,232
LONGWOOD COLLEGE	PUB-FG	364,161	204,829	25,448	11,737	59,931	34,995	2,827	4,127	9,277	10,990
LYNCHBURG COLLEGE	PRI-FG	273,363	121,037	16,500	13,145	66,387	19,320	2,947	4,908	6,066	23,053
MARY BALDWIN COLLEGE	PRI-FN	151,098	62,454	0	759	43,103	23,879	0	0	2,810	18,093
MARYMOUNT COLLEGE OF VA	PRI-FG	217,481	133,227	17,320	0	44,832	8,398	1,156	1,825	3,345	7,378
MARY WASHINGTON COLLEGE	PUB-FN	459,743	220,255	24,372	23,151	89,588	47,864	5,074	352	6,726	42,361
NATIONAL BUSINESS COLLEGE	PRI-T	17,846	B	B	0	1,218	233	0	0	0	B
NORFOLK STATE UNIVERSITY	PUB-FG	682,520	384,194	49,611	54,696	47,833	78,866	0	0	0	67,320
OLD DOMINION UNIVERSITY	PUB-FG	1,535,817	590,002	65,585	96,364	277,056	301,019	9,631	977	37,062	158,121
PRESB SCH OF CHRISTIAN ED	PRI-FG				SEE UNION THEOL SEM JOINT LIB						
PROT EPIS THEOL SEM IN VA	PRI-FG	155,900	71,361	28,724	4,818	26,920	7,592	0	0	4,914	11,571
RADFORD UNIVERSITY	PUB-FG	626,818	259,886	36,297	93,347	159,126	15,316	13,463	7,674	988	40,721
RANDOLPH-MACON COLLEGE	PRI-FG	147,646	65,631	8,133	8,684	29,862	17,385	1,280	2,118	1,957	12,596
RANDOLPH-MACON WOMAN'S C	PRI-FN	193,503	98,216	0	13,662	44,122	29,949	1,736	0	2,330	3,488
ROANOKE COLLEGE	PRI-FN	201,710	106,454	15,137	3,963	35,391	16,213	0	5,057	5,220	14,275
SAINT PAUL'S COLLEGE	PRI-FN	109,132	46,750	4,790	35,040	11,772	3,425	1,143	1,715	1,492	3,005
SHENANDOAH C-CONSV MUSIC	PRI-FN	206,871	80,268	4,335	0	72,588	13,697	8,681	5,106	2,489	19,707
SOUTHERN SEM JR COLLEGE	PRI-T	29,716	B	0	1,019	10,615	1,376	0	2,250	479	B
SWEET BRIAR COLLEGE	PRI-FN	227,522	108,047	17,739	11,935	54,665	24,799	1,116	11	5,500	3,910
UNION THEOL SEM IN VA	PRI FG				SEE UNION THEOL SEM JOINT LIB						
UNION THEOL SEM JOINT LIB	PRI-FG	346,412	177,008	44,945	15,708	57,635	9,982	3,258	9,006	3,210	25,660
UNIVERSITY OF RICHMOND	PRI-FG	772,916	310,753	50,763	34,443	166,161	98,645	800	27,926	11,627	71,798
U OF VIRGINIA ALL CAM											
U OF VIRGINIA MAIN CAMPUS	PUB-U	6,981,313	2,932,936	314,402	348,255	1,199,198	1,111,171	185,286	32,070	154,233	703,762
U VA CLINCH VLY COLLEGE	PUB-FN	245,994	105,346	14,186	3,776	38,074	13,427	5,295	8,352	10,708	46,830
VIRGINIA COLLEGE	PRI-T	A	A	A	A	A	A	A	A	A	A
VIRGINIA COMMONWEALTH U	PUB-U	2,871,473	1,255,916	133,126	129,565	459,421	576,260	10,050	0	36,000	271,135
VA INTERMONT COLLEGE	PRI-FN	112,027	42,335	7,650	5,580	16,382	8,802	2,062	7,485	1,949	19,782
VIRGINIA MILITARY INST	PUB-FN	427,783	217,060	26,484	6,319	66,158	38,648	1,467	0	10,071	61,576
VA POLY INST AND STATE U	PUB-U	4,296,090	1,816,041	0	152,281	927,119	791,928	97,572	6,275	140,975	363,899
VIRGINIA STATE UNIV	PUB-FG	611,607	356,264	40,667	6,459	105,478	68,215	8,427	143	7,406	18,548
VA STATE CC SYS ALL INST											
BLUE RIDGE CMTY COLLEGE	PUB-T	109,171	69,241	7,610	0	28,700	0	0	0	2,020	1,600
CENTRAL VA CMTY COLLEGE	PUB-T	100,642	70,679	7,453	0	12,489	4,580	1,390	29	0	4,022
DABNEY S LANCASTER CC	PUB-T	99,821	57,532	7,414	0	13,026	7,172	2,102	4,299	38	8,238
DANVILLE CMTY COLLEGE	PUB-T	221,716	124,148	16,594	10,140	28,800	6,000	7,905	11,211	342	16,576
ESTN SHORE CMTY COLLEGE	PUB-T	58,340	B	B	0	10,720	2,691	1,013	1,744	0	B
GERMANNA CMTY COLLEGE	PUB-T	55,673	B	B	0	9,366	2,890	1,025	300	1,420	B
J SARGEANT REYNOLDS CC	PUB-T	430,343	252,080	30,392	0	92,184	24,093	9,528	3,398	703	17,965
JOHN TYLER CMTY COLLEGE	PUB-T	121,850	82,008	8,722	0	14,520	5,962	4,214	4,757	1,180	487
LORD FAIRFAX CMTY COLLEGE	PUB-T	189,810	127,867	11,751	0	19,828	8,159	2,293	6,356	0	13,556
MTN EMPIRE CMTY COLLEGE	PUB-T	122,246	60,196	12,003	0	8,706	5,017	27,191	2,310	314	6,509
NEW RIVER CMTY COLLEGE	PUB-T	234,789	131,195	12,020	0	25,438	4,270	9,289	3,493	200	48,884
NORTHERN VA CMTY COLLEGE	PUB-T	4,269,578	1,458,353	218,753	26,004	131,465	60,986	14,621	66,136	646	2,292,614
PATRICK HENRY CC	PUB-T	113,648	62,734	7,780	0	16,274	5,600	9,783	3,853	0	7,624
PAUL D CAMP CMTY COLLEGE	PUB-T	134,321	76,900	11,103	0	13,705	6,190	1,108	9,359	0	15,956
PIEDMONT VA CMTY COLLEGE	PUB-T	165,579	111,252	13,536	2,716	10,510	9,562	3,068	4,186	162	10,587
RAPPAHANNOCK CMTY COLLEGE	PUB-T	82,059	68,037	0	0	9,444	1,626	1,174	0	0	1,778
SOUTHSIDE VA CMTY COLLEGE	PUB-T	99,332	63,353	7,278	0	10,917	6,604	499	2,476	100	8,105
SOUTHWEST VA CMTY COLLEGE	PUB-T	94,176	67,479	8,165	0	7,589	6,858	582	31	0	3,472
THOMAS NELSN CMTY COLLEGE	PUB-T	248,985	150,766	17,589	0	28,246	16,670	3,614	16,714	477	14,909
TIDEWATER CMTY COLLEGE	PUB-T	766,660	457,355	59,432	60,084	60,457	27,030	10,985	31,173	1,023	59,121
VA HIGHLANDS CMTY COLLEGE	PUB-T	103,576	71,868	8,421	0	10,474	4,632	1,080	42	0	7,059
VA WESTERN CMTY COLLEGE	PUB-T	196,555	105,505	7,385	0	58,205	14,562	966	475	2,410	7,047

SEE FOOTNOTES AT END OF TABLE

Table 2. – Library Operating Expenditures (in Dollars) of College and University Libraries, by Category of Expenditure and by State or Other Area and Institution: Aggregate United States, 1978-79 – Continued

| STATE OR OTHER AREA AND INSTITUTION | CON- TROL AND TYPE OF IN- STITU- TION | TOTAL | SALARIES AND WAGES | | | BOOK- STOCK | PERIOD- ICALS | MICRO- FORMS | AUDIO- VISUAL | BIND- ING AND RE- BIND- ING | ALL OTHER OPER- ATING EXPEND- ITURES |
			LIBRARY STAFF	FRINGE BENEFITS	STUDENTS ON HOURLY BASIS						
(1)	(2)	(3)	(4)	(5)	(6)	(7)	(8)	(9)	(10)	(11)	(12)
VIRGINIA	--CONTINUED										
WYTHEVILLE CMTY COLLEGE	PUB-T	78,614	53,364	5,914	0	9,596	6,605	1,046	453	261	975
VIRGINIA UNION UNIVERSITY	PRI-FG	182,873	80,853	16,979	40,617	19,343	9,070	4,740	361	4,033	6,877
VIRGINIA WESLEYAN COLLEGE	PRI-FN	153,260	69,927	10,153	11,014	33,314	13,849	492	1,176	3,248	10,087
WASHINGTON AND LEE U[2/]	PRI-FG	518,833	177,194	32,417	25,073	98,236	123,302	0	0	14,236	48,375
WASHINGTON											
BELLEVUE CMTY COLLEGE	PUB-T	434,658	281,894	45,838	28,017	19,352	12,177	2,356	10,300	0	34,724
BIG BEND CMTY COLLEGE	PUB-T	132,162	69,158	12,312	815	17,747	8,376	3,106	4,160	100	16,398
CENTRALIA COLLEGE	PUB-T	143,224	64,583	11,696	6,307	12,681	5,251	1,731	7,669	125	33,181
CENTRAL WASH UNIVERSITY	PUB-FG	1,694,848	833,485	169,154	85,338	260,250	80,000	0	81,424	19,967	165,230
CITY COLLEGE[1/]	PRI-FG			NO LIBRARY FACILITIES							
CLARK COLLEGE	PUB-T	156,177	87,231	15,650	4,292	13,503	9,502	491	4,265	210	21,033
COLUMBIA BASIN CC	PUB-T	246,254	133,337	20,928	13,727	20,000	9,406	3,341	3,705	669	41,141
CORNISH INSTITUTE	PRI-FN	33,012	B	B	0	9,500	1,000	0	0	400	B
EASTERN WASH UNIVERSITY	PUB-FG	1,332,913	601,082	133,336	110,108	100,065	220,177	0	13,916	24,809	129,420
EVERGREEN STATE COLLEGE	PUB-FN	1,158,242	563,263	106,946	43,953	144,058	114,480	21,720	25,041	3,099	135,682
FORT STEILACOOM CC	PUB-T	358,404	238,864	41,780	12,965	25,010	6,672	147	6,109	0	26,857
FORT WRIGHT C HOLY NAMES	PRI-FG	47,021	B	B	2,983	7,778	3,572	0	829	0	B
GONZAGA UNIVERSITY	PRI-FG	688,761	242,863	34,395	62,402	64,980	182,130	27,181	0	12,538	62,272
GRAYS HARBOR COLLEGE	PUB-T	142,376	69,831	11,418	835	8,635	10,298	140	11,944	966	28,309
GREEN RIVER CMTY COLLEGE	PUB-T	259,136	159,155	32,041	7,991	10,562	11,502	0	10,002	0	27,883
GRIFFIN COLLEGE	PRI-FN	A	A	A	A	A	A	A	A	A	A
HIGHLINE CMTY COLLEGE	PUB-T	317,393	195,953	36,430	29,171	24,171	9,621	3,621	4,708	320	13,398
LOWER COLUMBIA COLLEGE	PUB-T	173,705	98,959	18,145	7,701	17,550	5,000	350	2,000	500	23,500
LUTH BIBLE INST SEATTLE	PRI-FN	35,902	B	B	5,281	2,409	1,184	0	0	0	B
NTHWST C ASSEMBLIES GOD	PRI-FN	68,019	B	B	6,044	10,003	4,022	3,906	40	300	B
OLYMPIA TECH CMTY COLLEGE	PUB-T	114,890	47,367	8,616	0	16,172	3,236	1,287	12,430	0	25,782
OLYMPIC COLLEGE	PUB-T	291,257	169,822	27,027	11,747	24,971	6,473	5,110	2,725	0	43,382
PACIFIC LUTH UNIVERSITY	PRI-FG	470,965	160,251	29,453	43,992	93,092	66,470	2,266	7,440	4,019	63,982
PENINSULA COLLEGE	PUB-T	145,949	83,821	11,310	1,196	14,924	7,089	2,256	738	128	24,507
PUGET SOUND C OF BIBLE	PRI-FN	34,544	B	B	5,418	6,347	1,585	1,297	50	530	B
SAINT MARTIN'S COLLEGE	PRI-FN	74,252	37,316	866	15,983	12,647	5,566	0	688	0	1,186
SEATTLE CC DIST ALL CAM NORTH SEATTLE CC	PUB-T	417,159	225,883	33,589	44,625	22,722	8,323	2,062	10,081	1,506	68,368
SEATTLE CC CENTRAL CAMPUS	PUB-T	390,783	251,041	37,330	2,800	25,000	11,000	5,000	6,000	0	52,612
SEATTLE CC SOUTH CAMPUS	PUB-T	258,337	158,774	23,609	9,838	17,078	8,257	2,117	9,124	1,014	28,526
SEATTLE PACIFIC U	PRI-FG	279,643	141,808	36,664	13,864	26,854	29,316	2,000	1,413	1,525	26,199
SEATTLE UNIVERSITY	PRI-FG	418,252	227,631	20,130	27,014	75,469	35,170	7,420	0	3,324	22,094
SHORELINE CMTY COLLEGE	PUB-T	492,756	282,584	52,396	13,367	28,396	14,449	4,928	42,159	0	54,477
SKAGIT VALLEY COLLEGE	PUB-T	265,467	162,786	25,962	22,800	13,197	9,254	1,531	12,834	1,281	15,822
TACOMA COMMUNITY COLLEGE	PUB-T	261,147	94,870	24,608	20,326	10,500	11,151	1,778	4,515	0	93,399
UNIVERSITY OF PUGET SOUND	PRI-FG	928,870	347,850	79,508	73,924	99,024	170,559	21,149	8,044	14,726	114,086
UNIVERSITY OF WASHINGTON	PUB-U	10,061,186	4,604,193	804,909	726,824	968,969	1,124,320	345,974	32,445	319,378	1,134,174
WALLA WALLA COLLEGE	PRI-FG	272,718	125,088	24,685	25,722	45,374	22,877	0	0	8,931	20,041
WALLA WALLA CMTY COLLEGE	PUB-T	348,258	163,580	31,752	3,814	15,538	9,812	9,452	2,675	0	111,635
WASH ST CC DIST 5 ALLINST EDMONDS COMMUNITY COLLEGE	PUB-T	281,134	172,734	30,386	6,500	18,000	6,700	800	13,000	0	33,014
EVERETT CMTY COLLEGE	PUB-T	385,647	207,540	37,157	31,324	21,243	10,664	6,113	4,946	1,292	65,368
WASH ST CC DIST 17 ALL SPOKANE COMMUNITY COLLEGE	PUB-T	358,499	147,284	26,323	0	0	23,086	13,192	9,894	0	138,720
SPOKANE FLS CMTY COLLEGE	PUB-T	596,246	246,561	44,064	0	48,326	22,952	2,277	23,546	500	208,020
WASHINGTON ST UNIVERSITY	PUB-U	4,745,569	2,124,370	495,269	274,967	371,848	876,815	0	26,972	94,333	480,994
WENATCHEE VALLEY COLLEGE	PUB-T	226,674	121,430	18,584	11,920	32,891	12,404	0	7,447	0	21,998
WESTERN WASH UNIVERSITY	PUB-FG	1,738,397	805,163	169,084	111,422	258,178	271,430	19,901	2,828	23,860	76,531
WHATCOM CMTY COLLEGE	PUB-T	119,864	81,272	15,245	1,091	13,224	3,513	0	0	0	5,519
WHITMAN COLLEGE	PRI-FN	350,547	129,498	19,428	36,907	70,172	47,669	7,846	0	6,206	32,821
WHITWORTH COLLEGE	PRI-FG	212,927	93,422	3,489	17,503	39,761	30,191	1,170	0	3,393	23,998
YAKIMA VALLEY CC	PUB-T	177,310	113,827	21,855	4,272	14,000	5,000	0	15,399	1,200	1,757
WEST VIRGINIA											
ALDERSON BROADDUS COLLEGE	PRI-FN	160,471	85,156	11,920	1,898	23,134	11,521	770	3,869	284	21,919
APPALACHIAN BIBLE COLLEGE	PRI-FN	25,145	B	0	0	3,362	870	0	0	0	B
BECKLEY COLLEGE	PRI-T	39,871	B	B	1,689	5,258	1,932	0	3,687	0	B
BETHANY COLLEGE	PRI-FN	216,975	71,839	6,252	19,157	29,775	24,946	3,976	5,536	1,091	54,403
BLUEFIELD STATE COLLEGE	PUB-FN	167,699	69,345	9,982	10,759	27,039	10,999	2,448	10,759	1,199	25,169

SEE FOOTNOTES AT END OF TABLE

Table 2. — Library Operating Expenditures (in Dollars) of College and University Libraries, by Category of Expenditure and by State or Other Area and Institution: Aggregate United States, 1978-79 — Continued

STATE OR OTHER AREA AND INSTITUTION	CON- TROL AND TYPE OF IN- STITU- TION	TOTAL	SALARIES AND WAGES			BOOK- STOCK	PERIOD- ICALS	MICRO- FORMS	AUDIO- VISUAL	BIND- ING AND RE- BIND- ING	ALL OTHER OPER- ATING EXPEND- ITURES
			LIBRARY STAFF	FRINGE BENEFITS	STUDENTS ON HOURLY BASIS						
(1)	(2)	(3)	(4)	(5)	(6)	(7)	(8)	(9)	(10)	(11)	(12)
WEST VIRGINIA	--CONTINUED										
CONCORD COLLEGE	PUB-FN	276,306	119,052	21,429	32,871	36,155	20,999	3,974	3,906	2,672	35,248
DAVIS AND ELKINS COLLEGE	PRI-FN	104,621	54,116	10,556	920	19,393	15,940	1,806	627	0	1,263
FAIRMONT STATE COLLEGE	PUB-FN	350,041	201,980	25,988	10,698	60,357	21,294	2,173	11,758	2,837	12,956
GLENVILLE STATE COLLEGE	PUB-FN	229,089	99,839	16,658	17,653	29,226	24,765	6,885	12,538	5,742	15,783
MARSHALL UNIVERSITY	PUB-FG	1,027,708	503,612	20,730	43,912	165,794	167,364	26,757	17,403	5,291	76,845
OHIO VALLEY COLLEGE	PRI-T	31,051	B	0	2,460	8,196	1,383	148	664	0	B
PARKERSBURG CMTY COLLEGE	PUB-T	436,599	402,595	0	0	17,648	4,322	5,181	1,426	789	4,638
POTOMAC STATE COLLEGE	PUB-T	100,663	55,860	4,583	0	11,980	2,553	1,210	3,606	622	20,249
SALEM COLLEGE ALL CAM											
SALEM COLLEGE MAIN CAMPUS	PRI-FG	96,085	54,200	5,500	0	17,000	10,000	1,000	2,100	500	5,785
SALEM COLLEGE CLARKSBURG	PRI-T	6,050	B	B	0	600	550	0	0	0	B
SHEPHERD COLLEGE	PUB-FN	283,042	141,275	22,045	13,210	68,501	17,871	7,819	2,959	0	9,362
SOUTHERN W VA CC ALL CAM											
STHN W VA CC-LOGAN CAM	PUB-T	73,794	40,585	1,614	0	7,395	6,401	3,453	6,574	0	7,772
STHN W VA CC-WILLIAMSON	PUB-T	71,574	30,330	1,218	0	15,599	4,148	1,760	6,795	0	11,724
U OF CHARLESTON	PRI-FG	172,760	91,523	13,728	10,525	33,161	10,196	659	493	5,943	6,532
WEST LIBERTY ST COLLEGE	PUB-FN	280,743	153,636	36,872	11,000	33,000	30,000	3,000	4,300	500	8,435
W VA COLLEGE GRAD STUDIES	PUB-FG	257,447	133,000	19,950	17,460	30,439	33,657	4,808	0	562	17,571
WEST VA INST TECHNOLOGY	PUB-FG	304,161	178,227	5,041	7,461	43,660	35,965	14,319	558	3,631	15,299
WEST VIRGINIA NORTHERN CC	PUB-T	115,886	86,790	4,236	6,540	7,087	5,611	1,215	1,008	0	3,399
W VA SCH OSTEOPATHIC MED	PUB-FG	128,270	42,592	0	808	23,307	20,560	0	29,549	339	11,115
W VA STATE COLLEGE	PUB-FN	343,759	170,878	9,981	41,972	55,250	29,423	4,646	0	7,980	23,629
WEST VIRGINIA UNIVERSITY	PUB-U	1,875,076	827,083	0	94,975	280,922	422,786	30,000	42,890	59,000	117,420
WEST VA WESLEYAN COLLEGE	PRI-FG	203,873	114,897	24,100	0	26,966	21,500	4,704	0	575	11,131
WHEELING COLLEGE	PRI-FG	131,154	65,150	8,638	2,279	19,556	17,502	4,290	0	1,868	11,871
WISCONSIN											
ALVERNO COLLEGE	PRI-FN	282,312	158,845	11,004	12,313	32,268	22,387	2,232	17,619	2,497	23,147
BELOIT COLLEGE	PRI-FG	175,230	72,480	0	17,500	44,000	28,000	0	0	3,000	10,250
BLACKHAWK TECHNICAL INST	PUB-T	129,882	54,357	13,452	0	12,367	6,802	0	34,739	0	8,165
CARDINAL STRITCH COLLEGE	PRI-FG	96,553	60,825	650	2,500	17,911	6,741	80	486	1,390	5,970
CARROLL COLLEGE	PRI-FN	191,659	81,685	17,962	13,363	45,291	20,492	770	21	4,512	7,563
CARTHAGE COLLEGE	PRI-FG	211,028	112,217	12,612	2,783	41,534	21,603	1,613	0	4,618	14,048
CONCORDIA COLLEGE	PRI-FN	64,657	40,560	5,273	6,010	5,715	2,807	1,318	1,706	145	1,123
DISTRICT ONE TECH INST	PUB-T	190,465	76,880	19,774	0	29,753	19,955	1,528	39,221	50	3,304
EDGEWOOD COLLEGE	PRI-FN	69,276	B	B	4,118	16,044	7,122	0	0	1,086	B
FOX VALLEY TECH INST	PUB-T	114,216	B	B	0	20,805	10,950	700	28,500	0	B
GATEWAY TECH INST ALL CAM											
GATEWAY TECH INST-KENOSHA	PUB-T	159,950	114,141	18,386	0	13,600	4,898	0	2,093	0	6,832
GATEWAY TECH INST-RACINE	PUB-T	85,288	47,809	15,043	0	11,127	4,007	0	1,712	0	5,590
HOLY REDEEMER COLLEGE	PRI-FN	39,150	B	B	0	5,249	3,391	164	171	305	B
INSTITUTE PAPER CHEMISTRY	PRI-FG	108,430	45,956	6,100	0	9,817	42,219	0	0	2,428	1,910
LAKELAND COLLEGE	PRI-FN	86,252	34,140	6,528	0	22,935	5,973	932	188	0	15,556
LAKESHORE TECHNICAL INST	PUB-T	85,754	49,944	11,157	0	8,230	3,500	400	3,318	0	9,205
LAWRENCE UNIVERSITY	PRI-FN	390,174	144,800	19,550	28,721	82,115	57,738	7,193	723	5,548	43,786
MADISON AREA TECH COLLEGE	PUB-T	322,559	160,836	39,389	8,311	24,797	12,559	2,481	9,049	700	64,437
MADISON BUSINESS COLLEGE	PRI-T	7,154	B	B	0	475	596	0	0	0	B
MARIAN C OF FOND DU LAC	PRI-FN	74,579	47,422	3,292	981	8,929	6,814	165	874	0	6,102
MARQUETTE UNIVERSITY	PRI-U	1,883,265	733,663	108,149	111,302	220,629	524,482	0	0	44,378	140,662
MEDICAL COLLEGE OF WIS	PRI-FG	458,658	205,216	34,815	17,477	42,500	125,000	0	0	13,500	20,150
MID-STATE TECHNICAL INST	PUB-T	86,627	33,130	6,522	1,226	26,744	10,219	0	2,140	0	6,646
MILTON COLLEGE	PRI-FN	71,505	B	B	8,584	11,167	4,083	925	0	0	B
MILWAUKEE AREA TECH C	PUB-T	311,645	213,629	46,999	0	33,241	9,731	0	0	50	7,995
MILWAUKEE SCH OF THE ARTS	PRI-FN	A	A	A	A	A	A	A	A	A	B
MILWAUKEE SCH ENGINEERING	PRI-FG	95,219	B	B	11,872	24,114	12,705	2,208	842	291	B
MILWAUKEE STRATTON C	PRI-T	A	A	A	A	A	A			800	7,000
MORAINE PARK TECH INST	PUB-T	120,350	64,550	15,000	0	18,000	15,000	0	0	800	7,000
MOUNT MARY COLLEGE	PRI-FN	122,717	62,100	2,367	15,181	16,307	8,365	343	5,140	5,417	7,497
MOUNT SENARIO COLLEGE	PRI-FN	98,045	53,301	7,142	0	16,732	4,422	698	2,149	131	13,470
NASHOTAH HOUSE	PRI-FG	92,123	35,456	7,074	6,164	25,477	7,642	0	23	216	10,071
NICOLET COLLEGE-TECH INST	PUB-T	202,111	97,330	22,261	4,332	23,024	15,054	900	16,175	200	22,835
NORTH CENTRAL TECH INST	PUB-T	129,988	63,514	15,872	0	21,167	8,773	896	13,300	0	6,466
NORTHEAST WIS TECH INST	PUB-T	48,500	0	0	0	33,000	12,000	3,500	0	0	0
NORTHLAND COLLEGE	PRI-FN	72,382	29,680	5,342	9,570	12,939	9,193	480	100	884	4,194
NORTHWESTERN COLLEGE	PRI-FN	A	A	A	A	A	A	A	A	A	

SEE FOOTNOTES AT END OF TABLE

Table 2. — Library Operating Expenditures (in Dollars) of College and University Libraries, by Category of Expenditure and by State or Other Area and Institution: Aggregate United States, 1978-79 — Continued

STATE OR OTHER AREA AND INSTITUTION	CONTROL AND TYPE OF INSTITUTION	TOTAL	SALARIES AND WAGES			BOOK-STOCK	PERIODICALS	MICRO-FORMS	AUDIO-VISUAL	BINDING AND RE-BINDING	ALL OTHER OPERATING EXPENDITURES
			LIBRARY STAFF	FRINGE BENEFITS	STUDENTS ON HOURLY BASIS						
(1)	(2)	(3)	(4)	(5)	(6)	(7)	(8)	(9)	(10)	(11)	(12)
WISCONSIN	--CONTINUED										
RIPON COLLEGE	PRI-FN	198,418	88,495	11,888	14,648	32,663	20,972	1,528	0	5,986	22,238
SACRED HEART SCH THEOLOGY	PRI-FG	41,072	10,000	0	0	11,900	2,998	400	2,000	2,274	B
SNT FRANCIS DE SALES C	PRI-FN	24,544	B	0	0	3,850	3,300	294	0	0	B
SNT FRAN SEM PSTL MINSTRY	PRI-FG	50,688	B	B	0	10,285	5,366	20	445	666	B
SAINT NORBERT COLLEGE	PRI-FN	309,044	144,984	17,461	21,907	49,085	20,674	4,416	22,585	2,217	25,715
SILVER LAKE COLLEGE	PRI-FN	78,515	61,252	2,007	473	7,461	2,217	180	2,717	280	1,928
STHWST WIS VOC TECH INST	PUB-T	A	A	A	A	A	A	A	A		A
U OF WIS SYS ALL INST											
U OF WISCONSIN EAU CLAIRE	PUB-FG	949,925	414,556	88,007	85,897	202,254	84,057	15,118	9,886	4,005	45,345
U OF WISCONSIN GREEN BAY	PUB-FG	733,038	316,242	71,300	61,485	90,000	110,000	20,000	9,500	2,208	52,303
U OF WISCONSIN LA CROSSE	PUB-FG	894,509	391,707	95,339	26,428	154,453	114,775	28,366	0	9,855	73,586
U OF WISCONSIN MADISON	PUB-U	9,696,889	4,407,038	1,044,724	679,686	1,122,179	1,485,372	0	0	227,173	730,717
U OF WISCONSIN MILWAUKEE1/	PUB-FG	3,627,621	1,225,448	0	318,147	637,066	463,416	92,508	11,086	51,361	828,589
U OF WISCONSIN OSHKOSH	PUB-FG	1,252,611	611,326	133,833	48,701	187,958	97,484	1,975	13,443	10,491	147,400
U OF WISCONSIN PARKSIDE	PUB-FG	845,040	358,266	78,818	80,056	109,000	121,000	24,500	7,000	1,600	64,800
U OF WISCONSIN PLATTEVL	PUB-FG	787,789	334,986	74,457	99,393	120,555	55,142	12,782	4,347	5,006	81,121
U OF WISCONSIN RIVER FLS	PUB-FG	631,101	311,263	69,129	24,432	124,181	49,875	3,581	609	6,340	41,691
U OF WISCONSIN STEVNS PNT	PUB-FG	1,164,823	634,724	141,664	74,129	112,253	110,369	4,100	19,350	11,660	56,574
U OF WISCONSIN STOUT	PUB-FG	686,021	279,429	65,429	45,362	119,000	68,800	9,500	22,000	1,500	75,001
U OF WISCONSIN SUPERIOR	PUB-FG	346,396	161,453	37,536	32,500	44,932	35,182	0	0	3,553	31,240
U OF WISCONSIN WHITEWATER	PUB-FG	1,173,209	625,322	134,324	70,383	115,914	61,259	9,800	25,000	14,000	117,207
U OF WISCONSIN CTR SYS	PUB-T	1,030,502	539,553	115,591	68,435	126,746	70,226	8,317	7,662	2,039	91,933
VITERBO COLLEGE	PRI-FN	113,043	79,802	0	8,160	10,354	6,245	43	370	1,617	6,452
WAUKESHA COUNTY TECH INST	PUB-T	96,444	44,725	12,956	5,945	22,516	2,169	3,500	2,170	0	2,463
WESTERN WIS TECH INST	PUB-T	108,552	64,122	16,030	0	15,000	7,000	1,500	0	0	4,900
WISCONSIN CONSV OF MUSIC	PRI-FG	A	A	A	A	A	A	A	A	A	A
WISCONSIN LUTHERAN C	PRI-T	43,192	B	B	0	9,149	1,506	0	125	175	B
WYOMING											
CASPER COLLEGE	PUB-T	211,993	122,123	19,904	0	43,391	19,097	0	0	0	7,478
CENTRAL WYOMING COLLEGE	PUB-T	70,919	32,989	4,559	0	15,355	3,988	600	2,003	600	10,825
EASTERN WYOMING COLLEGE	PUB-T	77,426	55,796	8,133	1,344	5,118	3,000	822	1,500	0	1,713
LARAMIE CO CMTY COLLEGE	PUB-T	124,291	65,095	10,253	0	13,433	6,337	0	14,099	132	14,942
NORTHWEST CMTY COLLEGE	PUB-T	54,814	29,288	4,918	5,608	7,158	6,376	480	0	498	488
SHERIDAN COLLEGE	PUB-T	62,585	30,487	3,217	0	7,396	5,399	1,413	12,336	400	1,937
UNIVERSITY OF WYOMING2/	PUB-U	1,775,200	715,738	0	33,830	406,696	498,930	0	9,980	35,434	74,592
WESTERN WYO CMTY COLLEGE	PUB-T	157,400	105,600	18,500	0	14,000	5,000	1,200	2,200	0	10,900
U.S. SERVICE SCHOOLS											
AIR FORCE INST TECHNOLOGY	PUB-FG	339,866	204,801	5,887	0	16,410	107,466	187	0	4,365	750
CC OF THE AIR FORCE	PUB-T	A	A	A	A	A	A	A		A	A
NAVAL POSTGRADUATE SCHOOL	PUB-FG	771,395	408,980	36,808	20,508	89,928	131,900	6,807	0	9,819	66,645
UNIFORMED SERV U HLTH SCI	PUB-FG	A	A	A	A	A	A	A	A	A	A
US AIR FORCE ACADEMY	PUB-FN	1,109,248	691,759	53,051	451	158,033	138,042	6,527	1,647	23,600	36,138
US ARMY CMND-GEN STAFF C	PUB-FG	A	A	A	A	A	A	A	A	A	A
US COAST GUARD ACADEMY	PUB-FN	235,000	115,000	11,500	4,000	60,000	30,000	3,000	1,000	4,000	6,500
US MERCHANT MARINE ACAD	PUB-FN	192,709	138,734	0	0	30,419	10,319	1,500	0	1,081	10,656
US MILITARY ACADEMY	PUB-FN	1,411,995	888,881	84,507	37,677	188,670	77,270	43,630	7,490	18,860	65,010
US NAVAL ACADEMY	PUB-FN	1,362,984	797,417	79,741	14,101	155,559	168,734	10,474	0	48,527	88,431
AMERICAN SAMOA											
AMER SAMOA CMTY COLLEGE	PUB-T	68,959	43,177	6,045	0	8,900	2,250	387	5,000	0	3,200
CANAL ZONE											
PANAMA CANAL COLLEGE	PUB-FN	162,339	B	B	38,685	10,000	2,577	3,344	10,000	6,000	B
GUAM											
UNIVERSITY OF GUAM	PUB-FG	405,574	259,170	28,349	0	91,432	0	0	0	0	26,623
PUERTO RICO											
AMERICAN C PUERTO RICO	PRI-FN	73,300	42,800	0	0	20,000	5,500	0	0	0	5,000
ANTILLIAN COLLEGE	PRI-FN	148,838	73,116	0	12,413	49,576	5,144	0	6,366	2,223	0
BAYAMON CEN UNIVERSITY	PRI-FN	372,245	171,560	12,969	87,943	44,067	7,492	734	6,281	0	41,199
CAGUAS CITY COLLEGE	PRI-T	33,688	20,124	264	0	10,200	1,500	0	1,300	300	0

SEE FOOTNOTES AT END OF TABLE

Table 2. — Library Operating Expenditures (in Dollars) of College and University Libraries, by Category of Expenditure and by State or Other Area and Institution: Aggregate United States, 1978-79 — Continued

STATE OR OTHER AREA AND INSTITUTION (1)	CONTROL AND TYPE OF INSTITUTION (2)	TOTAL (3)	SALARIES AND WAGES			BOOK-STOCK (7)	PERIOD-ICALS (8)	MICRO-FORMS (9)	AUDIO-VISUAL (10)	BINDING AND RE-BINDING (11)	ALL OTHER OPER-ATING EXPEND-ITURES (12)
			LIBRARY STAFF (4)	FRINGE BENEFITS (5)	STUDENTS ON HOURLY BASIS (6)						
PUERTO RICO	--CONTINUED										
CARIBBEAN CTR ADV STUDIES	PRI-FG	A	A	A	A	A	A		A	A	A
CARIBBEAN U COLLEGE	PRI-FN	89,600	46,828	3,000	0	33,500	1,773	0	4,499	0	0
CATHOLIC U PUERTO RICO	PRI-FG	36,060	4,800	960	0	16,153	3,050	1,200	2,100	900	6,897
CONSERVATORY OF MUSIC PR	PUB-FN	48,733	B	B	2,633	16,054	598	0	3,849	1,300	B
EDP C OF PUERTO RICO	PRI-T	27,000	B	B	3,000	5,000	600	0	0	0	B
FUNDACION EDUCATIVA ALL											
COLEGIO U DEL TURABO	PRI-FN	340,984	256,174	30,150	0	20,000	5,000	0	8,500	1,000	20,160
PUERTO RICO JR COLLEGE	PRI-T	381,675	270,475	44,400	0	18,500	6,500	1,000	12,000	1,000	27,800
INST COMERCIAL DE PR JC	PRI-T	48,850	30,000	800	0	11,000	2,000	0	4,000	300	750
INST TECNICO COMERCIAL JC	PRI-T	18,600	17,400	0	1,056	0	0	0	0	0	144
INTER AMER U PR ALL CAM											
INTER AMER U METRO CAM	PRI-FG	609,944	374,216	49,110	5,000	75,000	30,000	7,500	25,000	4,500	39,618
INTER AMER U ARECIBO BR	PRI-FN	124,570	64,520	7,850	2,500	25,000	5,000	0	6,000	3,000	10,700
INTER AMER U BARNQUITS BR	PRI-T	77,860	41,960	4,900	0	15,000	3,000	0	3,000	2,100	7,900
INTER AMER SAN GERMAN CAM	PRI-FG	324,759	220,164	28,395	3,500	15,000	25,000	0	9,000	4,000	19,700
INTER AMER U AGUADILLA BR	PRI-T	160,850	90,940	12,210	1,000	15,000	8,000	0	8,500	3,600	21,600
INTER AMER U FAJARDO BR	PRI-T	A	A	A	A						A
INTER AMER U GUAYAMA BR	PRI-T	81,400	42,020	6,180	0	15,500	3,500	0	5,000	1,500	A
INTER AMER U PONCE BR	PRI-T	96,900	55,030	7,270	2,000	15,000	5,000	0	4,000	2,000	7,700
INTRATL INST WORLD U	PRI-FG	380,350	202,500	20,250	19,800	52,800	5,000	0	0	0	6,600
RAMIREZ C BUS AND TECHN	PRI-T	13,000	B	B	0	1,000	500	0	0	0	80,000
SAN JUAN TECHNOLOGICAL CC	PUB-T	89,653	68,147	0	0	21,506	500	0	500	0	B
UNIV POLITECNICA DE PR	PRI-FN	28,000	B	0	3,600	10,000	0	0	0	0	B
UNIVERSIDAD DE PONCE	PRI-T	29,400	B	0	0	900	400	0	250	1,200	B
U OF PUERTO RICO ALL CAM							432	0		200	B
U OF PR RIO PIEDRAS	PUB-U	3,118,425	2,017,438	268,215	219,600	214,514	285,386	28,118	3,700	25,699	55,755
U OF PR MAYAGUEZ	PUB-FG	938,096	542,562	116,428	11,406	111,735	130,577	7,725	963	3,145	13,555
U OF PR MEDICAL SCIENCES	PUB-FG	470,213	272,266	39,827	0	24,000	112,000	0	0	14,000	8,120
U PR CAYEY UNIVERSITY C	PUB-FN	360,071	242,076	33,605	0	43,866	23,790	640	3,719	2,985	9,390
U PR HUMACAO U COLLEGE	PUB-FN	377,052	209,112	32,307	0	42,871	51,575	770	0	5,000	35,417
U PR REG COLLEGES ADMIN	PUB-T	1,083,106	703,576	184,215	3,149	90,565	31,645	3,665	26,175	5,956	34,160
U OF THE SACRED HEART	PRI-FN	283,799	176,072	26,358	5,850	34,847	15,216	1,000	300	565	23,591
TRUST TERRITORY											
CMTY COLLEGE MICRONESIA	PUB-T	32,287	14,280	0	0	7,730	1,500	530	4,347	0	3,900
VIRGIN ISLANDS											
COLLEGE OF VIRGIN ISLANDS	PUB-FG	270,485	100,584	17,520	22,655	61,167	37,326	0	0	3,600	27,633

NOTE - COLUMN 12, "ALL OTHER OPERATING EXPENDITURES" INCLUDES ALL OTHER LIBRARY MATERIALS EXPENDITURES

A - DATA NOT PROVIDED

B - DATA SUPPRESSED TO MAINTAIN CONFIDENTIALITY

1/ - USES LOCAL LIBRARIES

2/ - EXCLUDES THE LAW LIBRARY

3/ - USES FACILITIES OF EMMANUEL COLLEGE

4/ - JESUIT SCHOOL OF THEOLOGY AT CHICAGO IS ALSO A MEMBER OF THE JKM JOINT LIBRARY

5/ - CONTRACTS FOR USE OF LIBRARY FACILITIES

6/ - EXCLUDES THE MEDICAL LIBRARY

7/ - SHARES FACILITIES OF OHIO STATE UNIVERSITY NEWARK BRANCH

8/ - SHARES FACILITIES OF OHIO STATE UNIVERSITY LIMA BRANCH

9/ - SHARES FACILITIES OF OHIO STATE UNIVERSITY MARION BRANCH

10/ - SHARES FACILITIES OF OHIO STATE UNIVERSITY MANSFIELD BRANCH

11/ - SHARES FACILITIES OF KENT STATE UNIVERSITY STARK COUNTY REGIONAL CAMPUS

12/ - THE TEXAS MEDICAL CENTER LIBRARY OF THE HOUSTON ACADEMY OF MEDICINE HOUSES COLLECTIONS AND PROVIDES LIBRARY SERVICES FOR:
BAYLOR COLLEGE OF MEDICINE
PRAIRIE VIEW A&M UNIVERSITY SCHOOL OF NURSING
TEXAS WOMEN'S UNIVERSITY SCHOOL OF NURSING AND HEALTH SCIENCES
UNIVERSITY OF HOUSTON COLLEGE OF PHARMACY
UNIVERSITY OF TEXAS HEALTH SCIENCE CENTER AT HOUSTON MEDICAL SCHOOL, GRADUATE SCHOOL OF BIOMEDICAL SCIENCES, SCHOOL OF ALLIED HEALTH, SPEECH AND HEARING INSTITUTE, AND SCHOOL OF NURSING

13/ - FRINGE BENEFITS NOT INCLUDED IN LIBRARY BUDGET

Table 3. — Indexes Concerning Operating Expenditures, 1978-79, Bookstock Held at End of Year, 1978-79, and Library Staff (FTE), Fall 1979, College and University Libraries, by State or Other Area and Institution: Aggregate United States – Continued

STATE OR OTHER AREA AND INSTITUTION	CONTROL AND TYPE OF INSTITUTION	TOTAL FTE OPENING FALL ENROLLMENT, FALL 1978	LIBRARY OPERATING EXPENDITURES (IN DOLLARS) 1978-79			BOOKSTOCK HELD AT END OF YEAR 1978-79		FTE STUDENTS PER FTE LIBRARY STAFF FALL 1979	
			PER FTE STUDENT, FALL 1978	PER FULL-TIME FACULTY MEMBER, 1978	AS PER-CENT OF GENERAL EXPENDI-TURES, 1978-79	VOLUMES PER FTE STUDENT, FALL 1978	TITLES (INCLU-DING MICRO-FORMS) PER FTE STUDENT 1978	TOTAL STAFF	PROFES-SIONAL STAFF
(1)	(2)	(3)	(4)	(5)	(6)	(7)	(8)	(9)	(10)
ALABAMA									
ALABAMA A & M UNIVERSITY	PUB-FG	3,751	157.8	2,358.8	3.4	66.2	71.3	121.0	288.5
ALABAMA CHRISTIAN COLLEGE	PRI-T	1,056	53.3	3,519.5	2.0	21.7	17.0	377.1	586.6
ALA LUTH ACAD AND COLLEGE	PRI-T	227	168.7	5,472.1	5.5	51.4	51.2	90.8	227.0
ALABAMA STATE UNIVERSITY	PUB-FG	4,229	172.5	4,449.5	7.0	40.4	32.8	143.3	234.9
ALEXANDER CITY STATE JC	PUB-T	913	153.5	3,789.4	7.0	35.3	30.7	107.4	228.2
ATHENS STATE COLLEGE	PUB-FN	949	103.7	2,525.5	3.5	66.1	52.7	189.8	316.3
AUBURN U ALL CAMPUSES									
AUBURN U MAIN CAMPUS	PUB-U	16,572	155.0	2,489.5	2.4	62.9	41.5	173.8	534.5
AUBURN U AT MONTGOMERY	PUB-FG	3,552	95.9	2,641.0	3.1	27.4	97.6	273.2	645.8
BIRMINGHAM STHN COLLEGE	PRI-FN	1,178	145.3	2,518.1	2.7	109.0	86.9	138.5	992.6
BOOKER T WASHINGTON BUS C	PRI-T	D	D	D	D	D	D	D	D
BREWER STATE JR COLLEGE	PUB-T	1,371	69.7	2,584.5	6.2	17.2	17.3	342.7	685.5
CHATTAHOOCHEE VALLEY CC	PUB-T	1,937	152.3	6,709.0	7.8	19.3	19.3	293.4	645.6
ENTERPRISE ST JR COLLEGE	PUB-T	1,524	135.7	5,910.8	7.5	20.3	20.3	217.7	304.8
FAULKNER STATE JR COLLEGE	PUB-T	1,386	82.4	3,088.6	4.3	23.7	22.3	346.5	1,386.0
GADSDEN STATE JR COLLEGE	PUB-T	3,046	73.0	1,986.6	3.8	18.3	14.5	276.9	1,015.3
GEO C WALLACE ST CC-DOTHN	PUB-T	1,550	106.8	3,066.1	6.9	20.9	20.7	221.4	387.5
GEO C WALLACE ST CC-HNCV	PUB-T	724	92.8	2,168.2	4.1	15.9	15.4	233.5	517.1
GEO C WALLACE ST CC-SELMA	PUB-T	1,462	79.7	2,243.0	3.8	14.9	13.6	292.4	417.7
HUNTINGDON COLLEGE	PRI-FN	626	168.6	2,707.7	4.2	154.8	145.2	118.1	145.5
JACKSONVL ST UNIVERSITY	PUB-FG	6,008	166.4	3,745.2	7.4	60.7	54.7	235.6	462.1
JEFFERSON DAVIS STATE JC	PUB-T	541	110.0	2,976.5	5.4	55.0	52.9	180.3	270.5
JEFFERSON ST JR COLLEGE	PUB-T	4,522	59.5	1,503.4	3.4	10.6	10.7	565.2	1,130.5
JOHN C CALHOUN ST CC	PUB-T	3,179	41.0	1,078.0	1.9	10.8	8.2	496.7	1,059.6
JUDSON COLLEGE	PRI-FN	308	166.4	1,831.0	3.7	171.6	168.6	68.4	308.0
LAWSON STATE CMTY COLLEGE	PUB-T	1,140	75.7	981.3	1.6	34.6	34.6	228.0	380.0
LIVINGSTON UNIVERSITY	PUB-FG	1,110	181.9	3,154.9	5.1	100.1	111.6	158.5	370.0
LOMAX-HANNON JC	PRI-T	160	77.2	2,059.5	2.7	69.9	66.0	133.3	160.0
LURLEEN B WALLACE ST JC	PUB-T	690	134.4	3,710.6	5.4	32.0	29.6	98.5	345.0
MARION MILITARY INSTITUTE	PRI-T	225	199.2	2,490.3	3.4	118.9	100.3	75.0	225.0
MILES COLLEGE	PRI-FN	1,149	151.4	A	2.9	68.2	67.3	127.6	383.0
MOBILE COLLEGE	PRI-FN	823	106.0	A	4.4	74.3	55.7	164.6	274.3
NTHEST ALA ST JR COLLEGE	PUB-T	1,223	68.4	3,807.9	3.8	31.1	29.0	436.7	679.4
NTHWST ALA ST JR COLLEGE	PUB-T	795	90.4	2,996.3	5.0	43.6	39.3	184.8	240.9
OAKWOOD COLLEGE	PRI-FN	1,229	165.4	3,280.6	A	66.6	64.0	133.5	307.2
PATRICK HENRY STATE JC	PUB-T	621	74.7	2,017.5	4.2	43.4	42.5	207.0	310.5
S D BISHOP ST JR COLLEGE	PUB-T	1,237	107.7	2,379.8	3.1	24.0	19.8	190.3	618.5
SAMFORD UNIVERSITY	PRI-FG	3,387	265.1	A	8.5	74.5	40.7	104.5	225.8
SELMA UNIVERSITY	PRI-FN	612	19.3	539.1	.7	24.4	54.1	197.4	612.0
SNEAD STATE JR COLLEGE	PUB-T	4,814	27.0	3,823.4	5.3	7.2	6.7	802.3	1,604.6
STHESTN BIBLE COLLEGE	PRI-FG	238	161.4	2,401.2	4.8	107.5	A	58.0	238.0
SOUTHERN JC OF BUSINESS	PRI-T	D	D	D	D	D	D	D	D
STHN UNION ST JR COLLEGE	PUB-T	1,116	96.2	3,356.0	4.6	51.3	51.7	180.0	558.0
STHN VOCATIONAL COLLEGE	PRI-T	D	D	D	D	D	D	D	D
SPRING HILL COLLEGE	PRI-FN	861	187.3	3,935.2	4.0	177.1	139.4	101.2	374.3
STILLMAN COLLEGE	PRI-FN	598	161.8	2,546.8	2.8	124.5	95.0	99.6	199.3
TALLADEGA COLLEGE	PRI-FN	679	137.0	2,068.0	2.5	100.6	97.8	157.9	339.5
TROY STATE U ALL CAM									
TROY STATE U MAIN CAMPUS	PUB-FG	5,565	83.9	2,582.1	4.0	32.6	30.7	229.9	795.0
TROY ST U DOTHN-FT RUCKER	PUB-FG	1,148	91.5	2,563.9	5.8	17.7	17.2	185.1	382.6
TROY STATE U MONTGOMERY	PUB-FG	1,786	33.7	1,673.0	3.0	5.5	4.1	714.4	893.0
TUSKEGEE INSTITUTE	PRI-FG	3,204	138.7	1,406.8	2.0	73.2	52.9	168.6	337.2
U OF ALABAMA ALL INST									
UNIVERSITY OF ALABAMA	PUB-U	15,365	149.4	3,494.8	3.0	68.4	23.6	162.5	432.8
U ALABAMA IN BIRMINGHAM	PUB-FG	10,069	220.0	3,775.4	1.7	61.5	32.7	128.7	370.1
U ALABAMA IN HUNTSVILLE	PUB-FG	3,433	205.3	4,170.6	3.9	72.2	67.0	117.9	429.1
UNIVERSITY OF MONTEVALLO	PUB-FG	2,455	98.1	1,839.7	2.6	60.8	59.0	306.8	613.7
U OF NORTH ALABAMA	PUB-FG	4,337	119.7	2,837.1	5.9	35.4	29.6	255.4	433.7
U OF SOUTH ALABAMA	PUB-FG	5,965	258.7	5,341.4	4.4	43.7	36.7	103.7	350.8
WALKER COLLEGE	PRI-T	552	91.9	2,538.9	5.2	35.2	34.6	276.0	276.0
ALASKA									
ALASKA BIBLE COLLEGE	PRI-FN	20	A	A	A	811.0	A	20.0	20.0
ALASKA PACIFIC UNIVERSITY	PRI FG		SEE U ALASKA ANCHORAGE JT LIB						
INUPIAT U OF THE ARCTIC	PRI-FN		NO LIBRARY FACILITIES						
SHELDON JACKSON COLLEGE	PRI-FN		SEE STRATTON JOINT LIBRARY						
STRATTON JOINT LIBRARY	PUB-T	D	D	D	D	D	D	D	D

SEE FOOTNOTES AT END OF TABLE

STATE OR OTHER AREA AND INSTITUTION (1)	CONTROL AND TYPE OF INSTITUTION (2)	TOTAL FTE OPENING FALL ENROLLMENT, FALL 1978 (3)	LIBRARY OPERATING EXPENDITURES (IN DOLLARS) 1978-79			BOOKSTOCK HELD AT END OF YEAR 1978-79		FTE STUDENTS PER FTE LIBRARY STAFF FALL 1979	
			PER FTE STUDENT, FALL 1978 (4)	PER FULL-TIME FACULTY MEMBER, 1978 (5)	AS PERCENT OF GENERAL EXPENDITURES, 1978-79 (6)	VOLUMES PER FTE STUDENT, FALL 1978 (7)	TITLES (INCLUDING MICROFORMS) PER FTE STUDENT 1978 (8)	TOTAL STAFF (9)	PROFESSIONAL STAFF (10)
ALASKA --CONTINUED									
U ALASKA ALL INSTITUTION									
U ALAS FAIRBANKS ALL CAM									
U ALASKA FAIRBANKS CAMPUS	PUB-U	2,522	879.5	8,434.2	3.2	173.0	A	47.5	148.3
U OF ALASKA TANANA VLY CC	PUB-T								
U ALAS ANCHORAGE ALL CAM			NO LIBRARY FACILITIES						
U ALAS ANCHORAGE CAMPUS	PUB FG		SEE U ALASKA ANCHORAGE JT LIB						
U OF ALASKA ANCHORAI CC	PUB T		SEE U ALASKA ANCHORAGE JT LIB						
U OF ALASKA KENAI CC	PUB-T	587	140.6	5,505.4	3.1	21.0	17.1	987.0	587.0
U OF ALASKA KODIAK CC	PUB-T	122	534.7	13,048.6	5.1	68.0	67.3	81.3	122.0
U OF ALASKA KUSKOKWIM CC	PUB-T	315	346.0	4,994.5	3.1	32.2	31.7	197.5	315.0
U ALAS MATANUSKA-SUSITNA	PUB-T	151	513.3	15,503.2	7.5	74.3	74.4	75.5	151.0
U ALASKA STHESTN ALL CAM									
U ALAS STHESTN SENIOR C	PUB FG		SEE U ALASKA JUNEAU JT LIB						
U OF ALAS JUNEAU-OGLS CC	PUB T		SEE U ALASKA JUNEAU JT LIB						
U OF ALASKA KETCHIKAN CC	PUB-T	135	536.4	12,070.5	5.3	193.1	.1	67.5	135.0
U OF ALASKA SITKA CC	PUB T								
U ALASKA ANCHORAGE JT LIB	PUB-FG	D	SEE STRATTON JOINT LIBRARY						
U OF ALASKA JUNEAU JT LIB	PUB-FG	D	D	D	D	D	D	D	D
ARIZONA									
AMER GRAD SCH OF MGMT	PRI-FG	918	A	A	A	75.8	59.9	183.6	306.0
ARIZONA C OF THE BIBLE	PRI-FN	D	D	D		D	D	D	D
ARIZONA STATE UNIVERSITY	PUB-U	28,101	163.7	3,577.7	4.2	54.6	A	169.6	578.2
ARIZONA WESTERN COLLEGE	PUB-T	1,942	70.2	2,068.1	3.1	18.0	17.5	277.4	971.0
CENTRAL ARIZONA COLLEGE	PUB-T	2,606	113.1	3,349.8	4.0	27.4	40.2	236.9	521.2
COCHISE COLLEGE	PUB-T	2,046	92.2	2,776.6	3.4	23.3	19.5	196.7	465.0
COLLEGE OF GANADO	PRI-T	154	242.1	1,776.0	2.8	97.5	82.4	51.3	77.0
DEVRY INST OF TECHNOLOGY	PRI-FN	D	D	D	D	D	D	D	D
EASTERN ARIZONA COLLEGE	PUB-T	1,890	69.3	1,724.3	A	20.6	19.6	540.0	540.0
GRAND CANYON COLLEGE	PRI-FN	883	101.5	2,803.0	3.1	132.4	124.6	196.2	441.5
MARICPA CO CC SYS ALL INST									
GLENDALE CMTY COLLEGE	PUB-T	6,278	74.9	2,960.4	4.1	10.4	9.5	272.9	1,046.3
MARICOPA TECH CC	PUB-T	1,853	86.9	2,731.6	3.2	21.5	16.2	298.8	926.5
MESA COMMUNITY COLLEGE	PUB-T	4,861	87.0	2,503.5	3.6	10.1	8.9	215.0	1,056.7
PHOENIX COLLEGE	PUB-T	4,130	116.1	2,837.9	3.7	22.6	15.9	211.7	550.6
SCOTTSDALE CMTY COLLEGE	PUB-T	3,259	76.4	2,965.3	3.8	9.6	9.2	325.9	724.2
MOHAVE COMMUNITY COLLEGE	PUB-T	1,159	136.0	3,753.4	5.3	16.5	15.1	193.1	579.5
NAVAJO COMMUNITY COLLEGE	PUB-T	D	D	D	D	D	D	D	D
NORTHERN ARIZ UNIVERSITY	PUB-FG	10,626	135.1	3,206.0	4.3	45.4	77.8	253.0	590.3
NORTHLAND PIONEER COLLEGE	PUB-T	1,596	123.4	A	6.2	8.7	7.9	199.5	798.0
PIMA COMMUNITY COLLEGE	PUB-T	11,004	66.1	3,164.2	3.2	8.8	7.4	333.4	1,222.6
PRESCOTT CENTER COLLEGE	PRI-FN	67	141.4	1,579.5	2.4	62.1	61.1	74.4	95.7
STHWSTN BAPT BIBLE C	PRI-FN	178	144.5	4,287.5	A	92.0	91.1	178.0	178.0
UNIVERSITY OF ARIZONA	PUB-U	22,560	269.7	4,338.0	3.5	62.5	41.7	114.5	388.9
UNIVERSITY OF PHOENIX	PRI-FG	D	D	D	D	D	D	D	D
YAVAPAI COLLEGE	PUB-T	1,747	138.0	3,952.3	4.0	22.8	18.9	134.3	582.3
ARKANSAS									
AMERICAN C OF COMMERCE	PRI-T	D	D	D	D	D	D	D	D
ARKANSAS BAPTIST COLLEGE	PRI-FN	D	D	D	D	D	D	D	D
ARKANSAS COLLEGE	PRI-FN	444	248.2	3,340.1	3.9	144.6	A	261.1	634.2
ARKANSAS STATE U ALL CAM									
ARKANSAS STATE U MAIN CAM	PUB-FG	5,988	151.1	2,855.6	5.0	58.7	82.6	213.8	598.8
ARKANSAS STATE U BEEBE BR	PUB-T	704	96.8	2,524.1	3.9	50.4	67.8	234.6	352.0
ARKANSAS TECH UNIVERSITY	PUB-FG	2,294	122.7	2,366.3	4.4	63.8	57.5	229.4	573.5
CAPITAL CITY BUS COLLEGE	PRI-T	561	41.3	A	3.3	10.5	10.3	561.0	561.0
CENTRAL BAPTIST COLLEGE	PRI-FN	212	84.4	1,492.5	4.5	90.0	72.8	176.6	212.0
COLLEGE OF THE OZARKS	PRI-FN	518	116.2	2,508.1	3.0	132.0	89.6	207.2	345.3
CROWLEY'S RIDGE COLLEGE	PRI-T	60	163.6	1,636.0	3.2	199.1	199.0	60.0	60.0
EAST ARK CMTY COLLEGE	PUB-T	499	214.3	5,347.8	5.1	14.3	12.3	124.7	166.3
GARLAND CO CMTY COLLEGE	PUB-T	814	137.6	4,308.2	A	16.7	11.4	142.8	407.0
HARDING U ALL CAM									
HARDING U MAIN CAM	PRI-FG	2,774	99.9	2,116.3	3.4	53.2	37.0	229.2	495.3
HARDING GRAD SCH RELIGION	PRI-FG	178	509.2	12,949.8	11.2	328.3	264.0	44.9	89.0
HENDERSON ST UNIVERSITY	PUB-FG	2,608	157.6	2,816.7	5.4	59.3	67.3	121.8	434.6
HENDRIX COLLEGE	PRI-FM	990	206.8	3,863.9	5.6	128.0	90.5	126.9	330.0
JOHN BROWN UNIVERSITY	PRI-FN	696	156.6	2,180.1	3.4	99.5	104.0	232.0	348.0

SEE FOOTNOTES AT END OF TABLE

STATE OR OTHER AREA AND INSTITUTION (1)	CONTROL AND TYPE OF INSTITUTION (2)	TOTAL FTE OPENING FALL ENROLLMENT, FALL 1978 (3)	LIBRARY OPERATING EXPENDITURES (IN DOLLARS) 1978-79			BOOKSTOCK HELD AT END OF YEAR 1978-79		FTE STUDENTS PER FTE LIBRARY STAFF FALL 1979	
			PER FTE STUDENT, FALL 1978 (4)	PER FULL-TIME FACULTY MEMBER, 1978 (5)	AS PERCENT OF GENERAL EXPENDITURES, 1978-79 (6)	VOLUMES PER FTE STUDENT, FALL 1978 (7)	TITLES (INCLUDING MICROFORMS) PER FTE STUDENT 1978 (8)	TOTAL STAFF (9)	PROFESSIONAL STAFF (10)
ARKANSAS	--CONTINUED								
MISS CO CMTY COLLEGE	PUB-T	553	168.2	3,100.5	6.2	12.7	13.0	138.2	276.5
NORTH ARKANSAS CC	PUB-T	587	147.4	3,933.2	5.1	16.9	20.2	225.7	366.8
OUACHITA BAPT UNIVERSITY	PRI-FG	1,471	142.9	2,286.3	4.2	72.4	210.1	163.4	735.5
PHILANDER SMITH COLLEGE	PRI-FN	499	55.6	992.0	1.5	120.4	128.8	216.9	216.9
PHILLIPS CO CMTY COLLEGE	PUB-T	1,102	100.6	2,175.0	3.4	26.5	21.5	275.5	367.3
SHORTER COLLEGE	PRI-T	D	D	D	D	D	D	D	D
STHN ARK U ALL CAMPUSES									
STHN ARK U MAIN CAMPUS	PUB-FG	1,667	149.3	2,828.2	4.7	61.2	60.9	256.4	370.4
STHN ARK U EL DORADO BR	PUB-T	231	325.1	6,259.0	8.9	17.8	17.7	77.0	231.0
STHN ARK U STHWST TECH	PUB-T	400	134.5	1,416.7	A	28.0	23.0	400.0	400.0
SOUTHERN BAPTIST COLLEGE	PRI-T	353	163.6	4,126.3					
U OF ARKANSAS ALL CAM					6.2	134.5	101.2	88.2	235.3
U OF ARKANSAS MAIN CAMPUS	PUB-U	13,873	142.2	2,949.3	2.6	63.2	53.6	195.3	513.8
U OF ARK AT LITTLE ROCK	PUB-FG	6,232	207.5	4,158.4	7.2	48.5	30.9	167.9	404.6
U OF ARK MEDL SCI CAMPUS	PUB-FG	1,169	630.6	8,572.9	2.0	99.3	29.4	26.9	89.9
U OF ARKANSAS-MONTICELLO	PUB-FN	1,549	139.4	2,273.8	3.5	48.4	31.1	221.2	516.3
U OF ARKANSAS PINE BLUFF	PUB-FN	2,704	172.4	2,664.7	3.5	44.5	32.6	108.1	300.4
U OF CENTRAL ARKANSAS	PUB-FG	9,633	66.6	3,648.0	5.7	28.7	22.9	458.7	1,070.3
WESTARK COMMUNITY COLLEGE	PUB-T	2,144	74.9	1,673.6	3.7	17.2	16.7	285.8	536.0
CALIFORNIA									
ALLAN HANCOCK COLLEGE	PUB-T	3,480	88.6	2,658.6	2.8	12.9	12.7	366.3	1,392.0
AMER ACAD DRAMATIC ARTS-W	PRI-T	211	12.6	D	.4	3.3	2.1	263.7	422.0
AMER BAPT SEM OF WEST	PRI FG		SEE GRAD THEOL UN JT LIB						
AMERICAN CONSV THEATRE	PRI-FG	D	D	D	D	D	D	D	D
ANTELOPE VALLEY COLLEGE	PUB-T	4,055	42.7	2,192.0	3.4	9.8	9.1	579.2	2,027.5
ARMSTRONG COLLEGE	PRI-FG	533	43.5	D	2.1	32.0	20.0	533.0	533.0
ART CTR COLLEGE OF DESIGN	PRI-FG	1,183	76.3	2,579.4	2.2	16.7	16.1	197.1	591.5
AZUSA PACIFIC COLLEGE	PRI-FG	1,849	146.4	3,760.9	4.1	43.6	145.8	168.0	264.1
BAKERSFIELD COLLEGE	PUB-T	5,924	58.5	1,355.0	2.0	10.3	8.2	262.1	897.5
BARSTOW COLLEGE	PUB-T	876	135.8	3,401.0	4.0	35.0	34.3	203.7	876.0
BETHANY BIBLE COLLEGE	PRI-FN	478	217.4	5,471.5	6.7	95.6	73.9	103.9	239.0
BIOLA COLLEGE	PRI-FG	2,722	114.3	2,637.5	3.4	60.9	58.0	230.6	716.3
BROOKS COLLEGE	PRI-T	688	23.6	1,630.0	.6	2.1	2.1	344.0	344.0
BROOKS INSTITUTE	PRI-FG	724	52.4	A	1.7	5.4	4.5	344.7	1,206.6
BUTTE COLLEGE	PUB-T	3,325	87.4	2,968.4	A	14.4	12.8	270.3	1,007.5
CABRILLO COLLEGE	PUB-T	4,524	100.2	2,349.1	3.9	11.0	11.3	443.5	870.0
CAL BAPTIST COLLEGE	PRI-FN	691	168.5	3,234.6	4.3	166.1	166.2	92.1	197.4
CALIFORNIA CHRISTIAN C	PRI-FN	21	124.0	521.2	1.9	427.3	383.3	70.0	70.0
CAL COLLEGE ARTS & CRAFTS	PRI-FG	D				D	D		
CAL COLLEGE PODIATRIC MED	PRI-FG	377	246.6	5,812.5	3.2	36.1	21.2	94.2	188.5
CALIFORNIA INST OF ARTS	PRI-FG	702	418.5	4,197.6	4.3	97.7	84.5	58.5	117.0
CAL INST OF ASIAN STUDIES	PRI-FG	88	192.6	4,238.0	5.7	215.9	210.2	176.0	176.0
CAL INST OF TECHNOLOGY	PRI-FG	1,652	767.1	5,028.8	1.9	204.6	A	70.5	150.1
CAL LUTHERAN COLLEGE	PRI-FG	1,744	111.8	2,673.1	3.0	52.0	44.1	200.4	415.2
CALIFORNIA MARITIME ACAD	PUB-FN	484	193.6	3,905.0	2.3	37.8	32.5	161.3	242.0
CAL SCH PROF PSYC ALL CAM									
CAL SCH PSYC BERKELEY	PRI-FG								
CAL SCH PROF PSYC FRESNO	PRI-FG	247	226.4	D	4.5	60.7	40.5	123.5	247.0
CAL SCH PROF PSYC LOS ANG	PRI-FG	139	318.4	D	6.9	45.6	36.5	46.3	139.0
CAL SCH PROF PSYC SN DEGO	PRI-FG	261	203.3	3,121.6	4.1	37.7	36.8	124.2	163.1
		238	193.7	D	4.1	33.9	31.2	132.2	238.0
CAL ST U & C SYS ALL INST									
CAL ST COLLEGE-BAKERSFLD	PUB-FG								
CAL STATE C-SN BERNARDINO	PUB-FG	2,096	360.8	5,109.9	5.4	93.6	79.7	98.4	299.4
CAL ST COLLEGE-STANISLAUS	PUB-FG	2,993	322.2	5,388.9	5.6	100.8	80.9	103.2	374.1
CAL POLY ST U-SN LUIS OB	PUB-FG	2,350	340.0	4,701.2	5.4	82.2	74.0	106.8	293.7
		14,569	149.5	2,760.8	4.1	37.7	37.3	194.2	520.3
CAL STATE POLY U-POMONA	PUB-FG								
CAL STATE U-CHICO	PUB-FG	12,045	156.0	3,224.4	4.2	28.4	18.6	215.0	860.3
CAL STATE U-DOMINGUEZ HLS	PUB-FG	11,868	168.3	3,280.7	4.0	46.4	42.0	189.5	447.8
CAL STATE U-FRESNO	PUB-FG	5,928	244.5	9,407.6	6.1	41.6	68.5	141.7	394.8
CAL STATE U-FULLERTON	PUB-FG	12,374	183.6	3,495.8	4.7	46.5	29.9	183.3	458.2
		15,446	158.1	3,640.9	4.6	31.5	22.3	205.3	541.9
CAL STATE U-HAYWARD	PUB-FG								
CAL STATE U-LONG BEACH	PUB-FG	8,145	199.5	3,564.7	4.6	81.8	53.5	172.9	407.2
CAL STATE U-LOS ANGELES	PUB-FG	23,339	132.2	3,202.4	3.9	30.7	A	233.6	606.2
CAL STATE U-NORTHRIDGE	PUB-FG	16,185	161.1	3,473.7	3.9	46.3	30.9	208.0	578.0
CAL STATE U-SACRAMENTO	PUB-FG	20,847	129.5	3,193.9	4.2	33.1	22.4	225.3	641.4
		16,343	155.6	3,109.6	4.3	38.8	30.2	215.0	680.9
HUMBOLDT STATE U	PUB-FG	6,606	208.8	3,640.0	4.5	38.8	78.1	158.7	574.4

SEE FOOTNOTES AT END OF TABLE

STATE OR OTHER AREA AND INSTITUTION	CON-TROL AND TYPE OF IN-STITU-TION	TOTAL FTE OPENING FALL ENROLL-MENT, FALL 1978	LIBRARY OPERATING EXPENDITURES (IN DOLLARS) 1978-79			BOOKSTOCK HELD AT END OF YEAR 1978-79		FTE STUDENTS PER FTE LIBRARY STAFF FALL 1979	
			PER FTE STU-DENT, FALL 1978	PER FULL-TIME FAC-ULTY MEM-BER, 1978	AS PER-CENT OF GENERAL EXPENDI-TURES, 1978-79	VOLUMES PER FTE STUDENT, FALL 1978	TITLES (INCLU-DING MICRO-FORMS) PER FTE STUDENT 1978	TOTAL STAFF	PROFES-SIONAL STAFF
(1)	(2)	(3)	(4)	(5)	(6)	(7)	(8)	(9)	(10)
CALIFORNIA	--CONTINUED								
SAN DIEGO STATE U	PUB-FG	24,071	146.1	3,265.8	4.0	31.3	30.6	225.1	607.8
SAN FRANCISCO STATE U	PUB-FG	18,844	147.1	3,439.5	4.0	29.6	19.6	216.8	617.8
SAN JOSE STATE U	PUB-FG	20,955	133.7	3,020.7	3.7	33.2	23.7	206.4	469.8
SONOMA STATE UNIVERSITY	PUB-FG	4,436	261.4	4,113.1	4.7	64.7	113.3	132.4	328.5
CAL WESTERN SCHOOL OF LAW	PRI-FG	685	439.5	15,054.3	15.9	99.4	25.8	.0	A
CENTER FOR EARLY ED	PRI-FG	25	1,158.6	905.1	4.3	444.0	384.6	19.2	25.0
CERRITOS COLLEGE	PUB-T	8,335	72.7	2,306.4	2.9	8.0	7.1	368.8	1,634.3
CERRO COSO CMTY COLLEGE	PUB-T	1,419	120.7	7,141.8	5.8	11.2	10.3	157.6	567.6
CHABOT COLLEGE	PUB-T	7,342	127.8	3,831.9	5.9	14.8	14.7	244.7	772.8
CHAFFEY COLLEGE	PUB-T	5,888	41.7	1,241.7	1.6	11.3	9.8	600.8	1,369.3
CHAPMAN COLLEGE	PRI-FG	3,431	77.9	2,972.0	1.9	43.6	38.8	320.6	581.5
CHRIST COLLEGE IRVINE	PRI-FN	122	526.5	6,423.7	8.6	444.2	390.4	55.4	61.0
CHRISTIAN HERITAGE C	PRI-FN	464	185.3	6,616.0	5.2	76.7	69.5	77.3	232.0
CHURCH DIV SCH OF PACIFIC	PRI FG		SEE GRAD THEOL UN JT LIB						
CITRUS COLLEGE	PUB-T	4,358	65.0	2,360.8	2.9	17.4	16.2	269.0	1,281.7
CLAREMONT U SYS ALL INST									
CLAREMONT GRADUATE SCHOOL	PRI FG		SEE HONNOLD JOINT LIBRARY						
CLAREMONT MEN'S COLLEGE	PRI FN		SEE HONNOLD JOINT LIBRARY						
HARVEY MUDD COLLEGE	PRI FG		SEE HONNOLD JOINT LIBRARY						
PITZER COLLEGE	PRI FN		SEE HONNOLD JOINT LIBRARY						
POMONA COLLEGE	PRI FN		SEE HONNOLD JOINT LIBRARY						
SCRIPPS COLLEGE	PRI FN		SEE HONNOLD JOINT LIBRARY						
COAST CC SYS ALL INST									
COASTLINE CMTY COLLEGE1/	PUB-T		NO LIBRARY FACILITIES						
GOLDEN WEST COLLEGE	PUB-T	10,308	53.0	2,443.5	3.8	8.4	7.8	569.5	1,212.7
ORANGE COAST COLLEGE	PUB-T	13,292	41.0	1,727.8	2.5	6.9	6.0	626.9	1,329.2
COGSWELL COLLEGE	PRI-FN	374	89.0	1,585.0	1.6	25.1	23.6	311.6	374.0
COLEMAN COLLEGE	PRI-FN	424	69.7	A	2.0	8.6	8.4	192.7	385.4
COLLEGE OF THE CANYONS	PUB-T	1,263	188.7	6,811.6	5.8	28.1	28.0	138.7	631.5
COLLEGE OF THE DESERT	PUB-T	2,026	32.6	636.8	.7	22.8	A	440.4	1,266.2
COLLEGE OF MARIN	PUB-T	3,843	81.4	2,018.9	2.9	19.4	15.1	300.4	753.5
COLLEGE OF NOTRE DAME	PRI-FG	896	125.4	2,675.7	4.2	98.7	A	160.0	448.0
COLLEGE OSTEO MED PACIFIC	PRI-FG	36	1,498.2	D	7.8	50.0	41.6	20.0	36.0
COLLEGE OF THE REDWOODS	PUB-T	4,023	35.2	1,405.2	1.3	14.4	10.9	618.9	2,011.5
COLLEGE OF THE SEQUOIAS	PUB-T	3,876	49.8	1,583.7	2.1	18.2	16.2	680.0	1,550.4
COLLEGE OF THE SISKIYOUS	PUB-T	877	122.0	2,276.5	3.2	32.9	31.0	159.4	674.6
COLUMBIA COLLEGE	PUB-T	1,028	128.7	3,675.5	A	27.4	24.3	205.6	1,028.0
COMPTON CMTY COLLEGE	PUB-T	D	D	D	D	D	D	D	D
CNTR CSTA CC ALL INST									
CONTRA COSTA COLLEGE	PUB-T	4,220	72.1	2,294.5	2.6	13.7	13.6	468.8	844.0
DIABLO VALLEY COLLEGE	PUB-T	10,139	76.5	3,221.6	4.4	7.2	6.2	422.4	1,283.4
LOS MEDANOS COLLEGE	PUB-T	2,107	182.6	6,414.9	6.1	5.0	4.1	159.6	526.7
CRAFTON HILLS COLLEGE	PUB-T	1,358	111.5	5,222.7	4.8	49.1	39.7	301.7	679.0
CUESTA COLLEGE	PUB-T	2,686	106.4	3,970.2	4.5	12.3	11.1	209.8	624.6
CYPRESS COLLEGE	PUB-T	7,125	35.9	1,315.0	1.8	7.8	6.9	742.1	1,548.9
D-Q UNIVERSITY	PRI-T	D	D	D	D	D	D	D	D
DEEP SPRINGS COLLEGE	PRI-T	24	62.5	A	.7	750.0	666.6	48.0	48.0
DOMINICAN C OF SAN RAFAEL	PRI-FG	485	212.3	2,574.4	5.2	161.5	118.6	97.0	138.5
DOMINICAN SCH PHIL & THEO	PRI FG		SEE GRAD THEOL UN JT LIB						
DON BOSCO TECHNICAL INST	PRI-T	322	134.4	D	3.6	50.4	50.1	161.0	322.0
EL CAMINO COLLEGE	PUB-T	13,455	30.9	1,226.6	1.7	7.1	6.6	868.0	2,446.3
FASH INST DESIGN & MERCH	PRI-T	D	D	D	D	D	D	D	D
FIELDING INSTITUTE	PRI-FG	D	D	D	D	D	D	D	D
FOOTHL-DEANZA CC ALL INST			NO LIBRARY FACILITIES						
DE ANZA COLLEGE	PUB-T	9,050	81.7	2,824.7	3.3	8.1	6.2	309.9	1,587.7
FOOTHILL COLLEGE	PUB-T	7,206	73.2	2,867.9	3.0	14.1	11.9	389.5	1,310.1
FRANCISCAN SCH THEOLOGY	PRI FG		SEE GRAD THEOL UN JT LIB						
FRESNO PACIFIC COLLEGE	PRI FG		SEE MENNONITE-PACIFIC JT LIB						
FULLER THEOLOGICAL SEM	PRI-FG	1,298	204.1	7,572.7	4.8	86.6	78.4	133.8	350.8
FULLERTON COLLEGE	PUB-T	9,272	71.8	2,663.0	3.5	9.9	8.3	412.0	1,030.2
GAVILAN COLLEGE	PUB-T	1,301	92.3	2,224.4	2.6	31.4	29.6	302.5	650.5
GLENDALE CMTY COLLEGE	PUB-T	4,021	83.7	2,738.7	3.5	16.0	14.0	293.5	957.3
GOLDEN GATE BAPT SEMINARY	PRI-FG	D	D	D	D	D	D	D	D
GOLDEN GATE UNIVERSITY2/	PRI-FG	3,898	109.2	8,690.8	3.8	29.6	23.3	.0	A
GRADUATE THEOL UNION	PRI FG		SEE GRAD THEOL UN JT LIB						
GRAD THEOL UN JT LIBRARY	PRI-FG	D	D	D	D	D	D	D	D

SEE FOOTNOTES AT END OF TABLE

Table 3. – Indexes Concerning Operating Expenditures, 1978-79, Bookstock Held at End of Year, 1978-79, and Library Staff (FTE), Fall 1979, College and University Libraries, by State or Other Area and Institution: Aggregate United States – Continued

STATE OR OTHER AREA AND INSTITUTION (1)	CONTROL AND TYPE OF INSTITUTION (2)	TOTAL FTE OPENING FALL ENROLLMENT, FALL 1978 (3)	LIBRARY OPERATING EXPENDITURES (IN DOLLARS) 1978-79			BOOKSTOCK HELD AT END OF YEAR 1978-79		FTE STUDENTS PER FTE LIBRARY STAFF FALL 1979	
			PER FTE STUDENT, FALL 1978 (4)	PER FULL-TIME FACULTY MEMBER, 1978 (5)	AS PERCENT OF GENERAL EXPENDITURES, 1978-79 (6)	VOLUMES PER FTE STUDENT, FALL 1978 (7)	TITLES (INCLUDING MICROFORMS) PER FTE STUDENT 1978 (8)	TOTAL STAFF (9)	PROFESSIONAL STAFF (10)
CALIFORNIA	--CONTINUED								
GROSSMONT COLLEGE	PUB-T	7,652	114.6	4,156.8	5.1	11.5	A	249.2	1,048.2
HARTNELL COLLEGE	PUB-T	3,121	123.3	3,348.3	3.7	21.3	19.5	243.8	725.8
HEALD ENGR COLLEGE	PRI-FN	D	D	D	D	D	D	D	D
HOLY FAMILY COLLEGE	PRI-FN	70	475.7	D	25.4	525.9	394.9	38.6	46.6
HOLY NAMES COLLEGE	PRI-FG	437	194.3	1,807.4	3.0	200.5	172.9	87.4	124.8
HONNOLD JOINT LIBRARY	PRI-FG	D	D	D	D	D	D	D	D
HUMANISTIC PSYC INST	PRI-FG	D	D	D	D	D	D	D	D
HUMPHREYS COLLEGE	PRI-T	341	63.2	2,695.6	3.3	43.7	40.4	200.5	341.0
IMMACULATE HEART COLLEGE	PRI-FG	464	164.4	A	3.3	318.2	247.5	96.6	132.5
IMPERIAL VALLEY COLLEGE	PUB-T	2,688	76.1	2,177.9	2.5	16.5	15.0	316.2	1,344.0
INDIAN VALLEY COLLEGES	PUB-T	1,425	110.8	3,158.9	3.2	22.1	19.0	175.9	395.8
INTERNATIONAL COLLEGE	PRI-FG	NO LIBRARY FACILITIES							
JESUIT SCHOOL OF THEOLOGY	PRI FG	SEE GRAD THEOL UN JT LIB							
JOHN F KENNEDY UNIVERSITY	PRI-FG	734	139.8	25,654.0	6.3	34.5	20.3	122.3	367.0
LAKE TAHOE CMTY COLLEGE	PUB-T	516	331.3	11,399.0	A	34.0	30.7	129.0	516.0
LASSEN COLLEGE	PUB-T	1,224	117.0	3,332.5	3.6	10.7	10.5	235.3	1,224.0
LIFE BIBLE COLLEGE	PRI-FN	450	155.5	8,747.2	7.5	30.5	27.8	83.3	450.0
LINCOLN UNIVERSITY	PRI-FG	649	192.6	20,840.6	A	50.6	21.1	147.5	324.5
LOMA LINDA UNIVERSITY	PRI-FG	4,368	264.6	3,389.7	3.3	81.5	A	89.8	222.8
LONG BEACH CITY COLLEGE	PUB-T	13,017	38.1	A		9.4	A	1,009.0	1,759.0
LOS ANGELES BAPT COLLEGE	PRI-FN	366	128.7	1,963.7	3.9	82.7	78.9	166.3	366.0
LOS ANG C OF CHIROPRACTIC	PRI-FG	689	100.1	2,655.0	3.4	17.5	13.4	229.6	689.0
LOS ANG CC SYS ALL INST									
EAST LOS ANGELES COLLEGE	PUB-T	8,317	40.5	1,581.7	A	9.1	9.3	607.0	1,459.1
LOS ANGELES CITY COLLEGE	PUB-T	11,068	27.1	1,015.7	A	12.5	11.4	737.8	1,651.9
LOS ANG HARBOR COLLEGE	PUB-T	6,171	41.7	1,463.4	A	12.0	A	636.1	1,667.8
LOS ANGELES MISSION C	PUB-T	1,091	256.0	5,477.8	A	23.8	A	114.8	311.7
LOS ANG PIERCE COLLEGE	PUB-T	11,542	38.0	1,438.4	A	8.5	8.3	699.5	2,137.4
LOS ANG SOUTHWEST COLLEGE	PUB-T	3,562	68.9	2,758.9	A	17.5	18.4	299.3	516.2
LOS ANG TR TECH COLLEGE	PUB-T	8,325	37.9	1,321.4	A	10.6	9.7	756.8	1,387.5
LOS ANG VALLEY COLLEGE	PUB-T	11,055	28.6	1,169.4	A	10.4	9.5	789.6	1,650.0
WEST LOS ANGELES COLLEGE	PUB-T	4,689	87.9	4,338.9	A	10.4	10.2	275.8	721.3
LOS RIOS CC SYS ALL INST									
AMERICAN RIVER COLLEGE	PUB-T	11,027	32.4	1,242.2	2.0	6.7	A	706.8	1,670.7
COSUMNES RIVER COLLEGE	PUB-T	2,470	134.7	3,914.6	6.5	24.8	19.5	168.0	667.5
SACRAMENTO CITY COLLEGE	PUB-T	7,650	65.0	1,975.2	3.6	11.0	A	566.6	1,275.0
LOYOLA MARYMOUNT U	PRI-FG	10,271	121.0	5,625.3	6.6	37.4	23.3	216.2	586.9
MARYMOUNT PALOS VERDES C	PRI-T	337	173.3	9,733.8	4.5	94.5	90.1	112.3	168.5
MELODYLAND SCH THEOLOGY	PRI-FG	350	127.8	A	7.7	81.7	68.7	116.6	116.6
MENDOCINO COLLEGE	PUB-T	864	116.8	2,803.8	2.7	17.0	16.5	216.0	576.0
MENLO COLLEGE	PRI-FN	617	112.3	A	2.9	71.1	56.7	154.2	308.5
MENNONITE BRTHREN BIB SEM	PRI FG	SEE MENNONITE-PACIFIC JT LIB							
MENNONITE-PACIFIC JT LIB	PRI-FG	D	D	D	D	D	D	D	D
MERCED COLLEGE	PUB-T	3,885	72.3	2,361.0	3.4	9.3	8.6	287.7	1,554.0
MILLS COLLEGE	PRI-FG	955	310.1	4,855.4	4.0	194.4	122.7	98.4	191.0
MIRA COSTA COLLEGE	PUB-T	2,794	79.8	3,233.4	2.9	9.5	9.0	393.5	846.6
MODESTO JUNIOR COLLEGE	PUB-T	5,109	62.5	1,521.1	A	11.9	9.5	352.3	1,277.2
MONTEREY INTRNATL STDIES	PRI-FG	361	363.2	A	A	107.7	80.7	.0	A
MONTEREY PEN COLLEGE	PUB-T	3,698	42.9	1,498.1	1.7	17.5	20.3	462.2	1,607.8
MOUNT SNT MARY'S COLLEGE	PRI-FG	953	247.6	3,522.4	5.9	136.3	102.5	76.2	173.2
MOUNT SAN ANTONIO COLLEGE	PUB-T	9,595	117.0	4,099.1	5.1	9.3	7.5	195.4	799.5
MT SAN JACINTO COLLEGE	PUB-T	1,969	53.7	2,462.9	3.9	15.9	15.6	437.5	3,938.0
NAPA COLLEGE	PUB-T	2,749	117.4	3,937.4	4.5	15.7	19.7	654.5	2,290.8
NATIONAL UNIVERSITY	PRI-FG	3,033	66.4	15,506.0	2.8	3.1	2.9	356.8	758.2
NEW COLLEGE OF CALIFORNIA	PRI-FG	677	44.9	4,342.8	2.6	22.1	9.8	677.0	677.0
NORTHROP UNIVERSITY	PRI-FG	993	113.3	1,730.9	1.9	139.7	152.1	187.3	300.9
NYINGMA INSTITUTE	PRI-FG	D	D	D	D	D	D	D	D
OCCIDENTAL COLLEGE	PRI-FG	1,690	371.8	5,610.6	5.5	194.6	154.4	72.2	192.0
OHLONE COLLEGE	PUB-T	5,524	139.9	5,421.1	7.3	13.8	12.5	156.6	640.7
OTIS ART INST PARSON SCH	PRI-FG	173	359.0	A		A	A	86.5	86.5
PACIFIC CHRISTIAN COLLEGE	PRI-FG	556	139.2	5,529.7	4.1	74.7	65.0	222.4	278.0
PACIFIC LUTH THEOL SEM	PRI FG	SEE GRAD THEOL UN JT LIB							
PACIFIC OAKS COLLEGE	PRI-FG	116	411.6	2,652.9	3.8	205.1	203.4	38.6	116.0
PACIFIC SCH OF RELIGION	PRI-FG	SEE GRAD THEOL UN JT LIB							
PACIFIC UNION COLLEGE	PRI-FG	2,083	156.1	2,756.4	4.4	48.6	62.0	226.4	297.9
PALOMAR COLLEGE	PUB-T	7,638	89.7	3,625.5	3.4	16.3	A	209.8	942.9

SEE FOOTNOTES AT END OF TABLE

Table 3. — Indexes Concerning Operating Expenditures, 1978-79, Bookstock Held at End of Year, 1978-79, and Library Staff (FTE), Fall 1979, College and University Libraries, by State or Other Area and Institution: Aggregate United States — Continued

STATE OR OTHER AREA AND INSTITUTION	CON-TROL AND TYPE OF IN-STITU-TION	TOTAL FTE OPENING FALL ENROLL-MENT, FALL 1978	LIBRARY OPERATING EXPENDITURES (IN DOLLARS) 1978-79			BOOKSTOCK HELD AT END OF YEAR 1978-79		FTE STUDENTS PER FTE LIBRARY STAFF FALL 1979	
			PER FTE STU-DENT, FALL 1978	PER FULL-TIME FAC-ULTY MEM-BER, 1978	AS PER-CENT OF GENERAL EXPENDI-TURES, 1978-79	VOLUMES PER FTE STUDENT, FALL 1978	TITLES (INCLU-DING MICRO-FORMS) PER FTE STUDENT 1978	TOTAL STAFF	PROFES-SIONAL STAFF
(1)	(2)	(3)	(4)	(5)	(6)	(7)	(8)	(9)	(10)
CALIFORNIA	--CONTINUED								
PALO VERDE COLLEGE	PUB-T	351	152.5	3,149.8	4.9	42.1	42.1	140.4	140.4
PASADENA CITY COLLEGE	PUB-T	11,632	43.6	1,506.6	1.9	9.7	6.8	680.2	1,615.5
PASADENA COLLEGE CHIRO	PRI-FG	193	92.7	1,628.0	3.7	27.3	23.3	193.0	193.0
PATTEN COLLEGE	PRI-FN	79	308.0	8,112.0	15.8	221.6	A	39.5	39.5
PEPPERDINE UNIVERSITY2/	PRI-FG	5,723	119.7	3,827.4	1.8	38.8	34.5	332.7	743.2
PERALTA CC SYS ALL INST									
COLLEGE OF ALAMEDA	PUB-T	4,512	74.2	3,988.7	4.3	8.3	5.8	372.8	1,100.4
FEATHER RIVER COLLEGE	PUB-T	399	73.0	1,388.6	1.8	33.6	29.8	399.0	399.0
LANEY COLLEGE	PUB-T	6,142	68.2	2,216.6	3.1	11.0	9.9	438.7	944.9
MERRITT COLLEGE	PUB-T	4,634	67.1	2,117.5	3.3	12.6	12.7	382.9	926.8
VISTA COLLEGE	PUB-T	D	D	D	D	D	D	D	D
POINT LOMA COLLEGE	PRI-FG	1,655	351.7	7,013.9	A	97.8	49.1	132.6	236.2
PORTERVILLE COLLEGE	PUB-T	1,295	58.4	1,262.4	1.7	15.6	15.6	323.7	1,295.0
RAND GRAD INST POL STDIES	PRI-FG	42	18,483.9	D	A	1,995.0	5,418.0	1.3	4.6
RIO HONDO COLLEGE	PUB-T	3,889	108.5	1,945.9	3.4	19.2	17.0	216.0	598.3
RIVERSIDE CITY COLLEGE	PUB-T	7,794	50.7	2,299.1	2.9	9.4	8.5	526.6	1,146.1
SADDLEBACK CMTY COLLEGE	PUB-T	6,565	66.3	3,044.2	1.7	14.1	10.9	364.7	820.6
SAINT JOHN'S COLLEGE	PRI-FG	209	126.9	D	5.2	241.6	189.0	209.0	A
SNT MARY'S COLLEGE OF CAL	PRI-FG	1,993	84.6	2,908.2	A	64.3	63.0	255.5	398.6
SAINT PATRICK'S COLLEGE	PRI-FN	45	772.2	11,583.3	11.4	1,333.1	1,288.8	26.4	64.2
SAINT PATRICK'S SEMINARY	PRI-FG	78	546.2	.0	10.0	718.3	697.8	39.0	39.0
SN BERNARDINO VLY COLLEGE	PUB-T	7,241	51.7	1,835.3	2.6	16.0	11.2	482.7	1,448.2
SAN DIEGO CC ALL CAMPUSES									
SAN DIEGO CITY COLLEGE	PUB-T	3,357	140.1	2,997.6	4.8	16.6	A	197.4	588.9
SAN DIEGO EVENING C	PUB-T			NO LIBRARY FACILITIES					
SAN DIEGO MESA COLLEGE	PUB-T	6,234	63.0	1,763.0	3.4	13.3	10.1	331.5	1,176.2
SAN DIEGO MIRAMAR COLLEGE	PUB-T	465	130.6	3,791.5	3.5	6.5	6.5	155.0	465.0
SAN FERNANDO VALLEY C LAW	PRI-FG	264	675.7	11,893.2	13.9	155.1	70.3	132.0	132.0
SAN FRANCISCO ART INST	PRI-FG	755	137.2	3,453.5	3.6	30.0	26.7	132.4	279.6
SN FRISCO CC DISTRICT	PUB-T	D	D	D	D	D	D	D	D
SAN FRANCISCO CONSV MUSIC	PRI-FG	187	251.9	3,364.7	3.0	87.2	83.7	51.9	103.8
SAN FRANCISCO THEOL SEM	PRI FG		SEE GRAD THEOL UN JT LIB						
SAN JOAQUIN DELTA COLLEGE	PUB-T	3,989	110.9	2,148.8	2.7	17.1	A	249.3	797.8
SAN JOSE BIBLE COLLEGE	PRI-FN	169	204.7	4,325.5	7.2	172.4	150.0	112.6	112.6
SAN JOSE CC ALL INST									
EVERGREEN VALLEY COLLEGE	PUB-T	3,351	133.5	5,735.9	3.5	8.6	7.5	198.2	567.9
SAN JOSE CITY COLLEGE	PUB-T	6,321	58.2	2,750.0	2.1	10.6	9.4	501.6	1,108.9
SAN MATEO CC SYS ALL INST									
CANADA COLLEGE	PUB-T	3,141	76.5	2,641.2	3.0	14.8	14.4	345.1	1,047.0
COLLEGE OF SAN MATEO	PUB-T	7,299	31.1	1,037.5	1.4	15.0	13.7	912.3	1,824.7
SKYLINE COLLEGE	PUB-T	3,552	63.6	2,380.4	2.6	12.5	9.5	634.2	1,184.0
SANTA ANA COLLEGE	PUB-T	6,802	45.5	1,302.7	1.2	12.1	11.7	523.2	1,360.4
SANTA BARBARA CTY COLLEGE	PUB-T	5,249	53.6	1,863.7	2.0	15.0	13.0	546.7	1,141.0
SANTA MONICA COLLEGE	PUB-T	9,160	35.8	1,607.4	1.9	10.7	10.6	796.5	1,665.4
SANTA ROSA JUNIOR COLLEGE	PUB-T	6,371	45.6	1,546.7	1.4	13.0	11.7	606.7	1,592.7
SCH OF THEO AT CLAREMONT	PRI-FG	192	780.9	9,371.5	9.3	593.1	474.0	18.2	25.6
SHASTA COLLEGE	PUB-T	5,221	53.9	2,026.7	A	11.7	A	352.7	2,175.4
SIERRA COLLEGE	PUB-T	3,663	68.0	1,903.0	1.7	15.4	13.9	305.2	1,221.0
SIMPSON COLLEGE	PRI-FG	290	152.2	2,103.1	5.3	168.2	129.9	96.6	145.0
SOLANO COMMUNITY COLLEGE	PUB-T	4,420	26.6	942.4	1.1	7.6	7.0	884.0	2,210.0
SOUTHERN CAL COLLEGE	PRI-FN	601	131.6	3,043.9	4.3	97.2	78.3	162.4	273.1
STHN CAL C OF OPTOMETRY	PRI-FG	413	176.3	2,698.1	2.4	A	23.5	121.4	413.0
STHN CAL INSTITUTE ARCH	PRI-FG	318	94.6	1,672.8	4.3	4.8	4.6	318.0	318.0
SOUTHWESTERN COLLEGE	PUB-T	5,882	80.6	2,695.2	3.9	10.0	8.7	336.1	1,050.3
STHWSTN U SCHOOL OF LAW	PRI-FG	1,276	434.5	14,218.6	10.8	55.8	16.8	58.0	122.6
STANFORD UNIVERSITY	PRI-U	11,862	1,070.7	14,255.5	A	385.9	A	.0	A
STARR KNG SCH FOR MINSTRY	PRI FG		SEE GRAD THEOL UN JT LIB						
STATE CTR CC SYS ALL INST									
FRESNO CITY COLLEGE	PUB-T	8,344	49.4	1,840.5	2.8	5.8	5.8	397.3	1,668.8
REEDLEY COLLEGE	PUB-T	1,784	105.0	2,432.9	3.4	15.6	14.6	169.9	396.4
TAFT COLLEGE	PUB-T	421	161.7	3,405.8	1.7	60.4	56.0	65.7	421.0
US INTERNATIONAL U	PRI-FG	2,915	95.4	A	A	78.9	78.8	208.2	485.8
U CAL SYSW ADMIN ALL CAM									
U OF CAL-BERKELEY	PUB-U	27,564	526.8	9,616.4	5.2	197.3	143.0	63.3	179.8
U OF CAL-DAVIS	PUB-FG	16,882	445.3	8,400.9	3.8	90.3	53.7	67.4	253.8
U OF CAL HASTINGS C LAW	PUB-FG	1,490	399.8	A	8.5	132.4	23.9	119.2	212.8

SEE FOOTNOTES AT END OF TABLE

138

Table 3. — Indexes Concerning Operating Expenditures, 1978-79, Bookstock Held at End of Year, 1978-79, and Library Staff (FTE), Fall 1979, College and University Libraries, by State or Other Area and Institution: Aggregate United States — Continued

STATE OR OTHER AREA AND INSTITUTION	CONTROL AND TYPE OF INSTITUTION	TOTAL FTE OPENING FALL ENROLLMENT, FALL 1978	LIBRARY OPERATING EXPENDITURES (IN DOLLARS) 1978-79			BOOKSTOCK HELD AT END OF YEAR 1978-79		FTE STUDENTS PER FTE LIBRARY STAFF FALL 1979	
			PER FTE STUDENT, FALL 1978	PER FULL-TIME FACULTY MEMBER, 1978	AS PERCENT OF GENERAL EXPENDITURES, 1978-79	VOLUMES PER FTE STUDENT, FALL 1978	TITLES (INCLUDING MICROFORMS) PER FTE STUDENT 1978	TOTAL STAFF	PROFESSIONAL STAFF
(1)	(2)	(3)	(4)	(5)	(6)	(7)	(8)	(9)	(10)
CALIFORNIA	--CONTINUED								
U OF CAL-IRVINE	PUB-FG	9,430	539.2	12,744.1	5.6	94.0	65.3	75.5	230.0
U OF CAL-LOS ANGELES	PUB-U	30,475	434.5	8,381.5	3.5	134.8	A	78.2	213.8
U OF CAL-RIVERSIDE	PUB-FG	4,391	1,057.1	15,422.3	7.4	215.8	125.2	33.8	159.0
U OF CAL-SAN DIEGO	PUB-FG	10,507	611.1	12,868.0	3.4	A	84.5	55.2	229.4
U OF CAL-SAN FRANCISCO	PUB-FG	3,710	458.1	8,672.3	1.0	123.1	68.8	55.7	208.4
U OF CAL-SANTA BARBARA	PUB-FG	14,025	422.1	9,280.5	6.5	94.4	101.3	78.3	264.6
U OF CAL-SANTA CRUZ	PUB-FG	5,544	488.9	8,290.4	5.8	107.3	46.5	74.1	210.7
UNIVERSITY OF JUDAISM	PRI-FG	104	995.1	34,500.0	7.1	1,201.9	1,061.0	20.8	52.0
UNIVERSITY OF LA VERNE	PRI-FG	2,855	251.4	8,444.6	5.8	58.2	42.5	185.9	515.4
UNIVERSITY OF THE PACIFIC	PRI-U	5,670	147.2	2,364.4	2.4	A	A	185.9	515.4
UNIVERSITY OF REDLANDS	PRI-FG	3,247	114.6	2,953.3	3.7	79.1	58.5	263.9	541.1
UNIVERSITY OF SAN DIEGO2/	PRI-FG	3,294	282.9	6,131.5	6.6	104.4	57.7	110.5	253.3
U OF SAN FRANCISCO	PRI-FG	5,143	206.7	A	A	95.2	61.4	155.8	354.6
UNIVERSITY OF SANTA CLARA	PRI-U	5,712	223.6	5,604.1	6.0	63.0	39.3	150.3	317.3
U OF SOUTHERN CALIFORNIA	PRI-U	21,253	280.3	5,819.5	2.5	91.7	76.1	98.3	259.8
U OF WEST LOS ANGELES	PRI-FG	429	124.9	A	A	44.2	3.8	429.0	429.0
VENTURA CO CC SYS INST									
MOORPARK COLLEGE	PUB-T	4,572	31.9	1,228.6	1.5	12.5	12.2	774.9	2,078.1
OXNARD COLLEGE	PUB-T	2,014	68.1	3,193.7	2.7	10.4	10.4	402.8	1,007.0
VENTURA COLLEGE	PUB-T	6,571	50.1	2,257.6	2.5	10.0	7.4	.0	A
VICTOR VALLEY COLLEGE	PUB-T	1,552	90.1	2,497.6	3.3	19.6	16.7	337.3	970.0
WEST COAST BIBLE COLLEGE	PRI-FN	189	102.6	3,233.8	3.1	120.6	100.2	135.0	472.5
WEST COAST U ALL CAMPUSES									
WEST COAST U MAIN CAMPUS	PRI-FG	640	91.9	D	3.3	10.2	10.0	.0	A
W COAST U ORANGE CO CTR	PRI-FG	278	A	A	A	9.3	9.1	.0	A
WSTN STATES COLLEGE ENGR	PRI-FN	94	54.8	2,580.0	3.3	21.6	19.3	470.0	470.0
WSTN ST U C LAW ALL CAM									
WSTN ST U C LAW ORANGE CO	PRI-FG	826	A	A	A	44.9	A	.0	A
WSTN ST U C LAW SAN DIEGO	PRI-FG	853	A	A	A	31.9	A	.0	A
WEST HILLS COLLEGE	PUB-T	926	117.8	2,321.8	2.5	43.0	46.9	149.3	926.0
WESTMONT COLLEGE	PRI-FN	1,006	223.4	4,683.2	4.7	120.5	96.5	125.7	182.9
MISSION COLLEGE	PUB-T	1,204	306.6	A	7.8	A	11.1	75.2	240.8
WEST VALLEY COLLEGE	PUB-T	8,510	63.5	2,424.3	2.3	5.8	5.3	316.3	915.0
WHITTIER COLLEGE	PRI-FG	1,501	386.3	6,168.6	6.4	125.4	97.9	88.2	136.4
WOODBURY UNIVERSITY	PRI-FG	1,236	141.4	A	5.1	32.8	27.1	247.2	309.0
WORLD COLLEGE WEST	PRI-FN	46	205.1	1,348.0	2.5	217.3	213.0	230.0	460.0
THE WRIGHT INSTITUTE	PRI-FG	88	245.3	D	A	75.0	42.0	125.7	125.7
YESHIVA U OF LOS ANGELES	PRI-FG	D	D	D	D	D	D	D	D
YUBA COLLEGE	PUB-T	3,562	71.2	2,395.7	A	14.4	A	274.0	1,731.0
COLORADO									
ADAMS STATE COLLEGE	PUB-FG	1,970	112.0	2,121.6	3.4	95.8	A	218.8	394.0
AIMS COMMUNITY COLLEGE	PUB-T	2,194	40.5	1,058.4	1.8	14.3	11.5	626.8	2,194.0
ARAPAHOE CMTY COLLEGE	PUB-T	3,312	51.9	1,719.3	A	9.9	9.0	473.1	1,656.0
AURARIA JOINT LIBRARY	PUB-FN	D	D	D	D	D	D	D	D
BAPT BIBLE C OF DENVER	PRI-FG	D	D	D	D	D	D	D	D
COLORADO COLLEGE	PRI-FG	1,868	232.3	3,191.2	4.3	155.6	99.3	93.4	219.7
COLO MTN COLLEGE ALL CAM									
COLO MTN COLLEGE EAST CAM	PUB-T	688	107.6	A	3.1	25.7	24.0	191.1	382.2
COLO MTN COLLEGE WEST CAM	PUB-T	949	82.5	A	2.8	28.9	40.0	237.2	474.5
COLORADO NORTHWESTERN CC	PUB-T	822	78.7	2,023.5	2.5	17.0	14.3	249.0	822.0
COLORADO SCHOOL OF MINES	PUB-FG	2,487	224.0	3,505.0	3.0	56.8	23.8	130.8	310.8
COLORADO STATE UNIVERSITY	PUB-U	16,928	164.9	3,183.6	2.4	51.0	20.6	151.4	419.0
COLO TECHNICAL COLLEGE	PRI-FN	281	20.5	320.7	1.0	12.3	8.2	281.0	281.0
COLORADO WOMEN'S COLLEGE	PRI-FN	396	301.1	4,111.8	3.9	366.1	304.0	79.2	113.1
CC OF DENVER ALL CAM									
CC OF DENVER AURARIA CAM	PUB T	SEE AURARIA JOINT LIBRARY							
CC OF DENVER NORTH CAMPUS	PUB-T	3,735	103.2	3,571.8	5.3	9.2	7.6	261.1	933.7
CC OF DENVER RED ROCKS CAM	PUB-T	2,857	119.2	3,126.1	4.2	11.5	10.4	228.5	714.2
CONS BAPTIST THEOL SEM	PRI-FG	297	304.4	6,027.2	7.7	200.3	A	84.8	297.0
FORT LEWIS COLLEGE	PUB-FN	2,719	130.3	2,928.5	5.0	47.1	41.6	194.2	453.1
ILIFF SCHOOL OF THEOLOGY	PRI-FG	195	843.2	11,745.5	14.4	537.5	352.9	30.4	81.2
INTERMOUNTAIN BIBLE C	PRI-FN	60	138.0	2,071.0	3.0	200.0	192.9	60.0	60.0
LAMAR COMMUNITY COLLEGE	PUB-T	364	90.6	1,375.0	2.6	58.4	51.6	151.6	364.0
LORETTO HEIGHTS COLLEGE	PRI-FN	718	174.6	A	2.8	143.4	85.1	140.7	718.0
MESA COLLEGE	PUB-FN	2,631	87.6	1,801.3	3.7	35.3	20.9	279.8	657.7
METROPOLITAN ST COLLEGE	PUB FN	SEE AURARIA JOINT LIBRARY							

SEE FOOTNOTES AT END OF TABLE

Table 3. – Indexes Concerning Operating Expenditures, 1978-79, Bookstock Held at End of Year, 1978-79, and Library Staff (FTE), Fall 1979, College and University Libraries, by State or Other Area and Institution: Aggregate United States – Continued

STATE OR OTHER AREA AND INSTITUTION (1)	CONTROL AND TYPE OF INSTITUTION (2)	TOTAL FTE OPENING FALL ENROLLMENT, FALL 1978 (3)	LIBRARY OPERATING EXPENDITURES (IN DOLLARS) 1978-79			BOOKSTOCK HELD AT END OF YEAR 1978-79		FTE STUDENTS PER FTE LIBRARY STAFF FALL 1979	
			PER FTE STUDENT, FALL 1978 (4)	PER FULL-TIME FACULTY MEMBER, 1978 (5)	AS PERCENT OF GENERAL EXPENDITURES, 1978-79 (6)	VOLUMES PER FTE STUDENT, FALL 1978 (7)	TITLES (INCLUDING MICROFORMS) PER FTE STUDENT 1978 (8)	TOTAL STAFF (9)	PROFESSIONAL STAFF (10)
COLORADO	--CONTINUED					39.9	39.7	119.5	251.0
MORGAN COMMUNITY COLLEGE	PUB-T	251	120.7	2,526.2	3.8	51.8	46.0	147.8	488.0
NAZARENE BIBLE COLLEGE	PRI-T	488	119.0	3,418.4	8.0	35.5	A	116.1	1,161.0
NORTHEASTERN JR COLLEGE	PUB-T	1,161	70.7	1,347.5	2.6	D	D	D	D
OTERO JUNIOR COLLEGE	PUB-T	D	D	D	D	D	D	D	D
PARKS COLLEGE	PRI-T	D	D	D	D	D	D	D	D
PIKES PEAK CMTY COLLEGE	PUB-T	3,640	96.5	2,621.9	3.4	10.3	A	260.0	606.6
PUEBLO VOCATIONAL CC	PUB-T	D	D	D		69.5	49.4	104.6	308.7
REGIS COLLEGE	PRI-FG	1,235	133.5	2,999.3	3.8	117.2	99.7	161.4	161.4
ROCKMONT COLLEGE	PRI-FN	226	119.7	2,460.8	3.9	602.0	A	50.0	75.0
SAINT THOMAS SEMINARY	PRI-FG	150	531.3	9,962.7	7.7				
TRINIDAD STATE JR COLLEGE	PUB-T	943	101.2	1,871.7	2.6	62.1	A	188.6	471.5
U OF COLORADO ALL INST	PUB-U	19,649	209.5	4,657.7	4.1	92.2	A	151.9	556.6
U OF COLORADO AT BOULDER	PUB-FG	3,044	144.8	4,281.9	6.0	40.1	31.7	241.5	461.2
U OF COLO COLO SPRINGS	PUB-FG			SEE AURARIA JOINT LIBRARY					
U OF COLO AT DENVER	PUB FG								
U OF COLO MLTH SCI CENTER	PUB-FG	1,428	534.6	6,525.0	1.2	109.5	46.0	43.2	129.8
UNIVERSITY OF DENVER	PRI-U	5,927	297.5	3,945.8	3.4	137.6	A	79.3	290.5
U OF NORTHERN COLORADO	PUB-FG	10,068	155.8	3,525.1	4.3	38.6	A	130.2	451.4
U OF SOUTHERN COLORADO	PUB-FG	4,522	99.0	1,874.9	2.6	34.3	29.7	266.0	646.0
WESTERN BIBLE COLLEGE	PRI-FN	195	122.0	2,643.7	5.8	97.6	84.0	195.0	195.0
WESTERN ST COLLEGE COLO	PUB-FG	2,972	106.3	2,413.0	4.3	42.8	30.7	297.2	495.3
YESH TORAS CHAIM TALMUD	PRI-FG	D	D	D	D	D	D	D	D
CONNECTICUT									
ALBERTUS MAGNUS COLLEGE	PRI-FN	427	174.1	3,541.0	3.1	196.4	137.3	82.1	112.3
ANNHURST COLLEGE	PRI-FN	331	129.7	1,533.7	2.7	137.1	123.9	110.3	165.5
ASNUNTUCK CMTY COLLEGE	PUB-T	660	109.1	4,501.1	4.7	31.0	32.0	220.0	660.0
BAIS BINYOMIN ACADEMY	PRI-FG	D		NO LIBRARY FACILITIES		D	D	D	D
BOARD STATE ACAD AWARDS	PUB-T					47.6	A	70.0	70.0
BRIDGEPORT ENGR INSTITUTE	PRI-FN	210	27.1	D	1.4	33.8	30.6	306.6	435.7
CENTRAL ST COLLEGE	PUB-FG	8,280	85.3	1,678.1	3.6	198.5	174.1	83.7	162.8
CONNECTICUT COLLEGE	PRI-FG	1,726	335.0	4,518.5	5.3	46.6	33.4	159.9	345.0
EASTERN CONN ST COLLEGE	PUB-FG	2,415	139.9	3,448.6	5.3	44.3	33.8	164.1	439.0
FAIRFIELD UNIVERSITY	PRI-FG	3,512	127.7	2,654.1	3.5	22.8	26.0	348.2	606.2
GREATER HARTFORD CC	PUB-T	1,637	83.1	2,959.0	4.6				
GREATER NEW HAVEN TECH C1/	PUB-T			NO LIBRARY FACILITIES		295.4	289.5	123.5	173.0
HARTFORD COLLEGE WOMEN	PRI-T	173	228.1	7,901.0	5.4	56.1	53.5	150.4	188.0
HARTFORD GRADUATE CENTER	PRI-FG	376	173.9	4,672.8	2.3	D	D	D	D
HARTFORD SEM FOUNDATION	PRI-FG	D							
HARTFORD ST TECH COLLEGE	PUB-T	897	36.3	708.9	A	8.9	8.3	448.5	897.0
HOLY APOSTLES COLLEGE	PRI-FG	60	1,073.0	.0	28.6	517.2	503.5	16.2	25.0
HOUSATONIC REGIONAL CC	PUB-T	1,691	109.4	3,190.6	5.0	17.2	28.1	301.9	301.9
MANCHESTER CMTY COLLEGE	PUB-T	3,734	47.9	1,990.8	3.7	10.6	16.6	373.4	622.3
MATTATUCK CMTY COLLEGE	PUB-T	2,484	69.0	2,639.2	4.2	10.6	9.1	326.8	690.0
MIDDLESEX CMTY COLLEGE	PUB-T	1,536	61.4	2,006.8	3.7	23.1	20.2	341.3	512.0
MITCHELL COLLEGE	PRI-T	543	113.4	2,932.4	3.3	83.0	70.4	358.5	627.5
MOHEGAN COMMUNITY COLLEGE	PUB-T	1,255	75.4	2,959.7	3.5	16.2	14.6	63.3	63.3
MT SACRED HEART COLLEGE	PRI-T	19	261.6	D	49.7	747.7	747.7	4,242.5	5,939.5
NTHWSTN CONN CMTY COLLEGE	PUB-T	11,879	8.5	2,915.1	5.6	3.5	2.9		
NORWALK COMMUNITY COLLEGE	PUB-T	1,925	69.1	1,985.9	A	25.8	A	240.6	481.2
NORWALK ST TECH COLLEGE	PUB-T	954	57.9	1,228.2	2.8	14.2	A	477.0	954.0
POST COLLEGE	PRI-FN	1,017	60.7	2,288.0	2.1	21.2	19.7	508.5	508.5
QUINEBAUG VALLEY CC	PUB-T	381	415.7	17,600.5	20.6	38.1	40.7	95.2	190.5
QUINNIPIAC COLLEGE	PRI-FG	2,640	149.1	A	4.4	37.3	25.9	139.6	303.4
SACRED HEART UNIVERSITY	PRI-FG	1,797	116.6	3,082.0	3.7	62.8	56.1	152.2	449.2
SAINT ALPHONSUS COLLEGE	PRI-FN	50	256.8	.0	5.2	622.9	A	19.2	25.0
SAINT BASIL'S COLLEGE	PRI-FN	10	2,078.4	A	24.2	1,737.0	1,038.5	5.0	10.0
SAINT JOSEPH COLLEGE	PRI-FG	890	144.6	2,219.6	3.1	107.9	63.4	130.8	296.6
SAINT THOMAS SEMINARY	PRI-T	47	442.0	10,387.0	4.2	1,051.7	919.5	47.0	47.0
SOUTH CEN CMTY COLLEGE	PUB-T	1,334	115.2	4,391.7	6.7	16.4	15.0	190.5	333.5
SOUTHERN CONN ST COLLEGE	PUB-FG	8,526	84.6	1,685.4	3.4	43.6	41.2	275.0	355.2
THAMES VLY STATE TECH C	PUB-T	875	41.1	1,000.3	2.6	8.1	8.4	437.5	875.0
TRINITY COLLEGE	PRI-FG	1,818	363.1	5,039.5	5.3	281.9	212.8	69.1	121.2
TUNXIS COMMUNITY COLLEGE	PUB-T	1,505	72.3	3,109.0	4.2	13.0	A	334.4	602.0
UNIVERSITY OF BRIDGEPORT2/	PRI-FG	4,956	132.0	2,459.5	2.7	62.9	51.8	166.8	420.0
U OF CONN ALL CAMPUSES									

SEE FOOTNOTES AT END OF TABLE

Table 3. — Indexes Concerning Operating Expenditures, 1978-79, Bookstock Held at End of Year, 1978-79, and Library Staff (FTE), Fall 1979, College and University Libraries, by State or Other Area and Institution: Aggregate United States — Continued

STATE OR OTHER AREA AND INSTITUTION (1)	CONTROL AND TYPE OF INSTITUTION (2)	TOTAL FTE OPENING FALL ENROLLMENT, FALL 1978 (3)	LIBRARY OPERATING EXPENDITURES (IN DOLLARS) 1978-79			BOOKSTOCK HELD AT END OF YEAR 1978-79		FTE STUDENTS PER FTE LIBRARY STAFF FALL 1979	
			PER FTE STUDENT, FALL 1978 (4)	PER FULL-TIME FACULTY MEMBER, 1978 (5)	AS PERCENT OF GENERAL EXPENDITURES, 1978-79 (6)	VOLUMES PER FTE STUDENT, FALL 1978 (7)	TITLES (INCLUDING MICROFORMS) PER FTE STUDENT 1978 (8)	TOTAL STAFF (9)	PROFESSIONAL STAFF (10)
CONNECTICUT	--CONTINUED								
UNIVERSITY OF CONNECTICUT	PUB-U	18,268	204.7	3,240.5	3.6	87.3	A	127.3	250.2
U OF CONN HEALTH CENTER	PUB-FG	527	1,693.1	13,727.7	2.1	213.4	63.8	17.4	45.0
UNIVERSITY OF HARTFORD	PRI-FG	6,590	82.1	1,893.3	2.3	40.9	24.6	262.5	732.2
UNIVERSITY OF NEW HAVEN	PRI-FG	4,350	111.5	3,489.9	4.0	30.5	22.5	174.0	725.0
WATERBURY ST TECH COLLEGE	PUB-T	842	49.8	1,076.4	2.3	10.0	10.3	421.0	842.0
WESLEYAN UNIVERSITY	PRI-FG	2,646	436.5	4,548.0	4.5	297.9	196.5	63.7	165.3
WESTERN CONN ST COLLEGE	PUB-FG	3,589	113.7	2,386.4	4.9	38.8	27.2	247.5	341.8
YALE UNIVERSITY	PRI-U	9,598	1,291.6	15,438.9	5.9	736.8	460.5	16.3	61.2
DELAWARE									
BRANDYWINE C OF WIDENER U	PRI-T	820	85.3	2,916.2	3.2	44.5	35.6	273.3	410.0
DELAWARE STATE COLLEGE	PUB-FN	1,801	195.4	2,453.5	3.7	62.6	74.8	138.5	257.2
DEL TECH & CC ALL CAM									
DEL TECH & CC STHN CAM	PUB-T	949	128.0	1,814.4	2.7	26.7	24.8	169.4	263.6
DEL TECH & CC STANTON CAM	PUB-T	1,617	91.3	2,421.6	4.0	9.7	9.6	539.0	646.8
DEL TECH & CC TERRY CAM	PUB-T	778	158.0	3,978.4	4.6	17.0	17.1	172.8	311.2
DEL TECH & CC WILMINGTON	PUB-T	858	176.0	3,074.4	4.5	13.3	10.6	190.6	306.4
GOLDEY BEACON COLLEGE	PRI-FN	1,125	48.0	2,576.3	3.6	8.2	6.7	450.0	562.5
UNIVERSITY OF DELAWARE	PUB-U	15,580	167.3	3,291.2	3.0	75.3	42.3	192.3	662.9
WESLEY COLLEGE	PRI-FN	823	143.5	2,624.6	2.9	54.0	50.2	91.4	274.3
WILMINGTON COLLEGE	PRI-FG	462	116.9	4,501.8	3.3	115.9	65.7	-165.0	462.0
DISTRICT OF COLUMBIA									
AMERICAN UNIVERSITY	PRI-U	8,410	185.6	6,360.2	3.7	95.9	46.2	134.7	475.1
BEACON COLLEGE	PRI-FG		NO LIBRARY FACILITIES						
CATHOLIC U OF AMERICA	PRI-U	5,604	267.1	4,966.8	4.9	196.4	135.6	74.7	164.8
CORCORAN SCHOOL OF ART	PRI-FN	D	D	D	D	D	D	D	D
DOMINICAN HOUSE STUDIES	PRI-FG	38	1,617.9	D	20.2	1,286.1	842.3	13.1	20.0
GALLAUDET COLLEGE	PRI-FG	1,196	600.5	6,204.5	A	110.3	292.0	45.0	82.3
GEORGETOWN UNIVERSITY	PRI-U	10,461	372.5	A	4.4	113.4	49.1	77.7	206.7
GEORGE WASH UNIVERSITY	PRI-U	12,250	255.6	7,214.6	3.0	67.6	A	129.7	482.2
HOWARD UNIVERSITY	PRI-U	18,288	282.6	6,436.8	4.1	57.8	42.3	116.0	290.2
MOUNT VERNON COLLEGE	PRI-FN	677	261.1	6,596.1	5.6	55.0	56.7	79.5	190.8
OBLATE COLLEGE	PRI-FG	D	D	D	D	D	D	418.0	522.5
SOUTHEASTERN UNIVERSITY	PRI-FG	1,045	94.2	A	5.1	A	A	457.6	686.5
STRAYER COLLEGE	PRI-FN	1,373	42.8	1,368.1	2.2	11.7	11.4	108.4	123.6
TRINITY COLLEGE	PRI-FG	618	190.5	2,617.0	5.4	242.9	156.0	108.4	123.6
UNIVERSITY OF DC	PUB-FG	7,174	317.7	3,469.1	3.9	53.1	37.0	88.5	199.2
WASH INTRNATL COLLEGE1/	PRI-FN		NO LIBRARY FACILITIES						
WESLEY THEOLOGICAL SEM	PRI-FG	267	512.1	A	9.2	329.7	A	44.5	133.5
FLORIDA									
BARRY COLLEGE	PRI-FG	1,449	177.5	3,384.6	4.9	71.5	56.4	85.2	259.8
BAUDER FASHION COLLEGE	PRI-T	D	D	D	D	D	D	D	D
BETHUNE COOKMAN COLLEGE	PRI-FN	1,731	141.0	2,872.9	3.1	94.1	2.7	157.3	247.2
BISCAYNE COLLEGE	PRI-FG	1,814	64.6	A	1.9	46.0	42.2	266.7	431.9
BREVARD CMTY COLLEGE	PUB-T	8,888	110.5	3,941.6	A	28.3	14.6	209.6	478.9
BROWARD CMTY COLLEGE	PUB-T	9,981	106.3	8,940.9	5.1	17.2	16.0	173.1	551.1
CENTRAL FLA CMTY COLLEGE	PUB-T	1,812	130.7	2,507.4	4.1	26.6	22.2	190.7	453.0
CHIPOLA JUNIOR COLLEGE	PUB-T	838	225.9	3,063.3	6.5	55.1	95.0	104.7	209.5
CLEARWATER CHRISTIAN C	PRI-FN	164	88.2	1,607.4	2.7	170.2	129.2	164.0	164.0
COLLEGE OF BOCA RATON	PRI-T	436	56.2	2,229.0	2.0	63.7	59.4	272.5	272.5
DAYTONA BCH CMTY COLLEGE	PUB-T	9,638	159.9	3,613.3	4.4	14.8	14.1	133.7	586.7
ECKERD COLLEGE	PRI-FN	870	236.1	3,313.8	3.2	138.7	149.5	103.5	217.5
EDISON COMMUNITY COLLEGE	PUB-T	2,291	157.9	5,836.4	8.2	25.4	23.3	136.3	381.8
EDWARD WATERS COLLEGE	PRI-FN	625	233.5	4,423.2	4.7	120.1	119.2	80.1	156.2
EMBRY-RIDDLE AERON U	PRI-FG	5,434	56.3	2,294.6	1.8	6.4	5.1	418.0	1,086.8
FLAGLER COLLEGE	PRI-FN	711	174.3	A	5.5	69.6	56.5	118.5	237.0
FLORIDA BEACON COLLEGE	PRI-FG	D	D	D	D	D	D	D	D
FLORIDA COLLEGE	PRI-T	528	102.4	A	4.7	47.7	39.2	146.6	660.0
FLORIDA INST TECHNOLOGY	PRI-FG	3,899	81.1	2,550.8	2.5	32.3	16.2	229.3	779.8
FLA JR COLLEGE JACKSONVL	PUB-T	8,432	176.7	4,038.8	5.2	22.3	17.8	119.2	368.2
FLORIDA KEYS CMTY COLLEGE	PUB-T	885	129.2	3,821.6	4.4	28.4	39.8	147.5	885.0
FLORIDA MEMORIAL COLLEGE	PRI-FN	694	123.0	A	A	105.9	88.9	138.8	231.3
FLORIDA SOUTHERN COLLEGE	PRI-FN	1,878	124.1	3,087.1	3.8	85.2	47.9	197.0	374.4
FORT LAUDERDALE COLLEGE	PRI-FN	D	D	D	D	D	D	D	D
GULF COAST CMTY COLLEGE	PUB-T	2,334	129.0	4,633.1	6.1	19.0	16.8	194.5	466.8
MEED UNIVERSITY	PRI-FG	D	D	D	D	D	D	D	D

SEE FOOTNOTES AT END OF TABLE

141

Table 3. — Indexes Concerning Operating Expenditures, 1978-79, Bookstock Held at End of Year, 1978-79, and Library Staff (FTE), Fall 1979, College and University Libraries, by State or Other Area and Institution: Aggregate United States — Continued

STATE OR OTHER AREA AND INSTITUTION	CONTROL AND TYPE OF INSTITUTION	TOTAL FTE OPENING FALL ENROLLMENT, FALL 1978	LIBRARY OPERATING EXPENDITURES (IN DOLLARS) 1978-79			BOOKSTOCK HELD AT END OF YEAR 1978-79		FTE STUDENTS PER FTE LIBRARY STAFF FALL 1979	
			PER FTE STUDENT, FALL 1978	PER FULL-TIME FACULTY MEMBER, 1978	AS PERCENT OF GENERAL EXPENDITURES, 1978-79	VOLUMES PER FTE STUDENT, FALL 1978	TITLES (INCLUDING MICROFORMS) PER FTE STUDENT 1978	TOTAL STAFF	PROFESSIONAL STAFF
(1)	(2)	(3)	(4)	(5)	(6)	(7)	(8)	(9)	(10)
FLORIDA	--CONTINUED								
HILLSBOROUGH CMTY COLLEGE	PUB-T	5,542	55.4	1,774.7	2.3	5.3	4.8	527.8	2,216.8
HOREB SEMINARY	PRI-FN	D	D	D	D	D	D	D	D
INDIAN RIVER CMTY COLLEGE	PUB-T	2,779	77.9	2,488.4	2.5	15.6	14.0	463.1	694.7
INTERNATIONAL FINE ARTS C	PRI-T	D	D	D	D	D	D	D	D
JACKSONVILLE UNIVERSITY	PRI-FG	1,869	143.1	2,972.6	A	87.8	A	113.2	373.8
JONES COLLEGE ALL CAM		1,161	19.4	D	A	9.2	7.8	774.0	1,161.0
JONES COLLEGE JACKSONVL	PRI-FN	1,220	15.3	D	A	5.7	5.2	1,220.0	1,220.0
JONES COLLEGE ORLANDO	PRI-FN	1,572	141.0	3,038.4	4.5	18.2	22.8	191.7	524.0
LAKE CITY CMTY COLLEGE	PUB-T	1,110	137.7	4,023.7	6.3	41.3	.2	154.1	346.8
LAKE-SUMTER CMTY COLLEGE	PUB-T								
LAKELAND C BUS AND FASH	PRI-T	D	D	D	D	D	D	D	D
LUTHER RICE SEMINARY	PRI-FG	105	308.3	D		295.2	219.8	43.7	75.0
MANATEE JUNIOR COLLEGE	PUB-T	3,015	81.4	2,790.9	3.2	15.6	18.0	225.0	1,005.0
MIAMI CHRISTIAN COLLEGE	PRI-FN	188	430.0	A	8.7	131.2	107.3	36.1	188.0
MIAMI-DADE CMTY COLLEGE	PUB-T	26,232	72.4	2,410.7	3.0	11.8	9.5	352.1	846.1
MORRIS C OF BUSINESS	PRI-T	103	60.2	D	A	11.2	10.4	206.0	206.0
NORTH FLORIDA JR COLLEGE	PUB-T	633	164.9	2,748.2	4.2	52.9	37.9	111.0	287.7
NOVA UNIVERSITY	PRI-FG	5,411	110.1	8,056.3	3.7	16.8	5.9	355.9	702.7
OKALOOSA-WALTON JUNIOR C	PUB-T	2,156	137.4	4,004.0	6.4	30.6	27.0	134.7	431.2
PALM BCH ATLANTIC COLLEGE	PRI-FN	478	180.8	2,700.9	3.8	85.5	67.7	119.5	239.0
PALM BEACH JUNIOR COLLEGE	PUB-T	5,025	110.4	3,323.1	5.7	22.2	21.3	-173.2	628.1
PASCO-HERNANDO CC	PUB-T	1,361	195.1	6,035.0	6.6	22.2	33.1	146.3	302.4
PENSACOLA JUNIOR COLLEGE	PUB-T	5,128	129.1	2,122.0	3.8	20.2	15.2	160.2	512.8
POLK COMMUNITY COLLEGE	PUB-T	2,742	121.7	3,240.4	5.8	25.2	19.5	156.6	548.4
RINGLING SCHOOL OF ART	PRI-FN	507	140.2	3,743.6	9.4	19.5	15.7	144.8	253.5
ROLLINS COLLEGE	PRI-FG	3,256	111.8	3,536.4	3.5	56.4	49.5	142.8	465.1
SAINT JOHNS RIVER CC	PUB-T	969	121.6	2,563.0	5.1	51.1	34.1	138.4	346.0
SNT JOHN VIANNEY C SEM	PRI-FN	63	567.2	D	5.5	746.0	742.8	31.5	63.0
SAINT LEO COLLEGE	PRI-FN	1,004	141.9	3,237.9	2.4	66.4	50.4	77.2	251.0
SAINT PETERSBG JR COLLEGE	PUB-T	9,373	90.0	2,776.8	4.6	19.1	15.4	246.6	551.3
SANTA FE CMTY COLLEGE	PUB-T	4,991	50.6	1,044.7	2.0	8.6	6.7	375.2	1,247.7
SEM SAINT VINCENT DE PAUL	PRI-FG	69	774.9	.0	9.3	536.2	539.6	26.5	34.5
SEMINOLE CMTY COLLEGE	PUB-T	2,505	71.8	4,304.6	4.5	24.2	21.9	139.1	455.4
STHESTN C ASSEMBLIES GOD	PRI-FN	1,164	72.8	2,493.5	5.7	36.1	35.2	363.7	582.0
SOUTH FLORIDA JR COLLEGE	PUB-T	302	284.5	2,772.0	4.2	98.4	93.4	75.5	302.0
ST U SYS OF FLA ALL INST			259.4	5,369.2	5.3	58.7	57.8	147.2	429.3
FLA AGRICULTURAL C MECH U	PUB-U	5,152	284.2	5,774.1	6.3	105.0	A	101.3	334.5
FLA ATLANTIC UNIVERSITY	PUB-FG	5,018	445.4	8,992.6	8.8	49.5	47.2	91.7	242.2
FLORIDA INTERNATIONAL U	PUB-FG	6,541	304.4	6,470.1	6.5	70.6	40.9	135.8	354.6
FLORIDA STATE UNIVERSITY	PUB-U	19,150							
U OF CENTRAL FLORIDA	PUB-FG	8,075	236.3	5,485.2	6.2	37.0	26.4	141.6	475.0
UNIVERSITY OF FLORIDA	PUB-U	28,610	262.8	3,645.7	3.5	72.6	A	137.5	362.1
U OF NORTH FLORIDA	PUB-FG	2,724	521.1	10,212.9	10.8	78.1	59.1	76.7	194.5
U OF SOUTH FLORIDA	PUB-FG	16,849	255.1	5,374.7	5.6	46.0	30.3	112.1	439.9
U OF WEST FLORIDA	PUB-FG	4,513	327.9	6,789.8	7.5	73.8	49.1	121.9	300.8
STETSON UNIVERSITY	PRI-FG	2,643	120.3	2,445.9	3.2	75.6	64.6	159.2	440.5
TALLAHASSEE CMTY COLLEGE	PUB-T	2,194	124.5	4,203.8	7.7	24.9	26.4	175.5	548.5
TALMUDIC C OF FLORIDA	PRI-FG	D	D	D	D	D	D	D	D
TAMPA COLLEGE	PRI-FN	816	41.1	D	A	12.9	12.0	816.0	816.0
UNIVERSITY OF MIAMI	PRI-U	12,062	282.9	5,660.3	2.8	107.8	52.0	80.3	261.0
UNIVERSITY OF SARASOTA	PRI-FG	142	164.1	A	A	265.0	A	101.4	101.4
UNIVERSITY OF TAMPA	PRI-FG	1,882	165.2	3,886.6	3.8	88.1	70.3	123.8	313.6
VALENCIA CMTY COLLEGE	PUB-T	5,458	101.6	3,363.3	4.4	9.9	9.4	189.5	620.2
WARNER SOUTHERN COLLEGE	PRI-FN	245	312.2	5,100.4	7.6	209.5	164.4	94.2	122.5
WEBBER COLLEGE	PRI-FN	98	359.1	4,400.1	A	146.8	120.1	39.2	98.0
GEORGIA									
ABRAHAM BALDWIN AGRL C	PUB-T	2,206	75.9	1,691.8	3.2	24.3	21.6	275.7	551.5
AGNES SCOTT COLLEGE	PRI-FN	540	430.1	3,466.5	5.1	293.5	214.7	60.6	117.3
ALBANY JUNIOR COLLEGE	PUB-T	1,367	170.0	3,521.6	7.1	45.4	46.5	130.1	273.4
ALBANY STATE COLLEGE	PUB-FN	1,663	138.5	1,800.0	3.0	74.5	90.4	184.7	332.6
ANDREW COLLEGE	PRI-T	324	93.8	2,339.6	3.4	71.4	70.7	135.0	324.0
ARMSTRONG STATE COLLEGE	PUB-FG	2,593	122.2	2,383.5	2.4	43.0	39.9	169.4	432.1
ATLANTA CHRISTIAN COLLEGE	PRI-FN	194	139.7	3,011.4	4.4	100.7	70.6	149.2	194.0
ATLANTA COLLEGE OF ART	PRI-FN	241	232.7	3,116.6	4.9	41.4	32.6	80.3	120.5
ATLANTA JUNIOR COLLEGE	PUB-T	1,207	155.3	3,408.4	6.2	14.4	13.5	185.6	402.3
ATLANTA UNIVERSITY	PRI-FG	1,004	368.6	A	3.7	316.1	262.7	47.8	71.7

SEE FOOTNOTES AT END OF TABLE

Table 3. — Indexes Concerning Operating Expenditures, 1978-79, Bookstock Held at End of Year, 1978-79, and Library Staff (FTE), Fall 1979, College and University Libraries, by State or Other Area and Institution: Aggregate United States — Continued

STATE OR OTHER AREA AND INSTITUTION	CONTROL AND TYPE OF INSTITUTION	TOTAL FTE OPENING FALL ENROLLMENT, FALL 1978	LIBRARY OPERATING EXPENDITURES (IN DOLLARS) 1978-79			BOOKSTOCK HELD AT END OF YEAR 1978-79		FTE STUDENTS PER FTE LIBRARY STAFF FALL 1979	
			PER FTE STUDENT, FALL 1978	PER FULL-TIME FACULTY MEMBER, 1978	AS PERCENT OF GENERAL EXPENDITURES, 1978-79	VOLUMES PER FTE STUDENT, FALL 1978	TITLES (INCLUDING MICROFORMS) PER FTE STUDENT 1978	TOTAL STAFF	PROFESSIONAL STAFF
(1)	(2)	(3)	(4)	(5)	(6)	(7)	(8)	(9)	(10)
GEORGIA	--CONTINUED								
AUGUSTA COLLEGE	PUB-FG	2,876	166.5	3,281.5	6.6	81.6	54.9	198.3	410.
BAINBRIDGE JUNIOR COLLEGE	PUB-T	390	238.4	3,720.4	6.2	52.3	42.2	108.3	150.0
BERRY COLLEGE	PRI-FG	1,452	174.3	3,088.1	3.6	75.7	173.8	161.3	363.0
BRENAU COLLEGE	PRI-FG	965	65.3	1,371.4	1.9	52.1	45.6	241.2	482.5
BREWTON-PARKER COLLEGE	PRI-T	562	69.3	1,447.3	3.0	39.5	39.5	224.8	562.0
BRUNSWICK JUNIOR COLLEGE	PUB-T	985	200.1	3,865.2	7.5	43.4	41.6	123.1	328.3
CLARK COLLEGE	PRI-FN	1,831	86.5	1,415.2	2.1	36.9	32.3	281.6	457.7
CLAYTON JUNIOR COLLEGE	PUB-T	2,182	102.7	2,700.6	5.9	21.5	19.3	220.4	507.4
COLUMBIA THEOLOGICAL SEM	PRI-FG	195	463.0	5,643.5	5.9	396.6	309.0	48.7	65.0
COLUMBUS COLLEGE	PUB-FG	3,932	156.2	2,940.1	6.2	35.2	35.5	162.4	491.5
COVENANT COLLEGE	PRI-FN	510	203.1	3,837.0	4.5	112.9	A	170.0	255.0
CRANDALL COLLEGE	PRI-T	0	D	0	D	0	0	0	D
DALTON JUNIOR COLLEGE	PUB-T	1,067	179.9	2,909.5	6.6	53.6	92.7	152.4	355.6
DEKALB COMMUNITY COLLEGE	PUB-T	D	D	D	D	D	D	D	D
DRAUGHON'S JC BUSINESS	PRI-T	361	39.3	3,552.5	2.6	8.2	7.6	361.0	601.6
EMANUEL CO JUNIOR COLLEGE	PUB-T	278	307.2	5,023.8	8.3	83.7	77.9	69.5	278.0
EMMANUEL COLLEGE	PRI-T	361	116.1	3,495.4	4.6	72.5	60.6	180.5	180.5
EMMANUEL SCH MINISTRIES3/	PRI-FN		NO LIBRARY FACILITIES						
EMORY UNIVERSITY	PRI-U	7,163	525.6	9,160.9	4.7	191.0	117.0	48.9	125.0
FLOYD JUNIOR COLLEGE	PUB-T	1,097	182.3	4,015.9	7.1	35.7	30.4	105.7	264.2
FORT VALLEY STATE COLLEGE	PUB-FG	1,732	211.7	A	3.8	89.1	39.2	108.2	288.6
GAINESVILLE JR COLLEGE	PUB-T	1,154	102.7	2,419.6	4.3	37.1	46.8	192.3	577.0
GEORGIA COLLEGE	PUB-FG	2,844	145.5	2,779.0	5.8	49.3	39.5	177.7	406.2
GA INST TECHN ALL CAM									
GA INST OF TECHN MAIN CAM	PUB-FG	9,807	259.9	4,694.9	3.2	59.5	25.0	108.0	225.4
GA INST TECHN-STHN TECH	PUB-FN	1,825	103.2	2,298.9	4.5	36.3	33.1	304.1	608.3
GEORGIA MILITARY COLLEGE	PRI-T	1,166	30.0	3,189.5	1.8	24.5	24.5	388.6	1,166.0
GEORGIA SOUTHERN COLLEGE	PUB-FG	5,824	135.0	2,649.1	5.4	45.4	A	157.4	364.0
GA SOUTHWESTERN COLLEGE	PUB-FG	1,953	173.3	2,892.7	5.9	60.3	46.6	139.5	279.0
GEORGIA STATE UNIVERSITY	PUB-FG	16,248	161.8	3,789.6	5.0	39.1	26.2	184.6	624.9
GORDON JUNIOR COLLEGE	PUB-T	859	254.0	5,898.7	10.8	45.6	48.5	107.3	286.3
INTRODENOMINATL THEOL CTR	PRI-FG	273	244.8	4,456.7	4.5	293.3	287.8	71.8	136.5
KENNESAW COLLEGE	PUB-FN	2,928	121.7	2,874.5	7.3	26.0	A	234.2	532.3
LA GRANGE COLLEGE	PRI-FG	816	126.3	2,193.0	4.5	81.6	67.8	136.0	272.0
LIFE CHIROPRACTIC COLLEGE	PRI-FG	872	51.1	1,144.6	2.2	15.5	13.2	249.1	436.0
MACON JUNIOR COLLEGE	PUB-T	1,631	96.8	2,078.9	4.9	33.2	A	203.8	943.6
MEDICAL COLLEGE OF GA	PUB-FG	1,829	358.4	3,683.0	1.4	55.9	24.9	64.1	215.1
MERCER U ALL CAMPUSES									
MERCER U MAIN CAMPUS	PRI-FG	2,203	266.3	5,335.1	6.0	106.6	66.8	99.2	244.7
MERCER U IN ATLANTA	PRI-FG	964	174.5	4,313.5	6.6	49.4	66.8	130.2	321.3
MERCER U STHN SCHOOL PHAR	PRI-FG	322	247.8	2,100.4	4.6	30.0	13.6	161.0	161.0
MIDDLE GEORGIA COLLEGE	PUB-T	1,345	151.5	2,830.9	6.1	55.0	50.9	134.5	336.2
MOREHOUSE COLLEGE	PRI-FG	D	D	D	D	D	D	D	D
MORRIS BROWN COLLEGE	PRI-FN	1,678	87.6	1,516.1	2.3	35.9	A	258.1	372.8
NORTH GEORGIA COLLEGE	PUB-FG	1,543	156.8	2,814.1	5.1	76.3	76.5	154.3	308.6
OGLETHORPE UNIVERSITY	PRI-FG	793	131.0	3,148.7	3.5	77.6	74.4	144.1	240.3
PAINE COLLEGE	PRI-FN	803	129.1	1,728.3	2.4	82.3	74.1	146.0	401.5
PHILLIPS COLLEGE	PRI-T	D	D	D	D	D	D	D	D
PHILLIPS COLLEGE	PRI-T	D	D	D	D	D	D	D	D
PIEDMONT COLLEGE	PRI-FN	355	182.8	2,496.8	8.3	174.8	176.3	208.8	236.6
REINHARDT COLLEGE	PRI-T	498	142.8	5,082.1	6.4	57.8	45.8	97.6	199.2
SAVANNAH STATE COLLEGE	PUB-FG	2,037	128.1	2,194.0	3.4	63.8	42.5	127.3	407.4
SHORTER COLLEGE	PRI-FN	812	120.9	2,232.4	4.4	96.0	93.2	135.3	135.3
SOUTH GEORGIA COLLEGE	PUB-T	922	160.1	3,142.1	4.5	73.4	61.1	124.5	230.5
SPELMAN COLLEGE	PRI-FN	1,247	79.8	1,094.5	1.6	38.3	38.3	249.4	415.6
THOMAS COUNTY CC	PRI-T	126	152.8	4,816.0	5.7	115.6	114.1	63.0	126.0
TIFT COLLEGE	PRI-FN	660	113.0	2,407.1	4.0	89.5	74.8	220.0	330.0
TOCCOA FALLS COLLEGE	PRI-FN	405	141.8	2,393.4	3.3	113.8	104.3	168.7	202.5
TRUETT MCCONNELL COLLEGE	PRI-T	578	80.0	2,313.7	3.9	44.6	44.7	289.0	578.0
UNIVERSITY OF GEORGIA	PUB-U	20,530	261.9	3,859.9	3.2	92.2	A	95.1	281.2
VALDOSTA STATE COLLEGE	PUB-FG	4,243	174.3	3,393.0	7.3	48.4	36.3	151.5	471.4
WAYCROSS JUNIOR COLLEGE	PUB-T	282	377.9	7,106.2	10.0	53.9	41.4	70.5	141.0
WESLEYAN COLLEGE	PRI-FN	467	472.4	5,014.0	8.4	230.4	A	93.4	155.6
WEST GEORGIA COLLEGE	PUB-FG	4,018	150.7	2,293.9	4.9	53.9	47.0	133.9	287.0
YOUNG HARRIS COLLEGE	PRI-T	495	117.8	2,651.0	5.0	90.3	80.3	198.0	495.0
HAWAII									
CHAMINADE U OF HONOLULU	PRI-FG	1,612	77.3	2,833.3	3.5	31.0	24.8	230.2	403.0

SEE FOOTNOTES AT END OF TABLE

Table 3. — Indexes Concerning Operating Expenditures, 1978-79, Bookstock Held at End of Year, 1978-79, and Library Staff (FTE), Fall 1979, College and University Libraries, by State or Other Area and Institution: Aggregate United States — Continued

STATE OR OTHER AREA AND INSTITUTION	CONTROL AND TYPE OF INSTITUTION	TOTAL FTE OPENING FALL ENROLLMENT, FALL 1978	LIBRARY OPERATING EXPENDITURES (IN DOLLARS) 1978-79			BOOKSTOCK HELD AT END OF YEAR 1978-79		FTE STUDENTS PER FTE LIBRARY STAFF FALL 1979	
			PER FTE STUDENT, FALL 1978	PER FULL-TIME FACULTY MEMBER, FALL 1978	AS PERCENT OF GENERAL EXPENDITURES, 1978-79	VOLUMES PER FTE STUDENT, FALL 1978	TITLES (INCLUDING MICROFORKS) PER FTE STUDENT 1978	TOTAL STAFF	PROFESSIONAL STAFF
(1)	(2)	(3)	(4)	(5)	(6)	(7)	(8)	(9)	(10)
HAWAII	--CONTINUED								
HAWAII LOA COLLEGE	PRI-FN	262	293.8	5,499.9	6.7	137.1	126.3	131.0	131.0
HAWAII PACIFIC COLLEGE	PRI-FN	599	142.5	7,761.0	5.6	32.5	24.0	299.5	299.5
U OF HAWAII SYS ALL INST									
U OF HAWAII AT MANOA	PUB-U	17,857	302.0	5,426.5	4.3	98.0	49.4	111.2	268.5
U OF HAWAII AT HILO	PUB-FN	2,606	233.8	3,832.6	7.0	51.0	42.6	153.2	372.2
U OF HAWAII WEST OAHU C	PUB-FN	139	448.0	A	9.7	61.4	69.6	92.6	92.6
U OF HAWAII HONOLULU CC	PUB-T	3,277	108.3	3,141.3	5.2	11.8	20.1	217.0	385.1
U OF HAWAII KAPIOLANI CC	PUB-T	3,347	41.5	1,362.0	2.4	8.9	5.6	557.8	1,115.6
U OF HAWAII KAUAI CC	PUB-T	736	313.6	5,368.2	8.9	56.3	28.3	102.2	184.0
U OF HAWAII LEEWARD CC	PUB-T	4,201	70.2	2,219.1	3.8	13.4	10.5	300.0	840.2
U OF HAWAII MAUI CC	PUB-T	1,210	102.4	2,136.9	4.0	26.9	19.2	186.1	345.7
U OF HAWAII WINDWARD CC	PUB-T	922	131.3	3,905.4	6.2	23.9	20.4	204.8	614.6
IDAHO									
BOISE STATE UNIVERSITY	PUB-FG	6,781	182.0	3,845.1	5.3	35.7	30.2	143.3	423.8
COLLEGE OF IDAHO	PRI-FG	684	214.5	A	4.4	175.0	172.7	95.6	273.6
COLLEGE OF SOUTHERN IDAHO	PUB-T	2,118	78.9	1,838.4	2.6	42.4	37.3	.0	A
IDAHO STATE UNIVERSITY	PUB-FG	5,386	257.6	4,937.6	5.4	53.6	39.0	151.7	384.7
LEWIS-CLARK ST COLLEGE	PUB-FN	995	210.1	2,403.8	4.2	78.2	95.6	142.1	497.5
NORTH IDAHO COLLEGE	PUB-T	1,334	90.1	1,603.6	1.6	22.2	20.9	230.0	580.0
NTHWST NAZARENE COLLEGE	PRI-FG	1,165	147.0	3,060.1	4.3	86.7	80.3	194.1	388.3
RICKS COLLEGE	PRI-T	5,859	127.2	A	5.6	17.7	15.0	177.5	450.6
UNIVERSITY OF IDAHO	PUB-U	7,118	249.2	4,548.9	3.5	78.0	43.2	114.2	355.9
ILLINOIS									
AERO-SPACE INSTITUTE	PRI-FN	70	217.1	3,040.0	14.1	57.1	57.1	46.6	70.0
ALFRED ADLER INST CHICAGO	PRI-FG	51	167.5	D	2.6	88.2	85.2	102.0	102.0
AMERICAN ACADEMY OF ART	PRI-T		NO LIBRARY FACILITIES						
AMERICAN CONSV OF MUSIC	PRI-FG	316	126.5	1,537.9	2.7	17.9	14.0	158.0	316.0
AUGUSTANA COLLEGE	PRI-FG	2,262	154.5	3,066.6	4.1	90.7	62.7	176.7	348.0
AURORA COLLEGE	PRI-FN	693	178.0	3,163.5	3.8	125.2	99.1	99.0	157.5
BARAT COLLEGE	PRI-FN	494	237.8	2,731.9	3.6	150.5	101.0	98.8	164.6
BELLEVILLE AREA COLLEGE	PUB-T	4,084	47.9	1,451.7	1.9	12.6	10.6	492.0	1,237.5
BETHANY-NTHN BAPT JT LIB	PRI-FG	D	D	D	D	D	D	D	D
BETHANY THEOLOGICAL SEM	PRI FG		SEE BETHANY-NTHN BAPT JT LIB						
BLACKBURN COLLEGE	PRI-FN	431	223.8	2,473.6	4.7	161.2	157.9	119.7	215.5
BLACK HAWK C ALL CAMPUSES									
BLACK HAWK C EAST CAMPUS	PUB-T	588	107.0	2,419.8	3.9	21.4	20.5	183.7	588.0
BLACK HAWK C QUAD-CITIES	PUB-T	2,970	69.2	1,523.9	2.4	16.3	17.7	396.0	742.5
BRADLEY UNIVERSITY	PRI-U	4,650	119.7	2,184.5	3.2	65.6	A	202.1	516.6
BRISK RABBINICAL COLLEGE	PRI-FG	D	D	D	D	D	D	D	D
CARL SANDBURG COLLEGE	PUB-T	1,530	103.7	3,173.8	5.4	22.0	17.5	133.0	510.0
CATHOLIC THEOL UNION	PRI-FG	201	463.9	A	11.1	393.3	391.8	50.2	100.5
CENTRAL YMCA CMTY COLLEGE	PRI-T	3,389	36.5	1,490.5	1.1	9.1	8.8	513.4	1,129.6
CHGO C OSTEOPATHIC MED	PRI-FG	383	1,759.7	D	8.2	60.8	84.7	22.5	58.9
CHGO CONSERVATORY COLLEGE	PRI-FG	D	D	D	D	D	D	D	D
CHICAGO STATE UNIVERSITY	PUB-FG	5,171	205.7	4,106.9	4.6	44.2	33.1	94.0	258.5
CHICAGO THEOLOGICAL SEM	PRI-FG	91	914.3	6,933.6	8.1	989.0	769.3	36.4	60.6
CTY COLLEGES CHGO ALL CAM									
CITY C CHGO CITY-WIDE C1/	PUB-T		NO LIBRARY FACILITIES						
CITY C CHGO KENNEDY-KING	PUB-T	D	D	D	D	D	D	D	D
CITY C CHICAGO LOOP C	PUB-T	3,808	95.7	1,950.4	5.5	12.2	9.1	292.9	761.6
CITY C CHGO MALCOLM X C	PUB-T	4,627	39.1	934.9	2.4	8.6	8.3	578.3	925.4
CITY C CHGO OLIVE-HARVEY	PUB-T	3,513	66.3	1,371.6	3.5	13.5	12.3	351.3	702.6
CITY C CHICAGO DALEY C	PUB-T	3,222	80.9	1,863.0	5.3	11.8	9.8	306.8	716.0
CITY C CHGO TRUMAN C	PUB-T	3,988	62.7	1,636.6	3.5	12.8	11.1	443.1	997.0
CITY C CHICAGO WRIGHT C	PUB-T	4,455	73.7	1,675.9	4.4	15.7	8.4	218.4	742.5
COLLEGE OF DUPAGE	PUB-T	8,594	159.1	6,871.2	7.5	10.8	12.5	179.0	592.6
COLLEGE OF LAKE COUNTY	PUB-T	4,679	103.9	2,860.6	4.9	16.2	13.1	195.7	668.4
COLLEGE OF SAINT FRANCIS	PRI-FN	1,344	115.0	4,295.3	4.6	81.4	52.8	134.4	231.7
COLUMBIA COLLEGE	PRI-FN	2,315	83.3	6,031.8	3.9	15.8	13.5	463.0	578.7
CONCORDIA COLLEGE	PRI-FG	1,006	191.1	2,497.4	3.6	124.6	A	147.9	201.2
DANIEL HALE WILLIAMS U	PRI-FN		NO LIBRARY FACILITIES						
DANVILLE AREA CMTY C	PUB-T	1,724	92.1	1,847.8	3.9	17.3	13.0	215.5	431.0
DELOURDES COLLEGE	PRI-FN	148	250.0	.0	17.0	130.1	130.0	74.0	74.0
DEPAUL UNIVERSITY	PRI-U	10,350	167.3	4,934.9	6.4	33.1	19.6	120.9	361.8
DEVRY INST OF TECHNOLOGY	PRI-FN	2,134	9.8	A	A	3.4	3.4	2,134.0	2,134.0

SEE FOOTNOTES AT END OF TABLE

Table 3. — Indexes Concerning Operating Expenditures, 1978-79, Bookstock Held at End of Year, 1978-79, and Library Staff (FTE), Fall 1979, College and University Libraries, by State or Other Area and Institution: Aggregate United States — Continued

STATE OR OTHER AREA AND INSTITUTION	CONTROL AND TYPE OF INSTITUTION	TOTAL FTE OPENING FALL ENROLLMENT, FALL 1978	LIBRARY OPERATING EXPENDITURES (IN DOLLARS) 1978-79			BOOKSTOCK HELD AT END OF YEAR 1978-79		FTE STUDENTS PER FTE LIBRARY STAFF FALL 1979	
			PER FTE STUDENT, FALL 1978	PER FULL-TIME FACULTY MEMBER, 1978	AS PERCENT OF GENERAL EXPENDITURES, 1978-79	VOLUMES PER FTE STUDENT FALL 1978	TITLES (INCLUDING MICROFORMS) PER FTE STUDENT 1978	TOTAL STAFF	PROFESSIONAL STAFF
(1)	(2)	(3)	(4)	(5)	(6)	(7)	(8)	(9)	(10)
ILLINOIS	--CONTINUED								
EASTERN ILL UNIVERSITY	PUB-FG	9,461	139.9	2,798.6	4.4	42.9	30.9	152.8	454.8
ELGIN COMMUNITY COLLEGE	PUB-T	2,507	95.9	2,732.3	3.9	17.5	13.6	218.0	501.4
ELMHURST COLLEGE	PRI-FN	2,291	177.8	4,380.7	5.7	57.7	55.5	150.7	458.2
EUREKA COLLEGE	PRI-FN	418	181.6	2,617.9	3.2	181.6	154.4	97.2	167.2
FELICIAN COLLEGE	PRI-T	220	260.4	.0	16.5	199.6	156.2	37.9	110.0
GARRETT-EVANGELCL THEOL	PRI-FG	249	789.5	6,779.2	7.4	669.0	485.6	31.1	62.2
GEORGE WILLIAMS COLLEGE	PRI-FG	982	182.9	2,642.2	2.9	89.2	58.4	115.5	245.5
GOVERNORS ST UNIVERSITY	PUB-FG	1,975	443.7	A	6.0	86.3	58.3	47.7	159.2
GREENVILLE COLLEGE	PRI-FN	787	168.7	A	4.3	120.7	104.5	143.0	314.8
HARRINGTON INSTITUTE	PRI-T	D	D	D	D	D	D	D	D
HEBREW THEOL COLLEGE	PRI-FG	144	A	A	A	286.1	126.8	48.0	72.0
HIGHLAND CMTY COLLEGE	PUB-T	1,110	61.2	1,511.0	1.7	29.8	28.4	370.0	1,110.0
ILL BENEDICTINE COLLEGE	PRI-FG	1,285	210.1	4,218.7	4.7	87.5	A	128.5	233.6
ILLINOIS CENTRAL COLLEGE	PUB-T	5,349	88.0	2,573.9	3.8	11.8	9.1	281.5	668.6
ILLINOIS COLLEGE	PRI-FN	750	179.9	2,933.1	5.7	128.5	119.9	150.0	250.0
ILL COLLEGE OF OPTOMETRY	PRI-FG	592	141.4	3,220.1	3.7	21.3	9.7	137.6	296.0
ILL COLLEGE PODIATRIC MED	PRI-FG	632	121.4	D	A	14.3	4.7	158.0	316.0
ILL ESTN CC SYS ALL INST									
ILL ESTN CC FRONTIER CC	PUB-T	750	25.4	4,772.0	1.9	2.8	2.8	214.2	750.0
ILL ESTN LINCOLN TRAIL C	PUB-T	938	54.3	1,415.9	3.5	21.0	20.6	312.6	469.0
ILL ESTN CC OLNEY CEN C	PUB-T	1,101	63.5	1,794.0	3.8	24.8	24.2	211.7	500.4
ILL ESTN CC WABASH VLY C	PUB-T	1,672	72.8	2,173.6	4.3	10.4	A	334.4	1,672.0
ILLINOIS INST TECHNOLOGY	PRI-FG	4,636	208.3	3,631.0	3.5	53.5	30.2	174.9	356.6
ILLINOIS STATE UNIVERSITY	PUB-FG	17,678	157.0	3,419.5	4.8	46.1	32.2	163.6	519.9
ILLINOIS VLY CMTY COLLEGE	PUB-T	2,249	95.0	2,429.7	4.9	27.7	22.8	229.4	468.5
ILL WESLEYAN UNIVERSITY	PRI-FN	1,624	209.9	2,939.2	4.2	86.8	88.0	135.3	324.8
JKM JOINT LIBRARY4/	PRI-FG	D	D	D	D	D	D	D	D
JOHN A LOGAN COLLEGE	PUB-T	1,187	144.8	3,738.0	5.6	22.7	18.6	148.3	395.6
JOHN MARSHALL LAW SCHOOL	PRI-FG	1,212	511.7	14,423.1	9.3	70.1	27.7	91.1	228.6
JOHN WOOD CMTY COLLEGE5/	PUB-T	1,337	33.5	3,208.4	1.5	2.0	.6	.0	A
JOLIET JUNIOR COLLEGE	PUB-T	3,952	87.0	2,205.7	3.3	12.4	8.9	256.6	731.8
JUDSON COLLEGE	PRI-FN	413	254.8	5,263.6	4.4	114.3	151.8	103.2	206.5
KANKAKEE CMTY COLLEGE	PUB-T	1,537	101.6	2,947.8	3.1	12.7	24.4	174.6	768.5
KASKASKIA COLLEGE	PUB-T	1,422	105.8	3,010.0	4.7	30.0	14.9	241.0	592.5
KELLER GRAD SCHOOL MGMT	PRI-FG	288	7.2	D	A	2.0	2.0	.0	A
KENDALL COLLEGE	PRI-FN	319	107.7	1,636.0	2.2	84.6	83.1	177.2	177.2
KISHWAUKEE COLLEGE	PUB-T	1,460	58.7	1,361.0	2.8	20.2	17.1	292.0	436.6
KNOX COLLEGE	PRI-FN	998	303.5	3,834.0	4.7	191.9	170.4	103.9	237.6
LAKE FOREST COLLEGE	PRI-FG	1,051	285.7	3,900.6	3.9	163.3	135.0	104.0	198.3
LAKE LAND COLLEGE	PUB-T	2,391	33.6	854.7	1.4	12.4	12.3	597.7	1,195.5
LEWIS AND CLARK CC	PUB-T	2,305	82.0	2,148.9	3.2	14.1	10.5	213.4	1,280.5
LEWIS UNIVERSITY	PRI-FG	2,673	85.7	A	2.1	41.2	A	281.3	668.2
LINCOLN CHRISTIAN COLLEGE	PRI-FG	600	111.4	2,387.5	3.1	99.5	49.6	200.0	300.0
LINCOLN COLLEGE	PRI-T	564	136.9	2,145.0	3.6	65.6	69.1	97.2	313.3
LINCOLN LAND CMTY COLLEGE	PUB-T	3,030	133.9	3,073.6	5.8	21.8	18.7	173.1	505.0
LOYOLA U OF CHICAGO	PRI-U	9,897	201.3	3,577.2	3.4	70.9	44.8	149.0	366.5
LUTH SCH THEOLOGY CHICAGO	PRI FG		SEE JKM JOINT LIBRARY						
MACCORMAC COLLEGE	PRI-T	D	D	D	D	D	D	D	D
MACMURRAY COLLEGE	PRI-FN	661	211.6	2,690.7	4.2	200.3	140.4	110.1	220.3
MALLINCKRODT COLLEGE	PRI-T	112	355.8	3,985.2	12.0	249.0	248.5	56.0	56.0
MCCORMICK THEOLOGICAL SEM	PRI FG		SEE JKM JOINT LIBRARY						
MCHENRY COUNTY COLLEGE	PUB-T	1,432	204.4	7,140.4	8.8	17.6	16.7	127.8	255.7
MCKENDREE COLLEGE	PRI-FN	712	166.0	2,955.6	3.3	78.1	51.0	169.5	712.0
MEADVL-LOMBARD THEOL SCH	PRI-FG	27	885.1	11,950.0	4.4	3,336.1	3,150.2	11.2	33.7
MIDSTATE COLLEGE	PRI-T	304	32.9	834.3	A	22.5	21.5	.0	A
MIDWEST COLLEGE OF ENGR	PRI-FG	D	D	D	D	D	D	D	D
MILLIKIN UNIVERSITY	PRI-FN	1,440	156.9	2,378.6	3.4	103.7	71.5	144.0	298.0
MONMOUTH COLLEGE	PRI-FN	665	179.8	2,491.9	3.6	181.2	126.8	166.2	221.6
MOODY BIBLE INSTITUTE	PRI-FN	1,250	88.1	2 A	A	82.0	62.9	312.5	312.5
MORAINE VLY CMTY COLLEGE	PUB-T	5,365	62.5	2,194.6	3.2	12.3	10.0	339.5	851.5
MORRISON INST OF TECHN	PRI-T	174	2.2	50.0	.0	12.5	12.3	.0	A
MORTON COLLEGE	PUB-T	1,783	79.5	2,117.8	3.8	20.7	19.6	198.1	1,783.0
MUNDELEIN COLLEGE	PRI-FG	1,244	185.1	3,437.4	4.0	103.0	93.8	111.0	248.8
NATL COLLEGE CHIROPRACTIC	PRI-FG	878	183.5	A	A	20.2	A	195.1	439.0
NATL COLLEGE ED ALL CAM									
NATL COLLEGE ED MAIN CAM	PRI-FG	1,382	158.1	3,974.1	3.8	69.5	67.4	107.9	203.2

SEE FOOTNOTES AT END OF TABLE

Table 3. — Indexes Concerning Operating Expenditures, 1978-79, Bookstock Held at End of Year, 1978-79, and Library Staff (FTE), Fall 1979, College and University Libraries, by State or Other Area and Institution: Aggregate United States — Continued

STATE OR OTHER AREA AND INSTITUTION	CON-TROL AND TYPE OF IN-STITU-TION	TOTAL FTE OPENING FALL ENROLL-MENT, FALL 1978	LIBRARY OPERATING EXPENDITURES (IN DOLLARS) 1978-79			BOOKSTOCK HELD AT END OF YEAR 1978-79		FTE STUDENTS PER FTE LIBRARY STAFF FALL 1979	
			PER FTE STU-DENT, FALL 1978	PER FULL-TIME FAC-ULTY MEM-BER, 1978	AS PER-CENT OF GENERAL EXPENDI-TURES, 1978-79	VOLUMES PER FTE STUDENT, FALL 1978	TITLES (INCLU-DING MICRO-FORMS) PER FTE STUDENT 1978	TOTAL STAFF	PROFES-SIONAL STAFF
(1)	(2)	(3)	(4)	(5)	(6)	(7)	(8)	(9)	(10)
ILLINOIS	--CONTINUED								
NATL COLLEGE ED URBAN CAM	PRI-FG	199	355.0	5,047.0	5.1	120.1	124.4	55.2	124.3
NATIVE AMERICAN EDUC SERV	PRI-FN	20	671.8	A	19.6	21.2	19.4	.0	A
NORTH CENTRAL COLLEGE	PRI-FN	929	127.4	2,233.5	3.1	104.1	83.3	201.9	258.0
NTHESTN ILL UNIVERSITY	PUB-FG	6,845	192.7	4,010.8	5.6	46.5	32.7	130.3	351.0
NORTHERN BAPT THEOL SEM	PRI FG			SEE BETHANY-NTHN BAPT JT LIB					
NORTHERN ILL UNIVERSITY	PUB-U	19,237	171.6	A	4.7	50.3	33.2	134.7	377.1
NORTH PARK C & THEOL SEM	PRI-FG	1,301	201.4	2,978.4	4.0	112.2	82.8	98.5	236.5
NORTHWESTERN UNIVERSITY	PRI-U	12,710	578.1	9,197.5	4.5	197.1	131.4	56.9	127.1
OAKTON COMMUNITY COLLEGE	PUB-T	3,814	121.9	3,606.8	3.9	12.8	12.1	227.0	595.9
OLIVET NAZARENE COLLEGE	PRI-FG	1,828	120.8	2,693.8	3.9	63.3	61.6	157.5	351.5
PARKLAND COLLEGE	PUB-T	3,719	176.4	4,525.1	7.5	17.8	A	145.8	495.8
PRAIRIE STATE COLLEGE	PUB-T	2,778	60.0	1,812.9	2.5	17.1	16.2	205.7	1,111.2
PRINCIPIA COLLEGE	PRI-FN	867	307.1	4,590.7	A	155.8	130.3	72.2	216.7
QUINCY COLLEGE	PRI-FN	878	201.5	2,528.3	4.3	221.8	235.9	129.1	292.6
REND LAKE COLLEGE	PUB-T	1,454	72.5	1,648.7	2.7	18.5	16.0	220.3	727.0
RICHLAND CMTY COLLEGE	PUB-T	1,093	144.7	4,519.0	5.5	18.5	15.9	140.1	364.3
ROCKFORD COLLEGE	PRI-FG	D	D	D	D	D	D	D	D
ROCK VALLEY COLLEGE	PUB-T	3,528	49.1	1,470.1	2.7	14.1	14.2	371.3	1,008.0
ROOSEVELT UNIVERSITY	PRI-FG	D	D	D	D	D	D	D	D
ROSARY COLLEGE	PRI-FG	1,051	275.9	6,443.8	6.8	169.2	159.7	93.0	198.3
RUSH UNIVERSITY	PRI-FG	900	687.6	D	4.3	94.4	88.8	33.8	100.0
SNT MARY OF THE LAKE SEM	PRI-FG	126	481.5	.0	5.4	1,053.7	606.9	28.6	126.0
SAINT XAVIER COLLEGE	PRI-FG	1,463	129.7	1,957.5	3.5	44.3	35.0	157.3	365.7
SANGAMON STATE UNIVERSITY	PUB-FG	1,964	608.6	7,114.9	9.1	118.2	81.8	42.8	245.5
SAUK VALLEY COLLEGE	PUB-T	1,502	83.9	2,292.6	3.8	27.4	25.4	214.5	375.5
SCH ART INSTITUTE CHICAGO	PRI-FG	1,313	493.8	10,630.1	15.4	9.1	105.1	52.1	105.8
SEABURY-WESTERN THEOL SEM	PRI-FG	78	897.2	6,998.8	9.0	967.0	701.7	43.3	78.0
SHAWNEE COLLEGE	PUB-T	940	67.5	2,352.3	3.5	36.6	38.3	470.0	940.0
SHERWOOD MUSIC SCHOOL	PRI-FN	D	D	D	D	D	D	D	D
SHIMER COLLEGE	PRI-FN	D	D	D	D	D	D	D	D
SOUTHEASTERN ILL COLLEGE	PUB-T	1,116	61.6	1,250.2	2.3	22.4	20.6	279.0	558.0
STHN ILLINOIS U ALL INST									
STHN ILLINOIS U CARBONDL	PUB-U	20,664	261.7	5,146.4	4.4	79.5	51.5	112.6	313.0
STHN ILLINOIS U EDWARDSVL	PUB-FG	8,897	221.8	3,402.5	4.3	77.2	57.6	139.8	369.1
SPERTUS COLLEGE JUDAICA	PRI-FG	363	297.6	7,202.4	7.2	165.5	72.0	69.8	103.7
SPOON RIVER COLLEGE	PUB-T	815	180.1	3,968.4	6.3	28.3	26.1	135.8	407.5
SPRINGFLD COLLEGE IN ILL	PRI-T	410	101.0	2,959.3	5.1	74.5	68.3	164.0	410.0
STATE COMMUNITY COLLEGE	PUB-T	877	100.5	1,241.4	2.2	31.3	31.4	219.2	438.5
TELSHE YESHIVA-CHICAGO	PRI-FG	D	D	D	D	D	D	D	D
THORNTON CMTY COLLEGE	PUB-T	4,203	61.5	2,173.7	2.7	7.5	7.4	400.2	934.0
TRINITY CHRISTIAN COLLEGE	PRI-FN	351	167.3	2,448.1	4.3	122.5	176.6	167.1	351.0
TRINITY COLLEGE	PRI-FN	725	186.9	3,663.6	4.4	75.7	93.7	95.3	181.2
TRINITY EVANGELCL DIV SCH	PRI-FG	598	313.8	7,219.2	6.8	116.2	87.0	542.5	1,905.1
TRITON COLLEGE	PUB-T	8,192	53.4	1,937.5	2.0	9.1	6.7	A	123.3
UNIVERSITY OF CHICAGO	PRI-U	8,387	822.1	9,181.5	4.2	498.7	A	26.4	
U HLTH SCI-CHGO MEDL SCH	PRI-FG	600	471.1	12,291.8	2.4	60.3	28.5	44.1	100.0
U OF ILLINOIS ALL CAM									
U OF ILL CHICAGO CIRCLE	PUB-FG	18,088	169.9	3,411.4	4.2	37.6	22.1	160.2	509.5
U OF ILL MEDL CTR CHGO	PUB-FG	4,776	469.8	5,355.8	2.0	77.8	23.2	46.0	140.4
U OF ILL URBANA CAMPUS	PUB-U	32,148	310.8	4,617.8	3.6	179.1	65.8	80.8	235.8
VANDERCOOK C OF MUSIC	PRI-FG	79	297.0	2,133.0	8.2	227.8	A	60.7	79.0
WAUBONSEE CMTY COLLEGE	PUB-T	2,011	116.2	3,292.9	5.2	23.4	22.5	174.8	628.4
WESTERN ILL UNIVERSITY	PUB-FG	11,064	149.5	2,530.8	4.0	41.4	38.4	186.5	650.8
WHEATON COLLEGE	PRI-FG	2,262	178.2	2,900.7	3.0	64.4	A	133.0	282.7
WM RAINEY HARPER COLLEGE	PUB-T	6,980	98.4	3,258.0	4.9	13.7	10.0	198.2	634.5
INDIANA									
ANCILLA DOMINI COLLEGE	PRI-T	132	213.1	14,068.0	10.3	206.7	206.6	73.3	132.0
ANDERSON COLLEGE	PRI-FG	1,895	184.2	3,878.5	4.2	87.9	64.1	132.5	217.8
BALL STATE UNIVERSITY	PUB-U	14,657	206.5	3,408.6	5.2	68.6	46.5	111.0	325.7
BETHEL COLLEGE	PRI-FN	400	137.1	3,226.0	4.6	126.8	A	200.0	266.6
BUTLER UNIVERSITY	PRI-U	2,730	117.4	2,095.4	3.1	68.7	50.7	147.5	210.0
CALUMET COLLEGE	PRI-FN	897	129.1	4,632.6	5.7	108.2	88.1	140.1	448.5
CHRISTIAN THEOLOGICAL SEM	PRI-FG	147	657.9	8,792.4	7.2	640.8	496.4	31.9	49.0
CLARK COLLEGE	PRI-T	D	D	D	D	D	D	D	D
CONCORDIA THEOLOGICAL SEM	PRI-FG	487	309.7	5,387.0	7.3	197.6	188.9	69.5	162.3
DEPAUW UNIVERSITY	PRI-FG	2,224	155.1	2,430.5	3.4	98.9	66.2	107.9	296.5

SEE FOOTNOTES AT END OF TABLE

Table 3. — Indexes Concerning Operating Expenditures, 1978-79, Bookstock Held at End of Year, 1978-79, and Library Staff (FTE), Fall 1979, College and University Libraries, by State or Other Area and Institution: Aggregate United States — Continued

STATE OR OTHER AREA AND INSTITUTION	CON- TROL AND TYPE OF IN- STITU- TION	TOTAL FTE OPENING FALL ENROLL- MENT, FALL 1978	LIBRARY OPERATING EXPENDITURES (IN DOLLARS) 1978-79			BOOKSTOCK HELD AT END OF YEAR 1978-79		FTE STUDENTS PER FTE LIBRARY STAFF FALL 1979	
			PER FTE STU- DENT, FALL 1978	PER FULL- TIME FAC- ULTY MEM- BER, 1978	AS PER- CENT OF GENERAL EXPENDI- TURES, 1978-79	VOLUMES PER FTE STUDENT, FALL 1978	TITLES (INCLU- DING MICRO- FORMS) PER FTE STUDENT 1978	TOTAL STAFF	PROFES- SIONAL STAFF
(1)	(2)	(3)	(4)	(5)	(6)	(7)	(8)	(9)	(10)
INDIANA	--CONTINUED								
EARLHAM COLLEGE	PRI-FG	1,089	288.6	4,082.0	3.7	239.4	A	114.6	181.5
FORT WAYNE BIBLE COLLEGE	PRI-FN	444	140.5	2,836.0	4.0	111.4	100.6	94.4	222.0
FRANKLIN COLLEGE INDIANA	PRI-FN	649	201.3	3,438.2	3.7	154.0	152.5	101.4	216.3
GOSHEN BIBLICAL SEMINARY	PRI·FG	SEE MENNONITE BIB SEM JT LIB							
GOSHEN COLLEGE	PRI-FN	1,130	107.0	1,778.9	2.3	89.0	A	251.1	565.0
GRACE COLLEGE	PRI-FN	972	153.0	3,304.9	4.1	87.1	83.9	129.6	237.0
HANOVER COLLEGE	PRI-FN	D	D	D	D	D	D	D	D
HOLY CROSS JUNIOR COLLEGE	PRI-T	202	101.3	10,235.0	6.8	41.9	41.6	183.6	183.6
HUNTINGTON COLLEGE	PRI-FG	545	189.2	3,033.7	4.6	94.5	91.2	143.4	272.5
INDIANA CEN UNIVERSITY	PRI-FG	1,778	135.6	3,054.0	3.7	56.4	40.6	157.3	508.0
INDIANA C MORTUARY SCI	PRI-T	70	6.1	D	.4	20.4	A	.0	A
INDIANA INST TECHNOLOGY	PRI-FN	394	81.7	2,013.5	2.1	116.5	91.9	394.0	394.0
IND NTHN GRAD SCH MGMT	PRI-FG	33	124.8	D	6.1	231.8	231.8	55.0	A
INDIANA STATE U ALL CAM									
INDIANA STATE U MAIN CAM	PUB-U	9,594	178.1	2,621.4	3.9	83.5	41.5	128.7	330.8
INDIANA ST U EVANSVL CAM	PUB-FN	2,123	139.8	3,092.9	4.5	63.1	46.5	141.5	530.7
INDIANA U ALL CAMPUSES									
INDIANA U BLOOMINGTON2/	PUB-U	27,887	283.9	6,289.1	5.2	116.7	80.6	92.0	256.5
INDIANA UNIVERSITY EAST	PUB-T	670	149.6	4,177.0	5.1	40.2	42.1	167.5	335.0
INDIANA U AT KOKOMO	PUB-FN	1,144	170.9	3,761.2	6.4	69.4	54.0	163.4	286.0
INDIANA U NORTHWEST	PUB-FG	2,473	108.7	2,259.8	3.3	56.8	39.4	309.1	824.3
IND-PURDUE U INDIANAPOLIS	PUB-FG	12,096	175.4	3,468.5	2.3	46.2	18.0	145.9	361.0
INDIANA U AT SOUTH BEND	PUB-FG	3,033	134.0	3,081.0	4.5	54.3	A	219.7	481.4
INDIANA U SOUTHEAST	PUB-FG	2,363	108.2	3,236.4	4.6	36.6	24.6	196.9	590.7
IND-PURDUE U FORT WAYNE	PUB-FG	5,545	103.2	2,169.2	4.0	36.8	34.2	277.2	693.1
IND VOC TECH C ALL CAM									
IND VOC TECH C-CEN IND	PUB-T	2,404	28.7	908.6	1.5	2.9	2.1	649.7	12,020.0
IND VOC TECH C-COLUMBUS	PUB-T	816	39.7	981.9	1.9	2.1	1.5	408.0	408.0
IND VOC TECH C-KOKOMO	PUB-T	900	54.7	2,735.8	3.7	2.1	A	272.7	310.3
IND VOC TECH C-LAFAYETTE	PUB-T	498	131.2	2,178.8	5.1	11.7	7.8	108.2	249.0
IND VOC TECH C-NTH CEN	PUB-T	1,068	31.6	733.6	1.4	6.8	6.6	667.5	3,560.0
IND VOC TECH C NORTHEAST	PUB-T	1,130	26.6	971.8	1.7	4.4	4.1	753.3	753.3
IND VOC TECH C-STHCEN	PUB-T	662	99.5	2,747.2	4.1	5.3	5.2	220.6	331.0
IND VOC TECH C-SOUTHWEST	PUB-T	734	33.9	997.9	1.7	4.7	4.2	734.0	734.0
IND VOC TECH-WABASH VLY	PUB-T	753	71.2	1,375.3	3.2	4.9	4.5	376.5	753.0
INTERNATIONAL BUSINESS C	PRI-T	286	36.0	A	4.1	6.9	5.5	286.0	286.0
LOCKYEAR COLLEGE	PRI-T	534	49.3	A	A	13.9	11.0	267.0	267.0
MANCHESTER COLLEGE	PRI-FG	1,112	154.1	2,414.4	3.9	135.5	97.8	161.1	278.0
MARIAN COLLEGE	PRI-FN	494	172.9	2,670.2	3.1	206.7	145.5	123.5	123.5
MARION COLLEGE	PRI-FG	832	118.5	1,934.5	3.6	97.3	67.2	184.8	332.8
MENNONITE BIBLICAL SEM	PRI FG	SEE MENNONITE BIB SEM JT LIB							
MENNONITE BIB SEM JT LIB	PRI-FG	D	D	D	D	D	D	D	D
OAKLAND CITY COLLEGE	PRI-FN	485	102.0	2,061.9	2.8	125.9	131.0	373.0	373.0
PURDUE U ALL CAMPUSES									
PURDUE U MAIN CAMPUS	PUB-U	28,165	159.5	3,287.4	2.3	49.2	19.7	134.6	625.8
PURDUE U CALUMET CAMPUS	PUB-FG	3,762	112.0	2,096.8	3.9	33.2	24.5	221.2	627.0
PURDUE U NORTH CEN CAMPUS	PUB-T	1,101	97.0	2,180.9	3.4	35.8	24.9	211.7	5,505.0
ROSE-HULMAN INST OF TECHN	PRI-FG	1,169	78.3	1,366.1	1.5	43.5	42.2	194.8	1,169.0
SAINT FRANCIS COLLEGE	PRI-FG	763	96.1	2,446.3	3.6	88.7	241.4	162.3	254.3
SAINT JOSEPH'S COLLEGE	PRI-FG	946	186.0	5,334.1	3.6	154.5	102.1	106.2	350.3
SAINT MARY'S COLLEGE	PRI-FN	1,726	142.2	2,135.1	3.4	86.1	69.8	150.0	265.5
SAINT MARY-OF-THE-WOODS C	PRI-FN	496	172.6	2,670.2	2.2	265.7	166.2	99.2	124.0
SAINT MEINRAD COLLEGE	PRI FN	SEE SNT MEINRAD C JT LIBRARY							
SNT MEINRAD C JT LIBRARY	PRI-FN	D	D	D	D	D	D	D	D
SNT MEINRAD SCH THEOLOGY	PRI FG	SEE SNT MEINRAD C JT LIBRARY							
TAYLOR UNIVERSITY	PRI-FN	1,499	119.8	2,643.0	3.2	82.5	81.9	333.1	374.7
TRI-STATE UNIVERSITY	PRI-FN	1,218	98.0	1,592.5	2.9	74.1	42.8	174.0	1,218.0
UNIVERSITY OF EVANSVILLE	PRI-FG	3,595	145.5	2,655.9	4.1	54.4	70.1	173.6	599.1
UNIVERSITY OF NOTRE DAME	PRI-U	8,543	321.0	6,205.2	5.2	161.9	68.4	71.6	211.9
VALPARAISO UNIVERSITY	PRI-FG	3,926	138.7	2,161.5	3.6	77.9	49.7	183.4	408.9
VINCENNES UNIVERSITY	PUB-T	3,188	79.7	1,344.8	2.9	18.9	18.4	205.6	531.3
WABASH COLLEGE	PRI-FN	808	266.9	3,037.8	3.0	257.3	A	118.8	367.2
IOWA									
AMERICAN INSTITUTE BUS	PRI-T	D	D	D	D	D	D	D	D
AQUINAS INST OF THEOLOGY	PRI-FG	110	630.2	34,665.5	9.5	656.1	A	.0	A

SEE FOOTNOTES AT END OF TABLE

Table 3. — Indexes Concerning Operating Expenditures, 1978-79, Bookstock Held at End of Year, 1978-79, and Library Staff (FTE), Fall 1979, College and University Libraries, by State or Other Area and Institution: Aggregate United States — Continued

STATE OR OTHER AREA AND INSTITUTION	CONTROL AND TYPE OF INSTITUTION	TOTAL FTE OPENING FALL ENROLLMENT, FALL 1978	LIBRARY OPERATING EXPENDITURES (IN DOLLARS) 1978-79			BOOKSTOCK HELD AT END OF YEAR 1978-79		FTE STUDENTS PER FTE LIBRARY STAFF FALL 1979	
			PER FTE STUDENT, FALL 1978	PER FULL-TIME FACULTY MEMBER, 1978	AS PERCENT OF GENERAL EXPENDITURES, 1978-79	VOLUMES PER FTE STUDENT, FALL 1978	TITLES (INCLUDING MICROFORMS) PER FTE STUDENT 1978	TOTAL STAFF	PROFESSIONAL STAFF
(1)	(2)	(3)	(4)	(5)	(6)	(7)	(8)	(9)	(10)
IOWA	--CONTINUED								
BRIAR CLIFF COLLEGE	PRI-FN	991	84.3	1,705.9	3.3	82.0	82.0	341.7	495.5
BUENA VISTA COLLEGE	PRI-FN	1,024	117.5	2,508.0	3.5	71.1	71.3	.0	A
CENTRAL U OF IOWA	PRI-FN	1,448	136.0	2,735.8	3.1	82.8	62.1	258.5	804.4
CLARKE COLLEGE	PRI-FG	486	184.2	1,827.9	4.0	210.1	217.2	108.0	220.9
COE COLLEGE	PRI-FN	1,068	245.4	3,691.7	4.8	165.0	123.6	94.5	267.0
COLLEGE OSTED MED-SURGERY	PRI-FG	529	152.2	D	1.1	41.6	14.0	.0	A
CORNELL COLLEGE	PRI-FN	875	202.2	2,641.2	3.2	133.2	101.2	106.7	218.7
DES MOINES AREA CC	PUB-T	4,124	71.4	1,146.1	2.2	17.3	15.9	298.8	959.0
DIVINE WORD COLLEGE	PRI-FN	94	748.4	7,816.6	9.1	892.5	758.0	18.8	31.3
DORDT COLLEGE	PRI-FN	1,197	116.3	1,990.0	3.7	69.0	67.4	171.0	598.5
DRAKE UNIVERSITY	PRI-U	5,228	212.1	4,264.9	5.0	88.1	72.4	139.4	348.5
ESTN IOWA CC DIST ALL CAM									
CLINTON COMMUNITY COLLEGE	PUB-T	591	103.2	1,848.3	3.0	23.8	23.0	197.0	591.0
MUSCATINE CMTY COLLEGE	PUB-T	553	190.6	3,765.8	5.7	30.8	30.2	251.3	460.8
SCOTT COMMUNITY COLLEGE	PUB-T	1,039	102.0	1,860.7	2.9	21.4	17.7	173.1	519.5
ELLSWORTH CMTY COLLEGE	PUB-T	782	146.6	2,163.6	4.9	30.6	33.5	124.1	260.6
FAITH BAPT BIBLE COLLEGE	PRI-FN	500	115.4	2,749.2	5.6	70.5	65.5	138.8	138.8
GRACELAND COLLEGE	PRI-FN	1,200	126.2	1,741.7	2.9	73.3	55.1	127.6	600.0
GRAND VIEW COLLEGE	PRI-FN	1,021	119.3	2,342.9	4.8	64.0	45.6	196.3	510.5
GRINNELL COLLEGE	PRI-FN	1,245	319.2	3,784.8	4.6	202.7	144.1	84.6	276.6
HAWKEYE INST TECHNOLOGY	PUB-T	1,667	71.0	1,066.3	1.7	9.3	5.9	416.7	833.5
INDIAN HILLS CC	PUB-T	D	D	D	D	D	D	D	D
IOWA CENTRAL CC	PUB-T	1,958	93.9	2,419.8	2.8	30.9	29.2	230.3	489.5
IOWA LAKES CC ALL CAM									
IOWA LAKES CC NORTH CTR	PUB-T	453	218.6	3,961.0	4.9	49.1	46.4	100.6	453.0
IOWA LAKES CC SOUTH CTR	PUB-T	707	102.9	1,323.3	2.5	15.4	14.4	235.6	707.0
IOWA STATE U SCI & TECHN	PUB-U	21,691	199.9	3,620.8	3.2	59.7	32.1	86.6	156.0
IOWA WESLEYAN COLLEGE	PRI-FN	624	196.4	2,723.7	4.3	149.5	108.7	223.1	401.7
IOWA WESTERN CMTY COLLEGE	PUB-T	1,607	123.8	1,716.3	2.9	33.7	30.5	314.9	769.7
KIRKWOOD CMTY COLLEGE	PUB-T	3,464	45.6	764.1	.8	13.6	A		
LORAS COLLEGE	PRI-FG	1,506	122.1	2,629.0	3.7	130.5	116.2	251.0	430.2
LUTHER COLLEGE	PRI-FN	1,933	176.2	2,562.1	4.1	126.4	77.3	133.3	322.1
MAHARISHI INTRNATL U	PRI-FG	726	86.0	1,487.9	1.5	64.7	55.9	.0	A
MARSHALLTWN CMTY COLLEGE	PUB-T	840	122.9	2,401.0	4.1	32.7	31.2	168.0	420.0
MARYCREST COLLEGE	PRI-FG	691	168.8	2,201.0	4.3	136.9	120.3	106.3	172.7
MORNINGSIDE COLLEGE	PRI-FG	1,232	145.8	2,219.0	3.3	97.0	76.6	152.0	308.0
MOUNT MERCY COLLEGE	PRI-FN	860	158.4	2,391.1	4.9	73.1	69.5	97.2	97.2
MOUNT SAINT CLARE COLLEGE	PRI-FN	175	177.2	6,204.6	4.6	110.8	90.9	173.6	503.5
NTHEST IA TECH INSTITUTE	PUB-T	1,007	108.9	1,828.3	2.4	17.8	6.0	195.1	780.5
N IOWA AREA CMTY COLLEGE	PUB-T	1,561	142.8	2,534.5	3.2	21.0	16.9		
NTHWST IOWA TECH C	PUB-T	D	D	D	D	D	D	D	D
NORTHWESTERN COLLEGE	PRI-FN	773	192.1	3,454.0	4.6	105.3	74.1	154.6	429.4
OPEN BIBLE COLLEGE	PRI-FN	98	112.5	2,205.6	3.7	155.2	137.0	98.0	98.0
PALMER C OF CHIROPRACTIC	PRI-FG	1,823	97.3	1,908.3	2.4	7.6	5.8	202.5	455.7
SAINT AMBROSE COLLEGE	PRI-FN	1,377	119.4	2,990.9	3.3	73.7	63.0	178.8	459.0
SIMPSON COLLEGE	PRI-FN	783	152.5	1,957.6	2.7	139.9	112.0	130.5	391.5
SIOUX EMPIRE COLLEGE	PRI-T	364	54.3	D	2.2	38.4	34.3	242.6	364.0
SOUTHEASTERN CMTY COLLEGE	PUB-T	1,327	141.9	2,093.0	4.4	30.7	30.4	59.6	159.0
SOUTHWESTERN CMTY COLLEGE	PUB-T	477	260.1	3,447.5	5.9	35.0	35.1	224.8	262.3
UNIVERSITY OF DUBUQUE	PRI-FG	787	198.2	3,319.8	4.1	177.2	A		
UNIVERSITY OF IOWA	PUB-U	20,177	280.4	5,591.3	3.5	109.8	68.7	107.0	270.8
U OF NORTHERN IOWA	PUB-FG	9,039	188.9	3,167.9	4.8	55.6	51.1	154.5	410.8
UPPER IOWA UNIVERSITY	PRI-FN	534	136.0	2,271.1	2.8	148.0	103.7	97.0	534.0
VENNARD COLLEGE	PRI-FN	189	163.6	3,092.7	3.8	220.5	175.4	94.5	189.0
WALDORF COLLEGE	PRI-T	493	103.1	1,816.1	2.4	62.4	48.7	189.6	189.6
WARTBURG COLLEGE	PRI-FN	1,093	173.1	2,489.5	3.4	119.4	101.1	130.1	321.4
WARTBURG THEOLOGICAL SEM	PRI-FG	256	270.8	4,333.2	5.9	281.9	A	73.1	256.0
WESTERN IOWA TECH	PUB-T	1,299	135.2	2,143.1	3.7	7.8	6.7	216.5	433.0
WESTMAR COLLEGE	PRI-FN	603	127.1	2,017.5	3.4	148.2	A	134.0	301.5
WILLIAM PENN COLLEGE	PRI-FN	596	105.6	1,656.4	2.3	117.5	122.0	199.6	298.0
KANSAS									
ALLEN CO CMTY JR COLLEGE	PUB-T	552	81.6	1,878.5	5.2	69.2	66.5	368.0	552.0
BAKER UNIVERSITY	PRI-FG	938	116.9	2,109.1	3.3	102.5	64.0	170.5	469.0
BARTON CO CMTY JR COLLEGE	PUB-T	1,026	83.6	1,532.3	2.7	23.7	23.7	150.8	228.0
BENEDICTINE COLLEGE	PRI-FN	952	186.5	2,691.1	4.3	299.7	167.2	91.5	190.4
BETHANY COLLEGE	PRI-FN	740	157.0	2,582.4	3.8	104.7	72.1	194.7	246.6

SEE FOOTNOTES AT END OF TABLE

Table 3. – Indexes Concerning Operating Expenditures, 1978-79, Bookstock Held at End of Year, 1978-79, and Library Staff (FTE), Fall 1979, College and University Libraries, by State or Other Area and Institution: Aggregate United States – Continued

STATE OR OTHER AREA AND INSTITUTION	CONTROL AND TYPE OF INSTITUTION	TOTAL FTE OPENING FALL ENROLLMENT, FALL 1978	LIBRARY OPERATING EXPENDITURES (IN DOLLARS) 1978-79			BOOKSTOCK HELD AT END OF YEAR 1978-79		FTE STUDENTS PER FTE LIBRARY STAFF FALL 1979	
			PER FTE STUDENT, FALL 1978	PER FULL-TIME FACULTY MEMBER, 1978	AS PERCENT OF GENERAL EXPENDITURES, 1978-79	VOLUMES PER FTE STUDENT, FALL 1978	TITLES (INCLUDING MICROFORMS) PER FTE STUDENT 1978	TOTAL STAFF	PROFESSIONAL STAFF
(1)	(2)	(3)	(4)	(5)	(6)	(7)	(8)	(9)	(10)
KANSAS	--CONTINUED								
BETHEL COLLEGE	PRI-FN	583	177.4	2,796.5	4.0	166.5	136.7	112.1	342.9
BUTLER CO CMTY JR COLLEGE	PUB-T	967	78.6	1,492.1	2.3	31.6	24.9	241.7	967.0
CENTRAL BAPTIST THEOL SEM	PRI-FG	73	576.4	8,416.4	7.0	897.6	677.5	27.0	104.2
CENTRAL COLLEGE	PRI-T	240	112.6	1,931.0	2.4	75.1	75.0	184.6	184.6
CLOUD CO CMTY JR COLLEGE	PUB-T	772	82.5	2,054.6	A	23.9	19.4	145.6	772.0
COFFEYVL CMTY JR COLLEGE	PUB-T	648	142.5	3,552.6	6.0	39.5	36.7	190.0	648.0
COLBY COMMUNITY COLLEGE	PUB-T	880	102.5	1,504.6	3.7	31.5	28.7	179.5	179.5
COWLEY CO CMTY JR COLLEGE	PUB-T	896	87.5	2,064.4	4.3	20.9	16.8	298.6	896.0
DODGE CTY CMTY JR COLLEGE	PUB-T	953	140.8	A	4.7	33.8	31.9	136.1	953.0
DONNELLY COLLEGE	PRI-T	372	125.4	4,243.2	4.4	81.8	68.5	106.2	248.0
EMPORIA STATE UNIVERSITY	PUB-FG	4,699	199.6	3,767.3	5.8	131.7	96.6	206.0	398.2
FORT HAYS ST UNIVERSITY	PUB-FG	4,239	142.3	2,635.7	4.3	70.8	67.8	249.3	529.8
FT SCOTT CMTY JR COLLEGE	PUB-T	760	75.4	2,205.9	3.4	25.9	26.9	253.3	380.0
FRIENDS BIBLE COLLEGE	PRI-FN	102	358.7	3,326.2	6.8	180.1	125.4	102.0	102.0
FRIENDS UNIVERSITY	PRI-FN	771	136.3	A	3.2	105.8	74.2	157.3	257.0
GARDEN CITY COMMUNITY JC	PUB-T	682	97.9	1,027.5	2.3	44.8	34.5	227.3	682.0
HASKELL INDIAN JR COLLEGE	PUB-T	839	269.2	3,227.2	3.4	23.9	18.8	.0	A
HESSTON COLLEGE	PRI-T	671	72.1	1,307.6	2.0	42.7	38.4	479.2	671.0
HIGHLAND CMTY JR COLLEGE	PUB-T	732	56.6	2,183.2	2.5	34.1	28.9	281.5	732.0
HUTCHINSN CMTY JR COLLEGE	PUB-T	1,709	62.7	1,190.6	2.5	21.9	21.3	255.0	461.8
INDEPENDENCE COMMUNITY JC	PUB-T	518	90.3	1,509.0	3.8	53.8	38.8	172.6	259.0
JOHNSN CO CMTY JR COLLEGE	PUB-T	3,090	77.0	1,816.4	2.6	12.4	12.0	396.1	583.0
KANSAS CITY KANS CMTY JC	PUB-T	2,063	64.9	1,506.5	2.7	24.6	24.4	248.5	687.6
KANSAS NEWMAN COLLEGE	PRI-FN	512	173.4	2,864.6	4.5	133.4	128.9	116.3	256.0
KANSAS ST U AGR & APP SCI	PUB-U	15,699	149.2	2,623.7	2.6	54.7	70.2	215.0	490.5
KANSAS TECHNICAL INST	PUB-T	246	274.0	3,744.9	5.5	63.1	62.0	82.0	246.0
KANSAS WESLEYAN	PRI-FN	389	243.9	2,875.3	5.3	192.4	190.5	77.8	129.6
LABETTE CMTY COLLEGE	PUB-T	533	105.6	2,010.4	4.2	37.0	34.7	266.5	266.5
MANHATTAN CHRSTN COLLEGE	PRI-FN	207	103.0	1,939.5	2.2	107.1	114.3	103.5	207.0
MARYMOUNT COLLEGE KANSAS	PRI-FN	630	157.3	2,108.7	4.1	119.2	116.1	121.1	286.3
MCPHERSON COLLEGE	PRI-FN	440	198.8	2,651.3	3.9	151.9	147.1	146.6	440.0
MID-AMERICA NAZARENE C	PRI-FN	1,043	100.7	A	2.8	60.0	79.3	226.7	260.7
NEOSHO CO CMTY JR COLLEGE	PUB-T	414	147.2	2,177.3	5.1	50.0	49.0	138.0	414.0
OTTAWA UNIVERSITY	PRI-FN	833	87.2	A	1.8	107.4	70.3	333.2	416.5
PITTSBURG ST UNIVERSITY	PUB-FG	3,954	173.4	2,981.6	4.7	51.4	48.3	232.5	395.4
PRATT CMTY JUNIOR COLLEGE	PUB-T	426	115.0	1,690.3	3.0	56.2	54.5	142.0	213.0
SAINT JOHN'S COLLEGE	PRI-T	222	234.6	3,064.7	5.1	198.0	186.2	63.4	222.0
SAINT MARY COLLEGE	PRI-FN	535	163.0	8,722.4	4.1	205.9	139.2	95.5	107.1
SAINT MARY PLAINS COLLEGE	PRI-FN	543	161.9	2,144.2	4.4	105.8	69.8	108.6	155.1
SEWARD CO CMTY JR COLLEGE	PUB-T	389	151.6	2,358.9	3.6	52.0	50.5	194.5	194.5
SOUTHWESTERN COLLEGE	PRI-FN	593	135.8	2,013.7	3.5	156.2	126.0	169.4	593.0
STERLING COLLEGE	PRI-FN	515	158.3	2,329.3	3.5	150.6	147.7	147.1	257.5
TABOR COLLEGE	PRI-FN	405	168.7	2,356.6	3.4	134.2	132.9	101.2	202.5
U KANSAS ALL CAMPUSES									
U OF KANSAS MAIN CAMPUS	PUB-U	19,780	234.2	4,512.4	5.2	99.0	63.1	120.9	321.6
U OF KANS MEDICAL CENTER	PUB-FG	1,764	397.6	10,171.7	1.4	69.4	29.5	49.0	176.4
WASHBURN U OF TOPEKA	PUB-FG	4,310	150.5	3,795.3	6.2	58.0	43.6	184.9	324.0
WICHITA STATE UNIVERSITY	PUB-U	10,413	171.4	3,514.1	4.8	58.4	44.1	202.1	507.9
KENTUCKY									
ALICE LLOYD COLLEGE	PRI-T	168	339.0	5,695.7	3.1	173.5	182.3	39.0	73.0
ASBURY COLLEGE	PRI-FN	1,251	179.3	2,465.7	5.1	75.4	57.7	120.2	250.2
ASBURY THEOLOGICAL SEM	PRI-FG	671	358.2	6,868.4	8.9	175.9	126.8	51.6	134.2
BELLARMINE COLLEGE	PRI-FG	1,242	133.9	2,919.4	4.6	62.9	58.1	144.4	310.5
BEREA COLLEGE	PRI-FN	1,371	247.5	3,263.9	4.0	168.2	142.9	97.9	195.8
BRESCIA COLLEGE	PRI-FN	596	207.7	2,526.9	6.0	105.2	104.0	99.3	119.2
CAMPBELLSVILLE COLLEGE	PRI-FN	608	165.3	2,233.5	4.5	140.3	103.0	101.3	202.6
CENTRE COLLEGE OF KY	PRI-FN	749	295.4	3,882.5	5.8	173.9	140.9	78.8	187.2
CUMBERLAND COLLEGE	PRI-FN	1,888	85.8	1,953.4	3.1	46.3	42.3	162.7	286.0
DRAUGHON'S COLLEGE	PRI-T	314	31.8	A	A	8.9	4.4	241.5	241.5
EASTERN KY UNIVERSITY	PUB-FG	11,147	143.7	2,720.6	4.0	41.7	58.7	131.1	454.9
GEORGETOWN COLLEGE	PRI-FG	974	129.3	2,172.7	3.3	131.2	144.7	162.3	324.6
KENTUCKY BUSINESS COLLEGE	PRI-T	737	14.6	A	.9	4.8	4.3	1,229.3	1,228.3
KY CHRISTIAN COLLEGE	PRI-FN	412	27.4	808.7	1.1	57.2	39.8	412.0	412.0
KENTUCKY STATE UNIVERSITY	PUB-FG	1,697	234.1	2,900.4	3.2	79.6	92.5	84.8	212.1
KENTUCKY WESLEYAN COLLEGE	PRI-FN	696	170.4	2,372.8	4.1	127.5	89.4	99.4	139.2

SEE FOOTNOTES AT END OF TABLE

149

Table 3. — Indexes Concerning Operating Expenditures, 1978-79, Bookstock Held at End of Year, 1978-79, and Library Staff (FTE), Fall 1979, College and University Libraries, by State or Other Area and Institution: Aggregate United States — Continued

STATE OR OTHER AREA AND INSTITUTION	CONTROL AND TYPE OF INSTITUTION	TOTAL FTE OPENING FALL ENROLL-MENT, FALL 1978	LIBRARY OPERATING EXPENDITURES (IN DOLLARS) 1978-79			BOOKSTOCK HELD AT END OF YEAR 1978-79		FTE STUDENTS PER FTE LIBRARY STAFF FALL 1979	
			PER FTE STUDENT, FALL 1978	PER FULL-TIME FACULTY MEMBER, 1978	AS PERCENT OF GENERAL EXPENDITURES, 1978-79	VOLUMES PER FTE STUDENT, FALL 1978	TITLES (INCLUDING MICROFORMS) PER FTE STUDENT 1978	TOTAL STAFF	PROFESSIONAL STAFF
(1)	(2)	(3)	(4)	(5)	(6)	(7)	(8)	(9)	(10)
KENTUCKY	--CONTINUED								
LEES JUNIOR COLLEGE	PRI-T	239	183.9	1,911.7	3.7	113.7	108.2	85.3	119.5
LEXINGTON THEOL SEMINARY	PRI-FG	124	798.3	9,000.0	8.8	734.1	645.1	41.3	62.0
LINDSEY WILSON COLLEGE	PRI-T	288	98.3	2,574.4	3.3	65.4	42.5	144.0	288.0
LOUISVL PRESB THEOL SEM	PRI-FG	166	885.7	12,253.3	9.7	505.5	495.6	33.2	83.0
LOUISVILLE SCHOOL OF ART	PRI-FN	82	225.5	2,642.4	6.1	80.3	75.6	82.0	82.0
MIDWAY COLLEGE	PRI-T	277	124.6	1,501.1	1.6	99.1	91.8	277.0	277.0
MOREHEAD STATE UNIVERSITY	PUB-FG	5,564	169.6	3,156.1	4.0	67.4	76.8	117.1	214.0
MURRAY STATE UNIVERSITY	PUB-FG	6,375	157.4	2,795.5	3.3	74.3	35.6	155.4	354.1
NORTHERN KY UNIVERSITY	PUB-FG	4,862	285.3	6,605.9	7.7	51.7	52.2	127.9	277.8
OWENSBORO BUSINESS C	PRI-T	354	66.5	A	A	7.6	6.7	177.0	177.0
PIKEVILLE COLLEGE	PRI-FN	552	198.9	2,440.9	2.7	154.0	142.2	110.4	184.0
SAINT CATHARINE COLLEGE	PRI-T	133	194.6	6,472.5	6.7	124.6	114.6	88.6	88.6
SEMINARY OF SAINT PIUS X	PRI-FN	117	640.5	.0	11.2	282.8	255.0	30.0	68.8
SOUTHERN BAPT THEOL SEM	PRI-FG	1,744	238.7	A	A	153.2	102.1	85.0	290.6
SPALDING COLLEGE	PRI-FG	676	168.3	2,231.0	4.7	160.4	102.8	77.7	169.0
SUE BENNETT COLLEGE	PRI-T	226	103.4	2,126.2	5.0	157.1	157.1	150.6	150.6
SULLIVAN JC BUSINESS	PRI-T	805	32.2	1,620.4	1.8	5.4	5.1	473.5	805.0
THOMAS MORE COLLEGE	PRI-FN	886	96.2	2,243.3	3.5	90.1	71.2	118.1	136.3
TRANSYLVANIA UNIVERSITY	PRI-FN	740	170.7	2,256.6	2.9	126.0	108.9	92.5	185.0
UNION COLLEGE	PRI-FG	878	133.2	2,924.1	4.4	81.1	77.6	175.6	292.6
U KENTUCKY ALL CAMPUSES									
UNIVERSITY OF KENTUCKY	PUB-U	18,953	246.2	3,931.3	2.8	65.6	50.1	99.4	285.0
U OF KENTUCKY CC SYSTEM	PUB-T	10,799	108.6	2,222.4	5.6	32.2	26.9	156.7	415.3
UNIVERSITY OF LOUISVILLE	PUB-U	13,915	199.3	4,962.8	2.9	59.7	32.6	120.4	339.3
WATTERSON COLLEGE	PRI-T	D	D	D	D	D	D	D	D
WESTERN KY UNIVERSITY	PUB-FG	10,310	174.5	3,225.2	4.8	45.4	67.3	117.1	234.3
LOUISIANA									
BOSSIER PARISH CC	PUB-T	676	67.8	1,911.2	6.9	27.0	22.1	198.8	281.6
CENTENARY C OF LOUISIANA	PRI-FG	719	237.8	2,999.6	4.6	183.4	170.6	99.8	231.9
DELGADO COLLEGE	PUB-T	6,204	53.4	1,843.8	A	5.2	4.8	387.7	689.3
DILLARD UNIVERSITY	PRI-FN	1,210	170.0	2,742.7	3.6	99.2	96.0	134.4	201.6
GRAMBLING STATE U	PUB-FG	3,450	144.5	2,769.6	4.0	51.5	39.2	215.6	313.6
LOUISIANA COLLEGE	PRI-FN	1,132	125.2	2,779.4	4.4	84.9	62.2	174.1	293.0
LOUISIANA ST U ALL CAM									
LA STATE U AND A&M C	PUB-U	21,841	186.6	3,433.4	4.9	80.9	32.7	160.1	445.7
LA STATE U ALEXANDRIA	PUB-T	1,200	261.2	4,124.8	9.1	83.4	58.6	109.0	171.4
LA STATE U EUNICE	PUB-T	741	242.5	3,993.2	7.9	101.7	91.9	92.6	185.2
LA ST U MEDICAL CENTER	PUB-FG	2,325	266.7	3,299.0	.8	52.4	A	101.0	258.3
LA STATE U SHREVEPORT	PUB-FG	2,231	195.4	3,791.7	8.3	49.8	34.0	123.9	278.8
UNIVERSITY OF NEW ORLEANS	PUB-FG	10,715	126.3	3,075.6	4.6	34.5	46.1	184.7	446.4
LOUISIANA TECH UNIVERSITY	PUB-FG	8,584	95.7	2,220.5	3.8	28.3	28.0	252.4	536.5
LOYOLA U IN NEW ORLEANS	PRI-U	3,196	263.1	4,521.7	5.5	118.9	91.7	80.9	222.8
MCNEESE STATE UNIVERSITY	PUB-FG	4,414	146.4	2,966.2	5.4	44.8	30.9	133.7	367.8
NEW ORLS BAPT THEOL SEM	PRI-FG	1,094	128.6	A	A	133.4	101.0	84.1	364.6
NICHOLLS STATE UNIVERSITY	PUB-FG	5,223	121.9	2,895.5	5.3	35.3	57.1	212.3	348.2
NORTHEAST LOUISIANA U	PUB-FG	7,411	132.1	3,069.0	4.8	39.9	44.7	211.7	570.0
NTHWSTN ST U OF LA	PUB-FG	4,451	136.1	2,601.3	4.6	54.8	80.4	167.9	387.0
NOTRE DAME SEM SCH THEO	PRI-FG	51	1,050.5	7,653.8	12.2	1,432.4	A	25.5	25.5
OUR LADY OF HOLY CROSS C	PRI-FN	D	D	D	D	D	D	D	D
PHILLIPS C NEW ORLEANS	PRI-T	D	D	D	D	D	D	D	D
SAINT BERNARD PARISH CC	PUB-T	192	314.0	8,612.8	8.9	104.1	103.9	48.0	64.0
SAINT JOSEPH SEM COLLEGE	PRI-FN	125	186.9	D	4.7	504.0	500.1	125.0	125.0
SAINT MARY'S DOMINICAN C	PRI-FN	587	150.2	2,844.8	5.0	122.0	82.7	85.0	133.4
STHESTN LA UNIVERSITY	PUB-FG	6,336	100.0	2,597.5	4.6	32.9	A	301.7	792.0
SOUTHERN U A&M ALL CAM									
SOUTHERN U A&M C MAIN CAM	PUB-FG	7,294	94.5	1,398.9	2.6	38.4	19.2	211.4	383.8
STHN U IN NEW ORLEANS	PUB-FN	2,355	126.8	2,692.1	4.4	64.0	67.7	157.0	196.2
STHN U SHREVEPORT-BOSSIER	PUB-T	640	211.0	2,701.8	5.2	41.5	28.8	106.6	160.0
TULANE U OF LOUISIANA	PRI-U	8,317	330.7	7,374.9	3.7	161.9	75.6	66.8	237.6
U OF STHWSTN LOUISIANA	PUB-FG	11,094	99.2	2,189.7	A.E	40.0	23.9	264.1	693.3
XAVIER UNIVERSITY OF LA	PRI-FG	1,780	225.9	3,438.0	3.6	55.1	44.2	95.1	237.3
MAINE									
ANDOVER COLLEGE	PRI-T	287	23.8	762.0	1.3	16.2	11.9	410.0	410.0
BANGOR THEOLOGICAL SEM	PRI-FG	106	419.0	6,345.8	6.2	654.5	A	53.0	53.0
BATES COLLEGE	PRI-FN	1,359	401.8	5,688.3	7.1	174.5	137.9	60.4	123.5

SEE FOOTNOTES AT END OF TABLE

Table 3. – Indexes Concerning Operating Expenditures, 1978-79, Bookstock Held at End of Year, 1978-79, and Library Staff (FTE), Fall 1979, College and University Libraries, by State or Other Area and Institution: Aggregate United States – Continued

STATE OR OTHER AREA AND INSTITUTION (1)	CONTROL AND TYPE OF INSTITUTION (2)	TOTAL FTE OPENING FALL ENROLLMENT, FALL 1978 (3)	LIBRARY OPERATING EXPENDITURES (IN DOLLARS) 1978-79			BOOKSTOCK HELD AT END OF YEAR 1978-79		FTE STUDENTS PER FTE LIBRARY STAFF FALL 1979	
			PER FTE STUDENT, FALL 1978 (4)	PER FULL-TIME FACULTY MEMBER, 1978 (5)	AS PERCENT OF GENERAL EXPENDITURES, 1978-79 (6)	VOLUMES PER FTE STUDENT, FALL 1978 (7)	TITLES (INCLUDING MICROFORMS) PER FTE STUDENT 1978 (8)	TOTAL STAFF (9)	PROFESSIONAL STAFF (10)
MAINE	--CONTINUED								
BEAL COLLEGE	PRI-T	352	35.5	1,787.1	1.6	38.7	26.4	352.0	352.0
BOWDOIN COLLEGE	PRI-FN	1,370	486.5	6,409.3	5.5	299.7	217.9	61.9	155.6
CASCO BAY COLLEGE	PRI-T	0	D	D	D	D	D	D	D
COLBY COLLEGE	PRI-FN	1,634	434.5	6,120.5	7.0	219.1	A	69.5	204.2
COLLEGE OF THE ATLANTIC	PRI-FN	123	495.9	5,083.2	5.2	103.8	79.6	41.0	123.0
EASTERN ME VOC-TECH INST	PUB-T	545	42.9	519.7	1.3	27.8	24.7	545.0	545.0
HUSSON COLLEGE	PRI-FG	1,020	45.6	1,411.6	1.2	27.9	27.9	340.0	510.0
MAINE MARITIME ACADEMY	PUB-FN	643	321.2	5,436.1	5.3	71.6	91.4	80.3	214.3
NASSON COLLEGE	PRI-FN	649	168.5	A	4.2	188.0	188.8	108.1	216.3
NTHN ME VOC TECH INST	PUB-T	0	D	·D	D	D	D	0	D
PORTLAND SCHOOL OF ART	PRI-FN	198	139.5	2,763.7	3.7	53.7	49.5	198.0	198.0
SAINT JOSEPH'S COLLEGE	PRI-FN	430	171.4	2,234.0	3.1	114.0	98.1	505.2	960.0
SOUTHERN ME VOC TECH INST	PUB-T	960	12.5	153.0	A	16.2	15.1	350.6	350.6
THOMAS COLLEGE	PRI-FG	561	65.4	1,669.4	2.3	29.0	23.8	350.6	350.6
UNITY COLLEGE	PRI-FN	628	124.8	3,135.2	3.6	57.0	54.8	251.2	314.0
U OF MAINE ALL CAMPUSES								398.6	397.0
U OF MAINE AT AUGUSTA	PUB-T	1,794	61.0	1,921.5	2.2	17.3	15.2	193.5	548.3
U OF MAINE AT FARMINGTON	PUB-FN	1,645	94.2	1,891.0	2.5	52.5	46.8	78.6	177.0
U OF MAINE AT FORT KENT	PUB-FN	354	233.5	3,757.8	4.6	108.9	98.3	134.2	179.0
U OF MAINE AT MACHIAS	PUB-FN	537	187.9	3,154.3	4.5	110.3	108.0		
U OF MAINE AT ORONO	PUB-U	9,622	160.2	3,323.6	2.9	56.5	A	152.2	501.1
U OF ME AT PRESQUE ISLE	PUB-FN	1,070	111.0	2,285.3	2.9	63.8	56.5	267.5	356.6
U OF SOUTHERN MAINE	PUB-FG	5,372	106.1	2,469.6	2.7	51.5	47.0	188.4	383.7
UNIVERSITY OF NEW ENGLAND	PRI-FG	399	259.5	A	3.4	164.5	124.7	61.3	137.5
WESTBROOK COLLEGE	PRI-FN	628	110.9	1,883.8	2.6	A	37.3	139.5	251.2
MARYLAND									
ALLEGANY CMTY COLLEGE	PUB-T	1,283	87.7	1,160.1	A	31.9	31.2	200.4	916.4
ANNE ARUNDEL CMTY COLLEGE	PUB-T	3,528	71.2	1,504.6	2.9	22.9	22.3	261.3	784.0
BALTIMORE HEBREW COLLEGE	PRI-FG	158	A	A	A	191.6	151.0	33.6	79.0
BOWIE STATE COLLEGE	PUB-FG	1,807	240.9	4,268.5	4.4	83.7	90.6	90.3	225.8
CAPITOL INST TECHNOLOGY	PRI-FN	364	67.7	2,738.2	3.0	24.2	20.0	364.0	364.0
CATONSVILLE CMTY COLLEGE	PUB-T	5,340	132.5	3,146.3	4.9	19.2	14.5	159.4	534.0
CECIL COMMUNITY COLLEGE	PUB-T	587	162.1	3,807.8	6.0	30.2	29.4	146.7	293.5
CHARLES CO CMTY COLLEGE	PUB-T	1,739	163.2	7,277.5	5.4	18.9	16.6	119.1	395.2
CHESAPEAKE COLLEGE	PUB-T	766	103.9	2,488.1	3.3	35.8	38.9	186.8	306.4
COLLEGE OF NOTRE DAME MD	PRI-FN		SEE LOYOLA-NOTRE DAME JT LIB						
COLUMBIA UNION COLLEGE	PRI-FN	594	316.5	3,082.3	5.6	177.8	128.3	104.2	160.5
CMTY COLLEGE OF BALTIMORE	PUB-T	5,095	89.2	2,858.3	3.2	17.2	14.0	222.4	480.6
COPPIN STATE COLLEGE	PUB-FG	2,363	152.8	2,696.2	3.0	47.9	45.0	139.0	337.5
DE SALES HALL SCH THEO	PRI-FG	5	3,948.6	.0	10.8	7,163.4	7,140.0	4.1	5.0
DUNDALK CMTY COLLEGE	PUB-T	1,150	199.5	4,172.1	4.6	15.1	14.5	143.7	297.5
ESSEX COMMUNITY COLLEGE	PUB-T	4,989	70.4	2,043.6	2.8	17.2	15.1	293.4	1,247.2
FREDERICK CMTY COLLEGE	PUB-T	1,083	166.3	5,811.4	7.9	25.7	A	95.8	361.0
FROSTBURG STATE COLLEGE	PUB-FG	3,189	173.0	2,999.6	4.7	52.4	56.2	109.9	289.9
GARRETT COMMUNITY COLLEGE	PUB-T	368	318.1	5,854.8	6.1	56.4	50.1	61.3	368.0
GOUCHER COLLEGE	PRI-FG	926	283.4	3,696.6	3.7	219.6	118.6	71.2	205.7
HAGERSTOWN JUNIOR COLLEGE	PUB-T	1,320	134.0	3,050.3	5.0	33.3	36.3	146.6	440.0
HARFORD COMMUNITY COLLEGE	PUB-T	1,903	91.6	2,180.5	2.8	19.5	16.8	152.2	475.7
HOOD COLLEGE	PRI-FG	1,269	178.5	2,697.1	3.8	97.5	70.8	139.4	253.8
HOWARD COMMUNITY COLLEGE	PUB-T	1,190	181.5	5,269.2	6.4	22.7	20.0	82.0	340.0
JOHNS HOPKINS UNIVERSITY	PRI-U	6,205	729.4	8,095.8	2.5	356.8	227.0	35.2	120.9
LOYOLA COLLEGE	PRI-FG		SEE LOYOLA-NOTRE DAME JT LIB						
LOYOLA-NOTRE DAME JT LIB	PRI-FG	0	D	D	D	D	D	D	D
MARYLAND C ART AND DESIGN	PRI-T	69	213.3	4,907.6	5.9	92.1	91.8	46.0	46.0
MD INST COLLEGE OF ART	PRI-FG	810	152.2	A	3.2	48.1	43.2	119.1	231.4
MONTGOMERY C ALL CAMPUSES									
MONTGOMERY C GERMANTOWN	PUB-T	549	172.1	3,376.2	4.2	41.0	37.2	84.4	274.5
MONTGOMERY C ROCKVILLE	PUB-T	6,588	99.3	2,499.3	3.2	14.2	12.1	253.3	823.5
MONTGOMERY C TAKOMA PARK	PUB-T	1,715	159.8	3,263.7	5.2	30.6	28.1	171.5	428.7
MORGAN STATE UNIVERSITY	PUB-FG	4,310	222.7	3,000.4	4.8	45.7	34.6	163.6	232.9
MOUNT SNT MARY'S COLLEGE	PRI-FG	1,571	121.5	3,537.0	3.6	80.0	59.6		374.0
NER ISRAEL RAB COLLEGE	PRI-FG	275	54.4	998.8	1.2	61.7	52.0	275.0	550.0
PEABODY INST OF JHU	PRI-FG	358	222.4	1,244.4	2.1	182.9	77.4	89.5	89.5
PRINCE GEORGES CC	PUB-T	7,448	95.8	2,950.7	4.0	9.2	8.3	292.0	931.0
SAINT JOHN'S C ALL CAM									
SAINT JOHN'S C MAIN CAM	PRI-FG	369	208.9	2,084.3	2.7	213.1	102.0	123.0	123.0

SEE FOOTNOTES AT END OF TABLE

Table 3. — Indexes Concerning Operating Expenditures, 1978-79, Bookstock Held at End of Year, 1978-79, and Library Staff (FTE), Fall 1979, College and University Libraries, by State or Other Area and Institution: Aggregate United States — Continued

STATE OR OTHER AREA AND INSTITUTION	CONTROL AND TYPE OF INSTITUTION	TOTAL FTE OPENING FALL ENROLLMENT, FALL 1978	LIBRARY OPERATING EXPENDITURES (IN DOLLARS) 1978-79			BOOKSTOCK HELD AT END OF YEAR 1978-79		FTE STUDENTS PER FTE LIBRARY STAFF FALL 1979	
			PER FTE STUDENT, FALL 1978	PER FULL-TIME FACULTY MEMBER, 1978	AS PERCENT OF GENERAL EXPENDITURES, 1978-79	VOLUMES PER FTE STUDENT, FALL 1978	TITLES (INCLUDING MICROFORMS) PER FTE STUDENT 1978	TOTAL STAFF	PROFESSIONAL STAFF
(1)	(2)	(3)	(4)	(5)	(6)	(7)	(8)	(9)	(10)
MARYLAND	--CONTINUED								
SNT JOHN'S C SANTA FE NM	PRI-FG	296	322.5	2,808.2	3.8	149.6	93.2	74.0	148.0
SNT MARY'S COLLEGE OF MD	PUB-FN	1,163	273.8	4,752.9	7.3	66.6	60.6	96.9	387.6
SAINT MARY'S SEMINARY & U	PRI-FG	187	434.8	81,321.0	5.2	408.8	A	38.1	62.3
SALISBURY STATE COLLEGE	PUB-FG	3,362	141.7	2,722.3	4.8	50.5	49.6	168.1	336.2
TOWSON STATE UNIVERSITY	PUB-FG	11,329	107.4	2,601.7	4.0	28.9	A	263.4	666.4
UNIVERSITY OF BALTIMORE	PUB-FG	3,103	275.9	7,195.0	8.4	95.1	72.2	97.5	200.1
U MARYLAND SYS ALL INST									
U OF MARYLAND ALL CAM									
U OF MD COLLEGE PARK CAM	PUB-U	30,422	206.8	4,596.3	4.2	43.8	18.8	145.5	428.4
U OF MD BALTIMORE CO CAM	PUB-FG	4,788	261.3	4,757.8	5.9	61.3	67.5	101.0	451.6
U OF MD BALT PROF SCHOOLS	PUB-FG	4,108	388.2	4,265.0	1.9	89.4	28.6	65.2	164.3
U MD UNIVERSITY COLLEGE	PUB-FG		NO LIBRARY FACILITIES						
U OF MD-EASTERN SHORE	PUB-FG	940	309.7	3,882.0	3.5	115.5	137.3	58.3	117.5
VILLA JULIE COLLEGE	PRI-T	437	86.5	2,522.6	3.1	60.7	35.4	218.5	218.5
WASHINGTON BIBLE COLLEGE	PRI-FG	476	154.5	4,325.1	5.1	59.7	A	198.3	476.0
WASHINGTON COLLEGE	PRI-FG	747	261.1	3,483.7	5.3	139.7	122.3	74.7	249.0
WASHINGTON THEOL UNION	PRI-FG	D	D	D	D	D	D	D	D
WESTERN MARYLAND COLLEGE	PRI-FG	1,622	157.2	2,965.9	4.0	73.5	52.6	193.0	368.6
WOR-WIC TECH CMTY COLLEGE	PUB-T		NO LIBRARY FACILITIES						
MASSACHUSETTS									
AMERICAN INTRNATL COLLEGE	PRI-FG	1,691	64.7	1,563.9	2.1	71.2	43.5	281.8	845.5
AMHERST COLLEGE	PRI-FN	1,466	575.7	5,821.1	5.8	371.8	202.4	42.3	139.6
ANDOVER NEWTON THEOL SCH	PRI-FG	321	440.6	8,319.7	A	607.5	398.1	40.1	107.0
ANNA MARIA COLLEGE	PRI-FG	675	76.7	1,992.4	3.3	70.7	55.0	156.9	293.4
AQUINAS JC ALL CAMPUSES									
AQUINAS JC AT MILTON	PRI-T	404	47.2	1,910.5	2.7	20.6	17.5	404.0	404.0
AQUINAS JC AT NEWTON	PRI-T	296	88.8	6,577.5	3.9	37.3	37.3	155.7	296.0
ADL MGMT ED INSTITUTE	PRI-FG	69	9,902.8	D	69.0	565.2	522.6	3.5	8.1
ASSUMPTION COLLEGE	PRI-FG	1,658	96.7	2,292.4	2.5	89.9	50.1	259.0	552.6
ATLANTIC UNION COLLEGE	PRI-FN	579	202.7	2,608.2	4.2	166.7	A	144.7	289.5
BABSON COLLEGE	PRI-FG	2,003	185.6	4,706.4	4.5	40.4	28.6	129.2	174.1
BAY PATH JUNIOR COLLEGE	PRI-T	637	83.3	2,211.3	2.3	44.5	42.4	212.3	318.5
BAY STATE JC OF BUS	PRI-T	726	24.0	1,166.1	1.2	5.5	5.3	726.0	726.0
BECKER JC ALL INSTITUTION									
BECKER JC-LEICESTER	PRI-T	505	78.0	2,629.2	3.6	50.4	42.5	202.0	336.6
BECKER JC-WORCESTER	PRI-T	726	94.2	2,738.1	4.8	40.0	29.4	242.0	726.0
BENTLEY COLLEGE	PRI-FG	4,371	110.7	4,035.0	3.7	21.7	18.1	236.2	624.4
BERKLEE COLLEGE OF MUSIC	PRI-FN	2,602	31.7	661.8	1.7	9.9	9.6	867.3	867.3
BERKSHIRE CHRISTIAN C	PRI-FN	119	296.0	4,403.1	6.3	291.5	239.3	59.5	59.5
BLUE HILLS REG TECH INST	PUB-T		60.6	905.8	2.2	10.0	A	293.7	470.0
BOSTON COLLEGE	PRI-U	12,935	178.8	4,986.1	4.4	62.6	43.5 T	137.6	369.5
BOSTON CONSV OF MUSIC	PRI-FG	D	D	D	D	D	D	D	D
BOSTON UNIVERSITY	PRI-U	20,410	194.8	A	2.5	63.0	46.2	117.0	298.8
BRADFORD COLLEGE	PRI-FN	264	257.1	4,525.0	4.0	207.2	211.8	82.5	146.6
BRANDEIS UNIVERSITY	PRI-U	3,480	503.4	5,309.4	4.3	175.0	169.5	57.4	151.3
CEN NEW ENG COLLEGE TECHN	PRI FN		SEE WORCESTER JOINT LIBRARY						
CHAMBERLAYNE JR COLLEGE	PRI-T	771	19.4	787.3	A	32.6	32.4	771.0	771.0
CLARK UNIVERSITY	PRI-FG	2,449	251.2	4,807.1	4.1	142.0	85.5	102.8	257.7
COLLEGE OF THE HOLY CROSS	PRI-FG	2,574	175.8	2,777.6	3.8	141.5	90.1	119.7	286.0
COLLEGE OUR LADY OF ELMS	PRI-FN	398	285.4	9,468.0	7.9	175.4	107.0	49.7	99.5
CURRY COLLEGE	PRI-FN	937	149.3	2,221.2	3.1	84.2	71.2	170.3	468.5
DEAN JUNIOR COLLEGE	PRI-T	980	132.4	2,360.6	3.4	34.7	39.3	140.0	326.6
EASTERN NAZARENE COLLEGE	PRI-FG	716	147.8	2,301.4	4.7	115.9	105.8	159.1	286.4
EMERSON COLLEGE	PRI-FG	1,495	150.5	2,744.6	4.1	41.9	34.4	132.3	373.7
EMMANUEL COLLEGE	PRI-FG	765	170.9	2,615.5	2.9	156.3	149.6	136.6	212.5
ENDICOTT COLLEGE	PRI-T	881	101.8	2,137.4	3.3	54.3	52.4	129.5	400.4
EPISCOPAL DIVINITY SCHOOL	PRI-FG	116	896.3	5,472.5	6.8	885.7	695.3	13.8	30.5
ESSEX AGRL-TECH INST	PUB-T	702	98.2	1,379.0	2.4	18.9	26.8	234.0	702.0
FISHER JUNIOR COLLEGE	PRI-T	1,900	20.6	1,637.8	.8	11.6	10.8	950.0	950.0
FORSYTH SCH DENTL HYGNSTS	PRI-T	201	211.7	3,868.3	4.9	34.8	33.8	201.0	201.0
FRANKLIN INST OF BOSTON	PRI-T	560	28.2	405.5	.5	13.7	13.7	560.0	560.0
GORDON COLLEGE	PRI-FN	908	174.4	3,300.0	4.4	129.9	100.6	116.4	302.6
GORDON-CONWELL THEOL SEM	PRI-FG	618	248.2	6,135.7	6.8	152.8	132.2	88.2	206.0
HAMPSHIRE COLLEGE	PRI-FN	1,245	361.6	7,034.6	5.9	47.9	38.9	47.8	146.4
HARVARD UNIVERSITY	PRI-U	14,628	1,237.7	20,504.7	5.8	677.7	269.7	.0	A
HEBREW COLLEGE	PRI-FG	61	992.9	A	A	1,060.7	1,030.3	24.4	24.4

SEE FOOTNOTES AT END OF TABLE

STATE OR OTHER AREA AND INSTITUTION (1)	CONTROL AND TYPE OF INSTITUTION (2)	TOTAL FTE OPENING FALL ENROLLMENT, FALL 1978 (3)	LIBRARY OPERATING EXPENDITURES (IN DOLLARS) 1978-79			BOOKSTOCK HELD AT END OF YEAR 1978-79		FTE STUDENTS PER FTE LIBRARY STAFF FALL 1979	
			PER FTE STUDENT, FALL 1978 (4)	PER FULL-TIME FACULTY MEMBER, 1978 (5)	AS PERCENT OF GENERAL EXPENDITURES, 1978-79 (6)	VOLUMES PER FTE STUDENT, FALL 1978 (7)	TITLES (INCLUDING MICROFORMS) PER FTE STUDENT 1978 (8)	TOTAL STAFF (9)	PROFESSIONAL STAFF (10)
MASSACHUSETTS	--CONTINUED								
HELLENIC C-HOLY CROSS SCH	PRI-FG	146	600.3	4,869.3	5.6	471.6	A	36.5	73.0
KATHARINE GIBBS SCHOOL	PRI-T	461	8.1	198.6	A	3.8	2.5	1,536.6	4,610.0
LABOURE JUNIOR COLLEGE	PRI-T	402	137.5	1,974.9	4.5	21.3	17.3	134.0	201.0
LASELL JUNIOR COLLEGE	PRI-T	646	104.9	1,540.6	2.2	75.2	68.0	170.0	403.7
LESLEY COLLEGE	PRI-FG	1,404	186.9	5,833.2	3.9	51.4	46.9	130.0	242.0
MASS BOARD CC ALL INST									
BERKSHIRE CMTY COLLEGE	PUB-T	1,808	58.3	1,621.9	A	21.6	18.5	347.6	904.0
BRISTOL COMMUNITY COLLEGE	PUB-T	2,458	154.3	4,034.9	9.6	16.4	13.7	180.7	438.9
BUNKER HILL CMTY COLLEGE	PUB-T	3,348	70.1	2,397.6	4.2	6.2	5.3	372.0	837.0
CAPE COD CMTY COLLEGE	PUB-T	1,711	127.3	2,757.4	5.4	28.6	27.0	201.2	380.2
GREENFIELD CMTY COLLEGE	PUB-T	1,620	132.7	3,414.7	6.4	24.0	21.6	144.6	324.0
HOLYOKE COMMUNITY COLLEGE	PUB-T	3,525	59.5	1,841.5	3.6	13.3	8.9	345.5	839.2
MASS BAY CMTY COLLEGE	PUB-T	2,507	87.1	2,800.2	6.6	16.3	14.8	227.9	417.8
MASSASOIT CMTY COLLEGE	PUB-T	3,245	56.4	A	3.9	18.5	14.9	405.6	811.2
MIDDLESEX CMTY COLLEGE	PUB-T	2,468	59.5	2,490.9	4.9	13.3	13.1	448.7	725.8
MT WACHUSETT CMTY COLLEGE	PUB-T	1,894	51.0	1,511.2	2.7	28.0	25.1	430.4	631.3
NTHN ESSEX CMTY COLLEGE	PUB-T	3,315	60.1	1,717.8	3.3	14.6	14.9	473.5	1,105.0
NORTH SHORE CMTY COLLEGE	PUB-T	D	D	D	D	D	D	D	D
QUINSIGAMOND CMTY COLLEGE	PUB-T	2,697	35.3	1,071.4	2.3	19.7	A	539.4	899.0
ROXBURY COMMUNITY COLLEGE	PUB-T	514	232.0	3,975.8	4.0	2.8	2.0	102.8	128.5
SPRINGFIELD TECHNICAL CC	PUB-T	4,271	42.6	1,078.3	2.4	10.2	9.3	520.8	1,256.1
MASS C PHAR-HLTH SCI	PRI-FG	1,459	149.5	3,256.0	4.3	37.9	16.1	124.7	291.8
MASS INST OF TECHNOLOGY	PRI-U	8,606	503.4	4,624.0	1.8	204.5	65.4	43.4	144.6
MASS STATE C SYS ALL INST									
BOSTON STATE COLLEGE	PUB-FG	7,177	74.2	1,850.4	3.4	20.4	20.0	321.8	717.7
BRIDGEWATER STATE COLLEGE	PUB-FG	5,305	126.4	2,916.1	6.6	33.2	36.7	156.0	401.8
FITCHBURG STATE COLLEGE	PUB-FG	4,447	80.8	1,672.2	3.4	33.7	36.8	342.0	555.8
FRAMINGHAM STATE COLLEGE	PUB-FG	3,683	91.7	2,207.7	5.4	35.3	36.4	217.9	433.2
MASS COLLEGE OF ART	PUB-FG	1,405	116.9	3,572.7	5.5	45.7	38.4	281.0	702.5
MASS MARITIME ACADEMY	PUB-FN	886	131.6	2,430.8	3.0	40.0	32.4	147.6	221.5
NORTH ADAMS STATE COLLEGE	PUB-FG	2,398	114.2	2,795.9	4.7	47.4	38.1	255.1	705.2
SALEM STATE COLLEGE	PUB-FG	5,639	80.8	1,767.1	2.9	31.9	62.3	313.2	433.7
WESTFIELD STATE COLLEGE	PUB-FG	3,233	82.9	1,823.4	3.8	37.8	26.5	293.9	808.2
WORCESTER STATE COLLEGE	PUB-FG	3,922	122.2	2,592.3	6.0	37.3	30.6	145.2	356.5
MERRIMACK COLLEGE	PRI-FN	2,563	74.7	1,757.7	2.4	45.8	24.3	320.3	569.5
MOUNT HOLYOKE COLLEGE	PRI-FG	1,950	370.7	4,228.0	5.4	224.1	137.4	63.9	158.5
MOUNT IDA JUNIOR COLLEGE	PRI-T	675	75.4	1,376.3	2.5	38.3	33.0	270.0	450.0
NEWBURY JUNIOR COLLEGE	PRI-T	924	80.8	2,766.2	2.8	7.6	6.6	440.0	840.0
NEW ENGLAND C OPTOMETRY	PRI-FG	351	236.0	3,068.8	3.3	25.7	17.1	87.7	175.5
NEW ENG CONSV OF MUSIC	PRI-FG	738	236.6	3,063.8	3.6	54.2	36.7	92.2	184.5
NEW ENG INST APP ARTS-SCI	PRI-T	138	143.7	9,919.0	5.9	24.7	21.8	138.0	138.0
NEW ENGLAND SCHOOL OF LAW	PRI-FG	757	423.1	16,858.9	10.2	96.0	20.1	86.0	151.4
NICHOLS COLLEGE	PRI-FG	D	D	D	D	D	D	D	D
NORTHEASTERN UNIVERSITY[2]	PRI-U	24,350	98.4	3,515.1	2.9	17.8	30.7	219.3	593.9
PINE MANOR COLLEGE	PRI-FN	451	186.5	3,658.8	3.3	69.1	56.2	73.9	136.6
POPE JOHN XXIII NATL SEM	PRI-FG	D	D	D	D	D	D	D	D
QUINCY JUNIOR COLLEGE	PUB-T	1,644	54.4	3,198.1	6.9	4.3	4.2	548.0	548.0
RADCLIFFE COLLEGE	PRI-FN	3,937	76.6	A	A	6.0	7.8	252.3	1,968.5
REGIS COLLEGE	PRI-FG	911	169.8	6,448.6	4.2	131.0	126.2	140.1	260.2
SNT HYACINTH COLLEGE-SEM	PRI-FN	47	576.1	D	12.5	1,129.7	470.5	26.1	26.1
SAINT JOHN'S SEMINARY	PRI-FG	185	438.6	.0	4.7	649.8	A	61.6	185.0
SCH OF MUSEUM FINE ARTS	PRI-FG	641	46.3	A	A	10.4	9.0	641.0	641.0
SCH WORCESTER ART MUSEUM	PRI-T	116	351.6	3,708.7	10.8	273.8	132.8	50.4	58.0
SIMMONS COLLEGE	PRI-FG	2,313	203.9	3,187.1	3.6	68.2	58.5	116.8	167.6
SIMON'S ROCK EARLY C	PRI-FN	205	516.3	3,920.0	6.2	222.2	217.7	41.0	102.5
SMITH COLLEGE	PRI-FG	2,813	511.3	5,597.4	6.3	307.9	184.7	44.5	133.9
STHESTN MASS UNIVERSITY	PUB-FG	5,504	303.9	5,690.9	9.1	40.9	44.7	157.2	393.1
SPRINGFIELD COLLEGE	PRI-FG	2,488	91.7	1,811.9	2.6	54.4	45.7	163.6	622.0
STONEHILL COLLEGE	PRI-FN	2,007	124.2	3,370.5	4.1	54.7	37.1	182.4	409.5
SUFFOLK UNIVERSITY	PRI-FG	4,463	208.1	5,370.9	6.4	44.3	31.7	176.4	433.3
SWAIN SCHOOL OF DESIGN	PRI-FN	190	101.0	1,371.0	3.8	63.6	58.9	126.6	190.0
TUFTS UNIVERSITY	PRI-U	5,543	328.2	5,812.3	2.9	102.2	99.7	76.9	230.9
UNIVERSITY OF LOWELL	PUB-FG	8,694	168.2	3,666.6	6.8	32.1	21.5	220.1	434.7
U OF MASS ALL CAMPUSES									
U OF MASS AMHERST CAMPUS	PUB-U	21,609	167.4	2,942.1	3.0	58.2	46.5	145.9	431.3
U OF MASS BOSTON CAMPUS	PUB-FG	7,123	156.5	3,186.9	3.8	44.6	27.7	169.5	339.1

SEE FOOTNOTES AT END OF TABLE

153

Table 3. — Indexes Concerning Operating Expenditures, 1978-79, Bookstock Held at End of Year, 1978-79, and Library Staff (FTE), Fall 1979, College and University Libraries, by State or Other Area and Institution: Aggregate United States — Continued

STATE OR OTHER AREA AND INSTITUTION	CONTROL AND TYPE OF INSTITUTION	TOTAL FTE OPENING FALL ENROLLMENT, FALL 1978	LIBRARY OPERATING EXPENDITURES (IN DOLLARS) 1978-79			BOOKSTOCK HELD AT END OF YEAR 1978-79		FTE STUDENTS PER FTE LIBRARY STAFF FALL 1979	
			PER FTE STUDENT, FALL 1978	PER FULL-TIME FACULTY MEMBER, 1978	AS PERCENT OF GENERAL EXPENDITURES, 1978-79	VOLUMES PER FTE STUDENT, FALL 1978	TITLES (INCLUDING MICROFORMS) PER FTE STUDENT 1978	TOTAL STAFF	PROFESSIONAL STAFF
(1)	(2)	(3)	(4)	(5)	(6)	(7)	(8)	(9)	(10)
MASSACHUSETTS	--CONTINUED								
U MASS MEDL SCH-WORCESTER	PUB-FG	413	1,385.7	0	2.7	180.0	37.5	24.1	59.0
WELLESLEY COLLEGE	PRI-FN	2,042	471.5	5,015.5	4.7	265.3	144.7	49.6	145.8
WENTWORTH INST OF TECH	PRI-FN	2,033	66.6	1,102.3	1.4	24.8	19.2	508.2	677.6
WESTERN NEW ENG COLLEGE	PRI-FG	3,047	225.9	7,170.1	7.7	54.8	25.5	145.0	380.8
WHEATON COLLEGE	PRI-FN	1,330	399.3	6,399.5	6.8	154.8	97.6	62.7	130.3
WHEELOCK COLLEGE	PRI-FG	757	191.8	3,300.4	3.8	81.0	64.4	105.1	151.4
WILLIAMS COLLEGE	PRI-FG	1,990	358.5	4,008.1	4.5	246.4	119.5	80.8	234.1
WORCESTER JUNIOR COLLEGE	PRI-T		SEE WORCESTER JOINT LIBRARY						
WORCESTER JOINT LIBRARY	PRI-FN	0	0	0	0	0	0	0	0
WORCESTER POLY INSTITUTE	PRI-FG	2,788	180.7	2,947.5	2.5	62.9	34.4	154.8	371.7
MICHIGAN									
ADRIAN COLLEGE	PRI-FN	747	274.2	3,725.4	4.2	150.2	A	91.0	249.0
ALBION COLLEGE	PRI-FN	1,770	184.2	3,047.1	3.8	123.3	115.6	141.6	354.0
ALMA COLLEGE	PRI-FN	1,165	274.3	4,917.2	5.2	117.9	97.9	88.2	179.2
ALPENA COMMUNITY COLLEGE	PUB-T	1,115	98.9	1,935.6	3.1	26.0	A	278.7	1,115.0
ANDREWS UNIVERSITY	PRI-FG	2,591	334.5	A	7.0	147.8	A	82.5	199.3
AQUINAS COLLEGE	PRI-FG	1,266	203.1	5,249.9	5.1	83.5	80.1	126.6	253.2
BAKER JUNIOR COLLEGE BUS	PRI-T	1,154	30.2	2,184.1	2.4	2.5	2.4	461.6	461.6
BAY DE NOC CMTY COLLEGE	PUB-T	896	134.1	3,082.9	4.9	27.6	26.3	213.3	448.0
CALVIN COLLEGE	PRI-FG		SEE CALVIN COLLEGE JOINT LIB						
CALVIN COLLEGE JOINT LIB	PRI-FG	0	0	0	0	0	0	0	0
CALVIN THEOLOGICAL SEM	PRI-FG		SEE CALVIN COLLEGE JOINT LIB						
CTR FOR CREATIVE STUDIES	PRI-FN	641	54.3	893.4	1.5	16.2	16.0	641.0	641.0
CENTRAL MICH UNIVERSITY	PUB-FG	15,155	156.2	3,849.9	4.7	35.3	26.9	219.6	466.3
CHAS S MOTT CMTY COLLEGE	PUB-T	5,076	59.4	1,416.9	1.9	17.8	16.6	604.2	1,492.9
CLEARY COLLEGE	PRI-FN	275	71.0	0	3.1	38.9	A	343.7	550.0
CONCORDIA COLLEGE	PRI-FN	552	249.1	4,044.3	6.9	187.3	136.4	184.0	276.0
CRANBROOK ACADEMY OF ART	PRI-FG	144	163.1	2,937.5	1.9	140.1	137.0	144.0	144.0
DAVENPORT COLLEGE OF BUS	PRI-T	1,544	31.0	1,497.5	1.6	8.2	8.0	1,544.0	1,544.0
DELTA COLLEGE	PUB-T	5,058	73.9	1,898.3	2.2	16.7	18.0	459.8	1,011.6
DETROIT BIBLE COLLEGE	PRI-FN	190	359.0	6,821.7	9.1	206.6	165.3	59.3	190.0
DETROIT C OF BUS ADMIN	PRI-FN	1,602	43.1	3,639.1	2.9	11.3	10.9	1,335.0	1,335.0
DETROIT COLLEGE OF LAW	PRI-FG	550	510.4	12,206.3	13.6	95.4	176.7	68.7	137.5
DETROIT INST TECHNOLOGY	PRI-FN	651	95.0	2,577.2	1.7	94.3	71.8	162.7	325.5
EASTERN MICH UNIVERSITY	PUB-FG	12,700	136.2	2,907.4	3.4	36.6	26.2	204.8	470.3
FERRIS STATE COLLEGE	PUB-FG	10,020	109.8	2,452.0	3.2	18.6	15.7	225.1	607.2
GENERAL MOTORS INSTITUTE	PRI-FN	2,248	45.4	A	A	18.0	21.3	.0	A
GLEN OAKS CMTY COLLEGE	PUB-T	594	101.7	2,238.2	3.3	53.2	47.5	237.6	594.0
GOGEBIC COMMUNITY COLLEGE	PUB-T	791	120.5	1,986.3	3.6	27.6	23.7	197.7	791.0
GRACE BIBLE COLLEGE	PRI-FN	164	58.0	954.5	2.1	157.6	119.0	.0	A
GRAND RAPIDS BAPT C & SEM	PRI-FG	969	112.4	2,224.0	4.0	67.1	55.2	138.4	242.2
GRAND RAPIDS JR COLLEGE	PUB-T	4,905	51.6	1,121.6	2.1	9.9	8.7	485.6	961.7
GRAND RAPIDS SCH BIBLE	PRI-T	621	39.6	2,236.9	1.9	19.6	13.2	388.1	621.0
GRAND VALLEY ST COLLEGE	PUB-FG	5,428	98.4	2,323.1	2.6	38.2	29.5	310.1	775.4
GREAT LAKES BIBLE COLLEGE	PRI-FN	208	162.0	3,064.2	3.5	84.1	68.0	148.5	148.5
HENRY FORD CMTY COLLEGE	PUB-T	10,989	46.8	2,442.4	2.9	7.9	5.2	682.5	1,277.7
HIGHLAND PK CMTY COLLEGE	PUB-T	1,746	56.1	1,420.4	1.6	A	11.5	349.2	873.0
HILLSDALE COLLEGE	PRI-FN	1,006	207.1	3,722.1	3.6	85.1	A	167.6	251.5
HOPE COLLEGE	PRI-FN	2,201	183.0	2,721.8	4.1	85.9	74.7	174.6	550.2
JACKSON COMMUNITY COLLEGE	PUB-T	3,144	48.2	1,486.3	1.6	12.4	10.3	786.0	1,572.0
JOHN WESLEY COLLEGE	PRI-FN	209	225.4	2,771.5	5.5	172.2	173.4	209.0	209.0
JORDAN COLLEGE	PRI-FN	181	58.8	0	1.6	71.8	64.9	181.0	181.0
KALAMAZOO COLLEGE	PRI-FN	1,441	205.9	3,450.2	3.7	154.9	112.5	169.5	411.7
KALAMAZOO VALLEY CC	PUB-T	2,984	116.1	3,982.8	4.9	20.2	16.2	162.1	552.5
KELLOGG COMMUNITY COLLEGE	PUB-T	2,335	160.7	4,216.3	5.7	16.7	15.0	189.8	440.5
KENDALL SCH OF DESIGN	PRI-FN	0	0	0	0	0	0	0	0
KIRTLAND CMTY COLLEGE	PUB-T	730	132.2	4,388.4	3.6	41.1	34.0	280.7	730.0
LAKE MICHIGAN COLLEGE	PUB-T	1,701	100.0	3,210.4	4.1	41.1	26.7	340.2	567.0
LAKE SUPERIOR ST COLLEGE	PUB-FN	2,071	148.5	2,929.9	4.2	44.8	34.7	188.2	414.2
LANSING COMMUNITY COLLEGE	PUB-T	8,157	125.6	5,992.4	4.4	9.1	7.7	224.7	815.7
LAWRENCE INST TECHNOLOGY	PRI-FN	3,800	41.4	3,089.2	2.7	12.4	11.8	622.9	950.0
LEWIS C BUSINESS	PRI-T	510	14.9	0	.5	5.4	4.9	510.0	510.0
MACOMB CO CC ALL CAM									
MACOMB CO CC-CENTER CAM	PUB-T	2,906	152.0	4,417.6	7.0	19.7	11.8	195.0	440.3
MACOMB CO CC-SOUTH CAMPUS	PUB-T	8,804	103.0	3,734.1	4.5	10.7	6.5	306.7	733.6
MADONNA COLLEGE	PRI-FN	1,662	95.6	2,337.5	4.0	56.9	56.6	126.8	554.0

SEE FOOTNOTES AT END OF TABLE

Table 3. – Indexes Concerning Operating Expenditures, 1978-79, Bookstock Held at End of Year, 1978-79, and Library Staff (FTE), Fall 1979, College and University Libraries, by State or Other Area and Institution: Aggregate United States – Continued

STATE OR OTHER AREA AND INSTITUTION	CONTROL AND TYPE OF INSTITUTION	TOTAL FTE OPENING FALL ENROLLMENT, FALL 1978	LIBRARY OPERATING EXPENDITURES (IN DOLLARS) 1978-79			BOOKSTOCK HELD AT END OF YEAR 1978-79		FTE STUDENTS PER FTE LIBRARY STAFF FALL 1979	
			PER FTE STUDENT, FALL 1978	PER FULL-TIME FACULTY MEMBER, 1978	AS PERCENT OF GENERAL EXPENDITURES, 1978-79	VOLUMES PER FTE STUDENT, FALL 1978	TITLES (INCLUDING MICROFORMS) PER FTE STUDENT 1978	TOTAL STAFF	PROFESSIONAL STAFF
(1)	(2)	(3)	(4)	(5)	(6)	(7)	(8)	(9)	(10)
MICHIGAN	--CONTINUED								
MARYGROVE COLLEGE	PRI-FG	669	208.7	3,103.1	3.1	255.8	201.9	89.2	148.6
MERCY COLLEGE OF DETROIT	PRI-FN	1,685	141.0	3,047.6	4.0	70.0	59.6	153.1	271.7
MERRILL-PALMER INSTITUTE	PRI-FG	92	A	A	A	195.6	A	46.0	92.0
MICH CHRISTIAN COLLEGE	PRI-T	290	182.1	4,803.0	4.6	109.0	131.7	193.3	290.0
MICHIGAN STATE UNIVERSITY	PUB-U	40,521	138.2	2,875.7	2.1	47.0	32.4	200.5	536.7
MICHIGAN TECHNOLOGICAL U	PUB-FG	6,760	125.1	2,549.0	2.5	67.3	16.4	236.3	650.0
MID MICHIGAN CMTY COLLEGE	PUB-T	895	97.3	2,421.3	3.2	20.4	16.6	162.7	995.0
MONROE CO CMTY COLLEGE	PUB-T	1,144	180.9	A	5.6	39.7	35.8	137.8	381.3
MONTCALM CMTY COLLEGE	PUB-T	754	95.2	2,659.9	3.6	28.1	27.6	251.3	754.0
MUSKEGON BUSINESS COLLEGE	PRI-T	930	31.0	1,698.9	2.4	3.8	3.8	715.3	715.3
MUSKEGON CMTY COLLEGE	PUB-T	2,450	74.6	1,510.5	2.4	21.6	17.8	326.6	700.0
NAZARETH COLLEGE	PRI-FN	422	215.9	2,940.0	5.0	196.6	131.2	100.4	127.8
NORTH CEN MICH COLLEGE	PUB-T	840	60.0	1,527.9	2.4	25.2	25.0	420.0	840.0
NORTHERN MICH UNIVERSITY	PUB-FG	7,594	96.4	2,075.0	2.5	45.7	29.7	345.1	843.7
NORTHWESTERN MICH COLLEGE	PUB-T	1,982	115.3	2,458.9	A	22.3	23.2	198.2	330.3
NORTHWOOD INSTITUTE	PRI-FN	D	D	D	D	D	D	D	D
OAKLAND COMMUNITY COLLEGE	PUB-T	10,047	73.6	2,982.5	3.0	14.5	7.0	358.8	1,116.3
OAKLAND UNIVERSITY	PUB-FG	8,414	152.6	3,868.7	4.0	34.5	A	191.2	400.6
OLIVET COLLEGE	PRI-FG	651	210.1	3,257.9	4.5	114.1	105.1	81.3	144.6
REFORMED BIBLE COLLEGE	PRI-FN	205	208.0	4,264.0	6.3	168.1	139.2	102.5	205.0
SACRED HEART SEMINARY C	PRI-FN	73	651.1	15,845.0	5.9	698.0	700.1	36.5	73.0
SAGINAW VLY STATE COLLEGE	PUB-FG	2,301	154.1	3,512.3	3.9	38.0	35.7	225.5	442.5
SNT CLAIR CO CMTY COLLEGE	PUB-T	2,071	120.5	2,355.4	3.6	20.2	20.3	235.3	517.7
SNT JOHN PROVINCIAL SEM	PRI-FG	D	D	D	D	D	D	D	D
SAINT MARY'S COLLEGE	PRI-FN	138	452.2	20,801.6	8.6	352.5	3.3	28.7	138.0
SCHOOLCRAFT COLLEGE	PUB-T	4,313	78.6	2,406.2	2.9	16.1	15.3	435.6	695.6
SHAW COLLEGE AT DETROIT	PRI-FN	735	135.0	1,872.9	3.3	121.9	146.4	133.6	245.0
SIENA HEIGHTS COLLEGE	PRI-FG	841	148.3	3,371.5	4.1	90.9	81.9	125.5	271.2
SOUTHWESTERN MICH COLLEGE	PUB-T	1,437	61.7	2,219.5	2.6	17.3	17.4	463.5	1,437.0
SPRING ARBOR COLLEGE	PRI-FN	789	187.2	3,787.7	4.2	81.6	72.7	127.2	263.0
SUOMI COLLEGE	PRI-T	537	102.8	3,069.1	1.8	41.6	A	244.0	537.0
THOMAS M COOLEY LAW SCH	PRI-FN	D	D	D	D	D	D	D	D
UNIVERSITY OF DETROIT	PRI-U	5,489	210.8	4,286.6	4.0	81.9	84.9	104.3	234.5
U OF MICHIGAN ALL CAM									
U MICHIGAN-ANN ARBOR	PUB-U	32,434	315.9	5,892.3	3.0	156.5	114.7	70.0	214.9
U OF MICHIGAN-DEARBORN	PUB-FG	4,170	142.5	3,162.9	4.2	50.6	A	212.7	571.2
U OF MICHIGAN-FLINT	PUB-FG	2,679	214.9	4,682.3	5.2	35.4	A	148.8	297.6
WALSH C ACCTY & BUS ADMIN	PRI-FG	637	74.5	11,866.5	4.4	19.6	15.7	318.5	796.2
WASHTENAW CMTY COLLEGE	PUB-T	3,398	110.1	3,093.8	3.3	14.1	11.5	212.3	755.1
WAYNE COUNTY CMTY COLLEGE	PUB-T	9,288	64.7	3,250.5	1.9	4.5	1.4	418.3	928.8
WAYNE STATE UNIVERSITY	PUB-U	24,784	199.1	4,418.0	2.9	72.8	26.5	144.6	390.2
WESTERN MICH UNIVERSITY	PUB-FG	17,690	133.5	2,839.5	3.5	42.6	22.6	226.5	640.9
WESTERN THEOLOGICAL SEM	PRI-FG	113	718.1	6,762.2	10.5	663.5	469.3	36.4	102.7
WEST SHORE CMTY COLLEGE	PUB-T	566	124.0	2,265.2	3.3	20.0	19.0	161.7	283.0
MINNESOTA									
AUGSBURG COLLEGE	PRI-FN	1,470	159.3	2,723.0	3.7	89.4	73.3	196.0	267.2
BETHANY LUTHERAN COLLEGE	PRI-T	266	150.0	3,070.2	4.3	A	A	177.3	177.3
BETHEL C & SEM ALL CAM									
BETHEL COLLEGE	PRI-FN	1,791	149.2	3,072.0	4.0	69.7	62.6	168.9	275.5
BETHEL THEOL SEMINARY	PRI-FG	366	311.2	7,120.6	8.5	234.3	172.0	85.1	366.0
CARLETON COLLEGE	PRI-FN	1,814	335.1	4,864.2	5.3	143.3	117.1	104.2	362.8
COLLEGE OF SAINT BENEDICT	PRI-FN	1,750	193.0	3,838.0	4.8	58.1	45.2	173.2	500.0
COLLEGE OF SNT CATHERINE	PRI-FN	2,067	217.8	3,783.5	5.7	99.8	99.5	107.0	196.8
COLLEGE SAINT SCHOLASTICA	PRI-FG	1,101	149.7	2,748.7	3.7	73.7	69.2	148.7	282.3
COLLEGE OF SAINT TERESA	PRI-FN	865	209.0	2,259.8	4.1	150.9	151.8	112.3	247.1
COLLEGE OF SAINT THOMAS	PRI-FG	3,613	152.0	4,259.9	4.7	54.2	30.1	155.7	296.1
CONCORDIA C AT MOORHEAD	PRI-FN	2,636	171.7	3,100.8	4.1	77.4	80.6	155.9	376.5
CONCORDIA C-SAINT PAUL	PRI-FN	609	237.7	3,366.7	5.4	135.8	128.5	110.7	243.6
CROSIER SEMINARY	PRI-T	17	2,344.8	D	40.6	1,176.4	1,166.1	6.0	8.5
DR MARTIN LUTHER COLLEGE	PRI-FN	822	132.3	1,754.3	6.0	56.6	53.9	105.3	274.0
GOLDEN VLY LUTH COLLEGE	PRI-T	575	115.8	2,561.1	2.7	43.8	37.9	143.7	143.7
GUSTAVUS ADOLPHUS COLLEGE	PRI-FN	2,204	172.6	2,860.5	4.2	79.0	81.9	153.0	400.7
HAMLINE UNIVERSITY	PRI-FG	1,617	290.4	4,515.5	5.5	147.4	91.5	85.1	179.6
LUTHER NTHWSTN SEM JT LIB	PRI-FG	D	D	D	D	D	D	D	D
LUTHER THEOLOGICAL SEM	PRI-FG			SEE LUTHER NTHWSTN SEM JT LIB					
MACALESTER COLLEGE	PRI-FN	1,686	170.0	2,514.3	3.2	160.9	100.5	117.9	337.2

SEE FOOTNOTES AT END OF TABLE

Table 3. — Indexes Concerning Operating Expenditures, 1978-79, Bookstock Held at End of Year, 1978-79, and Library Staff (FTE), Fall 1979, College and University Libraries, by State or Other Area and Institution: Aggregate United States — Continued

STATE OR OTHER AREA AND INSTITUTION (1)	CONTROL AND TYPE OF INSTITUTION (2)	TOTAL FTE OPENING FALL ENROLLMENT, FALL 1978 (3)	LIBRARY OPERATING EXPENDITURES (IN DOLLARS) 1978-79			BOOKSTOCK HELD AT END OF YEAR 1978-79		FTE STUDENTS PER FTE LIBRARY STAFF FALL 1979	
			PER FTE STUDENT, FALL 1978 (4)	PER FULL-TIME FACULTY MEMBER, 1978 (5)	AS PERCENT OF GENERAL EXPENDITURES, 1978-79 (6)	VOLUMES PER FTE STUDENT, FALL 1978 (7)	TITLES (INCLUDING MICROFORMS) PER FTE STUDENT 1978 (8)	TOTAL STAFF (9)	PROFESSIONAL STAFF (10)
MINNESOTA	--CONTINUED								
MAYO MEDICAL SCHOOL	PRI-FG	162	274.8	D	1.3	15.8	7.5	81.0	162.0
MINNEAPOLIS C-ART DESIGN	PRI-FN	688	190.5	2,789.0	4.5	66.3	39.7	95.5	163.8
MINNESOTA BIBLE COLLEGE	PRI-FN	122	238.1	2,641.5	A	139.5	124.4	61.0	122.0
MINN CC SYSTEM ALL INST									
ANOKA-RAMSEY CMTY COLLEGE	PUB-T	1,806	78.2	2,317.4	3.8	16.1	16.1	361.2	602.0
AUSTIN COMMUNITY COLLEGE	PUB-T	677	145.5	2,526.8	4.1	31.6	34.0	218.3	376.1
BRAINERD CMTY COLLEGE	PUB-T	509	126.3	2,679.6	4.1	30.1	29.8	509.0	509.0
FERGUS FALLS CMTY COLLEGE	PUB-T	478	159.9	2,831.5	4.9	53.6	50.5	159.3	478.0
HIBBING COMMUNITY COLLEGE	PUB-T	498	151.0	2,594.6	4.8	47.2	33.1	142.2	498.0
INVER HILLS CMTY COLLEGE	PUB-T	1,795	87.4	2,705.0	4.0	16.2	15.4	326.3	598.3
ITASCA COMMUNITY COLLEGE	PUB-T	505	148.5	2,885.2	4.7	38.3	32.5	229.5	505.0
LAKEWOOD CMTY COLLEGE	PUB-T	2,096	86.4	2,745.6	4.4	12.7	12.3	361.3	524.0
MESABI COMMUNITY COLLEGE	PUB-T	579	89.4	1,785.0	2.9	48.5	47.7	445.3	445.3
METROPOLITAN CMTY COLLEGE	PUB-T	1,473	87.0	2,374.2	3.5	A	15.1	267.8	491.0
NORMANDALE CMTY COLLEGE	PUB-T	3,722	98.0	3,579.1	6.0	13.7	10.5	310.1	1,861.0
N HENNEPIN CMTY COLLEGE	PUB-T	2,748	103.9	3,662.4	5.5	9.8	8.8	319.5	763.3
NORTHLAND CMTY COLLEGE	PUB-T	377	122.1	2,707.9	3.9	32.4	31.1	221.7	314.1
RAINY RIVER CMTY COLLEGE	PUB-T	317	149.3	2,255.0	4.2	48.4	43.7	158.5	317.0
ROCHESTER CMTY COLLEGE	PUB-T	2,306	60.7	1,539.6	2.7	20.2	18.6	354.7	658.8
VERMILION CMTY COLLEGE	PUB-T	391	143.3	3,502.6	4.4	40.9	39.4	391.0	391.0
WILLMAR CMTY COLLEGE	PUB-T	685	82.7	2,099.8	3.3	26.8	26.8	380.5	685.0
WORTHINGTON CMTY COLLEGE	PUB-T	384	126.8	1,949.1	3.6	81.1	75.2	192.0	384.0
NORTH CEN BIBLE COLLEGE	PRI-FN	575	49.1	2,019.3	2.3	43.9	36.5	287.5	287.5
NORTHWESTERN COLLEGE	PRI-FN	675	120.9	2,551.1	A	71.4	59.3	168.7	225.0
NTHWSTN C CHIROPRACTIC	PRI-FG	385	161.5	A	5.3	15.8	15.6	96.2	192.5
NTHWSTN LUTH THEOL SEM	PRI-FG	SEE LUTHER NTHWSTN SEM JT LIB							
SAINT JOHN'S UNIVERSITY	PRI-FG	1,920	223.0	3,568.8	5.3	147.5	109.1	120.0	282.3
SAINT MARY'S COLLEGE	PRI-FG	1,229	163.2	2,572.7	3.7	111.7	112.4	163.8	273.1
SAINT MARY'S JR COLLEGE	PRI-T	740	78.6	1,163.6	2.0	33.1	29.8	284.6	462.5
SAINT OLAF COLLEGE	PRI-FN	2,919	144.8	2,224.6	3.3	109.4	75.5	179.0	351.6
SAINT PAUL BIBLE COLLEGE	PRI-FN	591	139.8	3,179.8	5.0	109.6	106.1	147.7	295.5
SAINT PAUL SEMINARY	PRI-FG	128	545.6	6,984.0	8.3	487.8	414.0	31.2	64.0
STATE U SYS MINN ALL INST									
BEMIDJI STATE U	PUB-FG	4,292	125.7	2,697.8	4.0	47.6	45.2	232.0	504.9
MANKATO STATE UNIVERSITY	PUB-FG	8,947	158.6	3,065.7	5.5	41.2	39.3	199.2	357.8
METROPOLITAN STATE U1/	PUB-FN	NO LIBRARY FACILITIES							
MOORHEAD STATE UNIVERSITY	PUB-FG	5,445	99.7	1,918.6	3.5	45.6	A	256.8	664.0
SAINT CLOUD ST UNIVERSITY	PUB-FG	9,873	143.3	3,245.9	5.7	48.3	32.0	205.6	429.2
STHWST STATE UNIVERSITY	PUB-FN	1,671	207.3	3,535.4	4.6	86.5	72.2	162.2	255.2
WINONA STATE UNIVERSITY	PUB-FG	3,995	129.5	2,890.9	4.7	42.6	27.4	210.2	499.3
UNITED THEOLOGICAL SEM	PRI-FG	261	245.6	6,412.4	7.4	203.6	203.7	104.4	130.5
U OF MINNESOTA ALL CAM									
U OF MINNESOTA DULUTH	PUB-FG	6,942	146.4	3,238.1	4.2	37.0	24.0	208.4	514.2
U MINN MAYO GRAD SCH MED	PRI-FG	433	1,942.2	D	1.7	507.3	158.2	15.1	30.9
U OF MINN MNPLS SNT PAUL	PUB-U	46,777	194.1	4,989.2	2.5	79.9	79.9	160.7	398.7
U OF MINNESOTA MORRIS	PUB-FN	1,435	216.7	3,418.6	4.4	78.0	70.2	144.9	287.0
U MINN TECH COL CROOKSTON	PUB-T	882	227.7	3,292.5	5.0	21.5	18.3	98.0	882.0
U OF MINN TECH C-WASECA	PUB-T	873	166.3	3,456.9	3.9	24.1	21.4	194.0	291.0
WM MITCHELL COLLEGE LAW	PRI-FG	1,157	304.8	14,108.0	13.5	61.7	15.0	107.1	289.2
MISSISSIPPI									
ALCORN STATE UNIVERSITY	PUB-FG	2,100	211.4	3,264.9	3.0	59.7	52.0	110.5	300.0
BELHAVEN COLLEGE	PRI-FN	551	154.5	3,154.1	4.5	101.9	100.7	110.2	183.6
BLUE MOUNTAIN COLLEGE	PRI-FN	284	185.2	2,023.4	5.8	157.4	97.6	167.0	189.3
CLARKE COLLEGE	PRI-T	179	112.0	1,253.3	3.4	100.4	87.6	179.0	179.0
COAHOMA JUNIOR COLLEGE	PUB-T	1,420	117.3	A	A	18.4	16.4	157.7	473.3
COPIAH-LINCOLN JR COLLEGE	PUB-T	1,195	93.7	1,578.4	3.1	32.7	31.8	163.6	341.4
DELTA STATE UNIVERSITY	PUB-FG	2,418	233.3	3,339.4	5.5	86.9	75.4	120.9	302.2
EAST CENTRAL JR COLLEGE	PUB-T	558	136.2	1,948.7	4.3	47.4	43.4	186.0	186.0
EAST MISS JUNIOR COLLEGE	PUB-T	729	76.2	1,134.7	2.2	28.1	24.0	243.0	364.5
HINDS JUNIOR COLLEGE	PUB-T	4,501	127.4	2,206.8	5.5	15.8	11.6	206.4	500.1
HOLMES JUNIOR COLLEGE	PUB-T	920	58.5	979.0	2.6	38.6	38.9	460.0	460.0
ITAWAMBA JUNIOR COLLEGE	PUB-T	1,146	158.9	1,718.5	5.5	31.7	30.5	143.2	382.0
JACKSON STATE UNIVERSITY	PUB-FG	6,665	137.5	2,745.2	4.3	47.2	66.9	196.0	555.4
JONES CO JUNIOR COLLEGE	PUB-T	2,047	134.4	2,202.0	5.7	24.2	23.9	255.8	409.4
MARY HOLMES COLLEGE	PRI-T	641	121.1	3,377.0	A	35.9	34.9	128.2	320.5
MERIDIAN JUNIOR COLLEGE	PUB-T	1,866	106.1	1,636.7	5.2	19.8	18.9	169.6	373.2

SEE FOOTNOTES AT END OF TABLE

Table 3. — Indexes Concerning Operating Expenditures, 1978-79, Bookstock Held at End of Year, 1978-79, and Library Staff (FTE), Fall 1979, College and University Libraries, by State or Other Area and Institution: Aggregate United States — Continued

STATE OR OTHER AREA AND INSTITUTION	CONTROL AND TYPE OF INSTITUTION	TOTAL FTE OPENING FALL ENROLLMENT, FALL 1978	LIBRARY OPERATING EXPENDITURES (IN DOLLARS) 1978-79			BOOKSTOCK HELD AT END OF YEAR 1978-79		FTE STUDENTS PER FTE LIBRARY STAFF FALL 1979	
			PER FTE STUDENT, FALL 1978	PER FULL-TIME FACULTY MEMBER, 1978	AS PERCENT OF GENERAL EXPENDITURES, 1978-79	VOLUMES PER FTE STUDENT, FALL 1978	TITLES (INCLUDING MICROFORMS) PER FTE STUDENT 1978	TOTAL STAFF	PROFESSIONAL STAFF
(1)	(2)	(3)	(4)	(5)	(6)	(7)	(8)	(9)	(10)
MISSISSIPPI	--CONTINUED								
MILLSAPS COLLEGE	PRI-FN	908	191.8	3,002.9	A	105.7	93.6	106.8	227.0
MINISTERIAL INST AND C	PRI-T	400	32.2	.0	A	17.5	16.7	133.3	400.0
MISSISSIPPI COLLEGE	PRI-FG	1,572	244.6	A	6.6	142.3	127.6	94.1	134.3
MISS DELTA JUNIOR COLLEGE	PUB-T	1,371	107.1	1,562.6	4.4	18.5	17.8	195.8	342.7
MISS GULF CST JC ALL CAM									
MISS GULF CST JC JACKSON	PUB-T	1,593	108.7	2,406.9	4.8	15.8	15.8	177.0	531.0
MISS GULF CST JC JEFF DAVIS	PUB-T	2,233	68.9	2,000.0	2.6	14.7	14.4	319.0	558.2
MISS GULF CST JC PERKNSTN	PUB-T	705	226.6	3,829.3	12.1	29.8	29.7	100.7	176.2
MISS INDUSTRIAL COLLEGE	PRI-FN	248	33.8	399.7	A	155.4	155.7	99.2	99.2
MISSISSIPPI ST UNIVERSITY	PUB-U	10,710	180.5	2,765.8	2.2	58.1	24.1	193.3	451.8
MISS UNIVERSITY FOR WOMEN	PUB-FG	2,234	177.7	2,720.5	3.8	98.8	58.7	116.3	279.2
MISS VLY ST UNIVERSITY	PUB-FG	2,720	169.5	3,073.7	4.4	36.1	36.3	113.3	247.2
NORTHEAST MISS JR COLLEGE	PUB-T	1,249	88.1	1,101.3	2.7	25.8	20.4	312.2	416.3
NORTHWEST MISS JR COLLEGE	PUB-T	2,179	57.7	873.4	2.3	13.2	12.5	363.1	435.8
PEARL RIVER JR COLLEGE	PUB-T	D	D	D	D	D	D	D	D
PHILLIPS COLLEGE	PRI-T	542	30.4	1,499.0	3.3	2.1	2.0	542.0	542.0
PRENTISS NORM-INDUS INST	PRI-T	81	313.6	2,823.1	3.9	77.8	62.8	40.5	40.5
REFORMED THEOLOGICAL SEM	PRI-FG	254	507.5	7,161.6	8.8	183.5	A	36.2	63.5
RUST COLLEGE	PRI-FN	675	225.5	4,758.6	4.2	95.7	90.5	135.0	225.0
SOUTHEASTERN BAPT COLLEGE	PRI-FN	38	280.4	A	A	242.9	A	130.0	130.0
SOUTHWEST MISS JR COLLEGE	PUB-T	986	90.8	A	A	25.4	17.9	246.5	328.6
TOUGALOO COLLEGE	PRI-FN	894	126.3	1,661.3	2.2	A	95.0	119.2	223.5
U OF MISSISSIPPI ALL CAM									
U OF MISSISSIPPI MAIN CAM	PUB-U	9,116	170.9	3,755.6	4.2	66.0	30.3	148.4	325.5
U OF MISSISSIPPI MEDL CTR	PUB-FG	1,476	349.6	4,868.9	1.6	72.5	18.6	68.6	105.4
U OF SOUTHERN MISSISSIPPI	PUB-FG	9,678	167.0	2,981.9	4.0	44.1	45.6	167.4	314.2
UTICA JUNIOR COLLEGE	PUB-T	823	142.8	1,992.7	3.6	31.2	31.3	117.5	205.7
WESLEY COLLEGE	PRI-FN	75	418.5	5,231.3	11.0	227.9	205.1	46.8	75.0
WHITWORTH BIBLE COLLEGE	PRI-FN	25	245.6	3,070.0	5.1	333.4	333.4	125.0	125.0
WILLIAM CAREY COLLEGE	PRI-FG	1,317	132.6	3,493.9	4.3	58.5	56.4	173.2	263.4
WOOD JUNIOR COLLEGE	PRI-T	223	156.7	3,177.3	5.7	113.1	107.6	111.5	111.5
MISSOURI									
ASSEMBLIES GOD GRAD SCH	PRI-FG	512	230.3	19,656.3	19.1	56.6	56.3	73.1	128.0
AVILA COLLEGE	PRI-FG	1,382	66.1	1,522.7	2.4	47.7	43.5	307.1	345.5
BAPTIST BIBLE COLLEGE	PRI-FN	2,150	47.0	1,805.5	2.9	13.8	A	.0	A
CALVARY BIBLE COLLEGE	PRI-FG	332	99.1	2,194.3	4.0	99.2	A	122.9	474.2
CARDINAL GLENNON COLLEGE	PRI-FN	91	411.9	9,371.2	5.7	690.4	A	91.0	91.0
CARDINAL NEWMAN COLLEGE	PRI-FN	53	758.4	8,040.0	4.9	112.9	93.5	26.5	53.0
CENTRAL BIBLE COLLEGE	PRI-FN	1,072	132.5	4,180.0	8.1	79.7	A	306.2	428.8
CEN CHRSTN C OF THE BIBLE	PRI-FN	D	D	D	D	D	D	D	D
CENTRAL METHODIST COLLEGE	PRI-FN	610	133.4	1,356.3	2.4	223.9	106.0	152.5	305.0
CENTRAL MO ST UNIVERSITY	PUB-FG	8,763	136.2	2,720.6	5.2	35.6	29.1	168.5	515.4
CHRIST SEMINARY-SEMINEX	PRI-FG	222	585.4	7,220.3	8.2	126.6	110.0	46.2	51.6
CLEVELAND CHIROPRACTIC C	PRI-FG	233	159.6	A	4.1	16.6	16.4	233.0	233.0
COLUMBIA COLLEGE	PRI-FN	2,424	49.1	2,247.1	1.7	15.6	20.2	484.8	808.0
CONCEPTION SEM COLLEGE	PRI-FN	89	466.9	13,852.6	9.6	977.6	839.8	22.2	29.6
CONCORDIA SEMINARY	PRI-FG	522	502.4	10,492.1	10.1	279.6	185.8	46.1	121.3
COTTEY COLLEGE	PRI-T	D	D	D	D	D	D	D	D
COVENANT THEOLOGICAL SEM	PRI-FG	155	440.2	6,203.6	7.8	230.9	201.1	32.2	77.5
CROWDER COLLEGE	PUB-T	739	86.6	3,049.7	4.2	35.7	32.4	230.9	615.8
CULVER-STOCKTON COLLEGE	PRI-FN	423	134.5	1,626.6	2.3	237.9	224.5	120.8	423.0
DRURY COLLEGE	PRI-FG	1,470	107.4	2,722.5	3.4	75.4	A	229.6	432.3
EAST CENTRAL MO DIST JC	PUB-T	944	74.4	1,527.9	2.8	20.0	18.8	236.0	944.0
EDEN THEOLOGICAL SEMINARY	PRI-FG	SEE EDEN-WEBSTER JT LIB							
EDEN-WEBSTER JT LIBRARIES	PRI-FG	D	D	D	D	D	D	D	D
EVANGEL COLLEGE	PRI-FN	1,370	89.6	2,273.2	2.8	64.1	62.9	214.0	456.6
FONTBONNE COLLEGE	PRI-FG	687	150.3	1,750.4	3.8	124.9	125.0	129.6	137.4
HANNIBAL-LAGRANGE COLLEGE	PRI-FN	302	95.1	A	2.7	82.7	60.8	167.7	302.0
HARRIS-STOWE STATE C	PUB-FN	893	88.7	1,761.7	2.7	62.2	78.8	288.0	297.6
JEFFERSON COLLEGE	PUB-T	1,188	99.3	1,475.2	3.4	33.4	31.4	199.0	594.0
KANSAS CITY ART INSTITUTE	PRI-FN	589	103.4	1,417.0	2.2	48.2	A	143.6	210.3
KANSAS CITY C OSTEO MED	PRI-FG	616	303.7	D	A	52.6	32.7	102.6	205.3
KEMPER MILITARY SCH AND C	PRI-T	60	189.7	3,795.6	.9	344.3	337.0	60.0	60.0
KENRICK SEMINARY	PRI-FG	149	381.1	.0	7.7	417.6	405.2	53.2	149.0
KIRKSVL COLLEGE OSTEO MED	PRI-FG	496	297.8	D	2.5	101.0	38.0	124.0	248.0

SEE FOOTNOTES AT END OF TABLE

Table 3. – Indexes Concerning Operating Expenditures, 1978-79, Bookstock Held at End of Year, 1978-79, and Library Staff (FTE), Fall 1979, College and University Libraries, by State or Other Area and Institution: Aggregate United States – Continued

STATE OR OTHER AREA AND INSTITUTION	CONTROL AND TYPE OF INSTITUTION	TOTAL FTE OPENING FALL ENROLLMENT, FALL 1978	LIBRARY OPERATING EXPENDITURES (IN DOLLARS) 1978-79			BOOKSTOCK HELD AT END OF YEAR 1978-79		FTE STUDENTS PER FTE LIBRARY STAFF FALL 1979	
			PER FTE STUDENT FALL 1978	PER FULL-TIME FACULTY MEMBER 1978	AS PERCENT OF GENERAL EXPENDITURES, 1978-79	VOLUMES PER FTE STUDENT, FALL 1978	TITLES (INCLUDING MICROFORMS) PER FTE STUDENT 1978	TOTAL STAFF	PROFESSIONAL STAFF
(1)	(2)	(3)	(4)	(5)	(6)	(7)	(8)	(9)	(10)
MISSOURI	--CONTINUED								
LINCOLN UNIVERSITY	PUB-FG	1,759	157.4	2,366.4	2.9	74.4	101.6	149.0	293.1
THE LINDENWOOD COLLEGES	PRI-FG	1,179	92.1	2,218.1	2.8	74.1	64.4	214.3	336.8
LOGAN C OF CHIROPRACTIC	PRI-FG	557	111.3	3,101.2	4.3	24.7	24.7	150.5	185.6
MARYVILLE C-SAINT LOUIS	PRI-FG	984	163.0	2,917.0	3.9	94.5	94.3	103.5	246.0
METRO CC ADMINV ALL INST									
LONGVIEW CMTY COLLEGE	PUB-T	2,355	48.7	1,882.8	2.1	9.7	9.6	373.8	905.7
MAPLE WOODS CMTY COLLEGE	PUB-T	1,278	72.2	2,429.8	3.2	14.2	11.0	297.2	555.6
PENN VALLEY CMTY COLLEGE	PUB-T	3,140	50.9	1,392.0	2.1	18.7	A	628.0	1,570.0
PIONEER COMMUNITY COLLEGE	PUB-T	351	45.1	1,320.3	1.3	2.0	2.0	351.0	351.0
MIDWESTERN BAPT THEOL SEM	PRI-FG	D	D	D	D	D	D	D	D
MINERAL AREA COLLEGE	PUB-T	779	103.5	1,646.2	4.4	29.6	24.2	194.7	389.5
MISSOURI BAPTIST COLLEGE	PRI-FN	296	181.6	2,688.0	5.0	114.0	107.0	98.6	98.6
MISSOURI INST TECHNOLOGY	PRI-FN	169	A	A	A	7.2	6.3	84.5	84.5
MISSOURI STHN ST COLLEGE	PUB-FN	3,011	196.6	3,974.0	8.4	42.9	125.7	215.0	430.1
MISSOURI VALLEY COLLEGE	PRI-FN	351	127.3	1,596.0	2.8	241.4	162.6	135.0	175.5
MISSOURI WSTN ST COLLEGE	PUB-FN	2,960	120.8	2,466.8	4.7	35.1	24.6	261.9	592.0
MOBERLY JUNIOR COLLEGE	PUB-T	549	82.1	1,961.6	4.6	26.2	23.8	183.0	549.0
NAZARENE THEOLOGICAL SEM	PRI-FG	426	176.2	4,693.2	8.3	126.5	101.1	142.0	213.0
NTHEST MO ST UNIVERSITY	PUB-FG	5,115	146.1	3,114.7	4.9	46.1	37.1	190.8	601.7
NTHWST MO ST UNIVERSITY	PUB-FG	3,567	127.7	1,899.4	3.5	57.8	40.9	178.3	509.5
PARK COLLEGE	PRI-FN	D	D	D	D	D	D	D	D
ROCKHURST COLLEGE	PRI-FG	1,861	72.8	2,377.3	2.1	54.7	A	310.1	620.3
SNT LOUIS CHRISTIAN C	PRI-FN	158	219.2	3,849.4	A	134.5	219.7	92.9	158.0
SNT LOUIS COLLEGE OF PHAR	PRI-FN	713	124.5	A	5.0	44.5	30.2	203.7	356.5
SNT LU CC CENTER ALL CAM	PRI-FG	D	D	D	D	D	D	D	D
SNT LU CC-FLORISSANT VLY	PUB-T	5,120	114.0	3,316.9	5.3	11.8	9.7	182.8	568.8
SNT LU CC-FOREST PARK	PUB-T	3,927	124.0	3,103.7	4.3	12.6	11.8	170.7	654.5
SAINT LOUIS CC-MERAMEC	PUB-T	5,566	92.4	3,120.3	4.7	10.5	8.9	231.9	795.1
SNT LOUIS CONSV OF MUSIC	PRI-FG	60	582.2	5,822.1	A	125.1	67.2	30.0	60.0
SAINT LOUIS RAB COLLEGE									
SAINT LOUIS U ALL CAM									
SAINT LOUIS U MAIN CAMPUS	PRI-U	7,123	185.7	3,366.4	2.4	109.5	62.7	110.6	293.7
SAINT LOUIS U-PARKS C	PRI-FN	808	72.0	1,354.6	2.1	41.8	22.9	404.0	808.0
SAINT MARY'S C D'FALLON	PRI-T	450	150.3	4,832.4	12.5	97.0	82.1	84.9	346.1
SAINT MARY'S SEM-COLLEGE	PRI-FN	52	664.6	A	6.3	1,094.5	727.1	26.0	34.6
SNT PAUL SCH OF THEOLOGY	PRI-FG	173	447.9	4,558.3	7.0	349.0	A	43.2	86.5
SAINT PAUL'S COLLEGE	PRI-T	141	404.7	3,170.2	11.4	230.6	211.7	70.5	141.0
SCHOOL OF THE OZARKS	PRI-FN	1,342	134.8	3,015.7	3.1	60.3	57.2	279.5	353.1
STHEST MO ST UNIVERSITY	PUB-FG	7,816	132.6	2,825.1	5.3	31.9	34.1	188.3	488.5
SOUTHWEST BAPTIST COLLEGE	PRI-FN	1,325	78.7	1,429.4	2.6	56.0	39.2	220.8	530.0
STHWST MO ST UNIVERSITY	PUB-FG	10,546	102.3	2,194.0	4.3	30.7	45.3	277.5	602.6
STATE FAIR CMTY COLLEGE	PUB-T	885	128.5	1,995.1	3.3	27.4	26.2	160.9	354.0
STEPHENS COLLEGE	PRI-FN	1,509	195.0	2,373.8	3.7	78.0	70.2	93.1	301.8
TARKIO COLLEGE	PRI-FN	577	70.1	1,305.9	1.6	113.7	112.7	288.5	288.5
THREE RIVERS CMTY COLLEGE	PUB-T	729	88.1	1,396.6	3.1	27.9	26.8	364.5	364.5
TRENTON JUNIOR COLLEGE	PUB-T	336	107.2	1,441.5	4.0	36.5	33.3	165.0	336.0
U OF MO CEN ADMIN ALL CAM									
U OF MISSOURI-COLUMBIA	PUB-U	21,084	213.1	4,751.1	2.9	100.0	61.0	126.6	363.5
U OF MISSOURI-KANSAS CITY	PUB-FG	7,380	232.6	3,716.0	3.2	86.0	94.5	98.7	240.3
U OF MISSOURI-ROLLA	PUB-FG	4,986	120.7	2,012.9	2.0	57.1	A	202.6	831.0
U OF MISSOURI-SAINT LOUIS	PUB-FG	8,026	154.4	3,614.3	4.5	43.2	35.5	189.2	573.2
WASHINGTON UNIVERSITY	PRI-U	8,690	476.8	7,533.8	2.6	201.9	119.3	50.3	183.3
WEBSTER COLLEGE	PRI-FG			SEE EDEN-WEBSTER JT LIB					
WENTWORTH MILITARY ACAD	PRI-T	176	57.6	1,014.6	2.4	91.3	83.9	176.0	176.0
WESTMINSTER COLLEGE	PRI-FN	633	175.5	2,268.0	3.9	83.7	80.2	102.0	171.0
WILLIAM JEWELL COLLEGE	PRI-FN	1,510	125.2	A	3.6	87.1	A	173.5	431.4
WILLIAM WOODS COLLEGE	PRI-FN	902	122.9	1,980.2	2.7	59.3	53.4	180.4	300.6
MONTANA									
CARROLL COLLEGE	PRI-FN	1,178	112.6	2,248.8	3.6	63.7	61.7	261.7	294.5
COLLEGE OF GREAT FALLS	PRI-FN	854	142.1	3,195.5	4.6	63.2	66.1	142.3	427.0
DAWSON COMMUNITY COLLEGE	PUB-T	306	144.8	1,773.5	4.4	57.7	51.6	153.0	306.0
FLATHEAD VLY CMTY COLLEGE	PUB-T	860	75.0	2,152.7	2.0	11.2	9.7	860.0	860.0
MILES COMMUNITY COLLEGE	PUB-T	342	181.1	2,581.0	5.4	32.8	31.0	148.6	342.0
MONTANA INST OF THE BIBLE	PRI-FN	234	106.5	A	3.9	73.4	72.9	117.0	234.0
MONTANA U SYSTEM ALL INST									

SEE FOOTNOTES AT END OF TABLE

Table 3. — Indexes Concerning Operating Expenditures, 1978-79, Bookstock Held at End of Year, 1978-79, and Library Staff (FTE), Fall 1979, College and University Libraries, by State or Other Area and Institution: Aggregate United States — Continued

STATE OR OTHER AREA AND INSTITUTION	CONTROL AND TYPE OF INSTITUTION	TOTAL FTE OPENING FALL ENROLLMENT, FALL 1978	LIBRARY OPERATING EXPENDITURES (IN DOLLARS) 1978-79			BOOKSTOCK HELD AT END OF YEAR 1978-79		FTE STUDENTS PER FTE LIBRARY STAFF FALL 1979	
			PER FTE STUDENT, FALL 1978	PER FULL-TIME FACULTY MEMBER, FALL 1978	AS PERCENT OF GENERAL EXPENDITURES, 1978-79	VOLUMES PER FTE STUDENT, FALL 1978	TITLES (INCLUDING MICROFORMS) PER FTE STUDENT 1978	TOTAL STAFF	PROFESSIONAL STAFF
(1)	(2)	(3)	(4)	(5)	(6)	(7)	(8)	(9)	(10)
MONTANA	--CONTINUED								
EASTERN MONTANA COLLEGE	PUB-FG	2,940	100.0	2,179.3	3.1	43.1	35.2	272.2	612.5
MONTANA C MINRL SCI-TECHN	PUB-FG	1,084	122.0	2,405.6	2.3	67.1	63.4	180.6	542.0
MONTANA STATE UNIVERSITY	PUB-U	9,356	119.9	2,120.5	2.7	42.2	19.1	179.2	528.5
NORTHERN MONTANA COLLEGE	PUB-FG	953	146.6	1,958.5	3.8	85.1	235.9	167.1	476.5
UNIVERSITY OF MONTANA	PUB-U	7,349	227.3	4,026.7	6.3	96.8	A	145.8	408.2
WESTERN MONTANA COLLEGE	PUB-FG	656	183.6	3,345.8	4.9	75.2	A	328.0	656.0
ROCKY MOUNTAIN COLLEGE	PRI-FN	492	154.5	3,306.6	4.1	118.4	107.3	164.0	492.0
NEBRASKA									
BELLEVUE COLLEGE	PRI-FN	1,625	61.9	3,727.3	5.5	26.5	27.1	541.6	650.0
CEN TECH CMTY C AREA	PUB-T	D	D	D	D	D	D	D	D
CHADRON STATE COLLEGE	PUB-FG	1,482	212.3	3,702.5	5.7	93.1	91.5	123.5	211.7
COLLEGE OF SAINT MARY	PRI-FN	492	138.5	1,585.2	3.1	125.5	125.2	246.0	492.0
CONCORDIA TCHRS COLLEGE	PRI-FG	1,070	197.6	2,323.6	4.6	112.5	112.1	142.6	305.7
CREIGHTON UNIVERSITY	PRI-U	4,671	250.2	4,548.5	3.9	84.3	61.8	93.0	311.4
DANA COLLEGE	PRI-FN	440	152.6	1,918.5	3.0	192.6	180.6	133.3	220.0
DOANE COLLEGE	PRI-FN	649	124.9	1,885.5	3.2	95.8	94.9	106.3	231.7
GRACE C OF THE BIBLE	PRI-FN	431	89.0	A	2.2	108.7	A	143.6	431.0
HASTINGS COLLEGE	PRI-FN	703	147.4	1,993.3	3.2	136.2	89.2	137.8	251.0
KEARNEY STATE COLLEGE	PUB-FG	4,486	146.8	2,745.5	5.9	29.1	38.3	179.4	345.0
METROPOLITAN TECHNICAL CC	PUB-T	2,803	144.4	4,174.2	4.5	8.5	6.4	169.8	560.6
MIDLAND LUTHERAN COLLEGE	PRI-FN	735	147.9	2,013.5	3.5	102.8	88.5	163.3	294.0
MID PLAINS CC ALL CAM									
MCCOOK COMMUNITY COLLEGE	PUB-T	340	206.5	3,511.5	7.8	58.9	53.1	75.5	340.0
MID PLAINS CC	PUB-T	920	52.6	934.7	1.6	17.5	16.7	460.0	920.0
NEBR CHRISTIAN COLLEGE	PRI-FN	132	74.6	1,094.2	2.5	151.7	A	.0	A
NEBR WESLEYAN UNIVERSITY	PRI-FN	1,059	155.8	2,088.7	4.0	170.8	116.4	151.2	353.0
NEBRASKA WESTERN COLLEGE	PUB-T	677	132.4	A	2.5	30.9	24.8	173.5	225.6
NORTHEAST TECHNICAL CC	PUB-T	1,094	79.0	1,217.5	1.9	20.9	20.8	352.9	1,094.0
PERU STATE COLLEGE	PUB-FN	614	345.0	4,414.3	8.0	133.3	90.5	87.7	153.5
PLATTE VLY BIBLE COLLEGE	PRI-FN	40	71.5	A	1.1	300.0	293.7	.0	A
STHESTN NEBR TECH ALL CAM									
STHEST CC FAIRBY-BEATRICE	PUB-T	334	159.5	2,219.7	3.9	31.8	31.4	107.7	303.6
SOUTHEAST CC LINCOLN CAM	PUB-T	1,017	96.0	1,284.7	1.8	14.2	11.5	254.2	1,017.0
SOUTHEAST CC MILFORD CAM	PUB-T	907	98.6	1,242.8	3.0	6.1	5.4	226.7	907.0
UNION COLLEGE	PRI-FN	824	176.0	A	4.5	140.3	127.7	206.0	274.6
U NEBR CEN ADMIN ALL INST									
U OF NEBRASKA-LINCOLN	PUB-U	19,655	201.5	3,244.1	3.4	73.4	32.7	126.2	377.5
U NEBRASKA MEDICAL CTR	PUB-FG	1,599	640.3	5,784.4	2.9	108.6	31.3	42.8	163.1
U OF NEBRASKA AT OMAHA	PUB-FG	9,379	159.1	3,817.0	5.1	38.7	38.2	155.0	586.1
WAYNE STATE COLLEGE	PUB-FG	2,037	176.6	3,964.8	6.3	71.6	50.4	130.4	347.8
YORK COLLEGE	PRI-T	290	230.5	4,457.8	5.4	87.9	85.8	67.4	290.0
NEVADA									
SIERRA NEVADA COLLEGE	PRI-FN	172	176.8	30,418.0	9.4	65.7	A	344.0	344.0
U OF NEVADA SYS ALL INST									
U OF NEVADA LAS VEGAS	PUB-FG	5,456	252.9	4,383.5	5.4	65.7	A	133.0	363.7
U OF NEVADA RENO	PUB-U	5,489	434.0	7,133.2	5.5	113.3	75.5	77.0	248.3
CLARK CO CMTY COLLEGE	PUB-T	3,358	85.7	3,787.4	4.6	6.8	5.8	239.8	559.6
NORTHERN NEV CMTY COLLEGE	PUB-T	482	197.8	8,670.5	9.8	49.4	47.7	160.6	482.0
WESTERN NEV CMTY COLLEGE	PUB-T	3,241	87.0	5,320.5	6.0	8.4	8.0	300.0	558.7
NEW HAMPSHIRE									
CASTLE JUNIOR COLLEGE	PRI-T	100	143.7	D	9.0	44.4	44.2	100.0	100.0
COLBY-SAWYER COLLEGE	PRI-FN	D	D	D	D	D	D	D	D
DANIEL WEBSTER COLLEGE	PRI-FN	434	83.8	2,800.9	3.3	40.4	39.6	173.6	620.0
DARTMOUTH COLLEGE	PRI-FG	4,137	749.7	9,149.8	4.6	325.6	262.6	31.2	129.2
FRANKLIN PIERCE COLLEGE	PRI-FN	1,016	91.8	1,830.7	2.2	A	45.2	307.8	1,016.0
FRANKLIN PIERCE LAW CTR	PRI-FG	251	748.1	13,413.5	A	230.5	26.7	43.2	96.5
MCINTOSH COLLEGE	PRI-T	89	.0	.0	.0	56.4	55.3	148.3	148.3
NATHANIEL HAWTHORNE C	PRI-FN	D	D	D	D	D	D	D	D
NEW ENGLAND COLLEGE	PRI-FN	1,514	149.2	3,052.9	3.4	53.9	48.0	116.4	302.8
NEW HAMPSHIRE COLLEGE	PRI-FG	3,404	79.0	5,848.2	3.7	15.8	11.0	340.4	680.8
NH TECHNICAL INSTITUTE	PUB-T	1,088	50.0	989.5	A	18.6	14.4	362.6	544.0
NH VOC-TECH C BERLIN	PUB-T	349	72.6	792.0	3.3	17.5	12.8	349.0	349.0
NH VOC-TECH C CLAREMONT	PUB-T	321	69.0	692.2	1.8	22.2	20.8	321.0	321.0
NH VOC-TECH C LACONIA	PUB-T	219	120.7	1,201.6	3.5	30.3	30.1	219.0	219.0
NH VOC-TECH C MANCHESTER	PUB-T	304	74.1	901.4	2.2	24.3	19.8	304.0	304.0

SEE FOOTNOTES AT END OF TABLE

Table 3. – Indexes Concerning Operating Expenditures, 1978-79, Bookstock Held at End of Year, 1978-79, and Library Staff (FTE), Fall 1979, College and University Libraries, by State or Other Area and Institution: Aggregate United States – Continued

STATE OR OTHER AREA AND INSTITUTION	CONTROL AND TYPE OF INSTITUTION	TOTAL FTE OPENING FALL ENROLLMENT, FALL 1978	LIBRARY OPERATING EXPENDITURES (IN DOLLARS) 1978-79			BOOKSTOCK HELD AT END OF YEAR 1978-79		FTE STUDENTS PER FTE LIBRARY STAFF FALL 1979	
			PER FTE STUDENT, FALL 1978	PER FULL-TIME FACULTY MEMBER, 1978	AS PERCENT OF GENERAL EXPENDITURES, 1978-79	VOLUMES PER FTE STUDENT, FALL 1978	TITLES (INCLUDING MICROFORMS) PER FTE STUDENT 1978	TOTAL STAFF	PROFESSIONAL STAFF
(1)	(2)	(3)	(4)	(5)	(6)	(7)	(8)	(9)	(10)
NEW HAMPSHIRE	--CONTINUED								
NH VOC-TECH C NASHUA	PUB-T	530	50.5	1,072.4	2.9	11.2	10.3	530.0	530.0
NH VOC-TECH C PORTSMOUTH	PUB-T	563	42.7	1,504.8	2.4	13.9	11.6	563.0	563.0
NOTRE DAME COLLEGE	PRI-FG	530	128.2	4,856.3	6.2	76.6	75.6	112.7	176.6
RIVIER COLLEGE	PRI-FG	1,112	89.0	2,476.9	5.1	81.4	72.3	176.5	258.6
SAINT ANSELM'S COLLEGE	PRI-FN	1,705	205.7	3,617.0	4.9	76.3	67.4	100.2	310.0
U SYS OF NH ALL INST									
U OF NEW HAMPSHIRE	PUB-U	10,470	197.7	4,182.3	3.3	74.5	53.9	120.3	418.8
U OF NH KEENE ST COLLEGE	PUB-FG	2,782	103.2	2,177.0	3.2	53.7	54.4	241.9	556.4
U NH PLYMOUTH ST COLLEGE	PUB-FG	2,808	172.8	3,594.6	5.7	61.0	38.1	127.6	255.2
WHITE PINES COLLEGE	PRI-T	69	231.8	16,000.0	8.8	256.5	176.1	46.0	69.0
NEW JERSEY									
ASSUMPTION C FOR SISTERS	PRI-T	29	1,106.1	D	24.2	684.4	683.2	9.6	9.6
ATLANTIC CMTY COLLEGE	PUB-T	2,382	80.7	1,658.9	2.9	32.9	28.2	253.4	595.5
BERGEN COMMUNITY COLLEGE	PUB-T	5,851	179.4	5,330.2	7.6	14.4	9.3	132.9	307.9
THE BERKELEY SCHOOL	PRI-T	438	131.4	3,598.1	4.3	65.0	64.4	292.0	292.0
BETH MEDRASH GOVOHA	PRI-FG	D	D	D	D	D	D	D	D
BLOOMFIELD COLLEGE	PRI-FN	1,880	93.3	3,310.5	3.4	61.1	38.7	177.3	437.2
BROOKDALE CMTY COLLEGE	PUB-T	5,034	244.0	8,413.5	8.7	12.8	7.9	75.0	405.9
BURLINGTON COUNTY COLLEGE	PUB-T	2,328	94.2	2,522.8	2.1	24.2	20.8	122.5	582.0
CALDWELL COLLEGE	PRI-FN	474	201.3	3,976.6	4.3	203.9	158.5	100.8	128.1
CAMDEN COUNTY COLLEGE	PUB-T	4,595	79.2	3,606.7	4.8	15.2	14.2	306.3	765.8
CENTENARY COLLEGE	PRI-FN	726	102.5	1,816.3	2.6	59.8	47.6	181.5	363.0
C MED & DENT OF NJ NEWARK	PUB-FG	1,575	527.7	14,332.0	1.3	63.4	28.5	54.3	105.0
COLLEGE OF SNT ELIZABETH	PRI-FN	539	297.7	10,031.6	5.8	270.5	173.0	62.6	96.2
COUNTY COLLEGE OF MORRIS	PUB-T	6,061	94.0	2,985.7	5.1	13.5	12.6	181.4	531.6
CUMBERLAND COUNTY COLLEGE	PUB-T	1,254	104.0	2,212.4	4.0	38.0	30.6	209.0	313.5
DON BOSCO COLLEGE	PRI-FN	83	263.6	A	A	612.8	586.8	39.5	48.8
DREW UNIVERSITY	PRI-FG	1,862	382.0	6,586.3	6.7	209.3	161.1	62.4	125.8
ESSEX COUNTY COLLEGE	PUB-T	4,986	112.8	2,603.8	3.2	14.4	13.3	231.9	498.6
FAIRLEIGH DCKSN U ALL CAM									
FARLGH DCKSN U EDW WMS C	PRI-T	502	38.9	1,397.0	1.7	19.9	14.4	502.0	A
FARLGH DCKSN MADISON CAM	PRI-FG	3,687	117.7	3,678.6	3.7	39.6	A	218.1	526.7
FARLGH DCKSN U RUTHERFD	PRI-FG	3,341	168.0	4,491.5	4.5	48.2	40.3	109.9	300.9
FARLGH DCKSN TEANECK CAM	PRI-FG	5,816	141.4	3,057.5	2.8	40.1	23.1	130.6	387.7
FELICIAN COLLEGE	PRI-FN	534	223.3	2,293.2	6.9	125.3	108.5	111.2	133.5
GEORGIAN COURT COLLEGE	PRI-FG	741	191.1	4,569.9	5.8	94.7	71.5	83.2	145.2
GLASSBORO STATE COLLEGE	PUB-FG	8,084	92.8	2,078.6	2.9	32.1	37.5	206.2	538.9
GLOUCESTER COUNTY COLLEGE	PUB-T	1,634	133.2	3,024.3	4.8	29.9	28.2	158.6	340.4
HUDSON CO CC COMMISSION5/	PUB-T	NO LIBRARY FACILITIES							
IMMACULATE CONCEPTION SEM	PRI-FG	162	569.1	.0	8.4	427.6	425.9	81.0	162.0
JERSEY CITY STATE COLLEGE	PUB-FG	7,173	92.1	2,146.5	3.3	31.3	49.4	251.6	512.3
KATHARINE GIBBS SCHOOL	PRI-T	454	8.5	A	A	7.0	4.3	.0	A
KEAN C OF NEW JERSEY	PUB-FG	8,762	98.0	2,359.3	3.8	32.8	25.2	223.5	580.2
MERCER CO CMTY COLLEGE	PUB-T	4,263	82.7	2,593.7	3.0	14.5	14.1	275.0	710.5
MIDDLESEX COUNTY COLLEGE	PUB-T	6,551	58.3	1,677.5	2.5	10.8	10.1	292.4	1,091.8
MONMOUTH COLLEGE	PRI-FG	2,809	164.8	3,237.2	4.0	74.3	56.1	130.6	468.1
MONTCLAIR STATE COLLEGE	PUB-FG	11,087	109.3	2,459.1	4.4	28.0	19.6	188.8	482.0
NEW BRUNSWICK THEOL SEM	PRI-FG	79	722.9	9,518.3	10.9	1,690.8	927.7	21.9	39.5
NJ INSTITUTE TECHNOLOGY	PUB-FG	4,019	134.6	2,026.4	2.7	31.2	22.5	240.6	502.3
NTHESTN BIBLE COLLEGE	PRI-FN	D	D	D	D	D	D	D	D
OCEAN COUNTY COLLEGE	PUB-T	3,335	118.5	4,163.1	4.8	19.9	19.0	202.1	513.0
PASSAIC CO CMTY COLLEGE	PUB-T	1,536	142.0	5,073.4	3.6	15.9	12.3	128.0	384.0
PRINCETON THEOLOGICAL SEM	PRI-FG	716	498.6	11,157.1	6.7	479.9	410.8	55.5	119.3
PRINCETON UNIVERSITY	PRI-U	5,934	1,224.1	11,659.5	8.2	534.5	A	18.2	64.5
RAB COLLEGE OF AMERICA	PRI-FN	225	86.5	1,622.5	1.3	26.6	5.1	112.5	112.5
RAMAPO C OF NEW JERSEY	PUB-FN	3,074	200.1	4,047.0	5.8	44.7	26.2	92.8	276.9
RIDER COLLEGE	PRI-FG	4,162	142.4	3,071.7	4.0	75.0	74.6	173.4	346.8
RUTGERS THE ST U ALL CAM									
RUTGERS U CAMDEN CAMPUS	PUB-FG	4,098	266.9	5,065.4	4.7	67.6	A	117.4	394.0
RUTGERS U NEWARK CAMPUS	PUB-FG	7,197	194.6	3,433.9	3.2	60.1	A	142.2	529.1
RUTGERS U NEW BRUNSWICK	PUB-U	27,082	246.7	4,643.7	4.7	53.7	A	124.2	390.2
SNT MICHAELS PASIONST MON	PRI-FG	22	705.8	D	A	863.6	681.8	16.9	16.9
SAINT PETERS COLLEGE	PRI-FG	3,118	160.0	4,025.7	4.3	76.1	51.9	141.7	346.4
SALEM COMMUNITY COLLEGE	PUB-T	1,068	72.1	2,485.1	3.8	17.2	16.5	232.1	534.0
SETON HALL UNIVERSITY2/	PRI-U	7,528	135.3	3,223.8	3.3	42.4	27.3	172.6	501.8
SOMERSET COUNTY COLLEGE	PUB-T	2,341	130.0	3,953.1	5.5	27.1	28.8	151.0	390.1

SEE FOOTNOTES AT END OF TABLE

Table 3. — Indexes Concerning Operating Expenditures, 1978-79, Bookstock Held at End of Year, 1978-79, and Library Staff (FTE), Fall 1979, College and University Libraries, by State or Other Area and Institution: Aggregate United States — Continued

STATE OR OTHER AREA AND INSTITUTION	CONTROL AND TYPE OF INSTITUTION	TOTAL FTE OPENING FALL ENROLLMENT, FALL 1978	LIBRARY OPERATING EXPENDITURES (IN DOLLARS) 1978-79			BOOKSTOCK HELD AT END OF YEAR 1978-79		FTE STUDENTS PER FTE LIBRARY STAFF FALL 1979	
			PER FTE STUDENT, FALL 1978	PER FULL-TIME FACULTY MEMBER, 1978	AS PERCENT OF GENERAL EXPENDITURES, 1978-79	VOLUMES PER FTE STUDENT, FALL 1978	TITLES (INCLUDING MICROFORMS) PER FTE STUDENT 1978	TOTAL STAFF	PROFESSIONAL STAFF
(1)	(2)	(3)	(4)	(5)	(6)	(7)	(8)	(9)	(10)
NEW JERSEY	--CONTINUED								
STEVENS INST TECHNOLOGY	PRI-FG	2,023	150.0	2,639.9	1.7	47.3	26.0	187.3	674.3
STOCKTON STATE COLLEGE	PUB-FN	4,235	247.0	6,419.6	9.9	24.8	25.4	89.1	338.8
TALMUD INST OF CEN JERSEY	PRI-FG	D	D	D	D	D	D	D	D
THOMAS A EDISON COLLEGE	PUB-FN		NO LIBRARY FACILITIES						
TRENTON STATE COLLEGE	PUB-FG	7,420	162.5	3,157.6	5.0	51.3	38.5	155.8	350.0
UNION COLLEGE	PRI-T	3,301	97.7	3,194.9	3.8	24.8	22.4	257.8	589.4
UNION CO TECHNICAL INST	PUB-T	1,598	63.9	1,548.2	2.8	11.7	10.6	532.6	799.0
UPSALA COLLEGE	PRI-FG	1,288	167.3	3,654.4	4.0	114.2	72.9	121.5	181.4
WESTMINSTER CHOIR COLLEGE	PRI-FG	437	315.9	3,633.0	4.7	72.0	65.9	49.6	121.3
WILLIAM PATERSON COLLEGE	PUB-FG	8,649	134.6	2,926.2	4.7	31.3	24.3	157.5	341.8
NEW MEXICO									
COLLEGE OF SANTA FE	PRI-FN	882	69.1	1,108.4	1.4	96.3	57.8	220.5	882.0
COLLEGE OF THE SOUTHWEST	PRI-FN	92	1,064.3	12,240.0	16.7	378.4	303.4	18.4	46.0
EASTERN NM U ALL CAMPUSES									
EASTERN NM U MAIN CAMPUS	PUB-FG	3,256	234.3	5,156.0	5.1	68.1	68.0	142.1	365.8
EASTERN NM U ROSWELL CAM	PUB-T	810	72.3	A	2.3	28.2	27.0	270.0	405.0
INST AMERICAN INDIAN ARTS	PUB-T	D	D	D	D	D	D	D	D
NEW MEXICO HIGHLANDS U	PUB-FG	1,759	268.1	3,931.0	5.5	94.7	86.8	114.2	251.2
NM INST OF MINING & TECHN	PUB-FG	944	223.1	2,735.2	2.3	54.7	A	134.8	472.0
NEW MEXICO JUNIOR COLLEGE	PUB-T	860	245.8	4,806.0	6.9	93.4	75.0	90.5	286.6
NEW MEXICO MILITARY INST	PUB-T	562	203.3	2,040.5	3.5	109.1	71.0	82.6	281.0
NM STATE U ALL CAMPUSES									
NM STATE U MAIN CAMPUS	PUB-U	10,419	175.3	4,023.7	2.6	58.7	54.8	138.1	359.2
NM STATE U ALAMOGORDO	PUB-T	663	131.2	4,835.9	9.6	41.4	41.0	118.3	315.7
NM STATE U CARLSBAD	PUB-T	314	115.9	3,640.1	6.0	55.2	46.5	157.0	314.0
NM STATE U GRANTS BRANCH	PUB-T	179	209.6	4,690.6	5.9	107.8	99.7	59.6	179.0
NM STATE U SAN JUAN	PUB-T	680	136.0	2,642.3	4.6	34.5	27.6	119.2	971.4
NTHN NM COMMUNITY COLLEGE	PUB-T	D	D	D	D	D	D	D	D
UNIVERSITY OF ALBUQUERQUE	PRI-FN	2,109	75.9	2,003.5	3.0	25.6	31.0	140.6	351.5
U OF NM ALL CAMPUSES									
U OF NM MAIN CAMPUS	PUB-U	16,808	274.4	6,102.4	5.5	68.0	40.0	82.1	263.4
U OF NM GALLUP BRANCH	PUB-T	381	133.8	3,641.7	5.1	38.7	34.6	127.0	381.0
WESTERN NM UNIVERSITY	PUB-FG	1,125	176.3	3,252.1	4.9	104.6	310.9	104.1	375.0
NEW YORK									
ACADEMY OF AERONAUTICS	PRI-T	1,437	63.9	1,612.2	3.4	17.1	16.7	359.2	479.0
ADELPHI UNIVERSITY	PRI-U	7,346	239.5	4,570.0	4.7	47.7	29.4	97.6	311.2
ALBANY BUSINESS COLLEGE	PRI-T	624	16.8	A	.9	6.5	6.4	1,248.0	1,248.0
ALBANY COLLEGE PHARMACY	PRI-FN	610	38.9	990.5	1.6	10.8	A	610.0	610.0
ALBANY LAW SCHOOL	PRI-FG	704	631.1	20,195.5	19.7	118.4	22.1	38.4	117.3
ALBANY MEDICAL COLLEGE	PRI-FG	566	821.7	D	1.6	146.5	109.1	22.0	70.7
ALFRED U ALL CAMPUSES									
ALFRED UNIVERSITY	PRI-FG	1,896	179.7	3,476.7	3.3	85.8	73.1	99.7	379.2
NY ST C CERAMICS ALFRED U	PUB-FG	659	475.0	8,696.0	6.5	87.8	51.4	54.0	126.7
AMER ACAD DRAMATIC ARTS	PRI-T	D	D	D	D	D	D	D	D
ASSOCD BETH RIVKAH SCHS	PRI-FN	D	D	D	D	D	D	D	D
BAIS YAAKOV SEMINARY	PRI-FN	D	D	D	D	D	D	D	D
BANK STREET COLLEGE OF ED	PRI-FG	477	436.4	8,006.5	3.0	194.0	451.1	58.1	170.3
BARD COLLEGE	PRI-FN	673	247.5	A	3.4	216.9	141.3	96.1	224.3
BE'ER SHMUEL TALMUD ACAD	PRI-FG	D	D	D	D	D	D	D	D
BELZER YESH-MACHZIKEI SEM	PRI-FG	D	D	D	D	D	D	D	D
BERK-CLAREMONT HICKSVL	PRI-T	279	7.6	265.6	.2	.8	.8	.0	A
BERK-CLAREMONT NY CITY	PRI-T	581	43.9	1,823.5	1.6	.6	.5	290.5	581.0
THE BERKELEY SCHOOL	PRI-T	D	D	D	D	D	D	D	D
BETH HMDRSH SHAAREI YOSH	PRI-FG	D	D	D	D	D	D	D	D
BETH HATALMUD RAB C	PRI-FG	D	D	D	D	D	D	D	D
BETH JACOB HEBREW TCHRS C	PRI-FN	D	D	D	D	D	D	D	D
BETH JOSEPH RAB SEMINARY	PRI-FG	D	D	D	D	D	D	D	D
BETH MEDRASH EMEK HALACHA	PRI-FG	D	D	D	D	D	D	D	D
BETH MDRASH EYUN HATALMUD	PRI-FN	D	D	D	D	D	D	D	D
BORICUA COLLEGE	PRI-FN	D	D	D	D	D	D	D	D
BRAMSON ORT TRAINING CTR	PRI-T	D	D	D	D	D	D	D	D
BROOKLYN LAW SCHOOL	PRI-FG	1,020	365.9	13,331.5	A	143.1	31.6	51.7	150.0
BRYANT-STRATTON BUS INST	PRI-T	519	10.5	546.4	.5	1.5	1.3	.0	A
BRYANT-STRATTON BUS INST	PRI-T	2,518	2.1	124.1	.1	.3	.2	.0	A
CANISIUS COLLEGE	PRI-FG	3,149	105.8	2,206.7	2.7	66.1	50.8	204.4	492.0

SEE FOOTNOTES AT END OF TABLE

161

Table 3. — Indexes Concerning Operating Expenditures, 1978-79, Bookstock Held at End of Year, 1978-79, and Library Staff (FTE), Fall 1979, College and University Libraries, by State or Other Area and Institution: Aggregate United States — Continued

STATE OR OTHER AREA AND INSTITUTION	CON-TROL AND TYPE OF IN-STITU-TION	TOTAL FTE OPENING FALL ENROLL-MENT, FALL 1978	LIBRARY OPERATING EXPENDITURES (IN DOLLARS) 1978-79			BOOKSTOCK HELD AT END OF YEAR 1978-79		FTE STUDENTS PER FTE LIBRARY STAFF FALL 1979	
			PER FTE STU-DENT, FALL 1978	PER FULL-TIME FAC-ULTY MEM-BER, 1978	AS PER-CENT OF GENERAL EXPENDI-TURES, 1978-79	VOLUMES PER FTE STUDENT, FALL 1978	TITLES (INCLU-DING MICRO-FORMS) PER FTE STUDENT 1978	TOTAL STAFF	PROFES-SIONAL STAFF
(1)	(2)	(3)	(4)	(5)	(6)	(7)	(8)	(9)	(10)
NEW YORK	--CONTINUED								
CTHDL C IMMAC CONCEPTION	PRI-FN	167	593.6	33,047.3	5.7	459.7	423.4	37.1	83.5
CAZENOVIA COLLEGE	PRI-T	477	113.6	3,189.2	2.7	73.7	62.9	119.2	238.5
CEN CITY BUSINESS INST	PRI-T		NO LIBRARY FACILITIES						
CEN YESH TOM TMIHIM LUBVZ	PRI-FG	D	D	D	D	D	D	37.4	37.4
CHRIST THE KING SEMINARY	PRI-FG	131	629.7	D	11.1	538.4	A	37.4	37.4
CITY U OF NY SYS ALL INST									
CUNY BERNARD BARUCH C	PUB-FG	10,234	88.1	2,212.3	2.5	24.6	16.1	241.9	591.5
CUNY BORO OF MANHATTAN CC	PUB-T	7,009	49.2	1,189.3	1.5	7.2	5.3	393.7	637.1
CUNY BRONX CMTY COLLEGE	PUB-T	6,002	89.5	1,784.9	2.2	12.8	A	240.0	645.3
CUNY BROOKLYN COLLEGE	PUB-FG	14,866	134.0	2,194.2	2.8	39.0	28.4	177.3	507.3
CUNY CITY COLLEGE	PUB-FG	11,345	174.0	2,557.9	3.3	82.6	48.3	164.1	365.9
CUNY C OF STATEN ISLAND	PUB-FG	7,611	101.9	2,143.0	2.4	22.0	47.4	241.6	555.5
CUNY GRAD SCH & U CENTER	PUB-FG	2,541	265.5	12,270.1	3.4	55.7	44.8	123.9	231.0
CUNY HOSTOS CMTY COLLEGE	PUB-T	2,549	101.1	2,833.9	2.7	10.5	8.1	293.2	509.8
CUNY HUNTER COLLEGE	PUB-FG	12,646	127.8	2,387.7	3.3	34.6	19.4	235.9	451.6
CUNY JOHN JAY C CRIM JUST	PUB-FG	5,217	94.5	2,211.0	2.4	22.8	17.4	240.4	511.4
CUNY KINGSBOROUGH CC	PUB-T	6,794	47.1	1,271.9	1.4	13.5	9.8	629.0	1,358.8
CUNY LA GUARDIA CC	PUB-T	5,671	76.1	2,821.5	2.3	8.0	7.6	276.6	472.5
CUNY LEHMAN COLLEGE	PUB-FG	7,347	125.4	2,038.6	2.9	49.5	38.2	202.3	459.1
CUNY MEDGAR EVERS COLLEGE	PUB-FN	2,310	149.4	3,167.8	3.5	32.9	37.4	132.7	316.4
CUNY NEW YORK CITY CC	PUB-T	9,404	51.1	A	1.4	12.6	8.6	427.4	783.6
CUNY QUEENSBOROUGH CC	PUB-T	8,643	79.6	1,874.6	2.6	13.7	11.2	347.1	785.7
CUNY QUEENS COLLEGE	PUB-FG	14,642	147.2	2,625.8	3.7	34.9	33.1	177.2	472.3
CUNY YORK COLLEGE	PUB-FN	3,105	102.2	1,888.9	2.2	38.4	38.8	215.6	463.4
CLARKSON COLLEGE OF TECHN	PRI-FG	3,354	140.5	2,740.0	2.6	26.1	43.0	195.0	455.8
COLG ROCH-BEXLEY-CROZER	PRI-FG	156	827.4	8,067.4	A	1,261.2	882.4	22.2	44.5
COLGATE UNIVERSITY	PRI-FG	2,362	298.0	4,292.9	4.3	137.7	171.4	100.0	262.4
COLLEGE FOR HUMAN SERVICE	PRI-FN	130	262.7	D	A	150.3	A	55.0	130.0
COLLEGE OF INSURANCE	PRI-FG	747	231.4	5,960.7	5.6	102.1	101.9	124.5	149.4
COLLEGE OF MT SNT VINCENT	PRI-FN	1,029	238.7	3,412.5	5.4	110.7	109.0	62.7	171.5
COLLEGE OF NEW ROCHELLE	PRI-FG	3,312	83.9	3,657.4	2.7	41.4	30.8	260.7	525.7
COLLEGE OF SAINT ROSE	PRI-FG	1,589	141.4	3,944.0	4.0	78.9	88.4	162.1	338.0
COLUMBIA U ALL CAMPUSES									
COLUMBIA U MAIN DIVISION	PRI-U	14,705	663.7	10,808.9	3.6	332.7	137.1	36.2	114.8
BARNARD COLLEGE	PRI-FN	2,250	343.9	5,774.8	5.9	65.2	A	132.3	281.2
COLUMBIA U TCHRS COLLEGE	PRI-FG	2,986	363.3	7,330.4	4.9	131.9	62.0	43.6	122.3
CONCORDIA COLLEGE	PRI-FN	433	210.0	2,674.5	4.3	94.3	129.1	108.2	144.3
COOPER UNION	PRI-FG	883	271.3	4,991.6	4.1	82.8	56.9	105.1	220.7
CORNELL U ALL CAMPUSES									
CORNEL U ENDOWED COLLEGES	PRI-U	10,060	722.0	8,575.3	5.1	352.3	A	33.4	109.3
CORNELL U MEDICAL CENTER	PRI-FG	616	1,280.5	D	2.2	165.4	63.0	22.8	64.8
CORNELL U STATUTORY C	PUB-FG	6,793	258.4	4,324.8	1.6	107.5	A	91.7	271.7
CULINARY INST OF AMERICA	PRI-T	1,417	58.0	1,083.0	.7	11.2	8.4	354.2	708.5
DAEMEN COLLEGE	PRI-FN	1,195	115.5	1,973.4	2.9	83.3	58.2	157.2	298.7
DERECH AYSON RAB SEMINARY	PRI-FG	D	D	D	D	D	D	D	D
DOMINICAN C OF BLAUVELT	PRI-FN	747	170.2	3,633.1	6.9	102.0	95.0	162.3	373.5
DOWLING COLLEGE	PRI-FG	1,836	158.8	A	3.5	47.9	125.1	137.0	340.0
D'YOUVILLE COLLEGE	PRI-FN	1,329	181.7	3,058.2	5.7	68.2	42.2	105.4	255.8
EISENHOWER COLLEGE	PRI-FN	480	331.2	3,613.5	3.7	165.6	116.0	68.5	240.0
ELIZABETH SETON COLLEGE	PRI-T	1,169	60.3	2,823.6	2.5	34.7	26.6	224.8	584.5
ELMIRA COLLEGE	PRI-FG	1,478	224.8	5,275.3	5.5	90.8	100.9	95.3	246.3
FIVE TOWNS COLLEGE	PRI-T	280	84.3	1,312.3	4.0	29.6	29.3	140.0	140.0
FORDHAM UNIVERSITY	PRI-U	10,655	200.4	4,583.8	5.3	117.2	85.0	129.9	394.6
FRIENDS WORLD COLLEGE	PRI-FN	D	D	D	D	D	D	D	D
GENERAL THEOLOGICAL SEM	PRI-FG	113	1,344.6	9,496.5	8.8	1,701.3	1,305.4	16.1	22.6
GRUSS GIRLS SEMINARY	PRI-FN	D	D	D	D	D	D	D	D
HADAR HATORAH RAB SEM	PRI-FN	D	D	D	D	D	D	D	D
HAMILTON COLLEGE	PRI-FN	1,577	390.2	4,697.3	5.3	221.5	129.4	57.7	242.6
HARRIMAN COLLEGE	PRI-T	354	110.7	6,536.6	3.1	92.9	89.2	177.0	354.0
HARTWICK COLLEGE	PRI-FN	1,400	218.5	2,593.1	3.6	111.7	82.9	135.9	325.5
HILBERT COLLEGE	PRI-T	446	190.3	4,716.2	6.7	96.5	96.7	111.5	143.6
HOBART-WM SMITH COLLEGES	PRI-FN	D	D	D	D	D	D	D	D
HOFSTRA UNIVERSITY	PRI-FG	7,980	232.9	5,566.5	5.1	99.6	51.0	92.4	296.6
HOLY TRINITY ORTHODOX SEM	PRI-FN	D	D	D	D	D	D	D	D
HOUGHTON COLLEGE	PRI-FN	1,164	170.4	A	4.9	141.4	A	127.9	323.3
INST OF DESIGN AND CONSTR	PRI-T		NO LIBRARY FACILITIES						

SEE FOOTNOTES AT END OF TABLE

Table 3. — Indexes Concerning Operating Expenditures, 1978-79, Bookstock Held at End of Year, 1978-79, and Library Staff (FTE), Fall 1979, College and University Libraries, by State or Other Area and Institution: Aggregate United States — Continued

STATE OR OTHER AREA AND INSTITUTION	CONTROL AND TYPE OF INSTITUTION	TOTAL FTE OPENING FALL ENROLLMENT, FALL 1978	LIBRARY OPERATING EXPENDITURES (IN DOLLARS) 1978-79			BOOKSTOCK HELD AT END OF YEAR 1978-79		FTE STUDENTS PER FTE LIBRARY STAFF FALL 1979	
			PER FTE STUDENT, FALL 1978	PER FULL-TIME FACULTY MEMBER, 1978	AS PER-CENT OF GENERAL EXPENDI-TURES, 1978-79	VOLUMES PER FTE STUDENT, FALL 1978	TITLES (INCLUDING MICRO-FORMS) PER FTE STUDENT 1978	TOTAL STAFF	PROFES-SIONAL STAFF
(1)	(2)	(3)	(4)	(5)	(6)	(7)	(8)	(9)	(10)
NEW YORK	--CONTINUED								
INTERBORO INSTITUTE	PRI-T	390	31.0	A	1.5	9.0	7.7	390.0	390.0
IONA COLLEGE	PRI-FG	4,204	105.1	3,134.0	3.5	40.6	A	289.9	467.1
ITHACA COLLEGE	PRI-FG	4,739	143.6	2,617.4	3.4	54.8	37.7	147.1	391.6
JAMESTWN BUSINESS COLLEGE	PRI-T	D	D	D	D	D	D	D	D
JEWISH THEOL SEM AMERICA	PRI-FG	D	D	D	D	D	D	D	D
THE JUILLIARD SCHOOL	PRI-FG	982	90.7	1,714.5	1.2	14.9	A	163.6	196.4
KATHARINE GIBBS SCHOOL	PRI-T	736	9.0	316.0	A	2.0	1.9	2,453.3	2,453.3
KEHILATH YAKOV RAB SEM	PRI-FG	D	D	D	D	D	D	D	D
KEUKA COLLEGE	PRI-FN	526	304.6	3,270.1	5.3	175.6	138.0	65.7	175.3
KING'S COLLEGE	PRI-FN	838	162.0	3,017:8	3.6	87.7	86.3	149.6	209.5
LAB INST OF MERCHANDISING	PRI-T	246	59.6	0	2.0	12.1	10.1	246.0	246.0
LADYCLIFF COLLEGE	PRI-FN	423	256.3	5,162.8	A	181.9	147.3	65.0	169.2
LE MOYNE COLLEGE	PRI-FN	1,879	127.8	2,402.9	3.7	76.7	48.6	170.8	469.7
LONG IS C HOSP SCH NURS	PRI-T	94	1,714.5	16,116.8	32.3	160.3	57.1	18.8	31.3
LONG IS SEM JEWISH STDIES	PRI-FN	D	D	D	D	D	D	D	D
LONG IS U ALL CAMPUSES									
LONG IS U BROOKLYN CENTER	PRI-FG	4,542	122.1	2,746.0	2.3	48.2	54.1	176.0	302.8
LONG IS U C W POST CENTER	PRI-U	7,917	217.2	4,885.4	4.8	48.9	37.4	107.5	222.3
LONG IS U SOUTHAMPTON CTR	PRI-FG	1,337	161.2	5,014.3	3.0	77.7	65.1	139.2	334.2
MACHZIKEI HADATH RAB C	PRI-FG	D	D	D	D	D	D	D	D
MANHATTAN COLLEGE	PRI-FG	3,990	150.0	3,696.1	A	55.5	35.5	129.9	411.3
MANHATTAN SCHOOL OF MUSIC	PRI-FG	620	165.0	4,652.2	2.9	145.2	87.4	100.0	119.2
MANHATTANVILLE COLLEGE	PRI-FG	1,052	337.6	5,302.1	5.8	278.3	173.9	80.9	175.3
MANNES COLLEGE OF MUSIC	PRI-FN	296	148.7	3,387.3	3.2	75.3	A	98.6	148.0
MARIA COLLEGE OF ALBANY	PRI-T	456	82.2	1,072.1	3.6	93.6	94.8	134.1	325.7
MARIA REGINA COLLEGE	PRI-T	282	133.3	7,523.4	5.1	134.7	132.9	74.2	117.5
MARIST COLLEGE	PRI-FG	1,881	101.6	2,516.3	2.6	42.8	28.7	182.6	470.2
MARYKNOLL SCH OF THEOLOGY	PRI-FG	84	1,119.8	15,078.1	10.8	983.9	934.8	16.8	28.0
MARYMOUNT COLLEGE	PRI-FN	1,048	136.0	2,458.7	3.1	102.6	97.6	108.0	349.3
MARYMOUNT MANHATTAN C	PRI-FN	1,355	134.8	3,971.4	3.5	43.4	38.9	229.6	288.2
MATER DEI COLLEGE	PRI-T	195	296.7	4,450.8	6.6	240.4	156.4	65.0	97.5
MEDAILLE COLLEGE	PRI-FN	604	98.4	2,585.3	3.5	147.6	152.1	158.9	604.0
MERCY COLLEGE	PRI-FN	5,886	124.5	A	A	40.9	35.0	231.7	382.2
MESIVTA ESTN PKWY RAB SEM	PRI-FG	D	D	D	D	D	D	D	D
MES TORAH VODAATH SEM	PRI-FG	D	D	D	D	D	D	D	D
MESIVTHA TIFERETH JER AMR	PRI-FG	D	D	D	D	D	D	D	D
MIRRER YESHIVA CEN INST	PRI-FG	D	D	D	D	D	D	D	D
MOLLOY COLLEGE	PRI-FN	1,207	126.8	1,867.7	3.2	65.1	58.8	154.7	201.1
MONROE BUSINESS INSTITUTE	PRI-T	717	26.8	837.8	A	3.5	3.0	717.0	717.0
MOUNT SAINT ALPHONSUS SEM	PRI-FG	76	822.7	.0	7.3	952.7	848.9	23.0	50.6
MOUNT SAINT MARY COLLEGE	PRI-FN	826	204.5	3,448.1	5.8	89.5	89.5	93.8	206.5
SINAI SCH OF MED CUNY	PRI-FG	459	1,741.7	.0	1.6	71.4	A	13.7	41.7
NAZARETH C OF ROCHESTER	PRI-FG	1,772	186.4	4,526.9	5.1	101.1	95.7	103.6	272.6
NEW SCH FOR SOC RESEARCH	PRI-FG	2,105	244.1	10,277.3	3.0	51.8	46.7	157.0	526.2
N Y CHIROPRACTIC COLLEGE	PRI-FG	649	36.3	D	.8	7.7	7.7	649.0	649.0
NY COLLEGE PODIATRIC MED	PRI-FG	439	118.1	D	1.8	13.3	7.0	146.3	219.5
NY INST TECHN ALL CAM									
NY INST TECHN MAIN CAMPUS	PRI-FG	6,017	106.6	5,052.3	3.1	14.1	9.3	225.3	449.0
NY INST TECHN NY CTY CAM	PRI-FG	2,031	75.7	4,804.6	2.4	18.7	14.9	350.1	725.3
NEW YORK LAW SCHOOL	PRI-FG	1,167	346.9	10,944.0	9.6	102.5	19.3	142.3	212.1
NEW YORK MEDICAL COLLEGE	PRI-FG	873	423.2	C	.8	114.5	63.5	124.7	291.0
NY SCH OF INTERIOR DESIGN	PRI-FN	248	56.4	0	1.3	7.9	6.7	248.0	248.0
NEW YORK THEOL SEMINARY	PRI-FG	80	445.6	0	7.1	211.1	202.8	40.0	40.0
NEW YORK UNIVERSITY	PRI-U	21,142	316.4	5,863.0	2.7	127.7	A	87.8	314.1
NIAGARA UNIVERSITY	PRI-FG	4,073	121.1	2,851.3	4.5	40.4	29.8	193.9	484.8
NYACK COLLEGE	PRI-FG	714	167.0	4,113.8	5.2	89.5	70.6	129.8	238.0
OHEL SHMUEL YESHIVA	PRI-FG	D	D	D	D	D	D	D	D
OHR HAMEIR THEOL SEM	PRI-FG	D	D	D	D	D	D	D	D
OHR YISROEL RAB COLLEGE	PRI-FN	D	D	D	D	D	D	D	D
OLEAN BUSINESS INSTITUTE	PRI-T	181	48.3	1,750.0	4.0	9.0	8.7	181.0	181.0
PACE UNIVERSITY ALL CAM									
PACE U C OF WHITE PLAINS	PRI-FG	1,261	429.8	15,057.9	12.2	120.8	56.2	69.6	109.6
PACE UNIVERSITY NEW YORK	PRI-FG	6,457	84.0	2,535.1	2.1	40.4	29.5	233.1	529.2
PACE U PLSNTVL-BRCLF CAM	PRI-FG	3,250	101.8	3,036.6	3.1	59.6	48.5	200.6	353.2
PARSONS SCHOOL OF DESIGN	PRI-FG	1,572	83.1	5,447.5	1.7	20.6	18.4	224.5	786.0
PAUL SMITH'S C ARTS & SCI	PRI-T	1,038	86.0	1,276.7	2.0	31.9	31.0	188.7	519.0

SEE FOOTNOTES AT END OF TABLE

Table 3. – Indexes Concerning Operating Expenditures, 1978-79, Bookstock Held at End of Year, 1978-79, and Library Staff (FTE), Fall 1979, College and University Libraries, by State or Other Area and Institution: Aggregate United States – Continued

STATE OR OTHER AREA AND INSTITUTION	CONTROL AND TYPE OF INSTITUTION	TOTAL FTE OPENING FALL ENROLLMENT, FALL 1978	LIBRARY OPERATING EXPENDITURES (IN DOLLARS) 1978-79			BOOKSTOCK HELD AT END OF YEAR 1978-79		FTE STUDENTS PER FTE LIBRARY STAFF FALL 1979	
			PER FTE STUDENT, FALL 1978	PER FULL-TIME FACULTY MEMBER, 1978	AS PERCENT OF GENERAL EXPENDITURES, 1978-79	VOLUMES PER FTE STUDENT, FALL 1978	TITLES (INCLUDING MICROFORMS) PER FTE STUDENT 1978	TOTAL STAFF	PROFESSIONAL STAFF
(1)	(2)	(3)	(4)	(5)	(6)	(7)	(8)	(9)	(10)
NEW YORK	--CONTINUED								
POLYTECHNIC INST NEW YORK	PRI-FG	5,142	107.9	2,488.1	A	50.1	20.1	262.3	612.1
POWELSON BUSINESS INST	PRI-T	418	20.8	869.6	1.1	2.8	2.7	2,090.0	2,090.0
PRATT INSTITUTE	PRI-U	3,691	138.3	3,927.7	3.0	60.0	A	160.4	369.1
RABBI ISAAC ELCHANAN SEM	PRI-FG	169	86.6	1,830.0	A	37.8	A	169.0	169.0
RAB AC MES RAB CHAIM BRLN	PRI-FG	D	D	D	D	D	D	D	D
RAB COLLEGE BETH SHRAGA	PRI-FG	D	D	D	D	D	D	D	D
RAB C BOBOVER B'NEI ZION	PRI-FG	D	D	D	D	D	D	D	D
RAB C CH'SAN SOFER NY	PRI-FG	D	D	D	D	D	D	D	D
RAB C OF KAMENITZ YESHIVA	PRI-FN	D	D	D	D	D	D	D	D
RAB COLLEGE LONG ISLAND	PRI-FG	D	D	D	D	D	D	D	D
RAB COLLEGE OF SANZ	PRI-FG	D	D	D	D	D	D	D	D
RABBINICAL C OF TASH	PRI-FG	D	D	D	D	D	D	D	D
RAB SEMINARY ADAS YEREIM	PRI-FN	D	D	D	D	D	D	D	D
RABBINICAL SEM OF AMERICA	PRI-FG	D	D	D	D	D	D	D	D
RAB SEM BETH YIT D'SPINKA	PRI-FG	D	D	D	D	D	D	D	D
RAB SEMINARY M'KOR CHAIM	PRI-FG	D	D	D	D	D	D	D	D
RABBINICAL SEM OF MUNKACS	PRI-FG	D	D	D	D	D	D	D	D
RAB SEM OF NEW SQUARE	PRI-FG	D	D	D	D	D	D	D	D
RENSSELAER POLY INSTITUTE	PRI-U	5,565	168.5	2,758.7	2.0	51.1	38.5	142.3	459.9
RIKA BREUER TEACHERS SEM	PRI-FN	D	D	D	D	D	D	D	D
ROBERTS WESLEYAN COLLEGE	PRI-FN	601	208.4	2,784.5	5.0	130.1	95.1	100.1	200.3
ROCHESTER BUS INSTITUTE	PRI-T	123	13.1	268.8	.6	18.5	13.6	615.0	A
ROCHESTER INST TECHNOLOGY	PRI-FG	8,690	119.1	1,855.7	1.9	20.9	15.9	255.5	579.3
ROCKEFELLER UNIVERSITY	PRI-FG	98	5,998.9	2,114.7	1.5	1,914.2	A	4.6	32.6
RUSSELL SAGE C ALL CAM									
RUSSELL SAGE C MAIN CAM	PRI-FG	2,120	191.1	3,405.5	4.4	86.2	44.2	100.9	353.3
RUSSELL SAGE JC OF ALBANY	PRI-T	912	249.8	5,697.3	8.8	81.5	53.8	114.0	228.0
SAINT BERNARD'S SEMINARY	PRI-FG	77	936.0	16,415.0	A	836.5	426.5	22.0	77.0
SAINT BONAVENTURE U	PRI-FG	2,397	164.2	3,052.4	4.7	102.5	113.4	115.7	239.7
SAINT FRANCIS COLLEGE	PRI-FN	2,436	95.0	3,354.2	3.6	50.1	50.3	293.4	459.6
SAINT JOHN FISHER COLLEGE	PRI-FN	1,633	197.0	4,369.0	5.3	73.7	48.2	201.6	233.2
SAINT JOHN'S UNIVERSITY	PRI-U	13,672	125.7	3,515.0	4.0	64.5	45.0	167.7	396.2
SNT JOSEPHS C ALL CAM									
SNT JOSEPH'S C MAIN CAM	PRI-FN	1,209	77.8	2,296.6	3.7	89.0	66.9	215.8	403.0
SNT JOSEPHS C SUFFOLK CAM	PRI-FN	308	360.2	12,328.5	13.4	147.4	116.8	61.6	308.0
SNT JOSEPHS SEM & COLLEGE	PRI-FG	73	1,180.6	.0	9.0	1,269.0	667.2	26.0	36.5
SAINT LAWRENCE UNIVERSITY	PRI-FG	2,385	206.2	3,152.9	3.5	117.9	85.3	118.6	397.5
SAINT THOMAS AQUINAS C	PRI-FN	830	165.1	3,917.2	5.9	94.5	72.9	100.0	230.5
SNT VLADMR ORTH THEOL SEM	PRI-FG	80	499.4	A	A	462.5	402.3	34.7	40.0
SARAH LAWRENCE COLLEGE	PRI-FG	907	337.5	4,710.7	4.9	171.6	138.5	51.2	113.3
SARA SCHENIRER TCHRS SEM	PRI-FN	D	D	D	D	D	D	D	D
SCHOOL OF VISUAL ARTS	PRI-FN	2,377	46.6	3,956.0	A	8.4	6.7	432.1	792.3
SEM IMMAC CONCEPTION	PRI-FG	145	366.7	.0	5.8	301.3	289.6	72.5	72.5
SH'OR YOSHUV RAB COLLEGE	PRI-FG	D	D	D	D	D	D	D	D
SIENA COLLEGE	PRI-FN	2,499	134.5	3,113.2	4.2	67.3	31.7	192.2	357.0
SKIDMORE COLLEGE	PRI-FN	2,163	231.8	3,299.6	4.1	101.0	87.1	105.5	270.3
STATE U NY SYS ALL INST									
SUNY AT ALBANY	PUB-U	12,548	291.1	5,287.8	4.4	70.0	40.5	94.9	286.4
SUNY AT BINGHAMTON	PUB-FG	8,647	340.0	7,155.2	5.8	94.8	119.8	81.8	240.1
SUNY AT BUFFALO ALL CAM									
SUNY AT BUFFALO MAIN CAM	PUB-U	17,531	277.1	5,597.5	3.2	96.8	58.1	90.9	282.7
SUNY HEALTH SCI CTR BFLO	PUB-FG	2,622	307.6	4,772.6	4.0	71.4	26.7	79.9	238.3
SUNY AT STONY BK ALL CAM									
SUNY AT STONY BK MAIN CAM	PUB-U	11,999	290.0	5,551.2	2.8	84.9	41.6	82.1	272.7
SUNY HLTH SCI CTR STNY BK	PUB-FG	1,215	624.5	5,197.2	6.8	131.0	29.6	60.7	173.5
SUNY DOWNSTATE MEDL CTR	PUB-FG	1,366	631.8	3,958.9	1.9	174.0	29.2	39.0	91.0
SUNY UPSTATE MEDICAL CTR	PUB-FG	837	799.9	13,948.8	2.0	149.9	76.8	38.9	111.6
SUNY COLLEGE AT BROCKPORT	PUB-FG	8,118	162.3	2,804.4	3.3	43.9	31.5	172.7	405.9
SUNY COLLEGE AT BUFFALO	PUB-FG	8,922	152.0	2,535.6	3.0	45.7	38.1	148.7	356.8
SUNY COLLEGE AT CORTLAND	PUB-FG	5,276	157.1	2,809.7	3.5	46.5	73.8	138.4	376.8
SUNY COLLEGE AT FREDONIA	PUB-FG	4,410	179.3	3,151.3	3.8	71.1	60.7	132.8	367.5
SUNY COLLEGE AT GENESEO	PUB-FG	4,889	175.3	3,008.0	3.6	66.5	66.6	128.6	325.9
SUNY COLLEGE AT NEW PALTZ	PUB-FG	5,045	174.6	2,517.6	3.2	58.5	46.8	132.7	360.3
SUNY COLLEGE OLD WESTBURY	PUB-FN	1,833	328.8	7,631.0	5.7	57.7	48.9	70.5	183.3
SUNY COLLEGE AT ONEONTA	PUB-FG	5,779	178.6	3,138.2	4.0	63.3	42.8	128.4	2,889.5
SUNY COLLEGE AT OSWEGO	PUB-FG	6,978	162.2	3,019.6	3.5	42.4	33.2	142.4	332.2

SEE FOOTNOTES AT END OF TABLE

Table 3. — Indexes Concerning Operating Expenditures, 1978-79, Bookstock Held at End of Year, 1978-79, and Library Staff (FTE), Fall 1979, College and University Libraries, by State or Other Area and Institution: Aggregate United States — Continued

STATE OR OTHER AREA AND INSTITUTION	CONTROL AND TYPE OF INSTITUTION	TOTAL FTE OPENING FALL ENROLLMENT, FALL 1978	LIBRARY OPERATING EXPENDITURES (IN DOLLARS) 1978-79			BOOKSTOCK HELD AT END OF YEAR 1978-79		FTE STUDENTS PER FTE LIBRARY STAFF FALL 1979	
			PER FTE STUDENT, FALL 1978	PER FULL-TIME FACULTY MEMBER, 1978	AS PERCENT OF GENERAL EXPENDITURES, 1978-79	VOLUMES PER FTE STUDENT, FALL 1978	TITLES (INCLUDING MICROFORMS) PER FTE STUDENT 1978	TOTAL STAFF	PROFESSIONAL STAFF
(1)	(2)	(3)	(4)	(5)	(6)	(7)	(8)	(9)	(10)
NEW YORK	--CONTINUED								
SUNY COLLEGE PLATTSBURGH	PUB-FG	5,439	162.8	3,054.9	3.6	41.7	87.1	147.0	418.3
SUNY COLLEGE AT POTSDAM	PUB-FG	3,984	193.9	3,018.4	3.7	74.5	56.5	122.5	274.7
SUNY COLLEGE AT PURCHASE	PUB-FN	2,284	296.9	5,606.0	4.1	64.7	52.9	98.8	240.4
SUNY C OF TECH UTICA-ROME	PUB-FG	1,723	245.4	7,048.9	4.7	53.0	A	132.5	246.1
SUNY EMPIRE STATE COLLEGE	PUB-FN	1,860	18.5	359.5	.2	2.3	6.4	.0	A
SUNY C ENVRNMTL SCI-FORS	PUB-FG	1,701	215.7	3,562.2	2.1	44.1	18.5	113.4	243.0
SUNY MARITIME COLLEGE	PUB-FG	1,021	297.1	4,667.0	4.7	64.1	53.8	77.9	167.3
SUNY STATE C OF OPTOMETRY	PUB-FG	221	585.6	3,156.6	1.9	80.6	44.9	49.1	110.5
SUNY AGRL & TECH C ALFRED	PUB-T	3,999	62.9	1,186.9	1.5	13.6	9.1	312.4	666.5
SUNY AGRL & TECH C CANTON	PUB-T	2,354	67.9	1,367.6	1.6	14.5	13.8	336.2	588.5
SUNY AGRL TECH C COBLESKL	PUB-T	2,586	127.9	2,330.9	3.0	24.3	18.8	142.0	431.0
SUNY AGRL & TECH C DELHI	PUB-T	2,511	84.3	1,681.0	2.0	17.8	13.3	279.0	627.7
SUNY AGRL TECH C FARMNGDL	PUB-T	8,929	65.0	2,053.0	1.8	9.7	8.4	335.6	797.2
SUNY AGRL TECH C MORRISVL	PUB-T	2,772	77.7	1,562.4	1.8	26.9	22.9	216.5	554.4
ADIRONDACK CMTY COLLEGE	PUB-T	1,443	91.2	1,936.0	3.7	30.7	30.8	192.4	412.2
BROOME COMMUNITY COLLEGE	PUB-T	3,563	83.6	2,069.3	3.4	14.6	13.1	225.5	445.3
CAYUGA CO CMTY COLLEGE	PUB-T	1,893	74.3	1,876.1	3.0	33.1	31.9	332.1	511.6
CLINTON COMMUNITY COLLEGE	PUB-T	1,001	202.0	5,777.9	7.2	33.4	29.8	217.6	500.5
COLUMBIA-GREENE CC	PUB-T	799	192.7	4,162.8	6.1	38.2	33.4	153.6	799.0
CMTY COLLEGE FINGER LAKES	PUB-T	1,587	111.8	2,572.0	3.8	25.6	17.5	151.1	396.7
CORNING COMMUNITY COLLEGE	PUB-T	2,125	158.2	3,232.5	4.7	31.1	25.5	105.1	303.5
DUTCHESS CMTY COLLEGE	PUB-T	3,810	76.1	2,232.0	2.6	20.0	16.8	317.5	635.0
ERIE COMMUNITY COLLEGE	PUB-T	7,952	75.7	A	3.3	13.7	12.5	467.7	883.5
FASHION INST TECHNOLOGY	PUB-FN	5,370	133.8	4,303.9	3.5	10.1	9.1	189.0	516.3
FULTON-MONTGOMERY CC	PUB-T	1,133	124.0	2,555.4	3.8	47.4	45.3	174.3	377.6
GENESEE COMMUNITY COLLEGE	PUB-T	1,332	126.9	2,523.6	3.3	34.9	32.8	214.8	493.3
HERKIMER CO CMTY COLLEGE	PUB-T	1,559	141.0	3,489.3	6.5	33.6	26.7	154.3	519.6
HUDSON VLY CMTY COLLEGE	PUB-T	5,400	128.2	2,972.8	4.6	17.0	19.5	166.1	600.0
JAMESTOWN CMTY COLLEGE	PUB-T	2,170	104.5	2,061.6	4.1	21.6	14.3	206.6	723.3
JEFFERSON CMTY COLLEGE	PUB-T	1,057	131.3	3,155.3	5.0	53.2	49.2	132.1	264.2
MOHAWK VLY CMTY COLLEGE	PUB-T	4,522	67.2	2,187.8	3.0	14.3	12.4	282.6	595.6
MONROE COMMUNITY COLLEGE	PUB-T	6,592	54.5	1,253.5	1.8	11.2	8.1	515.0	1,098.6
NASSAU COMMUNITY COLLEGE	PUB-T	13,001	81.9	2,389.0	2.7	10.6	7.7	315.5	849.7
NIAGARA CO CMTY COLLEGE	PUB-T	2,910	130.6	3,276.3	4.4	12.5	11.9	151.5	319.7
N COUNTRY CMTY COLLEGE	PUB-T	917	115.8	3,124.5	3.7	33.3	28.4	183.4	458.5
ONONDAGA CMTY COLLEGE	PUB-T	4,078	129.1	2,910.2	4.5	19.2	18.4	171.3	485.4
ORANGE CO CMTY COLLEGE	PUB-T	3,313	82.9	2,080.7	2.7	20.8	17.0	236.6	602.3
ROCKLAND CMTY COLLEGE	PUB-T	5,287	91.0	3,648.4	3.4	24.0	31.1	284.2	1,762.3
SCHENECTADY COUNTY CC	PUB-T	1,452	192.6	7,362.2	7.5	26.9	25.9	122.0	345.7
SUFFOLK CO CMTY COLLEGE	PUB-T	12,146	85.9	2,670.3	3.6	11.8	10.8	244.8	572.9
SULLIVAN CO CMTY COLLEGE	PUB-T	1,461	127.1	2,902.7	3.8	29.3	26.6	162.3	429.7
TOMPKINS-CORTLAND CC	PUB-T	1,750	125.5	4,576.4	5.0	16.4	14.1	156.2	372.3
ULSTER CO CMTY COLLEGE	PUB-T	1,924	134.8	3,016.5	4.1	35.8	31.0	165.8	481.0
WESTCHESTER CMTY COLLEGE	PUB-T	5,345	105.1	3,070.2	3.9	16.3	12.9	227.4	427.6
STENOTYPE INSTITUTE	PRI-T	D	D	D	D	D	D	D	D
SYRACUSE U ALL CAMPUSES									
SYRACUSE U MAIN CAMPUS	PRI-U	15,957	241.4	4,362.9	3.8	114.1	68.5	83.9	301.0
UTICA C OF SYRACUSE U	PRI-FN	1,522	198.3	3,510.4	4.8	76.5	50.6	96.3	253.6
TALMUDICAL INST UPST NY	PRI-FN	D	D	D	D	D	D	D	D
TALMUD SEM OHOLEI TORAH	PRI-FG	D	D	D	D	D	D	D	D
TAYLOR BUSINESS INSTITUTE	PRI-T	1,379	17.9	1,052.7	A	1.5	1.1	1,379.0	1,379.0
TECH CAREER INSTITUTES	PRI-T	841	17.5	328.6	.3	2.4	2.2	8,410.0	8,410.0
TOBE-COBURN SCH FASH CARS	PRI-T	170	57.4	1,628.1	3.6	13.3	A	170.0	170.0
TOURO COLLEGE	PRI-FG	1,402	125.9	4,528.2	4.2	85.5	60.7	250.3	250.3
TROCAIRE COLLEGE	PRI-T	508	254.2	3,689.9	7.6	74.7	60.4	84.6	169.3
UNION COLLEGE	PRI-FG	2,448	295.7	5,322.8	4.7	156.6	79.3	85.5	178.6
UNION THEOLOGICAL SEM	PRI-FG	D	D	D	D	D	D	D	D
UNITED TALMUDICAL ACADEMY	PRI-FG	D	D	D	D	D	D	D	D
UNIVERSITY OF ROCHESTER	PRI-U	6,783	565.8	7,094.6	3.0	270.6	107.1	48.2	133.0
U ST NY REGENTS EXTNL DEG	PUB-FN		NO LIBRARY FACILITIES						
UTICA SCHOOL OF COMMERCE	PRI-T	245	30.5	1,497.2	A	6.0	A	204.1	490.0
VASSAR COLLEGE	PRI-FG	2,313	460.3	5,755.4	6.4	224.2	121.5	53.4	185.0
VILLA MARIA COLLEGE BFLO	PRI-T	422	188.3	4,183.5	6.6	109.0	96.9	65.9	124.1
WADHAMS HALL SEM-COLLEGE	PRI-FN	75	756.7	18,918.6	12.7	1,062.3	848.6	25.0	37.5
WAGNER COLLEGE	PRI-FG	2,109	147.2	3,043.9	3.3	119.0	98.6	139.6	383.4
WEBB INST OF NAVAL ARCH	PRI-FN	80	679.4	4,941.7	5.4	401.7	353.4	40.0	80.0

SEE FOOTNOTES AT END OF TABLE

Table 3. – Indexes Concerning Operating Expenditures, 1978-79, Bookstock Held at End of Year, 1978-79, and Library Staff (FTE), Fall 1979, College and University Libraries, by State or Other Area and Institution: Aggregate United States – Continued

STATE OR OTHER·AREA AND INSTITUTION	CON-TROL AND TYPE OF IN-STITU-TION	TOTAL FTE OPENING FALL ENROLL-MENT, FALL 1978	LIBRARY OPERATING EXPENDITURES (IN DOLLARS) 1978-79			BOOKSTOCK HELD AT END OF YEAR 1978-79		FTE STUDENTS PER FTE LIBRARY STAFF FALL 1979	
			PER FTE STU-DENT, FALL 1978	PER FULL-TIME FAC-ULTY MEM-BER, 1978	AS PER-CENT OF GENERAL EXPENDI-TURES, 1978-79	VOLUMES PER FTE STUDENT, FALL 1978	TITLES (INCLU-DING MICRO-FORMS) PER FTE STUDENT 1978	TOTAL STAFF	PROFES-SIONAL STAFF
(1)	(2)	(3)	(4)	(5)	(6)	(7)	(8)	(9)	(10)
NEW YORK	--CONTINUED								
WELLS COLLEGE	PRI-FN	531	345.8	3,747.5	4.4	367.4	213.9	65.5	129.5
WESTCHESTER INSTITUTE	PRI-FG	D	D	D	D	D	D	D	D
THE WOOD SCHOOL	PRI-T	500	10.7	446.5	.4	1.0	.9	1,250.0	A
YESH BETH HILLEL KRASNA	PRI-FG	D	D	D	D	D	D	D	D
YESH BETH SHEARM RAB INST	PRI-FG	D	D	D	D	D	D	D	D
YESH CHOFETZ CHAIM RADUN	PRI-FG	D	D	D	D	D	D	D	D
YESH·KARLIN STOLIN INST	PRI-FG	D	D	D	D	D	D	D	D
YESHIVA NACHLAS HALEVIYIM	PRI-FG	D	D	D	D	D	D	D	D
YESH OF NITRA RAB COLLEGE	PRI-FN	D	D	D	D	D	D	D	D
YESHIVA SHAAR HATORAH	PRI-FG	D	D	D	D	D	D	D	D
YESHIVA UNIVERSITY	PRI-U	3,640	524.0	9,883.6	1.7	211.7	119.7	48.6	103.4
YESH MIKDASH MELECH	PRI-FN	D	D	D	D	D	D	D	D
YESHIVATH VIZHITZ	PRI-FG	D	D	D	D	D	D	D	D
YESHIVATH ZICHRON MOSHE	PRI-FG	D	D	D	D	D	D	D	D
NORTH CAROLINA									
ANSON TECHNICAL COLLEGE	PUB-T	361	284.6	5,409.2	7.0	34.6	35.1	68.1	156.9
ASHEBORO COLLEGE	PRI-T	D	D	D	D	D	D	D	D
ASHEVL BUNCOMBE TECH C	PUB-T	1,689	65.6	1,499.1	2.7	14.6	14.3	281.5	844.5
ATLANTIC CHRISTIAN C	PRI-FN	1,512	88.2	1,515.9	3.6	61.5	A	.0	A
BARBER-SCOTIA COLLEGE	PRI-FN	399	162.1	2,941.3	2.9	169.2	128.6	133.0	399.0
BEAUFORT CO CMTY COLLEGE	PUB-T	706	87.2	1,811.8	2.8	23.0	22.8	196.1	271.5
BELMONT ABBEY COLLEGE	PRI-FN	666	149.7	3,562.8	4.8	119.6	89.6	90.0	237.8
BENNETT COLLEGE	PRI-FN	611	262.9	3,651.3	5.9	129.1	68.6	81.4	152.7
BLADEN TECHNICAL INST	PUB-T	317	183.6	3,064.6	5.2	43.4	A	64.6	317.0
BLANTONS JUNIOR COLLEGE	PRI-T	180	49.9	D	3.7	29.2	27.7	.0	A
BLUE RIDGE TECHNICAL C	PUB-T	599	112.9	2,942.3	3.8	24.2	25.0	239.6	399.3
BREVARD COLLEGE	PRI-T	648	99.6	1,655.0	3.3	58.3	35.5	147.2	648.0
CALDWELL CC AND TECH INST	PUB-T	1,041	119.2	2,342.0	3.6	20.9	20.9	130.1	520.5
CAMPBELL UNIVERSITY2/	PRI-FG	2,182	124.3	2,608.7	3.4	15.8	13.9	112.7	727.3
CAPE FEAR TECHNICAL INST	PUB-T	1,184	166.5	3,129.4	4.1	15.8	13.9	112.7	394.6
CARTERET TECHNICAL INST	PUB-T	798	176.3	4,140.0	7.8	21.3	19.6	114.0	399.0
CATAWBA COLLEGE	PRI-FN	938	165.7	2,355.3	4.3	129.8	95.7	111.6	223.3
CATAWBA VALLEY TECH C	PUB-T	1,519	92.2	2,060.5	3.9	17.0	15.7	217.0	759.5
CECILS JUNIOR COLLEGE	PRI-T	251	65.6	16,480.0	A	25.5	23.3	119.5	125.5
CEN CAROLINA TECH C	PUB-T	1,503	162.4	3,815.2	6.5	12.6	11.1	115.6	214.7
CEN PIEDMONT CMTY COLLEGE	PUB-T	8,475	47.2	1,556.5	2.2	7.9	7.6	513.6	1,540.9
CHOWAN COLLEGE	PRI-T	1,050	124.8	2,520.3	4.0	59.5	44.3	210.0	350.0
CLEVELAND CO TECH INST	PUB-T	1,010	134.3	2,423.5	5.1	20.7	18.6	202.0	505.0
COASTAL CAROLINA CC	PUB-T	1,598	83.1	1,845.2	3.5	16.4	18.2	399.5	532.6
COLLEGE OF THE ALBEMARLE	PUB-T	837	94.6	1,885.5	3.8	40.5	31.8	194.6	558.0
CRAVEN COMMUNITY COLLEGE	PUB-T	1,004	83.5	1,864.7	3.9	17.8	17.6	251.0	334.6
DAVIDSON COLLEGE	PRI-FN	1,348	353.6	5,125.7	6.0	185.9	128.4	81.2	192.5
DAVIDSON CO CMTY COLLEGE	PUB-T	1,611	106.1	2,311.2	5.3	21.6	20.3	268.5	537.0
DUKE UNIVERSITY	PRI-U	9,528	615.7	A	A	317.2	A	37.9	113.0
DURHAM COLLEGE	PRI-T	D	D	D	D	D	D	D	D
DURHAM TECHNICAL INST	PUB-T	2,286	61.9	1,839.5	3.0	8.3	7.7	408.2	879.2
EDGECOMBE TECH INST	PUB-T	631	257.9	4,283.3	7.4	25.4	20.4	63.1	210.3
ELON COLLEGE	PRI-FN	2,181	78.6	2,171.9	2.8	55.9	34.0	272.6	454.3
FAYETTEVILLE TECH INST	PUB-T	4,106	69.1	1,917.4	3.2	7.2	5.6	273.7	586.5
FORSYTH TECHNICAL INST	PUB-T	2,107	71.7	1,467.5	3.0	12.6	12.7	351.1	1,053.5
GARDNER-WEBB COLLEGE	PRI-FN	1,275	190.8	3,160.1	5.9	82.6	81.6	127.5	318.7
GASTON COLLEGE	PUB-T	1,778	71.3	1,565.8	3.1	23.5	21.5	355.6	444.5
GREENSBORO COLLEGE	PRI-FN	655	116.9	2,016.4	2.4	112.4	103.1	163.7	327.5
GUILFORD COLLEGE	PRI-FN	1,474	143.5	2,784.2	3.7	97.4	102.0	145.9	320.4
GUILFORD TECHNICAL INST	PUB-T	2,468	147.8	3,200.8	5.7	14.8	14.7	135.6	329.0
HALIFAX CMTY COLLEGE	PUB-T	841	107.0	1,800.6	4.3	24.2	20.9	210.2	420.5
HAMILTON COLLEGE	PRI-T	469	32.7	A	A	12.7	12.6	469.0	469.0
HARDBARGER JC BUSINESS	PRI-T	D	D	D	D	D	D	D	D
HAYWOOD TECHNICAL INST	PUB-T	723	184.4	2,469.3	4.6	28.3	27.7	120.5	144.6
HIGH POINT COLLEGE	PRI-FN	1,031	126.6	2,374.6	4.3	99.5	96.5	206.2	343.6
ISOTHERMAL CMTY COLLEGE	PUB-T	846	106.6	2,818.4	4.7	32.5	31.3	211.5	423.0
JAMES SPRUNT INSTITUTE	PUB-T	613	142.9	2,037.6	4.1	35.1	30.9	153.2	613.0
JEFFERSON COLLEGE	PRI-T	412	33.8	1,392.7	5.4	13.0	13.0	.0	A
JOHNSN C SMITH UNIVERSITY	PRI-FN	1,452	129.3	2,761.3	3.2	63.9	38.9	121.0	264.0
JOHNSTON TECHNICAL INST	PUB-T	999	85.0	1,148.5	2.8	12.5	12.4	249.7	999.0
JOHN WESLEY COLLEGE	PRI-FN	53	206.4	3,647.0	5.5	305.5	291.1	35.3	35.3

SEE FOOTNOTES AT END OF TABLE

Table 3. — Indexes Concerning Operating Expenditures, 1978-79, Bookstock Held at End of Year, 1978-79, and Library Staff (FTE), Fall 1979, College and University Libraries, by State or Other Area and Institution: Aggregate United States — Continued

STATE OR OTHER AREA AND INSTITUTION (1)	CONTROL AND TYPE OF INSTITUTION (2)	TOTAL FTE OPENING FALL ENROLLMENT, FALL 1978 (3)	LIBRARY OPERATING EXPENDITURES (IN DOLLARS) 1978-79 — PER FTE STUDENT, FALL 1978 (4)	PER FULL-TIME FACULTY MEMBER, 1978 (5)	AS PERCENT OF GENERAL EXPENDITURES, 1978-79 (6)	BOOKSTOCK HELD AT END OF YEAR 1978-79 — VOLUMES PER FTE STUDENT, FALL 1978 (7)	TITLES (INCLUDING MICROFORMS) PER FTE STUDENT 1978 (8)	FTE STUDENTS PER FTE LIBRARY STAFF FALL 1979 — TOTAL STAFF (9)	PROFESSIONAL STAFF (10)
		D	D	D	D	D	D	D	D
NORTH CAROLINA --CONTINUED									
KING'S C-CHARLOTTE	PRI-T	722	67.3	3,239.4	A	15.8	7.6	313.9	313.9
KING'S COLLEGE-RALEIGH	PRI-T	672	54.4	2,033.3	A	8.0	A	480.0	480.0
LAFAYETTE COLLEGE	PRI-T			2,059.0	3.5	A	77.4	145.6	364.0
LEES-MCRAE COLLEGE	PRI-T	728	101.8		4.9	31.7	A	152.2	369.7
LENOIR CMTY COLLEGE	PUB-T	1,294	135.5	2,402.1					
LENOIR-RHYNE COLLEGE	PRI-FN	1,223	174.0	2,391.3	4.8	81.3	73.6	113.2	214.5
LIVINGSTONE COLLEGE	PRI-FN	839	119.9	2,053.5	2.3	82.5	88.3	119.8	209.7
LOUISBURG COLLEGE	PRI-T	670	97.2	2,101.0	3.9	69.8	64.4	148.8	223.3
MARS HILL COLLEGE	PRI-FN	1,647	98.1	1,650.3	2.2	38.1	36.5	130.7	343.1
MARTIN COMMUNITY COLLEGE	PUB-T	545	143.7	2,008.5	4.2	29.5	22.1	181.6	272.5
MAYLAND TECHNICAL INST	PUB-T	442	141.1	2,310.2	5.0	29.4	27.4	119.4	442.0
MCDOWELL TECHNICAL INST	PUB-T	455	98.2	1,719.6	3.9	31.1	32.9	227.5	455.0
MEREDITH COLLEGE	PRI-FN	1,401	175.8	3,519.6	5.3	63.1	A	172.9	368.6
METHODIST COLLEGE	PRI-FN	830	118.8	2,293.6	4.5	78.6	60.4	150.9	276.6
MITCHELL CMTY COLLEGE	PUB-T	839	115.2	2,249.6	4.5	34.2	32.3	139.8	839.0
MONTGOMERY TECH INSTITUTE	PUB-T	188	245.0	1,771.9	4.4	46.7	42.7	62.6	188.0
MONTREAT-ANDERSON COLLEGE	PRI-T	418	211.8	4,428.4	6.2	106.1	85.2	87.0	232.2
MOUNT OLIVE COLLEGE	PRI-T	99	513.3	2,823.5	3.6	291.9	A	33.0	49.5
NASH TECHNICAL INSTITUTE	PUB-T	712	176.0	4,177.7	7.7	25.3	21.7	178.0	178.0
NC WESLEYAN COLLEGE	PRI-FN	654	139.2	2,461.0	3.8	85.4	65.6	148.6	654.0
PAMLICO TECHNICAL C	PUB-T	133	560.5	6,778.0	10.7	81.4	81.2	29.5	133.0
PEACE COLLEGE	PRI-T	505	88.6	1,864.3	2.8	63.0	61.1	202.0	505.0
PFEIFFER COLLEGE	PRI-FN	884	173.4	2,893.0	3.8	105.1	89.7	105.2	276.2
PIEDMONT BIBLE COLLEGE	PRI-FN	384	61.8	1,188.1	A	101.9	80.9	76.8	384.0
PIEDMONT TECHNICAL INST	PUB-T	536	260.1	3,984.5	6.7	28.1	28.6	67.0	178.6
PITT CMTY COLLEGE	PUB-T	1,298	158.2	3,160.4	6.3	21.6	20.6	144.2	324.5
QUEENS COLLEGE	PRI-FN	416	267.4	3,007.4	3.6	237.6	178.0	67.0	104.0
RANDOLPH TECHNICAL C	PUB-T	625	134.3	2,709.2	5.0	30.8	27.5	156.2	312.5
RICHMOND TECHNICAL INST	PUB-T	845	129.3	2,733.2	4.6	27.2	A	187.7	338.0
ROANOKE BIBLE COLLEGE	PRI-FN	171	135.2	A	6.3	116.0	107.8	.0	A
ROANOKE-CHOWAN TECH INST	PUB-T	595	251.7	5,350.6	6.2	37.7	32.9	95.9	297.5
ROBESON TECHNICAL INST	PUB-T	1,033	87.4	2,258.3	3.3	28.2	27.4	229.5	344.3
ROCKINGHAM CMTY COLLEGE	PUB-T	1,005	132.1	2,826.6	5.1	28.6	23.0	173.2	502.5
ROWAN TECHNICAL INSTITUTE	PUB-T	1,341	85.2	2,198.2	A	15.6	15.5	243.8	536.4
SACRED HEART COLLEGE	PRI-FN	262	193.7	2,986.4	4.1	183.3	183.5	65.5	87.3
SNT ANDREWS PRESB COLLEGE	PRI-FN	583	252.9	3,138.1	3.4	157.6	123.4	83.2	291.5
SAINT AUGUSTINES COLLEGE	PRI-FN	1,735	118.6	2,900.3	3.3	57.4	A	192.7	347.0
SAINT MARY'S COLLEGE	PRI-T	300	274.5	2,422.1	4.5	100.8	79.4	68.1	115.3
SALEM COLLEGE	PRI-FN	593	244.5	2,500.1	5.0	178.8	144.6	114.0	185.3
SAMPSON TECHNICAL C	PUB-T	804	113.8	2,614.2	4.6	19.5	17.8	201.0	268.0
SANDHILLS CMTY COLLEGE	PUB-T	1,472	80.6	1,318.9	2.9	28.6	28.4	245.3	736.0
SHAW UNIVERSITY	PRI-FN	1,240	83.4	1,668.9	2.5	64.0	56.6	248.0	310.0
STHESTN BAPTIST THEOL SEM	PRI-FG	646	371.7	7,505.0	8.4	179.2	241.7	58.7	129.2
SOUTHEASTERN CMTY COLLEGE	PUB-T	1,240	194.6	4,309.6	7.4	31.9	29.8	90.5	620.0
SOUTHWESTERN TECH C	PUB-T	748	75.2	1,563.3	2.3	27.0	23.5	249.3	748.0
STANLY TECHNICAL C	PUB-T	494	176.8	3,235.7	5.3	32.4	32.4	149.6	247.0
SURRY COMMUNITY COLLEGE	PUB-T	1,154	92.5	2,054.3	4.3	24.0	20.3	209.8	577.0
TECH C OF ALAMANCE	PUB-T	1,001	95.3	2,121.3	3.2	21.9	19.0	250.2	500.5
TRI-COUNTY COMMUNITY C	PUB-T	443	204.0	3,227.7	7.2	34.7	34.7	147.6	443.0
U OF NC ALL CAMPUSES									
APPALACHIAN ST UNIVERSITY	PUB-FG	8,782	191.3	3,465.2	5.9	45.2	65.1	179.2	462.0
EAST CAROLINA UNIVERSITY	PUB-FG	11,621	236.7	4,430.9	5.8	49.7	59.2	112.2	283.4
ELIZABETH CITY STATE U	PUB-FN	1,488	217.9	3,276.3	4.2	59.2	60.7	96.0	297.6
FAYETTEVL ST UNIVERSITY	PUB-FN	2,043	207.1	3,002.1	4.4	55.2	55.1	127.6	291.8
NC AGRL & TECH STATE U	PUB-FG	4,910	221.2	3,670.6	A	58.7	46.1	124.9	350.7
NC CENTRAL UNIVERSITY	PUB-FG	4,275	292.1	4,804.0	7.3	101.6	100.5	101.7	194.3
NC SCHOOL OF THE ARTS	PUB-FN	434	574.7	3,464.7	5.7	175.5	131.7	43.8	144.6
NC STATE U RALEIGH	PUB-U	16,194	224.7	4,242.8	2.9	54.9	25.8	129.5	558.4
PEMBROKE STATE UNIVERSITY	PUB-FG	1,939	239.6	3,574.7	7.0	78.1	91.2	129.2	277.0
U OF NC AT ASHEVILLE	PUB-FN	1,249	262.3	4,551.7	7.0	86.3	60.5	99.9	312.2
U OF NC AT CHAPEL HILL	PUB-U	18,852	338.6	5,862.7	2.8	122.8	57.1	76.6	228.5
U OF NC AT CHARLOTTE	PUB-FG	7,321	267.9	4,915.9	8.5	38.8	64.0	121.0	443.6
U OF NC AT GREENSBORO	PUB-FG	8,354	228.7	3,525.0	6.2	66.0	63.5	106.0	331.5
U OF NC AT WILMINGTON	PUB-FG	3,690	201.6	3,876.1	7.0	48.4	34.4	153.7	410.0
WSTN CAROLINA UNIVERSITY	PUB-FG	5,783	224.7	4,179.3	6.1	51.0	59.2	165.2	578.3
WINSTON-SALEM STATE U	PUB-FN	2,042	174.5	2,679.7	3.8	70.6	52.0	120.1	340.3

SEE FOOTNOTES AT END OF TABLE

Table 3. — Indexes Concerning Operating Expenditures, 1978-79, Bookstock Held at End of Year, 1978-79, and Library Staff (FTE), Fall 1979, College and University Libraries, by State or Other Area and Institution: Aggregate United States — Continued

STATE OR OTHER AREA AND INSTITUTION	CONTROL AND TYPE OF INSTITUTION	TOTAL FTE OPENING FALL ENROLLMENT, FALL 1978	LIBRARY OPERATING EXPENDITURES (IN DOLLARS) 1978-79			BOOKSTOCK HELD AT END OF YEAR 1978-79		FTE STUDENTS PER FTE LIBRARY STAFF FALL 1979	
			PER FTE STUDENT, FALL 1978	PER FULL-TIME FACULTY MEMBER, 1978	AS PERCENT OF GENERAL EXPENDITURES, 1978-79	VOLUMES PER FTE STUDENT, FALL 1978	TITLES (INCLUDING MICROFORMS) PER FTE STUDENT 1978	TOTAL STAFF	PROFESSIONAL STAFF
(1)	(2)	(3)	(4)	(5)	(6)	(7)	(8)	(9)	(10)
NORTH CAROLINA --CONTINUED									
VANCE-GRANVL CMTY COLLEGE	PUB-T	996	83.2	1,973.0	3.1	20.4	18.8	343.4	664.0
WAKE FOREST UNIVERSITY	PRI-U	4,523	458.3	9,013.1	3.7	149.9	104.4	166.7	608.5
WAKE TECHNICAL INSTITUTE	PUB-T	1,217	109.2	1,493.8	3.4	22.6	16.2	107.1	116.6
WARREN WILSON COLLEGE	PRI-FN	525	235.8	3,641.7	4.7	137.3	111.0		
WAYNE COMMUNITY COLLEGE	PUB-T	1,983	143.3	2,992.1	6.5	16.9	16.8	198.3	495.7
WESTERN PIEDMONT CC	PUB-T	1,009	184.6	3,653.6	6.4	30.9	29.0	112.1	336.3
WILKES COMMUNITY COLLEGE	PUB-T	1,253	160.5	2,794.1	5.5	31.3	A	100.2	417.6
WILSON CO TECHNICAL INST	PUB-T	823	205.8	3,683.3	6.4	30.1	22.1	94.5	274.3
WINGATE COLLEGE	PRI-FN	1,345	104.7	2,236.0	4.0	56.8	45.0	269.0	448.3
WINSALM COLLEGE	PRI-T	247	39.0	A	A	22.6	22.2	247.0	247.0
NORTH DAKOTA									
BISMARCK JUNIOR COLLEGE	PUB-T	1,690	66.5	1,209.6	3.1	18.1	16.5	338.0	845.0
DICKINSON STATE COLLEGE	PUB-FN	1,029	140.5	2,159.1	A	60.6	59.2	223.6	270.7
JAMESTOWN COLLEGE	PRI-FN	488	128.0	1,688.5	2.5	135.3	131.7	122.0	488.0
LAKE REGION JR COLLEGE	PUB-T	543	57.4	779.8	2.0	36.0	35.6	.0	A
MARY COLLEGE	PRI-FN	762	97.3	1,613.2	2.0	50.2	49.7	762.0	762.0
MAYVILLE STATE COLLEGE	PUB-FN	727	159.9	2,528.6	4.3	95.7	66.2	207.7	290.8
MINOT STATE COLLEGE	PUB-FG	2,195	113.4	A	3.9	54.7	41.2	219.5	645.5
ND STATE SCHOOL SCIENCE	PUB-T	3,302	68.8	1,402.3	2.5	17.0	19.3	340.4	600.3
ND STATE U ALL CAMPUSES									
ND STATE U MAIN CAMPUS	PUB-U	7,342	163.7	3,865.1	3.0	45.3	22.9	186.8	489.4
ND STATE U BOTTINEAU BR	PUB-T	521	140.5	2,712.5	4.2	48.4	50.0	260.5	260.5
NORTHWEST BIBLE COLLEGE	PRI-FN	146	230.6	4,810.8	11.7	183.3	129.8	146.0	146.0
STANDING ROCK CC	PRI-T	106	284.4	D	5.3	52.1	48.7	.0	A
TRINITY BIBLE INSTITUTE	PRI-FN	391	121.5	3,656.8	6.2	113.1	84.2	97.7	260.6
U OF ND ALL CAMPUSES									
U OF ND MAIN CAMPUS b/	PUB-U	8,648	153.0	3,567.3	2.9	60.6	34.7	213.5	455.1
U OF ND WILLISTON BRANCH	PUB-T	496	49.7	771.5	2.0	21.0	17.0	354.2	496.0
VALLEY CITY STATE COLLEGE	PUB-FN	964	148.4	2,751.6	4.6	73.6	63.2	214.2	385.6
OHIO									
ANTIOCH UNIVERSITY	PRI-FG	D	D	D	D	D	D	D	D
ART ACADEMY OF CINCINNATI	PRI-FN	148	488.3	6,570.7	12.9	289.2	279.9	32.8	74.0
ASHLAND COLLEGE	PRI-FG	1,992	118.6	2,110.2	3.2	86.5	59.5	144.3	423.8
ATHENAEUM OF OHIO	PRI-FG	235	448.4	.0	6.5	448.9	392.7	78.3	117.5
BALDWIN-WALLACE COLLEGE	PRI-FG	2,422	150.6	2,806.0	3.3	71.6	50.2	130.9	302.7
BELMONT TECHNICAL COLLEGE	PUB-T	506	49.7	1,049.4	1.9	8.8	7.7	337.3	722.8
BLUFFTON COLLEGE	PRI-FN	592	214.9	3,181.3	5.2	150.4	115.2	125.9	190.9
BORROMEO COLLEGE OF OHIO	PRI-FN	84	306.9	2,148.3	7.3	733.2	684.5	56.0	84.0
BOWLING GRN ST U ALL CAM									
BOWLING GRN ST U MAIN CAM	PUB-U	15,167	173.8	3,647.4	4.8	41.8	21.0	209.7	645.4
BOWLING GRN ST U FIRELDS	PUB-T	659	139.1	2,865.1	5.6	46.0	40.0	146.4	219.6
CAPITAL UNIVERSITY	PRI-FG	2,355	213.8	3,815.6	4.9	104.1	62.3	116.5	210.2
CASE WESTERN RESERVE U	PRI-U	6,617	494.3	5,862.7	3.3	203.4	A	44.2	113.1
CEDARVILLE COLLEGE	PRI-FN	1,158	144.2	3,094.1	4.7	65.5	57.0	130.1	463.2
CENTRAL OHIO TECHNICAL c/	PUB-T	NO LIBRARY FACILITIES							
CENTRAL STATE UNIVERSITY	PUB-FN	2,199	175.0	3,597.9	3.5	62.8	58.1	109.9	274.8
CHATFIELD COLLEGE	PRI-T	33	325.8	.0	A	521.1	464.2	33.0	33.0
CINCINNATI BIBLE SEMINARY	PRI-FG	D	D	D	D	D	D	D	D
CINCINNATI TECH COLLEGE	PUB-T	2,110	70.7	1,604.6	2.3	6.6	6.6	383.6	422.0
CIRCLEVILLE BIBLE COLLEGE	PRI-FN	209	103.2	1,961.0	4.7	86.7	86.8	130.6	130.6
CLARK TECHNICAL COLLEGE	PUB-T	1,292	134.5	3,279.5	5.2	18.3	17.7	230.7	358.8
CLEVELAND C JEWISH STDIES	PRI-FG	D	D	D	D	D	D	.0	D
CLEVELAND INST OF ART	PRI-FN	624	142.4	2,469.8	3.6	53.7	40.6	145.1	240.0
CLEVELAND INST OF MUSIC	PRI-FG	254	313.4	A	3.5	165.9	A	68.6	94.0
CLEVELAND ST UNIVERSITY	PUB-FG	11,753	216.4	4,864.3	6.0	48.3	25.6	166.7	470.1
C MT SNT JCS-ON-THE-OHIO	PRI-FN	1,038	110.4	1,880.1	3.2	102.0	57.3	207.6	415.2
COLLEGE OF STEUBENVILLE	PRI-FN	680	139.2	2,705.9	3.6	255.6	220.7	170.0	340.0
COLLEGE OF WOOSTER	PRI-FN	1,847	241.0	3,372.7	4.2	146.5	128.0	121.5	439.7
COLUMBUS C ART AND DESIGN	PRI-FN	752	96.0	1,719.0	3.2	22.1	21.8	214.8	376.0
COLUMBUS TECHNICAL INST	PUB-T	4,011	130.9	3,596.6	5.3	4.2	3.4	246.0	573.0
CUYAHOGA CC DISTRICT	PUB-T	D	D	D	D	D	D	.0	A
DAVIS JUNIOR COLLEGE	PRI-T	396	20.0	1,136.4	1.4	8.0	7.9	112.8	225.6
DEFIANCE COLLEGE	PRI-FN	677	227.8	3,281.5	4.4	122.7	88.3	127.2	339.3
DENISON UNIVERSITY	PRI-FN	2,036	197.8	2,650.4	3.9	116.8	93.5	257.1	600.0
DYKE COLLEGE	PRI-FN	900	73.4	3,304.9	2.9	11.2	10.5		
EDGECLIFF COLLEGE	PRI-FN	652	141.2	2,246.8	4.7	109.9	107.3	163.0	326.0

SEE FOOTNOTES AT END OF TABLE

Table 3. — Indexes Concerning Operating Expenditures, 1978-79, Bookstock Held at End of Year, 1978-79, and Library Staff (FTE), Fall 1979, College and University Libraries, by State or Other Area and Institution: Aggregate United States — Continued

STATE OR OTHER AREA AND INSTITUTION	CONTROL AND TYPE OF INSTITUTION	TOTAL FTE OPENING FALL ENROLLMENT, FALL 1978	LIBRARY OPERATING EXPENDITURES (IN DOLLARS) 1978-79			BOOKSTOCK HELD AT END OF YEAR 1978-79		FTE STUDENTS PER FTE LIBRARY STAFF FALL 1979	
			PER FTE STUDENT, FALL 1978	PER FULL-TIME FACULTY MEMBER, 1978	AS PERCENT OF GENERAL EXPENDITURES, 1978-79	VOLUMES PER FTE STUDENT, FALL 1978	TITLES (INCLUDING MICROFORMS) PER FTE STUDENT 1978	TOTAL STAFF	PROFESSIONAL STAFF
(1)	(2)	(3)	(4)	(5)	(6)	(7)	(8)	(9)	(10)
OHIO	--CONTINUED								
EDISON STATE CMTY COLLEGE	PUB-T	768	58.2	2,131.0	3.0	21.9	21.8	307.2	768.0
FINDLAY COLLEGE	PRI-FN	771	211.9	2,918.0	4.5	134.4	88.7	113.3	257.0
FRANKLIN UNIVERSITY	PRI-FN	2,938	85.6	6,137.3	5.6	14.8	13.4	481.6	576.0
HEBREW UNION C ALL CAM								5.6	15.7
HEBREW UNION C MAIN CAM	PRI-FG	132	3,668.8	21,055.9	10.3	2,233.4	A		
HEBREW UNION C CAL BRANCH	PRI-FG	83	1,008.1	9,297.4	6.2	756.0	714.9	20.7	83.0
HEBREW UNION C NY BRANCH	PRI-FG	D	D	D	D	D	D	D	D
HEIDELBERG COLLEGE	PRI-FN	875	185.1	2,218.6	2.9	140.6	112.8	121.5	273.4
HIRAM COLLEGE	PRI-FN	1,038	196.2	2,790.7	2.9	146.3	145.3	120.6	519.0
HOCKING TECHNICAL COLLEGE	PUB-T	1,773	61.0	1,386.7	2.3	8.2	8.1	322.3	886.5
JEFFERSON TECHNICAL C	PUB-T	942	109.6	2,347.7	4.3	19.4	18.5	269.1	942.0
JOHN CARROLL UNIVERSITY	PRI-FG	3,070	100.8	2,092.8	3.0	113.9	58.4	210.2	479.6
KENT STATE U ALL CAMPUSES									
KENT STATE U MAIN CAMPUS	PUB-U	15,115	162.2	3,190.0	4.1	70.3	40.7	172.5	581.3
KENT ST ASHTABULA REG CAM	PUB-T	631	164.2	3,140.0	5.8	67.0	41.6	157.7	631.0
KENT ST E LIVERPL REG CAM	PUB-T	374	100.3	2,346.7	4.0	77.3	75.6	249.3	374.0
KENT ST U SALEM REG CAM	PUB-T	338	95.0	1,690.6	3.4	64.0	63.9	338.0	338.0
KENT ST STARK CO REG CAM	PUB-T	1,303	121.2	2,324.2	4.9	46.8	43.1	162.8	434.3
KENT ST TRUMBULL REG CAM	PUB-T	1,145	124.4	2,907.7	5.2	38.0	30.6	229.0	572.5
KENT ST TUSCARAWS REG CAM	PUB-T	572	128.3	2,532.2	4.6	64.4	62.7	286.0	572.0
KENYON COLLEGE	PRI-FN	1,465	222.2	3,323.1	4.1	133.4	89.1	118.1	332.9
KETTERING C MEDICAL ARTS	PRI-T	371	548.9	5,989.5	16.5	123.9	62.3	47.5	123.6
LAKE ERIE COLLEGE	PRI-FG	890	108.3	1,785.0	2.0	96.1	60.0	148.3	222.5
LAKELAND CMTY COLLEGE	PUB-T	2,844	57.7	1,610.2	1.8	23.5	21.8	546.9	888.7
LIMA TECHNICAL COLLEGE8/	PUB-T	NO LIBRARY FACILITIES							
LORAIN CO CMTY COLLEGE	PUB-T	3,285	75.6	2,511.1	3.5	25.3	20.6	295.6	746.5
LOURDES COLLEGE	PRI-T	265	119.0	2,868.0	7.2	222.5	A	88.3	176.6
MALONE COLLEGE	PRI-FN	710	213.9	3,996.9	5.1	129.5	96.1	109.2	355.0
MARIETTA COLLEGE	PRI-FG	1,416	176.6	2,476.9	3.8	167.0	150.8	123.1	472.0
MARION TECHNICAL COLLEGE9/	PUB-T	NO LIBRARY FACILITIES							
MEDL COLLEGE OHIO-TOLEDO	PUB-FG	394	1,239.8	16,283.9	2.1	188.2	62.0	20.7	65.6
METHODIST THEOL SCH OHIO	PRI-FG	234	548.7	7,134.2	10.0	305.8	278.2	46.8	117.0
MIAMI-JACOBS JC BUSINESS	PRI-T	616	16.7	1,149.1	1.3	3.1	2.7	410.6	1,232.0
MIAMI UNIVERSITY ALL CAM									
MIAMI U HAMILTON CAMPUS	PUB-T	769	246.3	4,620.1	7.3	72.4	65.2	.0	A
MIAMI U MIDDLETOWN CAMPUS	PUB-T	889	173.4	3,505.0	9.5	73.1	65.0	161.6	296.3
MIAMI UNIV OXFORD CAM	PUB-U	13,874	173.8	3,563.5	4.8	66.6	42.1	167.1	495.5
MICHAEL J OWENS TECH C	PUB-T	2,116	119.1	3,360.4	4.7	16.8	15.8	371.2	516.0
MOUNT UNION COLLEGE	PRI-FN	1,193	158.2	2,697.5	4.0	155.1	96.2	183.5	298.2
MOUNT VERNON NAZARENE C	PRI-FN	864	148.2	3,123.8	4.1	62.5	58.7	160.0	254.1
MUSKINGUM AREA TECH C	PUB-T	D	D	D	D	D	D	D	D
MUSKINGUM COLLEGE	PRI-FN	D	D	D	D	D	D	D	D
NORTH CEN TECH COLLEGE10/	PUB-T	NO LIBRARY FACILITIES							
NTHESTN OHIO U C MED	PUB-FG	95	3,408.6	12,952.8	A	207.8	89.2	9.5	23.7
NORTHWEST TECH COLLEGE	PUB-T	483	73.9	1,428.8	2.3	18.2	16.5	483.0	483.0
NOTRE DAME COLLEGE	PRI-FN	391	209.4	6,824.7	4.8	252.0	150.3	64.0	130.3
OBERLIN COLLEGE	PRI-FG	2,683	420.1	5,368.4	5.3	299.1	180.1	46.3	153.3
OHIO C PODIATRIC MEDICINE	PRI-FG	561	186.8	5,822.6	3.1	15.1	10.9	112.2	280.5
OHIO DOMINICAN COLLEGE	PRI-FN	699	272.0	4,527.3	6.3	131.1	121.8	84.2	107.5
OHIO INST OF TECHNOLOGY	PRI-FN	2,229	13.5	A	A	2.2	A	2,229.0	2,229.0
OHIO NORTHERN UNIVERSITY	PRI-FG	2,603	244.5	4,515.5	6.7	92.9	42.8	104.1	260.3
OHIO STATE U ALL CAMPUSES									
OHIO STATE U MAIN CAMPUS	PUB-U	46,154	173.6	4,446.9	2.8	71.8	32.0	154.7	506.6
OHIO ST U AGRL TECH INST	PUB-T	748	129.0	3,114.3	3.5	15.8	9.5	166.2	748.0
OHIO STATE U LIMA BR	PUB-T	742	231.3	4,517.3	9.0	68.7	39.8	185.5	371.0
OHIO STATE U MANSFIELD BR	PUB-T	898	154.8	3,972.4	6.2	45.7	24.8	224.5	449.0
OHIO STATE U MARION BR	PUB-T	597	139.3	3,467.0	5.9	49.0	26.8	298.5	597.0
OHIO STATE U NEWARK BR	PUB-T	749	178.8	4,784.3	7.1	53.9	30.4	149.8	374.5
OHIO U ALL CAMPUSES									
OHIO U MAIN CAMPUS	PUB-U	12,492	166.7	3,274.8	3.8	58.9	53.4	158.5	567.8
OHIO U BELMONT CO BRANCH	PUB-T	461	108.1	2,768.7	4.2	78.8	65.5	219.5	354.6
OHIO U CHILLICOTHE BR	PUB-T	672	110.7	3,544.0	5.0	68.3	55.4	224.0	672.0
OHIO U IRONTON BRANCH	PUB-T	356	8.5	D	.5	27.2	A	.0	A
OHIO U LANCASTER BRANCH	PUB-T	846	171.8	5,193.5	7.2	55.8	53.6	169.2	423.0
OHIO U ZANESVILLE BRANCH	PUB-T	546	213.4	3,885.5	7.2	99.0	88.0	202.2	546.0
OHIO WESLEYAN UNIVERSITY	PRI-FN	2,255	183.0	2,580.0	3.5	168.0	151.2	172.1	425.4

SEE FOOTNOTES AT END OF TABLE

Table 3. – Indexes Concerning Operating Expenditures, 1978-79, Bookstock Held at End of Year, 1978-79, and Library Staff (FTE), Fall 1979, College and University Libraries, by State or Other Area and Institution: Aggregate United States – Continued

STATE OR OTHER AREA AND INSTITUTION	CONTROL AND TYPE OF INSTITUTION	TOTAL FTE OPENING FALL ENROLLMENT, FALL 1978	LIBRARY OPERATING EXPENDITURES (IN DOLLARS) 1978-79			BOOKSTOCK HELD AT END OF YEAR 1978-79		FTE STUDENTS PER FTE LIBRARY STAFF FALL 1979	
			PER FTE STUDENT, FALL 1978	PER FULL-TIME FACULTY MEMBER, 1978	AS PERCENT OF GENERAL EXPENDITURES, 1978-79	VOLUMES PER FTE STUDENT, FALL 1978	TITLES (INCLUDING MICROFORMS) PER FTE STUDENT 1978	TOTAL STAFF	PROFESSIONAL STAFF
(1)	(2)	(3)	(4)	(5)	(6)	(7)	(8)	(9)	(10)
OHIO	--CONTINUED								
OTTERBEIN COLLEGE	PRI-FN	1,368	150.8	2,344.4	3.5	85.9	64.6	152.0	342.0
PAYNE THEOLOGICAL SEM	PRI-FG	21	677.4	A	A	808.3	478.5	21.0	21.0
PONTIFICAL C JOSEPHINUM	PRI-FG	182	434.8	4,396.3	5.8	506.7	332.2	60.6	91.0
RABBINICAL COLLEGE TELSHE	PRI-FG	NO LIBRARY FACILITIES							
RIO GRANDE COLLEGE	PRI-FN	891	129.9	2,270.8	3.6	65.8	68.0	156.3	240.8
SAINT MARY SEMINARY	PRI-FG	67	499.1	.0	8.8	597.8	572.8	44.6	67.0
SHAWNEE ST CMTY COLLEGE	PUB-T	1,313	83.2	1,852.4	3.4	46.5	45.7	.0	A
SINCLAIR CMTY COLLEGE	PUB-T	6,813	76.3	2,420.4	3.7	10.5	9.7	469.8	908.4
SOUTHERN OHIO COLLEGE	PRI-T	D	D	D	D	D	D	D	D
STHN ST GEN-TECH COLLEGE	PUB-T	641	186.2	4,422.7	6.6	28.0	23.4	97.1	160.2
STARK TECHNICAL COLLEGE11/	PUB-T	NO LIBRARY FACILITIES							
TERRA TECHNICAL COLLEGE	PUB-T	1,278	134.8	3,068.4	5.6	9.3	6.8	149.8	424.6
TIFFIN UNIVERSITY	PRI-FN	377	104.9	4,397.7	5.9	24.7	25.7	188.5	377.0
TRINITY LUTHERAN SEMINARY	PRI-FG	402	338.1	7,552.2	11.6	185.4	192.7	57.4	134.0
UNION EXPERIMENTING C & U	PRI-FG	NO LIBRARY FACILITIES							
UNITED THEOLOGICAL SEM	PRI-FG	276	451.7	7,792.9	8.1	329.1	A	55.2	92.0
U OF AKRON ALL CAMPUSES									
U OF AKRON MAIN CAMPUS	PUB-U	16,010	165.7	4,260.3	5.0	43.2	45.2	194.0	653.4
U AKRON WAYNE GEN-TECH C	PUB-T	387	97.7	2,522.0	3.2	48.8	38.5	258.0	387.0
U OF CINCINNATI ALL CAM									
U OF CINCINNATI MAIN CAM	PUB-U	23,343	202.9	4,274.9	3.2	50.3	19.1	123.5	399.7
U CINCIN CLERMNT GEN-TECH	PUB-T	538	182.0	5,761.3	8.1	23.5	21.6	269.0	538.0
U CINCIN RAYMND WALTERS C	PUB-T	1,821	147.6	3,238.7	6.2	16.6	14.5	165.5	607.0
UNIVERSITY OF DAYTON2/	PRI-FG	8,417	101.9	2,459.4	2.1	50.5	47.7	194.3	480.9
UNIVERSITY OF TOLEDO2/	PUB-U	12,518	182.4	4,041.5	5.2	40.9	24.2	169.1	338.3
URBANA COLLEGE	PRI-FN	582	158.0	4,180.0	3.9	90.9	80.5	145.5	582.0
URSULINE COLLEGE	PRI-FN	607	123.6	1,787.6	3.9	108.2	80.0	129.1	303.5
WALSH COLLEGE	PRI-FN	512	139.0	2,738.0	3.7	130.7	104.6	111.3	256.0
WASHINGTON TECH COLLEGE	PUB-T	339	102.1	2,662.5	3.5	30.8	29.6	339.0	339.0
WILBERFORCE UNIVERSITY	PRI-FN	1,026	113.9	2,489.9	A	37.0	A	171.0	342.0
WILMINGTON COLLEGE	PRI-FN	524	163.9	2,456.6	3.3	129.1	A	99.2	294.2
WITTENBERG UNIVERSITY	PRI-FG	2,352	193.5	3,182.8	3.7	122.7	74.4	138.3	336.0
WOOSTER BUSINESS COLLEGE	PRI-T	D	D	D	D	D	D	D	D
WRIGHT ST U ALL CAMPUSES									
WRIGHT ST U MAIN CAMPUS	PUB-FG	9,938	273.4	6,290.4	5.6	42.2	A	106.0	321.6
WRIGHT ST U WSTN OHIO BR	PUB-T	424	149.0	3,160.8	4.9	49.4	49.3	212.0	424.0
XAVIER UNIVERSITY	PRI-FG	3,774	104.6	2,615.4	3.2	52.3	43.5	281.6	589.6
YOUNGSTOWN ST UNIVERSITY	PUB-FG	14,040	90.9	3,061.3	3.8	29.7	36.2	334.2	1,002.8
OKLAHOMA									
BACONE COLLEGE	PRI-T	407	129.8	1,468.4	2.3	63.0	62.6	135.6	203.5
BARTLESVILLE WESLEYAN C	PRI-FN	455	152.6	2,104.8	4.0	100.5	135.2	252.7	303.3
BETHANY NAZARENE COLLEGE	PRI-FG	1,152	118.2	2,390.3	4.4	82.2	62.0	164.5	384.0
CAMERON UNIVERSITY	PUB-FN	3,675	86.9	1,890.5	4.3	42.4	39.4	282.6	525.0
CARL ALBERT JR COLLEGE	PUB-T	865	70.5	2,651.9	3.4	14.2	6.8	432.5	865.0
CENTRAL STATE UNIVERSITY	PUB-FG	8,081	136.9	3,363.2	6.6	33.0	28.7	168.7	489.7
CLAREMORE JUNIOR COLLEGE	PUB-T	1,425	48.5	1,442.6	2.8	15.7	15.7	431.8	475.0
CONNORS STATE COLLEGE	PUB-T	987	116.2	2,731.4	5.8	30.5	22.9	580.5	580.5
EAST CENTRAL OKLA STATE U	PUB-FG	2,970	105.9	2,401.1	4.6	56.1	105.9	247.5	495.0
EASTERN OKLA ST COLLEGE	PUB-T	1,337	61.7	1,214.4	2.9	26.5	26.5	445.6	1,337.0
EL RENO JUNIOR COLLEGE	PUB-T	625	87.0	2,175.2	A	21.2	20.0	240.3	390.6
FLAMING RAINBOW U	PRI-FN	D	D	D	D	D	D	D	D
HILLSDL FREE WILL BAPT C	PRI-FN	159	61.9	2,463.0	1.8	64.7	62.9	159.0	159.0
LANGSTON UNIVERSITY	PUB-FN	833	130.0	1,525.7	2.9	157.2	126.4	119.0	277.6
MIDWEST CHRISTIAN COLLEGE	PRI-FN	105	219.0	5,749.0	4.7	173.2	169.8	25.0	25.0
MURRAY STATE COLLEGE	PUB-T	893	106.7	2,443.3	4.8	20.1	17.3	137.3	446.5
NTHESTN OKLA AGRL-MECH C	PUB-T	2,332	90.2	2,239.0	4.7	22.0	18.8	194.3	583.0
NORTHEASTERN OKLA STATE U	PUB-FG	4,280	142.1	3,270.0	4.8	42.1	59.0	203.8	428.0
NORTHERN OKLAHOMA COLLEGE	PUB-T	1,372	66.8	1,871.6	4.1	20.8	18.7	381.1	457.3
NTHWSTN OKLA STATE U	PUB-FG	1,478	78.3	1,808.7	4.0	77.4	65.0	335.9	335.9
OKLAHOMA BAPT UNIVERSITY	PRI-FN	1,436	136.6	2,109.6	3.6	85.1	73.4	151.1	359.0
OKLA CHRISTIAN COLLEGE	PRI-FN	1,355	68.4	2,060.8	2.5	64.3	62.9	271.0	677.5
OKLAHOMA CTY STHWSTN C	PRI-T	528	78.2	1,589.7	2.0	77.3	66.1	211.2	211.2
OKLAHOMA CITY UNIVERSITY	PRI-FG	5,644	62.3	A	4.5	37.5	21.3	376.2	627.1
OKLA C OSTED MED AND SURG	PUB-FG	237	850.0	D	4.6	30.9	29.0	33.8	79.0
OKLA PANHANDLE STATE U	PUB-FN	887	131.1	2,475.5	4.5	84.9	85.0	591.3	857.0

SEE FOOTNOTES AT END OF TABLE

Table 3. — Indexes Concerning Operating Expenditures, 1978-79, Bookstock Held at End of Year, 1978-79, and Library Staff (FTE), Fall 1979, College and University Libraries, by State or Other Area and Institution: Aggregate United States

STATE OR OTHER AREA AND INSTITUTION	CON- TROL AND TYPE OF IN- STITU- TION	TOTAL FTE OPENING FALL ENROLL- MENT, FALL 1978	LIBRARY OPERATING EXPENDITURES (IN DOLLARS) 1978-79			BOOKSTOCK HELD AT END OF YEAR 1978-79		FTE STUDENTS PER FTE LIBRARY STAFF FALL 1979	
			PER FTE STU- DENT, FALL 1978	PER FULL- TIME FAC- ULTY MEM- BER, 1978	AS PER- CENT OF GENERAL EXPENDI- TURES, 1978-79	VOLUMES PER FTE STUDENT, FALL 1978	TITLES (INCLU- DING MICRO- FORMS) PER FTE STUDENT 1978	TOTAL STAFF	PROFES- SIONAL STAFF
(1)	(2)	(3)	(4)	(5)	(6)	(7)	(8)	(9)	(10)
OKLAHOMA --CONTINUED									
OKLA SCH BUS ACCT LAW FIN	PRI-T	D	D	D	D	D	D	D	D
OKLA STATE U ALL CAMPUSES	PUB-U								
OKLA STATE U MAIN CAMPUS	PUB-U	20,477	100.0	2,401.5	2.4	62.8	A	262.5	620.5
OKLA STATE U TECH INST	PUB-T	1,414	49.1	1,449.1	2.3	8.4	7.4	353.5	707.0
ORAL ROBERTS UNIVERSITY	PRI-FG	3,628	569.2	A	8.0	136.1	130.7	68.4	196.1
OSCAR ROSE JUNIOR COLLEGE	PUB-T	5,015	99.2	3,363.8	5.9	11.3	10.1	191.4	576.4
PHILLIPS UNIVERSITY	PRI-FG	1,082	248.5	3,683.9	6.6	207.1	196.2	85.1	360.6
SAINT GREGORY'S COLLEGE	PRI-T	256	124.9	3,199.2	3.5	190.8	A	196.9	196.9
SAYRE JUNIOR COLLEGE	PUB-T	225	107.7	2,020.5	6.5	29.4	29.3	225.0	225.0
SEMINOLE JUNIOR COLLEGE	PUB-T	1,054	72.9	1,507.4	4.1	19.4	30.4	329.3	527.0
STHESTN OKLA STATE U	PUB-FG	3,389	44.6	1,103.7	2.0	36.4	23.6	564.8	1,129.6
SOUTH OKLA CTY JR COLLEGE	PUB-T	2,494	96.5	2,561.7	4.0	7.5	6.2	259.7	623.5
STHWSTN OKLA STATE U	PUB-FG	4,082	101.2	2,108.1	4.6	48.1	44.6	291.5	650.3
TULSA JUNIOR COLLEGE	PUB-T	4,576	110.5	3,748.5	4.5	10.7	9.7	217.9	572.0
U OF OKLAHOMA ALL CAM									
U OF OKLA HEALTH SCI CTR	PUB-FG	2,183	298.7	3,047.2	1.6	58.9	37.1	75.2	174.6
U OF OKLAHOMA NORMAN CAM	PUB-U	17,228	147.9	3,720.5	3.9	90.7	43.1	183.0	550.4
U OF SCI & ARTS OF OKLA	PUB-FN	892	151.3	2,499.3	4.0	91.2	54.9	148.6	297.3
UNIVERSITY OF TULSA	PRI-U	4,902	346.3	5,977.5	7.7	105.0	143.8	106.5	233.4
WESTERN OKLAHOMA STATE C	PUB-T	1,006	92.6	2,218.9	5.9	30.3	30.3	251.5	503.0
OREGON									
BASSIST INSTITUTE	PRI-T	D	D	D	D	D	D	D	D
BLUE MTN CMTY COLLEGE	PUB-T	1,192	159.1	2,964.6	4.7	29.7	30.4	163.2	340.5
CENTRAL OREG CMTY COLLEGE	PUB-T	1,154	70.3	1,248.6	1.9	31.1	30.7	164.8	577.0
CHEMEKETA CMTY COLLEGE	PUB-T	4,462	51.4	1,274.8	1.6	9.9	8.3	446.2	1,274.8
CLACKAMAS CMTY COLLEGE	PUB-T	3,411	57.1	1,510.0	1.8	12.0	10.1	415.9	1,065.9
CLATSOP COMMUNITY COLLEGE	PUB-T	906	149.0	3,008.8	4.0	36.1	27.7	164.7	226.5
COLEGIO CESAR CHAVEZ	PRI-FN	D	D	D	D	D	D	D	D
COLUMBIA CHRISTIAN C	PRI-FN	273	117.7	2,922.2	2.0	122.2	159.9	136.5	273.0
CONCORDIA COLLEGE	PRI-FN	291	224.9	3,850.2	4.4	137.8	140.0	97.0	145.5
GEORGE FOX COLLEGE	PRI-FN	670	159.4	3,141.5	4.0	98.3	74.4	121.8	268.0
JUDSON BAPTIST COLLEGE	PRI-T	231	145.5	2,101.5	3.3	109.7	94.9	231.0	231.0
LANE COMMUNITY COLLEGE	PUB-T	4,967	62.3	1,295.0	1.6	10.7	9.1	354.7	1,241.7
LEWIS AND CLARK COLLEGE	PRI-FG	2,656	318.0	6,033.7	6.0	90.0	49.5	106.2	204.3
LINFIELD COLLEGE	PRI-FG	974	167.3	2,432.1	3.4	100.1	94.4	147.5	374.6
LINN-BENTON CMTY COLLEGE	PUB-T	2,504	125.5	2,664.6	3.3	15.3	13.3	185.4	626.0
MARYLHURST ED CENTER	PRI-FN	233	375.2	D	A	462.6	323.4	41.6	75.1
MOUNT ANGEL SEMINARY	PRI-FG	101	1,088.7	10,996.3	A	1,029.7	792.8	16.8	101.0
MOUNT HOOD CMTY COLLEGE	PUB-T	5,272	39.6	1,290.4	1.6	10.2	9.8	554.9	1,817.9
MULTNOMAH SCHOOL OF BIBLE	PRI-FG	643	132.5	3,044.4	4.0	42.0	35.7	136.8	321.5
MUSEUM ART SCHOOL	PRI-FN	169	210.7	2,226.5	6.5	65.3	61.0	112.6	112.6
NTHWST CHRISTIAN COLLEGE	PRI-FN	254	285.4	5,578.0	6.1	177.0	129.0	57.7	127.0
OREGON GRADUATE CENTER	PRI-FG	38	2,352.4	3,724.6	2.5	228.0	156.8	19.0	38.0
OR ST HI ED SYS ALL INST									
EASTERN OREGON ST COLLEGE	PUB-FG	1,418	266.3	4,970.1	6.6	60.7	41.0	111.6	337.6
OREGON COLLEGE OF ED	PUB-FG	2,541	150.3	2,433.5	3.5	63.7	62.4	185.4	423.5
OREGON INST OF TECHNOLOGY	PUB-FN	1,861	112.4	1,453.2	2.7	28.0	14.7	248.1	930.5
OREGON STATE UNIVERSITY	PUB-U	15,717	172.1	3,882.8	2.4	53.7	24.7	197.4	513.6
PORTLAND STATE UNIVERSITY	PUB-FG	10,245	238.8	4,973.8	6.5	56.0	31.3	111.1	335.9
STHN OREGON ST COLLEGE	PUB-FG	3,610	166.8	3,041.3	5.3	50.0	72.1	141.5	361.0
U OF OREGON ALL CAM									
U OF OREGON MAIN CAMPUS	PUB-U	14,642	261.2	5,432.7	5.9	97.3	54.1	118.1	347.7
U OF OREGON HLTH SCI CTR	PUB-FG	1,424	536.0	A	1.7	112.7	37.0	47.3	131.8
PACIFIC UNIVERSITY	PRI-FG	1,014	268.5	3,630.3	4.1	120.5	A	69.4	169.0
PORTLAND CMTY COLLEGE	PUB-T	10,193	55.9	1,857.0	2.0	6.6	3.5	340.9	1,698.0
REED COLLEGE	PRI-FG	1,127	298.9	3,584.0	4.6	243.2	145.2	.0	A
ROGUE COMMUNITY COLLEGE	PUB-T	1,350	66.7	1,766.2	2.4	21.4	20.0	337.5	1,350.0
STHWSTN OREG CMTY COLLEGE	PUB-T	1,277	202.1	4,231.2	6.5	37.2	31.0	128.9	327.4
TREASURE VLY CMTY COLLEGE	PUB-T	1,095	53.6	1,276.1	1.9	24.5	23.6	331.8	608.3
UMPQUA COMMUNITY COLLEGE	PUB-T	1,089	119.5	2,367.7	2.9	39.3	37.9	213.5	544.5
UNIVERSITY OF PORTLAND	PRI-U	2,185	118.1	2,412.1	3.0	82.1	98.0	190.0	435.5
WARNER PACIFIC COLLEGE	PRI-FG	405	217.3	2,839.3	3.4	123.4	112.9	135.0	202.5
WESTERN BAPTIST COLLEGE	PRI-FN	399	168.8	3,963.1	4.3	100.9	76.2	124.6	199.5
WESTERN CONS BAPTIST SEM	PRI-FG	354	267.5	3,507.4	5.2	101.4	81.1	56.1	177.0
WSTN EVANGELICAL SEM	PRI-FG	177	330.8	14,640.0	12.0	207.5	138.0	47.8	147.5
WSTN STATES CHIRPRCTC C	PRI-FG	511	125.4	3,051.8	4.1	13.6	12.0	127.7	255.5

SEE FOOTNOTES AT END OF TABLE

Table 3. — Indexes Concerning Operating Expenditures, 1978-79, Bookstock Held at End of Year, 1978-79, and Library Staff (FTE), Fall 1979, College and University Libraries, by State or Other Area and Institution: Aggregate United States — Continued

STATE OR OTHER AREA AND INSTITUTION (1)	CONTROL AND TYPE OF INSTITUTION (2)	TOTAL FTE OPENING FALL ENROLLMENT, FALL 1978 (3)	LIBRARY OPERATING EXPENDITURES (IN DOLLARS) 1978-79			BOOKSTOCK HELD AT END OF YEAR 1978-79		FTE STUDENTS PER FTE LIBRARY STAFF FALL 1979	
			PER FTE STUDENT, FALL 1978 (4)	PER FULL-TIME FACULTY MEMBER, 1978 (5)	AS PERCENT OF GENERAL EXPENDITURES, 1978-79 (6)	VOLUMES PER FTE STUDENT, FALL 1978 (7)	TITLES (INCLUDING MICROFORMS) PER FTE STUDENT 1978 (8)	TOTAL STAFF (9)	PROFESSIONAL STAFF (10)
OREGON	--CONTINUED								
WILLAMETTE UNIVERSITY2/	PRI-FG	1,803	302.9	5,056.9	5.9	111.2	80.4	85.8	212.1
PENNSYLVANIA									
ACADEMY OF THE NEW CHURCH	PRI-FG	146	607.6	4,436.0	10.2	672.3	465.3	28.6	52.1
ALBRIGHT COLLEGE	PRI-FN	1,360	174.8	2,830.7	4.6	90.1	97.8	129.5	388.5
ALLEGHENY COLLEGE	PRI-FG	1,900	161.4	2,377.9	3.9	138.5	89.5	158.3	380.0
ALLNTWN C SNT FRAN DESALS	PRI-FN	·624	211.3	3,381.1	4.9	148.6	90.7	135.6	312.0
ALLIANCE COLLEGE	PRI-FN	195	262.9	2,229.4	3.9	341.0	253.4	48.7	97.5
ALVERNIA COLLEGE	PRI-FN	384	167.5	5,360.4	6.6	136.6	125.1	69.8	192.0
AMERICAN COLLEGE	PRI-FN	165	270.8	D	A	76.3	52.2	41.2	82.5
BAPT BIBLE COLLEGF OF PA	PRI-FG	762	183.3	3,776.1	5.3	84.9	A	95.2	254.0
BEAVER COLLEGE	PRI-FG	1,006	196.6	4,037.0	3.1	117.8	106.9	89.0	335.3
BLOOMSBURG STATE COLLEGE	PUB-FG	5,317	190.4	3,433.2	4.5	54.9	45.3	221.5	483.3
BRYN MAWR COLLEGE	PRI-FG	1,457	803.0	9,140.8	8.3	376.2	249.0	38.3	81.3
BUCKNELL UNIVERSITY	PRI-FG	3,139	289.4	4,187.2	5.1	125.9	83.3	83.0	224.2
BUCKS COUNTY CMTY COLLEGE	PUB-T	5,376	81.4	2,328.3	3.9	19.1	19.0	260.9	840.0
BUTLER CO CMTY COLLEGE	PUB-T	1,040	127.6	2,709.1	3.7	36.8	30.1	148.5	346.6
CABRINI COLLEGE	PRI-FN	457	162.0	3,220.0	3.3	125.9	117.4	103.8	169.2
CALIFORNIA STATE COLLEGE	PUB-FG	3,658	177.4	2,035.1	3.4	61.9	116.2	166.2	332.5
CARLOW COLLEGE	PRI-FN	810	133.8	2,463.9	2.7	127.0	90.6	94.1	162.0
CARNEGIE-MELLON U	PRI-U	5,060	180.3	2,157.6	1.6	91.9	A	101.2	341.8
CEDAR CREST COLLEGE	PRI-FN	752	234.9	2,995.0	5.0	137.2	101.7	82.6	170.9
CENTER FOR DEGREE STUDIES	PRI-T	D	D	241.5	.2	D	D	D	D
CEN PA BUSINESS SCHOOL	PRI-T	D	D	D	D	D	D	D	D
CHATHAM COLLEGE	PRI-FN	612	196.7	2,562.2	2.8	192.9	136.1	102.0	204.0
CHESTNUT HILL COLLEGE	PRI-FN	706	173.6	6,131.2	4.9	131.2	92.0	108.6	235.3
CHEYNEY STATE COLLEGE	PUB-FG	2,298	178.5	2,229.4	3.4	54.2	62.6	135.1	459.6
CLARION STATE C ALL CAM									
CLARION STATE C MAIN CAM	PUB-FG	4,415	214.3	3,943.2	5.3	67.8	47.9	145.6	310.9
CLARION ST C VENANGO CAM	PUB-T	264	345.6	4,344.79	8.6	88.7	A	85.1	125.7
COLLEGE MISERICORDIA	PRI-FN	828	229.3	2,435.0	5.3	123.6	92.6	80.3	207.0
COMBS COLLEGE OF MUSIC	PRI-FG	86	472.8	A	A	139.5	143.0	86.0	86.0
CC ALLEGHENY CO ALL CAM									
CC ALLEGHENY CO ALLEG CAM	PUB-T	4,696	66.3	1,997.0	2.8	15.5	15.6	229.0	853.8
CC ALLEGHENY CO BOYCE CAM	PUB-T	2,154	63.4	1,731.1	2.4	24.8	18.4	287.2	718.0
CC ALLEGHENY CO NORTH CAM	PUB-T	987	169.3	6,964.0	4.2	12.0	10.8	141.0	329.0
CC ALLEGHENY CO SOUTH CAM	PUB-T	2,090	93.4	2,381.5	3.4	20.2	17.5	240.2	497.6
CMTY COLLEGE OF BEAVER ·CO	PUB-T	1,427	60.1	1,383.7	2.2	24.7	A	407.7	570.8
CMTY COLLEGE DELAWARE CO	PUB-T	3,772	53.8	2,072.1	2.6	13.6	18.9	423.8	943.0
CMTY COLLEGE PHILADELPHIA	PUB-T	8,258	87.2	2,222.5	3.3	9.2	8.4	211.7	688.1
CURTIS INSTITUTE OF MUSIC	PRI-FG	140	570.2	D	A	273.5	245.0	38.8	46.6
DELAWARE VLY C SCI & AGR	PRI-FN	1,438	89.7	1,676.1	2.7	33.3	32.9	167.2	334.4
DICKINSON COLLEGE	PRI-FN	1,710	299.4	4,741.1	5.5	143.6	93.5	83.4	244.2
DICKINSON SCHOOL OF LAW	PRI-FG	471	560.2	21,991.6	18.7	196.6	25.2	72.4	94.2
DREXEL UNIVERSITY	PRI-FG	8,535	141.0	4,269.4	3.2	45.2	29.8	156.6	502.0
THE DROPSIE UNIVERSITY	PRI-FG	52	1,425.1	12,351.3	14.3	2,500.0	2,211.5	18.5	18.5
DUQUESNE UNIVERSITY	PRI-U	6,030	136.3	3,079.8	3.6	78.5	1.5	198.3	538.3
EASTERN BAPTIST THEOL SEM	PRI-FG	191	393.8	6,838.3	7.1	440.6	319.9	47.7	63.6
EASTERN COLLEGE	PRI-FN	615	140.1	2,394.9	2.8	104.8	106.8	120.5	307.5
EAST STROUDSBG ST COLLEGE	PUB-FG	3,479	223.3	3,393.8	5.0	87.6	246.0	165.6	347.9
EDINBORO STATE COLLEGE	PUB-FG	4,953	221.8	2,767.7	4.6	68.0	46.1	159.7	275.1
ELIZABETHTOWN COLLEGE	PRI-FN	1,546	153.7	2,451.0	3.9	82.4	56.0	181.8	454.7
FAITH THEOLOGICAL SEM	PRI-FG	44	44.7	328.0	1.8	510.3	507.3	.0	A
FRANKLIN AND MARSHALL C	PRI-FG	2,279	194.3	3,304.8	3.7	111.7	.4	108.5	284.8
GANNON COLLEGE	PRI-FG	2,554	151.7	4,123.9	4.2	60.5	66.3	154.7	425.6
GENEVA COLLEGE	PRI-FN	1,145	191.2	3,774.8	4.8	104.1	121.6	146.7	266.2
GETTYSBURG COLLEGE	PRI-FN	1,958	216.0	3,088.1	4.7	125.9	108.9	89.0	326.3
GRATZ COLLEGE	PRI-FG	154	312.9	A	A	181.8	162.3	.0	A
GROVE CITY COLLEGE	PRI-FN	2,234	32.7	A	A	56.9	A	167.0	306.3
GWYNEDD-MERCY COLLEGE	PRI-FN	919	132.7	1,768.2	4.8	63.2	63.1	100.8	290.8
HAHNEMANN MEDL C AND HOSP	PRI-FG	1,745	207.3	D	A	39.1	14.4	187.6	238.3
HARCUM JUNIOR COLLEGE	PRI-T	882	64.8	1,788.5	2.7	34.4	33.7	214.7	460.1
HARRISBURG AREA CC	PUB-T	·3,221	116.0	2,790.2	5.4	26.9	A	214.7	460.1
HAVERFORD COLLEGE	PRI-FN	955	546.1	7,345.9	0.6	433.5	375.8	41.5	112.3
HOLY FAMILY COLLEGE	PRI-FN	693	134.0	3,870.2	5.0	127.6	100.7	97.6	231.0
IMMACULATA COLLEGE	PRI-FN	760	184.8	10,035.7	5.3	151.8	132.2	84.4	190.0

SEE FOOTNOTES AT END OF TABLE

172

Table 3. — Indexes Concerning Operating Expenditures, 1978-79, Bookstock Held at End of Year, 1978-79, and Library Staff (FTE), Fall 1979, College and University Libraries, by State or Other Area and Institution: Aggregate United States — Continued

STATE OR OTHER AREA AND INSTITUTION	CONTROL AND TYPE OF INSTITUTION	TOTAL FTE OPENING FALL ENROLLMENT, FALL 1978	LIBRARY OPERATING EXPENDITURES (IN DOLLARS) 1978-79			BOOKSTOCK HELD AT END OF YEAR 1978-79		FTE STUDENTS PER FTE LIBRARY STAFF FALL 1979	
			PER FTE STUDENT, FALL 1978	PER FULL-TIME FACULTY MEMBER, FALL 1978	AS PER-CENT OF GENERAL EXPENDITURES, 1978-79	VOLUMES PER FTE STUDENT, FALL 1978	TITLES (INCLUDING MICROFORMS) PER FTE STUDENT 1978	TOTAL STAFF	PROFESSIONAL STAFF
(1)	(2)	(3)	(4)	(5)	(6)	(7)	(8)	(9)	(10)
PENNSYLVANIA	--CONTINUED								
INDIANA U OF PENNSYLVANIA	PUB-FG	10,819	145.4	2,810.9	4.0	44.4	30.2	327.8	540.9
JUNIATA COLLEGE	PRI-FN	1,125	185.9	3,032.0	3.5	114.6	91.8	132.3	281.2
KEYSTONE JUNIOR COLLEGE	PRI-T	721	107.7	2,158.8	2.6	46.3	44.3	138.6	360.5
KING'S COLLEGE	PRI-FN	1,797	176.7	3,528.7	4.9	83.7	71.8	108.9	359.4
KUTZTOWN STATE COLLEGE	PUB-FG	4,297	180.9	2,944.9	4.5	62.2	25.2	195.3	358.0
LACKAWANNA JUNIOR COLLEGE	PRI-T	1,092	67.0	2,713.1	4.4	21.9	15.4	248.1	420.0
LAFAYETTE COLLEGE	PRI-FN	2,159	277.8	3,973.3	4.8	163.6	156.4	89.1	227.2
LANCASTER BIBLE COLLEGE	PRI-FN	401	144.0	A	5.3	65.3	A	111.3	154.2
LANCASTER THEOLOGICAL SEM	PRI-FG	162	649.3	10,519.2	12.3	755.5	754.2	40.5	81.0
LA ROCHE COLLEGE	PRI-FN	775	180.7	4,668.4	5.7	64.5	48.4	110.7	387.5
LA SALLE COLLEGE	PRI-FG	4,831	114.6	3,111.1	4.0	51.9	37.3	185.0	513.9
LEBANON VALLEY COLLEGE	PRI-FN	1,056	166.7	2,200.6	3.8	104.6	101.2	182.0	352.0
LEHIGH CO CMTY COLLEGE	PUB-T	1,878	66.9	1,876.5	2.3	22.2	18.1	275.1	939.0
LEHIGH UNIVERSITY	PRI-FG	5,326	226.7	3,692.7	3.3	131.3	52.7	102.4	295.8
LINCOLN UNIVERSITY	PUB-FG	1,113	254.8	4,298.4	4.0	122.2	102.0	73.2	139.1
LOCK HAVEN STATE COLLEGE	PUB-FG	2,158	223.1	3,127.0	4.7	131.8	80.5	143.8	269.7
LUTH THEOL SEM GETTYSBURG	PRI-FG	251	507.2	8,487.7	10.9	471.2	340.1	37.4	125.5
LUTHERAN THEOL SEM PHILA	PRI-FG	172	735.7	9,734.5	12.0	739.7	592.4	29.6	43.0
LUZERNE CO CMTY COLLEGE	PUB-T	2,120	76.7	2,502.5	3.3	24.5	22.9	286.4	1,060.0
LYCOMING COLLEGE	PRI-FN	1,130	197.7	3,060.4	4.9	117.0	84.1	118.9	322.8
MANOR JUNIOR COLLEGE	PRI-T	212	140.5	2,483.6	3.9	102.0	10.3	141.3	212.0
MANSFIELD STATE COLLEGE	PUB-FG	2,404	277.1	3,347.9	4.9	73.0	51.3	104.5	184.9
MARY IMMACULATE SEMINARY	PRI-FG	52	956.9	D	10.5	1,089.4	692.7	34.6	52.0
MARYWOOD COLLEGE	PRI-FG	2,188	168.3	3,758.2	4.9	69.8	50.6	100.8	218.8
THE MEDL COLLEGE OF PA	PRI-FG	568	445.2	D	1.3	54.5	A	52.1	81.1
MERCYHURST COLLEGE	PRI-FG	1,148	88.4	1,209.2	2.0	66.0	66.2	176.6	382.6
MESSIAH COLLEGE	PRI-FN	1,048	188.9	3,883.7	4.4	91.5	80.4	180.6	349.3
MILLERSVILLE ST COLLEGE	PUB-FG	5,081	183.0	3,196.1	4.6	60.4	43.5	188.1	317.5
MONTGOMERY CO COMMUNITY C	PUB-T	4,168	91.9	2,456.3	4.3	18.3	17.2	177.3	453.0
MOORE COLLEGE OF ART	PRI-FN	520	201.5	2,757.5	4.6	59.6	44.2	96.2	260.0
MORAVIAN COLLEGE	PRI-FN	1,412	169.4	2,990.5	4.1	114.1	90.1	.0	A
MOUNT ALOYSIUS JR COLLEGE	PRI-T	482	212.3	3,010.5	5.1	62.7	57.3	64.2	241.0
MUHLENBERG COLLEGE	PRI-FN	1,572	188.1	3,286.1	4.2	112.3	76.3	141.6	341.7
NEW SCHOOL OF MUSIC	PRI-FN	83	188.4	3,129.0	3.5	18.4	15.1	83.0	166.0
NORTHAMPTON CO AREA CC	PRI-T	2,442	106.0	2,909.3	4.4	21.0	16.8	257.0	610.5
NORTHEASTERN CHRISTIAN JC	PRI-T	193	286.3	4,605.1	6.1	130.8	113.4	107.2	128.6
OUR LADY ANGELS COLLEGE	PRI-FN	489	304.1	8,262.7	8.5	133.1	103.6	56.8	163.0
PEIRCE JUNIOR COLLEGE	PRI-T	1,239	105.2	2,835.2	3.9	28.1	27.6	154.8	309.7
PA COLLEGE OF OPTOMETRY	PRI-FG	572	103.7	1,799.0	1.3	25.0	7.8	286.0	572.0
PA COLLEGE PODIATRIC MED	PRI-FG	463	200.7	3,442.4	2.0	25.4	15.2	132.2	231.5
PA STATE U ALL CAMPUSES									
PA STATE U MAIN CAMPUS	PUB-U	32,420	195.3	4,270.2	3.2	48.0	37.4	121.8	450.2
PA STATE U ALLENTOWN CAM	PUB-T	336	197.9	6,649.7	5.6	68.8	58.4	224.0	336.0
PA STATE U ALTOONA CAM	PUB-T	1,731	66.2	1,592.3	2.7	23.3	19.8	346.2	865.5
PA STATE U BEAVER CAMPUS	PUB-T	1,082	75.8	1,784.2	2.8	26.7	22.6	541.0	1,082.0
PA ST U BEHREND COLLEGE	PUB-FG	1,522	91.4	1,617.8	3.0	33.3	28.3	304.4	761.0
PA STATE U BERKS CAMPUS	PUB-T	923	108.6	2,572.2	4.0	32.5	27.6	230.7	461.5
PA STATE U CAPITOL CAMPUS	PUB-FG	2,040	196.7	3,344.4	4.6	68.4	64.7	2,040.0	4,080.0
PA STATE U DELAWARE CAM	PUB-T	1,237	60.7	1,598.5	2.3	21.8	18.5	412.3	618.5
PA STATE U DU BOIS CAMPUS	PUB-T	598	83.5	1,783.9	3.2	47.0	39.9	299.0	598.0
PA STATE U FAYETTE CAMPUS	PUB-T	745	115.6	2,208.4	3.4	43.4	36.9	186.2	745.0
PA STATE U HAZLETON CAM	PUB-T	958	92.5	2,161.7	3.8	33.8	28.7	239.5	958.0
PA ST U HERSHEY MEDL CTR	PUB-FG	495	741.8	D	1.7	168.6	31.7	38.0	123.7
PA STATE U MCKEESPORT CAM	PUB-T	1,199	57.8	1,387.2	2.2	22.8	19.4	399.6	1,199.0
PA STATE U MONT ALTO CAM	PUB-T	803	89.6	2,180.3	3.6	34.9	29.7	267.6	803.0
PA ST U NEW KENSINGTN CAM	PUB-T	986	79.8	2,020.0	2.9	25.3	21.5	328.6	986.0
PA STATE U OGONTZ CAMPUS	PUB-T	2,209	54.6	1,723.5	2.3	20.0	17.0	368.1	1,104.5
PA ST U RADNOR CENTER	PUB-FG	126	469.7	11,838.4	10.5	81.0	68.7	126.0	126.0
PA STATE U SCHUYLKILL CAM	PUB-T	645	90.2	2,156.2	3.3	40.9	34.7	322.5	645.0
PA ST U SHENANGO VLY CAM	PUB-T	670	86.7	1,659.9	2.9	25.5	20.2	223.3	670.0
PA ST U WILKES-BARRE CAM	PUB-T	545	74.3	1,501.4	2.3	27.6	23.5	545.0	A
PA ST U WRTHGTN SCRTN CAM	PUB-T	892	86.2	1,972.9	3.5	33.2	28.2	297.3	892.0
PA STATE U YORK CAMPUS	PUB-T	839	68.5	1,798.1	2.6	22.3	19.0	419.5	839.0
PHILA COLLEGE OF ART	PRI-FG	1,153	113.0	1,916.4	2.3	38.9	29.8	128.1	384.3
PHILA COLLEGE OF BIBLE	PRI-FN	498	173.9	3,207.6	4.4	88.7	73.9	124.5	166.0
PHILA COLLEGE OSTEO MED	PRI-FG	818	360.2	D	2.6	48.8	18.7	81.3	409.0

SEE FOOTNOTES AT END OF TABLE

Table 3. — Indexes Concerning Operating Expenditures, 1978-79, Bookstock Held at End of Year, 1978-79, and Library Staff (FTE), Fall 1979, College and University Libraries, by State or Other Area and Institution: Aggregate United States — Continued

STATE OR OTHER AREA AND INSTITUTION (1)	CONTROL AND TYPE OF INSTITUTION (2)	TOTAL FTE OPENING FALL ENROLLMENT, FALL 1978 (3)	LIBRARY OPERATING EXPENDITURES (IN DOLLARS) 1978-79			BOOKSTOCK HELD AT END OF YEAR 1978-79		FTE STUDENTS PER FTE LIBRARY STAFF FALL 1979	
			PER FTE STUDENT, FALL 1978 (4)	PER FULL-TIME FACULTY MEMBER, 1978 (5)	AS PERCENT OF GENERAL EXPENDITURES, 1978-79 (6)	VOLUMES PER FTE STUDENT, FALL 1978 (7)	TITLES (INCLUDING MICROFORMS) PER FTE STUDENT 1978 (8)	TOTAL STAFF (9)	PROFESSIONAL STAFF (10)
PENNSYLVANIA	--CONTINUED								
PHILA C PERFORMING ARTS	PRI-FG	314	296.6	7,763.1	1.9	44.5	40.5	62.8	62.8
PHILA COLLEGE PHAR & SCI	PRI-FG	1,093	344.9	5,712.8	6.9	66.2	23.8	76.4	176.2
PHILA C TEXTILES AND SCI	PRI-FG	1,934	104.1	2,518.1	3.4	33.4	33.7	203.5	429.7
PINEBROOK JUNIOR COLLEGE	PRI-T	76	565.1	42,951.0	12.3	372.1	289.4	76.0	76.0
PITTSBURGH THEOL SEMINARY	PRI-FG	220	714.7	6,837.1	8.3	848.7	A	36.6	220.0
POINT PARK COLLEGE	PRI-FN	1,550	84.5	1,725.3	2.1	63.7	46.1	221.4	387.5
READING AREA CMTY COLLEGE	PUB-T	898	119.2	4,117.0	3.3	16.2	14.4	256.5	449.0
REFORMED PRESB THEOL SEM	PRI-FG	39	396.3	3,864.7	10.3	524.4	418.4	32.5	39.0
ROBERT MORRIS COLLEGE	PRI-FG	3,225	148.0	5,616.9	6.4	26.2	19.6	136.6	424.3
ROSEMONT COLLEGE	PRI-FN	532	239.2	3,535.7	4.9	242.8	150.4	74.9	152.0
SNT CHARLES BORROMEO SEM	PRI-FG	278	655.8	60,777.6	A	629.4	598.9	25.5	55.6
SAINT FRANCIS COLLEGE	PRI-FG	1,292	148.2	3,039.4	4.6	111.2	76.9	103.3	323.0
SAINT JOSEPH'S UNIVERSITY	PRI-FG	3,778	123.1	3,693.4	4.1	47.9	38.1	145.8	406.2
SAINT VINCENT COLLEGE	PRI-FN		SEE SNT VINCENT C-SEM JT LIB						
SNT VINCENT C-SEM JT LIB	PRI-FN	D	D	D	D	D	D	D	D
SAINT VINCENT SEMINARY	PRI-FG		SEE SNT VINCENT C-SEM JT LIB						
SETON HILL COLLEGE	PRI-FN	786	140.5	2,253.8	3.0	85.9	72.7	151.1	262.0
SHIPPENSBURG ST COLLEGE	PUB-FG	4,906	180.1	3,237.1	4.4	69.9	68.3	158.2	408.8
SLIPPERY ROCK ST COLLEGE	PUB-FG	5,247	201.6	3,435.3	4.9	77.7	68.3	190.8	437.2
SPRING GARDEN COLLEGE	PRI-FN	799	82.0	1,141.0	1.9	22.8	21.6	396.5	396.5
SUSQUEHANNA UNIVERSITY	PRI-FN	1,490	199.1	2,937.3	4.6	72.5	57.8	120.1	372.5
SWARTHMORE COLLEGE	PRI-FG	1,251	676.6	6,133.9	7.6	358.7	253.2	33.0	96.2
TALMUD YESHIVA OF PHILA	PRI-FG	D	D	D	D	D	D	D	D
TEMPLE UNIVERSITY	PUB-U	23,728	208.1	3,521.0	3.0	69.0	44.4	110.3	296.2
THEOL SEM REFORMD EPIS CH	PRI-FG	75	145.6	2,730.5	10.2	268.8	240.9	75.0	75.0
THIEL COLLEGE	PRI-FN	1,068	166.8	2,969.2	A	100.7	77.8	152.5	267.0
THOMAS JEFF UNIVERSITY	PRI-FG	1,670	424.7	9,585.8	1.9	70.4	30.3	54.5	167.0
UNITED WESLEYAN COLLEGE	PRI-FN	204	69.5	886.6	2.0	137.6	120.6	156.9	185.4
U OF PENNSYLVANIA	PRI-U	17,147	447.8	7,851.3	3.1	177.4	99.8	63.9	188.4
U OF PITTSBG ALL CAMPUSES									
U OF PITTSBG MAIN CAMPUS	PUB-U	21,780	253.5	4,018.6	3.2	87.8	61.8	87.8	228.5
U OF PITTSBG BRADFORD CAM	PUB-FN	669	145.2	2,259.7	4.5	70.1	64.6	176.0	371.6
U OF PITTSBG GREENSBG CAM	PUB-T	781	118.1	2,977.4	6.1	59.6	58.5	260.3	390.5
U OF PITTSBG JOHNSTWN CAM	PUB-FN	2,553	123.7	2,678.0	4.7	29.0	23.7	145.8	729.4
U OF PITTSBG TITUSVL CAM	PUB-T	390	127.5	3,826.6	5.0	70.7	54.8	229.4	229.4
UNIVERSITY OF SCRANTON	PRI-FG	3,566	101.2	2,655.1	3.6	53.1	32.7	181.0	396.2
URSINUS COLLEGE	PRI-FN	1,273	166.1	3,065.4	4.5	108.2	80.2	123.5	212.1
VALLEY FORGE CHRISTIAN C	PRI-FN	571	71.3	3,702.8	2.5	51.3	44.2	190.3	571.0
VALLEY FORGE MILITARY JC	PRI-T	114	502.5	8,185.0	10.8	519.4	516.5	38.0	57.0
VILLA MARIA COLLEGE	PRI-FN	493	107.6	1,360.3	2.2	86.5	86.5	176.0	246.5
VILLANOVA UNIVERSITY	PRI-U	7,554	170.2	3,239.5	4.4	84.3	51.4	140.4	295.0
WASHINGTON JEFF COLLEGE	PRI-FG	1,095	176.1	2,572.2	3.8	153.0	125.5	128.8	365.0
WAYNESBURG COLLEGE	PRI-FN	787	172.5	2,771.0	4.0	143.2	128.3	196.7	262.3
WEST CHESTER ST COLLEGE	PUB-FG	7,203	173.0	2,658.0	4.2	51.4	44.1	234.6	490.0
WESTMINSTER COLLEGE	PRI-FG	1,696	191.8	3,159.2	4.5	110.1	74.1	128.4	339.2
WESTMINSTER THEOL SEM	PRI-FG	327	415.8	12,362.7	11.3	255.3	246.3	61.6	163.5
WESTMORELAND COUNTY CC	PUB-T	1,492	112.1	3,485.5	4.4	17.9	18.8	204.3	497.3
WIDENER C OF WIDENER U	PRI-FG	2,860	139.4	3,798.8	3.7	53.7	29.0	133.0	336.4
WILKES COLLEGE	PRI-FG	2,260	164.4	2,545.6	3.8	73.1	74.0	135.3	358.7
WILLIAMSPORT AREA CC	PUB-T	2,830	57.4	973.7	1.4	14.8	12.1	353.7	707.5
WILSON COLLEGE	PRI-FN	209	526.0	2,681.4	4.7	725.4	502.7	53.5	104.5
YESHIVATH BETH MOSHE	PRI-FG	D	D	D	D	D	D	D	D
YORK COLLEGE PENNSYLVANIA	PRI-FG	2,044	129.6	2,944.2	5.4	49.3	44.1	163.5	511.0
RHODE ISLAND									
BARRINGTON COLLEGE	PRI-FN	476	110.3	1,500.0	2.0	137.6	129.5	190.4	215.3
BROWN UNIVERSITY	PRI-FG	6,637	519.9	7,668.0	5.7	246.5	A	52.8	144.9
BRYANT C BUSINESS ADMIN	PRI-FG	3,683	74.7	3,201.9	2.8	24.1	17.2	409.2	736.6
JOHNSON & WALES COLLEGE	PRI-FN	4,545	16.3	A	.8	3.1	2.9	2,272.5	2,272.5
NEW ENG INST TECHNOLOGY	PRI-T	476	43.2	1,143.0	2.0	23.3	16.9	476.0	476.0
PROVIDENCE COLLEGE	PRI-FG	4,482	122.2	3,534.6	A	50.7	30.5	169.1	574.6
RHODE ISLAND COLLEGE	PUB-FG	5,805	149.0	2,403.1	A	41.3	35.8	207.3	645.0
RHODE ISLAND JR COLLEGE	PUB-T	6,622	78.2	1,798.4	2.7	10.9	9.5	323.0	513.3
RI SCHOOL OF DESIGN	PRI-FG	1,438	126.4	2,392.4	A	39.6	22.3	139.6	479.3
ROGER WILLIAMS C ALL CAM									
ROGER WILLIAMS C MAIN CAM	PRI-FN	1,880	143.6	3,376.5	5.0	37.8	33.0	151.6	376.0

SEE FOOTNOTES AT END OF TABLE

174

Table 3. — Indexes Concerning Operating Expenditures, 1978-79, Bookstock Held at End of Year, 1978-79, and Library Staff (FTE), Fall 1979, College and University Libraries, by State or Other Area and Institution: Aggregate United States — Continued

STATE OR OTHER AREA AND INSTITUTION	CONTROL AND TYPE OF INSTITUTION	TOTAL FTE OPENING FALL ENROLLMENT, FALL 1978	LIBRARY OPERATING EXPENDITURES (IN DOLLARS) 1978-79			BOOKSTOCK HELD AT END OF YEAR 1978-79		FTE STUDENTS PER FTE LIBRARY STAFF FALL 1979	
			PER FTE STUDENT, FALL 1978	PER FULL-TIME FACULTY MEMBER, FALL 1978	AS PERCENT OF GENERAL EXPENDITURES, 1978-79	VOLUMES PER FTE STUDENT, FALL 1978	TITLES (INCLUDING MICROFORMS) PER FTE STUDENT 1978	TOTAL STAFF	PROFESSIONAL STAFF
(1)	(2)	(3)	(4)	(5)	(6)	(7)	(8)	(9)	(10)
RHODE ISLAND	--CONTINUED								
ROGER WILLIAMS C PROV BR	PRI-FN		NO LIBRARY FACILITIES			55.6	40.9	167.0	401.0
SALVE REGINA-NEWPORT C	PRI-FG	1,203	95.7	2,172.3	2.9	60.4	59.8	168.9	475.7
U OF RHODE ISLAND	PUB-U	11,086	171.2	2,692.5	2.6				
SOUTH CAROLINA									
AIKEN TECHNICAL COLLEGE	PUB-T	776	102.6	A	3.9	18.2	15.9	115.8	298.4
ALLEN UNIVERSITY	PRI-FN	408	140.8	A		94.8	74.0	170.0	255.0
ANDERSON COLLEGE	PRI-T	1,077	73.2	1,877.6	3.4	25.3	23.2	239.3	538.5
BAPT COLLEGE AT CHASTN	PRI-FN	1,776	205.1	4,671.4	5.6	53.1	48.4	77.2	222.0
BEAUFORT TECH COLLEGE	PUB-T	733	127.8	1,912.4	4.3	17.3	16.4	146.6	366.5
BENEDICT COLLEGE	PRI-FN	1,753	165.4	2,762.5	A	68.3	64.9	146.0	194.7
BOB JONES UNIVERSITY	PRI-FG	4,179	37.0	A	A	39.1	29.7	225.8	398.0
CENTRAL WESLEYAN COLLEGE	PRI-FN	377	211.7	3,193.6	5.8	126.2	122.6	78.5	150.8
CHESTERFLD-MARLBORO TECH	PUB-T	429	94.6	1,623.6	3.4	35.7	33.2	195.0	429.0
CITADEL MILITARY C OF SC	PUB-FG	2,502	169.4	2,717.7	3.7	66.0	84.0	147.1	500.4
CLAFLIN COLLEGE	PRI-FN	847	277.7	3,856.6	6.6	137.6	132.0	73.6	211.7
CLEMSON UNIVERSITY	PUB-U	10,023	197.4	3,111.4	2.4	49.6	28.9	132.7	527.5
CLINTON JUNIOR COLLEGE	PRI-T	122	79.0	A		24.5	21.3	61.0	61.0
COKER COLLEGE	PRI-FN	278	243.7	1,993.2	2.8	218.1	178.9	81.7	139.0
COLLEGE OF CHARLESTON	PUB-FG	4,177	148.1	3,814.8	4.8	47.2	A	126.5	298.3
COLUMBIA BIBLE COLLEGE	PRI-FG	675	191.9	A	6.4	72.9	56.4	84.3	337.5
COLUMBIA COLLEGE	PRI-FN	905	216.0	3,314.6	5.9	112.6	76.9	37.8	226.2
COLUMBIA JUNIOR C	PRI-T	927	14.7	A	2.2	4.5	2.5	713.0	713.0
CONVERSE COLLEGE	PRI-FG	815	229.6	2,793.7	4.3	138.6	133.8	85.7	163.0
DENMARK TECHNICAL COLLEGE	PUB-T	491	157.4	1,756.8	5.6	27.6	16.9	122.7	245.5
ERSKINE C AND SEMINARY	PRI-FG	692	170.7	2,461.3	4.6	160.1	A	130.5	629.0
FLORENCE DARLINGTON TECH	PUB-T	1,934	41.7	939.8	1.9	13.3	12.5	483.5	967.0
FRANCIS MARION COLLEGE	PUB-FG	2,020	274.4	6,025.1	8.9	79.4	99.8	96.1	252.5
FRIENDSHIP COLLEGE	PRI-T	165	416.2	6,244.3	8.9	57.1	56.3	41.2	55.0
FURMAN UNIVERSITY	PRI-FG	2,507	175.2	3,230.5	4.0	98.7	66.7	147.4	358.1
GREENVILLE TECH COLLEGE	PUB-T	3,706	53.1	1,185.8	1.9	8.8	7.5	390.1	823.5
HORRY-GEORGETOWN TECH C	PUB-T	1,048	70.5	1,803.8	3.2	16.6	14.3	436.6	748.5
LANDER COLLEGE	PUB-FN	1,445	245.4	4,171.8	7.8	60.3	60.8	111.1	321.1
LIMESTONE COLLEGE	PRI-FN	1,075	50.6	1,755.3	2.1	49.2	39.6	275.6	537.5
LUTHERAN THEOL STHN SEM	PRI-FG	130	685.2	8,907.9	11.2	526.3	A	65.0	65.0
MEDICAL UNIVERSITY OF SC	PUB-GA	2,044	441.9	5,611.1	1.5	62.6	48.9	59.2	151.4
MIDLANDS TECH COLLEGE	PUB-T	4,248	51.7	1,099.5	2.1	11.2	10.8	369.3	566.4
MORRIS COLLEGE	PRI-FN	634	199.7	3,724.8	4.8	96.8	72.0	105.6	211.3
NEWBERRY COLLEGE	PRI-FN	799	202.9	3,059.0	4.6	79.8	57.7	96.2	242.1
NORTH GREENVILLE COLLEGE	PRI-T	518	109.0	2,092.6	4.1	65.2	55.4	129.5	259.0
ORANGEBURG CALHOUN TECH C	PUB-T	1,115	140.3	3,328.5	5.3	21.9	22.1	119.8	318.5
PIEDMONT TECH COLLEGE	PUB-T	1,436	81.7	2,553.1	4.2	12.2	11.8	191.4	478.6
PRESBYTERIAN COLLEGE	PRI-FN	873	185.5	3,520.4	4.4	125.1	116.9	124.7	436.5
RICE COLLEGE	PRI-T	D	D	D	D	D	D	D	D
RUTLEDGE COLLEGE	PRI-T	D	D	D	D	D	D	D	D
SC STATE COLLEGE	PUB-FG	3,060	139.3	2,002.3	3.0	70.0	59.0	218.5	332.5
SPARTANBURG METH COLLEGE	PRI-T	950	60.9	2,068.6	2.6	28.3	21.2	271.4	475.0
SPARTANBURG TECH COLLEGE	PUB-T	1,352	56.6	1,196.4	A	15.9	14.8	386.2	1,352.0
SUMTER AREA TECH COLLEGE	PUB-T	1,068	70.9	1,762.8	3.0	17.2	17.2	427.2	712.0
TRI-COUNTY TECH COLLEGE	PUB-T	1,747	74.4	1,757.2	2.6	17.2	17.2	207.9	873.5
TRIDENT TECHNICAL COLLEGE	PUB-T	3,714	72.8	2,529.2	3.3	12.2	A	281.3	599.0
U OF SC ALL CAMPUSES									
U OF SC AT AIKEN	PUB-FN	1,290	273.2	4,763.8	8.7	44.0	38.1	135.7	430.0
U OF SC AT BEAUFORT	PUB-T	300	283.7	5,674.5	12.2	97.7	A	100.0	200.0
U OF SC COASTAL CAROLINA	PUB-FN	1,542	143.3	2,600.1	4.9	37.0	A	220.2	514.0
U OF SC AT COLUMBIA	PUB-U	19,823	203.5	4,459.6	4.2	66.6	32.8	123.8	353.9
U OF SC AT LANCASTER	PUB-T	508	118.6	2,152.1	4.8	63.5	51.8	153.9	508.0
U OF SC AT SALKEHATCHIE	PUB-T	243	198.3	4,820.3	5.5	104.9	79.3	162.0	243.0
U OF SC AT SPARTANBURG	PUB-FN	1,751	153.0	3,842.7	4.9	29.5	28.1	159.1	350.2
U OF SC AT SUMTER	PUB-T	642	155.9	4,005.2	7.3	A	A	142.6	321.0
U OF SC AT UNION	PUB-T	195	246.5	4,370.6	8.0	126.8	105.1	97.5	195.0
VOORHEES COLLEGE	PRI-FN	794	149.4	2,580.0	2.8	96.8	95.1	158.8	264.6
WILLIAMSBURG TECH C	PUB-T	373	180.2	2,490.5	4.6	25.9	22.9	106.5	373.0
WINTHROP COLLEGE	PUB-FG	3,675	201.8	3,726.8	5.5	73.8	53.3	118.5	282.6
WOFFORD COLLEGE	PRI-FN	963	213.0	3,871.0	A	129.6	101.8	101.3	175.0
YORK TECHNICAL COLLEGE	PUB-T	1,235	47.7	1,092.8	2.3	13.5	13.3	494.0	1,235.0

SEE FOOTNOTES AT END OF TABLE

175

Table 3. — Indexes Concerning Operating Expenditures, 1978-79, Bookstock Held at End of Year, 1978-79, and Library Staff (FTE), Fall 1979, College and University Libraries, by State or Other Area and Institution: Aggregate United States — Continued

STATE OR OTHER AREA AND INSTITUTION (1)	CONTROL AND TYPE OF INSTITUTION (2)	TOTAL FTE OPENING FALL ENROLLMENT, FALL 1978 (3)	LIBRARY OPERATING EXPENDITURES (IN DOLLARS) 1978-79			BOOKSTOCK HELD AT END OF YEAR 1978-79		FTE STUDENTS PER FTE LIBRARY STAFF FALL 1979	
			PER FTE STUDENT, FALL 1978 (4)	PER FULL-TIME FACULTY MEMBER, 1978 (5)	AS PERCENT OF GENERAL EXPENDITURES, 1978-79 (6)	VOLUMES PER FTE STUDENT, FALL 1978 (7)	TITLES (INCLUDING MICROFORMS) PER FTE STUDENT 1978 (8)	TOTAL STAFF (9)	PROFESSIONAL STAFF (10)
SOUTH DAKOTA									
AUGUSTANA COLLEGE	PRI-FG	2,037	163.6	2,732.9	3.9	73.8	61.6	185.1	407.4
BLACK HILLS STATE COLLEGE	PUB-FG	2,706	69.1	2,079.5	2.9	37.9	35.9	281.8	751.6
DAKOTA STATE COLLEGE	PUB-FN	767	149.6	2,495.4	4.1	100.0	96.6	153.4	255.6
DAKOTA WESLEYAN U	PRI-FN	475	146.5	2,175.3	4.4	143.1	136.8	158.3	316.6
FREEMAN JUNIOR COLLEGE	PRI-T	46	587.1	2,701.1	7.6	315.9	281.2	30.6	30.6
HURON COLLEGE	PRI-FN	290	90.6	973.5	2.2	206.6	206.4	161.1	193.3
MOUNT MARTY COLLEGE	PRI-FN	516	218.0	3,515.5	5.0	133.4	110.9	103.2	172.0
NATIONAL COLLEGE	PRI-FN	2,640	39.3	3,714.5	2.0	7.7	6.8	613.9	2,640.0
NORTH AMERICAN BAPT SEM	PRI-FG	101	556.6	6,246.8	7.3	522.7	A	36.0	72.1
NORTHERN STATE COLLEGE	PUB-FG	2,075	123.8	2,215.1	3.6	58.3	58.9	230.5	415.0
OGLALA SIOUX CC	PUB-T	D	D	D	D	D	D	D	D
PRESENTATION COLLEGE	PRI-T	298	171.1	2,039.7	3.7	107.6	92.2	99.3	149.0
SINTE GLESKA COLLEGE	PRI-FN	216	480.4	A	6.2	78.7	78.7	43.2	43.2
SIOUX FALLS COLLEGE	PRI-FN	624	135.3	2,558.4	4.2	122.3	109.0	178.2	312.0
SD SCH MINES & TECHNOLOGY	PUB-FG	1,586	143.5	2,528.9	2.7	54.1	32.2	178.2	793.0
SD STATE UNIVERSITY	PUB-U	6,321	124.0	2,614.7	2.2	48.8	28.0	245.9	590.7
U OF SD ALL CAMPUSES									
U OF SD MAIN CAMPUS	PUB-U	5,503	225.2	4,490.2	4.4	81.2	40.3	107.0	314.4
U OF SD AT SPRINGFIELD	PUB-FN	771	224.6	2,886.5	5.6	103.4	98.8	171.3	428.3
YANKTON COLLEGE	PRI-FN	268	188.5	1,742.2	3.1	241.2	147.3	103.0	268.0
TENNESSEE									
AMER BAPT THEOL SEM	PRI-FN	114	118.8	3,388.2	3.1	141.3	A	67.0	81.4
AQUINAS JUNIOR COLLEGE	PRI-T	206	248.1	7,303.4	A	103.3	102.9	103.0	103.0
BELMONT COLLEGE	PRI-FN	1,098	121.8	2,090.0	3.6	68.6	57.8	189.3	274.5
BETHEL COLLEGE	PRI-FN	324	189.7	3,074.7	4.1	207.2	151.0	95.2	162.0
BRISTOL COLLEGE	PRI-T	168	A	A	A	12.0	A	.0	A
BRYAN COLLEGE	PRI-FN	530	150.7	2,496.2	4.1	114.1	94.4	132.5	265.0
CARSON-NEWMAN COLLEGE	PRI-FN	1,566	103.5	1,843.4	3.3	87.5	68.9	208.8	348.0
CHRISTIAN BROS COLLEGE	PRI-FN	1,160	79.6	1,514.9	2.4	68.6	58.2	210.9	290.0
CUMBERLAND COLLEGE TENN	PRI-T	333	127.9	2,663.1	4.4	85.7	85.4	158.5	302.7
DAVID LIPSCOMB COLLEGE	PRI-FN	2,098	115.7	2,556.3	4.0	50.5	A	196.0	349.6
DRAUGHON'S JR COLLEGE	PRI-T	849	12.0	A	A	1.7	1.6	849.0	849.0
DRAUGHON'S JC BUSINESS	PRI-T	D	D	D	D	D	D	D	D
DRAUGHONS JC BUSINESS	PRI-T	395	22.8	A	1.4	5.7	4.9	453.7	453.7
EDMONDSON JR COLLEGE	PRI-T	363	30.5	A	A	2.7	2.6	453.7	453.7
EMMANUEL SCH OF RELIGION	PRI-FG	85	729.6	7,752.6	A	518.7	318.3	24.2	42.5
FISK UNIVERSITY	PRI-FG	D	D	D	D	D	D	D	D
FREED-HARDEMAN COLLEGE	PRI-FN	1,372	142.7	3,263.7	4.9	61.4	52.7	137.2	343.0
FREE WILL BAPTIST BIBLE C	PRI-FN	511	107.6	2,751.4	5.4	58.9	A	.0	A
HIWASSEE COLLEGE	PRI-T	505	122.4	2,576.2	4.1	69.2	68.8	.0	A
JOHN A GUPTON COLLEGE	PRI-T	60	123.4	3,704.0	7.4	79.2	77.2	60.0	60.0
JOHNSON BIBLE COLLEGE	PRI-FN	355	194.1	5,743.0	4.4	102.3	67.9	88.7	355.0
KING COLLEGE	PRI-FN	300	205.7	2,285.7	3.0	246.8	A	103.4	157.8
KNOXVILLE BUSINESS C	PRI-T	473	21.8	A	5.0	6.4	6.2	473.0	473.0
KNOXVILLE COLLEGE	PRI-FN	670	130.3	A	2.0	117.0	A	89.3	335.0
LAMBUTH COLLEGE	PRI-FN	705	142.9	1,799.3	3.4	111.8	68.6	108.4	235.0
LANE COLLEGE	PRI-FN	660	175.2	2,820.9	3.9	122.0	88.8	82.5	110.0
LEE COLLEGE	PRI-FN	1,248	135.9	A	4.7	66.8	58.3	102.2	265.5
LE MOYNE-OWEN COLLEGE	PRI-FN	974	85.3	1,732.3	2.5	81.2	71.6	194.8	324.6
LINCOLN MEM UNIVERSITY	PRI-FN	889	80.1	1,827.2	2.7	62.3	62.2	222.2	296.3
MARTIN COLLEGE	PRI-T	223	184.4	2,057.0	5.5	92.2	83.1	111.5	223.0
MARYVILLE COLLEGE	PRI-FN	608	167.4	2,262.2	3.0	180.5	173.9	95.0	202.6
MCKENZIE COLLEGE	PRI-T	500	75.1	A	A	.4	A	333.3	500.0
MEHARRY MEDICAL COLLEGE	PRI-FG	1,033	499.8	.0	2.8	38.9	A	64.5	516.5
MEMPHIS ACADEMY OF ARTS	PRI-FN	203	179.2	2,139.8	4.0	82.9	61.5	101.5	101.5
MEMPHIS THEOLOGICAL SEM	PRI-FG	120	640.2	12,805.1	21.7	564.8	366.6	40.0	40.0
MID AMERICA BAPT SEMINARY	PRI-FG	D	D	D	D	D	D	D	D
MID-SOUTH BIBLE COLLEGE	PRI-FN	88	448.9	6,585.1	8.0	217.8	158.3	44.0	88.0
MILLIGAN COLLEGE	PRI-FN	714	106.0	1,682.3	A	118.7	131.4	204.0	357.0
MORRISTOWN COLLEGE	PRI-T	148	823.0	8,120.2	16.5	153.5	131.6	37.0	148.0
NASHVILLE STATE TECH INST	PUB-T	2,078	87.2	2,553.3	4.4	9.4	8.2	230.8	346.3
O'MORE SCH INTERIOR DESIGN	PRI-T	D	D	D	D	D	D	D	D
SCARRITT COLLEGE	PRI-FG	117	620.5	4,270.5	4.2	449.8	328.9	39.0	117.0
STHN COLLEGE OF OPTOMETRY	PRI-FG	616	153.2	2,145.4	2.4	23.8	20.6	166.4	308.0
STHN MISSIONARY COLLEGE	PRI-FN	1,603	169.9	2,523.1	5.1	70.0	67.9	102.1	281.2
SOUTHWESTERN AT MEMPHIS	PRI-FN	1,018	262.2	3,216.3	4.6	169.7	113.5	107.1	145.4

SEE FOOTNOTES AT END OF TABLE

STATE OR OTHER AREA AND INSTITUTION	CONTROL AND TYPE OF INSTITUTION	TOTAL FTE OPENING FALL ENROLLMENT, FALL 1978	LIBRARY OPERATING EXPENDITURES (IN DOLLARS) 1978-79			BOOKSTOCK HELD AT END OF YEAR 1978-79		FTE STUDENTS PER FTE LIBRARY STAFF FALL 1979	
			PER FTE STUDENT, FALL 1978	PER FULL-TIME FACULTY MEMBER, FALL 1978	AS PERCENT OF GENERAL EXPENDITURES, 1978-79	VOLUMES PER FTE STUDENT, FALL 1978	TITLES (INCLUDING MICROFORMS) PER FTE STUDENT 1978	TOTAL STAFF	PROFESSIONAL STAFF
(1)	(2)	(3)	(4)	(5)	(6)	(7)	(8)	(9)	(10)
TENNESSEE	--CONTINUED								
STATE TECH INST KNOXVILLE	PUB-T	983	69.1	2,517.4	3.9	5.3	5.2	327.6	4 .5
STATE TECH INST MEMPHIS	PUB-T	3,654	45.0	1,551.7	2.2	8.2	6.8	456.7	913.3
ST U-CC SYS TENN ALL INST									
AUSTIN PEAY ST UNIVERSITY	PUB-FG	3,706	165.2	3,257.7	5.2	49.6	39.7	142.5	308.8
EAST TENN ST UNIVERSITY	PUB-FG	8,109	145.8	2,688.2	3.5	68.9	74.5	180.2	506.8
MEMPHIS STATE UNIVERSITY	PUB-FG	15,706	143.1	2,993.2	4.4	55.2	35.9	140.6	547.2
MIDDLE TENN ST UNIVERSITY	PUB-FG	8,623	127.6	2,745.9	4.4	46.8	31.9	226.9	538.9
TENNESSEE ST UNIVERSITY	PUB-FG	5,087	181.8	3,364.7	4.2	68.5	72.3	113.0	226.0
TENNESSEE TECHNOLOGICAL U	PUB-FG	6,156	120.5	2,550.5	3.7	54.8	103.9	219.8	513.0
CHATTANOOGA ST TECH CC	PUB-T	3,372	43.9	1,808.3	2.9	8.5	9.0	636.2	1,124.0
CLEVELAND ST CMTY COLLEGE	PUB-T	1,928	119.1	2,610.3	4.7	24.3	21.1	148.3	482.0
COLUMBIA ST CMTY COLLEGE	PUB-T	1,246	138.1	3,019.5	5.3	34.8	31.2	178.0	311.5
DYERSBURG ST CMTY COLLEGE	PUB-T	642	122.5	2,538.9	4.7	42.4	34.6	.0	A
JACKSON ST CMTY COLLEGE	PUB-T	1,514	107.3	2,389.2	4.7	31.2	25.6	189.0	378.5
MOTLOW STATE CMTY COLLEGE	PUB-T	1,052	153.0	3,743.7	6.0	29.4	27.5	150.2	350.6
ROANE STATE CMTY COLLEGE	PUB-T	1,758	103.7	2,570.0	4.1	16.3	18.1	219.7	879.0
SHELBY STATE CMTY COLLEGE	PUB-T	15,926	16.6	1,893.3	3.1	2.7	2.5	1,447.8	3,185.2
VOLUNTEER ST CMTY COLLEGE	PUB-T	1,526	94.1	1,730.3	3.7	20.5	18.1	153.9	508.6
WALTERS ST CMTY COLLEGE	PUB-T	1,934	89.9	2,174.8	4.1	18.8	17.1	175.8	429.7
STEED COLLEGE	PRI-FN	684	37.3	1,417.5	2.6	10.7	10.3	684.0	684.0
TENNESSEE TEMPLE U	PRI-FG	2,206	101.7	A	3.9	32.3	32.8	200.5	668.4
TENN WESLEYAN COLLEGE	PRI-FN	393	233.1	3,817.7	6.7	164.1	152.3	71.4	196.5
TOMLINSON COLLEGE	PRI-T	272	134.7	2,618.7	6.5	93.7	67.9	90.6	136.0
TREVECCA NAZARENE COLLEGE	PRI-FN	1,279	80.0	3,101.5	2.6	57.1	69.3	131.8	272.1
TUSCULUM COLLEGE	PRI-FN	436	171.2	2,665.9	3.2	126.8	102.1	103.8	145.3
UNION UNIVERSITY	PRI-FN	1,065	122.3	2,207.7	4.0	68.4	68.0	177.5	266.2
UNIVERSITY OF THE SOUTH	PRI-FG	1,073	436.9	5,717.1	6.1	306.6	206.8	46.2	134.1
U OF TENNESSEE ALL CAM									
U OF TENN CTR HEALTH SCI	PUB-FG	2,127	356.6	4,436.3	1.3	64.8	16.4	60.5	150.8
U OF TENN AT CHATTANOOGA	PUB-FG	5,039	154.9	3,213.7	4.8	54.0	40.7	162.5	387.6
U OF TENNESSEE KNOXVILLE	PUB-U	25,232	168.5	3,302.4	2.9	57.7	A	131.7	502.6
U OF TENNESSEE AT MARTIN	PUB-FG	4,364	132.2	2,646.7	4.4	47.4	53.3	181.8	436.4
VANDERBILT UNIVERSITY	PRI-U	7,216	541.8	8,232.3	4.9	216.2	132.9	48.3	150.9
TEXAS									
ABILENE CHRSTN UNIVERSITY	PRI-FG	4,345	106.5	2,722.8	4.6	54.2	53.9	181.7	452.2
ALVIN COMMUNITY COLLEGE	PUB-T	2,010	54.7	1,294.4	1.8	16.9	15.7	335.0	670.0
AMARILLO COLLEGE	PUB-T	2,868	124.7	2,130.2	3.8	22.6	25.5	147.8	531.1
AMERICAN TECHNOLOGICAL U	PRI-FG	525	108.1	6,311.5	1.9	26.3	27.6	262.5	525.0
ANGELINA COLLEGE	PUB-T	1,431	72.9	1,800.7	3.7	20.1	16.9	286.2	477.0
ANGELO STATE UNIVERSITY	PUB-FG	4,765	98.3	2,966.7	4.6	35.4	61.1	272.2	794.1
AUSTIN COLLEGE	PRI-FG	1,103	189.7	2,616.0	3.3	115.3	102.8	137.8	367.6
AUSTIN COMMUNITY COLLEGE	PUB-T	4,540	124.0	3,994.6	5.3	5.8	4.4	148.8	363.2
AUSTIN PRESB THEOL SEM	PRI-FG	159	581.8	6,608.5	1.9	686.9	537.7	45.4	106.0
BAYLOR COLLEGE DENTISTRY	PRI-FG	508	257.7	1,407.7	1.5	100.5	86.9	84.6	169.3
BAYLOR COLLEGE MEDICINE12/	PRI-FG		SEE TEXAS MEDL CTR JOINT LIB						
BAYLOR UNIVERSITY	PRI-U	9,068	182.9	4,107.0	6.3	91.8	65.1	171.0	465.0
BEE COUNTY COLLEGE	PUB-T	1,558	88.1	1,854.8	3.3	22.1	19.6	259.6	519.3
BISHOP COLLEGE	PRI-FN	1,203	112.1	1,822.7	2.0	139.2	A	218.7	343.7
BLINN COLLEGE	PUB-T	2,049	103.1	4,495.4	6.8	31.4	30.3	512.2	683.0
BRAZOSPORT COLLEGE	PUB-T	2,270	71.5	2,223.8	3.8	18.8	16.9	324.2	1,135.0
CENTRAL TEXAS COLLEGE	PUB-T	2,822	83.5	2,875.3	2.5	16.3	32.8	434.1	806.2
CISCO JUNIOR COLLEGE	PUB-T	1,201	51.5	1,125.8	2.7	22.4	22.3	240.2	1,201.0
CLARENDON COLLEGE	PUB-T	512	76.8	1,873.8	4.7	39.6	32.4	256.0	512.0
COLLEGE OF THE MAINLAND	PUB-T	1,362	263.0	18,859.7	5.2	29.5	24.8	89.0	272.4
CONCORDIA LUTH COLLEGE	PRI-T	236	217.7	3,953.3	6.8	93.8	A	118.0	236.0
COOKE COUNTY COLLEGE	PUB-T	981	113.5	1,688.0	4.1	34.9	26.1	245.2	490.5
DALLAS BAPTIST COLLEGE	PRI-FN	749	273.4	4,096.6	6.1	183.3	214.5	94.8	133.7
DALLAS BIBLE COLLEGE	PRI-FN	192	147.8	2,838.3	5.5	150.3	130.2	96.0	192.0
DALLAS CHRISTIAN COLLEGE	PRI-FN	116	284.9	4,131.5	6.6	208.0	158.6	.0	A
DALLAS CO CC DIST ALLINST									
BROOKHAVEN COLLEGE	PUB-T	0	0	0	0	0	0	0	0
CEDAR VALLEY COLLEGE	PUB-T	826	307.8	6,519.3	7.2	15.7	A	86.9	110.1
EASTFIELD COLLEGE	PUB-T	3,722	179.2	4,978.1	7.4	11.7	10.4	129.6	744.4
EL CENTRO COLLEGE	PUB-T	2,897	146.6	2,672.3	5.2	20.0	20.1	137.2	432.3
MOUNTAIN VIEW COLLEGE	PUB-T	2,465	195.6	5,608.9	7.1	14.6	13.2	125.7	493.0

SEE FOOTNOTES AT END OF TABLE

Table 3. — Indexes Concerning Operating Expenditures, 1978-79, Bookstock Held at End of Year, 1978-79, and Library Staff (FTE), Fall 1979, College and University Libraries, by State or Other Area and Institution: Aggregate United States — Continued

STATE OR OTHER AREA AND INSTITUTION	CONTROL AND TYPE OF INSTITUTION	TOTAL FTE OPENING FALL ENROLLMENT, FALL 1978	LIBRARY OPERATING EXPENDITURES (IN DOLLARS) 1978-79			BOOKSTOCK HELD AT END OF YEAR 1978-79		FTE STUDENTS PER FTE LIBRARY STAFF FALL 1979	
			PER FTE STUDENT, FALL 1978	PER FULL-TIME FACULTY MEMBER, 1978	AS PERCENT OF GENERAL EXPENDITURES, 1978-79	VOLUMES PER FTE STUDENT, FALL 1978	TITLES (INCLUDING MICROFORMS) PER FTE STUDENT 1978	TOTAL STAFF	PROFESSIONAL STAFF
(1)	(2)	(3)	(4)	(5)	(6)	(7)	(8)	(9)	(10)
TEXAS	--CONTINUED								
NORTH LAKE COLLEGE	PUB-T	1,760	135.4	4,182.8	4.4	8.6	8.7	352.0	880.0
RICHLAND COLLEGE	PUB-T	5,245	221.8	7,411.2	10.8	9.5	A	143.3	582.7
DALLAS THEOL SEMINARY	PRI-FG	D	D	D	D	D	D	D	D
DEL MAR COLLEGE	PUB-T	5,253	92.8	1,981.9	3.6	20.9	18.8	247.7	709.8
DEVRY INST OF TECHNOLOGY	PRI-FN	D	D	D	D	D	D	D	D
EAST TEXAS BAPT COLLEGE	PRI-FN	754	194.0	3,657.5	6.1	117.8	92.0	53.8	251.3
EAST TEXAS ST UNIVERSITY	PUB-FG	6,742	177.2	A	5.1	76.9	80.4	158.6	385.2
EL PASO CO CMTY COLLEGE	PUB-T	7,200	53.2	2,255.2	2.5	5.7	5.7	347.8	827.5
EPIS THEOL SEM SOUTHWEST	PRI-FG	62	1,242.0	12,834.3	10.8	1,287.4	980.9	16.3	31.0
FRANK PHILLIPS COLLEGE	PUB-T	513	119.9	2,279.2	4.2	56.3	41.6	.0	A
GALVESTON COLLEGE	PUB-T	1,040	241.1	3,858.3	7.2	32.8	30.1	86.6	260.0
GRAYSON CO JUNIOR COLLEGE	PUB-T	2,190	90.0	1,843.1	4.1	22.1	A	273.7	730.0
GULF COAST BIBLE COLLEGE	PRI-FN	310	237.1	5,654.6	6.6	113.0	150.9	62.0	155.0
HARDIN-SIMMONS UNIVERSITY	PRI-FG	1,375	183.5	2,900.1	4.7	112.2	95.1	105.7	196.4
HAROLD R. YEARY JT LIB	PUB-FG	D	D	D	D	D	D	D	D
HENDERSON CO JR COLLEGE	PUB-T	1,603	61.1	1,582.2	2.9	17.4	4.7	534.3	1,603.0
HILL JUNIOR COLLEGE	PUB-T	570	89.4	1,645.1	3.5	43.6	A	285.0	285.0
HOUSTON BAPT UNIVERSITY	PRI-FG	1,647	113.1	2,025.7	3.4	57.1	44.8	156.8	329.4
HOUSTON COMMUNITY COLLEGE	PUB-T	6,750	131.9	3,906.0	3.4	6.1	4.2	142.7	379.2
HOWARD C AT BIG SPRING	PUB-T	680	87.4	1,607.8	2.4	45.6	42.9	183.7	340.0
HOWARD PAYNE UNIVERSITY	PRI-FN	1,147	131.3	1,956.1	3.6	104.4	A	191.1	229.4
HUSTON-TILLOTSON COLLEGE	PRI-FN	587	212.6	3,671.0	4.2	103.6	85.3	101.2	146.7
INCARNATE WORD COLLEGE	PRI-FG	1,122	221.9	3,557.4	4.9	106.5	76.5	102.0	187.0
JACKSONVILLE COLLEGE	PRI-T	255	126.8	3,233.4	6.2	73.7	49.1	127.5	255.0
JARVIS CHRISTIAN COLLEGE	PRI-FN	473	260.0	2,860.6	2.7	117.0	104.5	59.1	94.6
KILGORE COLLEGE	PUB-T	2,742	115.5	2,436.8	5.9	21.5	17.9	182.8	685.5
LAMAR UNIVERSITY	PUB-FG	9,757	120.3	2,769.7	5.7	38.6	25.1	206.2	696.9
LAREDO JUNIOR COLLEGE	PUB-T		SEE HAROLD R. YEARY JT LIB						
LEE COLLEGE	PUB-T	2,639	138.5	3,293.1	4.6	34.3	21.2	182.0	527.8
LETOURNEAU COLLEGE	PRI-FN	882	173.7	3,064.9	4.5	109.6	118.5	129.7	176.4
LON MORRIS COLLEGE	PRI-T	296	209.7	3,448.5	6.1	71.4	51.5	197.3	296.0
LUBBOCK CHRISTIAN COLLEGE	PRI-FN	1,016	100.8	1,601.4	2.6	66.1	48.6	169.3	508.0
MCLENNAN CMTY COLLEGE	PUB-T	2,260	74.8	1,444.9	2.9	29.6	22.9	240.4	753.3
MCMURRY COLLEGE	PRI-FN	999	138.5	2,563.0	3.3	136.1	97.8	142.7	333.0
MIDLAND COLLEGE	PUB-T	1,505	102.1	2,402.0	3.8	13.9	12.4	167.2	501.6
MIDWESTERN ST UNIVERSITY	PUB-FG	3,476	132.2	3,307.5	4.8	62.0	A	248.2	869.0
NAVARRO COLLEGE	PUB-T	1,197	70.8	2,651.9	2.2	27.7	26.3	299.2	598.5
NORTH HARRIS CO COLLEGE	PUB-T	2,574	108.5	3,070.9	5.8	8.9	8.8	240.5	858.0
NORTH TEXAS ST UNIVERSITY	PUB-U	13,725	173.4	3,505.4	4.6	59.6	42.4	140.7	450.0
OBLATE COLLEGE OF STHWST	PRI-FG	48	686.5	.0	7.6	775.8	527.3	26.6	48.0
ODESSA COLLEGE	PUB-T	1,641	180.6	2,179.2	3.5	36.8	33.1	117.2	328.2
OUR LADY OF LAKE U	PRI-FG	1,284	359.9	5,374.6	6.6	80.1	64.0	64.2	116.7
PAN AMERICAN UNIVERSITY	PUB-FG	6,542	123.4	2,844.0	4.2	28.5	29.9	198.2	545.1
PANOLA JUNIOR COLLEGE	PUB-T	683	72.0	1,756.8	3.9	36.7	29.2	227.6	683.0
PARIS JUNIOR COLLEGE	PUB-T	1,329	136.9	2,303.7	4.6	126.9	23.9	189.8	443.0
PAUL QUINN COLLEGE	PRI-FN	403	117.5	1,578.7	3.3	220.5	A	100.7	403.0
RANGER JUNIOR COLLEGE	PUB-T	577	72.4	1,817.1	3.7	36.3	38.0	240.4	240.4
RICE UNIVERSITY	PRI-U	3,597	602.5	6,300.8	5.6	250.7	126.8	47.6	156.3
SAINT EDWARD'S UNIVERSITY	PRI-FG	1,653	80.0	1,889.2	1.8	50.6	A	236.1	472.2
SNT MARY'S U SAN ANTONIO	PRI-FG	2,928	173.5	5,185.9	5.6	95.3	50.5	84.8	136.1
SAM HOUSTON ST UNIVERSITY	PUB-FG	9,755	107.6	3,282.6	4.6	60.5	A	314.6	975.5
SN ANTO DIST JC ALL CAM									
SAINT PHILIP'S COLLEGE	PUB-T	5,253	68.5	2,093.4	3.6	10.5	11.7	350.2	875.5
SAN ANTONIO COLLEGE	PUB-T	14,091	127.0	4,004.7	7.0	14.4	13.1	227.2	671.0
SAN JACINTO C ALL CAM									
SAN JACINTO C CENTRAL CAM	PUB-T	5,370	44.0	1,149.1	2.1	19.1	14.2	394.8	1,732.2
SAN JACINTO C NORTH CAM	PUB-T	1,269	79.1	1,732.4	3.1	23.4	19.3	244.0	1,269.0
SCHREINER COLLEGE	PRI-T	352	121.4	2,375.8	2.9	44.8	41.8	234.6	234.6
SOUTHERN BIBLE COLLEGE	PRI-FN	96	93.3	2,240.2	3.7	188.2	183.0	160.0	192.0
SOUTHERN METH UNIVERSITY	PRI-U	7,334	313.1	5,184.7	5.2	150.4	95.8	105.0	240.4
SOUTH PLAINS COLLEGE	PUB-T	2,010	65.3	1,427.9	2.7	23.6	23.5	402.0	670.0
SOUTH TEXAS COLLEGE LAW	PRI-FG	1,036	292.4	20,200.0	A	78.1	51.4	172.6	345.3
STHWSTN ADVENTIST COLLEGE	PRI-FN	650	215.7	A	4.2	147.5	172.0	147.7	216.6
SOUTHWESTERN ASSEMB GOD C	PRI-FN	759	69.0	3,276.1	3.4	74.1	50.8	189.7	379.5
STHWSTN BAPT THEOL SEM	PRI-FG	D	D	D	D	D	D	D	D
STHWSTN CHRISTIAN COLLEGE	PRI-T	464	116.1	3,592.8	3.9	42.2	41.9	232.0	232.0

SEE FOOTNOTES AT END OF TABLE

| STATE OR OTHER AREA AND INSTITUTION (1) | CONTROL AND TYPE OF INSTITUTION (2) | TOTAL FTE OPENING FALL ENROLLMENT, FALL 1978 (3) | LIBRARY OPERATING EXPENDITURES (IN DOLLARS) 1978-79 | | | BOOKSTOCK HELD AT END OF YEAR 1978-79 | | FTE STUDENTS PER FTE LIBRARY STAFF FALL 1979 | |
			PER FTE STUDENT, FALL 1978 (4)	PER FULL-TIME FACULTY MEMBER, 1978 (5)	AS PERCENT OF GENERAL EXPENDITURES, 1978-79 (6)	VOLUMES PER FTE STUDENT, FALL 1978 (7)	TITLES (INCLUDING MICROFORMS) PER FTE STUDENT 1978 (8)	TOTAL STAFF (9)	PROFESSIONAL STAFF (10)
TEXAS	--CONTINUED								
SOUTHWESTERN UNIVERSITY	PRI-FN	926	210.8	3,426.1	3.9	142.2	106.8	88.1	308.6
SOUTHWEST TEX JR COLLEGE	PUB-T	1,356	94.1	2,201.8	3.5	24.1	24.2	193.7	452.0
STHWST TEX ST UNIVERSITY	PUB-FG	13,038	116.2	3,246.2	5.3	28.0	A	239.2	736.6
STEPHEN F AUSTIN STATE U	PUB-FG	9,347	129.6	3,124.0	5.0	35.7	30.1	198.8	491.9
SUL ROSS STATE UNIVERSITY	PUB-FG	1,853	258.2	5,563.9	8.8	103.7	82.6	13?.3	231.6
TARRANT CO JUNIOR COLLEGE	PUB-T	9,762	175.6	4,464.2	7.4	13.1	11.8	118.9	554.6
TEMPLE JUNIOR COLLEGE	PUB-T	1,537	54.7	1,168.3	2.6	19.4	18.2	512.3	768.5
TEXARKANA CMTY COLLEGE	PUB-T	2,232	54.9	1,074.8	2.5	13.5	12.5	318.8	1,116.0
TEXAS A&M U SYS ALL INST									
PRAIRIE VIEW A&M U12/	PUB-FG	D	D	D	D	D	D	D	D
TARLETON STATE UNIVERSITY	PUB-FG	2,893	143.7	3,353.7	4.8	49.8	65.0	222.5	578.6
TEXAS A&M U ALL CAMPUSES									
TEXAS A&M U MAIN CAMPUS	PUB-U	28,263	128.8	2,986.4	1.6	43.2	32.4	184.0	640.8
TEX A&M U AT GALVESTON	PUB-FN	577	412.0	7,670.3	7.7	38.3	29.6	64.1	192.3
TEXAS CHIROPRACTIC C	PRI-FG	311	127.3	4,949.5	5.3	9.6	6.5	155.5	311.0
TEXAS CHRISTIAN U	PRI-U	5,102	253.1	4,035.8	4.4	166.4	A	115.4	250.0
TEXAS COLLEGE	PRI-FN	468	153.3	1,840.0	3.1	214.2	A	78.0	187.2
TEXAS COLLEGE OSTEO MED	PUB-FG	299	3,986.3	18,337.1	8.9	122.2	41.1	11.8	29.9
TEXAS LUTHERAN COLLEGE	PRI-FN	958	134.6	2,224.7	3.4	93.5	79.3	127.7	319.3
TEXAS MEDL CTR JOINT LIB12/	PUB-FG	D	D	D	D	D	D	D	D
TEXAS SOUTHERN UNIVERSITY	PUB-FG	7,317	142.3	2,740.9	4.0	46.0	65.5	141.5	472.0
TEXAS SOUTHMOST COLLEGE	PUB-T	2,770	112.2	2,704.1	5.4	39.6	28.9	155.6	692.5
TEX ST TECH INST ALL CAM									
TEX ST TECH AMARILLO CAM	PUB-T	584	146.7	1,587.3	2.5	19.0	17.2	146.0	584.0
TEX ST TECH-HARLINGEN CAM	PUB-T	1,067	99.3	1,324.7	3.5	12.7	9.7	177.8	533.5
TEX ST TECH INST WACO CAM	PUB-T	3,284	103.0	1,332.8	2.7	15.6	12.7	218.9	821.0
TEXAS TECH UNIVERSITY	PUB-U	20,345	171.2	4,033.2	5.3	56.6	44.5	160.4	385.3
TEXAS WESLEYAN COLLEGE	PRI-FN	1,163	203.4	3,154.6	4.3	108.3	91.6	94.5	176.2
TEXAS WOMAN'S UNIVERSITY12/	PUB-U	6,383	151.1	2,249.5	3.5	81.7	72.4	159.5	455.9
TRINITY UNIVERSITY	PRI-FG	3,021	321.5	5,139.6	5.7	95.0	86.6	60.4	215.7
TYLER JUNIOR COLLEGE	PUB-T	4,609	53.5	1,032.9	3.3	13.0	A	443.1	1,152.2
UNIVERSITY OF DALLAS	PRI-FG	1,615	131.0	2,580.5	3.3	81.6	98.3	185.6	293.6
U OF HOUSTON ALL CAMPUSES									
U OF HOUSTON CEN CAMPUS12/	PUB-U	21,504	173.5	3,630.1	3.5	55.6	23.7	140.4	551.3
U HOUSTON CLEAR LAKE CITY	PUB-FG	2,737	185.4	3,817.3	4.5	79.6	59.7	122.7	329.7
U OF HOUSTON DOWNTOWN C	PUB-FN	3,541	133.3	4,629.7	5.4	25.8	24.9	128.7	472.1
U HOUSTON VICTORIA CAMPUS	PUB FG			SEE VC UHVC JOINT LIB					
U OF MARY HARDIN-BAYLOR	PRI-FN	840	113.0	1,758.3	2.8	100.2	117.2	152.7	280.0
UNIVERSITY OF SNT THOMAS	PRI-FG	4,020	64.2	3,109.6	6.5	30.0	24.7	222.0	574.2
U SYS S TEXAS ALL INST									
CORPUS CHRISTI STATE U	PUB-FG	1,694	267.6	5,038.0	6.9	93.6	236.2	110.7	319.6
LAREDO STATE UNIVERSITY	PUB FG			SEE HAROLD R. YEARY JT LIB					
TEXAS A&I UNIVERSITY	PUB-FG	5,078	125.8	2,754.7	3.8	76.0	74.5	253.9	634.7
U OF TEXAS SYS ALL INST									
U OF TEXAS AT AUSTIN	PUB-U	40,263	231.5	5,341.9	4.0	98.6	48.4	87.6	341.7
U OF TEXAS AT ARLINGTON	PUB-FG	15,559	97.1	2,695.0	3.3	28.2	21.1	233.2	720.3
U OF TEXAS AT DALLAS	PUB-FG	2,937	684.2	11,041.8	8.0	65.9	125.6	57.7	147.5
U OF TEXAS AT EL PASO	PUB-FG	12,702	134.1	3,906.9	5.7	37.4	33.4	191.5	651.3
U TEX HLTH SCI CTR DALLAS	PUB-FG	1,271	733.2	19,019.3	1.1	123.3	35.4	34.9	85.8
U TEX HLTH SCI CTR HOUSTN12/	PUB FG			SEE TEXAS MEDL CTR JOINT LIB					
U TEX HLTH SCI SN ANTO	PUB-FG	1,755	510.1	3,909.8	1.4	64.3	A	39.4	130.0
U TEX MEDL BR GALVESTON	PUB-FG	1,538	A	A	A	152.6	45.6	22.9	80.9
U OF TEXAS PERMIAN BASIN	PUB-FG	757	394.5	4,977.3	5.6	213.1	201.9	73.4	229.3
U OF TEXAS SAN ANTONIO	PUB-FG	6,927	118.5	3,601.1	4.3	36.9	39.7	179.9	692.7
U OF TEXAS AT TYLER	PUB-FG	D	D	D	D	D	D	D	D
VERNON REG JUNIOR COLLEGE	PUB-T	788	107.6	A	3.9	25.5	25.4	225.1	394.0
VICTORIA COLLEGE	PUB T			SEE VC UHVC JOINT LIB					
VC UHVC JOINT LIBRARY	PUB-T	D	D	D	D	D	D	D	D
WAYLAND BAPTIST COLLEGE	PRI-FN	921	116.5	A	2.8	84.5	57.6	279.0	307.0
WEATHERFORD COLLEGE	PUB-T	1,065	91.4	2,562.3	4.9	43.7	39.9	213.0	1,065.0
WESTERN TEXAS COLLEGE	PUB-T	772	131.2	2,303.2	3.4	42.7	41.6	96.5	257.3
WEST TEXAS ST UNIVERSITY	PUB-FG	5,506	114.7	2,771.8	4.1	44.1	33.2	159.7	509.6
WHARTON CO JR COLLEGE	PUB-T	1,657	131.6	2,370.3	5.0	31.0	27.1	184.1	414.1
WILEY COLLEGE	PRI-FN	601	158.9	A	A	96.2	76.5	100.1	200.3
UTAH									
BRIGHAM YOUNG U ALL CAM									

SEE FOOTNOTES AT END OF TABLE

Table 3. – Indexes Concerning Operating Expenditures, 1978-79, Bookstock Held at End of Year, 1978-79, and Library Staff (FTE), Fall 1979, College and University Libraries, by State or Other Area and Institution: Aggregate United States – Continued

STATE OR OTHER AREA AND INSTITUTION	CONTROL AND TYPE OF INSTITUTION	TOTAL FTE OPENING FALL ENROLLMENT, FALL 1978	LIBRARY OPERATING EXPENDITURES (IN DOLLARS) 1978-79			BOOKSTOCK HELD AT END OF YEAR 1978-79		FTE STUDENTS PER FTE LIBRARY STAFF FALL 1979	
			PER FTE STUDENT, FALL 1978	PER FULL-TIME FACULTY MEMBER, 1978	AS PERCENT OF GENERAL EXPENDITURES, 1978-79	VOLUMES PER FTE STUDENT, FALL 1978	TITLES (INCLUDING MICROFORMS) PER FTE STUDENT 1978	TOTAL STAFF	PROFESSIONAL STAFF
(1)	(2)	(3)	(4)	(5)	(6)	(7)	(8)	(9)	(10)
UTAH	--CONTINUED								
BRIGHAM YOUNG U MAIN CAM	PRI-U	25,535	A	A	A	56.2	A	91.1	405.3
BRIGHAM YOUNG U-HAWA CAM	PRI-FN	1,758	348.1	A	A	54.7	A	39.9	109.8
LATTER-DAY SAINTS BUS C	PRI-T	692	27.7	A	A	5.5	5.2	692.0	692.0
STEVENS HENAGER COLLEGE	PRI-T	365	3.6	A	.3	6.1	5.6	3,650.0	3,650.0
UTAH HI ED SYS ALL INST									
UNIVERSITY OF UTAH	PUB-U	18,061	261.6	5,598.1	3.4	117.3	A	74.9	298.0
UTAH STATE UNIVERSITY	PUB-U	8,137	184.6	3,066.7	2.4	38.3	31.3	140.5	557.3
SOUTHERN UTAH ST COLLEGE	PUB-FN	1,650	227.1	3,904.1	5.3	83.1	78.5	170.1	226.0
WEBER STATE COLLEGE	PUB-FG	6,866	177.5	3,773.1	4.5	34.0	31.1	221.4	624.1
COLLEGE OF EASTERN UTAH	PUB-T	586	147.8	2,063.0	2.5	42.3	34.5	225.3	366.2
DIXIE COLLEGE	PUB-T	1,136	69.8	A	2.2	42.2	41.2	252.4	568.0
SNOW COLLEGE	PUB-T	902	76.5	1,570.1	1.8	31.8	29.7	214.7	451.0
UTAH TECH COLLEGE PROVO	PUB-T	2,642	63.3	1,146.0	1.8	A	6.8	240.1	1,321.0
UTAH TECH COLLEGE SALT LK	PUB-T	3,581	43.6	958.9	1.5	4.7	4.3	795.7	1,790.5
WESTMINSTER COLLEGE	PRI-FG	1,086	70.3	1,273.4	1.7	51.8	43.1	264.8	543.0
VERMONT									
BENNINGTON COLLEGE	PRI-FG	656	249.6	2,924.5	2.4	123.1	103.6	82.0	328.0
BURLINGTON COLLEGE1/	PRI-FN		NO LIBRARY FACILITIES						
CHAMPLAIN COLLEGE	PRI-T	902	62.7	1,663.9	2.1	29.6	23.3	300.6	902.0
C SNT JOSEPH THE PROVIDER	PRI-FG	226	133.5	4,310.1	4.6	89.3	89.4	113.0	1130.0
GODDARD COLLEGE	PRI-FG	1,553	97.0	2,842.7	3.0	45.5	42.2	155.3	517.6
GREEN MOUNTAIN COLLEGE	PRI-FN	431	247.1	3,944.8	4.5	147.8	174.1	61.5	143.6
MARLBORO COLLEGE	PRI-FN	216	240.7	2,363.8	3.5	197.1	179.7	144.0	216.0
MIDDLEBURY COLLEGE	PRI-FG	1,906	351.5	5,583.2	5.3	144.7	101.4	63.1	232.4
NORWICH U ALL CAM									
NORWICH U MAIN CAM	PRI-FG	1,585	156.2	2,476.5	3.9	75.7	86.8	186.4	792.5
VERMONT COLLEGE	PRI-FG	392	149.6	2,173.2	3.4	71.3	67.2	112.0	392.0
SAINT MICHAEL'S COLLEGE	PRI-FG	1,631	153.4	2,607.0	4.2	63.0	54.4	115.6	319.8
SCH FOR INTRNATL TRAINING	PRI-FG	502	92.3	858.7	1.7	46.7	38.9	193.0	251.0
SOUTHERN VERMONT COLLEGE	PRI-FN	314	109.7	2,870.8	3.1	47.7	47.7	314.0	314.0
TRINITY COLLEGE	PRI-FN	396	251.0	3,975.9	6.2	132.4	137.1	61.8	127.7
U VT & STATE AGRL COLLEGE	PUB-U	8,905	242.5	4,137.8	3.2	78.5	73.6	108.9	424.0
VERMONT LAW SCHOOL	PRI-FG	324	660.5	15,286.5	15.1	172.1	22.1	49.0	90.0
VERMONT ST C ALL INST									
CASTLETON STATE COLLEGE	PUB-FG	1,629	112.7	2,267.8	4.3	39.8	37.5	232.7	814.5
CMTY COLLEGE OF VERMONT1/	PUB-T		NO LIBRARY FACILITIES						
JOHNSON STATE COLLEGE	PUB-FG	955	181.4	3,397.9	4.5	86.0	A	159.1	238.7
LYNDON STATE COLLEGE	PUB-FG	2,057	65.2	2,314.1	3.9	26.4	21.7	307.0	2,057.0
VERMONT TECHNICAL COLLEGE	PUB-T	687	160.4	2,345.2	4.5	61.1	56.9	127.2	343.5
VIRGINIA									
AVERETT COLLEGE	PRI-FG	868	159.5	2,946.6	5.8	68.3	58.0	144.6	289.3
BLUEFIELD COLLEGE	PRI-FN	279	162.3	2,058.5	5.2	171.9	151.8	69.7	279.0
BRIDGEWATER COLLEGE	PRI-FN	881	181.4	3,074.6	5.1	120.7	103.1	146.8	293.6
C WILLIAM & MARY ALL CAM									
C OF WILLIAM AND MARY	PUB-FG	5,676	314.6	5,177.0	7.3	144.6	86.3	83.4	276.8
CHRISTOPHER NEWPORT C	PUB-FN	2,355	181.3	3,918.7	7.5	55.0	28.5	161.3	392.5
RICHARD BLAND C WM & MARY	PUB-T	706	123.6	2,910.5	5.0	66.5	60.3	176.5	353.0
ESTN MENNONITE C AND SEM	PRI-FG	1,073	216.9	3,063.0	4.8	85.8	82.2	127.7	315.5
EASTERN VA MEDL SCHOOL	PRI-FG	215	1,551.8	12,357.7	4.6	130.2	A	16.5	43.0
EMORY AND HENRY COLLEGE	PRI-FN	813	208.0	3,074.7	5.6	115.9	108.8	95.6	406.5
FERRUM COLLEGE	PRI-FN	1,489	139.9	3,360.9	5.2	43.0	33.8	186.1	248.1
GEORGE MASON UNIVERSITY	PUB-FG	7,342	146.9	2,956.3	5.4	24.2	25.1	181.2	444.9
HAMPDEN-SYDNEY COLLEGE	PRI-FN	734	222.7	3,336.6	4.0	93.0	93.4	107.0	349.6
HAMPTON INSTITUTE	PRI-FG	2,622	154.7	1,979.2	2.7	153.8	113.1	78.2	159.1
HOLLINS COLLEGE	PRI-FG	939	314.4	4,407.3	4.9				
INST TEXTILE TECHNOLOGY	PRI-FG	D	D	D	D	D	D	D	D
JAMES MADISON UNIVERSITY	PUB-FG	7,465	112.2	2,018.2	4.0	36.6	26.5	201.7	481.6
LIBERTY BAPTIST COLLEGE	PRI-FN	2,169	142.2	2,488.3	6.1	37.0	36.7	114.1	361.5
LONGWOOD COLLEGE	PUB-FG	2,287	159.2	2,304.8	5.6	78.4	66.0	104.9	381.1
LYNCHBURG COLLEGE	PRI-FG	1,868	146.3	2,554.7	4.2	58.3	50.8	156.9	381.2
MARY BALDWIN COLLEGE	PRI-FN	713	211.9	3,214.8	3.3	169.0	107.2	101.8	237.6
MARYMOUNT COLLEGE OF VA	PRI-FG	820	265.2	4,627.2	7.9	64.2	45.8	66.1	128.1
MARY WASHINGTON COLLEGE	PUB-FN	2,092	219.7	3,677.9	7.5	121.7	94.1	118.8	261.5
NATIONAL BUSINESS COLLEGE	PRI-T	804	22.1	849.8	A	6.9	4.9	472.9	472.9
NORFOLK STATE UNIVERSITY	PUB-FG	6,213	109.8	1,966.9	3.7	38.9	31.2	172.5	621.3
OLD DOMINION UNIVERSITY	PUB-FG	10,654	144.1	2,732.7	4.7	41.6	28.1	168.5	532.7

SEE FOOTNOTES AT END OF TABLE

Table 3. — Indexes Concerning Operating Expenditures, 1978-79, Bookstock Held at End of Year, 1978-79, and Library Staff (FTE), Fall 1979, College and University Libraries, by State or Other Area and Institution: Aggregate United States — Continued

STATE OR OTHER AREA AND INSTITUTION	CONTROL AND TYPE OF INSTITUTION	TOTAL FTE OPENING FALL ENROLLMENT, FALL 1978	LIBRARY OPERATING EXPENDITURES (IN DOLLARS) 1978-79			BOOKSTOCK HELD AT END OF YEAR 1978-79		FTE STUDENTS PER FTE LIBRARY STAFF FALL 1979	
			PER FTE STUDENT, FALL 1978	PER FULL-TIME FACULTY MEMBER, 1978	AS PER-CENT OF GENERAL EXPENDITURES, 1978-79	VOLUMES PER FTE STUDENT, FALL 1978	TITLES (INCLUDING MICRO-FORMS) PER FTE STUDENT 1978	TOTAL STAFF	PROFES-SIONAL STAFF
(1)	(2)	(3)	(4)	(5)	(6)	(7)	(8)	(9)	(10)
VIRGINIA	--CONTINUED								
PRESB SCH OF CHRISTIAN ED	PRI FG			SEE UNION THEOL SEM JOINT LIB					
PROT EPIS THEOL SEM IN VA	PRI-FG	169	922.4	7,423.8	8.0	591.7	A	33.8	84.5
RADFORD UNIVERSITY	PUB-FG	4,936	126.9	2,230.6	5.3	38.3	26.5	214.6	548.4
RANDOLPH-MACON COLLEGE	PRI-FN	926	159.4	2,636.5	3.5	117.9	99.3	156.9	308.6
RANDOLPH-MACON WOMAN'S C	PRI-FN	687	281.6	3,121.0	3.8	201.2	A	58.7	105.6
ROANOKE COLLEGE	PRI-FN	1,125	179.2	3,103.2	4.2	114.8	80.0	146.1	225.0
SAINT PAUL'S COLLEGE	PRI-FN	607	179.7	2,871.8	3.1	63.8	55.3	151.7	202.3
SHENANDOAH C-CONSV MUSIC	PRI-FN	749	276.1	2,873.2	7.0	74.8	60.7	85.1	110.1
SOUTHERN SEM JR COLLEGE	PRI-T	236	125.9	1,564.0	2.8	141.9	137.6	138.8	236.0
SWEET BRIAR COLLEGE	PRI-FN	663	343.1	3,297.4	A	263.2	A	51.0	165.7
UNION THEOL SEM IN VA	PRI FG	0		SEE UNION THEOL SEM JOINT LIB					
UNION THEOL SEM JOINT LIB	PRI-FG	0	0	0	0	0	0	0	0
UNIVERSITY OF RICHMOND	PRI-FG	3,370	229.3	3,984.1	5.6	83.8	76.2	104.3	306.3
U OF VIRGINIA ALL CAM	PUB-U	15,150	460.8	7,960.4	6.0	152.6	68.7	55.8	189.3
U OF VIRGINIA MAIN CAMPUS									
U VA CLINCH VLY COLLEGE	PUB-FN	723	340.2	5,999.8	7.0	113.4	80.7	65.7	241.0
VIRGINIA COLLEGE	PRI-T	0	0	0	0	0	0	0	0
VIRGINIA COMMONWEALTH U	PUB-U	13,417	214.0	3,447.1	3.0	40.2	29.3	118.5	432.8
VA INTERMONT COLLEGE	PRI-FN	624	179.5	2,667.3	4.8	89.7	71.1	124.8	312.0
VIRGINIA MILITARY INST	PU3-FN	1,321	323.8	4,599.8	6.2	185.2	130.6	71.4	330.2
VA POLY INST AND STATE U	PUB-U	18,739	229.2	3,335.4	3.3	61.7	38.4	116.3	340.7
VIRGINIA STATE UNIV	PUB-FG	3,803	160.8	2,476.1	3.2	51.8	37.6	152.1	316.9
VA STATE CC SYS ALL INST									
BLUE RIDGE CMTY COLLEGE	PUB-T	1,122	97.3	2,481.1	5.1	32.4	31.3	215.7	561.0
CENTRAL VA CMTY COLLEGE	PUB-T	1,879	53.5	1,437.7	2.5	20.0	20.2	417.5	751.6
DABNEY S LANCASTER CC	PUB-T	615	162.3	2,935.9	4.6	52.2	49.5	87.8	205.0
DANVILLE CMTY COLLEGE	PUB-T	1,534	144.5	3,079.3	6.8	23.8	21.4	170.4	255.6
ESTN SHORE CMTY COLLEGE	PUB-T	215	271.3	3,431.7	4.7	87.4	83.7	71.6	215.0
GERMANNA CMTY COLLEGE	PUB-T	573	97.1	1,795.9	3.9	35.0	A	191.0	573.0
J SARGEANT REYNOLDS CC	PUB-T	4,112	104.6	2,301.2	4.0	10.4	7.7	257.0	411.2
JOHN TYLER CMTY COLLEGE	PUB-T	1,865	65.3	1,542.4	2.8	14.6	A	333.0	621.6
LORD FAIRFAX CMTY COLLEGE	PUB-T	846	224.3	5,582.6	9.2	34.6	46.2	94.0	423.0
MTN EMPIRE CMTY COLLEGE	PUB-T	780	156.7	4,527.6	7.0	25.5	20.3	130.0	390.0
NEW RIVER CMTY COLLEGE	PUB-T	1,426	164.6	3,913.1	5.7	16.3	13.3	134.5	475.3
NORTHERN VA CMTY COLLEGE	PUB-T	15,645	272.9	8,471.3	13.5	12.7	A	150.8	481.3
PATRICK HENRY CC	PUB-T	659	172.4	4,371.0	6.7	43.1	33.4	119.8	659.0
PAUL D CAMP CMTY COLLEGE	PUB-T	698	192.4	3,950.6	7.3	28.2	23.1	99.7	349.0
PIEDMONT VA CMTY COLLEGE	PUB-T	1,367	121.1	3,379.1	6.0	13.8	12.1	158.9	683.5
RAPPAHANNOCK CMTY COLLEGE	PUB-T	689	119.0	2,413.5	3.2	57.7	56.3	114.8	229.6
SOUTHSIDE VA CMTY COLLEGE	PUB-T	896	110.8	2,365.0	4.1	30.1	28.2	149.3	448.0
SOUTHWEST VA CMTY COLLEGE	PUB-T	1,318	71.4	1,744.0	2.8	25.4	33.2	263.6	439.3
THOMAS NELSN CMTY COLLEGE	PUB-T	3,183	78.2	1,915.4	3.8	14.5	10.8	230.6	795.7
TIDEWATER CMTY COLLEGE	PUB-T	7,886	97.2	3,103.8	5.3	13.4	12.3	183.3	563.2
VA HIGHLANDS CMTY COLLEGE	PUB-T	940	110.1	2,030.9	4.2	25.1	21.2	188.0	470.0
VA WESTERN CMTY COLLEGE	PUB-T	2,900	67.7	1,611.1	3.1	14.6	12.8	329.5	966.6
WYTHEVILLE CMTY COLLEGE	PUB-T	1,048	75.0	1,604.3	2.3	28.0	24.4	249.5	524.0
VIRGINIA UNION UNIVERSITY	PRI-FG	1,136	160.9	2,230.1	2.9	108.5	61.3	123.4	270.4
VIRGINIA WESLEYAN COLLEGE	PRI-FN	760	201.6	3,831.5	6.0	86.4	69.5	108.5	253.3
WASHINGTON AND LEE U2/	PRI-FG	1,721	301.4	3,553.6	4.5	149.1	116.2	93.3	301.9
WASHINGTON									
BELLEVUE CMTY COLLEGE	PUB-T	4,519	96.1	4,575.3	5.7	8.4	6.5	243.2	717.3
BIG BEND CMTY COLLEGE	PUB-T	991	133.3	3,146.7	1.3	36.4	36.7	186.9	495.5
CENTRALIA COLLEGE	PUB-T	1,887	75.9	2,469.3	2.8	16.0	13.1	410.2	943.5
CENTRAL WASH UNIVERSITY	PUB-FG	5,845	289.9	6,277.2	7.5	51.7	133.1	101.1	382.0
CITY COLLEGE1/	PRI-FG			NO LIBRARY FACILITIES					
CLARK COLLEGE	PUB-T	3,941	39.6	1,432.8	2.1	A	A	532.5	1,970.5
COLUMBIA BASIN CC	PUB-T	3,189	77.2	2,438.1	4.2	11.4	9.7	303.7	708.6
CORNISH INSTITUTE	PRI-FN	340	97.0	2,063.2	2.4	10.6	10.5	170.0	340.0
EASTERN WASH UNIVERSITY	PUB-FG	5,868	227.1	3,967.0	5.2	53.4	91.1	123.5	434.6
EVERGREEN STATE COLLEGE	PUB-FN	2,059	562.5	9,899.5	10.5	65.8	78.1	59.1	294.1
FORT STEILACOOM CC	PUB-T	4,955	72.3	4,167.4	5.0	6.2	5.5	307.7	1,152.3
FORT WRIGHT C HOLY NAMES	PRI-FG	274	171.6	2,765.9	2.3	258.4	254.3	91.3	137.0
GONZAGA UNIVERSITY	PRI-FG	2,969	231.9	6,559.6	6.2	106.6	50.7	114.1	269.9
GRAYS HARBOR COLLEGE	PUB-T	1,260	112.9	3,029.2	4.6	32.2	29.0	237.7	630.0
GREEN RIVER CMTY COLLEGE	PUB-T	2,872	90.2	2,617.5	A	12.1	10.6	206.6	776.2
GRIFFIN COLLEGE	PRI-FN	0	0	0	0	0	0	0	0

SEE FOOTNOTES AT END OF TABLE

181

Table 3. — Indexes Concerning Operating Expenditures, 1978-79, Bookstock Held at End of Year, 1978-79, and Library Staff (FTE), Fall 1979, College and University Libraries, by State or Other Area and Institution: Aggregate United States — Continued

STATE OR OTHER AREA AND INSTITUTION	CONTROL AND TYPE OF INSTITUTION	TOTAL FTE OPENING FALL ENROLLMENT, FALL 1978	LIBRARY OPERATING EXPENDITURES (IN DOLLARS) 1978-79			BOOKSTOCK HELD AT END OF YEAR 1978-79		FTE STUDENTS PER FTE LIBRARY STAFF FALL 1979	
			PER FTE STUDENT, FALL 1978	PER FULL-TIME FACULTY MEMBER, 1978	AS PERCENT OF GENERAL EXPENDITURES, 1978-79	VOLUMES PER FTE STUDENT, FALL 1978	TITLES (INCLUDING MICROFORMS) PER FTE STUDENT 1978	TOTAL STAFF	PROFESSIONAL STAFF
(1)	(2)	(3)	(4)	(5)	(6)	(7)	(8)	(9)	(10)
WASHINGTON	--CONTINUED								
HIGHLINE CMTY COLLEGE	PUB-T	4,827	65.7	2,251.0	3.8	13.3	7.6	305.5	709.8
LOWER COLUMBIA COLLEGE	PUB-T	1,859	93.4	2,592.6	3.5	13.8	12.4	247.8	1,239.3
LUTH BIBLE INST SEATTLE	PRI-FN	168	213.7	3,263.8	3.3	119.0	98.5	88.4	88.4
NTHWST C ASSEMBLIES GOD	PRI-FN	672	101.2	3,579.9	A	71.2	71.2	224.0	336.0
OLYMPIA TECH CMTY COLLEGE	PUB-T	1,282	89.6	2,671.8	3.3	5.3	4.4	377.0	915.7
OLYMPIC COLLEGE	PUB-T	3,346	87.0	2,672.0	3.9	14.4	13.5	283.5	576.8
PACIFIC LUTH UNIVERSITY	PRI-FG	2,888	163.0	2,427.6	3.6	71.3	45.4	191.2	1,444.0
PENINSULA COLLEGE	PUB-T	1,107	131.8	3,394.1	5.2	29.1	27.9	194.2	461.2
PUGET SOUND C OF BIBLE	PRI-FN	165	209.3	5,757.3	6.1	130.3	122.2	110.0	330.0
SAINT MARTIN'S COLLEGE	PRI-FN	553	134.2	2,320.3	3.5	160.8	160.7	110.6	184.3
SEATTLE CC DIST ALL CAM NORTH SEATTLE CC	PUB-T	3,499	119.2	4,534.3	4.6	9.4	7.7	271.2	647.9
SEATTLE CC CENTRAL CAMPUS	PUB-T	5,093	76.7	2,195.4	2.7	10.7	10.0	292.7	795.7
SEATTLE CC SOUTH CAMPUS	PUB-T	2,545	101.5	3,491.0	3.3	6.3	4.9	215.6	591.8
SEATTLE PACIFIC U	PRI-FG	2,040	137.0	3,006.9	2.9	56.7	51.2	180.5	425.0
SEATTLE UNIVERSITY	PRI-FG	2,831	147.7	2,715.9	3.6	64.4	43.9	136.7	353.8
SHORELINE CMTY COLLEGE	PUB-T	4,742	103.9	3,596.7	A	14.3	12.3	244.4	790.3
SKAGIT VALLEY COLLEGE	PUB-T	2,753	96.4	3,847.3	A	21.3	15.6	250.2	550.6
TACOMA COMMUNITY COLLEGE	PUB-T	3,498	74.6	2,967.5	3.4	19.7	17.7	257.2	832.8
UNIVERSITY OF PUGET SOUND	PRI-FG	3,508	264.7	5,954.2	5.4	93.0	61.9	105.0	337.3
UNIVERSITY OF WASHINGTON	PUB-U	31,597	318.4	5,967.4	3.3	91.8	A	96.2	280.8
WALLA WALLA COLLEGE	PRI-FG	1,688	161.5	2,164.4	3.7	81.8	63.8	135.0	281.3
WALLA WALLA CMTY COLLEGE	PUB-T	2,854	122.0	3,744.7	5.9	11.2	10.5	203.8	951.3
WASH ST CC DIST 5 ALLINST EDMONDS COMMUNITY COLLEGE	PUB-T	2,795	100.5	4,462.4	5.6	10.7	7.5	207.0	621.1
EVERETT CMTY COLLEGE	PUB-T	3,826	100.7	2,696.8	5.2	12.1	8.4	273.2	765.2
WASH ST CC DIST 17 ALL SPOKANE COMMUNITY COLLEGE	PUB-T	5,342	67.1	1,917.1	2.9	4.9	4.9	434.3	1,335.5
SPOKANE FLS CMTY COLLEGE	PUB-T	5,707	104.4	4,289.5	5.2	6.7	5.6	320.6	781.7
WASHINGTON ST UNIVERSITY	PUB-U	15,764	301.0	6,335.8	4.2	75.4	A	93.7	321.7
WENATCHEE VALLEY COLLEGE	PUB-T	1,615	140.3	3,383.1	5.2	15.8	A	179.4	375.5
WESTERN WASH UNIVERSITY	PUB-FG	8,899	195.3	4,033.4	5.7	42.0	34.3	160.0	635.6
WHATCOM CMTY COLLEGE	PUB-T	900	133.1	6,659.1	5.3	10.8	9.8	150.0	450.0
WHITMAN COLLEGE	PRI-FN	1,158	302.7	4,437.3	5.3	136.9	115.9	95.7	231.6
WHITWORTH COLLEGE	PRI-FG	1,444	147.4	3,379.7	3.2	51.0	40.8	195.1	361.0
YAKIMA VALLEY CC	PUB-T	2,647	66.9	1,477.5	2.8	14.2	13.9	294.1	756.2
WEST VIRGINIA									
ALDERSON BROADDUS COLLEGE	PRI-FN	855	187.6	2,325.6	4.3	91.1	91.1	127.6	213.7
APPALACHIAN BIBLE COLLEGE	PRI-FN	223	112.7	4,190.8	2.6	120.7	A	74.3	223.0
BECKLEY COLLEGE	PRI-T	845	47.1	2,658.0	4.9	13.7	10.3	422.5	422.5
BETHANY COLLEGE	PRI-FN	923	235.0	3,556.9	A	144.0	137.0	116.8	242.8
BLUEFIELD STATE COLLEGE	PUB-FN	1,486	112.8	2,020.4	4.7	73.5	A	203.5	495.3
CONCORD COLLEGE	PUB-FN	1,651	167.3	3,733.8	6.2	73.4	64.8	137.5	412.7
DAVIS AND ELKINS COLLEGE	PRI-FN	888	117.8	1,973.9	2.5	91.8	72.0	123.3	222.0
FAIRMONT STATE COLLEGE	PUB-FN	3,523	99.3	2,134.3	4.4	44.5	A	220.1	503.2
GLENVILLE STATE COLLEGE	PUB-FN	1,258	182.1	2,899.8	5.8	76.6	88.4	139.7	251.6
MARSHALL UNIVERSITY	PUB-FG	8,237	124.7	2,800.2	4.6	40.6	A	196.1	549.1
OHIO VALLEY COLLEGE	PRI-T	236	131.5	2,587.5	3.8	80.4	80.3	118.0	118.0
PARKERSBURG CMTY COLLEGE	PUB-T	1,641	266.0	5,260.2	10.9	24.1	24.1	96.5	547.0
POTOMAC STATE COLLEGE	PUB-T	841	119.6	2,581.1	4.1	45.2	41.3	168.2	420.5
SALEM COLLEGE ALL CAM SALEM COLLEGE MAIN CAMPUS	PRI-FG	901	106.6	1,685.7	2.0	106.5	A	145.3	281.5
SALEM COLLEGE CLARKSBURG	PRI-T	145	41.7	D	3.6	131.0	A	290.0	290.0
SHEPHERD COLLEGE	PUB-FN	2,097	134.9	2,695.6	6.5	58.8	66.4	163.8	524.2
SOUTHERN W VA CC ALL CAM STHN W VA CC-LOGAN CAM	PUB-T	818	90.2	2,306.0	4.2	30.9	24.7	185.9	818.0
STHN W VA CC-WILLIAMSON	PUB-T	440	162.6	3,253.3	6.7	52.0	45.7	100.0	440.0
U OF CHARLESTON	PRI-FG	1,154	149.7	A	A	73.9	52.4	132.6	384.6
WEST LIBERTY ST COLLEGE	PUB-FN	2,266	123.8	1,963.2	4.5	75.8	53.7	167.8	412.0
W VA COLLEGE GRAD STUDIES	PUB-FG	1,057	243.5	5,363.4	6.7	45.1	36.5	81.3	264.2
WEST VA INST TECHNOLOGY	PUB-FN	2,546	119.4	2,188.2	4.2	51.4	48.3	134.7	391.6
WEST VIRGINIA NORTHERN CC	PUB-T	1,636	70.8	1,899.7	2.0	17.1	12.2	175.9	409.0
W VA SCH OSTEOPATHIC MED	PUB-FG	203	631.8	4,581.0	4.1	39.4	29.5	45.1	203.0
W VA STATE COLLEGE	PUB-FN	2,459	139.7	2,546.3	5.0	65.8	59.0	153.6	351.2
WEST VIRGINIA UNIVERSITY	PUB-U	17,962	104.3	1,961.3	1.7	43.3	26.7	183.2	598.7

SEE FOOTNOTES AT END OF TABLE

182

Table 3. – Indexes Concerning Operating Expenditures, 1978-79, Bookstock Held at End of Year, 1978-79, and Library Staff (FTE), Fall 1979, College and University Libraries, by State or Other Area and Institution: Aggregate United States – Continued

STATE OR OTHER AREA AND INSTITUTION	CON-TROL AND TYPE OF IN-STITU-TION	TOTAL FTE OPENING FALL ENROLL-MENT, FALL 1978	LIBRARY OPERATING EXPENDITURES (IN DOLLARS) 1978-79			BOOKSTOCK HELD AT END OF YEAR 1978-79		FTE STUDENTS PER FTE LIBRARY STAFF FALL 1979	
			PER FTE STU-DENT, FALL 1978	PER FULL-TIME FAC-ULTY MEM-BER, FALL 1978	AS PER-CENT OF GENERAL EXPENDI-TURES, 1978-79	VOLUMES PER FTE STUDENT, FALL 1978	TITLES (INCLU-DING MICRO-FORMS) PER FTE STUDENT 1978	TOTAL STAFF	PROFES-SIONAL STAFF
(1)	(2)	(3)	(4)	(5)	(6)	(7)	(8)	(9)	(10)
WEST VIRGINIA	--CONTINUED								
WEST VA WESLEYAN COLLEGE	PRI-FG	1,742	117.0	1,853.3	2.9	70.7	A	161.2	435.5
WHEELING COLLEGE	PRI-FG	902	145.4	2,571.6	3.4	115.4	101.1	150.3	451.0
WISCONSIN									
ALVERNO COLLEGE	PRI-FN	946	298.4	4,151.6	6.7	77.2	A	72.7	236.5
BELOIT COLLEGE	PPI-FG	999	175.4	2,367.9	3.2	225.2	A	142.7	249.7
BLACKHAWK TECHNICAL INST	PUB-T	1,412	91.9	1,731.7	2.8	9.2	8.4	282.4	706.0
CARDINAL STRITCH COLLEGE	PRI-FG	694	139.1	4,827.6	3.8	100.1	100.1	108.4	157.7
CARROLL COLLEGE	PRI-FN	1,177	162.8	2,489.0	3.6	132.5	97.2	.0	A
CARTHAGE COLLEGE	PRI-FG	1,245	169.5	2,542.5	4.5	89.0	66.8	113.1	311.2
CONCORDIA COLLEGE	PRI-FN	333	194.1	2,586.2	4.7	125.6	113.4	97.9	175.2
DISTRICT ONE TECH INST	PUB-T	2,124	89.6	1,360.4	2.0	18.6	18.1	283.2	424.8
EDGEWOOD COLLEGE	PRI-FN	379	182.7	5,328.9	4.0	157.5	135.4	157.9	189.5
FOX VALLEY TECH INST	PUB-T	3,004	38.0	634.5	.8	9.0	7.7	1,001.3	1,502.0
GATEWAY TECH INST ALL CAM									
GATEWAY TECH INST-KENOSHA	PUB-T	1,562	102.4	1,523.3	1.9	18.2	18.0	173.5	390.5
GATEWAY TECH INST-RACINE	PUB-T	759	112.3	1,705.7	1.4	17.4	17.4	205.1	379.5
HOLY REDEEMER COLLEGE	PRI-FN	54	725.0	9,787.5	5.1	591.2	404.4	27.0	54.0
INSTITUTE PAPER CHEMISTRY	PRI-FG	99	1,095.2	3,011.9	1.5	393.9	A	16.5	33.0
LAKELAND COLLEGE	PRI-FN	525	164.2	3,194.5	3.6	91.6	110.8	131.2	262.5
LAKESHORE TECHNICAL INST	PUB-T	1,513	56.6	1,008.8	1.4	14.7	14.3	432.2	756.5
LAWRENCE UNIVERSITY	PRI-FN	1,157	337.2	3,680.8	4.6	193.7	A	110.1	289.2
MADISON AREA TECH COLLEGE	PUB-T	5,055	63.8	1,231.1	A	10.2	7.1	443.4	2,527.5
MADISON BUSINESS COLLEGE	PRI-T	240	29.8	1,022.0	1.5	31.0	A	480.0	480.0
MARIAN C OF FOND DU LAC	PRI-FN	451	165.3	3,389.9	4.7	159.6	160.5	90.2	225.5
MARQUETTE UNIVERSITY	PRI-U	9,541	197.3	3,796.9	4.5	67.0	36.8	139.6	352.0
MEDICAL COLLEGE OF WIS	PRI-FG	686	668.5	0	1.2	139.5	134.2	36.1	76.2
MID-STATE TECHNICAL INST	PUB-T	959	90.3	1,312.5	1.7	28.1	26.0	126.1	959.0
MILTON COLLEGE	PRI-FN	537	133.1	2,979.3	A	116.5	116.5	268.5	A
MILWAUKEE AREA TECH C	PUB-T	8,741	35.6	498.6	.6	5.6	4.9	582.7	2,185.2
MILWAUKEE SCH OF THE ARTS	PRI-FN	0	0	0	0	0	0	0	0
MILWAUKEE SCH ENGINEERING	PRI-FG	1,654	57.5	1,560.9	1.5	17.6	17.6	551.3	827.0
MILWAUKEE STRATTON C	PRI-T	0	0	0	0	0	0	0	0
MORAINE PARK TECH INST	PUB-T	1,771	67.9	1,074.5	1.5	13.5	9.0	276.7	1,771.0
MOUNT MARY COLLEGE	PRI-FN	907	135.2	4,231.6	3.7	117.4	78.6	151.1	251.9
MOUNT SENARIO COLLEGE	PRI-FN	347	282.5	3,770.9	3.7	112.7	94.7	69.4	86.7
NASHOTAH HOUSE	PRI-FG	93	990.5	11,515.3	9.9	621.1	A	20.6	46.5
NICOLET COLLEGE-TECH INST	PUB-T	609	331.8	5,052.7	3.9	48.8	38.9	75.1	203.0
NORTH CENTRAL TECH INST	PUB-T	1,815	71.6	1,092.3	1.5	15.2	14.2	307.6	1,815.0
NORTHEAST WIS TECH INST	PUB-T	2,188	22.1	321.1	.5	5.9	4.6	218.8	729.3
NORTHLAND COLLEGE	PRI-FN	648	111.7	1,956.2	2.3	103.4	93.1	185.1	432.0
NORTHWESTERN COLLEGE	PRI-FN	0	0	0	0	0	0	0	0
RIPON COLLEGE	PRI-FN	921	215.4	3,100.2	4.0	118.7	80.7	131.5	230.2
SACRED HEART SCH THEOLOGY	PRI-FG	112	366.7	4,107.2	5.1	433.5	A	48.6	50.9
SNT FRANCIS DE SALES C	PRI-FN	83	295.7	24,544.0	7.8	337.5	A	83.0	83.0
SNT FRAN SEM PSTL MINSTRY	PRI-FG	92	550.9	A	A	625.0	624.5	36.8	41.8
SAINT NORBERT COLLEGE	PRI-FN	1,512	204.3	4,414.9	5.3	83.1	79.2	112.8	343.6
SILVER LAKE COLLEGE	PRI-FN	243	323.1	11,216.4	5.5	247.2	239.8	54.0	59.4
STHWST WIS VOC TECH INST	PUB-T	0	0	0	0	0	0	0	0
U OF WIS SYS ALL INST									
U OF WISCONSIN EAU CLAIRE	PUB-FG	9,504	99.9	2,410.9	3.2	42.6	34.1	320.0	792.0
U OF WISCONSIN GREEN BAY	PUB-FG	2,642	277.4	4,919.7	4.3	106.6	105.1	105.6	313.3
U OF WISCONSIN LA CROSSE	PUB-FG	7,710	116.0	2,830.7	3.6	41.2	30.2	310.8	771.0
U OF WISCONSIN MADISON	PUB-U	35,109	276.1	6,757.4	3.0	99.7	45.5	104.8	312.3
U OF WISCONSIN MILWAUKEE	PUB-FG	17,746	204.4	4,705.0	4.4	65.8	40.1	205.8	566.9
U OF WISCONSIN OSHKOSH	PUB-FG	7,867	159.2	2,840.3	4.1	38.9	53.9	194.2	476.7
U OF WISCONSIN PARKSIDE	PUB-FG	3,398	248.6	5,121.4	5.6	83.7	58.5	131.7	276.2
U OF WISCONSIN PLATTEVL	PUB-FG	4,202	187.4	3,647.1	5.0	44.9	37.3	178.0	407.9
U OF WISCONSIN RIVER FLS	PUB-FG	4,544	138.8	3,093.6	3.3	41.3	91.8	207.4	432.7
U OF WISCONSIN STEVNS PNT	PUB-FG	8,038	144.9	3,065.3	4.4	32.3	20.1	174.3	451.5
U OF WISCONSIN STOUT	PUB-FG	6,429	106.7	2,227.3	2.6	26.7	28.4	259.2	691.2
U OF WISCONSIN SUPERIOR	PUB-FG	1,844	187.8	2,727.5	3.1	114.5	223.5	163.1	368.8
U OF WISCONSIN WHITEWATER	PUB-FG	7,705	152.2	3,214.2	4.8	39.5	26.3	199.0	423.3
U OF WISCONSIN CTR SYS	PUB-T	5,978	172.3	3,170.7	5.6	68.2	61.4	148.3	251.0
VITERBO COLLEGE	PRI-FN	893	126.5	2,355.0	2.7	74.9	57.3	193.4	223.2
WAUKESHA COUNTY TECH INST	PUB-T	2,374	40.6	803.7	.7	8.3	5.4	474.8	2,374.0

SEE FOOTNOTES AT END OF TABLE

Table 3. — Indexes Concerning Operating Expenditures, 1978-79, Bookstock Held at End of Year, 1978-79, and Library Staff (FTE), Fall 1979, College and University Libraries, by State or Other Area and Institution: Aggregate United States — Continued

STATE OR OTHER AREA AND INSTITUTION (1)	CONTROL AND TYPE OF INSTITUTION (2)	TOTAL FTE OPENING FALL ENROLLMENT, FALL 1978 (3)	LIBRARY OPERATING EXPENDITURES (IN DOLLARS) 1978-79			BOOKSTOCK HELD AT END OF YEAR 1978-79		FTE STUDENTS PER FTE LIBRARY STAFF FALL 1979	
			PER FTE STUDENT, FALL 1978 (4)	PER FULL-TIME FACULTY MEMBER, 1978 (5)	AS PERCENT OF GENERAL EXPENDITURES, 1978-79 (6)	VOLUMES PER FTE STUDENT, FALL 1978 (7)	TITLES (INCLUDING MICROFORMS) PER FTE STUDENT 1978 (8)	TOTAL STAFF (9)	PROFESSIONAL STAFF (10)
WISCONSIN	--CONTINUED								
WESTERN WIS TECH INST	PUB-T	2,788	38.9	593.1	.9	8.7	7.2	557.6	1,394.0
WISCONSIN CONSV OF MUSIC	PRI-FG	D	D	D	D	D	D	D	D
WISCONSIN LUTHERAN C	PRI-T	D	D	D	D	D	D	D	D
WYOMING									
CASPER COLLEGE	PUB-T	1,882	112.6	1,766.6	3.2	28.7	21.4	168.0	855.4
CENTRAL WYOMING COLLEGE	PUB-T	423	167.6	2,026.2	3.2	55.1	45.6	.0	A
EASTERN WYOMING COLLEGE	PUB-T	427	181.3	3,097.0	4.6	47.8	44.6	85.4	142.3
LARAMIE CO CMTY COLLEGE	PUB-T	1,321	94.0	1,497.4	2.7	14.9	13.0	203.2	1,321.0
NORTHWEST CMTY COLLEGE	PUB-T	789	69.4	961.6	1.9	41.0	40.7	239.0	789.0
SHERIDAN COLLEGE	PUB-T	593	105.5	1,691.4	3.0	60.6	36.1	160.2	593.0
UNIVERSITY OF WYOMING2/	PUB-U	8,030	221.0	2,595.3	3.2	81.5	49.1	102.9	349.1
WESTERN WYO CMTY COLLEGE	PUB-T	645	244.0	3,839.0	4.5	29.3	27.6	100.7	215.0
U.S. SERVICE SCHOOLS									
AIR FORCE INST TECHNOLOGY	PUB-FG	546	622.4	7,724.2	3.1	139.7	61.1	45.5	109.2
CC OF THE AIR FORCE	PUB-T	D	D	D	D	D	D	D	D
NAVAL POSTGRADUATE SCHOOL	PUB-FG	1,211	636.9	3,383.3	2.8	152.5	95.9	41.0	100.9
UNIFORMED SERV U HLTH SCI	PUB-FG	D	D	D	D	D	D	D	D
US AIR FORCE ACADEMY	PUB-FN	4,491	246.9	A	A	80.8	48.3	95.5	299.4
US ARMY CMND-GEN STAFF C	PUB-FN	D	D	D	D	D	D	D	D
US COAST GUARD ACADEMY	PUB-FN	909	258.5	A	1.1	132.0	147.4	113.6	191.8
US MERCHANT MARINE ACAD	PUB-FN	1,125	171.2	2,470.6	1.5	79.0	61.3	187.5	375.0
US MILITARY ACADEMY	PUB-FN	4,277	330.1	27,686.1	1.3	89.3	122.1	80.6	194.4
US NAVAL ACADEMY	PUB-FN	4,400	309.7	5,262.4	1.4	81.6	46.1	84.6	231.5
AMERICAN SAMOA									
AMER SAMOA CMTY COLLEGE	PUB-T	526	131.1	A	6.8	34.2	31.3	103.1	526.0
CANAL ZONE									
PANAMA CANAL COLLEGE	PUB-FN	747	217.3	6,243.8	10.0	45.6	44.7	249.0	373.5
GUAM									
UNIVERSITY OF GUAM	PUB-FG	2,144	189.1	2,583.2	4.2	41.9	38.6	103.5	261.4
PUERTO RICO									
AMERICAN C PUERTO RICO	PRI-FN	1,105	66.3	2,443.3	2.8	9.9	7.7	221.0	368.3
ANTILLIAN COLLEGE	PRI-FN	686	216.9	3,816.3	A	42.9	35.8	84.6	221.2
BAYAMON CEN UNIVERSITY	PRI-FN	2,522	147.5	9,306.1	4.2	13.6	12.1	86.9	252.2
CAGUAS CITY COLLEGE	PRI-T	651	51.7	D	3.9	6.4	5.0	.0	A
CARIBBEAN CTR ADV STUDIES	PRI-FG	D	D	D	D	D	D	D	D
CARIBBEAN U COLLEGE	PRI-FN	1,093	81.9	7,466.6	6.2	9.6	7.0	176.2	546.5
CATHOLIC U PUERTO RICO	PRI-FG	9,461	3.8	155.4	.2	31.1	27.0	166.5	397.5
CONSERVATORY OF MUSIC PR	PUB-FN	192	253.8	1,804.9	5.5	77.2	72.3	80.0	80.0
EDP C OF PUERTO RICO	PRI-T	1,211	22.2	1,687.5	4.0	1.6	A	484.4	807.3
FUNDACION EDUCATIVA ALL									
COLEGIO U DEL TURABO	PRI-FN	5,238	65.0	4,158.3	5.0	6.6	5.6	187.0	654.7
PUERTO RICO JR COLLEGE	PRI-T	7,257	52.5	3,180.6	3.9	4.8	3.2	220.5	748.1
INST COMERCIAL DE PR JC	PRI-T	1,727	28.2	921.6	3.7	3.5	3.5	.0	A
INST TECNICO COMERCIAL JC	PRI-T	1,277	14.5	A	1.7	2.1	.0	.0	A
INTER AMER U PR ALL CAM									
INTER AMER U METRO CAM	PRI-FG	6,849	89.0	3,004.6	5.3	13.1	8.5	153.2	622.6
INTER AMER U ARECIBO BR	PRI-FN	2,086	59.7	3,460.2	9.0	13.6	11.0	208.6	521.5
INTER AMER U BARNQUITS BR	PRI-T	919	84.7	4,097.8	11.4	21.2	16.1	153.1	919.0
INTER AMER U SAN GERMAN CAM	PRI-FG	5,583	58.1	2,336.3	5.2	16.2	10.8	206.7	558.3
INTER AMER U AGUADILLA BR	PRI-T	1,938	82.9	4,347.2	9.2	17.1	15.3	176.1	1,938.0
INTER AMER U FAJARDO BR	PRI-T	1,398	A	A	A	13.4	11.5	139.8	699.0
INTER AMER U CUAYAMA BR	PRI-T	868	93.7	3,391.6	9.3	20.0	18.2	124.0	868.0
INTER AMER U PONCE BR	PRI-T	1,542	62.8	3,230.0	8.7	10.2	9.0	171.3	1,542.0
INTRATL INST WORLD U	PRI-FG	3,951	96.2	1,960.5	3.6	17.9	15.5	176.3	493.8
RAMIREZ C BUS AND TECHN	PRI-T	583	22.2	D	1.8	4.9	4.0	647.7	647.7
SAN JUAN TECHNOLOGICAL CC	PUB-T	834	107.4	1,338.1	A	3.9	A	166.8	208.5
UNIV POLITECNICA DE PR	PRI-FN	123	227.6	D	A	12.1	10.9	102.5	123.0
UNIVERSIDAD DE PONCE	PRI-T	341	86.2	3,266.6	...	15.5	16.1	170.5	170.5
U OF PUERTO RICO ALL CAM									
U OF PR RIO PIEDRAS	PUB-U	19,268	161.8	2,653.9	4.4	55.8	34.8	88.8	212.2
U OF PR MAYAGUEZ	PUB-FG	7,977	117.6	1,730.8	1.7	25.0	12.7	135.2	498.5
U OF PR MEDICAL SCIENCES	PUB-FG	2,476	189.9	936.0	1.3	17.6	17.1	91.3	309.5
U PR CAYEY UNIVERSITY C	PUB-FN	2,408	149.5	3,243.8	4.8	31.6	25.8	89.1	218.9
U PR HUMACAO U COLLEGE	PUB-FN	2,490	151.4	2,371.3	4.5	19.5	A	118.5	498.0

SEE FOOTNOTES AT END OF TABLE

Table 3. — Indexes Concerning Operating Expenditures, 1978-79, Bookstock Held at End of Year, 1978-79, and Library Staff (FTE), Fall 1979, College and University Libraries, by State or Other Area and Institution: Aggregate United States — Continued

STATE OR OTHER AREA AND INSTITUTION	CONTROL AND TYPE OF INSTITUTION	TOTAL FTE OPENING FALL ENROLLMENT, FALL 1978	LIBRARY OPERATING EXPENDITURES (IN DOLLARS) 1978-79			BOOKSTOCK HELD AT END OF YEAR 1978-79		FTE STUDENTS PER FTE LIBRARY STAFF FALL 1979		
			PER FTE STUDENT, FALL 1978	PER FULL-TIME FACULTY MEMBER, 1978	AS PER-CENT OF GENERAL EXPENDI-TURES, 1978-79	VOLUMES PER FTE STUDENT, FALL 1978	TITLES (INCLUDING MICRO-FORMS) PER FTE STUDENT 1978	TOTAL STAFF	PROFES-SIONAL STAFF	
(1)	(2)	(3)	(4)	(5)	(6)	(7)	(8)	(9)	(10)	
PUERTO RICO	--CONTINUED									
U PR REG COLLEGES ADMIN	PUB-T	6,661	162.6	3,312.2	4.5	18.6	14.6	117.6	294.7
U OF THE SACRED HEART	PRI-FN	4,656	60.9	3,262.0	3.0	15.2	9.9	211.6	291.0
TRUST TERRITORY										
CMTY COLLEGE MICRONESIA	PUB-T	285	113.2	1,793.7	5.8	31.5	24.9	89.0	237.5
VIRGIN ISLANDS										
COLLEGE OF VIRGIN ISLANDS	PUB-FG	1,058	255.6	4,584.4	3.5	67.1	61.2	132.2	302.2

A - DATA NOT PROVIDED

D - DATA NOT AVAILABLE IN ALL DATA SOURCES. RATIOS CANNOT BE CALCULATED.

1/ - USES LOCAL LIBRARIES

2/ - EXCLUDES THE LAW LIBRARY

3/ - USES FACILITIES OF EMMANUEL COLLEGE

4/ - JESUIT SCHOOL OF THEOLOGY AT CHICAGO IS ALSO A MEMBER OF THE JKM JOINT LIBRARY

5/ - CONTRACTS FOR USE OF LIBRARY FACILITIES

6/ - EXCLUDES THE MEDICAL LIBRARY

7/ - SHARES FACILITIES OF OHIO STATE UNIVERSITY NEWARK BRANCH

8/ - SHARES FACILITIES OF OHIO STATE UNIVERSITY LIMA BRANCH

9/ - SHARES FACILITIES OF OHIO STATE UNIVERSITY MARION BRANCH

10/ - SHARES FACILITIES OF OHIO STATE UNIVERSITY MANSFIELD BRANCH

11/ - SHARES FACILITIES OF KENT STATE UNIVERSITY STARK COUNTY REGIONAL CAMPUS

12/ - THE TEXAS MEDICAL CENTER LIBRARY OF THE HOUSTON ACADEMY OF MEDICINE HOUSES COLLECTIONS AND PROVIDES LIBRARY SERVICES FOR:
BAYLOR COLLEGE OF MEDICINE
PRAIRIE VIEW A&M UNIVERSITY SCHOOL OF NURSING
TEXAS WOMEN'S UNIVERSITY SCHOOL OF NURSING AND HEALTH SCIENCES
UNIVERSITY OF HOUSTON COLLEGE OF PHARMACY
UNIVERSITY OF TEXAS HEALTH SCIENCE CENTER AT HOUSTON MEDICAL SCHOOL, GRADUATE SCHOOL OF BIOMEDICAL SERVICES, SCHOOL OF ALLIED HEALTH, SPEECH AND HEARING INSTITUTE, AND SCHOOL OF NURSING